The Portable

STEINBECK

The Portable
STEINBECK

Revised, Selected,
and Introduced by
PASCAL COVICI, JR.

THE VIKING PRESS
NEW YORK

94-693

Originally published in 1943

Reissued in new format in 1980 by Viking Penguin, Inc.
40 West 23rd Street
New York, N.Y. 10010

Printed and bound in the United States of America

ISBN 0-517-61063-9

h g f e d c b a

To the memory
of Pascal Covici
and John Steinbeck,
their friendship
and their work

CONTENTS

Chapter titles and titles of short excerpts
are the editor's, not the author's

CONTENTS

INTRODUCTION

More than a quarter of a century ago, when my father was making selections for the first Viking *Portable Steinbeck*, he wrote of his friend John Steinbeck, whose publisher he had been since 1935: "We can enjoy him. His great, intuitive feeling for folklore, his magnificent use of the vernacular, his use of simple themes, and his poetic rhythms recall to me the Homeric spirit in American prose." The gusto of Homer and of Whitman is indeed here, along with the thoughtfulness of Emerson, that philosophical presence which more and more readers have been finding woven into the sturdiest strands of American literature. A humor sometimes sly and often carelessly robust finds its way onto Steinbeck's pages too, along with other qualities so diverse that perhaps the best that the editor of this Portable can do is to describe some of the satisfactions that John Steinbeck's work provides and then try to include samples that inform, satisfy, and frustrate the reader into wanting more.

One begins with the sense (I quote my father) that "literature, when creative, is an expression of the joy of living." With his words, I can explain my own choice of the following selections: "They stimulated my imagination, and stirred emotions and thoughts within me which I was glad to have." Now, why they did so is largely a subjective matter. Each of us enjoys an author for many reasons, most of them having more to do with what we bring to his works than with what the works may themselves offer. But I want to try to say why I think that John Steinbeck provides satisfactions not so much unique as, rather, uniquely perceptible in his writings. Primarily, I find in those writings a focus of interest more implicit than realized in the very early works, then gradually emerging into sharpened consciousness until it becomes a matter of articulated intention in the "log" that Steinbeck kept for 1951, during the composition of *East of Eden* (1952), the book he then saw as the culmination of all that he had previously done. Steinbeck wrote in that daily "log": "Very few people ever mature. It is enough if they flower and reseed. . . . But sometimes . . . awareness takes place—not very often and always inexplainable. There are no words for it because there is no one ever to tell. This is a secret not kept a secret, but locked in wordlessness. The craft or art of writing is the clumsy attempt to find symbols for the wordlessness."

The sense that some sort of "awareness" has taken place is precisely what Steinbeck's best work—perhaps what most good writing—leaves with a reader. Without trying to push this admirable definition of the art of writing to the limits of its applicability, one can advance the suspicion that Steinbeck's memorable characters linger in one's imagination primarily as they struggle toward various sorts of "awareness." Still, the directions of the struggle are so various that one can understand why earlier reviewers and critics were at a loss how to approach Steinbeck's work. Not only was there lots of it, but it seemed to be heading in too many, and too contradictory, directions at once to be contained within any viable critical frame. To be sure, certain recurring elements in the fiction have been identified and explored. A concern for common, human values, for warmth, love, and understanding, leads to a view of Steinbeck the sentimentalist. The social relevance of his writing reveals him as a reformer. His tender evocation of the land itself, his celebration of its fertility and of his characters' concern for the bringing forth of life, implies an interest first called "primitive" and then seen as "mythic." His capacity to make both his characters and his country come alive has been traced to his increasing mastery of vernacular as counterweight to the sonorous, almost mystical, rhythms of his frequently incantatory language. Finally, his explicit discussion, in *Sea of Cortez* (1941), of what he called "non-teleological thinking" confirms what for many has been the primary motif of his fictional writing, his conception of man as a biological mechanism, purposeless as well as animal-like. The proponents of this view of Steinbeck find in the half-witted Lennie (*Of Mice and Men*), the retarded Tularecito (*The Pastures of Heaven*), and the moronic Johnny Bear (*The Long Valley*)—the three most frequently cited— an obsession with human approximations of the animal. Others, equally struck by the pointed absence of didactic moralizing, have seen in the stories and novels a pseudo-scientific concern to record without judging ("is-thinking" was to become a Steinbeck synonym for "non-teleological thinking"), to present specimens simply for the reader's contemplation.

These and other insights into Steinbeck's work are necessary and useful; they alert one to the many currents of feeling and implication that run through the books. One other way of approaching this flow would be to examine some of the people Steinbeck has created, and to see how he has gone about "unlocking" the wordless secret by forging his own particular language of awareness. The selections in this Portable may help the reader to begin this rewarding process.

After sketching the pathetic disillusion of Henry Morgan, in *Cup of Gold* (1929), as he comes to recognize but not to accept his betrayal of his early dreams of conquest and understanding (a kind of story that the author was to tell with immensely greater impact in *The Winter of Our Discontent,* more than thirty years later), Steinbeck introduced his readers to his own imaginatively possessed territory of the Salinas Valley in California, and to the characters—also his own— that would come to inhabit it in increasing variety and complexity. "Deep down it's mine, right to the center of the world," says Joseph Wayne of the land he has just bought at the start of *To a God Unknown.*

Of the kinds of awareness that Steinbeck's stronger characters bring to their confrontation of life, this sense of an intimate and even overpowering connection between man and land becomes the most pervasive, the most elemental. Even unaware characters feel it, all unknowingly, so that Grandpa Joad, comic relief and all, is said to have died as soon as the Joad caravan leaves the Oklahoma farm where he had his roots, although Grandpa's body breathes until long after. The rhythm of the seasons makes the texture of *The Grapes of Wrath;* what potentially is simply an "angry" book is as much a paean to the succeeding seasons and their effect upon the physical terrain as it is a compassionate presentation of the lives of oppressed Okies in California. The land wildly blossoms in springtime (or else unnaturally does not), quietly gestates during the summer, yields its harvest in the fall, and then lies bare and dead during winter, only to give birth once more. So, too, the lives of Steinbeck's people are presented not simply as a complex pattern of action and desire, but also as variations on the simple pattern that Eliot's

Apeneck Sweeney tersely identified as "birth, copulation, and death."

The imagery of sexuality in Steinbeck's books generally derives from the progression of the seasons as it influences the implicitly related fertility of the soil and desire of the characters. The *paisanos* in *To a God Unknown* copulate ecstatically in response to much-needed rain; the inevitability of sexuality in *The Grapes of Wrath* is like that of any other natural succession: "Might as well stop the fall from comin', and might as well stop the sap from movin' in the trees." And in the same integrated way, Ma comforts Rose of Sharon, pregnant in the midst of death, with the assurance that "bearin' and dyin' is two pieces of the same thing." Jody's Red Pony lives through its mother's death, the human emotions encasing both events being—once more—"two pieces of the same thing."

But the awareness of nature and of nature's processes that Steinbeck's fiction engenders in a reader remains secondary, although poignant and vital. The people, the characters, even more than the soil, the rocks, and the trees—one cannot speak of Steinbeck's "landscape," for the word's connotations of superficiality belie the psychological weight that the author imparts to the natural environment of his stories—live in a reader's imagination not only because of what they do but because of what they feel, and because of their struggles to understand their own unique positions upon the earth. This uniqueness emerges as a function not so much of their psychological and spiritual identity as of their participation in the lives of other people and simultaneously in their own destinies. Steinbeck's main characters in the early books repeatedly feel themselves to be somehow "different" from others, and the reader

sees this difference as existing not at all in their isola-
tion—which is what they themselves see—but rather in
their oceanic sense of involvement with all humanity.
Only as they become aware of this sense of community
do they cease to feel so tortured, so alone, so painfully
unique; yet it is this very communion that, for the
reader, sets them apart from the mass of men who feel
readily enough their own self-important loneliness but
who cannot break through the walls of narcissism that
keep them from being, instead of merely seeing themselves as being, specially important in the universe.

This seeming paradox, this state of feeling that com-
bines lonely aloofness with a burgeoning sense of com-
munal participation in the human race, Steinbeck implies as early as *Cup of Gold* and articulates in *To a God
Unknown*, where Joseph Wayne wants, without quite
knowing it, to be himself the whole, the all, the giver
and guardian of life. Searching for water to save his
thirsting cattle in a time of drought, he comes upon
an old man who sacrifices "every night some creature"
to the setting sun, as if the sun could not go down without the old man's controlling magic. "'This man has
discovered a secret,' Joseph said to himself. 'He must
tell me if he can.'" But neither the old man, nor anyone
else, can put the secret into words; it is the first avatar
of that awareness "locked in wordlessness" that flickers
through all of Steinbeck's work. The old man can say
only, "I do this because it makes me glad."

Unaware himself, but deeply in touch with the cycle
of the sun, the old man has found a peacefulness that,
simple-minded and even imbecilic, haunts Joseph for
the rest of his life. Even as he dies, giving his own blood
in dark propitiation of the unknown God that can send
the rain, Joseph thinks of those nightly offerings. The
reader, on the other hand, is not attracted to the old

man's mystical nature-worship, whose ritual has no words. Too much is symbol; not enough has been made human. The problem confronting Steinbeck here at the start of his career—a problem that he solved and partially solved in many books, but that returned to trouble him in such unlike works as *The Moon Is Down* (1942) and *Burning Bright* (1950)—is that of finding ways for his characters to reveal levels of their experience and awareness that people do not naturally put into words. Human beings, as Steinbeck was to emphasize specifically in *East of Eden* (1952), have consciousness, choice, and awareness as animals do not. Yet people are also animals. How create a full sense of the human without overstating it, and without belying the ignorance and the reserve of the shy animal behind the articulate man? So at Joseph Wayne's wedding, the new father-in-law speaks as surely few, if any, men have ever spoken: "It's because you're stronger than I am that I hate you. Here I'm wanting to like you, and I can't because I'm a weak man." As Joseph points out, no weak man could bring himself to say what McGreggor has said—but then, neither could any sort of man at all. Not until Doc Burton and Jim Nolan of *In Dubious Battle* (1937) does Steinbeck find a way to present persuasively the insight and awareness of articulate, knowing people.

But meanwhile, *Tortilla Flat* (1935) provided a short cut through the problem by presenting very simple people—Danny and his *paisano* friends—whose range of awareness is narrow without being unbelievable. Although some critics have refused to enjoy life on the Flat, offended by the author's refusal to hew mercilessly to a consideration of "social conditions," most readers have found rare satisfaction in the characters: fully aware of undercurrents of feeling and motivation, their awareness emerges both realistically (that is, convincingly) and completely. Through dialogue, through perfect rendition of the spoken language, Steinbeck makes his reader believe in the world of petty chicanery, mildly corrupt poverty, loyalty, and unambitious gusto that is Tortilla Flat. The humor of the book lies primarily in the rationalizations that reveal the very awareness of motive that the characters pretend to hide. Pilon, deciding to steal Big Joe Portagee's pants, indulges in mental gymnastics that exemplify much of the book's flavor: "If, with one action, he could avenge Danny, discipline Big Joe, teach an ethical lesson, and get a little wine, who in the world could criticize him?" Big Joe, having stolen Danny's blanket, must himself learn how it feels to be robbed. Pilon will trade the pants for wine. Fooling no one, least of all himself or the reader, each character reasons in similar fashion about such things as the gaps in Mrs. Morales's fence, through which chickens may be encouraged to slip, a bottle of wine that might endanger the health of a friend, or the rent that—if paid—might corrupt a kind landlord.

But the complex human qualities emerging through the story's Arthurian overtones, as well as through *The Pastures of Heaven* and *The Long Valley* (both written earlier in the 1930s, despite the publication date of the latter), suggest that the simplicities of humanity could not subsume the author's total interest. Even *Of Mice and Men*, the first of Steinbeck's experiments in constructing a novel in as close to dramatic form as possible, allowed neither the preoccupation with direct presentation nor the limitations of the idiot, Lennie, to hold the impact of the story to that of simplicity starkly rendered. Slim, whose "ear heard more than was said to him, and [whose] slow speech had overtones not of thought, but of understanding beyond thought," becomes the only character to sense the reciprocity in the relationship between George and Lennie, and thus continues the sequence of Steinbeck's isolated and aware men that Doc Burton in *In Dubious Battle* and Tom Joad in *The Grapes of Wrath* most successfully exemplify. This type brings into focus the major impact of Steinbeck's work during the 1930s.

The social issue, of course, is crucially relevant; it is no coincidence that *In Dubious Battle* concerns a strike of California fruit-pickers and that *The Grapes of Wrath* had its origins in *Their Blood Is Strong*, a series of articles Steinbeck did for the San Francisco *News* in 1936, so titled when it was published in book form in April of 1938. For the book he added an "Epilogue" that boils with controlled indignation. The last sentence of this grim description of what California was doing to the Okies anticipates the vintage from the grapes of wrath: "Must the hunger become anger and the anger fury before anything will be done?" Steinbeck the man cared deeply about the immediate social issues of corporate tyranny and the material lot of migrant workers. But, without attempting to account for the motives of the man, the books themselves present with equal vividness the loneliness, the capacity for choice, and —in Tom Joad—the development of the character whose awareness evades articulation but infuses a felt quality into his life. The "sad-eyed" Doc Burton, detached observer, who says, "I simply want to see as much as I can, Mac, with the means that I have," believes not at all in the "cause," the strike of the workers, but in men: "I guess I just believe they're men, not animals." Jim Nolan's development from socially "useless" involvement with suffering people into a man with the capacity to "use" people for the purposes of the group counterpoints, especially in the brutality of

Jim's death, Doc's notion that "the end is never very different in its nature from the means."

Jim dies for his cause, illuminating in his death not only the mob behavior of "group man" but also a human being's capacity to choose his destiny. Tom Joad, two years later, goes on to develop his sensitive awareness of people into an involved responsibility, predicated upon Tom's acceptance of Jim Casy's discovery that "maybe all men got one big soul ever'body's a part of." Like Doc, Tom seeks understanding. Like Jim, he has the capacity for involved sacrifice; but his sacrifice is not self-destruction, nor is his understanding distant observation. The qualities of that understanding emerge with special clarity through the episode in which Tom shares breakfast and then finds work with a small family, an event presented almost word for word in "Breakfast," a first-person fragment that appeared in *The Long Valley*. Apart from the sheer joy that it generates in a reader, "Breakfast" makes apparent what were to become the warmly human facets of Tom Joad that appear to have merged with the cool intelligence of Doc Burton to form characters in a number of subsequent books, among them *The Moon Is Down* and *Cannery Row*. The reader will discover, however, that the differences between Tom Joad's experience and that of the narrator in "Breakfast" clarify Steinbeck's emphasis, the felt thought behind the work, even more sharply than do the similarities. Both passages emphasize the impact of having work to do, upon the feelings, especially the pride, of people. This psychological facet of work informs all of *The Grapes of Wrath* and is spelled out explicitly in the first part of Chapter 14. Tom Joad's participation in these feelings, as well as in the total experience of the family with whom he shares breakfast, contrasts with the narrator's separation from the family and from any anxiety about finding work, and from the joy in doing it. One sees here how the writer's own feelings in real life, moving and powerful in themselves, become unimportant and seem almost trivial when subsumed by the fuller, because richly imagined, context of the fictional Tom Joad in the novel. This seemingly slight excerpt from what were really working notes for the novel, a distillation of the author's own experience and observation, therefore fixes with some precision the direction and force that feelings about work and about commitment take in Steinbeck's writings with *In Dubious Battle* and *The Grapes of Wrath*.

In both these novels, despite the rhythms of social action and of seasonal change, the primary emotional counterpoint is that between "group man," the organism that has a life independent of its members, and those individuals who have, or who struggle toward, awareness, while retaining their communion with and commitment to the life of the group, which itself derives significance and satisfaction from the work that people do. The awareness at issue here is by no means to be mistaken for a merely verbal intellectualism. But even though it cannot be reduced to words, even though education and social status appear in these works as absolute obstacles to achieving it, neither is it made to seem the natural heritage of any hypothetical "common man." Perhaps here is the most invigorating paradox behind all the books Steinbeck has written. On one hand, the democratic assumption that all men are potentially of the psychological and social elect does battle—generally embodied in conflicts between characters—with the equally egalitarian sense that all men share a basic, animalistic nature, more buried in some than in others but always to be found. On the other hand, the elitist assumption that only some men can understand their dilemma, their situation, and by understanding it affect it, becomes embodied in the characters who struggle to order with their minds the chaos of feeling and matter that they encounter. "Sometimes . . . awareness takes place."

John Steinbeck's initial achievement was to present not only the land, with the people and the social forces that make life upon it so engrossing and sometimes so terrifying, but also the struggle of individuals toward the awareness "locked in wordlessness." That casual entry into the "log" for 1951 does seem to be not only an accurate summing up of what the author had previously been doing but also a clear anticipation both of the work it accompanied and of the author's subsequent work. Yet a distinction must be made. John Steinbeck seems to turn away from the man whose awareness is a matter of discovering himself to be in harmony with a universal world spirit, Preacher Casy's "one big soul," and to become concerned instead with characters who can find within themselves the power to free themselves from the conditioning of unthinking experience in order to choose deliberately actions which they know to be right. *East of Eden* itself consists primarily of an effort to explore a special kind of awareness, that of Lee, and a special kind of unawareness, that of Kate. The other characters arrange themselves along a spectrum of which these two form the extremes. Kate can only use people; she has no sense that emotions are "good" for anything besides exploitation, a lack that blinds her to the very existence of a full humanity. Lee, on the other hand, knows both in feeling and in thought what heights—and depths—man is capable of experiencing. Through exposure to and reaction against the two of them, various members of the Hamilton and Trask families · receive an education in what it can mean to be human.

This humanity defines itself through a felt connection between responsibility and freedom, and through the exercise of both. The social outrage behind *The Grapes of Wrath* comes back again and again to impersonal "conditions"; there is no one responsible, no one a dispossessed farmer can shoot. But in *East of Eden* people make their own fate, if they choose to; and if they choose not to, the responsibility is their own. It is not that Steinbeck's people in the later books are more aware than are their predecessors; rather, they are aware in different ways. "You don't know what you're a-doin'," mourns Preacher Casy as he is struck down. "You can call sin ignorance," explains Lee. Both sorts of unawareness, the psychological as well as the social, result in failure to accept—in Cathy-Kate's case, even to perceive—any responsibility for the effect of one's actions on one's fellows. By presenting Kate as a genetically conditioned freak (a "monster," he calls her), John Steinbeck manages to suggest irresponsibility of an almost casebook quality, an infantile megalomania that seems plausible enough in the light of World War II but still difficult to reconcile with the worlds of Steinbeck's earlier work. "I think you will find that Cathy as Kate fascinates people though," wrote Steinbeck in his "log" for March 30, 1951. "People are always interested in evil even when they pretend their interest is clinical. And they will mull Kate over. They will forget I said she was bad. And they will hate her because while she is a monster, she is a little piece of the monster in all of us. It won't be because she is foreign that people will be interested but because she is not." Kate becomes totally isolated from the rest of the book's humanity because she lacks all awareness that she can be connected to others either in Preacher Casy's sense of participation in common experience or in Lee's sense of freely chosen responsibility.

Any interested reader can develop further, for himself, this particular perspective on John Steinbeck's works. Certainly an awareness of the author's concern for awareness is part of the enjoyment in reading these stories. Even a grim confrontation with school segregation—see the "Cheerleaders" in "Southern Troubles," from *Travels with Charley* (1962)—manages to raise implications for all humanity through an implicit concern for the qualities of experience as human beings perceive it, each in his own way. But another aspect of the satisfaction gained from reading Steinbeck lies in his frequently humorous tone. Curiously, most readers would not immediately think of Steinbeck if they were asked to mention American humorists. Mark Twain suffered from having his deeply felt insights received as humor only; it may well be that John Steinbeck has equally suffered—or possibly his readers have—from a widespread misapprehension that he is at all times serious to the point of solemnity. If "The Affair at 7, rue de M——" can satisfy only the science-fiction buff, or if its parody of Poe obscures its other excellences from any reader, then, I suppose, the frog-hunt from *Cannery Row* must be read as a sociologically significant depiction of middle-class fantasies in conflict with classless realities—which, to be sure, it is, but one pities the reader who can follow Mac and the boys without experiencing more than an observer's intellectual curiosity. Most delicious of all may well be the delicate irony of the Thanksgiving in Texas, from *Travels with Charley*: are those Texans really deca-

Steinbeck presses more directly upon the pulses of tragedy than anywhere else in his work, and yet the humor, as much as any other element, helps to shape the book's moral core.

In their humor, their morality, their protest, and their evocation of man's potential for brotherhood, how curiously contemporary are John Steinbeck's three major works (*The Grapes of Wrath* [1938], *East of Eden* [1952], and *The Winter of Our Discontent* [1961]). The "one big soul" that Preacher Casy talks about, that both Casy and Tom Joad come to participate in, approaches the consciousness of today's "flower children." In an era when the workers' power to strike no longer carries the same challenging overtones that it did in the strike-breaking 1930s, college students find *The Grapes of Wrath* as gripping as did their fathers. This makes excellent sense, given the insistence on personal involvement with the human condition that emerges as even more central to the book's thrust than any celebration of the working man. In *East of Eden*, Kate—an "incomplete" monster, the author calls her— appears today as an almost allegorical figure representing the incompleteness of a mechanical society which increasingly ignores the life of feelings, thus bringing ever closer its own destruction. Her very unreality emphasizes the shallowness of the existence that Kate stands for. Ethan Allen Hawley, whose appearance is still too recent to be surprising in its relevance, represents several of our ethical dilemmas in straightforwardly realistic terms. How can a father provide moral guidance for his son when he himself cannot adhere to the code he professes? What ought an honest man to do when his continued honesty promises primarily despair and not integrity? At what point do means themselves become ends? The young read Steinbeck with a real sense of immediacy, because he deals with the truths of today's spirit.

Now this is not to say that John Steinbeck's significance lies in any deliberate anticipation of America's social consciousness. It is indeed true that *The Grapes of Wrath* presents the rural issues of the 1930s in terms relevant to the urban issues of the 1960s and '70s. The resentment and wrath of the Okies near Bakersfield, California, do anticipate Watts, just as Casy and Tom suggest the hippies' beatific desire for "community" that led to short-lived Haight-Ashbury. But neither the common working stiffs nor the Preacher and Tom are prepared to scrap what my father called the author's "thoroughly Jeffersonian . . . political and economic concepts" as means toward realizing his "high hopes for a more realistic and riper humanity." Justice within the system, rather than destroying or resigning from the system, was the goal of Steinbeck's Okies. Still, to mention the difference underlines the continuities and suggests that, like all writers of lasting importance, John Steinbeck had the creative power to develop with sufficient fullness the implications of his characters so that they emerge as more than simply immediately appealing, or relevant, figures. The air they breathe fills the lungs of humanity everywhere, in an emotional sense and above all in a moral sense.

One may wonder what John Steinbeck's preoccupations might have become had he lived longer and, therefore, written more. The group and the "one big soul" of his earlier writings make one form of an American transcendentalism that Emerson and Whitman would recognize, especially in its monistic morality that stays clear of such dualistic absolutes as "sin" and "virtue," seeing instead what Preacher Casy calls the "stuff folks do." In his later work, beginning with *Burning*

Bright (1950), he concentrated his focus upon the smaller group of the family and came to emphasize a responsibility less ecological than moral. Throughout his career, echoes of Malory's *Morte d'Arthur* are never far from his consciousness, most explicitly in the modernized version of the tales on which he worked through the late 1950s. Perhaps this particular interest would have carried him to some way of combining the sense of passionate commitment of *The Grapes of Wrath* with the passionate commitment to freedom of *East of Eden* and to responsibility of *The Winter of Our Discontent*. But any such speculation has value only in so far as it adds to a savoring of what John Steinbeck did in fact achieve. In literature, emotional truth, moral value, and social relevance all come down to life upon the page, to the author's capacity to create, and thus to vivify, the experience of being human. Because John Steinbeck had this capacity, his work should long give to his readers the delight in which all lasting art has its beginning and its end.

Pascal Covici, Jr.

BIOGRAPHICAL AND BIBLIOGRAPHICAL NOTES

BIOGRAPHICAL AND BIBLIOGRAPHICAL NOTES

I. BIOGRAPHY

The life may hold some clues to the art, but how young John Ernst Steinbeck, of Irish and German ancestry, moved from senior class president, contributor to *El Gabilan*, the Salinas, California, high-school newspaper, and member of the track and basketball teams, to an affinity for biological and ecological studies and investigation, for physical nature generally, and for the very poor, and then to the role of world traveler and almost dandified New Yorker, with walking-stick and brownstone house, must await a longer and more detailed telling than can be managed here.[1] A few facts, however, may be interesting.

Born in Salinas, Monterey County, California, John and his three sisters grew up in a small town that was close to the country that he later depicted in *The Red Pony*. His mother was a schoolteacher, and he came early to books, drawn to the Greek historians, to the Bible, and especially to Malory's *Morte d'Arthur*. But the countryside claimed him more compellingly than did books; the years from 1920 to 1925 found him in sporadic attendance at Stanford University, taking courses—primarily the biological sciences—that interested him, working on ranches and on roads as well as in laboratories, and finally wandering off without a de-

---

[1] See Bibliography, page xlii, for selected biographical studies.

gree, intent upon becoming a writer in the unrural canyons of New York City.

There, among other, less publicized activities, he helped build the "new" Madison Square Garden uptown on Eighth Avenue (since replaced by a newer one) and for a while reported for the now defunct New York *American*. Rejecting advertising as a means of support, and disappointed when a manuscript of short stories was turned down by the Robert McBride Company, he returned to California to write, and took a series of jobs of which the most memorable was that of caretaker for an isolated estate in the High Sierras near Lake Tahoe. When a tree crashed through the roof, the caretaker was fired, but by then the writer was beginning to emerge. After false starts and after destroying at least one completed manuscript of another novel, Steinbeck published *Cup of Gold* in 1929. This novel was based on the life of Sir Henry Morgan the buccaneer, on Steinbeck's fascination with Malory, and on a sense that "all the world's great have been little boys who wanted the moon; running and climbing, they sometimes caught a firefly. But if one grows to a man's mind, that mind must see that it cannot have the moon and would not want it if it could—and so it catches no fireflies."

In 1930 Steinbeck married Carol Henning, his father provided a house in Pacific Grove for them, and hers provided $25.00 a month. Little if any money was coming in from the writing. The depression was beginning; *The Pastures of Heaven,* in 1932, and *To a God Unknown,* completed earlier but published in 1933, joined *Cup of Gold* in helping their respective publishers toward insolvency without improving either the critical or the monetary fortunes of the author. But all that Steinbeck has publicly said about this period suggests that his work and his relationships—particularly the friendship with Ed Ricketts—gave satisfactions that outweighed poverty and obscurity. Also, McIntosh & Otis, the new literary agency with which Steinbeck allied himself (also in 1930), believed in his work, and two parts of *The Red Pony* and several short stories appeared in the *North American Review*. In 1934, "The Murder" was chosen as an O. Henry Prize story. Then the long association with publisher Pascal (Pat) Covici began, when Ben Abramson, the Chicago bookman, introduced Covici to Steinbeck's two recent novels. He was particularly impressed with *The Pastures of Heaven*, a novel in the form of related episodes centering on the destructive impact of one family's insensitivity upon the lives of others in a seemingly "heavenly" valley. In 1935, Covici published Steinbeck's *Tortilla Flat*, which won the author wide, if not always favorable, critical attention, and three or four thousand dollars for film rights. In several letters Steinbeck refers appreciatively, and wonderingly, to the effects of this relative fortune upon his style of life.

He now came increasingly into the public eye, or rather his work did, for he attempted personal invisibility for many years. *In Dubious Battle* in 1936 (frequently called "America's best strike novel") led to numerous requests for his writings, the most significant commission being that of the San Francisco *News* for a series of articles on conditions in California's migrant labor camps. He was now in the thick of the social involvements implicit in such work, and in being the author of *Of Mice and Men*. When the novel was published in 1937, it became a Book-of-the-Month Club "dual selection" (with H. G. Wells's *The Croquet-Player*) and gave Steinbeck his first large popular audience to add to the critical success and more moderate sales of its two predecessors. But he valued commitment more than applause. Later in the year, when the play version opened in New York, he was living in a migrant workers' camp in California, having trekked from Oklahoma with some of its inhabitants. His concern over the lives of the migrant workers led him to attempt a satirical novel, tentatively titled *L'Affaire Lettuceburg*. But the serious writer was making strides even more significant than those of social commitment. In a letter to "Dear Elizabeth [Otis] and Pat," his agent and his publisher, he explained why the book "is a bad book and . . . can't be printed." One epithet he applied to it was "smart-alec." After publishing, instead, *The Long Valley*, stories written over the previous decade, he went back to rethink and recast the terms of his indignation and compassion, emerging with *The Grapes of Wrath*, the publication of which has been called "a national event." Attacked and praised, widely read and occasionally banned, awarded the Pulitzer Prize, it is now seen as a major American novel.

With money and fame came more travel and more concern, especially as war came closer. With his wife he had visited Ireland, Sweden, and Russia in 1937; now he turned to a collecting expedition along the Gulf of California with Ed Ricketts, reported in *Sea of Cortez* (1941), then to Mexico and the experiences that led to his film and book, *The Forgotten Village* (1941), about the life of a Mexican village beset by the plagues of harsh existence. The connections between all this travel—which included work with the Army Air Corps—and his divorce in 1942 may emerge in the future. In any case, he was busy, as the appended chronology attests, and his life was taking new directions: in 1943 he married Gwyn Conger and moved to New York City; by the time the marriage ended in divorce five years later, he had become a permanent Easterner and, even more important, the father of two sons. With his marriage to Elaine Scott in late 1950, he solidified his sense of himself as, among other things, a family man, Mrs. Scott's daughter becoming in feeling as well as in fact a part of the Steinbeck family.

Whatever the impact upon him, John Steinbeck found himself living in New York City, struggling with the problems of growing boys and of an adolescent stepdaughter, blessed with a wife with whom he could share as much of life as one person can share with another, and working in a variety of directions interesting and satisfying to him. Writing speeches for Adlai Stevenson's campaigns, then for Lyndon Johnson's; a radio script for the United Nations; reports from Europe and then from Vietnam; editorials for the *Saturday Review;* intensive research into Malory's texts and life; travel; handwork in the city and at the Sag Harbor retreat that helped provide the milieu for *The Winter of Our Discontent*: the catalogue could be extended; clearly John Steinbeck was involved in much more than the writing of fiction.

But always he was concerned with writing and in experimenting with fictional as well as with expository modes. He saw *East of Eden* (1952) not only as the story of his family, to which he added the story of mankind, but also as a synthesis of and an advance beyond all that he had previously learned about writing. The movie scripts for *Lifeboat,* during World War II, and then for *Viva, Zapata!* represent some of his finest work. For the stage, however, he became less successful, as *The Moon Is Down* and *Burning Bright* marked successively greater failures to bring off the play-novel form as movingly as he had in *Of Mice and Men.*

Yet the spirit of the man is as interesting as the work. Through these changes, he never lost the energy, the zest, and the craftsman's delight that he brought to all that he touched. As early as the trip that led to *Travels with Charley*, he sensed that he would not live long, and he kept his resolve always to live hard. The enthusiasms of the boy-man that he celebrated in *Cup of Gold* found expression not only in the faith in and commitment to mankind's capacity to survive and to grow that informs so much of his work but also in the daily rhythms of his life. "Pat, listen to this," he would say. And his editor and friend could never know in advance whether he was about to receive an outline for a new novel, play, or story, or a scheme for improving electric pencil-sharpeners. Samuel Hamilton, the exuberantly inventive patriarch of *East of Eden*, drawn factually from the author's grandfather, exemplifies the creative joy that the real-life grandson experienced in all that he did. The disappointments when a new experiment failed, whether with a gadget or in an attempt to make articulate and objectively verifiable the most fleetingly conscious of human feelings, came as part of the craftsman's ardor to attack a next new insight. Of the many threads contributing to an understanding of John Steinbeck's life and to a capturing of its flavor, perhaps none will turn out to be more important than his insistence —as he began to recover from the stroke that impaired his left arm and hand in July of 1968—that "I must make my hand clever again." With his awareness of mass society and his dream of the self-sufficiency of the individual man, he will be an important American to understand. Both his character and his writing repay scrutiny.

CHRONOLOGY
AND
BIBLIOGRAPHY

II. CHRONOLOGY

1902 John Ernst Steinbeck born, February 27, Salinas, California.

1919 Graduates from Salinas High School.

1920 Enrolls at Stanford University.

1924 Publishes stories in Stanford *Spectator*.

1925 Leaves Stanford without a degree. In New York City as a construction worker and as reporter for the *American*.

1926 Back to California and a variety of jobs. Writing.

1929 *Cup of Gold* (pub. Robert M. McBride, New York).

1930 Marries Carol Henning and goes to live in Pacific Grove. Meets Edward Ricketts, marine biologist and immediate friend-for-life. Begins permanent association with the literary agency of McIntosh & Otis.

1932 Moves to Los Angeles. *The Pastures of Heaven* (pub. Brewer, Warren & Putnam, New York).

1933 Back to Pacific Grove. *To a God Unknown* (pub. Robert O. Ballou, New York); the first two parts of *The Red Pony* in the *North American Review*.

1934 Death of Olive Hamilton Steinbeck, the author's mother, in February. "The Murder" included in *O. Henry Prize Stories*. Ben Abramson brings *The Pastures of Heaven* and *To a God Unknown* to the attention of Pascal Covici.

1935 *Tortilla Flat* (pub. Covici-Friede, New York): California *paisanos* with Arthurian implications. Some money at last. Trip to Mexico.

1936 *In Dubious Battle,* after initial rejection by a

forgotten publisher's-reader on the grounds that
the book distorted Communist ideology. Moves
to Los Gatos. John Ernst Steinbeck [II], the author's father, dies in May. "The Harvest Gypsies," a series of eight articles in the San Francisco *News* (Oct. 5-12).

1937   *Of Mice and Men* (novel pub. in February;
play opens in November, winning Drama Critics'
Circle Award). *The Red Pony*, in three parts.
First trip to Europe. From Oklahoma to California with migrant workers.

1938   *The Long Valley* (pub. The Viking Press, New
York), including fourth part of *The Red Pony*.
Their Blood Is Strong, "The Harvest Gypsies"
plus an epilogue (pub. Simon J. Lubin Society
of California, Inc.).

1939   *The Grapes of Wrath*, Pulitzer Prize-winner.

1940   To Gulf of California on marine collecting expedition with Ed Ricketts. Filming of *The Forgotten Village* in Mexico.

1941   *Sea of Cortez: A Leisurely Journey of Travel
and Research* (with Ed Ricketts). *The Forgotten
Village* in book form. *Of Mice and Men* and
The Grapes of Wrath appear as films.

1942   *Bombs Away: The Story of a Bomber Team*
(for the Army Air Corps). *The Moon Is Down*
(novel and play). Divorce from Carol Henning.

1943   Marries Gwyndolen Conger in March.
After some months in the European war zone
as a correspondent for the New York *Herald
Tribune*, establishes residence in New York
City. First edition of *The Portable Steinbeck*,
selected and with a Foreword by Pascal Covici.

1944 Son Thom born. *Lifeboat* (film).

1945 *Cannery Row,* a novel of Pacific Grove, with a leading character drawn from Ed Ricketts. *The Red Pony* republished in four parts. "The Pearl of the World" in *Woman's Home Companion* (December).

1946 Son John [IV] born. Revised edition of *The Portable Steinbeck,* with an Introduction by Lewis Gannett.

1947 *The Wayward Bus. The Pearl.* Travels through Russia with Robert Capa.

1948 *A Russian Journal* (with pictures by Robert Capa). Election to American Academy of Letters. Divorce from Gwyndolen Conger. Death of Ed Ricketts.

1949 *The Red Pony* appears as film.

1950 *Viva, Zapata!* (film). *Burning Bright* (play and novel). Marries Elaine Scott in December.

1951 *The Log from the Sea of Cortez,* with a personal account "About Ed Ricketts." Moves into 206 East 72nd Street in New York City. Summers in Nantucket, writing *East of Eden.*

1952 *East of Eden.* March to September, in Europe, reporting for *Colliers,* with photographs by wife. Lively "battle" with the Communist press in Italy.

1953 *The Short Novels of John Steinbeck,* with an Introduction by Joseph Henry Jackson.

1954 *Sweet Thursday,* a novel about some of the *Cannery Row* characters. Nine months in Europe, four in Paris at 1 Avenue de Marigny. Writing for *Figaro* on a weekly basis.

1955 *Pipe Dream* (a musical comedy adapted by Richard Rodgers and Oscar Hammerstein II from *Sweet Thursday*). Editorials for the *Saturday Review*. Buys house in Sag Harbor, Long Island, for summers.

1957   *The Short Reign of Pippin IV: A Fabrication,* a comic novel of political satire. To Europe with sister Mary Dekker and his wife. Beginning of serious research into Malory and the *Morte d'Arthur,* including first trip into "Malory country."

1958   *Once There Was a War,* a collection of dispatches from England and the Mediterranean during World War II. June in England: more Malory explorations; involved with Malory scholarship and with Dr. Eugene Vinaver.

1959   Eleven months in England, living in Discove Cottage near Bruton, Somerset, working on modernization of the *Morte.* Later called this the happiest year of his life. Much planting and caulking as well as writing.

1960   Home. More work on the *Morte,* which ends in frustration, to be put off until "later." Summer at Sag Harbor, writing next novel. In autumn, the trip that will lead to *Travels with Charley.*

1961   *The Winter of Our Discontent.* After spring and summer at work, travels with wife, sons, and their tutor for ten months in Europe. In November, has what Elaine Steinbeck considers to have been his "first attack of heart failure."

1962   Home in June. *Travels with Charley in Search of America.* Receives the Nobel Prize for Literature.

1963   Cultural Exchange trip behind the Iron Curtain: The Steinbecks and Edward Albee.

1964   Receives Presidential Medal of Freedom. Death

of Pascal Covici, editor and friend, in October. To Ireland for Christmas.

1965   In London and Paris at start of year. Death of sister Mary Dekker. Christmas in Ireland.

1966   To Israel, writing articles for *Newsday*. *America and Americans,* a ruminative response to the search for America and for its essential meaning, as text for a book of photographs. In autumn, starts five-month trip through Southeast Asia, writing for *Newsday.* Condemns war in general, but supports American soldiers.

1967   Home from Asia May 1. Autumn: a back operation, then a spinal fusion.

1968   Memorial Day weekend, Sag Harbor, first medically diagnosed heart attack. July, New York City, major heart attack. Back to Sag Harbor for September and October. December 20, in New York City, death.

1969   *Journal of a Novel* (pub. in December, edited in deference to the feelings of living people), a memorial edition of what John Steinbeck called his "log," the daily letters to his editor that accompanied and commented upon the writing of *East of Eden.*

From Elaine Steinbeck, who supplied most of the chronology for the years 1950-1968, comes the following:

As you can see, during these years he traveled more than he worked. Yet he was *always* writing *something.* I think perhaps you can say that first and last and always writing was his passion. But he also wanted to see the world—he enjoyed our marriage—and who could write about (or who would be interested in reading about) his joy of life in Sag Harbor?

The work petered out—but never the excitement, the contentment, the joy, the love.

III. BIBLIOGRAPHY

John Steinbeck's own major works are included in the Chronology. Beginning with *Tortilla Flat* in 1935, his principal publisher was always the New York company with which Pascal Covici was associated, first Covici-Friede, which went out of business in 1938, and then The Viking Press. A useful introduction to the relationship between Steinbeck and Covici appears in Charles A. Madison's *Book Publishing in America* (New York: McGraw-Hill, 1966), pp. 305-10, partially reprinted in the *Saturday Review* of June 25, 1966. Full-scale critical and interpretative studies of Steinbeck's work include: Harry Thornton Moore's *The Novels of John Steinbeck: A First Critical Study* (Chicago: Normandie House, 1939); Peter Lisca's *The Wide World of John Steinbeck* (New Brunswick: Rutgers University Press, 1958); Warren French's *John Steinbeck* (New York: Twayne, 1961); F. W. Watt's *John Steinbeck* (New York: Grove Press; Edinburgh: Oliver and Boyd, 1962); Joseph Fontenrose's *John Steinbeck: An Introduction and Interpretation* (New York: Barnes & Noble, 1963). Salient biographical information can be found in the sketch done by Peter Lisca in 1957 for E. W. Tedlock, Jr., and C. V. Wicker's anthology, *Steinbeck and His Critics,* in Lewis Gannett's brief but very valuable biographical essays in 1939 and then in the 1946 revised edition of the Viking *Portable Steinbeck,* and in the first chapter of Warren French's *Steinbeck.*

FROM

The Long Valley

FLIGHT

THE SNAKE

THE HARNESS

THE CHRYSANTHEMUMS

Four complete stories from the author's only collected volume of short stories, published in 1938.

FLIGHT

A BOUT fifteen miles below Monterey, on the wild coast, the Torres family had their farm, a few sloping acres above a cliff that dropped to the brown reefs and to the hissing white waters of the ocean. Behind the farm the stone mountains stood up against the sky. The farm buildings huddled like little clinging aphids on the mountain skirts, crouched low to the ground as though the wind might blow them into the sea. The little shack, the rattling, rotting barn were gray-bitten with sea salt, beaten by the damp wind until they had taken on the color of the granite hills. Two horses, a red cow and a red calf, half a dozen pigs and a flock of lean, multicolored chickens stocked the place. A little corn was raised on the sterile slope, and it grew short and thick under the wind, and all the cobs formed on the landward sides of the stalks.

Mama Torres, a lean, dry woman with ancient eyes, had ruled the farm for ten years, ever since her husband tripped over a stone in the field one day and fell full length on a rattlesnake. When one is bitten on the chest there is not much that can be done.

Mama Torres had three children, two undersized black ones of twelve and fourteen, Emilio and Rosy, whom Mama kept fishing on the rocks below the farm when the sea was kind and when the truant officer was in some distant part of Monterey County. And there was Pepé, the tall smiling son of nineteen, a gentle, affectionate boy, but very lazy. Pepé had a tall head, pointed at the top, and from its peak, coarse black hair grew down like a thatch all around. Over his smiling little eyes Mama cut a straight bang so he could see. Pepé had sharp Indian cheek bones and an eagle nose, but his mouth was as sweet and shapely as a girl's mouth, and his chin was fragile and chiseled. He was loose and gangling, all legs and feet and wrists, and he was very lazy. Mama thought him fine and brave, but she never told him so. She said, "Some lazy cow must have got into thy father's family, else how could I have a son like thee." And she said, "When I carried thee, a sneaking lazy coyote came out of the brush and looked at me one day. That must have made thee so."

Pepé smiled sheepishly and stabbed at the ground with his knife to keep the blade sharp and free from rust. It was his inheritance, that knife, his father's knife. The long heavy blade folded back into the black handle. There was a button on the handle. When Pepé pressed the button, the blade leaped out ready for use. The knife was with Pepé always, for it had been his father's knife.

One sunny morning when the sea below the cliff was glinting and blue and the white surf creamed on the reef, when even the stone mountains looked kindly, Mama Torres called out the door of the shack, "Pepé, I have a labor for thee."

There was no answer. Mama listened. From behind the barn she heard a burst of laughter. She lifted her full long skirt and walked in the direction of the noise.

Pepé was sitting on the ground with his back against a box. His white teeth glistened. On either side of him stood the two black ones, tense and expectant. Fifteen feet away a redwood post was set in the ground. Pepé's right hand lay limply in his lap, and in the palm the big black knife rested. The blade was closed back into the handle. Pepé looked smiling at the sky.

Suddenly Emilio cried, "Ya!"

Pepé's wrist flicked like the head of a snake. The blade seemed to fly open in mid-air, and with a thump the point dug into the redwood post, and the black handle quivered. The three burst into excited laughter. Rosy ran to the post and pulled out the knife and brought it back to Pepé. He closed the blade and settled the knife carefully in his listless palm again. He grinned self-consciously at the sky.

"Ya!"

The heavy knife lanced out and sunk into the post again. Mama moved forward like a ship and scattered the play.

"All day you do foolish things with the knife, like a toy-baby," she stormed. "Get up on thy huge feet that eat up shoes. Get up!" She took him by one loose shoulder and hoisted at him. Pepé grinned sheepishly and came half-heartedly to his feet. "Look!" Mama cried. "Big lazy, you must catch the horse and put on him thy father's saddle. You must ride to Monterey. The medicine bottle is empty. There is no salt. Go thou now, Peanut! Catch the horse."

A revolution took place in the relaxed figure of Pepé. "To Monterey, me? Alone? Sí, Mama."

She scowled at him. "Do not think, big sheep, that you will buy candy. No, I will give you only enough for the medicine and the salt."

Pepé smiled. "Mama, you will put the hatband on the hat?"

She relented then. "Yes, Pepé. You may wear the hatband."

His voice grew insinuating, "And the green handkerchief, Mama?"

"Yes, if you go quickly and return with no trouble, the silk green handkerchief will go. If you make sure to take off the handkerchief when you eat so no spot may fall on it. . . ."

"*Sí*, Mama. I will be careful. I am a man."

"Thou? A man? Thou art a peanut."

He went into the rickety barn and brought out a rope, and he walked agilely enough up the hill to catch the horse.

When he was ready and mounted before the door, mounted on his father's saddle that was so old that the oaken frame showed through torn leather in many places, then Mama brought out the round black hat with the tooled leather band, and she reached up and knotted the green silk handkerchief about his neck. Pepé's blue denin coat was much darker than his jeans, for it had been washed much less often.

Mama handed up the big medicine bottle and the silver coins. "That for the medicine," she said, "and that for the salt. That for a candle to burn for the papa. That for *dulces* for the little ones. Our friend Mrs. Rodriguez will give you dinner and maybe a bed for the night. When you go to the church say only ten Paternosters and only twenty-five Ave Marias. Oh! I know, big coyote. You would sit there flapping your mouth over Aves all day while you looked at the candles and the holy pictures. That is not good devotion to stare at the pretty things."

The black hat, covering the high pointed head and black thatched hair of Pepé, gave him dignity and age. He sat the rangy horse well. Mama thought how handsome he was, dark and lean and tall. "I would not send thee now alone, thou little one, except for the medicine," she said softly. "It is not good to have no medicine, for who knows when the toothache will come, or the sadness of the stomach. These things are."

"Adios, Mama," Pepé cried. "I will come back soon. You may send me often alone. I am a man."

"Thou art a foolish chicken."

He straightened his shoulders, flipped the reins against the horse's shoulder and rode away. He turned once and saw that they still watched him, Emilio and Rosy and Mama. Pepé grinned with pride and gladness and lifted the tough buckskin horse to a trot.

When he had dropped out of sight over a little dip in the road, Mama turned to the black ones, but she spoke to herself. "He is nearly a man now," she said. "It will be a nice thing to have a man in the house again." Her eyes sharpened on the children. "Go to the rocks now. The tide is going out. There will be abalones to be found." She put the iron hooks into their hands and saw them down the steep trail to the reefs. She brought the smooth stone *metate* to the doorway and sat grinding her corn to flour and looking occasionally at the road over which Pepé had gone. The noonday came and then the afternoon, when the little ones beat the abalones on a rock to make them tender and Mama patted the tortillas to make them thin. They ate their dinner as the red sun was plunging down toward the ocean. They sat on the doorsteps and watched the big white moon come over the mountain tops.

Mama said, "He is now at the house of our friend Mrs. Rodriguez. She will give him nice things to eat and maybe a present."

Emilio said, "Some day I too will ride to Monterey for medicine. Did Pepé come to be a man today?"

Mama said wisely, "A boy gets to be a man when a man is needed. Remember this thing. I have known boys forty years old because there was no need for a man."

Soon afterwards they retired, Mama in her big oak bed on one side of the room, Emilio and Rosy in their boxes full of straw and sheepskins on the other side of the room.

The moon went over the sky and the surf roared on the rocks. The roosters crowed the first call. The surf subsided to a whispering surge against the reef. The moon dropped toward the sea. The roosters crowed again.

The moon was near down to the water when Pepé rode on a winded horse to his home flat. His dog bounced out and circled the horse yelping with pleasure. Pepé slid off the saddle to the ground. The weathered little shack was silver in the moonlight and the square shadow of it was black to the north and east. Against the east the piling mountains were misty with light; their tops melted into the sky.

Pepé walked wearily up the three steps and into the house. It was dark inside. There was a rustle in the corner.

Mama cried out from her bed. "Who comes? Pepé, is it thou?"

"Sí, Mama."

"Did you get the medicine?"

"Sí, Mama."

"Well, go to sleep, then. I thought you would be sleeping at the house of Mrs. Rodriguez." Pepé stood silently in the dark room. "Why do you stand there, Pepé? Did you drink wine?"

"Sí, Mama."

"Well, go to bed then and sleep out the wine."

His voice was tired and patient, but very firm. "Light the candle, Mama. I must go away into the mountains."

"What is this, Pepé? You are crazy." Mama struck a sulphur match and held the little blue burr until the flame spread up the stick. She set light to the candle on the floor beside her bed. "Now, Pepé, what is this you say?" She looked anxiously into his face.

He was changed. The fragile quality seemed to have gone from his chin. His mouth was less full than it had been, the lines of the lips were straighter, but in his eyes the greatest change had taken place. There was no laughter in them any more, nor any bashfulness. They were sharp and bright and purposeful.

He told her in a tired monotone, told her everything just as it had happened. A few people came into the kitchen of Mrs. Rodriguez. There was wine to drink. Pepé drank wine. The little quarrel—the man started toward Pepé and then the knife—it went almost by itself. It flew, it darted before Pepé knew it. As he talked, Mama's face grew stern, and it seemed to grow more lean. Pepé finished. "I am a man now, Mama. The man said names to me I could not allow."

Mama nodded. "Yes, thou art a man, my poor little Pepé. Thou art a man. I have seen it coming on thee. I have watched you throwing the knife into the post, and I have been afraid." For a moment her face had softened, but now it grew stern again. "Come! We must get you ready. Go. Awaken Emilio and Rosy. Go quickly."

Pepé stepped over to the corner where his brother and sister slept among the sheepskins. He leaned down and shook them gently. "Come, Rosy! Come, Emilio! The mama says you must arise."

The little black ones sat up and rubbed their eyes in the candlelight. Mama was out of bed now, her long black skirt over her nightgown. "Emilio," she cried. "Go up and catch the other horse for Pepé. Quickly, now! Quickly." Emilio put his legs in his overalls and stumbled sleepily out the door.

"You heard no one behind you on the road?" Mama demanded.

"No, Mama. I listened carefully. No one was on the road."

Mama darted like a bird about the room. From a nail on the wall she took a canvas water bag and threw it on the floor. She stripped a blanket from her bed and rolled it into a tight tube and tied the ends with string. From a

box beside the stove she lifted a flour sack half full of
black stringy jerky. "Your father's black coat, Pepé. Here,
put it on."

Pepé stood in the middle of the floor watching her activity. She reached behind the door and brought out the
rifle, a long 38-56, worn shiny the whole length of the
barrel. Pepé took it from her and held it in the crook of
his elbow. Mama brought a little leather bag and counted
the cartridges into his hand. "Only ten left," she warned.
"You must not waste them."

Emilio put his head in the door. " 'Qui 'st 'l caballo,
Mama."

"Put on the saddle from the other horse. Tie on the
blanket. Here, tie the jerky to the saddle horn."

Still Pepé stood silently watching his mother's frantic
activity. His chin looked hard, and his sweet mouth was
drawn and thin. His little eyes followed Mama about the
room almost suspiciously.

Rosy asked softly, "Where goes Pepé?"

Mama's eyes were fierce. "Pepé goes on a journey. Pepé
is a man now. He has a man's thing to do."

Pepé straightened his shoulders. His mouth changed
until he looked very much like Mama.

At last the preparation was finished. The loaded horse
stood outside the door. The water bag dripped a line of
moisture down the bay shoulder.

The moonlight was being thinned by the dawn and the
big white moon was near down to the sea. The family
stood by the shack. Mama confronted Pepé. "Look, my
son! Do not stop until it is dark again. Do not sleep even
though you are tired. Take care of the horse in order that
he may not stop of weariness. Remember to be careful
with the bullets—there are only ten. Do not fill thy stomach with jerky or it will make thee sick. Eat a little jerky

and fill thy stomach with grass. When thou comest to the high mountains, if thou seest any of the dark watching men, go not near to them nor try to speak to them. And forget not thy prayers." She put her lean hands on Pepé's shoulders, stood on her toes and kissed him formally on both cheeks, and Pepé kissed her on both cheeks. Then he went to Emilio and Rosy and kissed both of their cheeks.

Pepé turned back to Mama. He seemed to look for a little softness, a little weakness in her. His eyes were searching, but Mama's face remained fierce. "Go now," she said. "Do not wait to be caught like a chicken."

Pepé pulled himself into the saddle. "I am a man," he said.

It was the first dawn when he rode up the hill toward the little canyon which let a trail into the mountains. Moonlight and daylight fought with each other, and the two warring qualities made it difficult to see. Before Pepé had gone a hundred yards, the outlines of his figure were misty; and long before he entered the canyon, he had become a gray, indefinite shadow.

Mama stood stiffly in front of her doorstep, and on either side of her stood Emilio and Rosy. They cast furtive glances at Mama now and then.

When the gray shape of Pepé melted into the hillside and disappeared, Mama relaxed. She began the high, whining keen of the death wail. "Our beautiful—our brave," she cried. "Our protector, our son is gone." Emilio and Rosy moaned beside her. "Our beautiful—our brave, he is gone." It was the formal wail. It rose to a high piercing whine and subsided to a moan. Mama raised it three times and then she turned and went into the house and shut the door.

Emilio and Rosy stood wondering in the dawn. They

heard Mama whimpering in the house. They went out to sit on the cliff above the ocean. They touched shoulders. "When did Pepé come to be a man?" Emilio asked.

"Last night," said Rosy. "Last night in Monterey." The ocean clouds turned red with the sun that was behind the mountains.

"We will have no breakfast," said Emilio. "Mama will not want to cook." Rosy did not answer him. "Where is Pepé gone?" he asked.

Rosy looked around at him. She drew her knowledge from the quiet air. "He has gone on a journey. He will never come back."

"Is he dead? Do you think he is dead?"

Rosy looked back at the ocean again. A little steamer, drawing a line of smoke sat on the edge of the horizon. "He is not dead," Rosy explained. "Not yet."

Pepé rested the big rifle across the saddle in front of him. He let the horse walk up the hill and he didn't look back. The stony slope took on a coat of short brush so that Pepé found the entrance to a trail and entered it.

When he came to the canyon opening, he swung once in his saddle and looked back, but the houses were swallowed in the misty light. Pepé jerked forward again. The high shoulder of the canyon closed in on him. His horse stretched out its neck and sighed and settled to the trail.

It was a well-worn path, dark soft leaf-mould earth strewn with broken pieces of sandstone. The trail rounded the shoulder of the canyon and dropped steeply into the bed of the stream. In the shallows the water ran smoothly, glinting in the first morning sun. Small round stones on the bottom were as brown as rust with sun moss. In the sand along the edges of the stream the tall, rich wild mint grew, while in the water itself the cress, old and tough, had gone to heavy seed.

The path went into the stream and emerged on the other side. The horse sloshed into the water and stopped. Pepé dropped his bridle and let the beast drink of the running water.

Soon the canyon sides became steep and the first giant sentinel redwoods guarded the trail, great round red trunks bearing foliage as green and lacy as ferns. Once Pepé was among the trees, the sun was lost. A perfumed and purple light lay in the pale green of the underbrush. Gooseberry bushes and blackberries and tall ferns lined the stream, and overhead the branches of the redwoods met and cut off the sky.

Pepé drank from the water bag, and he reached into the flour sack and brought out a black string of jerky. His white teeth gnawed at the string until the tough meat parted. He chewed slowly and drank occasionally from the water bag. His little eyes were slumberous and tired, but the muscles of his face were hard set. The earth of the trail was black now. It gave up a hollow sound under the walking hoofbeats.

The stream fell more sharply. Little waterfalls splashed on the stones. Five-fingered ferns hung over the water and dripped spray from their fingertips. Pepé rode half over in his saddle, dangling one leg loosely. He picked a bay leaf from a tree beside the way and put it into his mouth for a moment to flavor the dry jerky. He held the gun loosely across the pommel.

Suddenly he squared in his saddle, swung the horse from the trail and kicked it hurriedly up behind a big redwood tree. He pulled up the reins tight against the bit to keep the horse from whinnying. His face was intent and his nostrils quivered a little.

A hollow pounding came down the trail, and a horseman rode by, a fat man with red cheeks and a white stubble beard. His horse put down its head and blubbered at the trail when it came to the place where Pepé had turned off. "Hold up!" said the man and he pulled up his horse's head.

When the last sound of the hoofs died away, Pepé came back into the trail again. He did not relax in the saddle any more. He lifted the big rifle and swung the lever to throw a shell into the chamber, and then he let down the hammer to half cock.

The trail grew very steep. Now the redwood trees were smaller and their tops were dead, bitten dead where the wind reached them. The horse plodded on; the sun went slowly overhead and started down toward the afternoon.

Where the stream came out of a side canyon, the trail left it. Pepé dismounted and watered his horse and filled up his water bag. As soon as the trail had parted from the stream, the trees were gone and only the thick brittle sage and manzanita and chaparral edged the trail. And the soft black earth was gone, too, leaving only the light tan broken rock for the trail bed. Lizards scampered away into the brush as the horse rattled over the little stones.

Pepé turned in his saddle and looked back. He was in the open now: he could be seen from a distance. As he ascended the trail the country grew more rough and terrible and dry. The way wound about the bases of great square rocks. Little gray rabbits skittered in the brush. A bird made a monotonous high creaking. Eastward the bare rock mountaintops were pale and powder-dry under the dropping sun. The horse plodded up and up the trail toward a little V in the ridge which was the pass.

Pepé looked suspiciously back every minute or so, and his eyes sought the tops of the ridges ahead. Once, on a white barren spur, he saw a black figure for a moment, but he looked quickly away, for it was one of the dark watchers. No one knew who the watchers were, nor where they lived, but it was better to ignore them and never to show interest in them. They did not bother one who stayed on the trail and minded his own business.

The air was parched and full of light dust blown by the breeze from the eroding mountains. Pepé drank sparingly from his bag and corked it tightly and hung it on the horn again. The trail moved up the dry shale hillside, avoiding rocks, dropping under clefts, climbing in and out of old water scars. When he arrived at the little pass he stopped and looked back for a long time. No dark watchers were to be seen now. The trail behind was empty. Only the high tops of the redwoods indicated where the stream flowed.

Pepé rode on through the pass. His little eyes were nearly closed with weariness, but his face was stern, relentless and manly. The high mountain wind coasted sighing through the pass and whistled on the edges of the big blocks of broken granite. In the air, a red-tailed hawk sailed over close to the ridge and screamed angrily. Pepé went slowly through the broken jagged pass and looked down on the other side.

The trail dropped quickly, staggering among broken rock. At the bottom of the slope there was a dark crease, thick with brush, and on the other side of the crease a little flat, in which a grove of oak trees grew. A scar of green grass cut across the flat. And behind the flat another mountain rose, desolate with dead rocks and starving little black bushes. Pepé drank from the bag again for the air was so dry that it encrusted his nostrils and burned his lips. He put the horse down the trail. The hooves slipped and struggled on the steep way, starting little stones that rolled off into the brush. The sun was gone behind the westward mountain now, but still it glowed brilliantly on the oaks and on the grassy flat. The rocks and the hillsides still sent up waves of the heat they had gathered from the day's sun.

Pepé looked up to the top of the next dry withered ridge. He saw a dark form against the sky, a man's figure standing on top of a rock, and he glanced away quickly not to appear curious. When a moment later he looked up again, the figure was gone.

Downward the trail was quickly covered. Sometimes the horse floundered for footing, sometimes set his feet and slid a little way. They came at last to the bottom where the dark chaparral was higher than Pepé's head. He held up his rifle on one side and his arm on the other to shield his face from the sharp brittle fingers of the brush.

Up and out of the crease he rode, and up a little cliff. The grassy flat was before him, and the round comfortable oaks. For a moment he studied the trail down which he had come, but there was no movement and no sound from it. Finally he rode out over the flat, to the green streak, and at the upper end of the damp he found a little spring welling out of the earth and dropping into a dug basin before it seeped out over the flat.

Pepé filled his bag first, and then he let the thirsty horse drink out of the pool. He led the horse to the clump of oaks, and in the middle of the grove, fairly protected from sight on all sides, he took off the saddle and the bridle and laid them on the ground. The horse stretched his jaws sideways and yawned. Pepé knotted the lead rope about the horse's neck and tied him to a sapling among the oaks, where he could graze in a fairly large circle.

When the horse was gnawing hungrily at the dry grass, Pepé went to the saddle and took a black string of jerky from the sack and strolled to an oak tree on the edge of the grove, from under which he could watch the trail. He sat down in the crisp dry oak leaves and automatically felt for his big black knife to cut the jerky, but he had no knife. He leaned back on his elbow and gnawed at the tough strong meat. His face was blank, but it was a man's face.

The bright evening light washed the eastern ridge, but the valley was darkening. Doves flew down from the hills to the spring, and the quail came running out of the brush and joined them, calling clearly to one another.

Out of the corner of his eye Pepé saw a shadow grow out of the bushy crease. He turned his head slowly. A big spotted wildcat was creeping toward the spring, belly to the ground, moving like thought.

Pepé cocked his rifle and edged the muzzle slowly around. Then he looked apprehensively up the trail and dropped the hammer again. From the ground beside him he picked an oak twig and threw it toward the spring. The quail flew up with a roar and the doves whistled away. The big cat stood up: for a long moment he looked at Pepé with cold yellow eyes, and then fearlessly walked back into the gulch.

The dusk gathered quickly in the deep valley. Pepé muttered his prayers, put his head down on his arm and went instantly to sleep.

The moon came up and filled the valley with cold blue light, and the wind swept rustling down from the peaks. The owls worked up and down the slopes looking for rabbits. Down in the brush of the gulch a coyote gabbled. The oak trees whispered softly in the night breeze.

Pepé started up, listening. His horse had whinnied. The moon was just slipping behind the western ridge, leaving the valley in darkness behind it. Pepé sat tensely gripping his rifle. From far up the trail he heard an answering whinny and the crash of shod hooves on the broken rock. He jumped to his feet, ran to his horse and led it under the trees. He threw on the saddle and cinched it tight for the steep trail, caught the unwilling head and forced the bit into the mouth. He felt the saddle to make sure the water bag and the sack of jerky were there. Then he mounted and turned up the hill.

It was velvet dark. The horse found the entrance to the trail where it left the flat, and started up, stumbling and slipping on the rocks. Pepé's hand rose up to his head. His hat was gone. He had left it under the oak tree.

The horse had struggled far up the trail when the first change of dawn came into the air, a steel grayness as light mixed thoroughly with dark. Gradually the sharp snaggled edge of the ridge stood out above them, rotten granite tortured and eaten by the winds of time. Pepé had dropped his reins on the horn, leaving direction to the horse. The brush grabbed at his legs in the dark until one knee of his jeans was ripped.

Gradually the light flowed down over the ridge. The starved brush and rocks stood out in the half light, strange and lonely in high perspective. Then there came warmth into the light. Pepé drew up and looked back, but he could see nothing in the darker valley below. The sky turned blue over the coming sun. In the waste of the mountainside, the poor dry brush grew only three feet high. Here and there, big outcroppings of unrotted granite stood up like mouldering houses. Pepé relaxed a little. He drank from his water bag and bit off a piece of jerky. A single eagle flew over, high in the light.

Without warning Pepé's horse screamed and fell on its side. He was almost down before the rifle crash echoed up from the valley. From a hole behind the struggling shoulder, a stream of bright crimson blood pumped and stopped and pumped and stopped. The hooves threshed on the ground. Pepé lay half stunned beside the horse. He looked slowly down the hill. A piece of sage clipped off beside his head and another crash echoed up from side to

side of the canyon. Pepé flung himself frantically behind
a bush.

He crawled up the hill on his knees and one hand. His
right hand held the rifle up off the ground and pushed it
ahead of him. He moved with the instinctive care of an
animal. Rapidly he wormed his way toward one of the
big outcroppings of granite on the hill above him. Where
the brush was high he doubled up and ran, but where the
cover was slight he wriggled forward on his stomach,
pushing the rifle ahead of him. In the last little distance
there was no cover at all. Pepé poised and then he darted
across the space and flashed around the corner of the rock.

He leaned panting against the stone. When his breath
came easier he moved along behind the big rock until he
came to a narrow split that offered a thin section of vision
down the hill. Pepé lay on his stomach and pushed the
rifle barrel through the slit and waited.

The sun reddened the western ridges now. Already the
buzzards were settling down toward the place where the
horse lay. A small brown bird scratched in the dead sage
leaves directly in front of the rifle muzzle. The coasting
eagle flew back toward the rising sun.

Pepé saw a little movement in the brush far below. His
grip tightened on the gun. A little brown doe stepped
daintily out on the trail and crossed it and disappeared
into the brush again. For a long time Pepé waited. Far
below he could see the little flat and the oak trees and the
slash of green. Suddenly his eyes flashed back at the trail
again. A quarter of a mile down there had been a quick
movement in the chaparral. The rifle swung over. The
front sight nestled in the v of the rear sight. Pepé studied
for a moment and then raised the rear sight a notch. The
little movement in the brush came again. The sight settled
on it. Pepé squeezed the trigger. The explosion crashed

down the mountain and up the other side, and came rattling back. The whole side of the slope grew still. No more
movement. And then a white streak cut into the granite of
the slit and a bullet whined away and a crash sounded up
from below. Pepé felt a sharp pain in his right hand. A
sliver of granite was sticking out from between his first
and second knuckles and the point protruded from his
palm. Carefully he pulled out the sliver of stone. The
wound bled evenly and gently. No vein nor artery was
cut.

Pepé looked into a little dusty cave in the rock and
gathered a handful of spider web, and he pressed the
mass into the cut, plastering the soft web into the blood.
The flow stopped almost at once.

The rifle was on the ground. Pepé picked it up, levered
a new shell into the chamber. And then he slid into the
brush on his stomach. Far to the right he crawled, and
then up the hill, moving slowly and carefully, crawling to
cover and resting and then crawling again.

In the mountains the sun is high in its arc before it
penetrates the gorges. The hot face looked over the hill
and brought instant heat with it. The white light beat on
the rocks and reflected from them and rose up quivering
from the earth again, and the rocks and bushes seemed to
quiver behind the air.

Pepé crawled in the general direction of the ridge peak,
zig-zagging for cover. The deep cut between his knuckles
began to throb. He crawled close to a rattlesnake before
he saw it, and when it raised its dry head and made a soft
beginning whirr, he backed up and took another way. The
quick gray lizards flashed in front of him, raising a tiny
line of dust. He found another mass of spider web and
pressed it against his throbbing hand.

Pepé was pushing the rifle with his left hand now.
Little drops of sweat ran to the ends of his coarse black

hair and rolled down his cheeks. His lips and tongue were growing thick and heavy. His lips writhed to draw saliva into his mouth. His little dark eyes were uneasy and suspicious. Once when a gray lizard paused in front of him on the parched ground and turned its head sideways he crushed it flat with a stone.

When the sun slid past noon he had not gone a mile. He crawled exhaustedly a last hundred yards to a patch of high sharp manzanita, crawled desperately, and when the patch was reached he wriggled in among the tough gnarly trunks and dropped his head on his left arm. There was little shade in the meager brush, but there was cover and safety. Pepé went to sleep as he lay and the sun beat on his back. A few little birds hopped close to him and peered and hopped away. Pepé squirmed in his sleep and he raised and dropped his wounded hand again and again.

The sun went down behind the peaks and the cool evening came, and then the dark. A coyote yelled from the hillside, Pepé started awake and looked about with misty eyes. His hand was swollen and heavy; a little thread of pain ran up the inside of his arm and settled in a pocket in his armpit. He peered about and then stood up, for the mountains were black and the moon had not yet risen. Pepé stood up in the dark. The coat of his father pressed on his arm. His tongue was swollen until it nearly filled his mouth. He wriggled out of the coat and dropped it in the brush, and then he struggled up the hill, falling over rocks and tearing his way through the brush. The rifle knocked against stones as he went. Little dry avalanches of gravel and shattered stone went whispering down the hill behind him.

After a while the old moon came up and showed the jagged ridge top ahead of him. By moonlight Pepé traveled more easily. He bent forward so that his throbbing arm hung away from his body. The journey uphill was made in dashes and rests, a frantic rush up a few yards and then a rest. The wind coasted down the slope rattling the dry stems of the bushes.

The moon was at meridian when Pepé came at last to the sharp backbone of the ridge top. On the last hundred yards of the rise no soil had clung under the wearing winds. The way was on solid rock. He clambered to the top and looked down on the other side. There was a draw like the last below him, misty with moonlight, brushed with dry struggling sage and chaparral. On the other side the hill rose up sharply and at the top the jagged rotten teeth of the mountain showed against the sky. At the bottom of the cut the brush was thick and dark.

Pepé stumbled down the hill. His throat was almost closed with thirst. At first he tried to run, but immediately he fell and rolled. After that he went more carefully. The moon was just disappearing behind the mountains when he came to the bottom. He crawled into the heavy brush feeling with his fingers for water. There was no water in the bed of the stream, only damp earth. Pepé laid his gun down and scooped up a handful of mud and put it in his mouth, and then he spluttered and scraped the earth from his tongue with his finger, for the mud drew at his mouth like a poultice. He dug a hole in the stream bed with his fingers, dug a little basin to catch water; but before it was very deep his head fell forward on the damp ground and he slept.

The dawn came and the heat of the day fell on the earth, and still Pepé slept. Late in the afternoon his head jerked up. He looked slowly around. His eyes were slits of wariness. Twenty feet away in the heavy brush a big tawny mountain lion stood looking at him. Its long thick tail waved gracefully, its ears were erect with interest, not laid back dangerously. The lion squatted down on its stomach and watched him.

Pepé looked at the hole he had dug in the earth. A half inch of muddy water had collected in the bottom. He tore the sleeve from his hurt arm, with his teeth ripped out a little square, soaked it in the water and put it in his mouth. Over and over he filled the cloth and sucked it.

Still the lion sat and watched him. The evening came down but there was no movement on the hills. No birds visited the dry bottom of the cut. Pepé looked occasionally at the lion. The eyes of the yellow beast drooped as though he were about to sleep. He yawned and his long thin red tongue curled out. Suddenly his head jerked around and his nostrils quivered. His big tail lashed. He stood up and slunk like a tawny shadow into the thick brush.

A moment later Pepé heard the sound, the faint far crash of horses' hooves on gravel. And he heard something else, a high whining yelp of a dog.

Pepé took his rifle in his left hand and he glided into the brush almost as quietly as the lion had. In the darkening evening he crouched up the hill toward the next ridge. Only when the dark came did he stand up. His energy was short. Once it was dark he fell over the rocks and slipped to his knees on the steep slope, but he moved on and on up the hill, climbing and scrabbling over the broken hillside.

When he was far up toward the top, he lay down and slept for a little while. The withered moon, shining on his face, awakened him. He stood up and moved up the hill. Fifty yards away he stopped and turned back, for he had forgotten his rifle. He walked heavily down and poked about in the brush, but he could not find his gun. At last he lay down to rest. The pocket of pain in his armpit had grown more sharp. His arm seemed to swell out and fall with every heartbeat. There was no position lying down where the heavy arm did not press against his armpit.

With the effort of a hurt beast, Pepé got up and moved again toward the top of the ridge. He held his swollen arm away from his body with his left hand. Up the steep hill he dragged himself, a few steps and a rest, and a few more steps. At last he was nearing the top. The moon showed the uneven sharp back of it against the sky.

Pepé's brain spun in a big spiral up and away from him. He slumped to the ground and lay still. The rock ridge top was only a hundred feet above him.

The moon moved over the sky. Pepé half turned on his back. His tongue tried to make words, but only a thick hissing came from between his lips.

When the dawn came, Pepé pulled himself up. His eyes were sane again. He drew his great puffed arm in front of him and looked at the angry wound. The black line ran up from his wrist to his armpit. Automatically he reached in his pocket for the big black knife, but it was not there. His eyes searched the ground. He picked up a sharp blade of stone and scraped at the wound, sawed at the proud flesh and then squeezed the green juice out in big drops. Instantly he threw back his head and whined like a dog. His whole right side shuddered at the pain, but the pain cleared his head.

In the gray light he struggled up the last slope to the ridge and crawled over and lay down behind a line of rocks. Below him lay a deep canyon exactly like the last, waterless and desolate. There was no flat, no oak trees, not even heavy brush in the bottom of it. And on the other side a sharp ridge stood up, thinly brushed with starving sage, littered with broken granite. Strewn over the hill there were giant outcroppings, and on the top the granite teeth stood out against the sky.

The new day was light now. The flame of the sun came over the ridge and fell on Pepé where he lay on the ground. His coarse black hair was littered with twigs and bits of spider web. His eyes had retreated back into his head. Between his lips the tip of his black tongue showed.

He sat up and dragged his great arm into his lap and nursed it, rocking his body and moaning in his throat. He threw back his head and looked up into the pale sky. A big black bird circled nearly out of sight, and far to the left another was sailing near.

He lifted his head to listen, for a familiar sound had come to him from the valley he had climbed out of; it was the crying yelp of hounds, excited and feverish, on a trail.

Pepé bowed his head quickly. He tried to speak rapid words but only a thick hiss came from his lips. He drew a shaky cross on his breast with his left hand. It was a long struggle to get to his feet. He crawled slowly and mechanically to the top of a big rock on the ridge peak. Once there, he arose slowly, swaying to his feet, and stood erect. Far below he could see the dark brush where he had slept. He braced his feet and stood there, black against the morning sky.

There came a ripping sound at his feet. A piece of stone flew up and a bullet droned off into the next gorge. The hollow crash echoed up from below. Pepé looked down for a moment and then pulled himself straight again.

His body jarred back. His left hand fluttered helplessly toward his breast. The second crash sounded from below. Pepé swung forward and toppled from the rock. His body struck and rolled over and over, starting a little avalanche. And when at last he stopped against a bush, the avalanche slid slowly down and covered up his head.

THE SNAKE

IT WAS almost dark when young Dr. Phillips swung his sack to his shoulder and left the tide pool. He climbed up over the rocks and squashed along the street in his rubber boots. The street lights were on by the time he arrived at his little commercial laboratory on the cannery street of Monterey. It was a tight little building, standing partly on piers over the bay water and partly on the land. On both sides the big corrugated-iron sardine canneries crowded in on it.

Dr. Phillips climbed the wooden steps and opened the door. The white rats in their cages scampered up and down the wire, and the captive cats in their pens mewed for milk. Dr. Phillips turned on the glaring light over the dissection table and dumped his clammy sack on the floor. He walked to the glass cages by the window where the rattlesnakes lived, leaned over and looked in.

The snakes were bunched and resting in the corners of the cage, but every head was clear; the dusty eyes seemed to look at nothing, but as the young man leaned over the cage the forked tongues, black on the ends and pink behind, twittered out and waved slowly up and down. Then the snakes recognized the man and pulled in their tongues.

Dr. Phillips threw off his leather coat and built a fire in the tin stove; he set a kettle of water on the stove and dropped a can of beans into the water. Then he stood staring down at the sack on the floor. He was a slight young man with the mild, preoccupied eyes of one who

26

looks through a microscope a great deal. He wore a short blond beard.

The draft ran breathily up the chimney and a glow of warmth came from the stove. The little waves washed quietly about the piles under the building. Arranged on shelves about the room were tier above tier of museum jars containing the mounted marine specimens the laboratory dealt in.

Dr. Phillips opened a side door and went into his bedroom, a book-lined cell containing an army cot, a reading light and an uncomfortable wooden chair. He pulled off his rubber boots and put on a pair of sheepskin slippers. When he went back to the other room the water in the kettle was already beginning to hum.

He lifted his sack to the table under the white light and emptied out two dozen common starfish. These he laid out side by side on the table. His preoccupied eyes turned to the busy rats in the wire cages. Taking grain from a paper sack, he poured it into the feeding troughs. Instantly the rats scrambled down from the wire and fell upon the food. A bottle of milk stood on a glass shelf between a small mounted octopus and a jellyfish. Dr. Phillips lifted down the milk and walked to the cat cage, but before he filled the containers he reached in the cage and gently picked out a big rangy alley tabby. He stroked her for a moment and then dropped her in a small black painted box, closed the lid and bolted it and then turned on a petcock which admitted gas into the killing chamber. While the short soft struggle went on in the black box he filled the saucers with milk. One of the cats arched against his hand and he smiled and petted her neck.

The box was quiet now. He turned off the petcock, for the airtight box would be full of gas.

On the stove the pan of water was bubbling furiously about the can of beans. Dr. Phillips lifted out the can with a big pair of forceps, opened it, and emptied the beans into a glass dish. While he ate he watched the starfish on the table. From between the rays little drops of milky fluid were exuding. He bolted his beans and when they were gone he put the dish in the sink and stepped to the equipment cupboard. From this he took a microscope and a pile of little glass dishes. He filled the dishes one by one with sea water from a tap and arranged them in a line beside the starfish. He took out his watch and laid it on the table under the pouring white light. The waves washed with little sighs against the piles under the floor. He took an eyedropper from a drawer and bent over the starfish.

At that moment there were quick soft steps on the wooden stairs and a strong knocking at the door. A slight grimace of annoyance crossed the young man's face as he went to open. A tall, lean woman stood in the doorway. She was dressed in a severe dark suit—her straight black hair, growing low on a flat forehead, was mussed as though the wind had been blowing it. Her black eyes glittered in the strong light.

She spoke in a soft throaty voice, "May I come in? I want to talk to you."

"I'm very busy just now," he said half-heartedly. "I have to do things at times." But he stood away from the door. The tall woman slipped in.

"I'll be quiet until you can talk to me."

He closed the door and brought the uncomfortable chair from the bedroom. "You see," he apologized, "the process is started and I must get to it." So many people wandered in and asked questions. He had little routines of explanations for the commoner processes. He could say them without thinking. "Sit here. In a few minutes I'll be able to listen to you."

The tall woman leaned over the table. With the eyedropper the young man gathered fluid from between the rays of the starfish and squirted it into a bowl of water, and then he drew some milky fluid and squirted it in the same bowl and stirred the water gently with the eye-dropper. He began his little patter of explanation.

"When starfish are sexually mature they release sperm and ova when they are exposed at low tide. By choosing mature specimens and taking them out of the water, I give them a condition of low tide. Now I've mixed the sperm and eggs. Now I put some of the mixture in each one of these ten watch glasses. In ten minutes I will kill those in the first glass with menthol, twenty minutes later I will kill the second group and then a new group every twenty minutes. Then I will have arrested the process in stages, and I will mount the series on microscope slides for biologic study." He paused. "Would you like to look at this first group under the microscope?"

"No, thank you."

He turned quickly to her. People always wanted to look through the glass. She was not looking at the table at all, but at him. Her black eyes were on him, but they did not seem to see him. He realized why—the irises were as dark as the pupils, there was no color line between the two. Dr. Phillips was piqued at her answer. Although answering questions bored him, a lack of interest in what he was doing irritated him. A desire to arouse her grew in him.

"While I'm waiting the first ten minutes I have something to do. Some people don't like to see it. Maybe you'd better step into that room until I finish."

"No," she said in her soft flat tone. "Do what you wish. I will wait until you can talk to me." Her hands rested side by side on her lap. She was completely at rest. Her eyes were bright but the rest of her was almost in a state of suspended animation. He thought, "Low metabolic rate, almost as low as a frog's, from the looks." The desire to shock her out of her inanition possessed him again.

He brought a little wooden cradle to the table, laid out scalpels and scissors and rigged a big hollow needle to a pressure tube. Then from the killing chamber he brought the limp dead cat and laid it in the cradle and tied its legs to hooks in the sides. He glanced sidewise at the woman. She had not moved. She was still at rest.

The cat grinned up into the light, its pink tongue stuck out between its needle teeth. Dr. Phillips deftly snipped open the skin at the throat; with a scalpel he slit through and found an artery. With flawless technique he put the needle in the vessel and tied it in with gut. "Embalming fluid," he explained. "Later I'll inject yellow mass into the venous system and red mass into the arterial system—for bloodstream dissection—biology classes."

He looked around at her again. Her dark eyes seemed veiled with dust. She looked without expression at the cat's open throat. Not a drop of blood had escaped. The incision was clean. Dr. Phillips looked at his watch. "Time for the first group." He shook a few crystals of menthol into the first watch-glass.

The woman was making him nervous. The rats climbed about on the wire of their cage again and squeaked softly. The waves under the building beat with little shocks on the piles.

The young man shivered. He put a few lumps of coal in the stove and sat down. "Now," he said. "I haven't anything to do for twenty minutes." He noticed how short her chin was between lower lip and point. She seemed to awaken slowly, to come up out of some deep pool of consciousness. Her head raised and her dark dusty eyes moved about the room and then came back to him.

"I was waiting," she said. Her hands remained side by side on her lap. "You have snakes?"

"Why, yes," he said rather loudly. "I have about two dozen rattlesnakes. I milk out the venom and send it to the anti-venom laboratories."

She continued to look at him but her eyes did not center on him, rather they covered him and seemed to see in a big circle all around him. "Have you a male snake, a male rattlesnake?"

"Well, it just happens I know I have. I came in one morning and found a big snake in—in coition with a smaller one. That's very rare in captivity. You see, I do know I have a male snake."

"Where is he?"

"Why, right in the glass cage by the window there."

Her head swung slowly around but her two quiet hands did not move. She turned back toward him. "May I see?"

He got up and walked to the case by the window. On the sand bottom the knot of rattlesnakes lay entwined, but their heads were clear. The tongues came out and flickered a moment and then waved up and down feeling the air for vibrations. Dr. Phillips nervously turned his head. The woman was standing beside him. He had not heard her get up from the chair. He had heard only the splash of water among the piles and the scampering of the rats on the wire screen.

She said softly, "Which is the male you spoke of?"

He pointed to a thick, dusty gray snake lying by itself in one corner of the cage. "That one. He's nearly five feet long. He comes from Texas. Our Pacific coast snakes are usually smaller. He's been taking all the rats, too. When I want the others to eat I have to take him out."

The woman stared down at the blunt dry head. The forked tongue slipped out and hung quivering for a long moment. "And you're sure he's a male."

"Rattlesnakes are funny," he said glibly. "Nearly every generalization proves wrong. I don't like to say anything definite about rattlesnakes, but—yes—I can assure you he's a male."

Her eyes did not move from the flat head. "Will you sell him to me?"

"Sell him?" he cried. "Sell him to you?"

"You do sell specimens, don't you?"

"Oh—yes. Of course I do. Of course I do."

"How much? Five dollars? Ten?"

"Oh! Not more than five. But—do you know anything about rattlesnakes? You might be bitten."

She looked at him for a moment. "I don't intend to take him. I want to leave him here, but—I want him to be mine. I want to come here and look at him and feed him and to know he's mine." She opened a little purse and took out a five-dollar bill. "Here! Now he is mine."

Dr. Phillips began to be afraid. "You could come to look at him without owning him."

"I want him to be mine."

"Oh, Lord!" he cried. "I've forgotten the time." He ran to the table. "Three minutes over. It won't matter much." He shook menthol crystals into the second watchglass. And then he was drawn back to the cage where the woman still stared at the snake.

She asked, "What does he eat?"

"I feed them white rats, rats from the cage over there."

"Will you put him in the other cage? I want to feed him."

"But he doesn't need food. He's had a rat already this week. Sometimes they don't eat for three or four months. I had one that didn't eat for over a year."

In her low monotone she asked, "Will you sell me a rat?"

He shrugged his shoulders. "I see. You want to watch how rattlesnakes eat. All right. I'll show you. The rat will cost twenty-five cents. It's better than a bullfight if you

look at it one way, and it's simply a snake eating his dinner if you look at it another." His tone had become acid.
He hated people who made sport of natural processes. He
was not a sportsman but a biologist. He could kill a thousand animals for knowledge, but not an insect for pleasure. He'd been over this in his mind before.

She turned her head slowly toward him and the beginning of a smile formed on her thin lips. "I want to feed my
snake," she said. "I'll put him in the other cage." She had
opened the top of the cage and dipped her hand in before
he knew what she was doing. He leaped forward and
pulled her back. The lid banged shut.

"Haven't you any sense," he asked fiercely. "Maybe he
wouldn't kill you, but he'd make you damned sick in spite
of what I could do for you."

"You put him in the other cage then," she said quietly.

Dr. Phillips was shaken. He found that he was avoiding the dark eyes that didn't seem to look at anything. He
felt that it was profoundly wrong to put a rat into the
cage, deeply sinful; and he didn't know why. Often he
had put rats in the cage when someone or other had
wanted to see it, but this desire tonight sickened him. He
tried to explain himself out of it.

"It's a good thing to see," he said. "It shows you how a
snake can work. It makes you have a respect for a rattlesnake. Then, too, lots of people have dreams about the
terror of snakes making the kill. I think because it is a
subjective rat. The person is the rat. Once you see it the
whole matter is objective. The rat is only a rat and the
terror is removed."

He took a long stick equipped with a leather noose
from the wall. Opening the trap he dropped the noose
over the big snake's head and tightened the thong. A
piercing dry rattle filled the room. The thick body writhed
and slashed about the handle of the stick as he lifted the

snake out and dropped it in the feeding cage. It stood ready to strike for a time, but the buzzing gradually ceased. The snake crawled into a corner, made a big figure eight with its body and lay still.

"You see," the young man explained, "these snakes are quite tame. I've had them a long time. I suppose I could handle them if I wanted to, but everyone who does handle rattlesnakes gets bitten sooner or later. I just don't want to take the chance." He glanced at the woman. He hated to put in the rat. She had moved over in front of the new cage; her black eyes were on the stony head of the snake again.

She said, "Put in a rat."

Reluctantly he went to the rat cage. For some reason he was sorry for the rat, and such a feeling had never come to him before. His eyes went over the mass of swarming white bodies climbing up the screen toward him. "Which one?" he thought. "Which one shall it be?" Suddenly he turned angrily to the woman. "Wouldn't you rather I put in a cat? Then you'd see a real fight. The cat might even win, but if it did it might kill the snake. I'll sell you a cat if you like."

She didn't look at him. "Put in a rat," she said. "I want him to eat."

He opened the rat cage and thrust his hand in. His fingers found a tail and he lifted a plump, red-eyed rat out of the cage. It struggled up to try to bite his fingers and, failing, hung spread out and motionless from its tail. He walked quickly across the room, opened the feeding cage and dropped the rat in on the sand floor. "Now, watch it," he cried.

The woman did not answer him. Her eyes were on the snake where it lay still. Its tongue flicking in and out rapidly, tasted the air of the cage.

The rat landed on its feet, turned around and sniffed at

its pink naked tail and then unconcernedly trotted across the sand, smelling as it went. The room was silent. Dr. Phillips did not know whether the water sighed among the piles or whether the woman sighed. Out of the corner of his eye he saw her body crouch and stiffen.

The snake moved out smoothly, slowly. The tongue flicked in and out. The motion was so gradual, so smooth that it didn't seem to be motion at all. In the other end of the cage the rat perked up in a sitting position and began to lick down the fine white hair on its chest. The snake moved on, keeping always a deep S curve in its neck.

The silence beat on the young man. He felt the blood drifting up in his body. He said loudly, "See! He keeps the striking curve ready. Rattlesnakes are cautious, almost cowardly animals. The mechanism is so delicate. The snake's dinner is to be got by an operation as deft as a surgeon's job. He takes no chances with his instruments."

The snake had flowed to the middle of the cage by now. The rat looked up, saw the snake and then unconcernedly went back to licking its chest.

"It's the most beautiful thing in the world," the young man said. His veins were throbbing. "It's the most terrible thing in the world."

The snake was close now. Its head lifted a few inches from the sand. The head weaved slowly back and forth, aiming, getting distance, aiming. Dr. Phillips glanced again at the woman. He turned sick. She was weaving too, not much, just a suggestion.

The rat looked up and saw the snake. It dropped to four feet and back up, and then—the stroke. It was impossible to see, simply a flash. The rat jarred as though under an invisible blow. The snake backed hurriedly into the corner from which it had come, and settled down, its tongue working constantly.

"Perfect!" Dr. Phillips cried. "Right between the shoulder blades. The fangs must almost have reached the heart."

The rat stood still, breathing like a little white bellows. Suddenly it leaped in the air and landed on its side. Its legs kicked spasmodically for a second and it was dead.

The woman relaxed, relaxed sleepily.

"Well," the young man demanded, "it was an emotional bath, wasn't it?"

She turned her misty eyes to him. "Will he eat it now?" she asked.

"Of course he'll eat it. He didn't kill it for a thrill. He killed it because he was hungry."

The corners of the woman's mouth turned up a trifle again. She looked back at the snake. "I want to see him eat it."

Now the snake came out of its corner again. There was no striking curve in its neck, but it approached the rat gingerly, ready to jump back in case it attacked. It nudged the body gently with its blunt nose, and drew away. Satisfied that it was dead, the snake touched the body all over with its chin, from head to tail. It seemed to measure the body and to kiss it. Finally it opened its mouth and unhinged its jaws at the corners.

Dr. Phillips put his will against his head to keep it from turning toward the woman. He thought, "If she's opening her mouth, I'll be sick. I'll be afraid." He succeeding in keeping his eyes away.

The snake fitted its jaws over the rat's head and then with a slow peristaltic pulsing, began to engulf the rat. The jaws gripped and the whole throat crawled up, and the jaws gripped again.

Dr. Phillips turned away and went to his work table. "You've made me miss one of the series," he said bitterly. "The set won't be complete." He put one of the watch glasses under a low-power microscope and looked at it, and then angrily he poured the contents of all the dishes into the sink. The waves had fallen so that only a wet whisper came up through the floor. The young man lifted a trapdoor at his feet and dropped the starfish down into the black water. He paused at the cat, crucified in the cradle and grinning comically into the light. Its body was puffed with embalming fluid. He shut off the pressure, withdrew the needle and tied the vein.

"Would you like some coffee?" he asked.

"No, thank you. I shall be going pretty soon."

He walked to her where she stood in front of the snake cage. The rat was swallowed, all except an inch of pink tail that stuck out of the snake's mouth like a sardonic tongue. The throat heaved again and the tail disappeared. The jaws snapped back into their sockets, and the big snake crawled heavily to the corner, made a big eight and dropped its head on the sand.

"He's asleep now," the woman said. "I'm going now. But I'll come back and feed my snake every little while. I'll pay for the rats. I want him to have plenty. And sometime—I'll take him away with me." Her eyes came out of their dusty dream for a moment. "Remember, he's mine. Don't take his poison. I want him to have it. Goodnight." She walked swiftly to the door and went out. He heard her footsteps on the stairs, but he could not hear her walk away on the pavement.

Dr. Phillips turned a chair around and sat down in front of the snake cage. He tried to comb out his thought as he looked at the torpid snake. "I've read so much about psychological sex symbols," he thought. "It doesn't seem to explain. Maybe I'm too much alone. Maybe I should kill the snake. If I knew—no, I can't pray to anything."

For weeks he expected her to return. "I will go out and

leave her alone here when she comes," he decided. "I won't see the damned thing again."

She never came again. For months he looked for her when he walked about in the town. Several times he ran after some tall woman thinking it might be she. But he never saw her again—ever.

* * *

Mysteries were constant at the laboratory. A thing happened one night which I later used as a short story. I wrote it just as it happened. I don't know what it means and do not even answer the letters asking what its philosophic intent is. It just happened. Very briefly, this is the incident. A woman came in one night wanting to buy a male rattlesnake. It happened that we had one and knew it was a male because it had recently copulated with another snake in the cage. The woman paid for the snake and then insisted that it be fed. She paid for a white rat to be given it. Ed put the rat in the cage. The snake struck and killed it and then unhinged its jaws preparatory to swallowing it. The frightening thing was that the woman, who had watched the process closely, moved her jaws and stretched her mouth just as the snake was doing. After the rat was swallowed, she paid for a year's supply of rats and said she would come back. But she never did come back. What happened or why I have no idea. Whether the woman was driven by a sexual, a religious, a zoophilic, or a gustatory impulse we never could figure. When I wrote the story just as it happened there were curious reactions. One librarian wrote that it was not only a bad story but the worst story she had ever read. A number of orders came in for snakes. I was denounced by a religious group for having a perverted imagination, and one man found symbolism of Moses smiting the rock in the account.

(From "About Ed Ricketts" (1951). See note on p. 519.)

THE HARNESS

PETER RANDALL was one of the most highly respected farmers of Monterey County. Once, before he was to make a little speech at a Masonic convention, the brother who introduced him referred to him as an example for young Masons of California to emulate. He was nearing fifty; his manner was grave and restrained, and he wore a carefully tended beard. From every gathering he reaped the authority that belongs to the bearded man. Peter's eyes were grave, too; blue and grave almost to the point of sorrowfulness. People knew there was force in him, but force held caged. Sometimes, for no apparent reason, his eyes grew sullen and mean, like the eyes of a bad dog; but that look soon passed, and the restraint and probity came back into his face. He was tall and broad. He held his shoulders back as though they were braced, and he sucked in his stomach like a soldier. Inasmuch as farmers are usually slouchy men, Peter gained an added respect because of his posture.

Concerning Peter's wife, Emma, people generally agreed that it was hard to see how such a little skin-and-bones woman could go on living, particularly when she was sick most of the time. She weighed eighty-seven pounds. At forty-five, her face was as wrinkled and brown as that of an old, old woman, but her dark eyes were feverish with a determination to live. She was a proud woman, who complained very little. Her father had been a thirty-third degree Mason and Worshipful Master of the

Grand Lodge of California. Before he died he had taken a great deal of interest in Peter's Masonic career.

Once a year Peter went away for a week, leaving his wife alone on the farm. To neighbors who called to keep her company she invariably explained, "He's away on a business trip."

Each time Peter returned from a business trip, Emma was ailing for a month or two, and this was hard on Peter, for Emma did her own work and refused to hire a girl. When she was ill, Peter had to do the housework.

The Randall ranch lay across the Salinas River, next to the foothills. It was an ideal balance of bottom and upland. Forty-five acres of rich level soil brought from the cream of the county by the river in old times and spread out as flat as a board; and eighty acres of gentle upland for hay and orchard. The white farmhouse was as neat and restrained as its owners. The immediate yard was fenced, and in the garden, under Emma's direction, Peter raised button dahlias and immortelles, carnations and pinks.

From the front porch one could look down over the flat to the river with its sheath of willows and cottonwoods, and across the river to the beet fields, and past the fields to the bulbous dome of the Salinas courthouse. Often in the afternoon Emma sat in a rocking-chair on the front porch, until the breeze drove her in. She knitted constantly, looking up now and then to watch Peter working on the flat or in the orchard, or on the slope below the house.

The Randall ranch was no more encumbered with mortgage than any of the others in the valley. The crops, judiciously chosen and carefully tended, paid the interest, made a reasonable living and left a few hundred dollars every year toward paying off the principal. It was no wonder that Peter Randall was respected by his neighbors, and that his seldom spoken words were given attention even when they were about the weather or the way things were going. Let Peter say, "I'm going to kill a pig Saturday," and nearly every one of his hearers went home and killed a pig on Saturday. They didn't know why, but if Peter Randall was going to kill a pig, it seemed like a good, safe, conservative thing to do.

Peter and Emma were married for twenty-one years. They collected a houseful of good furniture, a number of framed pictures, vases of all shapes, and books of a sturdy type. Emma had no children. The house was unscarred, uncarved, unchalked. On the front and back porches footscrapers and thick cocoa-fiber mats kept dirt out of the house.

In the intervals between her illnesses, Emma saw to it that the house was kept up. The hinges of doors and cupboards were oiled, and no screws were gone from the catches. The furniture and woodwork were freshly varnished once a year. Repairs were usually made after Peter came home from his yearly business trips.

Whenever the word went around among the farms that Emma was sick again, the neighbors waylaid the doctor as he drove by on the river road.

"Oh, I guess she'll be all right," he answered their questions. "She'll have to stay in bed for a couple of weeks."

The good neighbors took cakes to the Randall farm, and they tiptoed into the sickroom, where the little skinny bird of a woman lay in a tremendous walnut bed. She looked at them with her bright little dark eyes.

"Wouldn't you like the curtains up a little, dear?" they asked.

"No, thank you. The light worries my eyes."

"Is there anything we can do for you?"

"No, thank you. Peter does for me very well."

"Just remember, if there's anything you think of——"

Emma was such a tight woman. There was nothing you could do for her when she was ill, except to take pies and cakes to Peter. Peter would be in the kitchen, wearing a neat, clean apron. He would be filling a hot water bottle or making junket.

And so, one fall, when the news traveled that Emma was down, the farm-wives baked for Peter and prepared to make their usual visits.

Mrs. Chappell, the next farm neighbor, stood on the river road when the doctor drove by. "How's Emma Randall, doctor?"

"I don't think she's so very well, Mrs. Chappell. I think she's a pretty sick woman."

Because to Dr. Marn anyone who wasn't actually a corpse was well on the road to recovery, the word went about among the farms that Emma Randall was going to die.

It was a long, terrible illness. Peter himself gave enemas and carried bedpans. The doctor's suggestion that a nurse be employed met only beady, fierce refusal in the eyes of the patient; and, ill as she was, her demands were respected. Peter fed her and bathed her, and made up the great walnut bed. The bedroom curtains remained drawn.

It was two months before the dark, sharp bird eyes veiled, and the sharp mind retired into unconsciousness. And only then did a nurse come to the house. Peter was lean and sick himself, not far from collapse. The neighbors brought him cakes and pies, and found them uneaten in the kitchen when they called again.

Mrs. Chappell was in the house with Peter the afternoon Emma died. Peter became hysterical immediately. Mrs. Chappell telephoned the doctor, and then she called her husband to come and help her, for Peter was wailing like a crazy man, and beating his bearded cheeks with his fists. Ed Chappell was ashamed when he saw him.

Peter's beard was wet with his tears. His loud sobbing could be heard throughout the house. Sometimes he sat by the bed and covered his head with a pillow, and sometimes he paced the floor of the bedroom bellowing like a calf. When Ed Chappell self-consciously put a hand on his shoulder and said, "Come on, Peter, come on, now," in a helpless voice, Peter shook his hand off. The doctor drove out and signed the certificate.

When the undertaker came, they had a devil of a time with Peter. He was half mad. He fought them when they tried to take the body away. It was only after Ed Chappell and the undertaker held him down while the doctor stuck him with a hypodermic, that they were able to remove Emma.

The morphine didn't put Peter to sleep. He sat hunched in the corner, breathing heavily and staring at the floor.

"Who's going to stay with him?" the doctor asked. "Miss Jack?" to the nurse.

"I couldn't handle him, doctor, not alone."

"Will you stay, Chappell?"

"Sure, I'll stay."

"Well, look. Here are some triple bromides. If he gets going again, give him one of these. And if they don't work, here's some sodium amytal. One of these capsules will calm him down."

Before they went away, they helped the stupefied Peter into the sitting-room and laid him gently down on a sofa. Ed Chappell sat in an easy-chair and watched him. The bromides and a glass of water were on the table beside him.

The little sitting-room was clean and dusted. Only that morning Peter had swept the floor with pieces of damp newspaper. Ed built a little fire in the grate, and put on a couple of pieces of oak when the flames were well started. The dark had come early. A light rain spattered against the windows when the wind drove it. Ed trimmed the kerosene lamps and turned the flames low. In the grate the blaze snapped and crackled and the flames curled like hair over the oak. For a long time Ed sat in his easy-chair watching Peter where he lay drugged on the couch. At last Ed dozed off to sleep.

It was about ten o'clock when he awakened. He started up and looked toward the sofa. Peter was sitting up, looking at him. Ed's hand went out toward the bromide bottle, but Peter shook his head.

"No need to give me anything, Ed. I guess the doctor slugged me pretty hard, didn't he? I feel all right now, only a little dopey."

"If you'll just take one of these, you'll get some sleep."

"I don't want sleep." He fingered his draggled beard and then stood up. "I'll go out and wash my face, then I'll feel better."

Ed heard him running water in the kitchen. In a moment he came back into the living-room, still drying his face on a towel. Peter was smiling curiously. It was an expression Ed had never seen on him before, a quizzical, wondering smile. "I guess I kind of broke loose when she died, didn't I?" Peter said.

"Well—yes, you carried on some."

"It seemed like something snapped inside of me," Peter explained. "Something like a suspender strap. It made me all come apart. I'm all right, now, though."

Ed looked down at the floor and saw a little brown spider crawling, and stretched out his foot and stomped it.

Peter asked suddenly, "Do you believe in an after-life?"

Ed Chappell squirmed. He didn't like to talk about such things, for to talk about them was to bring them up in his mind and think about them. "Well, yes. I suppose if you come right down to it, I do."

"Do you believe that somebody that's—passed on—can look down and see what we're doing?"

"Oh, I don't know as I'd go that far—I don't know."

Peter went on as though he were talking to himself. "Even if she could see me, and I didn't do what she wanted, she ought to feel good because I did it when she was here. It ought to please her that she made a good man of me. If I wasn't a good man when she wasn't here, that'd prove she did it all, wouldn't it? I was a good man, wasn't I, Ed?"

"What do you mean, 'was'?"

"Well, except for one week a year I was good. I don't know what I'll do now. . . ." His face grew angry. "Except one thing." He stood up and stripped off his coat and his shirt. Over his underwear there was a web harness that pulled his shoulders back. He unhooked the harness and threw it off. Then he dropped his trousers, disclosing a wide elastic belt. He shucked this off over his feet, and then he scratched his stomach luxuriously before he put on his clothes again. He smiled at Ed, the strange, wondering smile, again. "I don't know how she got me to do things, but she did. She didn't seem to boss me, but she always made me do things. You know, I don't think I believe in an after-life. When she was alive, even when she was sick, I had to do things she wanted, but just the minute she died, it was—why like that harness coming off! I couldn't stand it. It was all over. I'm going to have to get used to going without that harness." He shook his finger in Ed's direction. "My stomach's going to stick out," he said positively. "I'm going to let it stick out. Why, I'm fifty years old."

Ed didn't like that. He wanted to get away. This sort of thing wasn't very decent. "If you'll just take one of these, you'll get some sleep," he said weakly.

Peter had not put his coat on. He was sitting on the sofa in an open shirt. "I don't want to sleep. I want to talk. I guess I'll have to put that belt and harness on for the funeral, but after that I'm going to burn them. Listen, I've got a bottle of whisky in the barn. I'll go get it."

"Oh no," Ed protested quickly. "I couldn't drink now, not at a time like this."

Peter stood up. "Well, I could. You can sit and watch me if you want. I tell you, it's all over." He went out the door, leaving Ed Chappell unhappy and scandalized. It was only a moment before he was back. He started talking as he came through the doorway with the whisky. "I only got one thing in my life, those trips. Emma was a pretty bright woman. She knew I'd've gone crazy if I didn't get away once a year. God, how she worked on my conscience when I came back!" His voice lowered confidentially. "You know what I did on those trips?"

Ed's eyes were wide open now. Here was a man he didn't know, and he was becoming fascinated. He took the glass of whisky when it was handed to him. "No, what did you do?"

Peter gulped his drink and coughed, and wiped his mouth with his hand. "I got drunk," he said. "I went to fancy houses in San Francisco. I was drunk for a week, and I went to a fancy house every night." He poured his glass full again. "I guess Emma knew, but she never said anything. I'd've *busted* if I hadn't got away."

Ed Chappell sipped his whisky gingerly. "She always said you went on business."

Peter looked at his glass and drank it, and poured it full again. His eyes had begun to shine. "Drink your drink, Ed. I know you think it isn't right—so soon, but no one'll know but you and me. Kick up the fire. I'm not sad."

Chappell went to the grate and stirred the glowing wood until lots of sparks flew up the chimney like little

shining birds. Peter filled the glasses and retired to the
sofa again. When Ed went back to the chair he sipped
from his glass and pretended he didn't know it was filled
up. His cheeks were flushing. It didn't seem so terrible,
now, to be drinking. The afternoon and the death had receded into an indefinite past.

"Want some cake?" Peter asked. "There's half a dozen
cakes in the pantry."

"No, I don't think I will thank you for some."

"You know," Peter confessèd, "I don't think I'll eat cake
again. For ten years, every time Emma was sick, people
sent cakes. It was nice of 'em, of course, only now cake
means sickness to me. Drink your drink."

Something happened in the room. Both men looked up,
trying to discover what it was. The room was somehow
different than it had been a moment before. Then Peter
smiled sheepishly. "It was that mantel clock stopped. I
don't think I'll start it any more. I'll get a little quick alarm
clock that ticks fast. That clack-clack-clack is too mournful." He swallowed his whisky. "I guess you'll be telling
around that I'm crazy, won't you?"

Ed looked up from his glass, and smiled and nodded.
"No, I will not. I can see pretty much how you feel about
things. I didn't know you wore that harness and belt."

"A man ought to stand up straight," Peter said. "I'm a
natural sloucher." Then he exploded: "I'm a natural fool!
For twenty years I've been pretending I was a wise, good
man—except for that one week a year." He said loudly,
"Things have been dribbled to me. My life's been dribbled out to me. Here, let me fill your glass. I've got another bottle out in the barn, way down under a pile of
sacks."

Ed held out his glass to be filled. Peter went on, "I
thought how it would be nice to have my whole river flat
in sweet peas. Think how it'd be to sit on the front porch

and see all those acres of blue and pink, just solid. And when the wind came up over them, think of the big smell. A big smell that would almost knock you over."

"A lot of men have gone broke on sweet peas. 'Course you get a big price for the seed, but too many things can happen to your crop."

"I don't give a damn," Peter shouted. "I want a lot of everything. I want forty acres of color and smell. I want fat women, with breasts as big as pillows. I'm hungry, I tell you, I'm hungry for everything, for a lot of everything."

Ed's face became grave under the shouting. "If you'd just take one of these, you'd get some sleep."

Peter looked ashamed. "I'm all right. I didn't mean to yell like that. I'm not just thinking these things for the first time. I been thinking about them for years, the way a kid thinks of vacation. I was always afraid I'd be too old. Or that I'd go first and miss everything. But I'm only fifty, I've got plenty of vinegar left. I told Emma about the sweet peas, but she wouldn't let me. I don't know how she made me do things," he said wonderingly. "I can't remember. She had a way of doing it. But she's gone. I can feel she's gone just like that harness is gone. I'm going to slouch, Ed—slouch all over the place. I'm going to track dirt into the house. I'm going to get a big fat housekeeper —a big fat one from San Francisco. I'm going to have a bottle of brandy on the shelf all the time."

Ed Chappell stood up and stretched his arms over his head. "I guess I'll go home now, if you feel all right. I got to get some sleep. You better wind that clock, Peter. It don't do a clock any good to stand not running."

The day after the funeral Peter Randall went to work on his farm. The Chappells, who lived on the next place, saw the lamp in his kitchen long before daylight, and they saw his lantern cross the yard to the barn half an hour before they even got up.

Peter pruned his orchard in three days. He worked from first light until he couldn't see the twigs against the sky any more. Then he started to shape the big piece of river flat. He plowed and rolled and harrowed. Two strange men dressed in boots and riding breeches came out and looked at his land. They felt the dirt with their fingers and ran a post-hole digger deep down under the surface, and when they went away they took little paper bags of the dirt with them.

Ordinarily, before planting time, the farmers did a good deal of visiting back and forth. They sat on their haunches, picking up handsful of dirt and breaking little clods between their fingers. They discussed markets and crops, recalled other years when beans had done well in a good market, and other years when field peas didn't bring enough to pay for the seed hardly. After a great number of these discussions it usually happened that all the farmers planted the same things. There were certain men whose ideas carried weight. If Peter Randall or Clark DeWitt thought they would put in pink beans and barley, most of the crops would turn out to be pink beans and barley that year; for, since such men were respected and fairly successful, it was conceded that their plans must be based on something besides chance choice. It was generally believed but never stated that Peter Randall and Clark DeWitt had extra reasoning powers and special prophetic knowledge.

When the usual visits started, it was seen that a change had taken place in Peter Randall. He sat on his plow and talked pleasantly enough. He said he hadn't decided yet what to plant, but he said it in such a guilty way that it was plain he didn't intend to tell. When he had rebuffed a few inquiries, the visits to his place stopped and the farmers went over in a body to Clark DeWitt. Clark was putting in Chevalier barley. His decision dictated the major part of the planting in the vicinity.

But because the questions stopped, the interest did not. Men driving by the forty-five acre flat of the Randall place studied the field to try to figure out from the type of work what the crop was going to be. When Peter drove the seeder back and forth across the land no one came in, for Peter had made it plain that his crop was a secret.

Ed Chappell didn't tell on him, either. Ed was a little ashamed when he thought of that night; ashamed of Peter for breaking down, and ashamed of himself for having sat there and listened. He watched Peter narrowly to see whether his vicious intentions were really there or whether the whole conversation had been the result of loss and hysteria. He did notice that Peter's shoulders weren't back and that his stomach stuck out a little. He went to Peter's house and was relieved when he saw no dirt on the floor and when he heard the mantel clock ticking away.

Mrs. Chappell spoke often of the afternoon. "You'd've thought he lost his mind the way he carried on. He just howled. Ed stayed with him part of the night, until he quieted down. Ed had to give him some whisky to get him to sleep. But," she said brightly, "hard work is the thing to kill sorrow. Peter Randall is getting up at three o'clock every morning. I can see the light in his kitchen window from my bedroom."

The pussywillows burst out in silver drops, and the little weeds sprouted up along the roadside. The Salinas River ran dark water, flowed for a month, and then subsided into green pools again. Peter Randall had shaped his land beautifully. It was smooth and black; no clod was larger than a small marble, and under the rains it looked purple with richness.

And then the little weak lines of green stretched out across the black field. In the dusk a neighbor crawled under the fence and pulled one of the tiny plants. "Some kind of legume," he told his friends. "Field peas, I guess. What did he want to be so quiet about it for? I asked him right out what he was planting, and he wouldn't tell me."

The word ran through the farms, "It's sweet peas. The whole God-damn' forty-five acres is in sweet peas!" Men called on Clark DeWitt then, to get his opinion.

His opinion was this: "People think because you can get twenty to sixty cents a pound for sweet peas you can get rich on them. But it's the most ticklish crop in the world. If the bugs don't get it, it might do good. And then come a hot day and bust the pods and lose your crop on the ground. Or it might come up a little rain and spoil the whole kaboodle. It's all right to put in a few acres and take a chance, but not the whole place. Peter's touched in the head since Emma died."

This opinion was widely distributed. Every man used it as his own. Two neighbors often said it to each other, each one repeating half of it. When too many people said it to Peter Randall he became angry. One day he cried, "Say, whose land is this? If I want to go broke, I've got a damn good right to, haven't I?" And that changed the whole feeling. Men remembered that Peter was a good farmer. Perhaps he had special knowledge. Why, that's who those two men in boots were—soil chemists! A good many of the farmers wished they'd put in a few acres of sweet peas.

They wished it particularly when the vines spread out, when they met each other across the rows and hid the dark earth from sight, when the buds began to form and it was seen the crop was rich. And then the blooms came; forty-five acres of color, forty-five acres of perfume. It was said that you could smell them in Salinas, four miles away. Busses brought the school children out to look at them. A group of men from a seed company spent all day looking at the vines and feeling the earth.

Peter Randall sat on his porch in a rocking-chair every afternoon. He looked down on the great squares of pink and blue, and on the mad square of mixed colors. When the afternoon breeze came up, he inhaled deeply. His blue shirt was open at the throat, as though he wanted to get the perfume down next his skin.

Men called on Clark DeWitt to get his opinion now. He said, "There's about ten things that can happen to spoil that crop. He's welcome to his sweet peas." But the men knew from Clark's irritation that he was a little jealous. They looked up over the fields of color to where Peter sat on his porch, and they felt a new admiration and respect for him.

Ed Chappell walked up the steps to him one afternoon. "You got a crop there, mister."

"Looks that way," said Peter.

"I took a look. Pods are setting fine."

Peter sighed. "Blooming's nearly over," he said. "I'll hate to see the petals drop off."

"Well, I'd be glad to see 'em drop. You'll make a lot of money, if nothing happens."

Peter took out a bandana handkerchief and wiped his nose, and jiggled it sideways to stop an itch. "I'll be sorry when the smell stops," he said.

Then Ed made his reference to the night of the death. One of his eyes drooped secretly. "Found somebody to keep house for you?"

"I haven't looked," said Peter. "I haven't had time." There were lines of worry about his eyes. But who wouldn't worry, Ed thought, when a single shower could ruin his whole year's crop.

If the year and the weather had been manufactured for sweet peas, they couldn't have been better. The fog lay close to the ground in the mornings when the vines were pulled. When the great piles of vines lay safely on spread canvasses, the hot sun shone down and crisped the pods for the threshers. The neighbors watched the long cotton sacks filling with round black seeds, and they went home and tried to figure out how much money Peter would make on his tremendous crop. Clark DeWitt lost a good part of his following. The men decided to find out what Peter was going to plant next year if they had to follow him around. How did he know, for instance, that this year'd be good for sweet peas? He *must* have some kind of special knowledge.

When a man from the upper Salinas Valley goes to San Francisco on business or for a vacation, he takes a room in the Ramona Hotel. This is a nice arrangement, for in the lobby he can usually find someone from home. They can sit in the soft chairs of the lobby and talk about the Salinas Valley.

Ed Chappell went to San Francisco to meet his wife's cousin who was coming out from Ohio for a trip. The train was not due until the next morning. In the lobby of the Ramona, Ed looked for someone from the Salinas Valley, but he could see only strangers sitting in the soft chairs. He went out to a moving picture show. When he returned, he looked again for someone from home, and still there were only strangers. For a moment he considered glancing over the register, but it was quite late. He sat down to finish his cigar before he went to bed.

There was a commotion at the door. Ed saw the clerk motion with his hand. A bellhop ran out. Ed squirmed around in his chair to look. Outside a man was being helped out of a taxicab. The bellhop took him from the driver and guided him in the door. It was Peter Randall. His eyes were glassy, and his mouth open and wet. He had no hat on his mussed hair. Ed jumped up and strode over to him.

"Peter!"

Peter was batting helplessly at the bellhop. "Let me alone," he explained. "I'm all right. You let me alone, and I'll give you two bits."

Ed called again, "Peter!"

The glassy eyes turned slowly to him, and then Peter fell into his arms. "My old friend," he cried. "Ed Chappell, my old, good friend. What you doing here? Come up to my room and have a drink."

Ed set him back on his feet. "Sure I will," he said. "I'd like a little night-cap."

"Night-cap, hell. We'll go out and see a show, or something."

Ed helped him into the elevator and got him to his room. Peter dropped heavily to the bed and struggled up to a sitting position. "There's a bottle of whisky in the bathroom. Bring me a drink, too."

Ed brought out the bottle and the glasses. "What you doing, Peter, celebrating the crop? You must've made a pile of money."

Peter put out his palm and tapped it impressively with a forefinger. "Sure I made money—but it wasn't a bit better than gambling. It was just like straight gambling."

"But you got the money."

Peter scowled thoughtfully. "I might've lost my pants," he said. "The whole time, all the year, I been worrying. It was just like gambling."

"Well, you got it, anyway."

Peter changed the subject, then. "I been sick," he said.

"I been sick right in the taxicab. I just came from a fancy house on Van Ness Avenue," he explained apologetically, "I just had to come up to the city. I'd'a busted if I hadn't come up and got some of the vinegar out of my system."

Ed looked at him curiously. Peter's head was hanging loosely between his shoulders. His beard was draggled and rough. "Peter—" Ed began, "the night Emma—passed on, you said you was going to—change things."

Peter's swaying head rose up slowly. He stared owlishly at Ed Chappell. "She didn't die dead," he said thickly. "She won't let me do things. She's worried me all year about those peas." His eyes were wondering. "I don't know how she does it." Then he frowned. His palm came out, and he tapped it again. "But you mark, Ed Chappell, I won't wear that harness, and I damn well won't ever wear it. You remember that." His head dropped forward again. But in a moment he looked up. "I been drunk," he said seriously. "I been to fancy houses." He edged out confidentially toward Ed. His voice dropped to a heavy whisper. "But it's all right, I'll fix it. When I get back, you know what I'm going to do? I'm going to put in electric lights. Emma always wanted electric lights." He sagged sideways on the bed.

Ed Chappell stretched Peter out and undressed him before he went to his own room.

THE CHRYSANTHEMUMS

THE high gray-flannel fog of winter closed off the Salinas Valley from the sky and from all the rest of the world. On every side it sat like a lid on the mountains and made of the great valley a closed pot. On the broad, level land floor the gang plows bit deep and left the black earth shining like metal where the shares had cut. On the foothill ranches across the Salinas River, the yellow stubble fields seemed to be bathed in pale cold sunshine, but there was no sunshine in the valley now in December. The thick willow scrub along the river flamed with sharp and positive yellow leaves.

It was a time of quiet and of waiting. The air was cold and tender. A light wind blew up from the southwest so that the farmers were mildly hopeful of a good rain before long; but fog and rain do not go together.

Across the river, on Henry Allen's foothill ranch there was little work to be done, for the hay was cut and stored and the orchards were plowed up to receive the rain deeply when it should come. The cattle on the higher slopes were becoming shaggy and rough-coated.

Elisa Allen, working in her flower garden, looked down across the yard and saw Henry, her husband, talking to two men in business suits. The three of them stood by the tractor shed, each man with one foot on the side of the little Fordson. They smoked cigarettes and studied the machine as they talked.

Elisa watched them for a moment and then went back to her work. She was thirty-five. Her face was lean and strong and her eyes were as clear as water. Her figure looked blocked and heavy in her gardening costume, a man's black hat pulled low down over her eyes, clod-hopper shoes, a figured print dress almost completely covered by a big corduroy apron with four big pockets to hold the snips, the trowel and scratcher, the seeds and the knife she worked with. She wore heavy leather gloves to protect her hands while she worked.

She was cutting down the old year's chrysanthemum stalks with a pair of short and powerful scissors. She looked down toward the men by the tractor shed now and then. Her face was eager and mature and handsome; even her work with the scissors was over-eager, over-powerful. The chrysanthemum stems seemed too small and easy for her energy.

She brushed a cloud of hair out of her eyes with the back of her glove, and left a smudge of earth on her cheek in doing it. Behind her stood the neat white farm house with red geraniums close-banked around it as high as the windows. It was a hard-swept looking little house, with hard-polished windows, and a clean mud-mat on the front steps.

Elisa cast another glance toward the tractor shed. The strangers were getting into their Ford coupe. She took off a glove and put her strong fingers down into the forest of new green chrysanthemum sprouts that were growing around the old roots. She spread the leaves and looked down among the close-growing stems. No aphids were there, no sowbugs or snails or cutworms. Her terrier fingers destroyed such pests before they could get started.

Elisa started at the sound of her husband's voice. He had come near quietly, and he leaned over the wire fence that protected her flower garden from cattle and dogs and chickens.

"At it again," he said. "You've got a strong new crop coming."

Elisa straightened her back and pulled on the gardening glove again. "Yes. They'll be strong this coming year." In her tone and on her face there was a little smugness.

"You've got a gift with things," Henry observed. "Some of those yellow chrysanthemums you had this year were ten inches across. I wish you'd work out in the orchard and raise some apples that big."

Her eyes sharpened. "Maybe I could do it, too. I've a gift with things, all right. My mother had it. She could stick anything in the ground and make it grow. She said it was having planters' hands that knew how to do it."

"Well, it sure works with flowers," he said.

"Henry, who were those men you were talking to?"

"Why, sure, that's what I came to tell you. They were from the Western Meat Company. I sold those thirty head of three-year-old steers. Got nearly my own price, too."

"Good," she said. "Good for you."

"And I thought," he continued, "I thought how it's Saturday afternoon, and we might go into Salinas for dinner at a restaurant, and then to a picture show—to celebrate, you see."

"Good," she repeated. "Oh, yes. That will be good."

Henry put on his joking tone. "There's fights tonight. How'd you like to go to the fights?"

"Oh, no," she said breathlessly. "No, I wouldn't like fights."

"Just fooling, Elisa. We'll go to a movie. Let's see. It's two now. I'm going to take Scotty and bring down those steers from the hill. It'll take us maybe two hours. We'll go in town about five and have dinner at the Cominos Hotel. Like that?"

"Of course I'll like it. It's good to eat away from home."

"All right, then. I'll go get up a couple of horses."

She said, "I'll have plenty of time to transplant some of these sets, I guess."

She heard her husband calling Scotty down by the barn. And a little later she saw the two men ride up the pale yellow hillside in search of the steers.

There was a little square sandy bed kept for rooting the chrysanthemums. With her trowel she turned the soil over and over, and smoothed it and patted it firm. Then she dug ten parallel trenches to receive the sets. Back at the chrysanthemum bed she pulled out the little crisp shoots, trimmed off the leaves of each one with her scissors and laid it on a small orderly pile.

A squeak of wheels and plod of hoofs came from the road. Elisa looked up. The country road ran along the dense bank of willows and cottonwoods that bordered the river, and up this road came a curious vehicle, curiously drawn. It was an old spring-wagon, with a round canvas top on it like the cover of a prairie schooner. It was drawn by an old bay horse and a little gray-and-white burro. A big stubble-bearded man sat between the cover flaps and drove the crawling team. Underneath the wagon, between the hind wheels, a lean and rangy mongrel dog walked sedately. Words were painted on the canvas, in clumsy, crooked letters. "Pots, pans, knives, sisors, lawn mores, Fixed." Two rows of articles, and the triumphantly definitive "Fixed" below. The black paint had run down in little sharp points beneath each letter.

Elisa, squatting on the ground, watched to see the crazy, loose-jointed wagon pass by. But it didn't pass. It turned into the farm road in front of her house, crooked old wheels skirling and squeaking. The rangy dog darted from between the wheels and ran ahead. Instantly the two ranch shepherds flew out at him. Then all three stopped, and with stiff and quivering tails, with taut straight legs, with ambassadorial dignity, they slowly circled, sniffing daintily. The caravan pulled up to Elisa's wire fence and stopped. Now the newcomer dog, feeling out-numbered, lowered his tail and retired under the wagon with raised hackles and bared teeth.

The man on the wagon seat called out, "That's a bad dog in a fight when he gets started."

Elisa laughed. "I see he is. How soon does he generally get started?"

The man caught up her laughter and echoed it heartily. "Sometimes not for weeks and weeks," he said. He climbed stiffly down, over the wheel. The horse and the donkey drooped like unwatered flowers.

Elisa saw that he was a very big man. Although his hair and beard were graying, he did not look old. His worn black suit was wrinkled and spotted with grease. The laughter had disappeared from his face and eyes the moment his laughing voice ceased. His eyes were dark, and they were full of the brooding that gets in the eyes of teamsters and of sailors. The calloused hands he rested on the wire fence were cracked, and every crack was a black line. He took off his battered hat.

"I'm off my general road, ma'am," he said. "Does this dirt road cut over across the river to the Los Angeles highway?"

Elisa stood up and shoved the thick scissors in her apron pocket. "Well, yes, it does, but it winds around and then fords the river. I don't think your team could pull through the sand."

He replied with some asperity, "It might surprise you what them beasts can pull through."

"When they get started?" she asked.

He smiled for a second. "Yes. When they get started."

"Well," said Elisa, "I think you'll save time if you go back to the Salinas road and pick up the highway there."

He drew a big finger down the chicken wire and made

it sing. "I ain't in any hurry, ma'am. I go from Seattle to San Diego and back every year. Takes all my time. About six months each way. I aim to follow nice weather."

Elisa took off her gloves and stuffed them in the apron pocket with the scissors. She touched the under edge of her man's hat, searching for fugitive hairs. "That sounds like a nice kind of a way to live," she said.

He leaned confidentially over the fence. "Maybe you noticed the writing on my wagon. I mend pots and sharpen knives and scissors. You got any of them things to do?"

"Oh, no," she said quickly. "Nothing like that." Her eyes hardened with resistance.

"Scissors is the worst thing," he explained. "Most people just ruin scissors trying to sharpen 'em, but I know how. I got a special tool. It's a little bobbit kind of thing, and patented. But it sure does the trick."

"No. My scissors are all sharp."

"All right, then. Take a pot," he continued earnestly, "a bent pot, or a pot with a hole. I can make it like new so you don't have to buy no new ones. That's a saving for you."

"No," she said shortly. "I tell you I have nothing like that for you to do."

His face fell to an exaggerated sadness. His voice took on a whining undertone. "I ain't had a thing to do today. Maybe I won't have no supper tonight. You see I'm off my regular road. I know folks on the highway clear from Seattle to San Diego. They save their things for me to sharpen up because they know I do it so good and save them money."

"I'm sorry," Elisa said irritably. "I haven't anything for you to do."

His eyes left her face and fell to searching the ground. They roamed about until they came to the chrysanthemum bed where she had been working. "What's them plants, ma'am?"

The irritation and resistance melted from Elisa's face. "Oh, those are chysanthemums, giant whites and yellows. I raise them every year, bigger than anybody around here."

"Kind of a long-stemmed flower? Looks like a quick puff of colored smoke?" he asked.

"That's it. What a nice way to describe them."

"They smell kind of nasty till you get used to them," he said.

"It's a good bitter smell," she retorted, "not nasty at all."

He changed his tone quickly. "I like the smell myself."

"I had ten-inch blooms this year," she said.

The man leaned farther over the fence. "Look. I know a lady down the road a piece, has got the nicest garden you ever seen. Got nearly every kind of flower but no chrysantheums. Last time I was mending a copper-bottom washtub for her (that's a hard job but I do it good), she said to me, 'If you ever run acrost some nice chrysanthemums I wish you'd try to get me a few seeds.' That's what she told me."

Elisa's eyes grew alert and eager. "She couldn't have known much about chrysanthemums. You *can* raise them from seed, but it's much easier to root the little sprouts you see there."

"Oh," he said. "I s'pose I can't take none to her, then."

"Why yes you can," Elisa cried. "I can put some in damp sand, and you can carry them right along with you. They'll take root in the pot if you keep them damp. And then she can transplant them."

"She'd sure like to have some, ma'am. You say they're nice ones?"

"Beautiful," she said. "Oh, beautiful." Her eyes shone. She tore off the battered hat and shook out her dark pretty hair. "I'll put them in a flower pot, and you can take them right with you. Come into the yard."

While the man came through the picket gate Elisa ran excitedly along the geranium-bordered path to the back of the house. And she returned carrying a big red flower pot. The gloves were forgotten now. She kneeled on the ground by the starting bed and dug up the sandy soil with her fingers and scooped it into the bright new flower pot. Then she picked up the little pile of shoots she had prepared. With her strong fingers she pressed them into the sand and tamped around them with her knuckles. The man stood over her. "I'll tell you what to do," she said. "You remember so you can tell the lady."

"Yes, I'll try to remember."

"Well, look. These will take root in about a month. Then she must set them out, about a foot apart in good rich earth like this, see?" She lifted a handful of dark soil for him to look at. "They'll grow fast and tall. Now remember this: In July tell her to cut them down, about eight inches from the ground."

"Before they bloom?" he asked.

"Yes, before they bloom." Her face was tight with eagerness. "They'll grow right up again. About the last of September the buds will start."

She stopped and seemed perplexed. "It's the budding that takes the most care," she said hesitantly. "I don't know how to tell you." She looked deep into his eyes, searchingly. Her mouth opened a little, and she seemed to be listening. "I'll try to tell you," she said. "Did you ever hear of planting hands?"

"Can't say I have, ma'am."

"Well, I can only tell you what it feels like. It's when you're picking off the buds you don't want. Everything goes right down into your fingertips. You watch your fingers work. They do it themselves. You can feel how it is.

They pick and pick the buds. They never make a mistake. They're with the plant. Do you see? Your fingers and the plant. You can feel that, right up your arm. They know. They never make a mistake. You can feel it. When you're like that you can't do anything wrong. Do you see that? Can you understand that?"

She was kneeling on the ground looking up at him. Her breast swelled passionately.

The man's eyes narrowed. He looked away self-consciously. "Maybe I know," he said. "Sometimes in the night in the wagon there——"

Elisa's voice grew husky. She broke in on him, "I've never lived as you do, but I know what you mean. When the night is dark—why, the stars are sharp-pointed, and there's quiet. Why, you rise up and up! Every pointed star gets driven into your body. It's like that. Hot and sharp and—lovely."

Kneeling there, her hand went out toward his legs in the greasy black trousers. Her hesitant fingers almost touched the cloth. Then her hand dropped to the ground. She crouched low like a fawning dog.

He said, "It's nice, just like you say. Only when you don't have no dinner, it ain't."

She stood up then, very straight, and her face was ashamed. She held the flower pot out to him and placed it gently in his arms. "Here. Put it in your wagon, on the seat, where you can watch it. Maybe I can find something for you to do."

At the back of the house she dug in the can pile and found two old and battered aluminum saucepans. She carried them back and gave them to him. "Here, maybe you can fix these."

His manner changed. He became professional. "Good as new I can fix them." At the back of his wagon he set a little anvil, and out of an oily tool box dug a small machine hammer. Elisa came through the gate to watch him while he pounded out the dents in the kettles. His mouth grew sure and knowing. At a difficult part of the work he sucked his under-lip.

"You sleep right in the wagon?" Elisa asked.

"Right in the wagon, ma'am. Rain or shine I'm dry as a cow in there."

"It must be nice," she said. "It must be very nice. I wish women could do such things."

"It ain't the right kind of a life for a woman."

Her upper lip raised a little, showing her teeth. "How do you know? How can you tell?" she said.

"I don't know, ma'am," he protested. "Of course I don't know. Now here's your kettles, done. You don't have to buy no new ones."

"How much?"

"Oh, fifty cents'll do. I keep my prices down and my work good. That's why I have all them satisfied customers up and down the highway."

Elisa brought him a fifty-cent piece from the house and dropped it in his hand. "You might be surprised to have a rival some time. I can sharpen scissors, too. And I can beat the dents out of little pots. I could show you what a woman might do."

He put his hammer back in the oily box and shoved the little anvil out of sight. "It would be a lonely life for a woman, ma'am, and a scarey life, too, with animals creeping under the wagon all night." He climbed over the singletree, steadying himself with a hand on the burro's white rump. He settled himself in the seat, picked up the lines. "Thank you kindly, ma'am," he said. "I'll do like you told me; I'll go back and catch the Salinas road."

"Mind," she called, "if you're long in getting there, keep the sand damp."

"Sand, ma'am? . . . Sand? Oh, sure. You mean around

the chrysantheums. Sure I will." He clucked his tongue. The beasts leaned luxuriously into their collars. The mongrel dog took his place between the back wheels. The wagon turned and crawled out the entrance road and back the way it had come, along the river.

Elisa stood in front of her wire fence watching the slow progress of the caravan. Her shoulders were straight, her head thrown back, her eyes half-closed, so that the scene came vaguely into them. Her lips moved silently, forming the words "Good-bye—good-bye." Then she whispered, "That's a bright direction. There's a glowing there." The sound of her whisper startled her. She shook herself free and looked about to see whether anyone had been listening. Only the dogs had heard. They lifted their heads toward her from their sleeping in the dust, and then stretched out their chins and settled asleep again. Elisa turned and ran hurriedly into the house.

In the kitchen she reached behind the stove and felt the water tank. It was full of hot water from the noonday cooking. In the bathroom she tore off her soiled clothes and flung them into the corner. And then she scrubbed herself with a little block of pumice, legs and thighs, loins and chest and arms, until her skin was scratched and red. When she had dried herself she stood in front of a mirror in her bedroom and looked at her body. She tightened her stomach and threw out her chest. She turned and looked over her shoulder at her back.

After a while she began to dress, slowly. She put on her newest underclothing and her nicest stockings and the dress which was the symbol of her prettiness. She worked carefully on her hair, penciled her eyebrows and rouged her lips.

Before she was finished she heard the little thunder of hoofs and the shouts of Henry and his helper as they drove the red steers into the corral. She heard the gate bang shut and set herself for Henry's arrival.

His step sounded on the porch. He entered the house calling, "Elisa, where are you?"

"In my room, dressing. I'm not ready. There's hot water for your bath. Hurry up. It's getting late."

When she heard him splashing in the tub, Elisa laid his dark suit on the bed, and shirt and socks and tie beside it. She stood his polished shoes on the floor beside the bed. Then she went to the porch and sat primly and stiffly down. She looked toward the river road where the willow-line was still yellow with frosted leaves so that under the high gray fog they seemed a thin band of sunshine. This was the only color in the gray afternoon. She sat unmoving for a long time. Her eyes blinked rarely.

Henry came banging out of the door, shoving his tie inside his vest as he came. Elisa stiffened and her face grew tight. Henry stopped short and looked at her. "Why —why, Elisa. You look so nice!"

"Nice? You think I look nice? What do you mean by 'nice'?"

Henry blundered on. "I don't know. I mean you look different, strong and happy."

"I am strong? Yes, strong. What do you mean 'strong'?"

He looked bewildered. "You're playing some kind of a game," he said helplessly. "It's a kind of a play. You look strong enough to break a calf over your knee, happy enough to eat it like a watermelon."

For a second she lost her rigidity. "Henry! Don't talk like that. You didn't know what you said." She grew complete again. "I'm strong," she boasted. "I never knew before how strong."

Henry looked down toward the tractor shed, and when he brought his eyes back to her, they were his own again.

"I'll get out the car. You can put on your coat while I'm starting."

Elisa went into the house. She heard him drive to the gate and idle down his motor, and then she took a long time to put on her hat. She pulled it here and pressed it there. When Henry turned the motor off she slipped into her coat and went out.

The little roadster bounced along on the dirt road by the river, raising the birds and driving the rabbits into the brush. Two cranes flapped heavily over the willow-line and dropped into the river-bed.

Far ahead on the road Elisa saw a dark speck. She knew.

She tried not to look as they passed it, but her eyes would not obey. She whispered to herself sadly, "He might have thrown them off the road. That wouldn't have been much trouble, not very much. But he kept the pot," she explained. "He had to keep the pot. That's why he couldn't get them off the road."

The roadster turned a bend and she saw the caravan ahead. She swung full around toward her husband so she could not see the little covered wagon and the mismatched team as the car passed them.

In a moment it was over. The thing was done. She did not look back.

She said loudly, to be heard above the motor, "It will be good, tonight, a good dinner."

"Now you're changed again," Henry complained. He took one hand from the wheel and patted her knee. "I ought to take you in to dinner oftener. It would be good for both of us. We get so heavy out on the ranch."

"Henry," she asked, "could we have wine at dinner?"

"Sure we could. Say! That will be fine."

She was silent for a while; then she said, "Henry, at

those prize fights, do the men hurt each other very much?"

"Sometimes a little, not often. Why?"

"Well, I've read how they break noses, and blood runs down their chests. I've read how the fighting gloves get heavy and soggy with blood."

He looked around at her. "What's the matter, Elisa? I didn't know you read things like that." He brought the car to a stop, then turned to the right over the Salinas River bridge.

"Do any women ever go to the fights?" she asked.

"Oh, sure, some. What's the matter, Elisa? Do you want to go? I don't think you'd like it, but I'll take you if you really want to go."

She relaxed limply in the seat. "Oh, no. No. I don't want to go. I'm sure I don't." Her face was turned away from him. "It will be enough if we can have wine. It will be plenty." She turned up her coat collar so he could not see that she was crying weakly—like an old woman.

◈◈◈◈◈◈◈◈◈◈◈◈◈◈◈◈◈◈◈◈◈◈◈◈◈◈◈◈◈◈◈◈◈◈◈◈

FROM

The Pastures of Heaven

TULARECITO

MOLLY MORGAN

PAT HUMBERT'S

Three stories of dwellers in a seemingly happy California valley, part of a recurring pattern in this episodic novel that tells of the innocent breaking-in upon and inadvertent twisting of lives by the newly arrived Munroe family. First published in 1932.

◈◈◈◈◈◈◈◈◈◈◈◈◈◈◈◈◈◈◈◈◈◈◈◈◈◈◈◈◈◈◈◈◈◈◈◈

TULARECITO

THE origin of Tularecito is cast in obscurity, while his discovery is a myth which the folks of the Pastures of Heaven refuse to believe, just as they refuse to believe in ghosts.

Franklin Gomez had a hired man, a Mexican Indian named Pancho, and nothing else. Once every three months, Pancho took his savings and drove into Monterey to confess his sins, to do his penance, and be shriven and to get drunk, in the order named. If he managed to stay out of jail, Pancho got into his buggy and went to sleep when the saloons closed. The horse pulled him home, arriving just before daylight, and in time for Pancho to have breakfast and go to work. Pancho was always asleep when he arrived; that is why he created so much interest on the ranch when, one morning, he drove into the corral at a gallop, not only awake, but shouting at the top of his voice.

Franklin Gomez put on his clothes and went out to interview his ranch hand. The story, when it was stretched out of its tangle of incoherencies, was this: Pancho had been driving home, very sober as always. Up near the Blake place, he heard a baby crying in the sage brush beside the road. He stopped the horse and went to investigate, for one did not often come upon babies like that. And sure enough he found a tiny child lying in a clear place in the sage. It was about three months old by the size of it, Pancho thought. He picked it up and lighted a match to see just what kind of a thing he had found, when

73

—horror of horrors!—the baby winked maliciously and said in a deep voice, "Look! I have very sharp teeth." Pancho did not look. He flung the thing from him, leaped into his buggy and galloped for home, beating the old horse with the butt end of the whip and howling like a dog.

Franklin Gomez pulled his whiskers a good deal. Pancho's nature, he considered, was not hysterical even under the influence of liquor. The fact that he had awakened at all rather proved there must be something in the brush. In the end, Franklin Gomez had a horse saddled, rode out and brought in the baby. It did not speak again for nearly three years; nor, on inspection, did it have any teeth, but neither of these facts convinced Pancho that it did not make that first ferocious remark.

The baby had short, chubby arms, and long, loose-jointed legs. Its large head sat without interval of neck between deformedly broad shoulders. The baby's flat face, together with its peculiar body, caused it automatically to be named Tularecito, Little Frog, although Franklin Gomez often called it Coyote, "For," he said, "there is in this boy's face that ancient wisdom one finds in the face of a coyote."

"But surely the legs, the arms, the shoulders, Señor," Pancho reminded him. And so Tularecito the name remained. It was never discovered who abandoned the misshapen little creature. Franklin Gomez accepted him into the patriarchate of his ranch, and Pancho took care of him. Pancho, however, could never lose a little fear of the boy. Neither the years nor a rigorous penance eradicated the effect of Tularecito's first utterance.

The boy grew rapidly, but after the fifth year his brain did not grow any more. At six Tularecito could do the work of a grown man. The long fingers of his hands were more dexterous and stronger than most men's fingers. On the ranch, they made use of the fingers of Tularecito. Hard knots could not long defy him. He had planting hands, tender fingers that never injured a young plant nor bruised the surfaces of a grafting limb. His merciless fingers could wring the head from a turkey gobbler without effort. Also Tularecito had an amusing gift. With his thumbnail he could carve remarkably correct animals from sandstone. Franklin Gomez kept many little effigies of coyotes and mountain lions, of chickens and squirrels, about the house. A two-foot image of a hovering hawk hung by wires from the ceiling of the dining room. Pancho, who had never quite considered the boy human, put his gift for carving in a growing category of diabolical traits definitely traceable to his supernatural origin.

While the people of the Pastures of Heaven did not believe in the diabolic origin of Tularecito, nevertheless they were uncomfortable in his presence. His eyes were ancient and dry; there was something troglodytic about his face. The great strength of his body and his strange and obscure gifts set him apart from other children and made men and women uneasy.

Only one thing could provoke anger in Tularecito. If any person, man, woman or child, handled carelessly or broke one of the products of his hands, he became furious. His eyes shone and he attacked the desecrator murderously. On three occasions when this had happened, Franklin Gomez tied his hands and feet and left him alone until his ordinary good nature returned.

Tularecito did not go to school when he was six. For five years thereafter, the county truant officer and the school superintendent sporadically worked on the case. Franklin Gomez agreed that he should go to school and even went so far as to start him off several times, but Tularecito never got there. He was afraid that school might prove unpleasant, so he simply disappeared for a day or so. It was not until the boy was eleven, with the shoulders of a weight lifter and the hands and forearms of a strangler that the concerted forces of the law gathered him in and put him in school.

As Franklin Gomez had known, Tularecito learned nothing at all, but immediately he gave evidence of a new gift. He could draw as well as he could carve in sandstone. When Miss Martin, the teacher, discovered his ability, she gave him a piece of chalk and told him to make a procession of animals around the blackboard. Tularecito worked long after school was dismissed, and the next morning an astounding parade was shown on the walls. All of the animals Tularecito had ever seen were there; all the birds of the hills flew above them. A rattlesnake crawled behind a cow; a coyote, his brush proudly aloft, sniffed at the heels of a pig. There were tomcats and goats, turtles and gophers, every one of them drawn with astonishing detail and veracity.

Miss Martin was overcome with the genius of Tularecito. She praised him before the class and gave a short lecture about each one of the creatures he had drawn. In her own mind she considered the glory that would come to her for discovering and fostering this genius.

"I can make lots more," Tularecito informed her.

Miss Martin patted his broad shoulder. "So you shall," she said. "You shall draw every day. It is a great gift that God has given you." Then she realized the importance of what she had just said. She leaned over and looked searchingly into his hard eyes while she repeated slowly, "It is a *great gift* that God has given you." Miss Martin glanced up at the clock and announced crisply, "Fourth grade arithmetic—at the board."

The fourth grade struggled out, seized erasers and began to remove the animals to make room for their numbers. They had not made two sweeps when Tularecito charged. It was a great day. Miss Martin, aided by the whole school, could not hold him down, for the enraged Tularecito had the strength of a man, and a madman at that. The ensuing battle wrecked the schoolroom, tipped over the desks, spilled rivers of ink, hurled bouquets of Teacher's flowers about the room. Miss Martin's clothes were torn to streamers, and the big boys, on whom the burden of the battle fell, were bruised and battered cruelly. Tularecito fought with hands, feet, teeth and head. He admitted no honorable rules and in the end he won. The whole school, with Miss Martin guarding its rear, fled from the building, leaving the enraged Tularecito in possession. When they were gone, he locked the door, wiped the blood out of his eyes and set to work to repair the animals that had been destroyed.

That night Miss Martin called on Franklin Gomez and demanded that the boy be whipped.

Gomez shrugged. "You really wish me to whip him, Miss Martin?"

The teacher's face was scratched; her mouth was bitter. "I certainly do," she said. "If you had seen what he did today, you wouldn't blame me. I tell you he needs a lesson."

Gomez shrugged again and called Tularecito from the bunk house. He took a heavy quirt down from the wall. Then, while Tularecito smiled blandly at Miss Martin, Franklin Gomez beat him severely across the back. Miss Martin's hand made involuntary motions of beating. When it was done, Tularecito felt himself over with long, exploring fingers, and still smiling, went back to the bunk house.

Miss Martin had watched the end of the punishment with horror. "Why, he's an animal," she cried. "It was just like whipping a dog."

Franklin Gomez permitted a slight trace of his con- ·

tempt for her to show on his face. "A dog would have cringed," he said. "Now you have seen, Miss Martin. You say he is an animal, but surely he is a good animal. You told him to make pictures and then you destroyed his pictures. Tularecito does not like that—"

Miss Martin tried to break in, but he hurried on.

"This Little Frog should not be going to school. He can work; he can do marvelous things with his hands, but he cannot learn to do the simple little things of the school. He is not crazy; he is one of those whom God has not quite finished.

"I told the Superintendent these things, and he said the law required Tularecito to go to school until he is eighteen years old. That is seven years from now. For seven years my Little Frog will sit in the first grade because the law says he must. It is out of my hands."

"He ought to be locked up," Miss Martin broke in. "This creature is dangerous. You should have seen him today."

"No, Miss Martin, he should be allowed to go free. He is not dangerous. No one can make a garden as he can. No one can milk so swiftly nor so gently. He is a good boy. He can break a mad horse without riding it; he can train a dog without whipping it, but the law says he must sit in the first grade repeating 'C-A-T, cat' for seven years. If he had been dangerous he could easily have killed me when I whipped him."

Miss Martin felt that there were things she did not understand and she hated Franklin Gomez because of them. She felt that she had been mean and he generous. When she got to school the next morning, she found Tularecito before her. Every possible space on the wall was covered with animals.

"You see?" he said, beaming over his shoulder at her.

"Lots more. And I have a book with others yet, but there is no room for them on the wall."

Miss Martin did not erase the animals. Class work was done on paper, but at the end of the term she resigned her position, giving ill health as her reason.

Miss Morgan, the new teacher, was very young and very pretty; too young and dangerously pretty, the aged men of the valley thought. Some of the boys in the upper grades were seventeen years old. It was seriously doubted that a teacher so young and so pretty could keep any kind of order in the school.

She brought with her a breathless enthusiasm for her trade. The school was astounded, for it had been used to ageing spinsters whose faces seemed to reflect consistently tired feet. Miss Morgan enjoyed teaching and made school an exciting place where unusual things happened.

From the first Miss Morgan was vastly impressed with Tularecito. She knew all about him, had read books and taken courses about him. Having heard about the fight, she laid off a border around the top of the blackboards for him to fill with animals, and, when he had completed his parade, she bought with her own money a huge drawing pad and a soft pencil. After that he did not bother with spelling. Every day he labored over his drawing board, and every afternoon presented the teacher with a marvelously wrought animal. She pinned his drawings to the schoolroom wall above the blackboards.

The pupils received Miss Morgan's innovations with enthusiasm. Classes became exciting, and even the boys who had made enviable reputations through teacher-baiting, grew less interested in the possible burning of the schoolhouse.

Miss Morgan introduced a practice that made the pupils adore her. Every afternoon she read to them for half an hour. She read by installments, *Ivanhoe* and *The Talisman;* fishing stories by Zane Grey, hunting stories of James Oliver Curwood; *The Sea Wolf, The Call of the Wild*—not baby stories about the little red hen and the fox and geese, but exciting, grown-up stories.

Miss Morgan read well. Even the tougher boys were won over until they never played hooky for fear of missing an installment, until they leaned forward gasping with interest.

But Tularecito continued his careful drawing, only pausing now and then to blink at the teacher and to try to understand how these distant accounts of the actions of strangers could be of interest to anyone. To him they were chronicles of actual events—else why were they written down. The stories were like the lessons. Tularecito did not listen to them.

After a time Miss Morgan felt that she had been humoring the older children too much. She herself liked fairy tales, liked to think of whole populations who believed in fairies and consequently saw them. Within the safe circle of her tried and erudite acquaintance, she often said that "part of America's cultural starvation was due to its boorish and superstitious denial of the existence of fairies." For a time she devoted the afternoon half hour to fairy tales..

Now a change came over Tularecito. Gradually, as Miss Morgan read about elves and brownies, fairies, pixies, and changelings, his interest centered and his busy pencil lay idly in his hand. Then she read about gnomes, and their lives and habits, and he dropped his pencil altogether and leaned toward the teacher to intercept her words.

After school Miss Morgan walked half a mile to the farm where she boarded. She liked to walk the way alone, cutting off thistle heads with a switch, or throwing stones into the brush to make the quail roar up. She thought she should get a bounding, inquisitive dog that could share her excitements, could understand the glamour of holes in the ground, and scattering pawsteps on dry leaves, of strange melancholy bird whistles and the gay smells that came secretly out of the earth.

One afternoon Miss Morgan scrambled high up the side of a chalk cliff to carve her initials on the white plane. On the way up she tore her finger on a thorn, and, instead of initials, she scratched: "Here I have been and left this part of me," and pressed her bloody finger against the absorbent chalk rock.

That night, in a letter, she wrote: "After the bare requisites to living and reproducing, man wants most to leave some record of himself, a proof, perhaps, that he has really existed. He leaves his proof on wood, on stone or on the lives of other people. This deep desire exists in everyone, from the boy who writes dirty words in a public toilet to the Buddha who etches his image in the race mind. Life is so unreal. I think that we seriously doubt that we exist and go about trying to prove that we do." She kept a copy of the letter.

On the afternoon when she had read about the gnomes, as she walked home, the grasses beside the road threshed about for a moment and the ugly head of Tularecito appeared.

"Oh! You frightened me," Miss Morgan cried. "You shouldn't pop up like that."

Tularecito stood up and smiled bashfully while he whipped his hat against his thigh. Suddenly Miss Morgan felt fear rising in her. The road was deserted—she had read stories of half-wits. With difficulty she mastered her trembling voice.

"What—what is it you want?"

Tularecito smiled more broadly and whipped harder with his hat.

"Were you just lying there, or do you want something?"

The boy struggled to speak, and then relapsed into his protective smile.

"Well, if you don't want anything, I'll go on." She was really prepared for flight.

Tularecito struggled again. "About those people—"

"What people?" she demanded shrilly. "About what people?"

"About those people in the book—"

Miss Morgan laughed with relief until she felt that her hair was coming loose on the back of her head. "You mean—you mean—gnomes?"

Tularecito nodded.

"What do you want to know about them?"

"I never saw any," said Tularecito. His voice neither rose nor fell, but continued on one low note.

"Why, few people do see them, I think."

"But I knew about them."

Miss Morgan's eyes squinted with interest. "You did? Who told you about them?"

"Nobody."

"You never saw them, and no one told you? How could you know about them then?"

"I just knew. Heard them, maybe. I knew them in the book all right."

Miss Morgan thought: "Why should I deny gnomes to this queer, unfinished child? Wouldn't his life be richer and happier if he did believe in them? And what harm could it possibly do?"

"Have you ever looked for them?" she asked.

"No, I never looked. I just knew. But I will look now."

Miss Morgan found herself charmed with the situation.

Here was paper on which to write, here was a cliff on which to carve. She could carve a lovely story that would be far more real than a book story ever could. "Where will you look?" she asked.

"I'll dig in holes," said Tularecito soberly.

"But the gnomes only come out at night, Tularecito. You must watch for them in the night. And you must come and tell me if you find any. Will you do that?"

"I'll come," he agreed.

She left him staring after her. All the way home she pictured him searching in the night. The picture pleased her. He might even find the gnomes, might live with them and talk to them. With a few suggestive words she had been able to make his life unreal and very wonderful, and separated from the stupid lives about him. She deeply envied him his searching.

In the evening Tularecito put on his coat and took up a shovel. Old Pancho came upon him as he was leaving the tool shed. "Where goest thou, Little Frog?" he asked.

Tularecito shifted his feet restlessly at the delay. "I go out into the dark. Is that a new thing?"

"But why takest thou the shovel? Is there gold, perhaps?"

The boy's face grew hard with the seriousness of his purpose. "I go to dig for the little people who live in the earth."

Now Pancho was filled with horrified excitement. "Do not go, Little Frog! Listen to your old friend, your father in God, and do not go! Out in the sage I found thee and saved thee from the devils, thy relatives. Thou art a little brother of Jesus now. Go not back to thine own people! Listen to an old man, Little Frog!"

Tularecito stared hard at the ground and drilled his old thoughts with this new information. "Thou hast said they are my people," he exclaimed. "I am not like the others at the school or here. I know that. I have loneliness for my own people who live deep in the cool earth. When I pass a squirrel hole, I wish to crawl into it and hide myself. My own people are like me, and they have called me. I must go home to them, Pancho."

Pancho stepped back and held up crossed fingers. "Go back to the devil, thy father, then. I am not good enough to fight this evil. It would take a saint. But see! At least I make the sign against thee and against all thy race." He drew the cross of protection in the air in front of him.

Tularecito smiled sadly, and turning, trudged off into the hills.

The heart of Tularecito gushed with joy at his homecoming. All his life he had been an alien, a lonely outcast, and now he was going home. As always, he heard the voices of the earth—the far-off clang of cow bells, the muttering of disturbed quail, the little whine of a coyote who would not sing this night, the nocturnes of a million insects. But Tularecito was listening for another sound, the movement of two-footed creatures, and the hushed voices of the hidden people.

Once he stopped and called, "My father, I have come home," and he heard no answer. Into squirrel holes he whispered, "Where are you, my people? It is only Tularecito come home." But there was no reply. Worse, he had no feeling that the gnomes were near. He knew that a doe and fawn were feeding near him; he knew a wildcat was stalking a rabbit behind a bush, although he could not see them, but from the gnomes he had no message.

A sugar-moon arose out of the hills.

"Now the animals will come out to feed," Tularecito said in the papery whisper of the half-witless. "Now the people will come out, too."

The brush stopped at the edge of a little valley and an

orchard took its place. The trees were thick with leaves, and the land finely cultivated. It was Bert Munroe's orchard. Often, when the land was deserted and ghost-ridden, Tularecito had come here in the night to lie on the ground under the trees and pick the stars with gentle fingers.

The moment he walked into the orchard he knew he was nearing home. He could not hear them, but he knew the gnomes were near. Over and over he called to them, but they did not come.

"Perhaps they do not like the moonlight," he said.

At the foot of a large peach tree he dug his hole—three feet across and very deep. All night he worked on it, stopping to listen awhile and then digging deeper and deeper into the cool earth. Although he heard nothing, he was positive that he was nearing them. Only when the daylight came did he give up and retire into the bushes to sleep.

In midmorning Bert Munroe walked out to look at a coyote trap and found the hole at the foot of the tree. "What the devil!" he said. "Some kids must have been digging a tunnel. That's dangerous! It'll cave in on them, or somebody will fall into it and get hurt." He walked back to the house, got a shovel and filled up the hole.

"Manny," he said to his youngest boy, "you haven't been digging in the orchard, have you?"

"Uh-uh!" said Manny.

"Well, do you know who has?"

"Uh-uh!" said Manny.

"Well, somebody dug a deep hole out there. It's dangerous. You tell the boys not to dig or they'll get caved in."

The dark came and Tularecito walked out of the brush to dig in his hole again. When he found it filled up, he growled savagely, but then his thought changed and he laughed. "The people were here," he said happily. "They didn't know who it was, and they were frightened. They filled up the hole the way a gopher does. This time I'll hide, and when they come to fill the hole, I'll tell them who I am. Then they will love me."

And Tularecito dug out the hole and made it much deeper than before, because much of the dirt was loose. Just before daylight, he retired into the brush at the edge of the orchard and lay down to watch.

Bert Munroe walked out before breakfast to look at his trap again, and again he found the open hole. "The little devils!" he cried. "They're keeping it up, are they? I'll bet Manny *is* in it after all."

He studied the hole for a moment and then began to push dirt into it with the side of his foot. A savage growl spun him around. Tularecito came charging down upon him, leaping like a frog on his long legs, and swinging his shovel like a club.

When Jimmie Munroe came to call his father to breakfast, he found him lying on the pile of dirt. He was bleeding at the mouth and forehead. Shovelfuls of dirt came flying out of the pit.

Jimmie thought someone had killed his father and was getting ready to bury him. He ran home in a frenzy of terror, and by telephone summoned a band of neighbors.

Half a dozen men crept up on the pit. Tularecito struggled like a wounded lion, and held his own until they struck him on the head with his own shovel. Then they tied him up and took him in to jail.

In Salinas a medical board examined the boy. When the doctors asked him questions, he smiled blandly at them and did not answer. Franklin Gomez told the board what he knew and asked the custody of him.

"We really can't do it, Mr. Gomez," the judge said

finally. "You say he is a good boy. Just yesterday he tried to kill a man. You must see that we cannot let him go loose. Sooner or later he will succeed in killing someone."

After a short deliberation, he committed Tularecito to the asylum for the criminal insane at Napa.

(Chapter IV)

MOLLY MORGAN

MOLLY MORGAN got off the train in Salinas and
waited three quarters of an hour for the bus. The
big automobile was empty except for the driver and
Molly.

"I've never been to the Pastures of Heaven, you know,"
she said. "Is it far from the main road?"

"About three miles," said the driver.

"Will there be a car to take me into the valley?"

"No, not unless you're met."

"But how do people get in there?"

The driver ran over the flattened body of a jack rabbit
with apparent satisfaction. "I only hit 'em when they're
dead," he apologized. "In the dark, when they get caught
in the lights, I try to miss 'em."

"Yes, but how am I going to get into the Pastures of
Heaven?"

"I dunno. Walk, I guess. Most people walk if they ain't
met."

When he set her down at the entrance to the dirt side-
road, Molly Morgan grimly picked up her suitcase and
marched toward the draw in the hills. An old Ford truck
squeaked up beside her.

"Goin' into the valley, ma'am?"

"Oh—yes, yes, I am."

"Well, get in, then. Needn't be scared. I'm Pat Humbert. I got a place in the Pastures."

Molly surveyed the grimy man and acknowledged his

introduction. "I'm the new schoolteacher, I mean, I think I am. Do you know where Mr. Whiteside lives?"

"Sure, I go right by there. He's clerk of the board. I'm on the school board myself, you know. We wondered what you'd look like." Then he grew embarrassed at what he had said, and flushed under his coating of dirt. " 'Course I mean what you'd *be* like. Last teacher we had gave a good deal of trouble. She was all right, but she was sick—I mean, sick and nervous. Finally quit because she was sick."

Molly picked at the fingertips of her gloves. "My letter says I'm to call on Mr. Whiteside. Is he all right? I don't mean that. I mean—is he—what kind of a man is he?"

"Oh, you'll get along with him all right. He's a fine old man. Born in that house he lives in. Been to college, too. He's a good man. Been clerk of the board for over twenty years."

When he put her down in front of the big old house of John Whiteside, she was really frightened. "Now it's coming," she said to herself. "But there's nothing to be afraid of. He can't do anything to me." Molly was only nineteen. She felt that this moment of interview for her first job was a tremendous inch in her whole existence.

The walk up to the door did not reassure her, for the path lay between tight little flower beds hedged in with clipped box, seemingly planted with the admonition, "Now grow and multiply, but don't grow too high, nor multiply too greatly, and above all things, keep out of this path!" There was a hand on those flowers, a guiding and a correcting hand. The large white house was very dignified. Venetian blinds of yellow wood were tilted down to keep out the noon sun. Halfway up the path she came in sight of the entrance. There was a veranda as broad and warm and welcoming as an embrace. Through her mind flew the thought, "Surely you can tell the hospitality of a house by its entrance. Suppose it had a little door and no porch." But in spite of the welcoming of the wide steps and the big doorway, her timidities clung to her when she rang the bell. The big door opened, and a large, comfortable woman stood smiling at Molly.

"I hope you're not selling something," said Mrs. Whiteside. "I never want to buy anything and I always do, and then I'm mad."

Molly laughed. She felt suddenly very happy. Until that moment she hadn't known how frightened she really was. "Oh, no," she cried. "I'm the new schoolteacher. My letter says I'm to interview Mr. Whiteside. Can I see him?"

"Well, it's noon, and he's just finishing his dinner. Did you have dinner?"

"Oh, of course. I mean, no."

Mrs. Whiteside chuckled and stood aside for her to enter. "Well, I'm glad you're sure." She led Molly into a large dining room, lined with mahogany, glass-fronted dish closets. The square table was littered with the dishes of a meal. "Why, John must have finished and gone. Sit down, young woman. I'll bring back the roast."

"Oh, no. Really, thank you, no, I'll just talk to Mr. Whiteside and then go along."

"Sit down. You'll need nourishment to face John."

"Is—is he very stern, with new teachers, I mean?"

"Well," said Mrs. Whiteside. "That depends. If they haven't had their dinner, he's a regular bear. He shouts at them. But when they've just got up from the table, he's only just fierce."

Molly laughed happily. "You have children," she said. "Oh, you've raised lots of children—and you like them."

Mrs. Whiteside scowled. "One child raised me. Raised me right through the roof. It was too hard on me. He's out raising cows now, poor devils. I don't think I raised him very high."

When Molly had finished eating, Mrs. Whiteside threw open a side door and called, "John, here's someone to see you." She pushed Molly through the doorway into a room that was a kind of a library, for big bookcases were loaded with thick, old, comfortable books, all filigreed in gold. And it was a kind of a sitting room. There was a fireplace of brick with a mantel of little red tile bricks and the most extraordinary vases on the mantel. Hung on a nail over the mantel, slung really, like a rifle on a shoulder strap, was a huge meerschaum pipe in the Jaeger fashion. Big leather chairs with leather tassels hanging to them, stood about the fireplace, all of them patent rocking chairs with the kind of springs that chant when you rock them. And lastly, the room was a kind of an office, for there was an old-fashioned roll-top desk, and behind it sat John Whiteside. When he looked up, Molly saw that he had at once the kindest and the sternest eyes she had ever seen, and the whitest hair, too. Real blue-white, silky hair, a great duster of it.

"I am Mary Morgan," she began formally.

"Oh, yes, Miss Morgan, I've been expecting you. Won't you sit down?"

She sat in one of the big rockers, and the springs cried with sweet pain. "I love these chairs," she said. "We used to have one when I was a little girl." Then she felt silly. "I've come to interview you about this position. My letter said to do that."

"Don't be so tense, Miss Morgan. I've interviewed every teacher we've had for years. And," he said, smiling, "I still don't know how to go about it."

"Oh—I'm glad, Mr. Whiteside. I never asked for a job before. I was really afraid of it."

"Well, Miss Mary Morgan, as near as I can figure, the

purpose of this interview is to give me a little knowledge of your past and of the kind of person you are. I'm supposed to know something about you when you've finished. And now that you know my purpose, I suppose you'll be self-conscious and anxious to give a good impression. Maybe if you just tell me a little about yourself, everything'll be all right. Just a few words about the kind of girl you are, and where you came from."

Molly nodded quickly. "Yes, I'll try to do that, Mr. Whiteside," and she dropped her mind back into the past.

There was the old, squalid, unpainted house with its wide back porch and the round washtubs leaning against the rail. High in the great willow tree her two brothers, Joe and Tom, crashed about crying, "Now I'm an eagle." "I'm a parrot." "Now I'm an old chicken." "Watch me!"

The screen door on the back porch opened, and their mother leaned tiredly out. Her hair would not lie smoothly no matter how much she combed it. Thick strings of it hung down beside her face. Her eyes were always a little red, and her hands and wrists painfully cracked. "Tom, Joe," she called. "You'll get hurt up there. Don't worry me so, boys! Don't you love your mother at all?" The voices in the tree were hushed. The shrieking spirits of the eagle and the old chicken were drenched in self-reproach. Molly sat in the dust, wrapping a rag around a stick and doing her best to imagine it a tall lady in a dress. "Molly, come in and stay with your mother. I'm so tired today."

Molly stood up the stick in the deep dust. "You, miss," she whispered fiercely. "You'll get whipped on your bare bottom when I come back." Then she obediently went into the house.

Her mother sat in a straight chair in the kitchen. "Draw up, Molly. Just sit with me for a little while. Love me, Molly! Love your mother a little bit. You are mother's good little girl, aren't you?" Molly squirmed on her chair. "Don't you love your mother, Molly?"

The little girl was very miserable. She knew her mother would cry in a moment, and then she would be compelled to stroke the stringy hair. Both she and her brothers knew they should love their mother. She did everything for them. They were ashamed that they hated to be near her, but they couldn't help it. When she called to them and they were not in sight, they pretended not to hear, and crept away, talking in whispers.

"Well, to begin with,•we were very poor," Molly said to John Whiteside. "I guess we were really poverty-stricken. I had two brothers a little older than I. My father was a traveling salesman, but even so, my mother had to work. She worked terribly hard for us."

About once in every six months a great event occurred. In the morning the mother crept silently out of the bedroom. Her hair was brushed as smoothly as it could be; her eyes sparkled, and she looked happy and almost pretty. She whispered, "Quiet, children! Your father's home."

Molly and her brothers sneaked out of the house, but even in the yard they talked in excited whispers. The news traveled quickly about the neighborhood. Soon the yard was filled with whispering children. "They say their father's home." "Is your father really home?" "Where's he been this time?" By noon there were a dozen children in the yard, standing in expectant little groups, cautioning one another to be quiet.

About noon the screen door on the porch sprang open and whacked against the wall. Their father leaped out. "Hi," he yelled. "Hi, kids!" Molly and her brothers flung themselves upon him and hugged his legs, while he plucked them off and hurled them into the air like kittens.

Mrs. Morgan fluttered about, clucking with excitement "Children, children. Don't muss your father's clothes."

The neighbor children threw handsprings and wrestled and shrieked with joy. It was better than any holiday.

"Wait till you see," their father cried. "Wait till you see what I brought you. It's a secret now." And when the hysteria had quieted a little he carried his suitcase out on the porch and opened it. There were presents such as no one had ever seen, mechanical toys unknown before—tin bugs that crawled, dancing wooden niggers and astounding steam shovels that worked in sand. There were superb glass marbles with bears and dogs right in their centres. He had something for everyone, several things for everyone. It was all the great holidays packed into one.

Usually it was midafternoon before the children became calm enough not to shriek occasionally. But eventually George Morgan sat on the steps, and they all gathered about while he told his adventures. This time he had been to Mexico while there was a revolution. Again he had gone to Honolulu, had seen the volcano and had himself ridden on a surfboard. Always there were cities and people, strange people; always adventures and a hundred funny incidents, funnier than anything they had ever heard. It couldn't all be told at one time. After school they had to gather to hear more and more. Throughout the world George Morgan tramped, collecting glorious adventures.

"As far as my home life went," Miss Morgan said, "I guess I almost didn't have any father. He was able to get home very seldom from his business trips."

John Whiteside nodded gravely.

Molly's hands rustled in her lap and her eyes were dim.

One time he brought a dumpy, woolly puppy in a box, and it wet on the floor immediately.

"What kind of a dog is it?" Tom asked in his most sophisticated manner.

Their father laughed loudly. He was so young! He looked twenty years younger than their mother. "It's a dollar and a half dog," he explained. "You get an awful lot of kinds of dog for a dollar and a half. It's like this. . . . Suppose you go into a candy store and say, 'I want a nickel's worth of peppermints and gumdrops and licorice and raspberry chews.' Well, I went in and said, 'Give me a dollar and a half's worth of mixed dog.' That's the kind it is. It's Molly's dog, and she has to name it."

"I'm going to name it George," said Molly.

Her father bowed strangely to her, and said, "Thank you, Molly." They all noticed that he wasn't laughing at her, either.

Molly got up very early the next morning and took George about the yard to show him the secrets. She opened the hoard where two pennies and a gold policeman's button were buried. She hooked his little front paws over the back fence so he could look down the street at the schoolhouse. Lastly she climbed into the willow tree, carrying George under one arm. Tom came out of the house and sauntered under the tree. "Look out you don't drop him," Tom called, and just at that moment the puppy squirmed out of her arms and fell. He landed on the hard ground with a disgusting little thump. One leg bent out at a crazy angle, and the puppy screamed long, horrible screams, with sobs between breaths. Molly scrambled out of the tree, dull and stunned by the accident. Tom was standing over the puppy, his face white and twisted with pain, and George, the puppy, screamed on and on.

"We can't let him," Tom cried. "We can't let him." He ran to the woodpile and brought back a hatchet. Molly was too stupefied to look away, but Tom closed his eyes and struck. The screams stopped suddenly. Tom threw the hatchet from him and leaped over the back fence. Molly saw him running away as though he were being chased.

At that moment Joe and her father came out of the back door. Molly remembered how haggard and thin and gray her father's face was when he looked at the puppy. It was something in her father's face that started Molly to crying. "I dropped him out of the tree, and he hurt himself, and Tom hit him, and then Tom ran away." Her voice sounded sulky. Her father hugged Molly's head against his hip.

"Poor Tom!" he said. "Molly, you must remember never to say anything to Tom about it, and never to look at him as though you remembered." He threw a gunny sack over the puppy. "We must have a funeral," he said. "Did I ever tell you about the Chinese funeral I went to, about the colored paper they throw in the air, and the little fat roast pigs on the grave?" Joe edged in closer, and even Molly's eyes took on a gleam of interest. "Well, it was this way. . . ."

Molly looked up at John Whiteside and saw that he seemed to be studying a piece of paper on his desk. "When I was twelve years old, my father was killed in an accident," she said.

The great visits usually lasted about two weeks. Always there came an afternoon when George Morgan walked out into the town and did not come back until late at night. The mother made the children go to bed early, but they could hear him come home, stumbling a little against the furniture, and they could hear his voice through the wall. These were the only times when his voice was sad and discouraged. Lying with held breaths, in their beds, the children knew what that meant. In the morning he would be gone, and their hearts would be gone with him.

They had endless discussions about what he was doing. Their father was a glad argonaut, a silver knight. Virtue and Courage and Beauty—he wore a coat of them. "Sometime," the boys said, "sometime when we're big, we'll go with him and see all those things."

"I'll go, too," Molly insisted.

"Oh, you're a girl. You couldn't go, you know."

"But he'd let me go, you know he would. Sometime he'll take me with him. You see if he doesn't."

When he was gone their mother grew plaintive again, and her eyes reddened. Querulously she demanded their love, as though it were a package they could put in her hand.

One time their father went away, and he never came back. He had never sent any money, nor had he ever written to them, but this time he just disappeared for good. For two years they waited, and then their mother said he must be dead. The children shuddered at the thought, but they refused to believe it, because no one so beautiful and fine as their father could be dead. Some place in the world he was having adventures. There was some good reason why he couldn't come back to them. Some day when the reason was gone, he would come. Some morning he would be there with finer presents and better stories than ever before. But their mother said he must have had an accident. He must be dead. Their mother was distracted. She read those advertisements which offered to help her make money at home. The children made paper flowers and shamefacedly tried to sell them. The boys tried to develop magazine routes, and the whole family nearly starved. Finally, when they couldn't stand it any longer, the boys ran away and joined the navy. After that Molly saw them as seldom as she had seen her father, and they were so changed, so hard and boisterous, that she didn't even care, for her brothers were strangers to her.

"I went through high school, and then I went to San Jose and entered Teachers' College. I worked for my board and room at the home of Mrs. Allen Morit. Before I finished school my mother died, so I guess I'm a kind of an orphan, you see."

"I'm sorry," John Whiteside murmured gently.

Molly flushed. "That wasn't a bid for sympathy, Mr. Whiteside. You said you wanted to know about me. Everyone has to be an orphan some time."

Molly worked for her board and room. She did the work of a full time servant, only she received no pay. Money for clothes had to be accumulated by working in a store during summer vacation. Mrs. Morit trained her girls. "I can take a green girl, not worth a cent," she often said, "and when that girl's worked for me six months, she can get fifty dollars a month. Lots of women know it, and they just snap up my girls. This is the first schoolgirl I've tried, but even she shows a lot of improvement. She reads too much though. I always say a servant should be asleep by ten o'clock, or else she can't do her work right."

Mrs. Morit's method was one of constant criticism and nagging, carried on in a just, firm tone. "Now, Molly, I don't want to find fault, but if you don't wipe the silver drier than that, it'll have streaks."—"The butter knife goes this way, Molly. Then you can put the tumbler here."

"I always give a reason for everything," she told her friends.

In the evening, after the dishes were washed, Molly sat on her bed and studied, and when the light was off, she lay on her bed and thought of her father. It was ridiculous to do it, she knew. It was a waste of time. Her father came up to the door, wearing a cutaway coat, and striped trousers and a top hat. He carried a huge bouquet of red roses in his hand. "I couldn't come before, Molly. Get on your coat quickly. First we're going down to get that evening dress in the window of Prussia's, but we'll have to hurry. I have tickets for the train to New York tonight. Hurry up, Molly! Don't stand there gawping." It was silly. Her father was dead. No, she didn't really believe he was dead. Somewhere in the world he lived beautifully, and sometime he would come back.

Molly told one of her friends at school, "I don't really believe it, you see, but I don't disbelieve it. If I ever knew he was dead, why it would be awful. I don't know what I'd do then. I don't want to think about *knowing* he's dead."

When her mother died, she felt little besides shame. Her mother had wanted so much to be loved, and she hadn't known how to draw love. Her importunities had bothered the children and driven them away.

"Well, that's about all," Molly finished. "I got my diploma, and then I was sent down here."

"It was about the easiest interview I ever had," John Whiteside said.

"Do you think I'll get the position, then?"

The old man gave a quick, twinkly glance at the big meerschaum hanging over the mantel.

"That's his friend," Molly thought. "He has secrets with that pipe."

"Yes, I think you'll get the job. I think you have it already. Now, Miss Morgan, where are you going to live? You must find board and room some place."

Before she knew she was going to say it, she had blurted, "I want to live here."

John Whiteside opened his eyes in astonishment. "But we never take boarders, Miss Morgan."

"Oh, I'm sorry I said that. I just like it so much here, you see."

He called, "Willa," and when his wife stood in the half-open door, "This young lady wants to board with us. She's the new teacher."

Mrs. Whiteside frowned. "Couldn't think of it. We never take boarders. She's too pretty to be around that fool of a Bill. What would happen to those cows of his? It'd be a lot of trouble. You can sleep in the third bedroom upstairs," she said to Molly. "It doesn't catch much sun anyway."

Life changed its face. All of a sudden Molly found she was a queen. From the first day the children of the school adored her, for she understood them, and what was more, she let them understand her. It took her some time to realize that she had become an important person. If two men got to arguing at the store about a point of history or literature or mathematics, and the argument deadlocked, it ended up, "Take it to the teacher! If she doesn't know, she'll find it." Molly was very proud to be able to decide such questions. At parties she had to help with the decorations and to plan refreshments.

"I think we'll put pine boughs around everywhere. They're pretty, and they smell so good. They smell like a party." She was supposed to know everything and to help with everything, and she loved it.

At the Whiteside home she slaved in the kitchen under the mutterings of Willa. At the end of six months, Mrs. Whiteside grumbled to her husband, "Now if Bill only had any sense. But then," she continued, "if *she* has any sense—" and there she left it.

At night Molly wrote letters to the few friends she had made in Teachers' College, letters full of little stories about her neighbors, and full of joy. She must attend every party because of the social prestige of her position.

On Saturdays she ran about the hills and brought back ferns and wild flowers to plant about the house.

Bill Whiteside took one look at Molly and scuttled back to his cows. It was a long time before he found the courage to talk to her very much. He was a big, simple young man who had neither his father's balance nor his mother's humor. Eventually, however, he trailed after Molly and looked after her from distances.

One evening, with a kind of feeling of thanksgiving for her happiness, Molly told Bill about her father. They were sitting in canvas chairs on the wide veranda, waiting for the moon. She told him about the visits, and then about the disappearance. "Do you see what I have, Bill?" she cried. "My lovely father is some place. He's mine. You think he's living, don't you, Bill?"

"Might be," said Bill. "From what you say, he was a kind of an irresponsible cuss, though. Excuse me, Molly. Still, if he's alive, it's funny he never wrote."

Molly felt cold. It was just the kind of reasoning she had successfully avoided for so long. "Of course," she said stiffly, "I know that. I have to do some work now, Bill."

High up on a hill that edged the valley of the Pastures of Heaven, there was an old cabin which commanded a view of the whole country and of all the roads in the vicinity. It was said that the bandit Vasquez had built the cabin and lived in it for a year while the posses went crashing through the country looking for him. It was a landmark. All the people of the valley had been to see it at one time or another. Nearly everyone asked Molly whether she had been there yet. "No," she said, "but I will go up some day. I'll go some Saturday. I know where the trail to it is." One morning she dressed in her new hiking boots and corduroy skirt. Bill sidled up and offered to accompany her. "No," she said. "You have work to do. I can't take you away from it."

"Work be hanged!" said Bill.

"Well, I'd rather go alone. I don't want to hurt your feelings, but I just want to go alone, Bill." She was sorry not to let him accompany her, but his remark about her father had frightened her. "I want to have an adventure," she said to herself. "If Bill comes along, it won't be an adventure at all. It'll just be a trip." It took her an hour and a half to climb up the steep trail under the oaks. The leaves on the ground were as slippery as glass, and the sun was hot. The good smell of ferns and dank moss and yerba buena filled the air. When Molly came at last to the ridge crest, she was damp and winded. The cabin stood in a small clearing in the brush, a little square wooden room with no windows. Its doorless entrance was a black shadow. The place was quiet, the kind of humming quiet that flies and bees and crickets make. The whole hillside sang softly in the sun. Molly approached on tiptoe. Her heart was beating violently.

"Now I'm having an adventure," she whispered. "Now I'm right in the middle of an adventure at Vasquez' cabin." She peered in at the doorway and saw a lizard scuttle out of sight. A cobweb fell across her forehead and seemed to try to restrain her. There was nothing at all in the cabin, nothing but the dirt floor and the rotting wooden walls, and the dry, deserted smell of the earth that has long been covered from the sun. Molly was filled with excitement. "At night he sat in there. Sometimes when he heard noises like men creeping up on him, he went out of the door like the ghost of a shadow, and just melted into the darkness." She looked down on the valley of the Pastures of Heaven. The orchards lay in dark green squares; the grain was yellow, and the hills behind, a light brown washed with lavender. Among the farms the roads twisted and curled, avoiding a field, looping around a huge tree, half circling a hill flank. Over the whole valley was stretched a veil of heat shimmer. "Unreal," Molly whispered, "fantastic. It's a story, a real story, and I'm having an adventure." A breeze rose out of the valley like the sigh of a sleeper, and then subsided.

"In the daytime that young Vasquez looked down on the valley just as I'm looking. He stood right here, and looked at the roads down there. He wore a purple vest braided with gold, and the trousers on his slim legs widened at the bottom like the mouths of trumpets. His spur rowels were wrapped with silk ribbons to keep them from clinking. Sometimes he saw the posses riding by on the road below. Lucky for him the men bent over their horses' necks, and didn't look up at the hilltops. Vasquez laughed, but he was afraid, too. Sometimes he sang. His songs were soft and sad because he knew he couldn't live very long."

Molly sat down on the slope and rested her chin in her cupped hands. Young Vasquez was standing beside her, and Vasquez had her father's gay face, his shining eyes as he came on the porch shouting, "Hi, Kids!" This was the kind of adventure her father had. Molly shook herself and stood up. "Now I want to go back to the first and think it all over again."

In the late afternoon Mrs. Whiteside sent Bill out to look for Molly. "She might have turned an ankle, you know," But Molly emerged from the trail just as Bill approached it from the road.

"We were beginning to wonder if you'd got lost," he said. "Did you go up to the cabin?"

"Yes."

"Funny old box, isn't it? Just an old woodshed. There are a dozen just like it down here. You'd be surprised, though, how many people go up there to look at it. The funny part is, nobody's sure Vasquez was ever there."

"Oh, I think he must have been there."

"What makes you think that?"

"I don't know."

Bill became serious. "Everybody thinks Vasquez was a kind of a hero, when really he was just a thief. He started in stealing sheep and horses and ended up robbing stages. He had to kill a few people to do it. It seems to me, Molly, we ought to teach people to hate robbers, not worship them."

"Of course, Bill," she said wearily. "You're perfectly right. Would you mind not talking for a little while, Bill? I guess I'm a little tired, and nervous, too."

The year wheeled around. Pussywillows had their kittens, and wild flowers covered the hills. Molly found herself wanted and needed in the valley. She even attended school board meetings. There had been a time when those secret and august conferences were held behind closed doors, a mystery and a terror to everyone. Now that Molly was asked to step into John Whiteside's sitting room, she found that the board discussed crops, told stories, and circulated mild gossip.

Bert Munroe had been elected early in the fall, and by the springtime he was the most energetic member. He it was who planned dances at the schoolhouse, who insisted upon having plays and picnics. He even offered prizes for the best report cards in the school. The board was coming to rely pretty much on Bert Munroe.

One evening Molly came down late from her room. As always, when the board was meeting, Mrs. Whiteside sat in the dining room. "I don't think I'll go in to the meeting," Molly said. "Let them have one time to themselves. Sometimes I feel that they would tell other kinds of stories if I weren't there."

"You go on in, Molly! They can't hold a board meeting without you. They're so used to you, they'd be lost. Besides, I'm not at all sure I want them to tell those other stories."

Obediently Molly knocked on the door and went into the sitting room. Bert Munroe paused politely in the story he was narrating. "I was just telling about my new farm hand, Miss Morgan. I'll start over again, 'cause it's kind of funny. You see, I needed a hay hand, and I picked this fellow up under the Salinas River bridge. He was pretty drunk, but he wanted a job. Now I've got him, I find he isn't worth a cent as a hand, but I can't get rid of him. That son of a gun has been every place. You ought to hear him tell about the places he's been. My kids wouldn't let me get rid of him if I wanted to. Why he can take the littlest thing he's seen and make a fine story out of it. My kids just sit around with their ears spread, listening to him. Well, about twice a month he walks into Salinas and goes on a bust. He's one of those dirty, periodic drunks. The Salinas cops always call me up when they find him in a gutter, and I have to drive in to get him. And you know, when he comes out of it, he's always got some kind of present in his pocket for my kid Manny. There's nothing you can do with a man like that. He disarms you. I don't get a dollar's worth of work a month out of him."

Molly felt a sick dread rising in her. The men were laughing at the story. "You're too soft, Bert. You can't afford to keep an entertainer on the place. I'd sure get rid of him quick."

Molly stood up. She was dreadfully afraid someone would ask the man's name. "I'm not feeling very well tonight," she said. "If you gentlemen will excuse me, I think I'll go to bed." The men stood up while she left the room. In her bed she buried her head in the pillow. "It's crazy," she said to herself. "There isn't a chance in the world. I'm forgetting all about it right now." But she found to her dismay that she was crying.

The next few weeks were agonizing to Molly. She was reluctant to leave the house. Walking to and from school she watched the road ahead of her. "If I see any kind of a stranger I'll run away. But that's foolish. I'm being a fool." Only in her own room did she feel safe. Her terror was making her lose color, was taking the glint out of her eyes.

"Molly, you ought to go to bed," Mrs. Whiteside insisted. "Don't be a little idiot. Do I have to smack you the way I do Bill to make you go to bed?" But Molly would not go to bed. She thought too many things when she was in bed.

The next time the board met, Bert Munroe did not appear. Molly felt reassured and almost happy at his absence.

"You're feeling better, aren't you, Miss Morgan?"

"Oh, yes. It was only a little thing, a kind of a cold. If I'd gone to bed I might have been really sick."

The meeting was an hour gone before Bert Munroe came in. "Sorry to be late," he apologized. "The same old thing happened. My so-called hay hand was asleep in the street in Salinas. What a mess! He's out in the car sleeping it off now. I'll have to hose the car out tomorrow."

Molly's throat closed with terror. For a second she thought she was going to faint. "Excuse me, I must go," she cried, and ran out of the room. She walked into the dark hallway and steadied herself against the wall. Then slowly and automatically she marched out of the front door and down the steps. The night was filled with whispers. Out in the road she could see the black mass that was Bert Munroe's car. She was surprised at the way her footsteps plodded down the path of their own volition. "Now I'm killing myself," she said. "Now I'm throwing everything away. I wonder why." The gate was under her hand, and her hand flexed to open it. Then a tiny breeze sprang up and brought to her nose the sharp foulness of vomit. She heard a blubbering, drunken snore. Instantly something whirled in her head. Molly spun around and ran frantically back to the house. In her room she locked the door and sat stiffly down, panting with the effort of her run. It seemed hours before she heard the men go out of the house, calling their good-nights. Then Bert's motor started, and the sound of it died away down the road. Now that she was ready to go she felt paralyzed.

John Whiteside was writing at his desk when Molly entered the sitting room. He looked up questioningly at her. "You aren't well, Miss Morgan. You need a doctor."

She planted herself woodenly beside the desk. "Could you get a substitute teacher for me?" she asked.

"Of course I could. You pile right into bed and I'll call a doctor."

"It isn't that, Mr. Whiteside. I want to go away to-night."

"What are you talking about? You aren't well."

"I told you my father was dead. I don't know whether he's dead or not. I'm afraid—I want to go away tonight."

He stared intently at her. "Tell me what you mean," he said softly.

"If I should see that drunken man of Mr. Munroe's—" she paused, suddenly terrified at what she was about to say.

John Whiteside nodded very slowly.

"No," she cried. "I don't think that. I'm sure I don't."

"I'd like to do something, Molly."

"I don't want to go, I love it here— But I'm afraid. It's so important to me."

John Whiteside stood up and came close to her and put his arm about her shoulders. "I don't think I understand, quite," he said. "I don't think I want to understand. That isn't necessary." He seemed to be talking to himself. "It wouldn't be quite courteous—to understand."

"Once I'm away I'll be able not to believe it," Molly whimpered.

He gave her shoulders one quick squeeze with his encircling arm. "You run upstairs and pack your things, Molly," he said. "I'll get out the car and drive you right in to Salinas now."

(Chapter VIII)

PAT HUMBERT'S

PAT HUMBERT'S parents were middle-aged when he was born; they had grown old and stiff and spiteful before he was twenty. All of Pat's life had been spent in an atmosphere of age, of the aches and illness, of the complaints and self-sufficiency of age. While he was growing up, his parents held his opinions in contempt because he was young. "When you've lived as long as we have, you'll see things different," they told him. Later, they found his youth hateful because it was painless. Their age, so they implied, was a superior state, a state approaching godhead in dignity and infallibility. Even rheumatism was desirable as a price for the great wisdom of age. Pat was led to believe that no young thing had any virtue. Youth was a clumsy, fumbling preparation for excellent old age. Youth should think of nothing but the duty it owed to age, of the courtesy and veneration due to age. On the other hand, age owed no courtesy whatever to youth.

When Pat was sixteen, the whole work of the farm fell upon him. His father retired to a rocking chair beside the airtight stove in the sitting room, from which he issued orders, edicts and criticisms.

The Humberts dwelt in an old, rambling farm house of five rooms: a locked parlor, cold and awful as doom, a hot, stuffy sitting room smelling always of pungent salves and patent medicines, two bedrooms and a large kitchen. The old people sat in cushioned rocking chairs and complained bitterly if Pat did not come in from the farm work to replenish the fire in the stove several times a day. Toward the end of their lives, they really hated Pat for being young.

They lived a long time. Pat was thirty when they died within a month of each other. They were unhappy and bitter and discontented with their lives, and yet each one clung tenaciously to the poor spark and only died after a long struggle.

There were two months of horror for Pat. For three weeks he nursed his mother while she lay rigid on the bed, her breath clattering in and out of her lungs. She watched him with stony, accusing eyes as he tried to make her comfortable. When she was dead, her eyes still accused him.

Pat unlocked the terrible parlor; the neighbors sat in rows before the coffin, a kind of audience, while the service went on. From the bedroom came the sound of old Mr. Humbert's peevish weeping.

The second period of nursing began immediately after the first funeral, and continued for three weeks more. Then the neighbors sat in rows before another coffin. Before the funerals, the parlor had always been locked except during the monthly cleaning. The blinds were drawn down to protect the green carpet from the sun. In the center of the room stood a gilt-legged marble-topped table which bore, on a tapestry of Millet's *Angelus*, a huge Bible with a deeply tooled cover. On either side of the Bible sat squat vases holding tight bouquets of everlasting flowers. There were four straight chairs in the parlor, one against each of the four walls—two for the coffin and two for the watchers. Three large pictures in gilt frames hung on the walls, colored, enlarged photographs of each of the old Humberts looking stern and dead, but so taken that their eyes followed an intruder about the room. The third picture showed the corpse of Elaine in its boat on the thin sad river. The shroud hung over the gunwale and dipped into the water. On a corner table stood a tall glass bell in which three stuffed orioles sat on a cherry branch. So cold and sepulchral was this parlor that it had never been entered except by corpses and their attendants. It was indeed a little private mortuary chamber. Pat had seen three aunts and an uncle buried from that parlor.

Pat stood quietly by the graveside while his neighbors shaped up a tent of earth. Already his mother's grave had sunk a little, leaving a jagged crack all around its mound. The men were patting the new mound now, drawing a straight ridgepole and smoothing the slope of the sides. They were good workmen with the soil; they liked to make a good job with it whether it be furrow or grave mound. After it was perfect, they still walked about patting it lightly here and there. The women had gone back to the buggies and were waiting for their husbands to come. Each man walked up to Pat and shook his hand and murmured some solemn friendly thing to him. The wagons and surreys and buggies were all moving away now, disappearing one by one in the distance. Still Pat stood in the cemetery staring at the two graves. He didn't know what to do now there was no one to demand anything of him.

Fall was in the air, the sharp smell of it and the little jerky winds of it breathing up and then dying in mid-blow. Wild doves sat in a line on the cemetery fence all facing one way, all motionless. A piece of old brown newspaper scudded along the ground and clung about Pat's ankles. He stooped and picked it off, looked at it for a moment and then threw it away. The sound of grating buggy wheels came from the road. T. B. Allen tied his horse to the fence and walked up to Pat. "We thought you'd be going someplace tonight," he said in an embarrassed voice. "If you feel like it, we'd like you to come to supper at our house—and stay the night, too."

Pat started out of the coma that had fallen on him. "I should be going away from here," he said. He fumbled for another thought. "I'm not doing any good here."

"It's better to get away from it," Allen said.

"It's hard to leave, Mr. Allen. It's a thing you'll sometimes want to remember, and other times you'll want to forget it, I guess. But it's hard to leave because then you know it's all over—forever."

"Well, why don't you come to supper over at our house?"

All of Pat's guards were down; he confessed, "I never had supper away from home in my life. They"—he nodded toward the graves—"they didn't like to be out after dark. Night air wasn't good for them."

"Then maybe it would be good for you to eat at our house. You shouldn't go back to the empty place, at least not tonight. A man ought to save himself a little." He took Pat's arm and swung him toward the gate. "You follow me in your wagon." And as they went out of the gate a little elegy escaped from him. "It's a fit thing to die in the fall," he said. "It wouldn't be good to die in the spring and never to know about the rainfall nor how the crops shaped. But in the fall everything's over."

"They wouldn't care, Mr. Allen. They didn't ever ask about the crops, and they hated the rain because of their rheumatism. They just wanted to live. I don't know why."

For supper there were cold cuts of beef, and potatoes fried raw with a few onions, and bread pudding with raisins. Mrs. Allen tried to help Pat in his trouble by speaking often of his parents, of how good and kind they were, of his father's honesty and his mother's famous cookery. Pat knew she was lying about them to help him, and he didn't need it. He was in no agony of grief. The thick lethargy still hung over him so that it was a great effort to move or to speak.

He was remembering something that had happened at the funeral. When the pallbearers lifted the casket from its two chairs, one of the men tripped against the marble-topped table. The accident tipped over one of the vases of everlastings and pushed the Bible askew on its tapestry. Pat knew that in decency he should restore the old order. The chairs should be pushed against their walls and the Bible set straight. Finally he should lock up the parlor again. The memory of his mother demanded these things of him.

The Allens urged him to stay the night, but after a little while, he bade them a listless good-night and dragged himself out to harness his horse. The sky was black and cold between the sharp stars, and the hills hummed faintly under a lowering temperature. Through his lethargy, Pat heard the clopping of the horse's hooves on the road, the crying of night birds and the whisk of wind through the drying leaves. But more real to him were his parents' voices sounding in his head. "There'll be frost," his father said. "I hate the frost worse than rats." And his mother chimed in, "Speaking of rats—I have a feeling there's rats in the cellar. I wonder if Pat has set the traps this year past. I told him to, but he forgets everything I tell him."

Pat answered the voices. "I put poison in the cellar. Traps aren't as good as poison."

"A cat is best," his mother's whining voice said. "I don't know why we never have a cat or two. Pat never has a cat."

"I get cats, mother, but they eat gophers and go wild and run away. I can't keep cats."

The house was black and unutterably dreary when he

arrived. Pat lighted the reflector lamp and built a fire in the stove to warm the kitchen. As the flame roared through the wood, he sank into a chair and found that he was very comfortable. It would be nice, he thought, to bring his bed into the kitchen and to sleep beside the stove. The straightening of the house could be done to-morrow, or any day for that matter.

When he threw open the door into the sitting room, a wave of cold, lifeless air met him. His nostrils were assailed by the smell of funeral flowers and age and medicine. He walked quickly to his bedroom and carried his cot into the warm and lighted kitchen.

After a while Pat blew out the light and went to bed. The fire cricked softly in the stove. For a time the night was still, and then gradually the house began to swarm with malignant life. Pat discovered that his body was tense and cold. He was listening for sounds from the sitting room, for the creak of the rocking chairs and for the loud breathing of the old people. The house cracked, and although he had been listening for sounds, Pat started violently. His head and legs became damp with perspiration. Silently and miserably he crept from his bed and locked the door into the sitting room. Then he went back to his cot and lay shivering under the covers. The night had become very still, and he was lonely.

The next morning Pat awakened with a cold sense of duty to be performed. He tried to remember what it was. Of course, it was the Bible lying off-center on its table. That should be put straight. The vase of everlastings should be set upright, and after that the whole house should be cleaned. Pat knew he should do these things in spite of the reluctance he felt for opening the door into the sitting room. His mind shrank from the things he would see when he opened the door—the two rocking chairs, one on either side of the stove; the pillows in the chair seats would be holding the impressions of his parents' bodies. He knew the odors of age and of unguents and of stale flowers that were waiting for him on the other side of the door. But the thing was a duty. It must be done.

He built a fire and made his breakfast. It was while he drank the hot coffee that a line of reasoning foreign to his old manner of life came to him. The unusual thoughts that thronged upon him astounded him at once for their audacity and for their simplicity.

"Why should I go in there?" he demanded. "There's no one to care, no one even to know. I don't have to go in there if I don't want to." He felt like a boy who breaks school to walk in a deep and satisfying forest. But to combat his freedom, his mother's complaining voice came to his ears. "Pat ought to clean the house. Pat never takes care of things."

The joy of revolt surged up in him. "You're dead!" he told the voice. "You're just something that's happening in my mind. Nobody can expect me to do things any more. Nobody will ever know if I don't do things I ought to. I'm not going in there, and I'm never going in there." And while the spirit was still strong in him, he strode to the door, plucked out the key and threw it into the tall weeds behind the house. He closed the shutters on all the windows except those in the kitchen, and nailed them shut with long spikes.

The joy of his new freedom did not last long. In the daytime the farm work kept him busy, but before the day was out, he grew lonely for the old duties which ate up the hours and made the time short. He knew he was afraid to go into the house, afraid of those impressions in the cushions and of the disarranged Bible. He had locked up two thin old ghosts, but he had not taken away their power to trouble him.

That night, after he had cooked his supper, he sat beside the stove. An appalling loneliness like a desolate fog fell upon him. He listened to the stealthy sounds in the old house, the whispers and little knockings. So tensely did he listen that after a while he could hear the chairs rocking in the other room, and once he made out the rasping sound of a lid being unscrewed from a jar of salve. Pat could not stand it any longer. He went to the barn, harnessed his horse and drove to the Pastures of Heaven General Store.

Three men sat around the fat-bellied stove, contemplating its corrugations with rapt abstraction. They made room for Pat to draw up a chair. None of the men looked at him, because a man in mourning deserves the same social immunities a cripple does. Pat settled himself in his chair and gazed at the stove. "Remind me to get some flour before I go," he said.

All of the men knew what he meant. They knew he didn't need flour, but each one of them, under similar circumstances, would have made some such excuse. T. B. Allen opened the stove door and looked in and then spat on the coals. "A house like that is pretty lonely at first," he observed. Pat felt grateful to him although his words constituted a social blunder.

"I'll need some tobacco and some shotgun shells, too, Mr. Allen," he said by way of payment.

Pat changed his habits of living after that. Determinedly he sought groups of men. During the daytime he worked on his farm, but at night he was invariably to be found where two or three people were gathered. When a dance or a party was given at the schoolhouse, Pat arrived early and stayed until the last man was gone. He sat at the house of John Whiteside; he arrived first at fires. On election days he stayed at the polls until they closed. Wherever a group of people gathered, Pat was sure to show up. From constant stalking of company he came to have almost an instinct for discovering excitements which would draw crowds.

Pat was a homely man, gangling, big-nosed and heavy-jawed. He looked very much like Lincoln as a young man. His figure was as unfitted for clothes as Lincoln's was. His nostrils and ears were large and full of hair. They looked as though furry little animals were hiding in them. Pat had no conversation; he knew he added little to the gatherings he frequented, and he tried to make up for his lack by working, by doing favors, by arranging things. He liked to be appointed to committees for arranging school dances, for then he could call on the other committeemen to discuss plans; he could spend evenings decorating the school or running about the valley borrowing chairs from one family and dishes from another. If on any evening he could find no gathering to join, he drove his Ford truck to Salinas and sat through two moving picture shows. After those first two nights of fearful loneliness, he never spent another evening in his closed-up house. The memory of the Bible, of the waiting chairs, or the years-old smells were terrifying to him.

For ten years Pat Humbert drove about the valley in search of company. He had himself elected to the school board; he joined the Masons and the Odd Fellows in Salinas and was never known to miss a meeting.

In spite of his craving for company, Pat never became a part of any group he joined. Rather he hung on the fringes, never speaking unless he was addressed. The people of the valley considered his presence inevitable. They used him unmercifully and hardly knew that he wished nothing better.

When the gatherings were over, when Pat was finally forced home, he drove his Ford into the barn and then rushed to bed. He tried with little success to forget the

terrible rooms on the other side of the door. The picture
of them edged into his mind sometimes. The dust would
be thick now, and the cobwebs would be strung in all the
corners and on all the furniture. When the vision invaded
and destroyed his defences before he could go to sleep,
Pat shivered in his bed and tried every little soporific
formula he knew.

Since he so hated his house, Pat took no care of it. The
old building lay moldering with neglect. A white Banksia
rose, which for years had been a stubby little bush, came
suddenly to life and climbed up the front of the house. It
covered the porch, hung festoons over the closed windows
and dropped long streamers from the eaves. Within the
ten years the house looked like a huge mound of roses.
People passing by on the county road paused to marvel
at its size and beauty. Pat hardly knew about the rose. He
refused to think about the house when he could refuse.

The Humbert farm was a good one. Pat kept it well and
made money from it, and, since his expenses were small,
he had quite a few thousand dollars in the bank. He loved
the farm for itself, but he also loved it because it kept him
from fear in the daytime. When he was working, the
terror of being solitary, the freezing loneliness, could not
attack him. He raised good fruit, but his berries were his
chief interest. The lines of supported vines paralleled the
county road. Every year he was able to market his berries
earlier than anyone in the valley.

Pat was forty years old when the Munroes came into
the valley. He welcomed them as his neighbors. Here was
another house to which he might go to pass an evening.
And since Bert Munroe was a friendly man, he liked to
have Pat drop in to visit. Pat was a good farmer. Bert
often asked his advice. Pat did not take very careful notice of Mae Munroe except to see, and to forget, that she
was a pretty girl. He did not often think of people as

individuals, but rather as antidotes for the poison of his loneliness, as escapes from the imprisoned ghosts.

One afternoon when the summer was dawning, Pat worked among his berry vines. He kneeled between the rows of vines and dug among the berry roots with a hoe. The berries were fast forming now, and the leaves were pale green and lovely. Pat worked slowly down the row. He was contented with the work, and he did not dread the coming night for he was to have supper at the Munroe house. As he worked he heard voices from the road. Although he was concealed among the vines, he knew from the tones that Mrs. Munroe and her daughter Mae were strolling by his house. Suddenly he heard Mae exclaim with pleasure.

"Mama, look at that!" Pat ceased his work to listen. "Did you ever see such a beautiful rose in your life, Mama?"

"It's pretty, all right," Mrs. Munroe said.

"I've just thought what it reminds me of," Mae continued. "Do you remember the post card of that lovely house in Vermont? Uncle Keller sent it. This house, with the rose over it, looks just like that house in the picture. I'd like to see the inside of it."

"Well, there isn't much chance of that. Mrs. Allen says no one in the valley has been in that house since Pat's father and mother died, and that's ten years ago. She didn't say whether it was pretty."

"With a rose like that on the outside, the inside must be pretty. I wonder if Mr. Humbert will let me see it sometime." The two women walked on out of hearing.

When they were gone, Pat stood up and looked at the great rose. He had never seen how beautiful it was—a haystack of green leaves and nearly covered with white roses. "It is pretty," he said. "And it's like a nice house in Vermont. It's like a Vermont house, and—well, it *is* pretty, a pretty bush." Then, as though he had seen through the bush and through the wall, a vision of the parlor came to him. He went quickly back to his work among the berries, struggling to put the house out of his mind. But Mae's words came back to him over and over again, "It must be pretty inside." Pat wondered what a Vermont house looked like inside. John Whiteside's solid and grand house he knew, and, with the rest of the valley, he had admired the plush comfort of Bert Munroe's house, but a pretty house he had never seen, that is, a house he could really call pretty. In his mind he went over all the houses he knew and not one of them was what Mae must have meant. He remembered a picture in a magazine, a room with a polished floor and white woodwork and a staircase; it might have been Mt. Vernon. That picture had impressed him. Perhaps that was what Mae meant.

He wished he could see the post card of the Vermont house, but if he asked to see it, they would know he had been listening. As he thought of it, Pat became obsessed with a desire to see a pretty house that looked like his. He put his hoe away and walked in front of his house. Truly the rose was marvelous. It dropped a canopy over the porch, hung awnings of white stars over the closed windows. Pat wondered why he had never noticed it before.

That night he did something he couldn't have contemplated before. At the Munroe door, he broke an engagement to spend an evening in company. "There's some business in Salinas I've got to attend to," he explained. "I stand to lose some money if I don't go right in."

In Salinas he went straight to the public library. "Have you got any pictures of Vermont houses—pretty ones?" he asked the librarian.

"You'll probably find some in the magazines. Come! I'll show you where to look."

They had to warn him when the library was about to

close. He had found pictures of interiors, but of interiors
he had never imagined. The rooms were built on a plan;
each decoration, each piece of furniture, even the floors
and walls were related, were a part of the plan. Some deep
and instinctive feeling in him for arrangement, for color
and line had responded to the pictures. He hadn't known
rooms could be like that—all in one piece. Every room he
had ever seen was the result of a gradual and accidental
accumulation. Aunt Sophie sent a vase, father bought a
chair. They put a stove in the fireplace because it threw
more heat; the Sperry Flour Company issued a big calendar and mother had its picture framed; a mail order
house advertised a new kind of lamp. That was the way
rooms were assembled. But in the pictures someone had
an idea, and everything in the room was a part of the
idea. Just before the library closed he came upon two pictures side by side. One showed a room like those he knew,
and right beside it was another picture of the same room
with all the clutter gone, and with the idea in it. It didn't
look like the same place at all. For the first time in his
life, Pat was anxious to go home. He wanted to lie in his
bed and to think, for a strange new idea was squirming
into being in the back of his mind.

Pat could not sleep that night. His head was too full of
plans. Once he got up and lighted the lamp to look in his
bank book. A little before daylight he dressed and cooked
his breakfast, and while he ate, his eyes wandered again
and again to the locked door. There was a light of malicious joy in his eyes. "It'll be dark in there," he said. "I
better rip open the shutters before I go in there."

When the daylight came at last, he took a crowbar and
walked around the house, tearing open the nailed shutters
as he went. The parlor windows he did not touch, for he
didn't want to disturb the rose bush. Finally he went back
into the kitchen and stood before the locked door. For a

moment the old vision stopped him. "But it will be just for a minute," he argued. "I'll start in tearing it to pieces right away." The crowbar poised and crashed on the lock. The door sprang open crying miserably on its dry hinges, and the horrible room lay before him. The air was foggy with cobwebs; a musty, ancient odor flowed through the door. There were the two rocking chairs on either side of the rusty stove. Even through the dust he could see the little hollows in their cushions. But these were not the terrible things. Pat knew where lay the center of his fears. He walked rapidly through the room, brushing the cobwebs from his eyes as he went. The parlor was still dark for its shutters were closed. Pat didn't have to grope for the table; he knew exactly where it was. Hadn't it haunted him for ten years? He picked up table and Bible together, ran out through the kitchen and hurled them into the yard.

Now he could go more slowly. The fear was gone. The windows were stuck so hard that he had to use the bar to pry them open. First the rocking chairs went out, rolling and jumping when they hit the ground, then the pictures, the ornaments from the mantel, the stuffed orioles. And when the movable furniture, the clothing, the rugs and vases were scattered about under the windows, Pat ripped up the carpets and crammed them out, too. Finally he brought buckets of water and splashed the walls and ceilings thoroughly. The work was an intense pleasure to him. He tried to break the legs from the chairs when he threw them out. While the water was soaking into the old dark wall paper, he collected all of the furniture from under the windows, piled it up and set fire to it. Old musty fabrics and varnished wood smoldered sullenly and threw out a foul stench of dust and dampness. Only when a bucket of kerosene was thrown over the pile did the flame

leap up. The tables and chairs cracked as they released
their ghosts into the fire. Pat surveyed the pile joyfully.

"You *would* sit in there all these years, wouldn't you?"
he cried. "You thought I'd never get up the guts to burn
you. Well, I just wish you could be around to see what
I'm going to do, you rotten stinking trash." The green
carpets burned through and left red, flaky coals. Old vases
and jars cracked to pieces in the heat. Pat could hear the
sizzle of mentholatum and painkiller gushing from containers and boiling into the fire. He felt that he was pre-
siding at the death of his enemy. Only when the pile had
burned down to coals did he leave it. The walls were
soaked thoroughly by now, so that the wall paper peeled
off in long, broad ribbons.

That afternoon Pat drove in to Salinas and bought all
the magazines on house decoration he could find. In the
evening, after dinner he searched the pages through. At
last, in one of the magazines, he found the perfect room.
There had been a question about some of the others;
there was none about this one. And he could make it quite
easily. With the partition between the sitting room and
the parlor torn out, he would have a room thirty feet long
and fifteen wide. The windows must be made wide, the
fireplace enlarged and the floor sandpapered, stained and
polished. Pat knew he could do all these things. His hands
ached to be at work. "Tomorrow I'll start," he said. Then
another thought stopped him. "She thinks it's pretty now.
I can't very well let her know I'm doing it now. Why,
she'd know I heard her say that about the Vermont house.
I can't let people know I'm doing it. They'd ask why I'm
doing it." He wondered why he was doing it. "It's none of
their darn business why," he explained to himself. "I don't
have to go around telling people why. I've got my reasons.
By God! I'll do it at night." Pat laughed softly to himself.

The idea of secretly changing his house delighted him. He could work here alone, and no one would know. Then, when it was all finished, he could invite a few people in and pretend it was always that way. Nobody would remember how it was ten years ago.

This was the way he ordered his life: During the day he worked on the farm, and at night rushed into the house with a feeling of joy. The picture of the completed room was tacked up in the kitchen. Pat looked at it twenty times a day. While he was building window seats, putting up the French-gray paper, coating the woodwork with cream-colored enamel, he could see the completed room before him. When he needed supplies, he drove to Salinas late in the evening and brought back his materials after dark. He worked until midnight and went to bed breathlessly happy.

The people of the valley missed him from their gatherings. At the store they questioned him, but he had his excuse ready. "I'm taking one of those mail courses," he explained. "I'm studying at night." The men smiled. Loneliness was too much for a man, they knew. Bachelors on farms always got a little queer sooner or later.

"What are you studying, Pat?"

"Oh! What? Oh! I'm taking some lessons in—building."

"You ought to get married, Pat. You're getting along in years."

Pat blushed furiously. "Don't be a damn fool," he said.

As he worked on the room, Pat was developing a little play, and it went like this: The room was finished and the furniture in place. The fire burned redly; the lamps threw misty reflections on the polished floor and on the shiny furniture. "I'll go to her house, and I'll say, offhand, 'I hear you like Vermont houses.' No! I can't say that. I'll say, 'Do you like Vermont houses? Well, I've got a room that's kind of like a Vermont room.'" The preliminaries were never quite satisfactory. He couldn't come on the perfect way for enticing her into his house. He ended by skipping that part. He could think it out later.

Now she was entering the kitchen. The kitchen wouldn't be changed, for that would make the other room a bigger surprise. She would stand in front of the door, and he would reach around her and throw it open. There was the room, rather dark, but full of dark light, really. The fire flowed up like a broad stream, and the lamps reflected on the floor. You could make out the glazed chintz hangings and the fat tiger of the overmantel hooked rug. The pewter glowed with a restrained richness. It was all so warm and snug. Pat's chest contracted with delight.

Anyway, she was standing in the door and—what would she say? Well, if she felt the way he did, maybe she wouldn't say anything. She might feel almost like crying. That was peculiar, the good full feeling as though you were about to cry. Maybe she'd stand there for a minute or two, just looking. Then Pat would say—"Won't you come in and sit for a while?" And of course that would break the spell. She would begin talking about the room in funny choked sentences. But Pat would be offhand about it all. "Yes, I always kind of liked it." He said this out loud as he worked. "Yes, I always thought it was kind of nice. It came to me the other day that you might like to see it."

The play ended this way: Mae sat in the wingback chair in front of the fire. Her plump pretty hands lay in her lap. As she sat there, a faraway look came into her eyes. . . . And Pat never went any farther than that, for at that point a self-consciousness overcame him. If he went farther, it would be like peeking in a window at two people who wanted to be alone. The electric moment, the palpitating moment of the whole thing was when he threw open the door; when she stood on the threshold, stunned by the beauty of the room.

At the end of three months the room was finished. Pat put the magazine picture in his wallet and went to San Francisco. In the office of a furniture company, he spread his picture on the desk. "I want furniture like that," he said.

"You don't mean originals, of course."

"What do you mean, originals?"

"Why, old pieces. You couldn't get them for under thirty thousand dollars."

Pat's face fell. His room seemed to collapse. "Oh!—I didn't know."

"We can get you good copies of everything here," the manager assured him.

"Why of course. That's good. That's fine. How much would the copies cost?"

A purchasing agent was called in. The three of them went over the articles in the picture and the manager made a list; pie-crust table, drop-leaf gate-leg table, chairs: one windsor, one rush seat ladderback, one wing-back, one fireplace bench; rag rugs, glazed chintz hangings, lamps with frosted globes and crystal pendants; one open-faced cupboard, pictorial bone-china, pewter candlesticks and sconces.

"Well, it will be around three thousand dollars, Mr. Humbert."

Pat frowned with thought. After all why should be save money? "How soon can you send it down?" he demanded.

While he waited for a notice that the furniture had arrived in Salinas, Pat rubbed the floor until it shone like a dull lake. He walked backward out of the room erasing his faint foot marks with a polisher. And then at last the crates arrived at the freight depot. It took four trips to Salinas in his truck to get them, trips made secretly in the night. There was an air of intrigue about the business.

Pat uncrated the pieces in the barn. He carried in chairs and tables, and, with a great many looks at the picture, arranged them in their exact places. That night the fire flowed up, and the frosted lamps reflected on the floor. The fat tiger on the hooked rug over the fireplace seemed to quiver in the dancing flame-light.

Pat went into the kitchen and closed the door. Then, very slowly he opened it again and stood looking in. The room glowed with warmth, with welcoming warmth. The pewter was even richer than he had thought it would be. The plates in the open-faced cupboard caught sparks on their rims. For a moment Pat stood in the doorway trying to get the right tone in his voice. "I always kind of liked it," he said in his most offhand manner. "It just came to me the other day that you might like to see it." He paused, for a horrible thought had come to him. "Why, she can't come here alone. A girl can't come to a single man's house at night. People would talk about her, and besides, she wouldn't do it." He was bitterly disappointed. "Her mother will have to come with her. But—maybe her mother won't get in the way. She can stand back here, kind of, out of the way."

Now that he was ready, a powerful reluctance stopped him. Evening after evening passed while he put off asking her to come. He went through his play until he knew exactly where she would stand, how she would look, what she would say. He had alternative things she might say. A week went by, and still he put off the visit that would bring her to see his room.

One afternoon he built up his courage with layers of will. "I can't put it off forever. I better go tonight." After dinner, he put on his best suit and set out to walk to the

Munroe house. It was only a quarter of a mile away. He wouldn't ask her for tonight. He wanted to have the fire burning and the lamps lighted when she arrived. The night was cold and very dark. When Pat stumbled in the dust of the road, he thought with dismay how his polished shoes would look.

There were a great many lights in the Munroe house. In front of the gate, a number of cars were parked. "It's a party," Pat said to himself. "I'll ask her some other night. I couldn't do it in front of a lot of people." For a moment he even considered turning back. "It would look funny though, if I asked her the first time I saw her in months. She might suspect something."

When he entered the house, Bert Munroe grasped him by the hand. "It's Pat Humbert," he shouted. "Where have you been keeping yourself, Pat?"

"I've been studying at night."

"Well it's lucky you came over. I was going to go over to see you tomorrow. You heard the news, of course!"

"What news?"

"Why, Mae and Bill Whiteside are going to get married next Saturday. I was going to ask you to help at the wedding. It'll just be a home affair with refreshments afterwards. You used to help at the schoolhouse all the time before you got this studying streak." He took Pat's arm and tried to lead him down the hall. The sound of a number of voices came from the room at the end of the hall.

Pat resisted firmly. He exerted all his training in the offhand manner. "That's fine, Mr. Munroe. Next Saturday, you say? I'd be glad to help. No, I can't stay now. I got to run to the store right away." He shook hands again and walked slowly out the door.

In his misery he wanted to hide for a while, to burrow into some dark place where no one could see him. His way was automatically homeward. The rambling house was

dark and unutterably dreary when he arrived. Pat went
into the barn and with deliberate steps climbed the short
ladder and lay down in the hay. His mind was shrunken
and dry with disappointment. Above all things he did not
want to go into the house. He was afraid he might lock up
the door again. And then, in all the years to come, two
puzzled spirits would live in the beautiful room, and in
his kitchen, Pat would understand how they gazed wist-
fully into the ghost of a fire.

(Chapter X)

FROM

Tortilla Flat

DANNY

PILON

THE PIRATE

THE TREASURE HUNT

TORTILLAS AND BEANS

Episodes from the lives of Danny and the boys, the carefree Mexican paisanos who inhabit an area on the outskirts of Monterey, California. The novel was first published in 1935. In a subsequent edition, the author spelled out his sense of the story's parallels with the cycle of Arthurian legend: the forming of the Table Round, the deeds of its members, the passing of Arthur, and the dissolution of the Fellowship. John Steinbeck later worked upon a modernization of Malory's fifteenth-century version of the tales, another testimony to a continuing fascination.

DANNY

HOW DANNY, HOME FROM THE WARS, FOUND HIMSELF AN HEIR, AND HOW HE SWORE TO PROTECT THE HELPLESS.

WHEN Danny came home from the army he learned that he was an heir and an owner of property. The viejo, that is the grandfather, had died leaving Danny the two small houses on Tortilla Flat.

When Danny heard about it he was a little weighed down with the responsibility of ownership. Before he ever went to look at his property he bought a gallon of red wine and drank most of it himself. The weight of responsibility left him then, and his very worst nature came to the surface. He shouted, he broke a few chairs in a poolroom on Alvarado Street; he had two short but glorious fights. No one paid much attention to Danny. At last his wavering bow-legs took him toward the wharf where, at this early hour in the morning, the Italian fishermen were walking down in rubber boots to go out to sea.

Race antipathy overcame Danny's good sense. He menaced the fishermen. "Sicilian bastards," he called them, and "Scum from the prison island," and "Dogs of dogs of dogs." He cried, *"Chinga tu madre, Piojo."* He thumbed his nose and made obscene gestures below his waist. The fishermen only grinned and shifted their oars and said, "Hello, Danny. When'd you get home? Come around tonight. We got new wine."

Danny was outraged. He screamed, *"Pon un condo a la cabeza."*

They called, "Good-by, Danny. See you tonight. And they climbed into their little boats and rowed out to the lampara launches and started their engines and chugged away.

Danny was insulted. He walked back up Alvarado Street, breaking windows as he went, and in the second block a policeman took him in hand. Danny's great respect for the law caused him to go quietly. If he had not just been discharged from the army after the victory over Germany, he would have been sentenced to six months. As it was, the judge gave him only thirty days.

And so for one month Danny sat on his cot in the Monterey city jail. Sometimes he drew obscene pictures on the walls, and sometimes he thought over his army career. Time hung heavy on Danny's hands there in his cell in the city jail. Now and then a drunk was put in for the night, but for the most part crime in Monterey was stagnant, and Danny was lonely. The bedbugs bothered him a little at first, but as they got used to the taste of him and he grew accustomed to their bites, they got along peacefully.

He started playing a satiric game. He caught a bedbug, squashed it against the wall, drew a circle around it with a pencil and named it "Mayor Clough." Then he caught others and named them after the City Council. In a little while he had one wall decorated with squashed bedbugs, each named for a local dignitary. He drew ears and tails on them, gave them big noses and mustaches. Tito Ralph, the jailer, was scandalized; but he made no complaint because Danny had not included either the justice of the peace who had sentenced him, nor any of the police force. He had a vast respect for the law.

One night when the jail was lonely, Tito Ralph came

into Danny's cell bearing two bottles of wine. An hour later he went out for more wine, and Danny went with him. It was cheerless in the jail. They stayed at Torrelli's, where they bought the wine, until Torrelli threw them out. After that Danny went up among the pines and fell asleep, while Tito Ralph staggered back and reported his escape.

When the brilliant sun awakened Danny about noon, he determined to hide all day to escape pursuit. He ran and dodged behind bushes. He peered out of the undergrowth like a hunted fox. And, at evening, the rules having been satisfied, he came out and went about his business.

Danny's business was fairly direct. He went to the back door of a restaurant. "Got any old bread I can give my dog?" he asked the cook. And while that gullible man was wrapping up the food, Danny stole two slices of ham, four eggs, a lamb chop and a fly swatter.

"I will pay you sometime," he said.

"No need to pay for scraps. I throw them away if you don't take them."

Danny felt better about the theft then. If that was the way they felt, on the surface he was guiltless. He went back to Torrelli's, traded the four eggs, the lamb chop and the fly swatter for a water glass of grappa and retired toward the woods to cook his supper.

The night was dark and damp. The fog hung like limp gauze among the black pines that guard the landward limits of Monterey. Danny put his head down and hurried for the shelter of the woods. Ahead of him he made out another hurrying figure; and as he narrowed the distance, he recognized the scuttling walk of his old friend Pilon. Danny was a generous man, but he recalled that he had sold all his food except the two slices of ham and the bag of stale bread.

"I will pass Pilon by," he decided. "He walks like a man who is full of roast turkey and things like that."

Then suddenly Danny noticed that Pilon clutched his coat lovingly across his bosom.

"Ai, Pilon, *amigo!*" Danny cried.

Pilon scuttled on faster. Danny broke into a trot. "Pilon, my little friend! Where goest thou so fast?"

Pilon resigned himself to the inevitable and waited. Danny approached warily, but his tone was enthusiastic. "I looked for thee, dearest of little angelic friends, for see, I have here two great steaks from God's own pig, and a sack of sweet white bread. Share my bounty, Pilon, little dumpling."

Pilon shrugged his shoulders. "As you say," he muttered savagely. They walked on together into the woods. Pilon was puzzled. At length he stopped and faced his friend. "Danny," he asked sadly, "how knewest thou I had a bottle of brandy under my coat?"

"Brandy?" Danny cried. "Thou hast brandy? Perhaps it is for some sick old mother," he said naïvely. "Perhaps thou keepest it for Our Lord Jesus when He comes again. Who am I, thy friend, to judge the destination of this brandy? I am not even sure thou hast it. Besides I am not thirsty. I would not touch this brandy. Thou art welcome to this big roast of pork I have, but as for thy brandy, that is thine own."

Pilon answered him sternly. "Danny, I do not mind sharing my brandy with you, half and half. It is my duty to see you do not drink it all."

Danny dropped the subject then. "Here in the clearing I will cook this pig, and you will toast the sugar cakes in this bag here. Put thy brandy here, Pilon. It is better here, where we can see it, and each other."

They built a fire and broiled the ham and ate the stale bread. The brandy receded quickly down the bottle. After they had eaten, they huddled near the fire and sipped delicately at the bottle like effete bees. And the fog came down upon them and grayed their coats with moisture. The wind sighed sadly in the pines about them.

And after a time, a loneliness fell upon Danny and Pilon. Danny thought of his lost friends.

"Where is Arthur Morales?" Danny asked, turning his palms up and thrusting his arms forward. "Dead in France," he answered himself, turning the palms down and dropping his arms in despair. "Dead for his country. Dead in a foreign land. Strangers walk near his grave and they do not know Arthur Morales lies there." He raised his hands palms upward again. "Where is Pablo, that good man?"

"In jail," said Pilon. "Pablo stole a goose and hid in the brush; and that goose bit Pablo and Pablo cried out and so was caught. Now he lies in jail for six months."

Danny sighed and changed the subject, for he realized that he had prodigally used up the only acquaintance in any way fit for oratory. But the loneliness was still on him and demanded an outlet. "Here we sit," he began at last.

"—broken hearted," Pilon added rhythmically.

"No, this is not a poem," Danny said. "Here we sit, homeless. We gave our lives for our country, and now we have no roof over our head."

"We never did have," Pilon added helpfully.

Danny drank dreamily until Pilon touched his elbow and took the bottle. "That reminds me," Danny said, "of a story of a man who owned two whore houses——" His mouth dropped open. "Pilon!" he cried. "Pilon! my little fat duck of a baby friend. I had forgotten! I am an heir! I own two houses."

"Whore houses?" Pilon asked hopefully. "Thou art a drunken liar," he continued.

"No, Pilon. I tell the truth. The viejo died. I am the heir. I, the favorite grandson."

"Thou art the only grandson," said the realist, Pilon. "Where are these houses?"

"You know the viejo's house on Tortilla Flat, Pilon?"

"Here in Monterey?"

"Yes, here in Tortilla Flat."

"Are they any good, these houses?"

Danny sank back, exhausted with emotion. "I do not know. I forgot I owned them."

Pilon sat silent and absorbed. His face grew mournful. He threw a handful of pine needles on the fire, watched the flames climb frantically among them and die. For a long time he looked into Danny's face with deep anxiety, and then Pilon sighed noisily, and again he sighed. "Now it is over," he said sadly. "Now the great times are done. Thy friends will mourn, but nothing will come of their mourning."

Danny put down the bottle, and Pilon picked it up and set it in his own lap.

"Now what is over?" Danny demanded. "What do you mean?"

"It is not the first time," Pilon went on. "When one is poor, one thinks, 'If I had money I would share it with my good friends.' But let that money come and charity flies away. So it is with thee, my once-friend. Thou art lifted above thy friends. Thou art a man of property. Thou wilt forget thy friends who shared everything with thee, even their brandy."

His words upset Danny. "Not I," he cried. "I will never forget thee, Pilon."

"So you think now," said Pilon coldly. "But when you have two houses to sleep in, then you will see. Pilon will be a poor paisano, while you eat with the mayor."

Danny arose unsteadily and held himself upright

against a tree. "Pilon, I swear, what I have is thine. While I have a house, thou hast a house. Give me a drink."

"I must see this to believe it," Pilon said in a discouraged voice. "It would be a world wonder if it were so. Men would come a thousand miles to look upon it. And besides, the bottle is empty."

(Chapter I)

PILON

HOW PILON WAS LURED BY GREED OF POSITION TO FORSAKE DANNY'S HOSPITALITY.

THE lawyer left them at the gate of the second house and climbed into his Ford and stuttered down the hill into Monterey.

Danny and Pilon stood in the front of the paintless picket fence and looked with admiration at the property, a low house streaked with old whitewash, uncurtained windows blank and blind. But a great pink rose of Castile was on the porch, and grandfather geraniums grew among the weeds in the front yard.

"This is the best of the two," said Pilon. "It is bigger than the other."

Danny held a new skeleton key in his hand. He tiptoed over the rickety porch and unlocked the front door. The main room was just as it had been when the viejo had lived there. The red rose calendar for 1906, the silk banner on the wall, with Fighting Bob Evans looking between the super-structures of a battleship, the bunch of red paper roses tacked up, the strings of dusty red peppers and garlic, the air-tight stove, the battered rocking chairs.

Pilon looked in the door. "Three rooms," he said breathlessly, "and a bed and a stove. We will be happy here, Danny."

Danny moved cautiously into the house. He had bitter memories of the viejo. Pilon darted ahead of him, and into the kitchen. "A sink with a faucet," he cried. He turned the handle. "No water. Danny, you must have the company turn on the water."

They stood and smiled at each other. Pilon noticed that the worry of property was settling on Danny's face. No more in life would that face be free of care. No more would Danny break windows now that he had windows of his own to break. Pilon had been right—he had been raised among his fellows. His shoulders had straightened to withstand the complexity of life. But one cry of pain escaped him before he left for all time his old and simple existence.

"Pilon," he said sadly, "I wish you owned it and I could come to live with you."

While Danny went to Monterey to have the water turned on, Pilon wandered into the weed-tangled back yard. Fruit trees were there, bony and black with age, and gnarled and broken from neglect. A few tent-like chicken coops lay among the weeds, a pile of rusty barrel hoops, a heap of ashes and a sodden mattress. Pilon looked over the fence into Mrs. Morales' chicken yard, and after a moment of consideration he opened a few small holes in the fence for the hens. "They will like to make nests in the tall weeds," he thought kindly. He considered how he could make a figure-four trap in case the roosters came in too and bothered the hens and kept them from the nests. "We will live happily," he thought again.

Danny came back indignant from Monterey. "That company wants a deposit," he said.

"Deposit?"

"Yes. They want three dollars before they will turn on the water."

"Three dollars," Pilon said severely, "is three gallons of wine. And when that is gone, we will borrow a bucket of water from Mrs. Morales, next door."

"But we haven't three dollars for wine."

"I know," Pilon said. "Maybe we can borrow a little wine from Mrs. Morales."

The afternoon passed. "Tomorrow we will settle down," Danny announced. "Tomorrow we will clean and scrub. And you, Pilon, will cut the weeds and throw the trash in the gulch."

"The weeds?" Pilon cried in horror. "Not *those* weeds." He explained his theory of Mrs. Morales' chickens.

Danny agreed immediately. "My friend," he said, "I am glad you have come to live with me. Now, while I collect a little wood, you must get something for dinner."

Pilon, remembering his brandy, thought this unfair. "I am getting in debt to him," he thought bitterly. "My freedom will be cut off. Soon I shall be a slave because of this Jew's house." But he did go out to look for some dinner.

Two blocks away, near the edge of the pine wood, he came upon a half-grown Plymouth Rock rooster scratching in the road. It had come to that adolescent age when its voice cracked, when its legs and neck and breast were naked. Perhaps because he had been thinking of Mrs. Morales' hens in a charitable vein, this little rooster engaged Pilon's sympathy. He walked slowly on toward the dark pine woods, and the chicken ran ahead of him.

Pilon mused, "Poor little bare fowl. How cold it must be for you in the early morning, when the dew falls and the air grows cold with the dawn. The good God is not always so good to little beasts." And he thought, "Here you play in the street, little chicken. Some day an auto-

mobile will run over you; and if it kills you, that will be
the best that can happen. If may only break your leg or
your wing. Then all of your life you will drag along in
misery. Life is too hard for you, little bird."

He moved slowly and cautiously. Now and then the
chicken tried to double back, but always there was
Pilon in the place it chose to go. At last it disappeared
into the pine forest, and Pilon sauntered after it.

To the glory of his soul be it said that no cry of pain
came from that thicket. That chicken, which Pilon had
prophesied might live painfully, died peacefully, or at
least quietly. And this is no little tribute to Pilon's technique.

Ten minutes later he emerged from the woods and
walked back toward Danny's house. The little rooster,
picked and dismembered, was distributed in his pockets.
If there was one rule of conduct more strong than any
other to Pilon, it was this: Never under any circum
stances bring feathers, head or feet home, for without
these a chicken cannot be identified.

In the evening they had a fire of cones in the air-tight
stove. The flames growled in the chimney. Danny and
Pilon, well-fed, warm and happy, sat in the rocking
chairs and gently teetered back and forth. At dinner
they had used a piece of candle, but now only the light
from the stove cracks dispelled the darkness of the room.
To make it perfect, rain began to patter on the roof.
Only a little leaked through, and that in places where
no one wanted to sit anyway.

"It is good, this," Pilon said. "Think of the nights
when we slept in the cold. This is the way to live."

"Yes, and it is strange," Danny said. "For years I
had no house. Now I have two. I cannot sleep in two
houses."

Pilon hated waste. "This very thing has been bothering me. Why don't you rent the other house?" he suggested.

Danny's feet crashed down on the floor. "Pilon," he
cried. "Why didn't I think of it!" The idea grew more
familiar. "But who will rent it, Pilon?"

"I will rent it," said Pilon. "I will pay ten dollars a
month in rent."

"Fifteen," Danny insisted. "It's a good house. It is
worth fifteen."

Pilon agreed grumbling. But he would have agreed
to much more, for he saw the elevation that came to a
man who lived in his own house; and Pilon longed to
feel that elevation.

"It is agreed, then," Danny concluded. "You will rent
my house. Oh, I will be a good landlord, Pilon. I will not
bother you."

Pilon, except for his year in the army, had never
possessed fifteen dollars in his life. But, he thought, it
would be a month before the rent was due, and who
could tell what might happen in a month.

They teetered contentedly by the fire. After a while
Danny went out for a few moments and returned with
some apples. "The rain would have spoiled them anyway," he apologized.

Pilon, not to be outdone, got up and lighted the
candle; he went into the bedroom and in a moment returned with a wash bowl and pitcher, two red glass vases
and a bouquet of ostrich plumes. "It is not good to have
so many breakable things around," he said. "When they
are broken you become sad. It is much better never to
have had them." He picked the paper roses from the
wall. "A compliment for Señora Torrelli," he explained
as he went out the door.

Shortly afterward he returned, wet through from the

rain, but triumphant in manner, for he had a gallon jug
of red wine in his hand.

They argued bitterly later, but neither cared who
won, for they were tired with the excitements of the
day. The wine made them drowsy, and they went to
sleep on the floor. The fire died down; the stove cricked
as it cooled. The candle tipped over and expired in its
own grease, with little blue, protesting flares. The house
was dark and quiet and peaceful.

(Chapter II)

THE PIRATE

HOW DANNY'S FRIENDS BECAME A FORCE FOR GOOD. HOW THEY SUCCORED THE POOR PIRATE.

A GREAT many people saw the Pirate every day, and some laughed at him, and some pitied him; but no one knew him very well, and no one interfered with him. He was a huge, broad man, with a tremendous black and bushy beard. He wore jeans and a blue shirt, and he had no hat. In town he wore shoes. There was a shrinking in the Pirate's eyes when he confronted any grown person, the secret look of an animal that would like to run away if it dared turn its back long enough. Because of this expression, the paisanos of Monterey knew that his head had not grown up with the rest of his body. They called him The Pirate because of his beard. Every day people saw him wheeling his barrow of pitchwood about the streets until he sold the load. And always in a cluster at his heels walked his five dogs.

Enrique was rather houndish in appearance, although his tail was bushy. Pajarito was brown and curly, and these were the only two things you could see about him. Rudolph was a dog of whom passers-by said, "He is an American dog." Fluff was a Pug and Señor Alec Thompson seemed to be a kind of an Airedale. They walked in a squad behind the Pirate, very respectful toward him, and very solicitous for his happiness. When he sat

down to rest from wheeling his barrow, they all tried
to sit in his lap and have their ears scratched.

Some people had seen the Pirate early in the morning on Alvarado Street; some had seen him cutting
pitchwood; some knew he sold kindling; but no one
except Pilon knew everything the Pirate did. Pilon
knew everybody and everything about everybody.

The Pirate lived in a deserted chicken house in the
yard of a deserted house on Tortilla Flat. He would
have thought it presumptuous to live in the house itself.
The dogs lived around and on top of him, and the
Pirate liked this, for his dogs kept him warm on the
coldest nights. If his feet were cold, he had only to put
them against the warm belly of Señor Alec Thompson.
The chicken house was so low that the Pirate had to
crawl in on his hands and knees.

Early every morning, well before daylight, the Pirate
crawled out of his chicken house, and the dogs followed
him, roughing their coats and sneezing in the cold air.
Then the party went down to Monterey and worked
along an alley. Four or five restaurants had their back
doors on this alley. The Pirate entered each one, into a
restaurant kitchen, warm and smelling of food. Grumbling cooks put packages of scraps in his hands at each
place. They didn't know why they did it.

When the Pirate had visited each back door and had
his arms full of parcels, he walked back up the hill to
Munroe Street and entered a vacant lot, and the dogs
excitedly swarmed about him. Then he opened the
parcels and fed the dogs. For himself he took bread or
a piece of meat out of each package, but he did not pick
the best for himself. The dogs sat down about him, licking
their lips nervously, and shifting their feet while they
waited for food. They never fought over it, and that was
a surprising thing. The Pirate's dogs never fought each

other, but they fought everything else that wandered the streets of Monterey on four legs. It was a fine thing to see the pack of five, hunting fox-terriers and Pomeranians like rabbits.

Daylight had come by the time the meal was over. The Pirate sat on the ground and watched the sky turn blue with the morning. Below him he saw the schooners put out to sea with deckloads of lumber. He heard the bell buoy ringing sweetly off China Point. The dogs sat about him and gnawed at the bones. The Pirate seemed to be listening to the day rather than seeing it, for while his eyes did not move about, there was an air of attentiveness in him. His big hands strayed to the dogs and his fingers worked soothingly in the coarse hair. After about half an hour, the Pirate went to the corner of the vacant lot, threw the covering of sacks from his wheelbarrow and dug up his ax out of the ground where he buried it every evening. Then up the hill he pushed the barrow, and into the woods, until he found a dead tree, full of pitch. By noon he had a load of fine kindling; and then, still followed by his dogs, he walked the streets until he had sold the load for twenty-five cents.

It was possible to observe all this, but what he did with the quarter, no one could tell. He never spent it. In the night, guarded from danger by his dogs, he went into the woods and hid the day's quarter with hundreds of others. Somewhere he had a great hoard of money.

Pilon, that acute man, from whom no details of the life of his fellows escaped, and who was doubly delighted to come upon those secrets that nestled deep in the brains of his acquaintances, discovered the Pirate's hoard by a logical process. Pilon reasoned thus: "Every day that Pirate has a quarter. If it is two dimes and a nickel, he takes it to a store and gets a twenty-five cent piece.

He never spends any money at all. Therefore, he must be hiding it."

Pilon tried to compute the amount of the treasure. For years the Pirate had been living in this way. Six days a week he cut pitchwood, and on Sundays he went to church. His clothes he got from the back doors of houses, his food at the back doors of restaurants. Pilon puzzled with the great numbers for a while, and then gave it up. "The Pirate must have at least a hundred dollars," he thought.

For a long time Pilon had considered these things. But it was only after the foolish and enthusiastic promise to feed Danny that the thought of the Pirate's hoard gained any personal significance to Pilon.

Before he approached the subject at all, Pilon put his mind through a long and stunning preparation. He felt very sorry for the Pirate. "Poor little half-formed one," he said to himself. "God did not give him all the brain he should have. That poor little Pirate cannot look after himself. For see, he lives in filth in an old chicken house. He feeds upon scraps fit only for his dogs. His clothes are thin and ragged. And because his brain is not a good one, he hides his money."

Now, with his groundwork of pity laid, Pilon moved on to his solution. "Would it not be a thing of merit," he thought, "to do those things for him which he cannot do for himself? To buy him warm clothes, to feed him food fit for a human? But," he reminded himself, "I have no money to do these things, although they lie squirming in my heart. How can these charitable things be accomplished?"

Now he was getting somewhere. Like the cat, which during a long hour closes in on a sparrow, Pilon was ready for his pounce. "I have it!" his brain cried. "It is like this: The Pirate has money, but he has not the brain to use it. I have the brain! I will offer my brain to his use. I will give freely of my· mind. That shall be my charity toward this poor little half-made man."

It was one of the finest structures Pilon had ever built. The urge of the artist to show his work to an audience came upon him. "I will tell it to Pablo," he thought. But he wondered whether he would dare do such a thing. Was Pablo strictly honest? Would he not want to divert some of this money to his own ends? Pilon decided not to take the chance, right then, anyway.

It is astounding to find that the belly of every black and evil thing is as white as snow. And it is saddening to discover how the concealed parts of angels are leprous. Honor and peace to Pilon, for he had discovered how to uncover and to disclose to the world the good that lay in every evil thing. Nor was he blind, as so many saints are, to the evil of good things. It must be admitted with sadness that Pilon had neither the stupidity, the self-righteousness nor the greediness for reward ever to become a saint. Enough for Pilon to do good and to be rewarded by the glow of human brotherhood accomplished.

That very night he paid a visit to the chicken house where the Pirate lived with his dogs. Danny, Pablo and Jesus Maria, sitting by the stove, saw him go and said nothing. For, they thought delicately, either a vapor of love had been wafted to Pilon or else he knew where he could get a little wine. In either case it was none of their business until he told them about it.

It was well after dark, but Pilon had a candle in his pocket, for it might be a good thing to watch the expression on the Pirate's face while he talked. And Pilon had a big round sugar cookie in a bag that Susie Francisco, who worked in a bakery, had given him in return for a formula for getting the love of Charlie Guzman.

Charlie was a Postal Telegraph messenger and rode a motorcycle; and Susie had a man's cap to put on backward in case Charlie should ever ask her to ride with him. Pilon thought the Pirate might like the sugar cookie.

The night was very dark. Pilon picked his way along a narrow street bordered with vacant lots and with weed-grown, neglected gardens.

Galvez' bad bulldog came snarling out of Galvez' yard, and Pilon spoke soothing compliments to him. "Nice dog," he said gently, and "Pretty dog," both of them palpable lies. They impressed the bulldog, however, for he retired into Galvez' yard.

Pilon came at last to the vacant property where the Pirate lived. And now he knew he must be careful, for the Pirate's dogs, if they suspected ill of anyone toward their master, were known to become defending furies. As Pilon stepped into the yard, he heard deep and threatening growls from the chicken house.

"Pirate," he called. "It is thy good friend Pilon, come to talk with thee."

There was silence. The dogs stopped growling.

"Pirate, it is only Pilon."

A deep surly voice answered him, "Go away. I am sleeping now. The dogs are sleeping. It is dark, Pilon. Go to bed."

"I have a candle in my pocket," Pilon called. "It will make a light as bright as day in thy dark house. I have a big sugar cookie for thee, too."

A faint scuffling sounded in the chicken house. "Come then," the Pirate said. "I will tell the dogs it is all right."

As he advanced through the weeds, Pilon could hear the Pirate talking softly to his dogs, explaining to them that it was only Pilon, who would do no harm. Pilon bent over in front of the dark doorway and scratched a match and lighted his candle.

The Pirate was seated on the dirt floor, and his dogs were all about him. Enrique growled, and had to be reassured again. "That one is not so wise as the others," the Pirate said pleasantly. His eyes were the pleased eyes of an amused child. When he smiled his big white teeth glistened in the candlelight.

Pilon held out the bag. "It is a fine cake for you," he said.

The Pirate took the bag and looked into it; then he smiled delightedly, and brought out the cookie. The dogs all grinned and faced him, and moved their feet and licked their lips. The Pirate broke his cookie into seven pieces. The first he gave to Pilon, who was his guest. "Now, Enrique," he said. "Now Fluff. Now Señor Alec Thompson." Each dog received his piece and gulped it and looked for more. Last, the Pirate ate his and held up his hands to the dogs. "No more, you see," he told them. Immediately the dogs lay down about him.

Pilon sat on the floor and stood the candle on the ground in front of him. The Pirate questioned him self-consciously with his eyes. Pilon sat silently, to let many questions pass through the Pirate's head. At length he said, "Thou art a worry to thy friends."

The Pirate's eyes filled with astonishment. "I? To my friends? What friends?"

Pilon softened his voice. "Thou hast many friends who think of thee. They do not come to see thee because thou art proud. They think it might hurt thy pride to have them see thee living in this chicken house, clothed in rags, eating garbage with thy dogs. But these friends of thine worry for fear the bad life may make thee ill."

The Pirate was following his words with breathless astonishment, and his brain tried to realize these new things he was hearing. It did not occur to him to doubt them, since Pilon was saying them. "I have all these friends?" he said in wonder. "And I did not know it. And I am a worry to those friends. I did not know, Pilon. I would not have worried them if I had known." He swallowed to clear his throat of emotion. "You see, Pilon, the dogs like it here. And I like it because of them. I did not think I was a worry to my friends." Tears came into the Pirate's eyes.

"Nevertheless," Pilon said, "thy mode of living keeps all thy friends uneasy."

The Pirate looked down at the ground and tried to think clearly, but as always, when he attempted to cope with a problem, his brain grew gray and no help came from it, but only a feeling of helplessness. He looked to his dogs for protection, but they had gone back to sleep, for it was none of their business. And then he looked earnestly into Pilon's eyes. "You must tell me what to do, Pilon. I did not know these things."

It was too easy. Pilon was a little ashamed that it should be so easy. He hesitated; nearly gave it up; but then he knew he would be angry with himself if he did. "Thy friends are poor," he said. "They would like to help thee, but they have no money. If thou hast money hidden, bring it out into the open. Buy thyself some clothes. Eat food that is not cast out by other people. Bring thy money out of its hiding place, Pirate."

Pilon had been looking closely at the Pirate's face while he spoke. He saw the eyes droop with suspicion and then with sullenness. In a moment Pilon knew two things certainly; first, that the Pirate had money hidden; and second, that it was not going to be easy to get at it. He was pleased at the latter fact. The Pirate had become a problem in tactics such as Pilon enjoyed.

Now the Pirate was looking at him again, and in his eyes was cunning, and on top of that, a studied ingenuousness. "I have no money anywhere," he said.

"But every day, my friend, I have seen thee get a quarter for thy wood, and never have I seen thee spend it."

This time the Pirate's brain came to his rescue. "I give it to a poor old woman," he said. "I have no money anywhere." And with his tone he closed a door tightly on the subject.

"So it must be guile," Pilon thought. So those gifts, that in him were so sharpened, must be called into play. He stood up and lifted his candle. "I only thought to tell thee how thy friends worry," he said critically. "If thou wilt not try to help, I can do nothing for thee."

The sweetness came back into the Pirate's eyes. "Tell them I am healthy," he begged. "Tell my friends to come and see me. I will not be too proud. I will be glad to see them any time. Wilt thou tell them for me, Pilon?"

"I will tell them," Pilon said ungraciously. "But thy friends will not be pleased when they see thou dost nothing to relieve their minds." Pilon blew out his candle and went away into the darkness. He knew that the Pirate would never tell where his hoard was. It must be found by stealth, taken by force and then all the good things given to the Pirate. It was the only way.

And so Pilon set himself to watch the Pirate. He followed him into the forest when he went to cut kindlings. He lay in wait outside the chicken house at night. He talked to him long and earnestly, and nothing came of it. The treasure was as far from discovery as ever. Either it lay buried in the chicken house or it was hidden deep in the forest, and was only visited at night.

The long and fruitless vigils wore out the patience of Pilon. He knew he must have help and advice. And who could better give it than those comrades, Danny, Pablo and Jesus Maria? Who could be so stealthy, so guileful? Who could melt to kindness with more ease?

Pilon took them into his confidence; but first he prepared them, as he had prepared himself: The Pirate's poverty, his helplessness, and finally—the solution. When he came to the solution, his friends were in a philanthropic frenzy. They applauded him. Their faces shone with kindness. Pablo thought there might be well over a hundred dollars in the hoard.

When their joy had settled to a working enthusiasm, they came to plans.

"We must watch him," Pablo said.

"But I have watched him," Pilon argued. "It must be that he creeps off in the night, and then one cannot follow too close, for his dogs guard him like devils. It is not going to be so easy."

"You've used every argument?" Danny asked.

"Yes. Every one."

In the end it was Jesus Maria, that humane man, who found the way out. "It is difficult while he lives in that chicken house," he said. "But suppose he lived here, with us? Either his silence would break under our kindness, or else it would be easier to know when he goes out at night."

The friends gave a good deal of thought to this suggestion. "Sometimes the things he gets out of restaurants are nearly new," mused Pablo. "I have seen him with a steak out of which only a little was missing."

"It might be as much as two hundred dollars," said Pilon.

Danny offered an objection. "But those dogs—he would bring his dogs with him."

"They are good dogs," said Pilon. "They obey him exactly. You may draw a line around a corner and say,

'Keep thy dogs within this line.' He will tell them, and those dogs will stay."

"I saw the Pirate one morning, and he had nearly half a cake, just a little bit damp with coffee," said Pablo.

The question settled itself. The house resolved itself into a committee, and the committee visited the Pirate.

It was a crowded place, that chicken house, when they all got inside. The Pirate tried to disguise his happiness with a gruff tone.

"The weather hás been bad," he said socially. And, "You wouldn't believe, maybe, that I found a tick as big as a pigeon's egg on Rudolph's neck." And he spoke disparagingly of his home, as a host should. "It is too small," he said. "It is not a fit place for one's friends to come. But it is warm and snug, especially for the dogs."

Then Pilon spoke. He told the Pirate that worry was killing his friends; but if he would go to live with them, then they could sleep again, with their minds at ease.

It was a very great shock to the Pirate. He looked at his hands. And he looked to his dogs for comfort, but they would not meet his glance. At last he wiped the happiness from his eyes with the back of his hand, and he wiped his hand on his big black beard.

"And the dogs?" he asked softly. "You want the dogs, too? Are you friends of the dogs?"

Pilon nodded. "Yes, the dogs, too. There will be a whole corner set aside for the dogs."

The Pirate had a great deal of pride. He was afraid he might not conduct himself well. "Go away now," he said pleadingly. "Go home now. Tomorrow I will come."

His friends knew how he felt. They crawled out of the door and left him alone.

"He will be happy with us, that one," said Jesus Maria.

"Poor little lonely man," Danny added. "If I had

known, I would have asked him long ago, even if he had no treasure."

A flame of joy burned in all of them.

They settled soon into the new relationship. Danny, with a piece of blue chalk, drew a segment of a circle, enclosing a corner of the living room, and that was where the dogs must stay when they were in the house. The Pirate slept in that corner too, with the dogs.

The house was beginning to be a little crowded, with five men and five dogs; but from the first, Danny and his friends realized that their invitation to the Pirate had been inspired by that weary and anxious angel who guarded their destinies and protected them from evil.

Every morning, long before his friends were awake, the Pirate arose from his corner and, followed by his dogs, he made the rounds of the restaurants and the wharves. He was one of those for whom every one feels a kindliness. His packages grew larger. The paisanos received his bounty and made use of it; fresh fish, half pies, untouched loaves of stale bread, meat that required only a little soda to take the green out. They began really to live.

And their acceptance of his gifts touched the Pirate more deeply than anything they could have done for him. There was a light of worship in his eyes as he watched them eat the food he brought.

In the evening, when they sat about the stove and discussed the doings of Tortilla Flat with the lazy voices of fed gods, the Pirate's eyes darted from mouth to mouth, and his own lips moved, whispering again the words his friends said. The dogs pressed in about him jealously.

These were his friends, he told himself in the night, when the house was dark, when the dogs snuggled close to him so that all might be warm. These men loved him so much that it worried them to have him live alone. The Pirate had often to repeat this to himself, for it was an astounding thing, an unbelievable thing. His wheelbarrow stood in Danny's yard now, and every day he cut his pitchwood and sold it. But so afraid was the Pirate that he might miss some word his friends said in the evening, might not be there to absorb some stream of the warm companionship, that he had not visited his hoard for several days to put the new coins there.

His friends were kind to him. They treated him with a sweet courtesy; but always there was some eye open and upon him. When he wheeled his barrow into the woods, one of the friends walked with him, and sat on a log while he worked. When he went into the gulch, the last thing at night, Danny or Pablo or Pilon or Jesus Maria kept him company. And in the night he must have been very quiet to have crept out without a shadow behind him.

For a week, the friends merely watched the Pirate. But at last the inactivity tired them. Direct action was out of the question, they knew. And so one evening the subject of the desirability of hiding one's money came up for discussion.

Pilon began it. "I had an uncle, a regular miser, and he hid his gold in the woods. And one time he went to look at it, and it was gone. Some one had found it and stolen it. He was an old man, then, and all his money was gone, and he hanged himself." Pilon noticed with some satisfaction, the look of apprehension that came upon the Pirate's face.

Danny noticed it, too; and he continued, "The viejo, my grandfather, who owned this house, also buried money. I do not know how much, but he was reputed a rich man, so there must have been three or four hundred dollars. The viejo dug a deep hole and put his money in it, and then he covered it up, and then he strewed pine needles over the ground until he thought no one could see that anything had been done there. But when he went back, the hole was open, and the money was gone."

The Pirate's lips followed the words. A look of terror had come into his face. His fingers picked among the neck hairs of Señor Alec Thompson. The friends exchanged a glance and dropped the subject for the time being. They turned to the love life of Cornelia Ruiz.

In the night the Pirate crept out of the house, and the dogs crept after him; and Pilon crept after all of them. The Pirate went swiftly into the forest, leaping with sure feet over logs and brush. Pilon floundered behind him. But when they had gone at least two miles, Pilon was winded, and torn by vines. He paused to rest a moment; and then he realized that all sounds ahead of him had ceased. He waited and listened and crept about, but the Pirate had disappeared.

After two hours, Pilon went back again, slowly and tiredly. There was the Pirate in the house, fast asleep among his dogs. The dogs lifted their heads when Pilon entered, and Pilon thought they smiled satirically at him for a moment.

A conference took place in the gulch the next morning. "It is not possible to follow him," Pilon reported. "He vanished. He sees in the dark. He knows every tree in the forest. We must find some other way."

"Perhaps one is not enough," Pablo suggested. "If all of us should follow him, then one might not loose track of him."

"We will talk again tonight," said Jesus Maria, "only worse. A lady I know is going to give me a little wine," he added modestly. "Maybe if the Pirate has a little wine in him, he will not disappear so easily." So it was left.

Jesus Maria's lady gave him a whole gallon of wine. What could compare with the Pirate's delight that evening when a fruit jar of wine was put into his hand, when he sat with his friends and sipped his wine and listened to the talk? Such joy had come rarely into the Pirate's life.

He wished he might clasp these dear people to his breast
and tell them how much he loved them. But that was not
a thing he could do, for they might think he was drunk.
He wished he could do some tremendous thing to show
them his love.

"We spoke last night of burying money," said Pilon.
"Today I remembered a cousin of mine, a clever man. If
any one in the world could hide money where it would
never be found, he could do it. So he took his money and
hid it. Perhaps you have seen him, that poor little one who
crawls about the wharf and begs fish heads to make soup
of. That is my cousin. Some one stole his buried money."

The worry came back into the Pirate's face.

Story topped story, and in each one all manner of evil
dogged the footsteps of those who hid their money.

"It is better to keep one's money close, to spend some
now and then, to give a little to one's friends," Danny
finished.

They had been watching the Pirate narrowly, and in
the middle of the worst story they had seen the worry go
from his face, and a smile of relief take its place. Now he
sipped his wine and his eyes glittered with joy.

The friends were in despair. All their plans had failed.
They were sick at heart. After all their goodness and their
charity, this had happened. The Pirate had in some way
escaped the good they had intended to confer upon him.
They finished their wine and went moodily to bed.

Few things could happen in the night without Pilon's
knowledge. His ears remained open while the rest of him
slept. He heard the stealthy exit of the Pirate and his dogs
from the house. He leaped to awaken his friends; and in a
moment the four were following the Pirate in the direction of the forest. It was very dark when they entered the
pine forest. The four friends ran into trees, tripped on

berry vines; but for a long time they could hear the Pirate marching on ahead of them. They followed as far as Pilon had followed the night before, and then, suddenly, silence, and the whispering forest and the vague night wind. They combed the woods and the brush patches, but the Pirate had disappeared again.

At last, cold and disconsolate, they came together and trudged wearily back toward Monterey. The dawn came before they got back. The sun was already shining on the bay. The smoke of the morning fires arose to them out of Monterey.

The Pirate walked out on the porch to greet them, and his face was happy. They passed him sullenly, and filed into the living room. There on the table lay a large canvas bag.

The Pirate followed them in. "I lied to thee, Pilon," he said. "I told thee I had no money, for I was afraid. I did not know about my friends, then. You have told how hidden money is so often stolen, and I am afraid again. Only last night did a way out come to me. My money will be safe with my friends. No one can steal it if my friends guard it for me."

The four men stared at him in horror. "Take thy money back to the woods and hide it," Danny said savagely. "We do not want to watch it."

"No," said the Pirate. "I would not feel safe to hide it. But I will be happy knowing my friends guard it for me. You would not believe it, but the last two nights some one followed me into the forest to steal my money."

Terrible as the blow was, Pilon, that clever man, tried to escape it. "Before this money is put into our hands, maybe you would like to take some out," he suggested smoothly.

The Pirate shook his head. "No. I cannot do that. It is

promised. I have nearly a thousand two-bitses. When I have a thousand I will buy a gold candle-stick for San Francisco de Assisi.

"Once I had a nice dog, and that dog was sick; and I promised a gold candle-stick of one thousand days if that dog would get well. And," he spread his great hands, "that dog got well."

"Is it one of these dogs?" Pilon demanded.

"No," said the Pirate. "A truck ran over him a little later."

So it was over, all hope of diverting the money. Danny and Pablo morosely lifted the heavy bag of silver quarters, took it in the other room and put it under the pillow of Danny's bed. In time they would take a certain pleasure in the knowledge that this money lay under the pillow, but now their defeat was bitter. There was nothing in the world they could do about it. Their chance had come, and it had gone.

The Pirate stood before them, and there were tears of happiness in his eyes, for he had proved his love for his friends.

"To think," he said, "all those years I lay in that chicken house, and I did not know any pleasure. But now," he added, "oh, now I am very happy."

(Chapter VII)

THE TREASURE HUNT

HOW DANNY'S FRIENDS SOUGHT MYSTIC
TREASURE ON ST. ANDREW'S EVE. HOW
PILON FOUND IT AND LATER HOW A
PAIR OF SERGE PANTS CHANGED OWN-
ERSHIP TWICE.

IF he had been a hero, the Portagee would have spent
a miserable time in the army. The fact that he was Big
Joe Portagee, with a decent training in the Monterey jail,
not only saved him the misery of patriotism thwarted, but
solidified his conviction that as a man's days are rightly
devoted half to sleeping and half to waking, so a man's
years are rightly spent half in jail and half out. Of the
duration of the war, Joe Portagee spent considerably more
time in jail than out.

In civilian life, one is punished for things one does; but
army codes add a new principle to this—they punish a
man for things he does not do. Joe Portagee never did
figure this out. He didn't clean his rifle; he didn't shave;
and once or twice, on leave, he didn't come back. Coupled
with these shortcomings was a propensity Big Joe had for
genial argument when he was taken to task.

Ordinarily, he spent half his time in jail; of two years in
the army, he spent eighteen months in jail. And he was
far from satisfied with prison life in the army. In the Monterey jail he was accustomed to ease and companionship.
In the army, he found only work. In Monterey, only one

charge was ever brought against him: Drunk and Dis-
orderly Conduct. The charges in the army bewildered him
so completely that the effect on his mind was probably
permanent.

When the war was over, and all the troops were dis-
banded, Big Joe still had six months' sentence to serve.
The charge had been: "Being drunk on duty. Striking a
sergeant with a kerosene can. Denying his identity (he
couldn't remember it, so he denied everything). Stealing
two gallons of cooked beans, and going A.W.O.L. on the
Major's horse."

If the Armistice had not already been signed, Big Joe
would probably have been shot. He came home to Monterey long after the other veterans had arrived and had
eaten up all the sweets of victory.

When Big Joe swung down from the train, he was
dressed in an army overcoat and tunic and a pair of blue
serge trousers.

The town hadn't changed much, except for prohibition;
and prohibition hadn't changed Torrelli's. Joe traded his
overcoat for a gallon of wine and went out to find his
friends:

True friends he found none that night, but in Monterey
he found no lack of those vile and false harpies and pimps
who are ever ready to lead men into the pit. Joe, who was
not very moral, had no revulsion for the pit; he liked it.

Before very many hours had passed, his wine was gone,
and he had no money; and then the harpies tried to get
Joe out of the pit, and he wouldn't go. He was comfortable
there.

When they tried to eject him by force, Big Joe, with a
just and terrible resentment, broke all the furniture and all
the windows, sent half-clothed girls screaming into the
night; and then, as an afterthought, set fire to the house. It

was not a safe thing to lead Joe into temptation; he had no resistance to it at all.

A policeman finally interfered and took him in hand. The Portagee sighed happily. He was home again.

After a short and juryless trial, in which he was sentenced to thirty days, Joe lay luxuriously on his leather cot and slept heavily for one tenth of his sentence.

The Portagee liked the Monterey jail. It was a place to meet people. If he stayed there long enough, all his friends were in and out. The time passed quickly. He was a little sad when he had to go, but his sadness was tempered with the knowledge that it was very easy to get back again.

He would have liked to go into the pit again, but he had no money and no wine. He combed the streets for his old friends, Pilon and Danny and Pablo, and could not find them. The police sergeant said he hadn't booked them for a long time.

"They must be dead," said the Portagee.

He wandered sadly to Torrelli's, but Torrelli was not friendly toward men who had neither money nor barterable property, and he gave Big Joe little solace; but Torrelli did say that Danny had inherited a house on Tortilla Flat, and that all his friends lived there with him.

Affection and a desire to see his friends came to Big Joe. In the evening he wandered up toward Tortilla Flat to find Danny and Pilon. It was dusk as he walked up the street, and on the way he met Pilon, hurrying by in a businesslike way.

"Ai, Pilon. I was just coming to see you."

"Hello, Joe Portagee," Pilon was brusque. "Where you been?"

"In the army," said Joe.

Pilon's mind was not on the meeting. "I have to go on."

"I will go with you," said Joe.

Pilon stopped and surveyed him. "Don't you remember what night it is?" he asked.

"No. What is it?"

"It is St. Andrew's Eve."

Then the Portagee knew; for this was the night when every paisano who wasn't in jail wandered restlessly through the forest. This was the night when all buried treasure sent up a faint phosphorescent glow through the ground. There was plenty of treasure in the woods, too. Monterey had been invaded many times in two hundred years, and each time valuables had been hidden in the earth.

The night was clear. Pilon had emerged from his hard daily shell, as he did now and then. He was the idealist tonight, the giver of gifts. This night he was engaged in a mission of kindness.

"You may come with me, Big Joe Portagee, but if we find any treasure I must decide what to do with it. If you do not agree, you can go by yourself and look for your own treasure."

Big Joe was not an expert at directing his own efforts. "I will go with you, Pilon," he said. "I don't care about the treasure."

The night came down as they walked into the forest. Their feet found the pine-needle beds. Now Pilon knew it for a perfect night. A high fog covered the sky, and behind it, the moon shone so that the forest was filled with a gauze-like light. There was none of the sharp outline we think of as reality. The tree trunks were not black columns of wood, but soft and unsubstantial shadows. The patches of brush were formless and shifting in the queer light. Ghosts could walk freely tonight, without fear of the disbelief of men; for this night was haunted, and it would be an insensitive man who did not know it.

Now and then Pilon and Big Joe passed other searchers who wandered restlessly, zig-zagging among the pines. Their heads were down and they moved silently and passed no greeting. Who could say whether all of them were really living men? Joe and Pilon knew that some were shades of those old folk who had buried the treasures; and who, on Saint Andrew's Eve, wandered back to the earth to see that their gold was undisturbed. Pilon wore his saint's medallion, hung around his neck, outside his clothes; so he had no fear of the spirits. Big Joe walked with his fingers crossed in the Holy Sign. Although they might be frightened, they knew they had protection more than adequate to cope with the unearthly night.

The wind arose as they walked, and drove the fog across the pale moon like a thin wash of gray water color. The moving fog gave shifting form to the forest, so that every tree crept stealthily along and the bushes moved soundlessly, like great dark cats. The tree-tops in the wind talked huskily, told fortunes and foretold deaths. Pilon knew it was not good to listen to the talking of the trees. No good ever came of knowing the future; and besides, this whispering was unholy. He turned the attention of his ears from the trees' talking.

He began a zig-zag path through the forest, and Big Joe walked beside him like a great alert dog. Lone silent men passed them, and went on without a greeting; and the dead passed them noiselessly, and went on without a greeting.

The fog siren began its screaming on the Point, far below them; and it wailed its sorrow for all the good ships that had drowned on the iron reef, and for all those others that would sometime die there.

Pilon shuddered and felt cold, although the night was warm. He whispered a Hail Mary under his breath.

They passed a gray man who walked with his head down, and who gave them no greeting.

An hour went by, and still Pilon and Big Joe wandered as restlessly as the dead who crowded the night.

Suddenly Pilon stopped. His hand found Big Joe's arm. "Do you see?" he whispered.

"Where?"

"Right ahead there."

"Ye-s—I think so."

It seemed to Pilon that he could see a soft pillar of blue light that shone out of the ground ten yards ahead of him.

"Big Joe," he whispered, "find two sticks about three or four feet long. I do not want to look away. I might lose it."

He stood like a pointing dog while Big Joe scurried off to find the sticks. Pilon heard him break two small dead limbs from a pine tree. And he heard the snaps as Big Joe broke the twigs from his sticks. And still Pilon stared at the pale shaft of nebulous light. So faint it was that sometimes it seemed to disappear altogether. Sometimes he was not sure he saw it at all. He did not move his eyes when Big Joe put the sticks in his hands. Pilon crossed the sticks at right angles and advanced slowly, holding the cross in front of him. As he came close, the light seemed to fade away, but he saw where it had come from, a perfectly round depression in the pine needles.

Pilon laid his cross over the depression, and he said, "All that lies here is mine by discovery. Go away, all evil spirits. Go away, spirits of men who buried this treasure, *In Nomen Patris et Filius et Spiritu Sancti*," and then he heaved a great sigh and sat down on the ground.

"We have found it, oh my friend, Big Joe," he cried. "For many years I have looked, and now I have found it."

"Let's dig," said Big Joe.

But Pilon shook his head impatiently. "When all the spirits are free? When even to be here is dangerous? You are a fool, Big Joe. We will sit here until morning; and then we will mark the place, and tomorrow night we will dig. No one else can see the light now that we have covered it with the cross. Tomorrow night there will be no danger."

The night seemed more fearful now that they sat in the pine needles, but the cross sent out a warmth of holiness and safety, like a little bonfire on the ground. Like a fire, however, it only warmed the front of them. Their backs were to the cold and evil things that wandered about in the forest.

Pilon got up and drew a big circle around the whole place, and he was inside when he closed the circle. "Let no evil thing cross this line, in the Name of the Most Holy Jesus," he chanted. Then he sat down again. Both he and Big Joe felt better. They could hear the muffled footsteps of the weary wandering ghosts; they could see the little lights that glowed from the transparent forms as they walked by; but their protecting line was impregnable. Nothing bad from this world or from any other world could cross into the circle.

"What are you going to do with the money?" Big Joe asked.

Pilon looked at him with contempt. "You have never looked for treasure, Big Joe Portagee, for you do not know how to go about it. I cannot keep this treasure for myself. If I go after it intending to keep it, then the treasure will dig itself down and down like a clam in the sand, and I shall never find it. No, that is not the way. I am digging this treasure for Danny."

All the idealism in Pilon came out then. He told Big Joe how good Danny was to his friends.

"And we do nothing for him," he said. "We pay no rent. Sometimes we get drunk and break the furniture. We fight with Danny when we are angry with him, and we call him names. Oh, we are very bad, Big Joe. And so all of us, Pablo and Jesus Maria and the Pirate and I talked and planned. We are all in the woods, tonight, looking for treasure. And the treasure is to be for Danny. He is so good, Big Joe. He is so kind; and we are so bad. But if we take a great sack of treasure to him, then he will be glad. It is because my heart is clean of selfishness that I can find this treasure?"

"Won't you keep any of it?" Big Joe asked, incredulous. "Not even for a gallon of wine?"

Pilon had no speck of the Bad Pilon in him this night. "No, not one scrap of gold! Not one little brown penny! It is all for Danny, every bit."

Joe was disappointed. "I walked all this way, and I won't even get a glass of wine for it," he mourned.

"When Danny has the money," Pilon said delicately, "it may be that he will buy a little wine. Of course I shall not suggest it, for this treasure is Danny's. But I think maybe he might buy a little wine. And then if you were good to him, you might get a glass."

Big Joe was comforted, for he had known Danny a long time. He thought it possible that Danny might buy a great deal of wine.

The night passed on over them. The moon went down and left the forest in muffled darkness. The fog siren screamed and screamed. During the whole night Pilon remained unspotted. He preached a little to Big Joe as recent converts are likely to do.

"It is worth while to be kind and generous," he said. "Not only do such actions pile up a house of joy in Heaven; but there is, too, a quick reward here on earth. One feels a golden warmth glowing like a hot enchilada in one's stomach. The Spirit of God clothes one in a coat as soft as camel's hair. I have not always been a good man, Big Joe Portagee. I confess it freely."

Big Joe knew it perfectly well.

"I have been bad," Pilon continued ecstatically. He was enjoying himself thoroughly. "I have lied and stolen. I have been lecherous. I have committed adultery and taken God's name in vain."

"Me too," said Big Joe happily.

"And what was the result, Big Joe Portagee? I have had a mean feeling. I have known I would go to Hell. But now I see that the sinner is never so bad that he cannot be forgiven. Although I have not yet been to confession, I can feel that the change in me is pleasing to God, for His grace is upon me. If you, too, would change your ways, Big Joe, if you would give up drunkenness and fighting and those girls down at Dora Williams' House, you too might feel as I do."

But Big Joe had gone to sleep. He never stayed awake very long when he was not moving about.

The grace was not quite so sharp to Pilon when he could not tell Big Joe about it, but he sat and watched the treasure place while the sky grayed and the dawn came behind the fog. He saw the pine trees take shape and emerge out of obscurity. The wind died down and the little blue rabbits came out of the brush and hopped about on the pine needles. Pilon was heavy-eyed but happy.

When it was light he stirred Big Joe Portagee with his foot. "It is time to go to Danny's house. The day has come." Pilon threw the cross away, for it was no longer needed, and he erased the circle. "Now," he said, "we must make no mark, but we must remember this by trees and rocks."

"Why don't we dig now?" Big Joe asked.

"And everybody in Tortilla Flat would come to help us," Pilon said sarcastically.

They looked hard at the surroundings, saying, "Now there are three trees together on the right, and two on the

left. That patch of brush is down there, and here is a
rock." At last they walked away from the treasure, mem-
orizing the way as they went.

At Danny's house they found tired friends. "Did you
find any?" the friends demanded.

"No," said Pilon quickly, to forestall Joe's confession.

"Well, Pablo thought he saw the light, but it disappeared before he got to it. And the Pirate saw the ghost of
an old woman, and she had his dog with her."

The Pirate broke into a smile. "That old woman told
me my dog was happy now," he said.

"Here is Big Joe Portagee, back from the army," announced Pilon.

"Hello, Joe."

"You got a nice place here," said the Portagee, and let
himself down easily into a chair.

"You keep out of my bed," said Danny, for he knew
that Joe Portagee had come to stay. The way he sat in a
chair and crossed his knees had an appearance of perma-
nence.

The Pirate went out, and took his wheelbarrow and
started into the forest to cut his kindlings; but the other
five men lay down in the sunshine that broke through the
fog, and in a little while they were asleep.

It was mid-afternoon before any of them awakened. At
last they stretched their arms and sat up and looked listlessly down at the bay below, where a brown oil tanker
moved slowly out to sea. The Pirate had left the bags on
the table, and the friends opened them and brought out
the food the Pirate had collected.

Big Joe walked down the path toward the sagging gate.
"See you later," he called to Pilon.

Pilon anxiously watched him until he saw that Big Joe
was headed down the hill to Monterey, not up toward the

pine forest. The four friends sat down and dreamily watched the evening come.

At dusk Joe Portagee returned. He and Pilon conferred in the yard, out of earshot of the house.

"We will borrow tools from Mrs. Morales," Pilon said. "A shovel and a pick-ax stand by her chicken house."

When it was quite dark they started. "We go to see some girls, friends of Joe Portagee's," Pilon explained. They crept into Mrs. Morales' yard and borrowed the tools. And then, from the weeds beside the road, Big Joe lifted out a gallon jug of wine.

"Thou hast sold the treasure," Pilon cried fiercely. "Thou art a traitor, oh dog of a dog."

Big Joe quieted him firmly. "I did not tell where the treasure was," he said with some dignity. "I told like this, 'We found a treasure,' I said, 'But it is for Danny. When Danny has it, I will borrow a dollar and pay for the wine.'"

Pilon was overwhelmed. "And they believed, and let you take the wine?" he demanded.

"Well—" Big Joe hesitated. "I left something to prove I would bring the dollar."

Pilon turned like lightning and took him by the throat. "What did you leave?"

"Only one little blanket, Pilon," Joe Portagee wailed. "Only one."

Pilon shook at him, but Big Joe was so heavy that Pilon only succeeded in shaking himself. "What blanket," he cried. "Say what blanket it was you stole."

Big Joe blubbered. "Only one of Danny's. Only one. He has two. I took only the little tiny one. Do not hurt me, Pilon. The other one was bigger. Danny will get it back when we find the treasure."

Pilon whirled him around and kicked him with accuracy and fire. "Pig," he said, "dirty thieving cow. You will get the blanket back or I will beat you to ribbons."

Big Joe tried to placate him. "I thought how we are working for Danny," he whispered. "I thought, 'Danny will be so glad, he can buy a hundred new blankets.'"

"Be still," said Pilon. "You will get that same blanket back or I will beat you with a rock." He took up the jug and uncorked it and drank a little to soothe his frayed sensibilities; moreover he drove the cork back and refused the Portagee even a drop. "For this theft you must do all the digging. Pick up those tools and come with me."

Big Joe whined like a puppy, and obeyed. He could not stand against the righteous fury of Pilon.

They tried to find the treasure for a long time. It was late when Pilon pointed to three trees in a row. "There!" he said.

They searched about until they found the depression in the ground. There was a little moonlight to guide them, for this night the sky was free of fog.

Now that he was not going to dig, Pilon developed a new theory for uncovering treasure. "Sometimes the money is in sacks," he said, "and the sacks are rotted. If you dig straight down you might lose some." He drew a generous circle around the hollow. "Now, dig a deep trench around, and then we will come *up* on the treasure."

"Aren't you going to dig?" Big Joe asked.

Pilon broke into fury. "Am I a thief of blankets?" he cried. "Do I steal from the bed of my friend who shelters me?"

"Well, I ain't going to do all the digging," Big Joe said.

Pilon picked up one of the pine limbs that only the night before had served as part of the cross. He advanced ominously toward Big Joe Portagee. "Thief," he snarled. "Dirty pig of an untrue friend. Take up that shovel."

Big Joe's courage flowed away, and he stooped for the

shovel on the ground. If Joe Portagee's conscience had not been bad, he might have remonstrated; but his fear of Pilon, armed with a righteous cause and a stick of pine wood, was great.

Big Joe abhorred the whole principle of shoveling. The line of the moving shovel was unattractive. The end to be gained, that of taking dirt from one place and putting it in another, was, to one who held the larger vision, silly and gainless. A whole lifetime of shoveling could accomplish practically nothing. Big Joe's reaction was a little more simple than this. He didn't like to shovel. He had joined the army to fight, and had done nothing but dig.

But Pilon stood over him, and the trench stretched around the treasure place. It did no good to profess sickness, hunger or weakness. Pilon was inexorable, and Joe's crime of the blanket was held against him. Although he whined, complained, held up his hands to show how they were hurt, Pilon stood over him and forced the digging.

Midnight came, and the trench was three feet down. The roosters of Monterey crowed. The moon sank behind the trees. At last Pilon gave the word to move in on the treasure. The bursts of dirt came slowly now; Big Joe was exhausted. Just before daylight, his shovel struck something hard.

"Ai," he cried. "We have it, Pilon."

The find was large and square. Frantically they dug at it in the dark, and they could not see it.

"Careful," Pilon cautioned. "Do not hurt it."

The daylight came before they had it out. Pilon felt metal and leaned down in the gray light to see. It was a good-sized square of concrete. On the top was a round brown plate. Pilon spelled out the words on it:

"United States Geodetic Survey + 1915 + Elevation 600 Feet."

Pilon sat down in the pit and his shoulders sagged in defeat.

"No treasure?" Big Joe asked plaintively.

Pilon did not answer him. The Portagee inspected the cement post and his brow wrinkled with thought. He turned to the sorrowing Pilon. "Maybe we can take this good piece of metal and sell it."

Pilon peered up out of his dejection. "Johnny Pom-pom found one," he said with a quietness of great disappointment. "Johnny Pom-pom took the metal piece and tried to sell it. It is a year in jail to dig one of these up," Pilon mourned. "A year in jail and two thousand dollar fine." In his pain, Pilon wanted only to get away from this tragic place. He stood up, found a weed in which to wrap the wine bottle, and started down the hill.

Big Joe trotted after him solicitously. "Where are we going?" he asked.

"I don't know," said Pilon.

The day was bright when they arrived at the beach; but even there Pilon did not stop. He trudged along the hard sand by the water's edge until Monterey was far behind and only the sand dunes of Seaside and the rippling waves of the bay were there to see his sorrow. At last he sat in the dry sand, with the sun warming him. Big Joe sat beside him, and he felt that in some way he was responsible for Pilon's silent pain.

Pilon took the jug out of its weed and uncorked it and drank deeply, and because sorrow is the mother of a general compassion, he passed Joe's wine to the miscreant Joe.

"How we build," Pilon cried. "How our dreams lead us. I had thought how we would carry bags of gold to Danny. I could see how his face would look. He would be surprised. For a long time he would not believe it." He took the bottle from Joe Portagee and drank colossally. "All this is gone, blown away in the night."

The sun was warming the beach now. In spite of his disappointment, Pilon felt a traitorous comfort stealing over him, a treacherous impulse to discover some good points in the situation.

Big Joe, in his quiet way, was drinking more than his share of the wine. Pilon took it indignantly and drank again and again.

"But after all," he said philosophically, "maybe if we had found gold, it might not have been good for Danny. He has always been a poor man. Riches might make him crazy."

Big Joe nodded solemnly. The wine went down and down in the bottle.

"Happiness is better than riches," said Pilon. "If we try to make Danny happy, it will be a better thing than to give him money."

Big Joe nodded again and took off his shoes. "Make him happy. That's the stuff."

Pilon turned sadly upon him. "You are only a pig, and not fit to live with men," he said gently. "You who stole Danny's blanket should be kept in a sty and fed potato peelings."

They were getting very sleepy in the warm sun. The little waves whispered along the beach. Pilon took off his shoes.

"Even Stephen," said Big Joe, and they drained the jug to the last drop.

The beach was swaying gently, heaving and falling with a movement like a ground-swell.

"You aren't a bad man," Pilon said. But Big Joe Portagee was already asleep. Pilon took off his coat and laid it over his face. In a few moments, he too was sleeping sweetly.

The sun wheeled over the sky. The tide spread up the beach, and then retreated. A squad of scampering kildeers inspected the sleeping men. A wandering dog sniffed them. Two elderly ladies, collecting seashells, saw the bodies and hurried past lest these men should awaken in passion, pursue and criminally assault them. It was a shame, they agreed, that the police did nothing to control such matters. "They are drunk," one said.

And the other stared back up the beach at the sleeping men. "Drunken beasts," she agreed.

When at last the sun went behind the pines of the hill in back of Monterey, Pilon awakened. His mouth was as dry as alum; his head ached and he was stiff from the hard sand. Big Joe snored on.

"Joe," Pilon cried, but the Portagee was beyond call. Pilon rested on his elbow and stared out to sea. "A little wine would be good for my dry mouth," he thought. He tipped up the jug and got not a single drop to soothe his dry tongue. Then he turned out his pockets in the hope that while he slept some miracle had taken place there; but none had. There was a broken pocket knife for which he had been refused a glass of wine at least twenty times. There was a fish-hook in a cork, a piece of dirty string, a dog's tooth and several keys that fit nothing Pilon knew of. In the whole lot was not a thing Torrelli would consider as worth having, even in a moment of insanity.

Pilon looked speculatively at Big Joe. "Poor fellow," he thought. "When Joe Portagee wakes up, he will feel as dry as I do. He will like it if I have a little wine for him." He pushed Big Joe roughly several times; and when the Portagee only mumbled, and then snored again, Pilon looked through his pockets. He found a brass pants button, a little metal disk which said "Good Eats at the Dutchman," four or five headless matches and a little piece of chewing tobacco.

Pilon sat back on his heels. So it was no use. He must wither here on the beach while his throat called lustily for wine.

He noticed the serge trousers the Portagee was wearing, and stroked them with his fingers. "Nice cloth," he thought. "Why should this dirty Portagee wear such good cloth when all his friends go about in jeans?" Then he remembered how badly the pants fit Big Joe, how tight the waist was even with two fly-buttons undone, how the cuffs missed the shoe tops by inches. "Some one of a decent size would be happy in those pants."

Pilon remembered Big Joe's crime against Danny, and he became an avenging angel. How did this big black Portagee dare to insult Danny so! "When he wakes up I will beat him! But," the more subtle Pilon argued, "his crime was theft. Would it not teach him a lesson to know how it feels to have something stolen? What good is punishment unless something is learned?" It was a triumphant position for Pilon. If, with one action, he could avenge Danny, discipline Big Joe, teach an ethical lesson and get a little wine, who in the world could criticize him?

He pushed the Portagee vigorously, and Big Joe brushed at him as though he were a fly. Pilon deftly removed the trousers, rolled them up and sauntered away into the sand dunes.

Torrelli was out, but Mrs. Torrelli opened the door to Pilon. He was mysterious in his manner, but at last he held up the pants for her inspection.

She shook her head decisively.

"But look," said Pilon. "You are seeing only the spots and the dirt. Look at this fine cloth underneath. Think, señora! You have cleaned the spots off and pressed the trousers! Torrelli comes in! He is silent; he is glum. And then you bring him these fine pants! See how his eyes grow bright! See how happy he is! He takes you on his

lap! Look how he smiles at you, señora! Is so much happiness too high at one gallon of red wine?"

"The seat of the pants is thin," she said.

He held them up to the light. "Can you see through
them? No! The stiffness, the discomfort is taken out of
them. They are in prime condition."

"No," she said firmly.

"You are cruel to your husband, señora. You deny him
happiness. I should not be surprised to see him going to
other women, who are not so heartless. For a quart,
then?"

Finally her resistance was beaten down and she gave
him the quart. Pilon drank it off immediately. "You try to
break down the price of pleasure," he warned her. "I
should have half a gallon."

Mrs. Torrelli was hard as stone. Not a drop more could
Pilon get. He sat there brooding in the kitchen. "Jewess,
that's what she is. She cheats me out of Big Joe's pants."

Pilon thought sadly of his friend out there on the beach.
What could he do? If he came into town he would be arrested. And what had this harpy done to deserve the
pants? She had tried to buy Pilon's friend's pants for a
miserable quart of miserable wine. Pilon felt himself dis-
solving into anger at her.

"I am going away in a moment," he told Mrs. Torrelli.
The pants were hung in a little alcove off the kitchen.

"Good-by," said Mrs. Torrelli over her shoulder. She
went into her little pantry to prepare dinner.

On his way out Pilon passed the alcove and lifted down
not only the pants, but Danny's blanket.

Pilon walked back down the beach, toward the place
where he had left Big Joe. He could see a bonfire burning
brightly on the sand, and as he drew nearer, a number of
small dark figures passed in front of the flame. It was very
dark now; he guided himself by the fire. As he came close,

he saw that it was a Girl Scout wienie bake. He approached warily.

For a while he could not see Big Joe, but at last he discovered him, lying half covered with sand, speechless with cold and agony. Pilon walked firmly up to him and held up the pants.

"Take them, Big Joe, and be glad you have them back."

Joe's teeth were chattering. "Who stole my pants, Pilon? I have been lying here for hours, and I could not go away because of those girls."

Pilon obligingly stood between Big Joe and the little girls who were running about the bonfire. The Portagee brushed the cold damp sand from his legs and put on his pants. They walked side by side along the dark beach toward Monterey, where the lights hung, necklace above necklace against the hill. The sand dunes crouched along the back of the beach like tired hounds, resting; and the waves gently practiced at striking, and hissed a little. The night was cold and aloof, and its warm life was withdrawn, so that it was full of bitter warnings to man that he is alone in the world, and alone among his fellows; that he has no comfort owing him from anywhere.

Pilon was still brooding, and Joe Portagee sensed the depth of his feeling. At last Pilon turned his head toward his friend. "We learn by this that it is great foolishness to trust a woman," he said.

"Did some woman take my pants?" Big Joe demanded excitedly. "Who was it? I'll kick the hell out of her!"

But Pilon shook his head as sadly as old Jehovah, who, resting on the seventh day, sees that his world is tiresome. "She is punished," Pilon said. "You might say she punished herself, and that is the best way. She had thy pants; she bought them with greed; and now she has them not."

These things were beyond Big Joe. They were mysteries it was better to let alone; and this was as Pilon wished it. Big Joe said humbly, "Thanks for getting my pants back, Pilon." But Pilon was so sunk in philosophy that even thanks were valueless.

"It was nothing," he said. "In the whole matter only the lesson we learn has any value."

They climbed up from the beach and passed the great silver tower of the gas works.

Big Joe Portagee was happy to be with Pilon. "Here is one who takes care of his friends," he thought. "Even when they sleep he is alert to see that no harm comes to them." He resolved to do something nice for Pilon sometime.

(Chapter VIII)

TORTILLAS AND BEANS

HOW DANNY'S FRIENDS THREW THEM-SELVES TO THE AID OF A DISTRESSED LADY.

SEÑORA TERESINA CORTEZ and her eight children and her ancient mother lived in a pleasant cottage on the edge of the deep gulch that defines the southern frontier of Tortilla Flat. Teresina was a good figure of a mature woman, nearing thirty. Her mother, that ancient, dried, toothless one, relict of a past generation, was nearly fifty. It was long since any one had remembered that her name was Angelica.

During the week work was ready to this vieja's hand, for it was her duty to feed, punish, cajole, dress and bed down seven of the eight children. Teresina was busy with the eighth, and with making certain preparations for the ninth.

On Sunday, however, the vieja, clad in black satin more ancient even than she, hatted in a grim and durable affair of black straw, on which were fastened two true cherries of enameled plaster, threw duty to the wind and went firmly to church, where she sat as motionless as the saints in their niches. Once a month, in the afternoon, she went to confession. It would be interesting to know what sins she confessed, and where she found the time to commit them, for in Teresina's house there were creepers, crawlers, stumblers, shriekers, cat-killers, fallers-out-of-trees;

and each one of these charges could be trusted to be rav-
enous every two hours.

Is it any wonder that the vieja had a remote soul and
nerves of steel? Any other kind would have gone screaming out of her body like little skyrockets.

Teresina was a mildly puzzled woman, as far as her
mind was concerned. Her body was one of those perfect
retorts for the distillation of children. The first baby, conceived when she was fourteen, had been a shock to her;
such a shock, that she delivered it in the ball park at night,
wrapped it in newspaper and left it for the night watchman to find. This is a secret. Even now Teresina might get
into trouble if it were known.

When she was sixteen, Mr. Alfred Cortez married her
and gave her his name and the two foundations of her
family, Alfredo and Ernie. Mr. Cortez gave her that name
gladly. He was only using it temporarily anyway. His
name, before he came to Monterey and after he left, was
Guggliemo. He went away after Ernie was born. Perhaps
he foresaw that being married to Teresina was not going
to be a quiet life.

The regularity with which she became a mother always astonished Teresina. It occurred sometimes that she
could not remember who the father of the impending
baby was; and occasionally she almost grew convinced
that no lover was necessary. In the time when she had
been under quarantine as a diphtheria carrier she conceived just the same. However, when a question became
too complicated for her mind to unravel, she usually laid
that problem in the arms of the Mother of Jesus, who, she
knew, had more knowledge of, interest in and time for
such things than she.

Teresina went often to confession. She was the despair
of Father Ramon. Indeed he had seen that while her
knees, her hands and her lips did penance for an old sin,

her modest and provocative eyes, flashing under drawn lashes, laid the foundations for a new one.

During the time I have been telling this, Teresina's ninth child was born, and for the moment she was unengaged. The vieja received another charge; Alfredo entered his third year in the first grade, Ernie his second, and Panchito went to school for the first time.

At about this time in California it became the stylish thing for school nurses to visit the classes and to catechize the children on intimate details of their home life. In the first grade, Alfredo was called to the principal's office, for it was thought that he looked thin.

The visiting nurse, trained in child psychology, said kindly, "Freddie, do you get enough to eat?"

"Sure," said Alfredo.

"Well, now. Tell me what you have for breakfast."

"Tortillas and beans," said Alfredo.

The nurse nodded her head dismally to the principal. "What do you have when you go home for lunch?"

"I don't go home."

"Don't you eat at noon?"

"Sure. I bring some beans wrapped up in a tortilla."

Actual alarm showed in the nurse's eyes, but she controlled herself: "At night what do you have to eat?"

"Tortillas and beans."

Her psychology deserted her. "Do you mean to stand there and tell me you eat nothing but tortillas and beans?"

Alfredo was astonished. "Jesus Christ," he said, "what more do you want?"

In due course the school doctor listened to the nurse's horrified report. One day he drove up to Teresina's house to look into the matter. As he walked through the yard the creepers, the crawlers and the stumblers were shrieking one terrible symphony. The doctor stood in the open kitchen door. With his own eyes he saw the vieja go to the stove, dip a great spoon into a kettle and sow the floor with boiled beans. Instantly the noise ceased. Creepers, crawlers and stumblers went to work with silent industry, moving from bean to bean, pausing only to eat them. The vieja went back to her chair for a few moments of peace. Under the bed, under the chairs, under the stove the children crawled with the intentness of little bugs. The doctor stayed two hours, for his scientific interest was piqued. He went away shaking his head.

He shook his head incredulously while he made his report. "I gave them every test I know of," he said, "teeth, skin, blood, skeleton, eyes, co-ordination. Gentlemen, they are living on what constitutes a slow poison, and they have from birth. Gentlemen, I tell you I have never seen healthier children in my life!" His emotion overcame him. "The little beasts," he cried. "I never saw such teeth in my life. I *never* saw such teeth!"

You will wonder how Teresina procured food for her family. When the bean threshers have passed, you will see, where they have stopped, big piles of bean chaff. If you will spread a blanket on the ground, and, on a windy afternoon, toss the chaff in the air over the blanket, you will understand that the threshers are not infallible. For an afternoon of work you may collect twenty or more pounds of beans.

In the autumn the vieja and those children who could walk went into the fields and winnowed the chaff. The landowners did not mind, for she did no harm. It was a bad year when the vieja did not collect three or four hundred pounds of beans.

When you have four hundred pounds of beans in the house, you need have no fear of starvation. Other things, delicacies such as sugar, tomatoes, peppers, coffee, fish or meat may come sometimes miraculously, through the intercession of the Virgin, sometimes through industry or cleverness; but your beans are there, and you are safe. Beans are a roof over your stomach. Beans are a warm cloak against economic cold.

Only one thing could threaten the lives and happiness of the family of the Señora Teresina Cortez; that was a failure of the bean crop.

When the beans are ripe, the little bushes are pulled and gathered into piles, to dry crisp for the threshers. Then is the time to pray that the rain may hold off. When the little piles of beans lie in lines, yellow against the dark fields, you will see the farmers watching the sky, scowling with dread at every cloud that sails over; for if a rain comes, the bean piles must be turned over to dry again. And if more rain falls before they are dry, they must be turned again. If a third shower falls, mildew and rot set in, and the crop is lost.

When the beans were drying, it was the vieja's custom to burn a candle to the Virgin.

In the year of which I speak, the beans were piled and the candle had been burned. At Teresina's house, the gunny sacks were laid out in readiness.

The threshing machines were oiled and cleaned.

A shower fell.

Extra hands rushed to the fields and turned the sodden hummocks of beans. The vieja burned another candle.

More rain fell.

Then the vieja bought two candles with a little gold piece she had kept for many years. The field hands turned over the beans to the sun again; and then came a downpour of cold streaking rain. Not a bean was harvested in all Monterey County. The soggy lumps were turned under by the plows.

Oh, then distress entered the house of Señora Teresina Cortez. The staff of life was broken; the little roof destroyed. Gone was that eternal verity, beans. At night the children cried with terror at the approaching starvation. They were not told, but they knew. The vieja sat in church, as always, but her lips drew back in a sneer when she looked at the Virgin. "You took my candles," she thought. "Ohee, yes. Greedy you are for candles. Oh, thoughtless one." And sullenly she transferred her allegiance to Santa Clara. She told Santa Clara of the injustice that had been done. She permitted herself a little malicious thought at the Virgin birth. "You know, sometimes Teresina can't remember either," she told Santa Clara viciously.

It has been said that Jesus Maria Corcoran was a great-hearted man. He had also that gift some humanitarians possess of being inevitably drawn toward those spheres where his instinct was needed. How many times had he not come upon young ladies when they needed comforting. Toward any pain or sorrow he was irresistibly drawn. He had not been to Teresinà's house for many months. If there is no mystical attraction between pain and humanitarianism, how did it happen that he went there to call on the very day when the last of the old year's beans was put in the pot?

He sat in Teresina's kitchen, gently brushing children off his legs. And he looked at Teresina with polite and pained eyes while she told of the calamity. He watched, fascinated, when she turned the last bean sack inside out to show that not one single bean was left. He nodded sympathetically when she pointed out the children, so soon to be skeletons, so soon to die of starvation.

Then the vieja told bitterly how she had been tricked by the Virgin. But upon this point, Jesus Maria was not sympathetic.

"What do you know, old one?" he said sternly. "Maybe the Blessed Virgin had business some place else."

"But four candles I burned," the vieja insisted shrilly.

Jesus Maria regarded her coldly. "What are four candles to Her?" he said. "I have seen one church where She had hundreds. She is no miser of candles."

But his mind burned with Teresina's trouble. That evening he talked mightily and piteously to the friends at Danny's house. Out of his great heart he drew a compelling oratory, a passionate plea for those little children who had no beans. And so telling was his speech·that the fire in his heart ignited the hearts of his friends. They leaped up. Their eyes glowed.

"The children shall not starve," they cried. "It shall be our trust!"

"We live in luxury," Pilon said.

"We shall give of our substance," Danny agreed. "And if they needed a house, they could live here."

"Tomorrow we shall start," Pablo exclaimed. "No more laziness! To work! There are things to be done!"

Jesus Maria felt the gratification of a leader with followers.

Theirs was no idle boast. Fish they collected. The vegetable patch of the Hotel Del Monte they raided. It was a glorious game. Theft robbed of the stigma of theft, crime altruistically committed— What is more gratifying?

The Pirate raised the price of kindlings to thirty cents and went to three new restaurants every morning. Big Joe stole Mrs. Palochico's goat over and over again, and each time it went home.

Now food began to accumulate in the house of Teresina. Boxes of lettuce lay on her porch, spoiled mackerel filled the neighborhood with a strong odor. And still the flame of charity burned in the friends.

If you could see the complaint book at the Monterey Police Department, you would notice that during this time there was a minor crime wave in Monterey. The police car hurried from place to place. Here a chicken was taken, there a whole patch of pumpkins. Paladini Company reported the loss of two one-hundred-pound cases of abalone steaks.

Teresina's house was growing crowded. The kitchen was stacked high with food. The back porch overflowed with vegetables. Odors like those of a packing house permeated Tortilla Flat. Breathlessly the friends dashed about at their larcenies, and long they talked and planned with Teresina.

At first Teresina was maddened with joy at so much food, and her head was turned by the compliment. After a week of it, she was not so sure. The baby was down with colic, Ernie had some kind of bowel trouble, Alfredo's face was flushed. The creepers and crawlers cried all the time. Teresina was ashamed to tell the friends what she must tell them. It took her several days to get her courage up; and during that time there arrived fifty pounds of celery and a crate of cantaloupes. At last she had to tell them. The neighbors were beginning to look at her with lifted brows.

She asked all of Danny's friends into her kitchen, and then she informed them of the trouble, modestly and carefully, that their feelings might not be hurt.

"Green things and fruit are not good for children," she explained. "Milk is constipating to a baby after it is weaned." She pointed to the flushed and irritable children. See, they were all sick. They were not getting the proper food.

"What is the proper food?" Pilon demanded.

"Beans," she said. "There you have something to trust, something that will not go right through you."

The friends went silently away. They pretended to themselves to be disheartened, but they knew that the first fire of their enthusiasm had been lacking for several days.

At Danny's house they held a conference.

This must not be told in some circles, for the charge might be serious.

Long after midnight, four dark forms who shall be nameless, moved like shadows through the town. Four indistinct shapes crept up on the Western Warehouse Company platform. The watchman said, afterward, that he heard sounds, investigated and saw nothing. He could not say how the thing was done, how a lock was broken and the door forced. Only four men know that the watchman was sound asleep, and they will never tell on him.

A little later the four shadows left the warehouse, and now they were bent under tremendous loads. Pantings and snortings came from the shadows.

At three o'clock in the morning Teresina was awakened by hearing her back door open. "Who is there?" she cried.

There was no answer, but she heard four great thumps that shook the house. She lighted a candle and went to the kitchen in her bare feet. There, against the wall, stood four one-hundred-pound sacks of pink beans.

Teresina rushed in and awakened the vieja. "A miracle!" she cried. "Come look in the kitchen."

The vieja regarded with shame the plump full sacks. "Oh, miserable dirty sinner am I," she moaned. "Oh, Holy Mother, look with pity on an old fool. Every month thou shalt have a candle, as long as I live."

At Danny's house, four friends were lying happily in their blankets. What pillow can one have like a good conscience? They slept well into the afternoon, for their work was done.

And Teresina discovered, by a method she had found to be infallible, that she was going to have a baby. As she poured a quart of the new beans into the kettle, she wondered idly which one of Danny's friends was responsible.

(Chapter XIII)

FROM

In Dubious Battle

A FUTURE WE CAN'T FORESEE

Part of Chapter 13 and the final chapter, containing the climax and developing the principal theme of the novel, first published in 1936. A story of the labor struggle on the California fruit farms, the characters and actions of this chapter are self-explanatory.

A FUTURE WE CAN'T
FORESEE

IN a moment London came into the tent, and the stranger followed him, a chunky, comfortable-looking man dressed in a gray business suit. His cheeks were pink and shaven, his hair nearly white. Wrinkles of good nature radiated from the corners of his eyes. On his mouth an open, friendly smile appeared every time he spoke. To London he said, "Are you the chairman of the camp?"

"Yeah," said London suspiciously. "I'm the elected boss."

Sam came in and took his place just behind London, his face dark and sullen. Mac squatted down on his haunches and balanced himself with his fingers. The newcomer smiled. His teeth were white and even. "My name's Bolter," he said simply. "I own a big orchard. I'm the new president of the Fruit Growers' Association of this valley."

"So what?" said London. "Got a good job for me if I'll sell out?"

The smile did not leave Bolter's face, but his clean, pink hands closed gently at his sides. "Let's try to get a better start than that," he begged. "I told you I was the *new* president. That means there's a change in policy. I don't believe in doing things the way they were being done." While he spoke Mac looked not at Bolter, but at London.

Some of the anger left London's face. "What you got to say?" he asked. "Spill it out."

Bolter looked around for something to sit on, and saw

195

nothing. He said, "I never could see how two men could get anything done by growling at each other. I've always had an idea that no matter how mad men were, if they could only get together with a table between them, something good would come out of it."

London snickered. "We ain't got a table."

"You know what I mean," Bolter continued. "Everybody in the Association said you men wouldn't listen to reason, but I told them I know American working men. Give American working men something reasonable to listen to, and they'll listen."

Sam spat out, "Well, we're listenin', ain't we? Go on an' give us somethin' reasonable."

Bolter's white teeth flashed. He looked around appreciatively. "There, you see? That's what I told them. I said, 'Let me lay our cards down on the table,' and then let them lay theirs down, and see if we can't make a hand. American working men aren't animals."

Mac muttered, "You ought to run for Congress."

"I beg your pardon?"

"I was talkin' to this here guy," said Mac. London's face had grown hard again.

Bolter went on, "That's what I'm here for, to lay our cards on the table. I told you I own an orchard, but don't think because of that I haven't your interests at heart. All of us know we can't make money unless the working man is happy." He paused, waiting for some kind of answer. None came. "Well, here's the way I figure it; you're losing money and we're losing money because we're sitting growling at each other. We want you to come back to work. Then you'll get your wages, and we'll get our apples picked. That way we'll both be happy. Will you come back to work? No questions, no grudges, just two people who figured things out over the table?"

London said, "Sure we'll go back to work, mister. Ain't we American working men? Just give us the raise we want and kick out the scabs and we'll be up in those old trees tomorrow morning."

Bolter smiled around at them, one at a time, until his smile had rested on each face. "Well, I think you ought to have a raise," he said. "And I told everybody I thought so. Well, I'm not a very good business man. The rest of the Association explained it all to me. With the price of apples what it is, we're paying the top price we can. If we pay any more, we lose money."

Mac grinned. "I guess we ain't American workin' men after all," he said. "None of this sounds reasonable to me. So far it's sounded like a sock full of crap."

Jim said, "The reason they can't pay the raise is because that'd mean we win the strike; and if we did that, a lot of other poor devils'd go on strike. Isn't that it, mister?"

Bolter's smile remained. "I thought from the first you deserved a raise, but I didn't have any power. I still believe it, and I'm the president of the Association. Now I've told the Association what I'm going to do. Some of 'em don't like it, but I insisted you men have to have a raise. I'm going to offer you twenty cents, and no questions and no grudges. And we'll expect you back at work tomorrow morning."

London looked around at Sam. He laughed at Sam's scowling face, and slapped the lean man on the shoulder. "Mr. Bolter," he said, "like Mac says, I guess we ain't American workin' men. You wanted cards laid down, and then you laid yours down backs up. Here's ours, and by Christ, she's a full house. Your God-damn apples got to be picked and we ain't picking 'em without our raise. Nor neither is nobody else pickin' 'em. What do you think of that, Mister Bolter?"

At last the smile had faded from Bolter's face. He said gravely, "The American nation has become great because everybody pitched in and helped. American labor is the best labor in the world, and the highest paid."

London broke in angrily, "S'pose a Chink does get half a cent a day, if he can eat on it? What the hell do we care how much we get, if we got to go hungry?"

Bolter put on his smile again. "I have a home and children," he said. "I've worked hard. You think I'm different from you. I want you to look on me as a working man, too. I've worked for everything I've got. Now we've heard that radicals are working among you. I don't believe it. I don't believe American men, with American ideals, will listen to radicals. All of us are in the same boat. Times are hard. We're all trying to get along, and we've got to help each other."

Suddenly Sam yelled, "Oh, for Christ's sake, lay off. If you got somethin' to say, say it; only cut out this God-damn speech."

Bolter looked very sad. "Will you accept half?"

"No," said London. "You wouldn't offer no half unless you was pressed."

"How do you know the men wouldn't accept, if you put it to a vote?"

"Listen, mister," London said, "them guys is so full of piss and vinegar they'll skin you if you show that slick suit outside. We're strikin' for our raise. We're picketin' your God-damn orchards, and we're kickin' hell out of any scabs you run in. Now come on through with your 'or else.' Turn your damn cards over. What you think you're goin' to do if we don't go back?"

"Turn the vigilantes loose," said Mac.

Bolter said hurriedly, "We don't know anything about any vigilantes. But if the outraged citizens band together to keep the peace, that's their affair. The Association knows nothing about that." He smiled again. "Can't you men see that if you attack our homes and our children we have to protect them? Wouldn't you protect your own children?"

"What the hell do you think we're doin'?" London cried. "We're trying to protect 'em from starving. We're usin' the only way a workin' stiff's got. Don't you go talkin' about no children, or we'll show you something."

"We only want to settle this thing peacefully," said Bolter. "American citizens demand order, and I assure you men we're going to have order if we have to petition the governor for troops."

Sam's mouth was wet. He shouted, "And you get order by shootin' our men from windows, you yellow bastard. And in 'Frisco you got order by ridin' down women. An' the newspapers says, 'This mornin' a striker was killed when he threw himself on a bayonet.' *Threw himself!*"

London wrapped his arm about the furious man and forced him slowly away from Bolter. "Lay off, Sam. Stop it, now. Just quiet yourself."

"Th' hell with you," Sam cried. "Stand there and take the lousy crap that big baloney hands you!"

London stiffened suddenly. His big fist lashed out and cracked into Sam's face, and Sam went down. London stood looking at him. Mac laughed hysterically. "A striker just threw himself into a fist," he said.

Sam sat up on the ground. "O.K., London. You win. I won't make no more fuss, but you wasn't in 'Frisco on Bloody Thursday."

Bolter stood where he was. "I hoped you would listen to reason," he said. "We have information that you're being influenced by radicals, sent here by red organizations. They are misleading you, telling you lies. They only want to stir up trouble. They're professional trouble-makers, paid to cause strikes."

Mac stood up from his haunches. "Well, the dirty rats," he said. "Misleadin' American workin' men, are they? Prob'ly gettin' paid by Russia, don't you think, Mr. Bolter?"

The man looked back at him for a long time, and the healthy red was gone from his cheeks. "You're going to make us fight, I guess," he said. "I'm sorry. I wanted peace. We know who the radicals are, and we'll have to take action against them." He turned imploringly to London. "Don't let them mislead you. Come back to work. We only want peace."

London was scowling. "I had enough o' this," he said. "You want peace. Well, what we done? Marched in two parades. An' what you done? Shot three of our men, burned a truck and a lunch wagon and shut off our food supply. I'm sick o' your God-damned lies, mister. I'll see you get out without Sam gets his hands on you, but don't send nobody else again till you're ready to talk straight."

Bolter shook his head sadly. "We don't want to fight you men," he said. "We want you to come back to work. But if we do have to fight, we have weapons. The health authorities are pretty upset about this camp. And the government doesn't like uninspected meat moving in this county. The citizens are pretty tired of all this riot. And of course we may have to call troops, if we need them."

Mac got up and went to the tent-flaps and looked out. Already the evening was coming. The camp was quiet, for the men stood watching London's tent. All the faces, white in the gathering evening, were turned in toward the tent. Mac yelled, "All right, boys. We ain't goin' to sell you out." He turned back into the tent. "Light the lamp, London. I want to tell this friend of man a few things."

London set a match to the tin lantern and hung it on the tent-pole, where it cast a pale, steady light. Mac took up a position in front of Bolter, and his muscled face broke into a derisive grin. "All right, Sonny Boy," he said. "You been talkin' big, but I know you been wettin' your pants the whole time. I admit you can do all the things you say you can, but look what happens after. Your health service burned the tents in Washington. And that was one of the reasons that Hoover lost the labor vote. You called out guardsmen in 'Frisco, and damn near the whole city went over to the strikers. Y' had to have the cops stop food from comin' in to turn public opinion against the strike. I'm not talkin' right an' wrong now, mister. I'm tellin' you what happens." Mac stepped back a pace. "Where do you think we're gettin' food and blankets an' medicine an' money? You know damn well where we're gettin' 'em. Your valley's lousy with sympathizers. Your 'outraged citizens' are a little bit outraged at you babies, and you know it. And you know, if you get too tough, the unions 'll go out. Truck drivers and restaurant men and field hands, everybody. And just because you do know it, you try to throw a bluff. Well, it don't work. This camp's cleaner'n the lousy bunk houses you keep for us on your ranches. You come here to try to scare us, an' it don't work."

Bolter was very pale. He turned away from Mac and faced London. "I've tried to make peace," he said. "Do you know that this man was sent out by red headquarters to start this strike? Watch out that when he goes to jail you don't go too. We have a right to protect our property, and we'll do it. I've tried to deal man to man with you, and you won't deal. From now on the roads are closed. An ordinance will go through tonight forbidding any parading on the county roads, or any gathering. The sheriff will deputize a thousand men, if he needs them."

London glanced quickly at Mac, and Mac winked at him. London said, "Jesus, mister, I hope we can get you out of here safe. When the guys out there hear what you just said, why they'll want to take you to pieces."

Bolter's jaw tightened and his eyelids drooped. He straightened his shoulders. "Don't get the idea you can scare me," he said. "I'll protect my home and my children with my life if I have to. And if you lay a hand on me we'll wipe out your strike before morning."

London's arms doubled, and he stepped forward, but Mac jumped in his way. "The guy's right, London. He don't scare. Plenty do, but he don't." He turned around. "Mister Bolter, we'll see you get out of the camp. We understand each other now. We know what to expect from you. And we know how careful you have to be when you use force. Don't forget the thousands of people that are sending us food and money. They'll do other things, if they have to. We been good, Mr. Bolter, but if you start any funny business, we'll show you a riot you'll remember."

Bolter said coldly, "That seems to be all. I'm sorry, but I'll have to report that you won't meet us halfway."

"Halfway?" Mac cried. "There ain't any halfway to nowhere." His voice dropped to softness. "London, you get on one side of him, and Sam on the other, and see that he gets away all right. Then I guess you'd better tell the guys what he said. But don't let 'em get out of hand. Tell 'em to tighten up the squads for trouble."

They surrounded Bolter and took him through the press of silent men, saw him into his coupe and watched him drive away down the road. When he was gone London raised his voice. "If you guys want to come over to the stand, I'll get up on it and tell you what the son-of-a-bitch said, and what we answered him back." He flailed his way through, and the men followed, excitedly. The cooks left the stoves where they were boiling beans and chunks of beef. The women crawled like rodents from the tents and followed. When London climbed up on the stand it was ringed closely with men, standing in the dusk looking up at him.

During the talk with Bolter Doc Burton had effaced himself, had been so quiet that he seemed to have disappeared, but when the group went out, leaving only Jim and Lisa sitting on the mattress, he came out of his corner and sat down on the edge of the mattress beside them. His face was worried. "It's going to be a mean one," he said.

"That's what we want, Doc," Jim told him. "The worse it is, the more effect it'll have."

Burton looked at him with sad eyes. "You see a way through," he said. "I wish I did. It all seems meaningless to me, brutal and meaningless."

"It has to go on," Jim insisted. "It can only stop when the men rule themselves and get the profits of their labor."

"Seems simple enough," Burton sighed. "I wish I thought it was so simple." He turned smiling to the girl. "What's your solution, Lisa?"

She started. "Huh?"

"I mean, what would you like to have to make you happy."

She looked self-consciously down at the baby. "I like to have a cow," she said. "I like to have butter an' cheese like you can make."

"Want to exploit a cow?"

"Huh?"

"I'm being silly. Did you ever have a cow, Lisa?"

"When I was a little kid we had one," she said. "Went out an' drunk it warm. Old man used to milk it into a cup-like, to drink. Tasted warm. That's what I like. Bet it would be good for the baby." Burton turned slowly away from her. She insisted, "Cow used to eat grass, an' sometimes hay. Not ever'body can milk 'em, neither. They kick."

Burton asked, "Did you ever have a cow, Jim?"

"No."

Burton said, "I never thought of cows as counter-revolutionary animals."

Jim asked, "What are you talking about, Doc, anyway?"

"Nothing. I'm kind of unhappy, I guess. I was in the army in the war. Just out of school. They'd bring in one of our men with his chest shot away, and they'd bring in a big-eyed German with his legs splintered off. I worked on 'em just as though they were wood. But sometimes, after it was all over, when I wasn't working, it made me unhappy, like this. It made me lonely."

Jim said, "Y'ought to think only of the end, Doc. Out of all this struggle a good thing is going to grow. That makes it worthwhile."

"Jim, I wish I knew it. But in my little experience the end is never very different in its nature from the means. Damn it, Jim, you can only build a violent thing with violence."

"I don't believe that," Jim said. "All great things have violent beginnings."

"There aren't any beginnings," Burton said. "Nor any ends. It seems to me that man has engaged in a blind and fearful struggle out of a past he can't remember, into a future he can't foresee nor understand. And man has met and defeated every obstacle, every enemy except one. He cannot win over himself. How mankind hates itself."

Jim said, "We don't hate ourselves, we hate the invested capital that keeps us down."

"The other side is made of men, Jim, men like you. Man hates himself. Psychologists say a man's self-love is balanced neatly with self-hate. Mankind must be the same. We fight ourselves and we can only win by killing every man. I'm lonely, Jim. I have nothing to hate. What are you going to get out of it, Jim?"

Jim looked startled. "You mean me?" He pointed a finger at his breast.

"Yes, you. What will you get out of all the mess?"

"I don't know; I don't care."

"Well, suppose blood-poisoning sets in in that shoulder, or you die of lockjaw and the strike gets broken? What then?"

"It doesn't matter," Jim insisted. "I used to think like you, Doc, but it doesn't matter at all."

"How do you get that way?" Burton asked. "What's the process?"

"I don't know. I used to be lonely, and I'm not any more. If I go out now it won't matter. The thing won't stop. I'm just a little part of it. It will grow and grow. This pain in the shoulder is kind of pleasant to me; and I bet before he died Joy was glad for a moment. Just in that moment I bet he was glad."

They heard a rough, monotonous voice outside, and then a few shouts, and then the angry crowd-roar, a bellow like an animal in fury. "London's telling them," said Jim. "They're mad. Jesus, how a mad crowd can fill the air with madness. You don't understand it, Doc. My old man used to fight alone. When he got licked, he was licked. I remember how lonely it was. But I'm not lonely any more, and I can't be licked, because I'm more than myself."

"Pure religious ecstasy. I can understand that. Partakers of the blood of the Lamb."

"Religion, hell!" Jim cried. "This is men, not God. This is something you know."

"Well, can't a group of men be God, Jim?"

Jim wrenched himself around. "You make too damn many words, Doc. You build a trap of words and then you fall into it. You can't catch me. Your words don't mean anything to me. I know what I'm doing. Argument doesn't have any effect on me."

"Steady down," Burton said soothingly. "Don't get so excited. I wasn't arguing, I was asking for information. All of you people get angry when you're asked a question."

As the dusk turned into night the lantern seemed to grow brighter, to find deeper corners of the tent with its yellow light. Mac came in quietly, as though he crept away from the noise and shouting outside. "They're wild," he said. "They're hungry again. Boiled meat and beans tonight. I knew they'd get cocky on that meat. They'd like to go out and burn houses right now."

"How does the sky look?" Burton asked. "Any more rain in it?"

"Clear and stars. It'll be good weather."

"Well, I want to talk to you, Mac. I'm low in supplies. I need disinfectant. Yes, and I could use some salvarsan. If any kind of epidemic should break out, we'd be out of luck."

"I know," Mac said. "I sent word to town how it was. Some of the boys are out trying to get money. They're trying to get money to bail Dakin out now. I'd just as soon he stayed in jail."

Burton stood up from his seat on the mattress. "You can tell London what to do, can't you. Dakin wouldn't take everything."

Mac studied him. "What's the matter, Doc? Don't you feel well?"

"What do you mean?"

"I mean your temper's going. You're tired. What is it, Doc?"

Burton put his hands in his pockets. "I don't know; I'm lonely, I guess. I'm awfully lonely. I'm working all alone, towards nothing. There's some compensation for you people. I only hear heartbeats through a stethoscope. You hear them in the air." Suddenly he leaned over and put his hand under Lisa's chin and raised her head up and looked into her shrinking eyes. Her hand came slowly up and pulled gently at his wrist. He let go and put his hand back in his pocket.

Mac said, "I wish I knew some woman you could go to, Doc, but I don't. I'm new around here. Dick could steer you, in town. He prob'ly has twenty lined up by now. But you might get caught and jailed, Doc; and if you weren't taking care of us, they'd bounce us off this land in a minute."

Burton said, "Sometimes you understand too much, Mac. Sometimes—nothing. I guess I'll go along and see Al Anderson. I haven't been there all day."

"O.K., Doc, if it'll make you feel any better. I'll keep Jim under cover tonight."

Doc looked down at Lisa once more, and then he went out.

(From Chapter 13)

THEY walked out into the clear yellow sunshine. The camp looked bedraggled and gray in the clean light. A litter had accumulated since Burton was gone, bits of paper, strings, overalls hung on the guy-ropes of the tents. Mac and Jim walked out of the camp and across the surrounding field, to the edge of the orchard. At the line of trees Mac stopped. His eyes moved slowly across the horizontal fields of vision. "Look close, Jim," he advised. "It's

probably a damn fool thing to go over alone. I know it
isn't good sense." He studied the orchard. The long, sun-
spotted aisles were silent. There was no movement. "It's
so quiet. Makes me suspicious. It's too quiet." He reached
to a limb and took down a small, misshapen apple the
pickers had left. "God, that tastes good. I'd forgot about
apples. Always forget what's so easy."

"I don't see anybody moving," said Jim. "Not a soul."

"Well look, we'll edge down in line with the trees. Anybody looking down a row won't see us, then." They
stepped slowly in under the big apple trees. Their eyes
moved restlessly about. They walked through shadows of
branches and leaves, and the sun struck them with soft,
warm blows.

Jim asked, "Mac, do you s'pose we could get a leave of
absence some time and go where nobody knows us, and
just sit down in an orchard?"

" 'Bout two hours of it, and you'd be raring to go
again."

"I never had time to look at things, Mac, never. I never
looked how leaves come out. I never looked at the way
things happen. This morning there was a whole line of
ants on the floor of the tent. I couldn't watch them. I was
thinking about something else. Some time I'd like to sit
all day and look at bugs, and never think of anything
else."

"They'd drive you nuts," said Mac. "Men are bad
enough, but bugs'd drive you nuts."

"Well, just once in a while you get that feeling—I
never look at anything. I never take time to see anything.
It's going to be over, and I won't know—even how an
apple grows."

They moved on slowly. Mac's restless eyes roved about
among the trees. "You can't see everything," he said. "I
took a leave and went into the woods in Canada. Say, in

a couple of days I came running out of there. I wanted trouble, I was hungry for a mess."

"Well, I'd like to try it sometime. The way old Dan talks about timber——"

"Damn it, Jim, you can't have everything! We've got something old Dan hasn't got. You can't have everything. In a few days we'll be back in town, and we'll be so damned anxious to get into another fuss we'll be biting our nails. You've got to take it easy till that shoulder heals. I'll take you to a flop-house where you can watch all the bugs you want. Keep back of the line of trees. You're standing out like a cow on a side-hill."

"It's nice out here," said Jim.

"It's too damn nice. I'm scared there's a trap someplace."

Through the trees they could see Anderson's little white house, and its picket fence, and the burning geraniums in the yard. "No one around," said Jim.

"Well, take it easy." At the last row Mac stopped again and let his eyes travel slowly across the open. The great black square on the ground, where the barn had been, still sent up a lazy, pungent smoke. The white tankhouse looked tall and lonely. "Looks O.K.," Mac said. "Let's go in the back way." He tried to open the picket gate quietly, but the latch clicked and the hinges growled. They walked up the short path to the porch with its yellowing passion vine. Mac knocked on the door.

A voice from inside called, "Who is it?"

"Is that you, Al?"

"Yeah."

"Are you alone?"

"Yeah. Who are you?"

"It's Mac."

"Oh, come on in, Mac. The door ain't locked."

They went into the kitchen. Al lay on his narrow bed

against the wall. He seemed to have grown gaunt in the few days. The skin hung loosely on his face. "Hi, Mac. I thought nobody'd ever come. My old man went out early."

"We tried to get over before, Al. How's all the hurts?"

"They hurt plenty," said Al. "And when you're all alone they hurt worse. Who burned the barn, Mac?"

"Vigilantes. We're sorry as hell, Al. We had guards here, but they got a fast one pulled on 'em."

"My old man just raised hell all night, Mac. Talked all night. Give me hell about four times an hour, all night."

"We're damn sorry."

Al cleared one hand from the bedclothes and scratched his cheek. "I'm still with you, Mac. But the old man wants to blast you. He went in this morning to get the sheriff to kick you off'n the place. Says you're trespassin', an' he wants you off. Says he's punished for listenin' to guys like you. Says I can go to hell if I string along with you. He was mad as a hornet, Mac."

"I was scared he would be, Al. Listen, we know you're with us, see? It don't do no good to make that old man any sorrier than he is. If it'd do any good, it'd be different. You just pretend to come around to his side. We'll understand that, Al. You can keep in touch with us. I'm awfully sorry for your old man."

Al sighed deeply. "I was scared you'd think I double-crossed you. If you know I ain't, I'll tell him t'hell with you."

"That's the stuff, Al. And we'll give you a boost in town, too. Oh, say, Al, did Doc look in on you last night?"

"No. Why?"

"Well, he started over here before the fire, an' he ain't been back."

"Jesus! What do you think happened to him?"

"I'm scared they snatched the poor devil."

"They been pushing you all around, ain't they?"

"Yeah. But our guys got in some good licks this morning. But if your old man turns us in, I guess they'll roll over us tomorrow."

"Whole thing flops, huh, Mac?"

"That don't mean anything. We done what we came to do. The thing goes right on, Al. You just make peace an' pretend you ain't ever goin' to get burned no more." He listened. "Is that somebody coming?" He ran through the kitchen and into the front of the house, and looked out a window.

"It's my old man, I recognize his step," said Al.

Mac returned. "I wanted to see if anybody was with him. He's all alone. We could make a sneak, I guess. I'd rather tell him I'm sorry."

"You better not," Al advised. "He won't listen to nothing from you. He hates your guts."

There were steps on the porch and the door burst open. Anderson stood, surprised and glaring. "God damn it," he shouted. "You bastards get out of here. I've been and turned you in. The sheriff's goin' kick the whole smear of you off my land." His chest swelled with rage.

Mac said, "We just wanted to tell you we're sorry. We didn't burn the barn. Some of the boys from town did."

"What th' hell do I care who burned it? It's burned, the crop's burned. What do you damn bums know about it? I'll lose the place sure, now." His eyes watered with rage. "You bastards never owned nothing. You never planted trees an' seen 'em grow an' felt 'em with your hands. You never owned a thing, never went out an' touched your own apple trees with your hands. What do you know?"

"We never had a chance to own anything," Mac said. "We'd like to own something and plant trees."

Anderson ignored his words. "I listened to your promises. Look what happened. The whole crop's burned, there's paper coming due."

Mac asked, "How about the pointers?"

Anderson's hands settled slowly to his sides. A look of cold, merciless hatred came into his eyes. He said slowly, softly, "The kennel was—against—the barn."

Mac turned to Al and nodded. For a moment Al questioned with his eyes, and then he scowled. "What he says goes. You guys get the hell out, and don't never come back."

Anderson ran to the bed and stood in front of it. "I could shoot you men now," he said, "but the sheriff's goin' to do it for me, an' damn quick."

Mac touched Jim on the arm, and they went out and shut the door. They didn't bother to look around when they went out the gate. Mac set out so rapidly that Jim had to stretch his stride to keep up. The sun was cutting downward now, and the shadows of whole trees lay between the rows, and the wind was stirring in the branches, so that both trees and ground seemed to quiver nervously.

"It keeps you hopping, keeping the picture," Mac said. "You see a guy hurt, or somebody like Anderson smashed, or you see a cop ride down a Jew girl, an' you think, what the hell's the use of it. An' then you think of the millions starving, and it's all right again. It's worth it. But it keeps you jumping between pictures. Don't it ever get you, Jim?"

"Not very much. It isn't long ago I saw my mother die; seems years, but it wasn't long ago. She wouldn't speak to me, she just looked at me. She was hurt so bad she didn't even want a priest. I guess I got something burned out of me that night. I'm sorry for Anderson, but what the hell. If I can give up my whole life, he ought to be able to give up a barn."

"Well, to some of those guys property's more important than their lives."

Jim said, "Slow down, Mac. What's your hurry? I seem to get tired easy."

Mac did slow his steps a little. "I thought that's what he went to town for. I want to get back before anything happens. I don't know what this sheriff'll do, but he'll be happy as hell to split us up." They walked silently over the soft, dark earth, and the shadows flickered on them. At the clearing they slowed down. Mac said, "Well, nothing's happened yet, anyway."

The smoke rose slowly from the stoves. Jim asked, "Where do you s'pose all the guys are?"

"In sleeping off the drunk, I guess. It wouldn't be a bad idea if we got some sleep, too. Prob'ly be up all night."

London moved over and met them. "Everything all right?" Mac asked.

"Just the same."

"Well, I was right. Anderson's been in and asked the sheriff to kick us off."

"Well?"

"Well, we wait. Don't tell the guys about it."

"Maybe you was right about that," London said, "but you was sure wrong about what them guys would eat. They cleaned us out. There ain't a damn drop o' beans left. I saved you a couple of cans, over in my tent."

"Maybe we won't need anything more to eat," said Mac.

"How do you mean?"

"We prob'ly won't any of us be here tomorrow."

In the tent London pointed to the two food cans on the box. "D'you s'pose the sheriff'll try to kick us off?" he asked.

"Damn right. He won't let a chance like that go by."

"Well, will he come shootin', d'you suppose? Or will he give the guys a warnin'?"

Mac said, "Hell, I don't know. Where's all the men?"

"All under cover, asleep."

Mac said, "I heard a car. May be our guys coming back."

London cocked his head. "Too big," he said. "That's one of them big babies."

They ran outside. Up the road from Torgas a huge Mack dump-truck rolled. It had a steel bed and sides, supported by two sets of double tires. It pulled up in front of the camp and stopped. A man stood up in the steel bed, and in his hands he held a submachine-gun with a big cartridge cylinder behind the forward grip. The heads of other men showed above the truck sides. Strikers began to boil out of the tents.

The standing man shouted, "I'm sheriff o' this county. If there's anyone in authority I want to see him." The mob approached closer and looked curiously at the truck.

Mac said softly, "Careful, London. They may pop us off. They could do it now if they wanted to." They walked forward, to the edge of the road, and stopped; and the mob was lining the road now, too.

London said, "I'm the boss, mister."

"Well, I've got a trespass complaint. We've been fair to you men. We've asked you to go back to work, or, if you wanted to strike, to do it peacefully. You've destroyed property and committed homicide. This morning you sent out men to destroy property. We had to shoot some of those men, and we caught the rest." He looked down at the men in the truck, and then up again. "Now we don't want any bloodshed, so we're going to let you out. You have all night tonight to get out. If you head straight for the county line, nobody'll bother you. But if this camp is here at daylight tomorrow, we're going through it."

The men stood silently and watched him. Mac whispered to London. London said, "Trespassin' don't give you no right to shoot guys."

"Maybe not, but resisting officers does. Now I'm talking fair with you, so you'll know what to expect. At daylight tomorrow a hundred men, in ten trucks like this, are coming out. Every man will have a gun, and we have three cases of Mills bombs. Some of you men who know can tell the others what a Mills bomb is. That's all. We're through fooling with you. You have till daylight to get out of the county. That's all." He turned forward. "Might as well drive along, Gus." He sank from sight behind the steel truck side. The wheels turned slowly, and gathered speed.

One of the strikers leaped into the shallow ditch and picked up a rock. And he stood holding it in his hand and looking at it as the truck rolled away. The men watched the truck go, and then they turned back into the camp.

London sighed. "Well, that sounds like orders. He didn't mean no funny business."

Mac said impatiently, "I'm hungry. I'm going to eat my beans." They followed him back into the tent. He gobbled his food quickly and hungrily. "Hope you got some, London."

"Me? Oh, sure. What we goin' to do now, Mac?"

"Fight," said Mac.

"Yeah, but if he brings the stuff he said, pineapples an' stuff, it ain't goin' to be no more fight than the stock yards."

"Bull," said Mac, and a little jet of chewed beans shot from his mouth. "If he had that stuff, he wouldn't need to tell us about it. He just hopes we'll get scattered so we can't put up a fight. If we move out tonight, they'll pick us off. They never do what they say."

London looked into Mac's face, hung on to his eyes.

"Is that straight, Mac? You said I was on your side. Are you puttin' somethin' over?"

Mac looked away. "We got to fight," he said. "If we get out without a scrap ever'thing we've been through'll be wasted."

"Yeah, but if we fight, a lot of guys that ain't done no harm is goin' get shot."

Mac put his unfinished food down on the box. "Look," he said. "In a war a general knows he's going to lose men. Now this is a war. If we get run out o' here without a fight, it's losing ground." For a moment he covered his eyes with his hand. "London," he said. "It's a hell of a responsibility. I know what we should do; you're the boss; for Christ's sake, do what you want. Don't make me take all the blame."

London said plaintively, "Yeah, but you know about things. You think we ought to fight, really?"

"Yes, we ought."

"Well, hell then, we'll fight—that is, if we can get the guys to fight."

"I know," said Mac. "They may run out on us, every one of 'em. The ones that heard the sheriff will tell the others. They may turn on us and say we caused the trouble."

London said, "Some ways, I hope they clear out. Poor bastards, they don't know nothing. But like you say, if they're ever goin' to get clear, they got to take it now. How about the hurt guys?" London went on, "Burke and old Dan, and the guy with the busted ankle?"

"Leave 'em," said Mac. "It's the only thing we can do. The county'll have to take care of 'em."

"I'm going to take a look around," London said. "I'm gettin' nervous as a cat."

"You ain't the only one," said Mac.

When he was gone, Jim glanced at Mac, and then began to eat the cold beans and strings of beef. "I wonder if they'll fight?" he asked. "D'you think they'd really let the guys through if they wanted to run?"

"Oh, the sheriff would. He'd be only too damn glad to get rid of 'em, but I don't trust the vigilante boys."

"They won't have anything to eat tonight, Mac. If they're scared already, there won't be any dinner to buck 'em up."

Mac scraped his can and set it down. "Jim," he said, "if I told you to do something, would you do it?"

"I don't know. What is it?"

"Well, the sun's going down pretty soon, and it'll be dark. They're going to lay for you and me, Jim. Don't make any mistake about that. They're going to want to get us, bad. I want you to get out, soon as it gets dark, get clear and go back to town."

"Why in hell should I do that?"

Mac's eyes slid over Jim's face and went to the ground again. "When I came out here, I thought I was hell on wheels. You're worth ten of me, Jim. I know that now. If anything happened to me, there's plenty of guys to take my place, but you've got a genius for the work. We can't spare you, Jim. If you was to get knocked off in a two-bit strike—well, it's bad economy."

"I don't believe it," said Jim. "Our guys are to be used, not saved. I couldn't run out. Y'said yourself this was a part of the whole thing. It's little, but it's important."

"I *want* you to go, Jim. You can't fight with that arm. You'd be no damn good here. You couldn't help at all."

Jim's face was rigid. "I won't go," he said. "I might be of some use here. You protect me all the time, Mac. And sometimes I get the feeling you're not protecting me for the Party, but for yourself."

Mac reddened with anger. "O.K., then. Get your can knocked off. I've told you what I think's the best thing.

Be pig-headed, if you want. I can't sit still. I'm going out. You do anything you damn please." He went out angrily.

Jim looked up at the back wall of the tent. He could see the outline of the red sun on the canvas. His hand stole up and touched his hurt shoulder, and pressed it gently, all around, in a circle that narrowed to the wound. He winced a little as his exploring fingers neared the hurt. For a long time he sat quietly.

He heard a step in the door and looked around. Lisa stood there, and her baby was in her arms. Jim could see past her, where the line of old cars stood against the road; and on the other side of the road the sun was on the treetops, but in the rows the shade had come. Lisa looked in, with a bird-like interest. Her hair was damp, plastered against her head, and little, uneven finger-waves were pressed into it. The short blanket that covered her shoulders was draped and held to one side with a kind of coquetry. "I seen you was alone," she said. She went to the mattress and sat down and arranged her gingham dress neatly over her legs. "I heard guys say the cops'll throw bombs, an' kill us all," she said lightly.

Jim was puzzled. "It doesn't seem to scare you much."

"No. I ain't never been ascared o' things like that."

"The cops wouldn't hurt you," Jim said. "I don't believe they'll do all that. It's a bluff. Do you want anything?"

"I thought I'd come an' set. I like to—just set here."

Jim smiled. "You like me, don't you, Lisa?"

"Yes."

"I like you, too, Lisa."

"You he'ped me with the baby."

Jim asked, "How's old Dan? Did you take care of him?"

"He's all right. Just lays there mumblin'."

"Mac helped you more than I did."

"Yes, but he don't look at me—nice. I like t'hear you talk. You're just a young kid, but you talk nice."

"I talk too much, Lisa. Too much talk, not enough do-ing things. Look how the evening's coming. We'll light the lantern before long. You wouldn't like to sit here in the dark with me."

"I wouldn' care," she said quickly.

He looked into her eyes again, and his face grew pleased. "Did you ever notice, in the evening, Lisa, how you think of things that happened a long time ago—not even about things that matter? One time in town, when I was a little kid, the sun was going down, and there was a board fence. Well, a gray cat went up and sat on that fence for a moment, long-haired cat, and that cat turned gold for a minute, a gold cat."

"I like cats," Lisa agreed softly. "I had two cats onct, two of them."

"Look. The sun's nearly gone, Lisa. Tomorrow we'll be somewhere else. I wonder where? You'll be on the move, I guess. Maybe I'll be in jail. I've been in jail before."

London and Mac came quietly into the tent together. London looked down at the girl. "What you doing here, Lisa? You better get out. We got business." Lisa got up and clutched her blanket close. She looked sideways at Jim as she passed. London said, "I don't know what's goin' on. There's about ten little meetin's out there, an' they don't want me at none o' them."

"Yeah, I know," Mac said. "The guys're scared. I don't know what they'll do, but they'll want to scram tonight." And then the conversation died. London and Mac sat down on boxes, facing Jim. They sat there while the sun went down and the tent grew a little dusky.

At last Jim said softly, "Even if the guys get out, it won't all be wasted. They worked together a little."

Mac roused himself. "Yeah, but we ought to make a last stand."

"How you goin' to get guys to fight when they want to run?" London demanded.

"I don't know. We can talk. We can try to make 'em fight talkin' to 'em."

"Talk don't do much good when they're scared."

"I know."

The silence fell again. They could hear the low talk of many voices outside, scattered voices that gradually drew together and made a babble like water. Mac said, "Got a match, London? Light the lantern."

"It ain't dark yet."

"Dark enough. Light it up. This God-damn half-light makes me nervous."

The shade screeched as London raised it, and screeched when he let it down.

Mac looked startled. "Something happened. What's wrong?"

"It's the men," said Jim. "They're quiet now. They've all stopped talking." The three men sat listening tensely. They heard footsteps coming closer. In the doorway the two short Italian men stood. Their teeth showed in self-conscious grins.

"C'n we come in?"

"Sure. Come on in, boys."

They stood in the tent like pupils preparing to recite. Each looked to the other to begin. One said, "The men out there—they want to call a meeting."

"Yeah? What for?"

The other answered quickly, "Those men say they vote the strike, they can vote again. They say, 'What's the use all the men get killed?' They say they can't strike no more." They were silent, waiting for London's answer.

London's eyes asked advice from Mac. "Of course you'll call a meeting," Mac said. "The men are the bosses. What they say goes " He looked up at the waiting emissaries. "Go out and tell the guys London calls a meeting in about half an hour, to vote whether we fight or run."

They looked at London for corroboration. He nodded his head slowly. "That's right," he said. "In a half hour. We do what the guys vote to do." The little men made foreign bows, and wheeled and left the tent.

Mac laughed loudly. "Why, that's fine," he said. "Why, that makes it better. I thought they might sneak out. But if they want to vote, that means they're still working together. Oh, that's fine. They can break up, if they do it by their own consent."

Jim asked, "But aren't you going to try to make them fight?"

"Oh, sure. We have to make plans about that. But if they won't fight, well anyway they don't just sneak off like dogs. It's more like a retreat, you see. It isn't just getting chased."

"What'll we do at the meeting?" London demanded.

"Well, let's see. It's just about dark now. You talk first, London. Tell 'em why they should fight, not run. Now I better not talk. They don't like me too well since I told 'em off this morning." His eyes moved to Jim. "You're it," he said. "Here's your chance. You do it. See if you can bring 'em around. Talk, Jim. Talk. It's the thing you've been wanting."

Jim's eyes shone with excitement. "Mac," he cried, "I can pull off this bandage and get a flow of blood. That might stir 'em up."

Mac's eyes narrowed and he considered the thought. "No—" he decided. "Stir 'em up that way, an' they got to hit something quick. If you make 'em sit around, they'll go way down. No, just talk, Jim. Tell 'em straight what a strike means, how it's a little battle in a whole war. You can do it, Jim."

Jim sprang up. "You're damn right I can do it. I'm near

choking, but I can do it." His face was transfigured. A
furious light of energy seemed to shine from it.

They heard running footsteps. A young boy ran into
the tent. "Out in the orchard," he cried. "There's a guy
says he's a doctor. He's all hurt."

The three started up. "Where?"

"Over the other side. Been lyin' there all day, he says."

"How'd you find him?" Mac demanded.

"I heard 'im yell. He says come and tell you."

"Show us the way. Come on now, hurry up."

The boy turned and plunged out. Mac shouted, "London, bring the lantern." Mac and Jim ran side by side.
The night was almost complete. Ahead, they saw the flying figure of the boy. Across the open space they tore.
The boy reached the line of trees and plunged among
them. They could hear him running ahead of them. They
dashed into the dark shadow of the trees.

Suddenly Mac reached for Jim. "Jim! Drop, for Christ'
sake!" There was a roar, and two big holes of light. Mac
had sprawled full length. He heard several sets of running footsteps. He looked toward Jim, but the flashes still
burned on his retinas. Gradually he made Jim out. He was
on his knees, his head down. "You sure got down quick,
Jim."

Jim did not move. Mac scrambled over to him, on his
knees. "Did you get hit, Jim?" The figure kneeled, and
the face was against the ground. "Oh, Christ!" Mac put
out his hand to lift the head. He cried out, and jerked his
hand away, and wiped it on his trousers, for there was no
face. He looked slowly around, over his shoulder.

The lantern bounced along toward him, lighting London's running legs. "Where are you?" London shouted.

Mac didn't answer. He sat back on his heels, sat very
quietly. He looked at the figure, kneeling in the position
of Moslem prayer.

London saw them at last. He came close, and stopped; and the lantern made a circle of light. "Oh," he said. He lowered the lantern and peered down. "Shot-gun?"

Mac nodded and stared at his sticky hand.

London looked at Mac, and shivered at his frozen face. Mac stood up, stiffly. He leaned over and picked Jim up and slung him over his shoulder, like a sack; and the dripping head hung down behind. He set off, stiff-legged, toward the camp. London walked beside him, carrying the lantern.

The clearing was full of curious men. They clustered around, until they saw the burden. And then they recoiled. Mac marched through them as though he did not see them. Across the clearing, past the stoves he marched, and the crowd followed silently behind him. He came to the platform. He deposited the figure under the handrail and leaped to the stand. He dragged Jim across the boards and leaned him against the corner post, and steadied him when he slipped sideways.

London handed the lantern up, and Mac set it carefully on the floor, beside the body, so that its light fell on the head. He stood up and faced the crowd. His hands gripped the rail. His eyes were wide and white. In front he could see the massed men, eyes shining in the lamplight. Behind the front row, the men were lumped and dark. Mac shivered. He moved his jaws to speak, and seemed to break the frozen jaws loose. His voice was high and monotonous. "This guy didn't want nothing for himself—" he began. His knuckles were white, where he grasped the rail. "Comrades! He didn't want nothing for himself——"

(Chapter 15)

Of Mice and Men

The complete novel, first published in 1937.

OF MICE AND MEN

A FEW miles south of Soledad, the Salinas River drops in close to the hillside bank and runs deep and green. The water is warm too, for it has slipped twinkling over the yellow sands in the sunlight before reaching the narrow pool. On one side of the river the golden foothill slopes curve up to the strong and rocky Gabilan mountains, but on the valley side the water is lined with trees—willows fresh and green with every spring, carrying in their lower leaf junctures the debris of the winter's flooding; and sycamores with mottled, white, recumbent limbs and branches that arch over the pool. On the sandy bank under the trees the leaves lie deep and so crisp that a lizard makes a great skittering if he runs among them. Rabbits come out of the brush to sit on the sand in the evening, and the damp flats are covered with the night tracks of 'coons, and with the spread pads of dogs from the ranches, and with the split-wedge tracks of deer that come to drink in the dark.

There is a path through the willows and among the sycamores, a path beaten hard by boys coming down from the ranches to swim in the deep pool, and beaten hard by tramps who come wearily down from the highway in the evening to jungle-up near water. In front of the low horizontal limb of a giant sycamore there is an ash pile made by many fires; the limb is worn smooth by men who have sat on it.

Evening of a hot day started the little wind to moving

among the leaves. The shade climbed up the hills toward
the top. On the sand banks the rabbits sat as quietly as
little gray, sculptured stones. And then from the direction
of the state highway came the sound of footsteps on crisp
sycamore leaves. The rabbits hurried noiselessly for cover.
A stilted heron labored up into the air and pounded down
river. For a moment the place was lifeless, and then two
men emerged from the path and came into the opening by
the green pool.

They had walked in single file down the path, and even
in the open one stayed behind the other. Both were
dressed in denim trousers and in denim coats with brass
buttons. Both wore black, shapeless hats and both carried
tight blanket rolls slung over their shoulders. The first
man was small and quick, dark of face, with restless eyes
and sharp, strong features. Every part of him was defined:
small, strong hands, slender arms, a thin and bony nose.
Behind him walked his opposite, a huge man, shapeless
of face, with large, pale eyes, and wide, sloping shoulders; and he walked heavily, dragging his feet a.little, the
way a bear drags his paws. His arms did not swing at his
sides, but hung loosely.

The first man stopped short in the clearing, and the follower nearly ran over him. He took off his hat and wiped
the sweat-band with his forefinger and snapped the moisture off. His huge companion dropped his blankets and
flung himself down and drank from the surface of the
green pool; drank with long gulps, snorting into the water
like a horse. The small man stepped nervously beside him.

"Lennie!" he said sharply. "Lennie, for God' sakes don't
drink so much." Lennie continued to snort into the pool.
The small man leaned over and shook him by the shoulder. "Lennie. You gonna be sick like you was last night."

Lennie dipped his whole head under, hat and all, and
then he sat up on the bank and his hat dripped down on

his blue coat and ran down his back. "That's good," he said. "You drink some, George. You take a good big drink." He smiled happily.

George unslung his bindle and dropped it gently on the bank. "I ain't sure it's good water," he said. "Looks kinda scummy."

Lennie dabbled his big paw in the water and wiggled his fingers so the water arose in little splashes; rings widened across the pool to the other side and came back again. Lennie watched them go. "Look, George. Look what I done."

George knelt beside the pool and drank from his hand with quick scoops. "Tastes all right," he admitted. "Don't really seem to be running, though. You never oughta drink water when it ain't running, Lennie," he said hopelessly. "You'd drink out of a gutter if you was thirsty." He threw a scoop of water into his face and rubbed it about with his hand, under his chin and around the back of his neck. Then he replaced his hat, pushed himself back from the river, drew up his knees and embraced them. Lennie, who had been watching, imitated George exactly. He pushed himself back, drew up his knees, embraced them, looked over to George to see whether he had it just right. He pulled his hat down a little more over his eyes, the way George's hat was.

George stared morosely at the water. The rims of his eyes were red with sun glare. He said angrily, "We could just as well of rode clear to the ranch if that bastard bus driver knew what he was talkin' about. 'Jes' a little stretch down the highway,' he says. 'Jes' a little stretch.' God damn near four miles, that's what it was! Didn't wanta stop at the ranch gate, that's what. Too God damn lazy to pull up. Wonder he isn't too damn good to stop in Soledad at all. Kicks us out and says 'Jes' a little stretch down the road.' I bet it was *more* than four miles. Damn hot day."

Lennie looked timidly over to him. "George?"

"Yeah, what ya want?"

"Where we goin', George?"

The little man jerked down the brim of his hat and scowled over at Lennie. "So you forgot that awready, did you? I gotta tell you again, do I? Jesus Christ, you're a crazy bastard!"

"I forgot," Lennie said softly. "I tried not to forget. Honest to God I did, George."

"O.K.—O.K. I'll tell ya again. I ain't got nothing to do. Might jus' as well spen' all my time tellin' you things and then you forget 'em, and I tell you again."

"Tried and tried," said Lennie, "but it didn't do no good. I remember about the rabbits, George."

"The hell with the rabbits. That's all you ever can remember is them rabbits. O.K! Now you listen and this time you got to remember so we don't get in no trouble. You remember settin' in that gutter on Howard street and watchin' that blackboard?"

Lennie's face broke into a delighted smile. "Why sure, George. I remember that . . . . but . . . . what'd we do then? I remember some girls come by and you says . . . . you say . . . ."

"The hell with what I says. You remember about us goin' in to Murray and Ready's, and they give us work cards and bus tickets?"

"Oh, sure, George. I remember that now." His hands went quickly into his side coat pockets. He said gently, "George . . . . I ain't got mine. I musta lost it." He looked down at the ground in despair.

"You never had none, you crazy bastard. I got both of 'em here. Think I'd let you carry your own work card?"

Lennie grinned with relief. "I . . . . . I thought I put it in my side pocket." His hand went into the pocket again.

George looked sharply at him. "What'd you take outa that pocket?"

"Ain't a thing in my pocket," Lennie said cleverly.

"I know there ain't. You got it in your hand. What you got in your hand—hidin' it?"

"I ain't got nothin', George. Honest."

"Come on, give it here."

Lennie held his closed hand away from George's direction. "It's on'y a mouse, George."

"A mouse? A live mouse?"

"Uh-uh. Jus' a dead mouse, George. I didn' kill it. Honest! I found it. I found it dead."

"Give it here!" said George.

"Aw, leave me have it, George."

"*Give it here!*"

Lennie's closed hand slowly obeyed. George took the mouse and threw it across the pool to the other side, among the brush. "What you want of a dead mouse, anyways?"

"I could pet it with my thumb while we walked along," said Lennie.

"Well, you ain't petting no mice while you walk with me. You remember where we're goin' now?"

Lennie looked startled and then in embarrassment hid his face against his knees. "I forgot again."

"Jesus Christ," George said resignedly. "Well—look, we're gonna work on a ranch like the one we come from up north."

"Up north?"

"In Weed."

"Oh, sure. I remember. In Weed."

"That ranch we're goin' to is right down there about a quarter mile. We're gonna go in an' see the boss. Now, look—I'll give him the work tickets, but you ain't gonna say a word. You jus' stand there and don't say nothing. If he finds out what a crazy bastard you are, we won't get no job, but if he sees ya work before he hears ya talk, we're set. Ya got that?"

"Sure, George. Sure I got it."

"O.K. Now when we go in to see the boss, what you gonna do?"

"I . . ., . I," Lennie thought. His face grew tight with thought. "I . . . . ain't gonna say nothin'. Jus' gonna stan' there."

"Good boy. That's swell. You say that over two, three times so you sure won't forget it."

Lennie droned to himself softly, "I ain't gonna say nothin' . . . . I ain't gonna say nothin' . . . . I ain't gonna say nothin'."

"O.K.," said George. "An' you ain't gonna do no bad things like you done in Weed, neither."

Lennie looked puzzled. "Like I done in Weed?"

"Oh, so ya forgot that too, did ya? Well, I ain't gonna remind ya, fear ya do it again."

A light of understanding broke on Lennie's face. "They run us outa Weed," he exploded triumphantly.

"Run us out, hell," said George disgustedly. "We run. They was lookin' for us, but they didn't catch us."

Lennie giggled happily. "I didn't forget that, you bet."

George lay back on the sand and crossed his hands under his head, and Lennie imitated him, raising his head to see whether he were doing it right. "God, you're a lot of trouble," said George. "I could get along so easy and so nice if I didn't have you on my tail. I could live so easy and maybe have a girl."

For a moment Lennie lay quiet, and then he said hopefully, "We gonna work on a ranch, George."

"Awright. You got that. But we're gonna sleep here because I got a reason."

The day was going fast now. Only the tops of the Gabilan mountains flamed with the light of the sun that had gone from the valley. A water snake slipped along on the pool, its head held up like a little periscope. The reeds jerked slightly in the current. Far off toward the highway a man shouted something, and another man shouted back. The sycamore limbs rustled under a little wind that died immediately.

"George—why ain't we goin' on to the ranch and get some supper? They got supper at the ranch."

George rolled on his side. "No reason at all for you. I like it here. Tomorra we're gonna go to work. I seen thrashin' machines on the way down. That means we'll be bucking grain bags, bustin' a gut. Tonight I'm gonna lay right here and look up. I like it."

Lennie got up on his knees and looked down at George. "Ain't we gonna have no supper?"

"Sure we are, if you gather up some dead willow sticks. I got three cans of beans in my bindle. You get a fire ready. I'll give you a match when you get the sticks together. Then we'll heat the beans and have supper."

Lennie said, "I like beans with ketchup."

"Well, we ain't got no ketchup. You go get wood. An' don't you fool around. It'll be dark before long."

Lennie lumbered to his feet and disappeared in the brush. George lay where he was and whistled softly to himself. There were sounds of splashings down the river in the direction Lennie had taken. George stopped whistling and listened. "Poor bastard," he said softly, and then went on whistling again.

In a moment Lennie came crashing back through the brush. He carried one small willow stick in his hand. George sat up. "Awright," he said brusquely. "Gi'me that mouse!"

But Lennie made an elaborate pantomime of innocence. "What mouse, George? I ain't got no mouse."

George held out his hand. "Come on. Give it to me.
You ain't puttin' nothing over."

Lennie hesitated, backed away, looked wildly at the
brush line as though he contemplated running for his freedom. George said coldly, "You gonna give me that mouse
or do I have to sock you?"

"Give you what, George?"

"You know God damn well what. I want that mouse."

Lennie reluctantly reached into his pocket. His voice
broke a little. "I don't know why I can't keep it. It ain't
nobody's mouse. I didn't steal it. I found it lyin' right beside the road."

George's hand remained outstretched imperiously.
Slowly, like a terrier who doesn't want to bring a ball to
its master, Lennie approached, drew back, approached
again. George snapped his fingers sharply, and at the
sound Lennie laid the mouse in his hand.

"I wasn't doin' nothing bad with it, George. Jus'
strokin' it."

George stood up and threw the mouse as far as he could
into the darkening brush, and then he stepped to the pool
and washed his hands. "You crazy fool. Don't you think I
could see your feet was wet where you went acrost the
river to get it?" He heard Lennie's whimpering cry and
wheeled about. "Blubberin' like a baby! Jesus Christ! A
big guy like you." Lennie's lip quivered and tears started
in his eyes. "Aw, Lennie!" George put his hand on Lennie's shoulder. "I ain't takin' it away jus' for meanness.
That mouse ain't fresh, Lennie; and besides, you've broke
it pettin' it. You get another mouse that's fresh and I'll let
you keep it a little while."

Lennie sat down on the ground and hung his head de-
jectedly. "I don't know where there is no other mouse. I

remember a lady used to give 'em to me—ever' one she got. But that lady ain't here."

George scoffed. "Lady, huh? Don't even remember who that lady was. That was your own Aunt Clara. An' she stopped givin' 'em to ya. You always killed 'em."

Lennie looked sadly up at him. "They was so little," he said, apologetically. "I'd pet 'em, and pretty soon they bit my fingers and I pinched their heads a little and then they was dead—because they was so little.

"I wish't we'd get the rabbits pretty soon, George. They ain't so little."

"The hell with the rabbits. An' you ain't to be trusted with no live mice. Your Aunt Clara give you a rubber mouse and you wouldn't have nothing to do with it."

"It wasn't no good to pet," said Lennie.

The flame of the sunset lifted from the mountaintops and dusk came into the valley, and a half darkness came in among the willows and the sycamores. A big carp rose to the surface of the pool, gulped air and then sank mysteriously into the dark water again, leaving widening rings on the water. Overhead the leaves whisked again and little puffs of willow cotton blew down and landed on the pool's surface.

"You gonna get that wood?" George demanded. "There's plenty right up against the back of that syca-more. Floodwater wood. Now you get it."

Lennie went behind the tree and brought out a litter of dried leaves and twigs. He threw them in a heap on the old ash pile and went back for more and more. It was almost night now. A dove's wings whistled over the water. George walked to the fire pile and lighted the dry leaves. The flame cracked up among the twigs and fell to work. George undid his bindle and brought out three cans of beans. He stood them about the fire, close in against the blaze, but not quite touching the flame.

"There's enough beans for four men," George said.

Lennie watched him from over the fire. He said patiently, "I like 'em with ketchup."

"Well, we ain't got any," George exploded. "Whatever we ain't got, that's what you want. God a'mighty, if I was alone I could live so easy. I could go get a job an' work, an' no trouble. No mess at all, and when the end of the month come I could take my fifty bucks and go into town and get whatever I want. Why, I could stay in a cat house all night. I could eat any place I want, hotel or any place, and order any damn thing I could think of. An' I could do all that every damn month. Get a gallon of whisky, or set in a pool room and play cards or shoot pool." Lennie knelt and looked over the fire at the angry George. And Lennie's face was drawn with terror. "An' whatta I got," George went on furiously. "I got you! You can't keep a job and you lose me ever' job I get. Jus' keep me shovin' all over the country all the time. An' that ain't the worst. You get in trouble. You do bad things and I got to get you out." His voice rose nearly to a shout. "You crazy son-of-a-bitch. You keep me in hot water all the time." He took on the elaborate manner of little girls when they are mimicking one another. "Jus' wanted to feel that girl's dress—jus' wanted to pet it like it was a mouse—— Well, how the hell did she know you jus' wanted to feel her dress? She jerks back and you hold on like it was a mouse. She yells and we got to hide in a irrigation ditch all day with guys lookin' for us, and we got to sneak out in the dark and get outta the country. All the time somethin' like that—all the time. I wisht I could put you in a cage with about a million mice an' let you have fun." His anger left him suddenly. He looked across the fire at Lennie's anguished face, and then he looked ashamedly at the flames.

It was quite dark now, but the fire lighted the trunks

of the trees and the curving branches overhead. Lennie crawled slowly and cautiously around the fire until he was close to George. He sat back on his heels. George turned the bean cans so that another side faced the fire. He pretended to be unaware of Lennie so close beside him.

"George," very softly. No answer. "George!"

"Whatta you want?"

"I was only foolin', George. I don't want no ketchup. I wouldn't eat no ketchup if it was right here beside me."

"If it was here, you could have some."

"But I wouldn't eat none, George. I'd leave it all for you. You could cover your beans with it and I wouldn't touch none of it."

George still stared morosely at the fire. "When I think of the swell time I could have without you, I go nuts. I never get no peace."

Lennie still knelt. He looked off into the darkness across the river. "George, you want I should go away and leave you alone?"

"Where the hell could you go?"

"Well, I could. I could go off in the hills there. Some place I'd find a cave."

"Yeah? How'd you eat. You ain't got sense enough to find nothing to eat."

"I'd find things, George. I don't need no nice food with ketchup. I'd lay out in the sun and nobody'd hurt me. An' if I foun' a mouse, I could keep it. Nobody'd take it away from me."

George looked quickly and searchingly at him. "I been mean, ain't I?"

"If you don' want me I can go off in the hills an' find a cave. I can go away any time."

"No—look! I was jus' foolin', Lennie. 'Cause I want you to stay with me. Trouble with mice is you always kill 'em." He paused. "Tell you what I'll do, Lennie. First chance I get I'll give you a pup. Maybe you wouldn't kill *it*. That'd be better than mice. And you could pet it harder."

Lennie avoided the bait. He had sensed his advantage. "If you don't want me, you only jus' got to say so, and I'll go off in those hills right there—right up in those hills and live by myself. An' I won't get no mice stole from me."

George said, "I want you to stay with me, Lennie. Jesus Christ, somebody'd shoot you for a coyote if you was by yourself. No, you stay with me. Your Aunt Clara wouldn't like you running off by yourself, even if she is dead."

Lennie spoke craftily, "Tell me—like you done before."

"Tell you what?"

"About the rabbits."

George snapped, "You ain't gonna put nothing over on me."

Lennie pleaded, "Come on, George. Tell me. Please, George. Like you done before."

"You get a kick outta that, don't you? Awright, I'll tell you, and then we'll eat our supper. . . ."

George's voice became deeper. He repeated his words rhythmically as though he had said them many times before. "Guys like us, that work on ranches, are the loneliest guys in the world. They got no family. They don't belong no place. They come to a ranch an' work up a stake and then they go into town and blow their stake, and the first thing you know they're poundin' their tail on some other ranch. They ain't got nothing to look ahead to."

Lennie was delighted. "That's it—that's it. Now tell how it is with us."

George went on. "With us it ain't like that. We got a future. We got somebody to talk to that gives a damn about us. We don't have to sit in no bar room blowin' in our jack jus' because we got no place else to go. If them other guys gets in jail they can rot for all anybody gives a damn. But not us."

Lennie broke in. *"But not us! An' why? Because . . . because I got you to look after me, and you got me to look after you, and that's why."* He laughed delightedly. "Go on now, George!"

"You got it by heart. You can do it yourself."

"No, you. I forget some a' the things. Tell about how it's gonna be."

"O.K. Someday—we're gonna get the jack together and we're gonna have a little house and a couple of acres an' a cow and some pigs and——"

"An' live off the fatta the lan'," Lennie shouted. "An' have *rabbits.* Go on, George! Tell about what we're gonna have in the garden and about the rabbits in the cages and about the rain in the winter and the stove, and how thick the cream is on the milk like you can hardly cut it. Tell about that, George."

"Why'n't you do it yourself? You know all of it."

"No . . . you tell it. It ain't the same if I tell it. Go on . . . George. How I get to tend the rabbits."

"Well," said George, "we'll have a big vegetable patch and a rabbit hutch and chickens. And when it rains in the winter, we'll just say the hell with goin' to work, and we'll build up a fire in the stove and set around it an' listen to the rain comin' down on the roof—Nuts!" He took out his pocket knife. "I ain't got time for no more." He drove his knife through the top of one of the bean cans, sawed out the top and passed the can to Lennie. Then he opened a second can. From his side pocket he brought out two spoons and passed one of them to Lennie.

They sat by the fire and filled their mouths with beans and chewed mightily. A few beans slipped out of the side of Lennie's mouth. George gestured with his spoon. "What you gonna say tomorrow when the boss asks you questions?"

Lennie stopped chewing and swallowed. His face was concentrated. "I . . . I ain't gonna . . . say a word."

"Good boy! That's fine, Lennie! Maybe you're gettin' better. When we get the coupla acres I can let you tend the rabbits all right. 'Specially if you remember as good as that."

Lennie choked with pride. "I can remember," he said.

George motioned with his spoon again. "Look, Lennie. I want you to look around here. You can remember this place, can't you? The ranch is about a quarter mile up that way. Just follow the river?"

"Sure," said Lennie. "I can remember this. Di'n't I remember about not gonna say a word?"

"'Course you did. Well, look. Lennie—if you jus' happen to get in trouble like you always done before, I want you to come right here an' hide in the brush."

"Hide in the brush," said Lennie slowly.

"Hide in the brush till I come for you. Can you remember that?"

"Sure I can, George. Hide in the brush till you come."

"But you ain't gonna get in no trouble, because if you do, I won't let you tend the rabbits." He threw his empty bean can off into the brush.

"I won't get in no trouble, George. I ain't gonna say a word."

"O.K. Bring your bindle over here by the fire. It's gonna be nice sleepin' here. Lookin' up, and the leaves. Don't build up no more fire. We'll let her die down."

They made their beds on the sand, and as the blaze dropped from the fire the sphere of light grew smaller; the curling branches disappeared and only a faint glimmer

showed where the tree trunks were. From the darkness
Lennie called, "George—you asleep?"

"No. Whatta you want?"

"Let's have different color rabbits, George."

"Sure we will," George said sleepily. "Red and blue
and green rabbits, Lennie. Millions of 'em."

"Furry ones, George, like I seen in the fair in Sacramento."

"Sure, furry ones."

"'Cause I can jus' as well go away, George, an' live
in a cave."

"You can jus' as well go to hell," said George. "Shut up
now."

The red light dimmed on the coals. Up the hill from
the river a coyote yammered, and a dog answered from
the other side of the stream. The sycamore leaves whispered in a little night breeze.

THE bunkhouse was a long, rectangular building.
Inside, the walls were whitewashed and the floor
unpainted. In three walls there were small, square windows, and in the fourth, a solid door with a wooden latch.
Against the walls were eight bunks, five of them made up
with blankets and the other three showing their burlap
ticking. Over each bunk there was nailed an apple box
with the opening forward so that it made two shelves
for the personal belongings of the occupant of the bunk.
And these shelves were loaded with little articles, soap
and talcum powder, razors and those Western magazines
ranch men love to read·and scoff at and secretly believe.
And there were medicines on the shelves, and little vials,
combs; and from nails on the box sides, a few neckties.
Near one wall there was a black cast-iron stove, its stove-

pipe going straight up through the ceiling. In the middle of the room stood a big square table littered with playing cards, and around it were grouped boxes for the players to sit on.

At about ten o'clock in the morning the sun threw a bright dust-laden bar through one of the side windows, and in and out of the beam flies shot like rushing stars.

The wooden latch raised. The door opened and a tall, stoop-shouldered old man came in. He was dressed in blue jeans and he carried a big push-broom in his left hand. Behind him came George, and behind George, Lennie.

"The boss was expectin' you last night," the old man said. "He was sore as hell when you wasn't here to go out this morning." He pointed with his right arm, and out of the sleeve came a round stick-like wrist, but no hand. "You can have them two beds there," he said, indicating two bunks near the stove.

George stepped over and threw his blankets down on the burlap sack of straw that was a mattress. He looked into his box shelf and then picked a small yellow can from it. "Say. What the hell's this?"

"I don't know," said the old man.

"Says 'positively kills lice, roaches and other scourges.' What the hell kind of bed you giving us, anyways. We don't want no pants rabbits."

The old swamper shifted his broom and held it between his elbow and his side while he held out his hand for the can. He studied the label carefully. "Tell you what—" he said finally, "last guy that had this bed was a blacksmith—hell of a nice fella and as clean a guy as you want to meet. Used to wash his hands even *after* he ate."

"Then how come he got graybacks?" George was working up a slow anger. Lennie put his bindle on the neighboring bunk and sat down. He watched George with open mouth.

"Tell you what," said the old swamper. "This here blacksmith—name of Whitey—was the kind of guy that would put that stuff around even if there wasn't no bugs —just to make sure, see? Tell you what he used to do— At meals he'd peel his boil' potatoes, an' he'd take out ever' little spot, no matter what kind, before he'd eat it. And if there was a red splotch on an egg, he'd scrape it off. Finally quit about the food. That's the kinda guy he was—clean. Used ta dress up Sundays even when he wasn't going no place, put on a necktie even, and then set in the bunkhouse."

"I ain't so sure," said George skeptically. "What did you say he quit for?"

The old man put the yellow can in his pocket, and he rubbed his bristly white whiskers with his knuckles. "Why . . . he . . . just quit, the way a guy will. Says it was the food. Just wanted to move. Didn't give no other reason but the food. Just says 'gimme my time' one night, the way any guy would."

George lifted his tick and looked underneath it. He leaned over and inspected the sacking closely. Immediately Lennie got up and did the same with his bed. Finally George seemed satisfied. He unrolled his bindle and put things on the shelf, his razor and bar of soap, his comb and bottle of pills, his liniment and leather wristband. Then he made his bed up neatly with blankets. The old man said, "I guess the boss'll be out here in a minute. He was sure burned when you wasn't here this morning. Come right in when we was eatin' breakfast and says, 'Where the hell's them new men?' An' he give the stable buck hell, too."

George patted a wrinkle out of his bed, and sat down. "Give the stable buck hell?" he asked.

"Sure. Ya see the stable buck's a nigger."

"Nigger, huh?"

"Yeah. Nice fella too. Got a crooked back where a horse kicked him. The boss gives him hell when he's mad. But the stable buck don't give a damn about that. He reads a lot. Got books in his room."

"What kind of a guy is the boss?" George asked.

"Well, he's a pretty nice fella. Gets pretty mad sometimes, but he's pretty nice. Tell ya what—know what he done Christmas? Brang a gallon of whisky right in here and says, 'Drink hearty boys. Christmas comes but once a year.'"

"The hell he did! Whole gallon?"

"Yes sir. Jesus, we had fun. They let the nigger come in that night. Little skinner name of Smitty took after the nigger. Done pretty good, too. The guys wouldn't let him use his feet, so the nigger got him. If he coulda used his feet, Smitty says he woulda killed the nigger. The guys said on account of the nigger's got a crooked back, Smitty can't use his feet." He paused in relish of the memory. "After that the guys went into Soledad and raised hell. I didn't go in there. I ain't got the poop no more."

Lennie was just finishing making his bed. The wooden latch raised again and the door opened. A little stocky man stood in the open doorway. He wore blue jean trousers, a flannel shirt, a black, unbuttoned vest and a black coat. His thumbs were stuck in his belt, on each side of a square steel buckle. On his head was a soiled brown Stetson hat, and he wore high-heeled boots and spurs to prove he was not a laboring man.

The old swamper looked quickly at him, and then shuffled to the door rubbing his whiskers with his knuckles as he went. "Them guys just come," he said, and shuffled past the boss and out the door.

The boss stepped into the room with the short, quick steps of a fat-legged man. "I wrote Murray and Ready I wanted two men this morning. You got your work slips?" George reached into his pocket and produced the slips and handed them to the boss. "It wasn't Murray and Ready's fault. Says right here on the slip that you was to be here for work this morning."

George looked down at his feet. "Bus driver give us a bum steer," he said. "We hadda walk ten miles. Says we was here when we wasn't. We couldn't get no rides in the morning."

The boss squinted his eyes. "Well, I had to send out the grain teams short two buckers. Won't do any good to go out now till after dinner." He pulled his time book out of his pocket and opened it where a pencil was stuck between the leaves. George scowled meaningfully at Lennie, and Lennie nodded to show that he understood. The boss licked his pencil. "What's your name?"

"George Milton."

"And what's yours?"

George said, "His name's Lennie Small."

The names were entered in the book. "Le's see, this is the twentieth, noon the twentieth." He closed the book. "Where you boys been working?"

"Up around Weed," said George.

"You, too?" to Lennie.

"Yeah, him too," said George.

The boss pointed a playful finger at Lennie. "He ain't much of a talker, is he?"

"No, he ain't, but he's sure a hell of a good worker. Strong as a bull."

Lennie smiled to himself. "Strong as a bull," he repeated.

George scowled at him, and Lennie dropped his head in shame at having forgotten.

The boss said suddenly, "Listen, Small!" Lennie raised his head. "What can you do?"

In a panic, Lennie looked at George for help. "He can do anything you tell him," said George. "He's a good skinner. He can rassel grain bags, drive a cultivator. He can do anything. Just give him a try."

The boss turned on George. "Then why don't you let him answer? What you trying to put over?"

George broke in loudly, "Oh! I ain't saying he's bright. He ain't. But I say he's a God damn good worker. He can put up a four hundred pound bale."

The boss deliberately put the little book in his pocket. He hooked his thumbs in his belt and squinted one eye nearly closed. "Say—what you sellin'?"

"Huh?"

"I said what stake you got in this guy? You takin' his pay away from him?"

"No, 'course I ain't. Why ya think I'm sellin' him out?"

"Well, I never seen one guy take so much trouble for another guy. I just like to know what your interest is."

George said, "He's my . . . cousin. I told his old lady I'd take care of him. He got kicked in the head by a horse when he was a kid. He's awright. Just ain't bright. But he can do anything you tell him."

The boss turned half away. "Well, God knows he don't need any brains to buck barley bags. But don't you try to put nothing over, Milton. I got my eye on you. Why'd you quit in Weed?"

"Job was done," said George promptly.

"What kinda job?"

"We . . . we was diggin' a cesspool."

"All right. But don't try to put nothing over, 'cause you can't get away with nothing. I seen wise guys before. Go on out with the grain teams after dinner. They're pickin' up barley at the threshing machine. Go out with Slim's team."

"Slim?"

"Yeah. Big tall skinner. You'll see him at dinner." He turned abruptly and went to the door, but before he went out he turned and looked for a long moment at the two men.

When the sound of his footsteps had died away, George turned on Lennie. "So you wasn't gonna say a word. You was gonna leave your big flapper shut and leave me do the talkin'. Damn near lost us the job."

Lennie stared hopelessly at his hands. "I forgot, George."

"Yeah, you forgot. You always forget, an' I got to talk you out of it." He sat down heavily on the bunk. "Now he's got his eye on us. Now we got to be careful and not make no slips. You keep your big flapper shut after this." He fell morosely silent.

"George."

"What you want now?"

"I wasn't kicked in the head with no horse, was I, George?"

"Be a damn good thing if you was," George said viciously. "Save ever'body a hell of a lot of trouble."

"You said I was your cousin, George."

"Well, that was a lie. An' I'm damn glad it was. If I was a relative of yours I'd shoot myself." He stopped suddenly, stepped to the open front door and peered out. "Say, what the hell you doin' listenin'?"

The old man came slowly into the room. He had his broom in his hand. And at his heels there walked a dragfooted sheepdog, gray of muzzle, and with pale, blind old eyes. The dog struggled lamely to the side of the room and lay down, grunting softly to himself and licking his grizzled, moth-eaten coat. The swamper watched him until he was settled. "I wasn't listenin'. I was jus' standin' in the shade a minute scratchin' my dog. I jus' now finished swampin' out the wash house."

"You was pokin' your big ears into our business," George said. "I don't like nobody to get nosey."

The old man looked uneasily from George to Lennie, and then back. "I jus' come there," he said. "I didn't hear nothing you guys was sayin'. I ain't interested in nothing you was sayin'. A guy on a ranch don't never listen nor he don't ast no questions."

"Damn right he don't," said George, slightly mollified, "not if he wants to stay workin' long." But he was reassured by the swamper's defense. "Come on in and set down a minute," he said. "That's a hell of an old dog."

"Yeah. I had 'em ever since he was a pup. God, he was a good sheep dog when he was younger." He stood his broom against the wall and he rubbed his white bristled cheek with his knuckles. "How'd you like the boss?" he asked.

"Pretty good. Seemed awright."

"He's a nice fella," the swamper agreed. "You got to take him right."

At that moment a young man came into the bunk house; a thin young man with a brown face, with brown eyes and a head of tightly curled hair. He wore a work glove on his left hand, and, like the boss, he wore high-heeled boots. "Seen my old man?" he asked.

The swamper said, "He was here jus' a minute ago, Curley. Went over to the cook house, I think."

"I'll try to catch him," said Curley. His eyes passed over the new men and he stopped. He glanced coldly at George and then at Lennie. His arms gradually bent at the elbows and his hands closed into fists. He stiffened and went into a slight crouch. His glance was at once calculating and pugnacious. Lennie squirmed under the look and shifted his feet nervously. Curley stepped gingerly close to him. "You the new guys the old man was waitin' for?"

"We just come in," said George.

"Let the big guy talk."

Lennie twisted with embarrassment.

George said, "S'pose he don't want to talk?"

Curley lashed his body around. "By Christ, he's gotta talk when he's spoke to. What the hell are you gettin' into it for?"

"We travel together," said George coldly.

"Oh, so it's that way."

George was tense, and motionless. "Yeah, it's that way."

Lennie was looking helplessly to George for instruction.

"An' you won't let the big guy talk, is that it?"

"He can talk if he wants to tell you anything." He nodded slightly to Lennie.

"We jus' come in," said Lennie softly.

Curley stared levelly at him. "Well, nex' time you answer when you're spoke to." He turned toward the door and walked out, and his elbows were still bent out a little.

George watched him out, and then he turned back to the swamper. "Say, what the hell's he got on his shoulder? Lennie didn't do nothing to him."

The old man looked cautiously at the door to make sure no one was listening. "That's the boss's son," he said quietly. "Curley's pretty handy. He done quite a bit in the ring. He's a lightweight, and he's handy."

"Well, let him be handy," said George. "He don't have to take after Lennie. Lennie didn't do nothing to him. What's he got against Lennie?"

The swamper considered. . . . "Well . . . tell you what. Curley's like a lot of little guys. He hates big guys. He's alla time picking scraps with big guys. Kind of like he's mad at 'em because he ain't a big guy. You seen little guys like that, ain't you? Always scrappy?"

"Sure," said George. "I seen plenty tough little guys. But this Curley better not make no mistakes about Lennie. Lennie ain't handy, but this Curley punk is gonna get hurt if he messes around with Lennie."

"Well, Curley's pretty handy," the swamper said skeptically. "Never did seem right to me. S'pose Curley jumps a big guy an' licks him. Ever'body says what a game guy Curley is. And s'pose he does the same thing and gets licked. Then ever'body says the big guy oughtta pick somebody his own size, and maybe they gang up on the big guy. Never did seem right to me. Seems like Curley ain't givin' nobody a chance."

George was watching the door. He said ominously, "Well, he better watch out for Lennie. Lennie ain't no fighter, but Lennie's strong and quick and Lennie don't know no rules." He walked to the square table and sat down on one of the boxes. He gathered some of the cards together and shuffled them.

The old man sat down on another box. "Don't tell Curley I said none of this. He'd slough me. He just don't give a damn. Won't ever get canned 'cause his old man's the boss."

George cut the cards and began turning them over, looking at each one and throwing it down on a pile. He said, "This guy Curley sounds like a son-of-a-bitch to me. I don't like mean little guys."

"Seems to me like he's worse lately," said the swamper. "He got married a couple of weeks ago. Wife lives over in the boss's house. Seems like Curley is cockier'n ever since he got married."

George grunted, "Maybe he's showin' off for his wife."

The swamper warmed to his gossip. "You seen that glove on his left hand?"

"Yeah. I seen it."

"Well, that glove's fulla vaseline."

"Vaseline? What the hell for?"

"Well, I tell ya what—Curley says he's keepin' that hand soft for his wife."

George studied the cards absorbedly. "That's a dirty thing to tell around," he said.

The old man was reassured. He had drawn a derogatory statement from George. He felt safe now, and he spoke more confidently. "Wait'll you see Curley's wife."

George cut the cards again and put out a solitaire lay, slowly and deliberately. "Purty?" he asked casually.

"Yeah. Purty . . . but——"

George studied his cards. "But what?"

"Well—she got the eye."

"Yeah? Married two weeks and got the eye? Maybe that's why Curley's pants is full of ants."

"I seen her give Slim the eye. Slim's a jerkline skinner. Hell of a nice fella. Slim don't need to wear no high-heeled boots on a grain team. I seen her give Slim the eye. Curley never seen it. An' I seen her give Carlson the eye."

George pretended a lack of interest. "Looks like we was gonna have fun."

The swamper stood up from his box. "Know what I think?" George did not answer. "Well, I think Curley's married . . . a tart."

"He ain't the first," said George. "There's plenty done that."

The old man moved toward the door, and his ancient dog lifted his head and peered about, and then got painfully to his feet to follow. "I gotta be settin' out the wash basins for the guys. The teams'll be in before long. You guys gonna buck barley?"

"Yeah."

"You won't tell Curley nothing I said?"

"Hell no."

"Well, you look her over, mister. You see if she ain't a tart." He stepped out the door into the brilliant sunshine. .

George laid down his cards thoughtfully, turned his piles of three. He built four clubs on his ace pile. The sun square was on the floor now, and the flies whipped through it like sparks. A sound of jingling harness and the croak of heavy-laden axles sounded from outside. From the distance came a clear call. "Stable Buck—ooh, staable Buck! And then, "Where the hell is that God damn nigger?"

George stared at his solitaire lay, and then he flounced the cards together and turned around to Lennie. Lennie was lying down on the bunk watching him.

"Look, Lennie! This here ain't no set up. I'm scared. You gonna have trouble with that Curley guy. I seen that kind before. He was kinda feelin' you out. He figures he's got you scared and he's gonna take a sock at you the first chance he gets."

Lennie's eyes were frightened. "I don't want no trouble," he said plaintively. "Don't let him sock me, George."

George got up and went over to Lennie's bunk and sat down on it. "I hate that kinda bastard," he said. "I seen plenty of 'em. Like the old guy says, Curley don't take no chances. He always wins." He thought for a moment. "If he tangles with you, Lennie, we're gonna get the can. Don't make no mistake about that. He's the boss's son. Look, Lennie. You try to keep away from him, will you? Don't never speak to him. If he comes in here you move clear to the other side of the room. Will you do that, Lennie?"

"I don't want no trouble," Lennie mourned. "I never done nothing to him."

"Well, that won't do you no good if Curley wants to plug himself up for a fighter. Just don't have nothing to do with him. Will you remember?"

"Sure, George. I ain't gonna say a word."

The sound of the approaching grain teams was louder, thud of big hooves on hard ground, drag of brakes and the jingle of trace chains. Men were calling back and forth from the teams. George, sitting on the bunk beside Lennie, frowned as he thought. Lennie asked timidly, "You ain't mad, George?"

"I ain't mad at you. I'm mad at this here Curley bastard. I hoped we was gonna get a little stake together—maybe a hundred dollars." His tone grew decisive. "You keep away from Curley, Lennie."

"Sure I will, George. I won't say a word."

"Don't let him pull you in—but—if the son-of-a-bitch socks you—let 'im have it."

"Let 'im have what, George?"

"Never mind, never mind. I'll tell you when. I hate that kind of a guy. Look, Lennie, if you get in any kind of trouble, you remember what I told you to do?"

Lennie raised up on his elbow. His face contorted with thought. Then his eyes moved sadly to George's face. "If I get in any trouble, you ain't gonna let me tend the rabbits."

"That's not what I meant. You remember where we slep' last night? Down by the river?"

"Yeah. I remember. Oh, sure I remember! I go there an' hide in the brush."

"Hide till I come for you. Don't let nobody see you. Hide in the brush by the river. Say that over."

"Hide in the brush by the river, down in the brush by the river."

"If you get in trouble."

"If I get in trouble."

A brake screeched outside. A call came, "Stable— Buck. Oh! Sta-able Buck."

George said, "Say it over to yourself, Lennie, so you won't forget it."

Both men glanced up, for the rectangle of sunshine in the doorway was cut off. A girl was standing there looking in. She had full, rouged lips and wide-spaced eyes, heavily made up. Her fingernails were red. Her hair hung in little rolled clusters, like sausages. She wore a cotton house dress and red mules, on the insteps of which were little bouquets of red ostrich feathers. "I'm lookin' for Curley," she said. Her voice had a nasal, brittle quality.

George looked away from her and then back. "He was in here a minute ago, but he went."

"Oh!" She put her hands behind her back and leaned against the door frame so that her body was thrown forward. "You're the new fellas that just come, ain't ya?"

"Yeah."

Lennie's eyes moved down over her body, and though she did not seem to be looking at Lennie she bridled a little. She looked at her fingernails. "Sometimes Curley's in here," she explained.

George said brusquely, "Well he ain't now."

"If he ain't, I guess I better look some place else," she said playfully.

Lennie watched her, fascinated. George said, "If I see him, I'll pass the word you was looking for him."

She smiled archly and twitched her body. "Nobody can't blame a person for lookin'," she said. There were footsteps behind her, going by. She turned her head. "Hi, Slim," she said.

Slim's voice came through the door. "Hi, Good-lookin'."

"I'm tryin' to find Curley, Slim."

"Well, you ain't tryin' very hard. I seen him goin' in your house."

She was suddenly apprehensive. "'Bye, boys," she called into the bunk house, and she hurried away.

George looked around at Lennie. "Jesus, what a tramp," he said. "So that's what Curley picks for a wife."

"She's purty," said Lennie defensively.

"Yeah, and she's sure hidin' it. Curley got his work ahead of him. Bet she'd clear out for twenty bucks."

Lennie still stared at the doorway where she had been. "Gosh, she was purty." He smiled admiringly. George looked quickly down at him and then he took him by an ear and shook him.

"Listen to me, you crazy bastard," he said fiercely. "Don't you even take a look at that bitch. I don't care what she says and what she does. I seen 'em poison before, but I never seen no piece of jail bait worse than her. You leave her be."

Lennie tried to disengage his ear. "I never done nothing, George."

"No, you never. But when she was standin' in the doorway showin' her legs, you wasn't lookin' the other way, neither."

"I never meant no harm, George. Honest I never."

"Well, you keep away from her, 'cause she's a rattrap if I ever seen one. You let Curley take the rap. He let himself in for it. Glove fulla vaseline," George said disgustedly. "An' I bet he's eatin' raw eggs and writin' to the patent medicine houses."

Lennie cried out suddenly—"I don' like this place,

George. This ain't no good place. I wanna get outa here."

"We gotta keep it till we get a stake. We can't help it, Lennie. We'll get out jus' as soon as we can. I don't like it no better than you do." He went back to the table and set out a new solitaire hand: "No, I don't like it," he said. "For two bits I'd shove out of here. If we can get jus' a few dollars in the poke we'll shove off and go up the American River and pan gold. We can make maybe a couple of dollars a day there, and we might hit a pocket."

Lennie leaned eagerly toward him. "Le's go, George. Le's get outa here. It's mean here."

"We gotta stay," George said shortly. "Shut up now. The guys'll be comin' in."

From the washroom nearby came the sound of running water and rattling basins. George studied the cards. "Maybe we oughtta wash up," he said. "But we ain't done nothing to get dirty."

A tall man stood in the doorway. He held a crushed Stetson hat under his arm while he combed his long, black, damp hair straight back. Like the others he wore blue jeans and a short denim jacket. When he had finished combing his hair he moved into the room, and he moved with a majesty only achieved by royalty and master craftsmen. He was a jerkline skinner, the prince of the ranch, capable of driving ten, sixteen, even twenty mules with a single line to the leaders. He was capable of killing a fly on the wheeler's butt with a bull whip without touching the mule. There was a gravity in his manner and a quiet so profound that all talk stopped when he spoke. His authority was so great that his word was taken on any subject, be it politics or love. This was Slim, the jerkline skinner. His hatchet face was ageless. He might have been thirty-five or fifty. His ear heard more than was said to him, and his slow speech had overtones not of thought, but of understanding beyond thought. His hands, large and lean, were as delicate in their action as those of a temple dancer.

He smoothed out his crushed hat, creased it in the middle and put it on. He looked kindly at the two in the bunk house. "It's brighter'n a bitch outside," he said gently. "Can't hardly see nothing in here. You the new guys?"

"Just come," said George.

"Gonna buck barley?"

"That's what the boss says."

Slim sat down on a box across the table from George. He studied the solitaire hand that was upside down to him. "Hope you get on my team," he said. His voice was very gentle. "I gotta pair of punks on my team that don't know a barley bag from a blue ball. You guys ever bucked any barley?"

"Hell, yes," said George. "I ain't nothing to scream about, but that big bastard there can put up more grain alone than most pairs can."

Lennie, who had been following the conversation back and forth with his eyes, smiled complacently at the compliment. Slim looked approvingly at George for having given the compliment. He leaned over the table and snapped the corner of a loose card. "You guys travel around together?" His tone was friendly. It invited confidence without demanding it.

"Sure," said George. "We kinda look after each other." He indicated Lennie with his thumb. "He ain't bright. Hell of a good worker, though. Hell of a nice fella, but he ain't bright. I've knew him for a long time."

Slim looked through George and beyond him. "Ain't many guys travel around together," he mused. "I don't know why. Maybe ever'body in the whole damn world is scared of each other."

"It's a lot nicer to go around with a guy you know," said George.

A powerful, big-stomached man came into the bunk house. His head still dripped water from the scrubbing and dousing. "Hi, Slim," he said, and then stopped and stared at George and Lennie.

"These guys jus' come," said Slim by way of introduction.

"Glad ta meet ya," the big man said. "My name's Carlson."

"I'm George Milton. This here's Lennie Small."

"Glad ta meet ya," Carlson said again. "He ain't very small." He chuckled softly at his joke. "Ain't small at all," he repeated. "Meant to ask you, Slim—how's your bitch? I seen she wasn't under your wagon this morning."

"She slang her pups last night," said Slim. "Nine of 'em. I drowned four of 'em right off. She couldn't feed that many."

"Got five left, huh?"

"Yeah, five. I kept the biggest."

"What kinda dogs you think they're gonna be?"

"I dunno," said Slim. "Some kinda shepherds, I guess. That's the most kind I seen around here when she was in heat."

Carlson went on, "Got five pups, huh. Gonna keep all of 'em?"

"I dunno. Have to keep 'em a while so they can drink Lulu's milk."

Carlson said thoughtfully, "Well, looka here, Slim. I been thinkin'. That dog of Candy's is so God damn old he can't hardly walk. Stinks like hell, too. Ever' time he comes into the bunk house I can smell him for two, three days. Why'n't you get Candy to shoot his old dog and give him one of the pups to raise up? I can smell that dog a mile away. Got no teeth, damn near blind, can't eat. Candy feeds him milk. He can't chew nothing else."

George had been staring intently at Slim. Suddenly a triangle began to ring outside, slowly at first, and then faster and faster until the beat of it disappeared into one ringing sound. It stopped as suddenly as it had started.

"There she goes," said Carlson

Outside, there was a burst of voices as a group of men went by.

Slim stood up slowly and with dignity. "You guys better come on while they's still something to eat. Won't be nothing left in a couple of minutes."

Carlson stepped back to let Slim precede him, and then the two of them went out the door.

Lennie was watching George excitedly. George rumpled his cards into a messy pile. "Yeah!" George said, "I heard him, Lennie. I'll ask him."

"A brown and white one," Lennie cried excitedly.

"Come on. Le's get dinner. I don't know whether he got a brown and white one."

Lennie didn't move from his bunk. "You ask him right away, George, so he won't kill no more of 'em."

"Sure. Come on now, get up on your feet."

Lennie rolled off his bunk and stood up, and the two of them started for the door. Just as they reached it, Curley bounced in.

"You seen a girl around here?" he demanded angrily.

George said coldly. ". 'Bout half an hour ago maybe."

"Well what the hell was she doin'?"

George stood still, watching the angry little man. He said insultingly, "She said—she was lookin' for you."

Curley seemed really to see George for the first time. His eyes flashed over George, took in his height, measured his reach, looked at his trim middle. "Well, which way'd she go?" he demanded at last.

"I dunno," said George. "I didn' watch her go."

Curley scowled at him, and turning, hurried out the door.

George said, "Ya know, Lennie, I'm scared I'm gonna tangle with that bastard myself. I hate his guts. Jesus Christ! Come on. They won't be a damn thing left to eat."

They went out the door. The sunshine lay in a thin line under the window. From a distance there could be heard a rattle of dishes.

After a moment the ancient dog walked lamely in through the open door. He gazed about with mild, half-blind eyes. He sniffed, and then lay down and put his head between his paws. Curley popped into the doorway again and stood looking into the room. The dog raised his head, but when Curley jerked out, the grizzled head sank to the floor again.

ALTHOUGH there was evening brightness showing through the windows of the bunkhouse, inside it was dusk. Through the open door came the thuds and occasional clangs of a horseshoe game, and now and then the sound of voices raised in approval or derision.

Slim and George came into the darkening bunk house together. Slim reached up over the card table and turned on the tin-shaded electric light. Instantly the table was brilliant with light, and the cone of the shade threw its brightness straight downward, leaving the corners of the bunk house still in dusk. Slim sat down on a box and George took his place opposite.

"It wasn't nothing," said Slim. "I would of had to drowned most of 'em anyways. No need to thank me about that."

George said, "It wasn't much to you, maybe, but it was a hell of a lot to him. Jesus Christ, I don't know how we're gonna get him to sleep in here. He'll want to sleep right out in the barn with 'em. We'll have trouble keepin' him from getting right in the box with them pups."

"It wasn't nothing," Slim repeated. "Say, you sure was right about him. Maybe he ain't bright, but I never seen such a worker. He damn near killed his partner buckin' barley. There ain't nobody can keep up with him. God awmighty I never seen such a strong guy."

George spoke proudly. "Jus' tell Lennie what to do an' he'll do it if it don't take no figuring. He can't think of nothing to do himself, but he sure can take orders."

There was a clang of horseshoe on iron stake outside and a little cheer of voices.

Slim moved back slightly so the light was not on his face. "Funny how you an' him string along together." It was Slim's calm invitation to confidence.

"What's funny about it?" George demanded defensively.

"Oh, I dunno. Hardly none of the guys ever travel together. I hardly never seen two guys travel together. You know how the hands are, they just come in and get their bunk and work a month, and then they quit and go out alone. Never seem to give a damn about nobody. It jus' seems kinda funny a cuckoo like him and a smart little guy like you travelin' together."

"He ain't no cuckoo," said George. "He's dumb as hell, but he ain't crazy. An' I ain't so bright neither, or I wouldn't be buckin' barley for my fifty and found. If I was bright, if I was even a little bit smart, I'd have my own little place, an' I'd be bringin' in my own crops, 'stead of doin' all the work and not getting what comes up outa the ground." George fell silent. He wanted to talk. Slim neither encouraged nor discouraged him. He just sat back quiet and receptive.

"It ain't so funny, him an' me goin' aroun' together,"

George said at last. "Him and me was both born in Auburn. I knowed his Aunt Clara. She took him when he was a baby and raised him up. When his Aunt Clara died, Lennie just come along with me out workin'. Got kinda used to each other after a little while."

"Umm," said Slim.

George looked over at Slim and saw the calm, God-like eyes fastened on him. "Funny," said George. "I used to have a hell of a lot of fun with 'im. Used to play jokes on 'im 'cause he was too dumb to take care of 'imself. But he was too dumb even to know he had a joke played on him. I had fun. Made me seem God damn smart alongside of him. Why he'd do any damn thing I tol' him. If I tol' him to walk over a cliff, over he'd go. That wasn't so damn much fun after a while. He never got mad about it, neither. I've beat the hell outa him, and he coulda bust every bone in my body jus' with his han's, but he never lifted a finger against me." George's voice was taking on the tone of confession. "Tell you what made me stop that. One day a bunch of guys was standin' around up on the Sacramento River. I was feelin' pretty smart. I turns to Lennie and says, 'Jump in.' An' he jumps. Couldn't swim a stroke. He damn near drowned before we could get him. An' he was so damn nice to me for pullin' him out. Clean forgot I told him to jump in. Well, I ain't done nothing like that no more."

"He's a nice fella," said Slim. "Guy don't need no sense to be a nice fella. Seems to me sometimes it jus' works the other way around. Take a real smart guy and he ain't hardly ever a nice fella."

George stacked the scattered cards and began to lay out his solitaire hand. The shoes thudded on the ground outside. At the windows the light of the evening still made the window squares bright.

"I ain't got no people," George said. "I seen the guys

that go around on the ranches alone. That ain't no good. They don't have no fun. After a long time they get mean. They get wantin' to fight all the time."

"Yeah, they get mean," Slim agreed. "They get so they don't want to talk to nobody."

" 'Course Lennie's a God damn nuisance most of the time," said George. "But you get used to goin' around with a guy an' you can't get rid of him."

"He ain't mean," said Slim. "I can see Lennie ain't a bit mean."

" 'Course he ain't mean. But he gets in trouble alla time because he's so God damn dumb. Like what happened in Weed——" He stopped, stopped in the middle of turning over a card. He looked alarmed and peered over at Slim. "You wouldn't tell nobody?"

"What'd he do in Weed?" Slim asked calmly.

"You wouldn' tell? . . . No, 'course you wouldn'."

"What'd he do in Weed?" Slim asked again.

"Well, he seen this girl in a red dress. Dumb bastard like he is, he wants to touch ever'thing he likes. Just wants to feel it. So he reaches out to feel this red dress an' the girl lets out a squawk, and that gets Lennie all mixed up, and he holds on 'cause that's the only thing he can think to do. Well, this girl squawks and squawks. I was jus' a little bit off, and I heard all the yellin', so I comes running, an' by that time Lennie's so scared all he can think to do is jus' hold on. I socked him over the head with a fence picket to make him let go. He was so scairt he couldn't let go of that dress, And he's so God damn strong, you know."

Slim's eyes were level and unwinking. He nodded very slowly. "So what happens?"

George carefully built his line of solitaire cards. "Well, that girl rabbits in an' tells the law she been raped. The guys in Weed start a party out to lynch Lennie. So we sit in a irrigation ditch under water all the rest of that day. Got on'y our heads sticking outa water, an' up under the grass that sticks out from the side of the ditch. An' that night we scrammed outa there."

Slim sat in silence for a moment. "Didn't hurt the girl none, huh?" he asked finally.

"Hell, no. He just scared her. I'd be scared too if he grabbed me. But he never hurt her. He jus' wanted to touch that red dress, like he wants to pet them pups all the time."

"He ain't mean," said Slim. "I can tell a mean guy a mile off."

" 'Course he ain't, and he'll do any damn thing I——"

Lennie came in through the door. He wore his blue denim coat over his shoulders like a cape, and he walked hunched way over.

"Hi, Lennie," said George. "How you like the pup now?"

Lennie said breathlessly, "He's brown an' white jus' like I wanted." He went directly to his bunk and lay down and turned his face to the wall and drew up his knees.

George put down his cards very deliberately. "Lennie," he said sharply.

Lennie twisted his neck and looked over his shoulder. "Huh? What you want, George?"

"I tol' you you couldn't bring that pup in here."

"What pup, George? I ain't got no pup."

George went quickly to him, grabbed him by the shoulder and rolled him over. He reached down and picked the tiny puppy from where Lennie had been concealing it against his stomach.

Lennie sat up quickly. "Give 'um to me, George."

George said, "You get right up an' take this pup back to the nest. He's gotta sleep with his mother. You want to kill him? Just born last night an' you take him out of the nest. You take him back or I'll tell Slim not to let you have him."

Lennie held out his hands pleadingly. "Give 'um to me, George. I'll take 'um back. I didn't mean no harm, George. Honest I didn't. I jus' wanted to pet 'um a little."

George handed the pup to him. "Awright. You get him back there quick, and don't you take him out no more. You'll kill him, the first thing you know." Lennie fairly scuttled out of the room.

Slim had not moved. His calm eyes followed Lennie out the door. "Jesus," he said. "He's jus' like a kid, ain't he."

"Sure he's jes' like a kid. There ain't no more harm in him than a kid neither, except he's so strong. I bet he won't come in here to sleep tonight. He'd sleep right alongside that box in the barn. Well—let 'im. He ain't doin' no harm out there."

It was almost dark outside now. Old Candy, the swamper, came in and went to his bunk, and behind him struggled his old dog. "Hello, Slim. Hello, George. Didn't neither of you play horseshoes?"

"I don't like to play ever' night," said Slim.

Candy went on, "Either you guys got a slug of whisky? I gotta gut ache."

"I ain't," said Slim. "I'd drink it myself if I had, an' I ain't got a gut ache neither."

"Gotta bad gut ache," said Candy. "Them God damn turnips give it to me. I knowed they was going to before I ever eat 'em."

The thick-bodied Carlson came in out of the darkening yard. He walked to the other end of the bunk house and turned on the second shaded light. "Darker'n hell in here," he said. "Jesus, how that nigger can pitch shoes."

"He's plenty good," said Slim.

"Damn right he is," said Carlson. "He don't give

nobody else a chance to win——" He stopped and sniffed the air, and still sniffing, looked down at the old dog. "God awmighty, that dog stinks. Get him outa here, Candy! I don't know nothing that stinks as bad as an old dog. You gotta get him out."

Candy rolled to the edge of his bunk. He reached over and patted the ancient dog, and he apologized, "I been around him so much I never notice how he stinks."

"Well, I can't stand him in here," said Carlson. "That stink hangs around even after he's gone. He walked over with his heavy-legged stride and looked down at the dog. "Got no teeth," he said. "He's all stiff with rheumatism. He ain't no good to you, Candy. An' he ain't no good to himself. Why'n't you shoot him, Candy?"

The old man squirmed uncomfortably. "Well—hell! I had him so long. Had him since he was a pup. I herded sheep with him." He said proudly, "You wouldn't think it to look at him now, but he was the best damn sheep dog I ever seen."

George said, "I seen a guy in Weed that had an Airedale could herd sheep. Learned it from the other dogs."

Carlson was not to be put off. "Look, Candy. This ol' dog jus' suffers hisself all the time. If you was to take him out and shoot him right in the back of the head—" he leaned over and pointed, "—right there, why he'd never know what hit him."

Candy looked about unhappily. "No," he said softly. "No, I couldn' do that. I had 'em too long."

"He don't have no fun," Carlson insisted. "And he stinks to beat hell. Tell you what. I'll shoot him for you. Then it won't be you that does it."

Candy threw his legs off his bunk. He scratched the white stubble whiskers on his cheek nervously. "I'm so used to him," he said softly. "I had him from a pup."

"Well, you ain't bein' kind to him keepin' him alive,"

said Carlson. "Look, Slim's bitch got a litter right now. I bet Slim would give you one of them pups to raise up, wouldn't you, Slim?"

The skinner had been studying the old dog with his calm eyes. "Yeah," he said. "You can have a pup if you want to." He seemed to shake himself free for speech "Carl's right, Candy. That dog ain't no good to himself. I wisht somebody's shoot me if I get old an' a cripple."

Candy looked helplessly at him, for Slim's opinions were law. "Maybe it'd hurt him," he suggested. "I don't mind takin' care of him."

Carlson said, "The way I'd shoot him, he wouldn't feel nothing. I'd put the gun right there." He pointed with his toe. "Right back of the head. He wouldn't even quiver."

Candy looked for help from face to face. It was quite dark outside by now. A young laboring man came in. His sloping shoulders were bent forward and he walked heavily on his heels, as though he carried the invisible grain bag. He went to his bunk and put his hat on his shelf. Then he picked a pulp magazine from his shelf and brought it to the light over the table. "Did I show you this, Slim?" he asked.

"Show me what?"

The young man turned to the back of the magazine, put it down on the table and pointed with his finger. "Right there, read that." Slim bent over it. "Go on," said the young man. "Read it out loud."

" 'Dear Editor' ": Slim read slowly. " 'I read your mag for six years and I think it is the best on the market. I like stories by Peter Rand. I think he is a whing-ding. Give us more like the Dark Rider. I don't write many letters. Just thought I would tell you I think your mag is the best dime's worth I ever spent.' "

Slim looked up questioningly. "What you want me to read that for?"

Whit said, "Go on. Read the name at the bottom."

Slim read, " 'Yours for success, William Tenner.' " He glanced up at Whit again. "What you want me to read that for?"

Whit closed the magazine impressively. "Don't you remember Bill Tenner? Worked here about three months ago?"

Slim thought. . . . "Little guy?" he asked. "Drove a cultivator?"

"That's him," Whit cried. "That's the guy!"

"You think he's the guy wrote this letter?"

"I know it. Bill and me was in here one day. Bill had one of them books that just come. He was lookin' in it and he says, 'I wrote a letter. Wonder if they put it in the book!' But it wasn't there. Bill says, 'Maybe they're savin' it for later.' An' that's just what they done. There it is."

"Guess you're right," said Slim. "Got it right in the book."

George held out his hand for the magazine. "Let's look at it?"

Whit found the place again, but he did not surrender his hold on it. He pointed out the letter with his forefinger. And then he went to his box shelf and laid the magazine carefully in. "I wonder if Bill seen it," he said. "Bill and me worked in that patch of field peas. Run cultivators, both of us. Bill was a hell of a nice fella."

During the conversation Carlson had refused to be drawn in. He continued to look down at the old dog. Candy watched him uneasily. At last Carlson said, "If you want me to, I'll put the old devil out of his misery right now and get it over with. Ain't nothing left for him. Can't eat, can't see, can't even walk without hurtin'."

Candy said hopefully, "You ain't got no gun."

"The hell I ain't. Got a Luger. It won't hurt him none at all."

Candy said, "Maybe tomorra. Le's wait till tomorra."

"I don't see no reason for it," said Carlson. He went to his bunk, pulled his bag from underneath it and took out a Luger pistol. "Le's get it over with," he said. "We can't sleep with him stinkin' around in here." He put the pistol in his hip pocket.

Candy looked a long time at Slim to try to find some reversal. And Slim gave him none. At last Candy said softly and hopelessly, "Awright—take 'im." He did not look down at the dog at all. He lay back on his bunk and crossed him arms behind his head and stared at the ceiling.

From his pocket Carlson took a little leather thong. He stooped over and tied it around the old dog's neck. All the men except Candy watched him. "Come boy. Come on, boy," he said gently. And he said apologetically to Candy, "He won't even feel it." Candy did not move nor answer him. He twitched the thong. "Come on, boy." The old dog got slowly and stiffly to his feet and followed the gently pulling leash.

Slim said, "Carlson."

"Yeah?"

"You know what to do."

"What ya mean, Slim?"

"Take a shovel," said Slim shortly.

"Oh, sure! I get you." He led the dog out into the darkness.

George followed to the door and shut the door and set the latch gently in its place. Candy lay rigidly on his bed staring at the ceiling.

Slim said loudly, "One of my lead mules got a bad hoof.

Got to get some tar on it." His voice trailed off. It was silent outside. Carlson's footsteps died away. The silence came into the room. And the silence lasted.

George chuckled, "I bet Lennie's right out there in the barn with his pup. He won't want to come in here no more now he's got a pup."

Slim said, "Candy, you can have any one of them pups you want."

Candy did not answer. The silence fell on the room again. It came out of the night and invaded the room. George said, "Anybody like to play a little euchre?"

"I'll play out a few with you," said Whit.

They took places opposite each other at the table under the light, but George did not shuffle the cards. He rippled the edge of the deck nervously, and the little snapping noise drew the eyes of all the men in the room, so that he stopped doing it. The silence fell on the room again. A minute passed, and another minute. Candy lay still, staring at the ceiling. Slim gazed at him for a moment and then looked down at his hands; he subdued one hand with the other, and held it down. There came a little gnawing sound from under the floor and all the men looked down toward it gratefully. Only Candy continued to stare at the ceiling.

"Sounds like there was a rat under there," said George. "We ought to get a trap down there."

Whit broke out, "What the hell's takin' him so long? Lay out some cards, why don't you? We ain't going to get no euchre played this way."

George brought the cards together tightly and studied the backs of them. The silence was in the room again.

A shot sounded in the distance. The men looked quickly at the old man. Every head turned toward him.

For a moment he continued to stare at the ceiling.

Then he rolled slowly over and faced the wall and lay silent.

George shuffled the cards noisily and dealt them. Whit drew a scoring board to him and set the pegs to start. Whit said, "I guess you guys really come here to work."

"How do ya mean?" George asked.

Whit laughed. "Well, ya come on a Friday. You got two days to work till Sunday."

"I don't see how you figure," said George.

Whit laughed again. "You do if you been around these big ranches much. Guy that wants to look over a ranch comes in Sat'day afternoon. He gets Sat'day night supper an' three meals on Sunday, and he can quit Monday mornin' after breakfast without turning his hand. But you come to work Friday noon. You got to put in a day an' a half no matter how you figure."

George looked at him levelly. "We're gonna stick aroun' a while," he said. "Me an' Lennie's gonna roll up a stake."

The door opened quietly and the stable buck put in his head; a lean negro head, lined with pain, the eyes patient. "Mr. Slim."

Slim took his eyes from old Candy. "Huh? Oh! Hello, Crooks. What's'a matter?"

"You told me to warm up tar for that mule's foot. I got it warm."

"Oh! Sure, Crooks. I'll come right out an' put it on."

"I can do it if you want, Mr. Slim."

"No. I'll come do it myself." He stood up.

Crooks said, "Mr. Slim."

"Yeah."

"That big new guy's messin' around your pups out in the barn."

"Well, he ain't doin' no harm. I give him one of them pups."

"Just thought I'd tell ya," said Crooks. "He's takin' 'em outa the nest and handlin' them. That won't do them no good."

"He won't hurt 'em," said Slim. "I'll come along with you now."

George looked up. "If that crazy bastard's foolin' around too much, jus' kick him out, Slim."

Slim followed the stable buck out of the room.

George dealt and Whit picked up his cards and examined them. "Seen the new kid yet?" he asked.

"What kid?" George asked.

"Why, Curley's new wife."

"Yeah, I seen her."

"Well, ain't she a looloo?"

"I ain't seen that much of her," said George.

Whit laid down his cards impressively. "Well, stick around an' keep your eyes open. You'll see plenty. She ain't concealin' nothing. I never seen nobody like her. She got the eye goin' all the time on everybody. I bet she even gives the stable buck the eye. I don't know what the hell she wants."

George asked casually, "Been any trouble since she got here?"

It was obvious that Whit was not interested in his cards. He laid his hand down and George scooped it in. George laid out his deliberate solitaire hand—seven cards, and six on top, and five on top of those.

Whit said, "I see what you mean. No, they ain't been nothing yet. Curley's got yella-jackets in his drawers but that's all so far. Ever' time the guys is around she shows up. She's lookin' for Curley, or she thought she lef' somethin' layin' around and she's lookin' for it. Seems like she can't keep away from guys. An' Curley's pants is just crawlin' with ants, but they ain't nothing come of it yet."

George said, "She's gonna make a mess. They's gonna be a bad mess about her. She's a jail bait all set on the trigger. That Curley got his work cut out for him. Ranch with a bunch of guys on it ain't no place for a girl, specially like her."

Whit said, "If you got idears, you ought ta come in town with us guys tomorra night."

"Why? What's doin'?"

"Jus' the usual thing. We go in to old Susy's place. Hell of a nice place. Old Susy's a laugh—always crackin' jokes. Like she says when we come up on the front porch las' Sat'day night. Susy opens the door and then she yells over her shoulder, 'Get yor coats on, girls, here comes the sheriff.' She never talks dirty, neither. Got five girls there."

"What's it set you back?" George asked.

"Two an' a half. You can get a shot for two bits. Susy got nice chairs to set in, too. If a guy don't want a flop, why he can just set in the chairs and have a couple or three shots and pass the time of day and Susy don't give a damn. She ain't rushin' guys through and kickin' 'em out if they don't want a flop."

"Might go in and look the joint over," said George.

"Sure. Come along. It's a hell of a lot of fun—her crackin' jokes all the time. Like she says one time, she says, 'I've knew people that if they got a rag rug on the floor an' a kewpie doll lamp on the phonograph they think they're running a parlor house.' That's Clara's house she's talkin' about. An' Susy says, 'I know what you boys want,' she says. 'My girls is clean,' she says, 'an' there ain't no water in my whisky,' she says. 'If any you guys wanta look at a kewpie doll lamp an' take your own chance gettin' burned, why you know where to go.' An' she says, 'There's guys around here walkin' bow-legged 'cause they like to look at a kewpie doll lamp.'"

George asked, "Clara runs the other house, huh?"

"Yeah," said Whit. "We don't never go there. Clara gets three bucks a crack and thirty-five cents a shot, and she don't crack no jokes. But Susy's place is clean and she got nice chairs. Don't let no goo-goos in, neither."

"Me an' Lennie's rollin' up a stake," said George. "I might go in an' set and have a shot, but I ain't puttin' out no two and a half."

"Well, a guy got to have some fun sometime," said Whit.

The door opened and Lennie and Carlson came in together. Lennie crept to his bunk and sat down, trying not to attract attention. Carlson reached under his bunk and brought out his bag. He didn't look at old Candy, who still faced the wall. Carlson found a little cleaning rod in the bag and a can of oil. He laid them on his bed and then brought out the pistol, took out the magazine and snapped the loaded shell from the chamber. Then he fell to cleaning the barrel with the little rod. When the ejector snapped, Candy turned over and looked for a moment at the gun before he turned back to the wall again.

Carlson said casually, "Curley been in yet?"

"No," said Whit. "What's eatin' on Curley?"

Carlson squinted down the barrel of his gun. "Lookin' for his old lady. I seen him going round and round outside."

Whit said sarcastically, "He spends half his time lookin' for her, and the rest of the time she's lookin' for him."

Curley burst into the room excitedly. "Any you guys seen my wife?" he demanded.

"She ain't been here," said Whit.

Curley looked threateningly about the room. "Where the hell's Slim?"

"Went out in the barn," said George. "He was gonna put some tar on a split hoof."

Curley's shoulders dropped and squared. "How long ago'd he go?"

"Five—ten minutes."

Curley jumped out the door and banged it after him.

Whit stood up. "I guess maybe I'd like to see this," he said. "Curley's just spoilin' or he wouldn't start for Slim. An' Curley's handy, God damn handy. Got in the finals for the Golden Gloves. He got newspaper clippings about it." He considered. "But jus' the same, he better leave Slim alone. Nobody don't know what Slim can do."

"Thinks Slim's with his wife, don't he?" said George.

"Looks like it," Whit said. " 'Course Slim ain't. Least I don't think Slim is. But I like to see the fuss if it comes off. Come on, le's go."

George said, "I'm stayin' right here. I don't want to get mixed up in nothing. Lennie and me got to make a stake."

Carlson finished the cleaning of the gun and put it in the bag and pushed the bag under his bunk. "I guess I'll go out and look her over," he said. Old Candy lay still, and Lennie, from his bunk, watched George cautiously.

When Whit and Carlson were gone and the door closed after them, George turned to Lennie. "What you got on your mind?"

"I ain't done nothing, George. Slim says I better not pet them pups so much for a while. Slim says it ain't good for them; so I come right in. I been good, George."

"I coulda told you that," said George.

"Well, I wasn't hurtin' 'em none. I jus' had mine in my lap pettin' it."

George asked, "Did you see Slim out in the barn?"

"Sure I did. He tol' me I better not pet that pup no more."

"Did you see that girl?"

"You mean Curley's girl?"

"Yeah. Did she come in the barn?"

"No. Anyways I never seen her."

"You never seen Slim talkin' to her?"

"Uh-uh. She ain't been in the barn."

"O.K.," said George. "I guess them guys ain't gonna see no fight. If there's any fightin', Lennie, you keep out of it."

"I don't want no fights," said Lennie. He got up from his bunk and sat down at the table, across from George. Almost automatically George shuffled the cards and laid out his solitaire hand. He used a deliberate, thoughtful, slowness.

Lennie reached for a face card and studied it, then turned it upside down and studied it. "Both ends the same," he said. "George, why is it both end's the same?"

"I don't know," said George. "That's jus' the way they make 'em. What was Slim doin' in the barn when you seen him?"

"Slim?"

"Sure. You seen him in the barn, an' he tol' you not to pet the pups so much."

"Oh, yeah. He had a can a' tar an' a paint brush. I don't know what for."

"You sure that girl didn't come in like she come in here today?"

"No. She never come."

George sighed. "You give me a good whore house every time," he said. "A guy can go in an' get drunk and get ever'thing outa his system all at once, an' no messes. And he knows how much it's gonna set him back. These here jail baits is just set on the trigger of the hoosegow."

Lennie followed his words admiringly, and moved his lips a little to keep up. George continued, "You remember Andy Cushman, Lennie? Went to grammar school?"

"The one that his old lady used to make hot cakes for the kids?" Lennie asked.

"Yeah. That's the one. You can remember anything if there's anything to eat in it." George looked carefully at the solitaire hand. He put an ace up on his scoring rack and piled a two, three and four of diamonds on it. "Andy's in San Quentin right now on account of a tart," said George.

Lennie drummed on the table with his fingers. "George?"

"Huh?"

"George, how long's it gonna be till we get that little place an' live on the fatta the lan'—an' rabbits?"

"I don' know," said George. "We gotta get a big stake together. I know a little place we can get cheap, but they ain't givin' it away."

Old Candy turned slowly over. His eyes were wide open. He watched George carefully.

Lennie said, "Tell about that place, George."

"I jus' tol' you, jus' las' night."

"Go on—tell again, George."

"Well, it's ten acres," said George. "Got a little win'mill. Got a little shack on it, an' a chicken run. Got a kitchen, orchard, cherries, apples, peaches, 'cots, nuts, got a few berries. They's a place for alfalfa and plenty water to flood it. They's a pig pen——"

"An' rabbits, George."

"No place for rabbits now, but I could easy build a few hutches and you could feed alfalfa to the rabbits."

"Damn right, I could," said Lennie. "You God damn right I could."

George's hands stopped working with the cards. His

voice was growing warmer. "An' we could have a few pigs. I could build a smoke house like the one gran'pa had, an' when we kill a pig we can smoke the bacon and the hams, and make sausage an' all like that. An' when the salmon run up river we could catch a hundred of 'em an' salt 'em down or smoke 'em. We could have them for breakfast. They ain't nothing so nice as smoked salmon. When the fruit come in we could can it—and tomatoes, they're easy to can. Ever' Sunday we'd kill a chicken or a rabbit. Maybe we'd have a cow or a goat, and the cream is so God damn thick you got to cut it with a knife and take it out with a spoon."

Lennie watched him with wide eyes, and old Candy watched him too. Lennie said softly, "We could live offa the fatta the lan'."

"Sure," said George. "All kin's a vegetables in the garden, and if we want a little whisky we can sell a few eggs or something, or some milk. We'd jus' live there. We'd belong there. There wouldn't be no more runnin' round the country and gettin' fed by a Jap cook. No, sir, we'd have our own place where we belonged and not sleep in no bunk house."

"Tell about the house, George," Lennie begged.

"Sure, we'd have a little house an' a room to ourself. Little fat iron stove, an' in the winter we'd keep a fire goin' in it. It ain't enough land so we'd have to work too hard. Maybe six, seven hours a day. We wouldn't have to buck no barley eleven hours a day. An' when we put in a crop, why, we'd be there to take the crop up. We'd know what come of our planting."

"An' rabbits," Lennie said eagerly. "An' I'd take care of 'em. Tell how I'd do that, George."

"Sure, you'd go out in the alfalfa patch an' you'd have a sack. You'd fill up the sack and bring it in an' put it in the rabbit cages."

"They'd nibble an' they'd nibble," said Lennie, "the way they do. I seen 'em."

"Ever' six weeks or so," George continued, "them does would throw a litter so we'd have plenty rabbits to eat an' to sell. An' we'd keep a few pigeons to go flyin' around the win'mill like they done when I was a kid." He looked raptly at the wall over Lennie's head. "An' it'd be our own, an' nobody could can us. If we don't like a guy we can say, 'Get the hell out,' and by God he's got to do it. An' if a fren' come along, why we'd have an extra bunk, an' we'd say, 'Why don't you spen' the night?' an' by God he would. We'd have a setter dog and a couple stripe cats, but you gotta watch out them cats don't get the little rabbits."

Lennie breathed hard. "You jus' let 'em try to get the rabbits. I'll break their God damn necks. I'll . . . I'll smash 'em with a stick." He subsided, grumbling to himself, threatening the future cats which might dare to disturb the future rabbits.

George sat entranced with his own picture.

When Candy spoke they both jumped as though they had been caught doing something reprehensible. Candy said, "You know where's a place like that?"

George was on guard immediately. "S'pose I do," he said. "What's that to you?"

"You don't need to tell me where it's at. Might be any place."

"Sure," said George. "That's right. You couldn't find it in a hundred years."

Candy went on excitedly, "How much they want for a place like that?"

George watched him suspiciously. "Well—I could get it for six hundred bucks. The ol' people that owns it is flat bust an' the ol' lady needs an operation. Say—what's it to you? You got nothing to do with us."

Candy said, "I ain't much good with on'y one hand. I lost my hand right here on this ranch. That's why they give me a job swampin'. An' they give me two hunderd an' fifty dollars 'cause I los' my hand. An' I got fifty more saved up right in the bank, right now. Tha's three hunderd, and I got fifty more comin' the end a the month. Tell you what——" He leaned forward eagerly. "S'pose I went in with you guys. Tha's three hunderd an' fifty bucks I'd put in. I ain't much good, but I could cook and tend the chickens and hoe the garden some. How'd that be?"

George half-closed his eyes. "I gotta think about that. We was always gonna do it by ourselves."

Candy interrupted him, "I'd make a will an' leave my share to you guys in case I kick off, 'cause I ain't got no relatives nor nothing. You guys got any money? Maybe we could do her right now?"

George spat on the floor disgustedly. "We got ten bucks between us." Then he said thoughtfully, "Look, if me an' Lennie work a month an' don't spen' nothing, we'll have a hunderd bucks. That'd be four fifty. I bet we could swing her for that. Then you an' Lennie could go get her started an' I'd get a job an' make up the res', an' you could sell eggs an' stuff like that."

They fell into a silence. They looked at one another, amazed. This thing they had never really believed in was coming true. George said reverently, "Jesus Christ! I bet we could swing her." His eyes were full of wonder. "I bet we could swing her," he repeated softly.

Candy sat on the edge of his bunk. He scratched the stump of his wrist nervously. "I got hurt four year ago," he said. "They'll can me purty soon. Jus' as soon as I can't swamp out no bunk houses they'll put me on the county. Maybe if I give you guys my money, you'll let me hoe in the garden even after I ain't no good at it. An' I'll wash dishes an' little chicken stuff like that. But I'll be on our own place, an' I'll be let to work on our own place." He said miserably, "You seen what they done to my dog tonight? They says he wasn't no good to himself nor nobody else. When they can me here I wisht somebody'd shoot me. But they won't do nothing like that. I won't have no place to go, an' I can't get no more jobs. I'll have thirty dollars more comin', time you guys is ready to quit."

George stood up. "We'll do her," he said. "We'll fix up that little old place an' we'll go live there." He sat down again. They all sat still, all bemused by the beauty of the thing, each mind was popped into the future when this lovely thing should come about.

George said wonderingly, "S'pose they was a carnival or a circus come to town, or a ball game, or any damn thing." Old Candy nodded in appreciation of the idea. "We'd just go to her," George said. "We wouldn't ask nobody if we could. Jus' say, 'We'll go to her,' an' we would. Jus' milk the cow and sling some grain to the chickens an' go to her."

"An' put some grass to the rabbits," Lennie broke in. "I wouldn't never forget to feed them. When we gon'ta do it, George?"

"In one month. Right squack in one month. Know what I'm gon'ta do? I'm gon'ta write to them old people that owns the place that we'll take it. An' Candy'll send a hunderd dollars to bind her."

"Sure will," said Candy. "They got a good stove there?"

"Sure, got a nice stove, burns coal or wood."

"I'm gonna take my pup," said Lennie. "I bet by Christ he likes it there, by Jesus."

Voices were approaching from outside. George said quickly, "Don't tell nobody about it. Jus' us three an' nobody else. They li'ble to can us so we can't make no stake. Jus' go on like we was gonna buck barley the rest of our lives, then all of a sudden some day we'll go get our pay an' scram outa here."

Lennie and Candy nodded, and they were grinning with delight. "Don't tell nobody," Lennie said to himself.

Candy said, "George."

"Huh?"

"I ought to of shot that dog myself, George. I shouldn't ought to of let no stranger shoot my dog."

The door opened. Slim came in, followed by Curley and Carlson and Whit. Slim's hands were black with tar and he was scowling. Curley hung close to his elbow.

Curley said, "Well, I didn't mean nothing, Slim. I just ast you."

Slim said, "Well, you been askin' me too often. I'm gettin' God damn sick of it. If you can't look after your own God damn wife, what you expect me to do about it? You lay offa me."

"I'm jus' tryin' to tell you I didn't mean nothing," said Curley. "I jus' thought you might of saw her."

"Why'n't you tell her to stay the hell home where she belongs?" said Carlson. "You let her hang around bunk houses and pretty soon you're gonna have som'pin on your hands and you won't be able to do nothing about it."

Curley whirled on Carlson. "You keep outta this les' you wanta step outside."

Carlson laughed. "You God damn punk," he said. "You tried to throw a scare into Slim, an' you couldn't make it stick. Slim throwed a scare into you. You're yella as a frog belly. I don't care if you're the best welter in the country. You come for me, an' I'll kick your God damn head off."

Candy joined the attack with joy. "Glove fulla vaseline," he said disgustedly. Curley glared at him. His eyes slipped on past and lighted on Lennie; and Lennie was still smiling with delight at the memory of the ranch.

Curley stepped over to Lennie like a terrier. "What the hell you laughin' at?"

Lennie looked blankly at him. "Huh?"

Then Curley's rage exploded. "Come on, ya big bastard. Get up on your feet. No big son-of-a-bitch is gonna laugh at me. I'll show ya who's yella."

Lennie looked helplessly at George, and then he got up and tried to retreat. Curley was balanced and poised. He slashed at Lennie with his left, and then smashed down his nose with a right. Lennie gave a cry of terror. Blood welled from his nose. "George," he cried. "Make 'um let me alone, George." He backed until he was against the wall, and Curley followed, slugging him in the face. Lennie's hands remained at his sides; he was too frightened to defend himself.

George was on his feet yelling, "Get him, Lennie. Don't let him do it."

Lennie covered his face with his huge paws and bleated with terror. He cried, "Make 'um stop, George." Then Curley attacked his stomach and cut off his wind.

Slim jumped up. "The dirty little rat," he cried, "I'll get 'um myself."

George put out his hand and grabbed Slim. "Wait a minute," he shouted. He cupped his hands around his mouth and yelled, "Get 'im, Lennie!"

Lennie took his hands away from his face and looked about for George, and Curley slashed at his eyes. The big face was covered with blood. George yelled again, "I said get him."

Curley's fist was swinging when Lennie reached for it. The next minute Curley was flopping like a fish on a line, and his closed fist was lost in Lennie's big hand. George ran down the room. "Leggo of him, Lennie. Let go."

But Lennie watched in terror the flopping little man whom he held. Blood ran down Lennie's face, one of his eyes was cut and closed. George slapped him in the face again and again, and still Lennie held on to the closed fist. Curley was white and shrunken by now, and his struggling had become weak. He stood crying, his fist lost in Lennie's paw.

George shouted over and over, "Leggo his hand, Lennie. Leggo. Slim, come help me while the guy got any hand left."

Suddenly Lennie let go his hold. He crouched cowering against the wall. "You tol' me to, George," he said miserably.

Curley sat down on the floor, looking in wonder at his crushed hand. Slim and Carlson bent over him. Then Slim straightened up and regarded Lennie with horror. "We got to get him in to a doctor," he said. "Looks to me like ever' bone in his han' is bust."

"I didn't wanta," Lennie cried. "I didn't wanta hurt him."

Slim said, "Carlson, you get the candy wagon hitched up. We'll take 'um into Soledad an' get 'um fixed up." Carlson hurried out. Slim turned to the whimpering Lennie. "It ain't your fault," he said. "This punk sure had it comin' to him. But—Jesus! He ain't hardly got no han' left." Slim hurried out, and in a moment returned with a tin cup of water. He held it to Curley's lips.

George said, "Slim, will we get canned now? We need the stake. Will Curley's old man can us now?"

Slim smiled wryly. He knelt down beside Curley. "You got your senses in hand enough to listen?" he asked. Curley nodded. "Well, then listen," Slim went on. "I think you got your han' caught in a machine. If you don't tell nobody what happened, we ain't going to. But you jus' tell an' try to get this guy canned and we'll tell ever'body, an' then will you get the laugh."

"I won't tell," said Curley. He avoided looking at Lennie.

Buggy wheels sounded outside. Slim helped Curley up. "Come on now. Carlson's gonna take you to a doctor." He helped Curley out the door. The sound of wheels drew away. In a moment Slim came back into the bunk house. He looked at Lennie, still crouched fearfully against the wall. "Le's see your hands," he asked.

Lennie stuck out his hands.

"Christ awmighty, I hate to have you mad at me," Slim said.

George broke in, "Lennie was jus' scairt," he explained. "He didn't know what to do. I told you nobody ought never to fight him. No, I guess it was Candy I told."

Candy nodded solemnly. "That's jus' what you done," he said. "Right this morning when Curley first lit intil your fren', you says, 'He better not fool with Lennie if he knows what's good for 'um.' That's jus' what you says to me."

George turned to Lennie. "It ain't your fault," he said. "You don't need to be scairt no more. You done jus' what I tol' you to. Maybe you better go in the wash room an' clean up your face. You look like hell."

Lennie smiled with his bruised mouth. "I didn't want no trouble," he said. He walked toward the door, but just before he came to it, he turned back. "George?"

"What you want?"

"I can still tend the rabbits, George?"

"Sure. You ain't done nothing wrong."

"I di'n't mean no harm, George."

"Well, get the hell out and wash your face."

CROOKS, the negro stable buck, had his bunk in
the harness room; a little shed that leaned off the
wall of the barn. On one side of the little room there was a
square four-paned window, and on the other, a narrow
plank door leading into the barn. Crooks' bunk was a long
box filled with straw, on which his blankets were flung.
On the wall by the window there were pegs on which
hung broken harness in process of being mended; strips
of new leather; and under the window itself a little bench
for leather-working tools, curved knives and needles and
balls of linen thread, and a small hand riveter. On pegs
were also pieces of harness, a split collar with the horse-
hair stuffing sticking out, a broken hame, and a trace
chain with its leather covering split. Crooks had his apple
box over his bunk, and in it a range of medicine bottles,
both for himself and for the horses. There were cans of
saddle soap and a drippy can of tar with its paint brush
sticking over the edge. And scattered about the floor were
a number of personal possessions; for, being alone, Crooks
could leave his things about, and being a stable buck and
a cripple, he was more permanent than the other men,
and he had accumulated more possessions than he could
carry on his back.

Crooks possessed several pairs of shoes, a pair of rubber boots, a big alarm clock and a single-barreled shotgun. And he had books, too; a tattered dictionary and a
mauled copy of the California civil code for 1905. There
were battered magazines and a few dirty books on a special shelf over his bunk. A pair of large gold-rimmed spectacles hung from a nail on the wall above his bed.

This room was swept and fairly neat, for Crooks was a
proud, aloof man. He kept his distance and demanded
that other people keep theirs. His body was bent over to
the left by his crooked spine, and his eyes lay deep in his

head, and because of their depth seemed to glitter with intensity. His lean face was lined with deep black wrinkles, and he had thin, pain-tightened lips which were lighter than his face.

It was Saturday night. Through the open door that led into the barn came the sound of moving horses, of feet stirring, of teeth champing on hay, of the rattle of halter chains. In the stable buck's room a small electric globe threw a meager yellow light.

Crooks sat on his bunk. His shirt was out of his jeans in back. In one hand he held a bottle of liniment, and with the other he rubbed his spine. Now and then he poured a few drops of the liniment into his pink-palmed hand and reached up under his shirt to rub again. He flexed his muscles against his back and shivered.

Noiselessly Lennie appeared in the open doorway and stood there looking in, his big shoulders nearly filling the opening. For a moment Crooks did not see him, but on raising his eyes he stiffened and a scowl came on his face. His hand came out from under his shirt.

Lennie smiled helplessly in an attempt to make friends.

Crooks said sharply, "You got no right to come in my room. This here's my room. Nobody got any right in here but me."

Lennie gulped and his smile grew more fawning. "I ain't doing nothing," he said. "Just come to look at my puppy. And I seen your light," he explained.

"Well, I got a right to have a light. You go on get outa my room. I ain't wanted in the bunk house, and you ain't wanted in my room."

"Why ain't you wanted?" Lennie asked.

" 'Cause I'm black. They play cards in there, but I can't play because I'm black. They say I stink. Well, I tell you, you all of you stink to me."

Lennie flapped his big hands helplessly. "Ever'body

went into town," he said. "Slim an' George an' ever'body. George says I gotta stay here an' not get in no trouble. I seen your light."

"Well, what do you want?"

"Nothing—I seen your light. I thought I could jus' come in an' set."

Crooks stared at Lennie, and he reached behind him and took down the spectacles and adjusted them over his pink ears and stared again. "I don't know what you're doin' in the barn anyway," he complained. "You ain't no skinner. They's no call for a bucker to come into the barn at all. You ain't no skinner. You ain't got nothing to do with the horses."

"The pup," Lennie repeated. "I come to see my pup."

"Well, go see your pup, then. Don't come in a place where you're not wanted."

Lennie lost his smile. He advanced a step into the room, then remembered and backed to the door again. "I looked at 'em a little. Slim says I ain't to pet 'em very much."

Crooks said, "Well, you been takin' 'em out of the nest all the time. I wonder the old lady don't move 'em someplace else."

"Oh, she don't care. She lets me." Lennie had moved into the room again.

Crooks scowled, but Lennie's disarming smile defeated him. "Come on in and set a while," Crooks said. " 'Long as you won't get out and leave me alone, you might as well set down." His tone was a little more friendly. "All the boys gone into town, huh?"

"All but old Candy. He just sets in the bunk house sharpening his pencil and sharpening and figuring."

Crooks adjusted his glasses. "Figuring? What's Candy figuring about?"

Lennie almost shouted, " 'Bout the rabbits."

"You're nuts," said Crooks. "You're crazy as a wedge. What rabbits you talkin' about?"

"The rabbits we're gonna get, and I get to tend 'em, cut grass an' give 'em water, an' like that."

"Jus' nuts," said Crooks. "I don't blame the guy you travel with for keepin' you outa sight."

Lennie said quietly, "It ain't no lie. We're gonna do it. Gonna get a little place an' live on the fatta the lan'."

Crooks settled himself more comfortably on his bunk. "Set down," he invited. "Set down on the nail keg."

Lennie hunched down on the little barrel. "You think it's a lie," Lennie said, "But it ain't no lie. Ever' word's the truth, an' you can ast George."

Crooks put his dark chin into his pink palm. "You travel aroun' with George, don't ya?"

"Sure. Me an' him goes ever' place together."

Crooks continued. "Sometimes he talks, and you don't know what the hell he's talkin' about. Ain't that so?" He leaned forward, boring Lennie with his deep eyes. "Ain't that so?"

"Yeah . . . . sometimes."

"Jus' talks on, an' you don't know what the hell it's all about?"

"Yeah . . . . sometimes. But . . . . not always."

Crooks leaned forward over the edge of the bunk. "I ain't a southern negro," he said. "I was born right here in California. My old man had a chicken ranch, 'bout ten acres. The white kids come to play at our place, an' sometimes I went to play with them, and some of them was pretty nice. My ol' man didn't like that. I never knew till long later why he didn't like that. But I know now." He hesitated, and when he spoke again his voice was softer. "There wasn't another colored family for miles around. And now there ain't a colored man on this ranch an' there's jus' one family in Soledad." He laughed. "If I say something, why it's just a nigger sayin' it."

Lennie asked, "How long you think it'll be before them pups will be old enough to pet?"

Crooks laughed again. "A guy can talk to you an' be sure you won't go blabbin'. Couple of weeks an' them pups'll be all right. George knows what he's about. Jus' talks, an' you don't understand nothing." He leaned forward excitedly. "This is just a nigger talkin', an' a busted-back nigger. So it don't mean nothing, see? You couldn't remember it anyways. I seen it over an' over—a guy talkin' to another guy and it don't make no difference if he don't hear or understand. The thing is, they're talkin', or they're settin' still not talkin'. It don't make no difference, no difference." His excitement had increased until he pounded his knee with this hand. "George can tell you screwy things, and it don't matter. It's just the talking. It's just bein' with another guy. That's all." He paused.

His voice grew soft and persuasive. "S'pose George don't come back no more. S'pose he took a powder and just ain't coming back. What'll you do then?"

Lennie's attention came gradually to what had been said. "What?" he demanded.

"I said s'pose George went into town tonight and you never heard of him no more." Crooks pressed forward some kind of private victory. "Jus' s'pose that," he repeated.

"He won't do it," Lennie cried. "George wouldn't do nothing like that. I been with George a long time. He'll come back tonight——" But the doubt was too much for him. "Don't you think he will?"

Crooks' face lighted with pleasure in his torture. "Nobody can't tell what a guy'll do," he observed calmly. "Le's say he wants to come back and can't. S'pose he gets killed or hurt so he can't come back."

Lennie struggled to understand. "George won't do nothing like that," he repeated. "George is careful. He won't get hurt. He ain't never been hurt, 'cause he's careful."

"Well, s'pose, jus' s'pose he don't come back. What'll you do then?"

Lennie's face wrinkled with apprehension. "I don' know. Say, what you doin' anyways?" he cried. "This ain't true. George ain't got hurt."

Crooks bored in on him. "Want me ta tell ya what'll happen? They'll take ya to the booby hatch. They'll tie ya up with a collar, like a dog."

Suddenly Lennie's eyes centered and grew quiet, and mad. He stood up and walked dangerously toward Crooks. "Who hurt George?" he demanded.

Crooks saw the danger as it approached him. He edged back on his bunk to get out of the way. "I was just supposin'," he said. "George ain't hurt. He's all right. He'll be back all right."

Lennie stood over him. "What you supposin' for? Ain't nobody goin' to suppose no hurt to George."

Crooks removed his glasses and wiped his eyes with his fingers. "Jus' set down," he said. "George ain't hurt."

Lennie growled back to his seat on the nail keg. "Ain't nobody goin' to talk no hurt to George," he grumbled.

Crooks said gently, "Maybe you can see now. You got George. You *know* he's goin' to come back. S'pose you didn't have nobody. S'pose you couldn't go into the bunk house and play rummy 'cause you was black. How'd you like that? S'pose you had to sit out here an' read books. Sure you could play horseshoes till it got dark, but then you got to read books. Books ain't no good. A guy needs somebody—to be near him." He whined, "A guy goes nuts if he ain't got nobody. Don't make no difference who the guy is, long's he's with you. I tell ya," he cried, "I tell ya a guy gets too lonely an' he gets sick."

"George gonna come back," Lennie reassured himself in a frightened voice. "Maybe George come back already. Maybe I better go see."

Crooks said, "I didn't mean to scare you. He'll come back. I was talkin' about myself. A guy sets alone out here at night, maybe readin' books or thinkin' or stuff like that. Sometimes he gets thinkin', an' he got nothing to tell him what's so an' what ain't so. Maybe if he sees somethin', he don't know whether it's right or not. He can't turn to some other guy and ast him if he sees it too. He can't tell. He got nothing to measure by. I seen things out here. I wasn't drunk. I don't know if I was asleep. If some guy was with me, he could tell me I was asleep, an' then it would be all right. But I jus' don't know." Crooks was looking across the room now, looking toward the window.

Lennie said miserably, "George wun't go away and leave me. I know George wun't do that."

The stable buck went on dreamily, "I remember when I was a little kid on my old man's chicken ranch. Had two brothers. They was always near me, always there. Used to sleep right in the same room, right in the same bed— all three. Had a strawberry patch. Had an alfalfa patch. Used to turn the chickens out in the alfalfa on a sunny morning. My brothers'd set on a fence rail an' watch 'em —white chickens they was."

Gradually Lennie's interest came around to what was being said. "George says we're gonna have alfalfa for the rabbits."

"What rabbits?"

"We're gonna have rabbits an' a berry patch."

"You're nuts."

"We are too. You ast George."

"You're nuts." Crooks was scornful. "I seen hunderds of men come by on the road an' on the ranches, with their bindles on their back an' that same damn thing in their heads. Hunderds of them. They come, an' they quit an' go on; an' every damn one of 'em's got a little piece of land in his head. An' never a God damn one of 'em ever gets it. Just like heaven. Ever'body wants a little piece of lan'. I read plenty of books out here. Nobody never gets to heaven, and nobody gets no land. It's just in their head. They're all the time talkin' about it, but it's jus' in their head." He paused and looked toward the open door, for the horses were moving restlessly and the halter chains clinked. A horse whinnied. "I guess somebody's out there," Crooks said. "Maybe Slim. Slim comes in sometimes two, three times a night. Slim's a real skinner. He looks out for his team." He pulled himself painfully upright and moved toward the door. "That you, Slim?" he called.

Candy's voice answered. "Slim went in town. Say, you seen Lennie?"

"Ya mean the big guy?"

"Yeah. Seen him around any place?"

"He's in here," Crooks said shortly. He went back to his bunk and lay down.

Candy stood in the doorway scratching his bald wrist and looking blindly into the lighted room. He made no attempt to enter. "Tell ya what, Lennie. I been figuring out about them rabbits."

Crooks said irritably, "You can come in if you want."

Candy seemed embarrassed. "I do' know. 'Course, if ya want me to."

"Come on in. If ever'body's comin' in, you might just as well." It was difficult for Crooks to conceal his pleasure with anger.

Candy came in, but he was still embarrassed. "You got a nice cozy little place in here," he said to Crooks. "Must be nice to have a room all to yourself this way."

"Sure," said Crooks. "And a manure pile under the window. Sure, it's swell."

Lennie broke in, "You said about them rabbits."

Candy leaned against the wall beside the broken collar while he scratched the wrist stump. "I been here a long time," he said. "An' Crooks been here a long time. This's the first time I ever been in his room."

Crooks said darkly, "Guys don't come into a colored man's room very much. Nobody been here but Slim. Slim an' the boss."

Candy quickly changed the subject. "Slim's as good a skinner as I ever seen."

Lennie leaned toward the old swamper. "About them rabbits," he insisted.

Candy smiled. "I got it figured out. We can make some money on them rabbits if we go about it right."

"But I get to tend 'em," Lennie broke in. "George says I get to tend 'em. He promised."

Crooks interrupted brutally. "You guys is just kiddin' yourself. You'll talk about it a hell of a lot, but you won't get no land. You'll be a swamper here till they take you out in a box. Hell, I seen too many guys. Lennie here'll quit an' be on the road in two, three weeks. Seems like ever' guy got land in his head."

Candy rubbed his cheek angrily. "You God damn right we're gonna do it. George says we are. We got the money right now."

"Yeah?" said Crooks. "An' where's George now? In town in a whore house. That's where your money's goin'. Jesus, I seen it happen too many times. I seen too many guys with land in their head. They never get none under their hand."

Candy cried, "Sure they all want it. Everybody wants a little bit of land, not much. Jus' som'thin' that was his. Som'thin' he could live on and there couldn't nobody throw him off of it. I never had none. I planted crops for damn near ever'body in this state, but they wasn't my crops, and when I harvested 'em, it wasn't none of my harvest. But we gonna do it now, and don't you make no mistake about that. George ain't got the money in town. That money's in the bank. Me an' Lennie an' George. We gonna have a room to ourself. We're gonna have a dog an' rabbits an' chickens. We're gonna have green corn an' maybe a cow or a goat." He stopped, overwhelmed with his picture.

Crooks asked, "You say you got the money?"

"Damn right. We got most of it. Just a little bit more to get. Have it all in one month. George got the land all picked out, too."

Crooks reached around and explored his spine with his hand. "I never seen a guy really do it," he said. "I seen guys nearly crazy with loneliness for land, but ever' time a whore house or a blackjack game took what it takes." He hesitated. ". . . . If you . . . . guys would want a hand to work for nothing—just his keep, why I'd come an' lend a hand. I ain't so crippled I can't work like a son-of-a-bitch if I want to."

"Any you boys seen Curley?"

They swung their heads toward the door. Looking in was Curley's wife. Her face was heavily made up. Her lips were slightly parted. She breathed strongly, as though she had been running.

"Curley ain't been here," Candy said sourly.

She stood still in the doorway, smiling a little at them, rubbing the nails of one hand with the thumb and forefinger of the other. And her eyes traveled from one face to another. "They left all the weak ones here," she said finally. "Think I don't know where they all went? Even Curley. I know where they all went."

Lennie watched her, fascinated; but Candy and Crooks were scowling down away from her eyes. Candy said, "Then if you know, why you want to ast us where Curley is at?"

She regarded them amusedly. "Funny thing," she said. "If I catch any one man, and he's alone, I get along fine with him. But just let two of the guys get together an' you won't talk. Jus' nothing but mad." She dropped her fingers and put her hands on her hips. "You're all scared of each other, that's what. Ever' one of you's scared the rest is goin' to get something on you."

After a pause Crooks said, "Maybe you better go along to your own house now. We don't want no trouble."

"Well, I ain't giving you no trouble. Think I don't like to talk to somebody ever' once in a while? Think I like to stick in that house alla time?"

Candy laid the stump of his wrist on his knee and rubbed it gently with his hand. He said accusingly, "You gotta husban'. You got no call foolin' aroun' with other guys, causin' trouble."

The girl flared up. "Sure I gotta husban'. You all seen him. Swell guy, ain't he? Spends all his time sayin' what he's gonna do to guys he don't like, and he don't like nobody. Think I'm gonna stay in that two-by-four house and listen how Curley's gonna lead with his left twict, and then bring in the ol' right cross? 'One-two' he says. 'Jus' the ol' one-two an' he'll go down.' " She paused and her face lost its sullenness and grew interested. "Say— what happened to Curley's han'?"

There was an embarrassed silence. Candy stole a look at Lennie. Then he coughed. "Why . . . . Curley . . . . he got his han' caught in a machine, ma'am. Bust his han'."

She watched for a moment, and then she laughed. "Baloney! What you think you're sellin' me? Curley started som'pin' he didn' finish. Caught in a machine—baloney! Why, he ain't give nobody the good ol' one-two since he got his han' bust. Who bust him?"

Candy repeated sullenly, "Got it caught in a machine."

"Awright," she said contemptuously. "Awright, cover 'im up if ya wanta. Whatta I care? You bindle bums think you're so damn good. Whatta ya think I am, a kid? I tell ya I could of went with shows. Not jus' one, neither. An' a guy tol' me he could put me in pitchers. . . ." She was breathless with indignation. "—Sat'iday night. Ever'body out doin' som'pin'. Ever'body! An' what am I doin'? Standin' here talkin' to a bunch of bindle stiffs—a nigger an' a dum-dum and a lousy ol' sheep—an' likin' it because they ain't nobody else."

Lennie watched her, his mouth half open. Crooks had retired into the terrible protective dignity of the Negro. But a change came over old Candy. He stood up suddenly and knocked his nail keg over backward. "I had enough," he said angrily. "You ain't wanted here. We told you you ain't. An' I tell ya, you got floozy idears about what us guys amounts to. You ain't got sense enough in that chicken head to even see that we ain't stiffs. S'pose you get us canned. S'pose you do. You think we'll hit the highway an' look for another lousy two-bit job like this. You don't know that we got our own ranch to go to, an' our own house. We ain't got to stay here. We gotta house and chickens an' fruit trees an' a place a hunderd time prettier than this. An' we got fren's, that's what we got. Maybe there was a time when we was scared of gettin' canned, but we ain't no more. We got our own lan', and it's ours, an' we c'n go to it."

Curley's wife laughed at him. "Baloney," she said. "I seen too many you guys. If you had two bits in the worl', why you'd be in gettin' two shots of corn with it and suckin' the bottom of the glass. I know you guys."

Candy's face had grown redder and redder, but before she was done speaking, he had control of himself. He was the master of the situation. "I might of knew," he said gently. "Maybe you just better go along an' roll your hoop. We ain't got nothing to say to you at all. We know what we got, and we don't care whether you know it or not. So maybe you better jus' scatter along now, 'cause Curley maybe ain't gonna like his wife out in the barn with us 'bindle stiffs.'"

She looked from one face to another, and they were all closed against her. And she looked longest at Lennie, until he dropped his eyes in embarrassment. Suddenly she said, "Where'd you get them bruises on your face?"

Lennie looked up guiltily. "Who—me?"

"Yeah, you."

Lennie looked to Candy for help, and then he looked at his lap again. "He got his han' caught in a machine," he said.

Curley's wife laughed. "O.K., Machine. I'll talk to you later. I like machines."

Candy broke in. "You let this guy alone. Don't you do no messing aroun' with him. I'm gonna tell George what you says. George won't have you messin' with Lennie."

"Who's George?" she asked. "The little guy you come with?"

Lennie smiled happily. "That's him," he said. "That's the guy, an' he's gonna let me tend the rabbits."

"Well, if that's all you want, I might get a couple rabbits myself."

Crooks stood up from his bunk and faced her. "I had enough," he said coldly. "You got no rights comin' in a colored man's room. You got no rights messing around in here at all. Now you jus' get out, an' get out quick. If you don't, I'm gonna ast the boss not to ever let you come in the barn no more."

She turned on him in scorn. "Listen, Nigger," she said. "You know what I can do to you if you open your trap?"

Crooks stared hopelessly at her, and then he sat down on his bunk and drew into himself.

She closed on him. "You know what I could do?"

Crooks seemed to grow smaller, and he pressed himself against the wall. "Yes, ma'am."

"Well, you keep your place then, Nigger. I could get you strung up on a tree so easy it ain't even funny."

Crooks had reduced himself to nothing. There was no personality, no ego—nothing to arouse either like or dislike. He said, "Yes, ma'am," and his voice was toneless.

For a moment she stood over him as though waiting for him to move so that she could whip at him again; but Crooks sat perfectly still, his eyes averted, everything that might be hurt drawn in. She turned at last to the other two.

Old Candy was watching her, fascinated. "If you was to do that, we'd tell," he said quietly. "We'd tell about you framin' Crooks."

"Tell an' be damned," she cried. "Nobody'd listen to you, an' you know it. Nobody'd listen to you."

Candy subsided. "No . . . ." he agreed. "Nobody'd listen to us."

Lennie whined, "I wisht George was here. I wisht George was here."

Candy stepped over to him. "Don't you worry none," he said. "I jus' heard the guys comin' in. George'll be in the bunk house right now, I bet." He turned to Curley's wife. "You better go home now," he said quietly. "If you go right now, we won't tell Curley you was here."

She appraised him coolly. "I ain't sure you heard nothing."

"Better not take no chances," he said. "If you ain't sure, you better take the safe way."

She turned to Lennie. "I'm glad you bust up Curley a little bit. He got it comin' to him. Sometimes I'd like to bust him myself." She slipped out the door and disappeared into the dark barn. And while she went through the barn, the halter chains rattled, and some horses snorted and some stamped their feet.

Crooks seemed to come slowly out of the layers of protection he had put on. "Was that the truth what you said about the guys come back?" he asked.

"Sure. I heard 'em."

"Well, I didn't hear nothing."

"The gate banged," Candy said, and he went on, "Jesus Christ, Curley's wife can move quiet. I guess she had a lot of practice, though."

Crooks avoided the whole subject now. "Maybe you guys better go," he said. "I ain't sure I want you in here no more. A colored man got to have some rights even if he don't like 'em."

Candy said, "That bitch didn't ought to of said that to you."

"It wasn't nothing," Crooks said dully. "You guys comin' in an' settin' made me forget. What she says is true."

The horses snorted out in the barn and the chains rang and a voice called, "Lennie. Oh, Lennie. You in the barn?"

"It's George," Lennie cried. And he answered, "Here, George. I'm right in here."

In a second George stood framed in the door, and he looked disapprovingly about. "What you doin' in Crooks' room. You hadn't ought to be here."

Crooks nodded. "I tol' 'em, but they come in anyways."

"Well, why'n't you kick 'em out?"

"I di'n't care much," said Crooks. "Lennie's a nice fella."

Now Candy aroused himself. "Oh, George! I been figurin' and figurin'. I got it doped out how we can even
make some money on them rabbits."

George scowled. "I thought I tol' you not to tell nobody
about that."

Candy was crestfallen. "Didn't tell nobody but Crooks."

George said, "Well you guys get outta here. Jesus,
seems like I can't go away for a minute."

Candy and Lennie stood up and went toward the door.
Crooks called, "Candy!"

"Huh?"

" 'Member what I said about hoein' and doin' odd
jobs?"

"Yeah," said Candy. "I remember."

"Well, jus' forget it," said Crooks. "I didn' mean it. Jus'
foolin'. I wouldn' want to go no place like that."

"Well, O.K., if you feel like that. Goodnight."

The three men went out of the door. As they went
through the barn the horses snorted and the halter chains
rattled.

Crooks sat on his bunk and looked at the door for a
moment, and then he reached for the liniment bottle. He
pulled out his shirt in back, poured a little liniment in his
pink palm and, reaching around, he fell slowly to rubbing his back.

ONE end of the great barn was piled high with new
hay and over the pile hung the four-taloned Jackson
fork suspended from its pulley. The hay came down like
a mountain slope to the other end of the barn, and there
was a level place as yet unfilled with the new crop. At the
sides the feeding racks were visible, and between the slats
the heads of horses could be seen.

It was Sunday afternoon. The resting horses nibbled

the remaining wisps of hay, and they stamped their feet and they bit the wood of the mangers and rattled the halter chains. The afternoon sun sliced in through the cracks of the barn walls and lay in bright lines on the hay. There was the buzz of flies in the air, the lazy afternoon humming.

From outside came the clang of horseshoes on the playing peg and the shouts of men, playing, encouraging, jeering. But in the barn it was quiet and humming and lazy and warm.

Only Lennie was in the barn, and Lennie sat in the hay beside a packing case under a manger in the end of the barn that had not been filled with hay. Lennie sat in the hay and looked at a little dead puppy that lay in front of him. Lennie looked at it for a long time, and then he put out his huge hand and stroked it, stroked it clear from one end to the other.

And Lennie said softly to the puppy, "Why do you got to get killed? You ain't so little as mice. I didn't bounce you hard." He bent the pup's head up and looked in its face, and he said to it, "Now maybe George ain't gonna let me tend no rabbits, if he fin's out you got killed."

He scooped a little hollow and laid the puppy in it and covered it over with hay, out of sight; but he continued to stare at the mound he had made. He said, "This ain't no bad thing like I got to go hide in the brush. Oh! no. This ain't. I'll tell George I foun' it dead."

•He unburied the puppy and inspected it, and he stroked it from ears to tail. He went on sorrowfully, "But he'll know. George always knows. He'll say, 'You done it. Don't try to put nothing over on me.' An' he'll say, 'Now jus' for that you don't get to tend no rabbits!' "

Suddenly his anger arose. "God damn you," he cried. "Why do you got to get killed? You ain't so little as mice." He picked up the pup and hurled it from him. He turned his back on it. He sat bent over his knees and he whispered, "Now I won't get to tend the rabbits. Now he won't let me." He rocked himself back and forth in his sorrow.

From outside came the clang of horseshoes on the iron stake, and then a little chorus of cries. Lennie got up and brought the puppy back and laid it on the hay and sat down. He stroked the pup again. "You wasn't big enough," he said. "They tol' me and tol' me you wasn't. I di'n't know you'd get killed so easy." He worked his fingers on the pup's limp ear. "Maybe George won't care," he said. "This here God damn little son-of-a-bitch wasn't nothing to George."

Curley's wife came around the end of the last stall. She came very quietly, so that Lennie didn't see her. She wore her bright cotton dress and the mules with the red ostrich feathers. Her face was made up and the little sausage curls were all in place. She was quite near to him before Lennie looked up and saw her.

In a panic he shoveled hay over the puppy with his fingers. He looked sullenly up at her.

She said, "What you got there, sonny boy?"

Lennie glared at her. "George says I ain't to have nothing to do with you—talk to you or nothing."

She laughed. "George giving you orders about everything?"

Lennie looked down at the hay. "Says I can't tend no rabbits if I talk to you or anything."

She said quietly, "He's scared Curley'll get mad. Well, Curley got his arm in a sling—an' if Curley gets tough, you can break his other han'. You didn't put nothing over on me about gettin' it caught in no machine."

But Lennie was not to be drawn. "No, sir. I ain't gonna talk to you or nothing."

She knelt in the hay beside him. "Listen," she said. "All

the guys got a horseshoe tenement goin' on. It's on'y about four o'clock. None of them guys is goin' to leave that tenement. Why can't I talk to you? I never get to talk to nobody. I get awful lonely."

Lennie said, "Well, I ain't supposed to talk to you or nothing."

"I get lonely," she said. "You can talk to people, but I can't talk to nobody but Curley. Else he gets mad. How'd you like not to talk to anybody?"

Lennie said, "Well, I ain't supposed to. George's scared I'll get in trouble."

She changed the subject. "What you got covered up there?"

Then all of Lennie's woe came back on him. "Jus' my pup," he said sadly. "Jus' my little pup." And he swept the hay from on top of it.

"Why, he's dead," she cried.

"He was so little," said Lennie. "I was jus' playin' with him . . . . an' he made like he's gonna bite me . . . . an' I made like I was gonna smack him . . . . an' . . . . an' I done it. An' then he was dead."

She consoled him. "Don't you worry none. He was jus' a mutt. You can get another one easy. The whole country is fulla mutts."

"It ain't that so much," Lennie explained miserably. "George ain't gonna let me tend no rabbits now."

"Why don't he?"

"Well, he said if I done any more bad things he ain't gonna let me tend the rabbits."

She moved closer to him and she spoke soothingly. "Don't you worry about talkin' to me. Listen to the guys yell out there. They got four dollars bet in that tenement. None of them ain't gonna leave till it's over."

"If George sees me talkin' to you he'll give me hell," Lennie said cautiously. "He tol' me so."

Her face grew angry. "Wha's the matter with me?" she cried. "Ain't I got a right to talk to nobody? Whatta they think I am, anyways? You're a nice guy. I don't know why I can't talk to you. I ain't doin' no harm to you."

"Well, George says you'll get us in a mess."

"Aw, nuts!" she said. "What kinda harm am I doin' to you? Seems like they ain't none of them cares how I gotta live. I tell you I ain't used to livin' like this. I coulda made somethin' of myself." She said darkly, "Maybe I will yet." And then her words tumbled out in a passion of communication, as though she hurried before her listener could be taken away. "I lived right in Salinas," she said. "Come there when I was a kid. Well, a show come through, an' I met one of the actors. He says I could go with that show. But my ol' lady wouldn' let me. She says because I was on'y fifteen. But the guy says I coulda. If I'd went, I wouldn't be livin' like this, you bet."

Lennie stroked the pup back and forth. "We gonna have a little place—an' rabbits," he explained.

She went on with her story quickly, before she should be interrupted. " 'Nother time I met a guy, an' he was in pitchers. Went out to the Riverside Dance Palace with him. He says he was gonna put me in the movies. Says I was a natural. Soon's he got back to Hollywood he was gonna write to me about it." She looked closely at Lennie to see whether she was impressing him. "I never got that letter," she said. "I always thought my ol' lady stole it. Well, I wasn't gonna stay no place where I couldn't get nowhere or make something of myself, an' where they stole your letters, I ast her if she stole it, too, an' she says no. So I married Curley. Met him out to the Riverside Dance Palace that same night." She demanded, "You listenin'?"

"Me? Sure."

"Well, I ain't told this to nobody before. Maybe I ought'n to. I don' *like* Curley. He ain't a nice fella." And because she had confided in him, she moved closer to Lennie and sat beside him. "Coulda been in the movies, an' had nice clothes—all them nice clothes like they wear. An' I coulda sat in them big hotels, an' had pitchers took of me. When they had them previews I coulda went to them, an' spoke in the radio, an' it wouldn'ta cost me a cent because I was in the pitcher. An' all them nice clothes like they wear. Because this guy says I was a natural." She looked up at Lennie, and she made a small grand gesture with her arm and hand to show that she could act. The fingers trailed after her leading wrist, and her little finger stuck out grandly from the rest.

Lennie sighed deeply. From outside came the clang of a horseshoe on metal, and then a chorus of cheers. "Somebody made a ringer," said Curley's wife.

Now the light was lifting as the sun went down, and the sun streaks climbed up the wall and fell over the feeding racks and over the heads of the horses.

Lennie said, "Maybe if I took this pup out and threw him away George wouldn't never know. An' then I could tend the rabbits without no trouble."

Curley's wife said angrily, "Don't you think of nothing but rabbits?"

"We gonna have a little place," Lennie explained patiently. "We gonna have a house an' a garden and a place for alfalfa, an' that alfalfa is for the rabbits, an' I take a sack and get it all fulla alfalfa and then I take it to the rabbits."

She asked, "What makes you so nuts about rabbits?"

Lennie had to think carefully before he could come to a conclusion. He moved cautiously close to her, until he was right against her. "I like to pet nice things. Once at a fair I seen some of them long-hair rabbits. An' they was nice, you bet. Sometimes I've even pet mice, but not when I could get nothing better."

Curley's wife moved away from him a little. "I think you're nuts," she said.

"No I ain't," Lennie explained earnestly. "George says I ain't. I like to pet nice things with my fingers, sof' things."

She was a little bit reassured. "Well, who don't?" she said. "Ever'body likes that. I like to feel silk an' velvet. Do you like to feel velvet?"

Lennie chuckled with pleasure. "You bet, by God," he cried happily. "An' I had some, too. A lady give me some, an' that lady was—my own Aunt Clara. She give it right to me—'bout this big a piece. I wisht I had that velvet right now." A frown came over his face. "I lost it," he said. "I ain't seen it for a long time."

Curley's wife laughed at him. "You're nuts," she said. "But you're a kinda nice fella. Jus' like a big baby. But a person can see kinda what you mean. When I'm doin' my hair sometimes I jus' set an' stroke it 'cause it's so soft." To show how she did it, she ran her fingers over the top of her head. "Some people got kinda coarse hair," she said complacently. "Take Curley. His hair is jus' like wire. But mine is soft and fine. 'Course I brush it a lot. That makes it fine. Here—feel right here." She took Lennie's hand and put it on her head. "Feel right aroun' there an' see how soft it is."

Lennie's big fingers fell to stroking her hair.

"Don't you muss it up," she said.

Lennie said, "Oh! That's nice," and he stroked harder "Oh, that's nice."

"Look out, now, you'll muss it." And then she cried angrily, "You stop it now, you'll mess it all up." She jerked her head sideways, and Lennie's fingers closed on her hair and hung on. "Let go," she cried. "You let go!"

Lennie was in a panic. His face was contorted. She screamed then, and Lennie's other hand closed over her mouth and nose. "Please don't," he begged. "Oh! Please don't do that. George'll be mad."

She struggled violently under his hands. Her feet battered on the hay and she writhed to be free; and from under Lennie's hand came a muffled screaming. Lennie began to cry with fright. "Oh! Please don't do none of that," he begged. "George gonna say I done a bad thing. He ain't gonna let me tend no rabbits." He moved his hand a little and her hoarse cry came out. Then Lennie grew angry. "Now don't," he said. "I don't want you to yell. You gonna get me in trouble jus' like George says you will. Now don't you do that." And she continued to struggle, and her eyes were wild with terror. He shook her then, and he was angry with her. "Don't you go yellin'," he said, and he shook her; and her body flopped like a fish. And then she was still, for Lennie had broken her neck.

He looked down at her, and carefully he removed his hand from over her mouth, and she lay still. "I don't want ta hurt you," he said, "but George'll be mad if you yell." When she didn't answer nor move he bent closely over her. He lifted her arm and let it drop. For a moment he seemed bewildered. And then he whispered in fright, "I done a bad thing. I done another bad thing."

He pawed up the hay until it partly covered her.

From outside the barn came a cry of men and the double clang of shoes on metal. For the first time Lennie became conscious of the outside. He crouched down in the hay and listened. "I done a real bad thing," he said. "I shouldn't of did that. George'll be mad. An' . . . . he said . . . . an' hide in the brush till he come. He's gonna be mad. In the brush till he come. Tha's what he said." Lennie went back and looked at the dead girl. The puppy lay close to her. Lennie picked it up. "I'll throw him away," he said. "It's bad enough like it is." He put the pup under his coat, and he crept to the barn wall and peered out between the cracks, toward the horseshoe game. And then he crept around the end of the last manger and disappeared.

The sun streaks were high on the wall by now, and the light was growing soft in the barn. Curley's wife lay on her back, and she was half covered with hay.

It was very quiet in the barn, and the quiet of the afternoon was on the ranch. Even the clang of the pitched shoes, even the voices of the men in the game seemed to grow more quiet. The air in the barn was dusky in advance of the outside day. A pigeon flew in through the open hay door and circled and flew out again. Around the last stall came a shepherd bitch, lean and long, with heavy, hanging dugs. Halfway to the packing box where the puppies were she caught the dead scent of Curley's wife, and the hair arose along her spine. She whimpered and cringed to the packing box, and jumped in among the puppies.

Curley's wife lay with a half-covering of yellow hay. And the meanness and the plannings and the discontent and the ache for attention were all gone from her face. She was very pretty and simple, and her face was sweet and young. Now her rouged cheeks and her reddened lips made her seem alive and sleeping very lightly The curls, tiny little sausages, were spread on the hay behind her head, and her lips were parted.

As happens sometimes, a moment settled and hovered and remained for much more than a moment. And sound stopped and movement stopped for much, much more than a moment.

Then gradually time awakened again and moved sluggishly on. The horses stamped on the other side of the feeding racks and the halter chains clinked. Outside, the mens' voices became louder and clearer.

From around the end of the last stall old Candy's voice came. "Lennie," he called. "Oh, Lennie! You in here? I been figuring some more. Tell you what we can do, Lennie." Old Candy appeared around the end of the last stall. "Oh, Lennie!" he called again; and then he stopped, and his body stiffened. He rubbed his smooth wrist on his white stubble whiskers. "I di'n't know you was here," he said to Curley's wife.

When she didn't answer, he stepped nearer. "You oughten to sleep out here," he said disapprovingly; and then he was beside her and—"Oh, Jesus Christ!" he looked about helplessly, and he rubbed his beard. And then he jumped up and went quickly out of the barn.

But the barn was alive now. The horses stamped and snorted, and they chewed the straw of their bedding and they clashed the chains of their halters. In a moment Candy came back, and George was with him.

George said, "What was it you wanted to see me about?"

Candy pointed at Curley's wife. George stared. "What's the matter with her?" he asked. He stepped closer, and then he echoed Candy's words. "Oh, Jesus Christ!" He was down on his knees beside her. He put his hand over her heart And finally, when he stood up, slowly and stiffly, his face was as hard and tight as wood, and his eyes were hard

Candy said, "What done it?"

George looked coldly at him. "Ain't you got any idear?" he asked. And Candy was silent. "I should of knew," George said hopelessly "I guess maybe way back in my head I did."

Candy asked, "What we gonna do now, George. What we gonna do now?"

George was a long time in answering. "Guess . . . . we gotta tell the . . . . guys. I guess we gotta get 'im an' lock 'im up. We can't let 'im get away. Why, the poor bastard'd starve." And he tried to reassure himself. "Maybe they'll lock 'im up an' be nice to 'im."

But Candy said excitedly, "We oughtta let 'im get away. You don't know that Curley. Curley gon'ta wanta get 'im lynched. Curley'll get 'im killed."

George watched Candy's lips. "Yeah," he said at last, "that's right, Curley will. An' the other guys will." And he looked back at Curley's wife.

Now Candy spoke his greatest fear. "You an' me can get that little place, can't we, George? You an' me can go there an' live nice, can't we, George? Can't we?"

Before George answered, Candy dropped his head and looked down at the hay. He knew.

George said softly, "—I think I knowed from the very first. I think I know'd we'd never do her. He usta like to hear about it so much I got to thinking maybe we would."

"Then—it's all off?" Candy asked sulkily.

George didn't answer his question. George said, "I'll work my month an' I'll take my fifty bucks an' I'll stay all night in some lousy cat house. Or I'll set in some poolroom till ever'body goes home. An' then I'll come back an' work another month an' I'll have fifty bucks more."

Candy said, "He's such a nice fella. I didn' think he'd do nothing like this."

George still stared at Curley's wife. "Lennie never done it in meanness," he said "All the time he done bad things, but he never done one of 'em mean." He straightened up and looked back at Candy. "Now listen. We gotta tell the guys. They got to bring him in, I guess. They ain't no way out. Maybe they won't hurt 'im." He said sharply, "I ain't gonna let 'em hurt Lennie. Now you listen. The guys might think I was in on it. I'm gonna go in the bunk house.

Then in a minute you come out and tell the guys about her, and I'll come along and make like I never seen her. Will you do that? So the guys won't think I was in on it?"

Candy said, "Sure, George. Sure I'll do that."

"O.K. Give me a couple minutes then, and you come runnin' out an' tell like you jus' found her. I'm going now." George turned and went quickly out of the barn.

Old Candy watched him go. He looked helplessly back at Curley's wife, and gradually his sorrow and his anger grew into words. "You God damn tramp," he said viciously. "You done it, di'n't you? I s'pose you're glad. Ever'body knowed you'd mess things up. You wasn't no good. You ain't no good now, you lousy tart." He sniveled, and his voice shook. "I could of hoed in the garden and washed dishes for them guys." He paused, and then went on in a singsong. And he repeated the old words: "If they was a circus or a baseball game . . . . we would of went to her . . . . jus' said 'ta hell with work,' an' went to her. Never ast nobody's say so. An' they'd of been a pig and chickens . . . . an' in the winter . . . . the little fat stove . . . . an' the rain comin' . . . . an' us jes' settin' there." His eyes blinded with tears and he turned and went weakly out of the barn, and he rubbed his bristly whiskers with his wrist stump.

Outside the noise of the game stopped. There was a rise of voices in question, a drum of running feet and the men burst into the barn. Slim and Carlson and young Whit and Curley, and Crooks keeping back out of attention range. Candy came after them, and last of all came George. George had put on his blue denim coat and buttoned it, and his black hat was pulled down low over his eyes. The men raced around the last stall. Their eyes found Curley's wife in the gloom, they stopped and stood still and looked.

Then Slim went quietly over to her, and he felt her

wrist. One lean finger touched her cheek, and then his hand went under her slightly twisted neck and his fingers explored her neck. When he stood up the men crowded near and the spell was broken.

Curley came suddenly to life. "I know who done it," he cried. "That big son-of-a-bitch done it. I know he done it. Why—ever'body else was out there playin' horseshoes." He worked himself into a fury. "I'm gonna get him. I'm going for my shot gun. I'll kill the big son-of-a-bitch myself. I'll shoot 'im in the guts. Come on, you guys." He ran furiously out of the barn. Carlson said, "I'll get my Luger," and he ran out too.

Slim turned quietly to George. "I guess Lennie done it, all right," he said. "Her neck's bust. Lennie coulda did that."

George didn't answer, but he nodded slowly. His hat was so far down on his forehead that his eyes were covered.

Slim went on, "Maybe like that time in Weed you was tellin' about."

Again George nodded.

Slim sighed. "Well, I guess we got to get him. Where you think he might of went?"

It seemed to take George some time to free his words. "He—would of went south," he said. "We come from north so he would of went south."

"I guess we gotta get 'im," Slim repeated.

George stepped close. "Couldn' we maybe bring him in an' they'll lock him up? He's nuts, Slim. He never done this to be mean."

Slim nodded. "We might," he said. "If we could keep Curley in, we might. But Curley's gonna want to shoot 'im. Curley's still mad about his hand. An' s'pose they lock him up an' strap him down and put him in a cage. That ain't no good, George."

"I know," said George, "I know."

Carlson came running in. "The bastard's stole my Luger," he shouted. "It ain't in my bag." Curley followed him, and Curley carried a shotgun in his good hand. Curley was cold now.

"All right, you guys," he said. "The nigger's got a shotgun. You take it, Carlson. When you see 'um, don't give 'im no chance. Shoot for his guts. That'll double 'im over."

Whit said excitedly, "I ain't got a gun."

Curley said, "You go in Soledad an' get a cop. Get Al Wilts, he's deputy sheriff. Le's go now." He turned suspiciously on George. "You're comin' with us, fella."

"Yeah," said George. "I'll come. But listen, Curley. The poor bastard's nuts. Don't shoot 'im. He di'n't know what he was doin'."

"Don't shoot 'im?" Curley cried. "He got Carlson's Luger. 'Course we'll shoot 'im."

George said weakly, "Maybe Carlson lost his gun."

"I seen it this morning," said Carlson. "No, it's been took."

Slim stood looking down at Curley's wife. He said, "Curley—maybe you better stay here with your wife."

Curley's face reddened. "I'm goin'," he said. "I'm gonna shoot the guts outa that big bastard myself, even if I only got one hand. I'm gonna get 'im."

Slim turned to Candy. "You stay here with her then, Candy. The rest of us better get goin'."

They moved away. George stopped a moment beside Candy and they both looked down at the dead girl until Curley called, "You George! You stick with us so we don't think you had nothin' to do with this."

George moved slowly after them, and his feet dragged heavily.

And when they were gone, Candy squatted down in

the hay and watched the face of Curley's wife. "Poor bastard," he said softly.

The sound of the men grew fainter. The barn was darkening gradually and, in their stalls, the horses shifted their feet and rattled the halter chains. Old Candy lay down in the hay and covered his eyes with his arm.

THE deep green pool of the Salinas River was still in the late afternoon. Already the sun had left the valley to go climbing up the slopes of the Gabilan mountains, and the hilltops were rosy in the sun. But by the pool among the mottled sycamores, a pleasant shade had fallen.

A water snake glided smoothly up the pool, twisting its periscope head from side to side; and it swam the length of the pool and came to the legs of a motionless heron that stood in the shallows. A silent head and beak lanced down and plucked it out by the head, and the beak swallowed the little snake while its tail waved frantically.

A far rush of wind sounded and a gust drove through the tops of the trees like a wave. The sycamore leaves turned up their silver sides, the brown, dry leaves on the ground scudded a few feet. And row on row of tiny wind waves flowed up the pool's green surface.

As quickly as it had come, the wind died, and the clearing was quiet again. The heron stood in the shallows, motionless and waiting. Another little water snake swam up the pool, turning its periscope head from side to side.

Suddenly Lennie appeared out of the brush, and he came as silently as a creeping bear moves. The heron pounded the air with its wings, jacked itself clear of the water and flew off down river. The little snake slid in among the reeds at the pool's side.

Lennie came quietly to the pool's edge. He knelt down and drank, barely touching his lips to the water. When a little bird skittered over the dry leaves behind him, his head jerked up and he strained toward the sound with eyes and ears until he saw the bird, and then he dropped his head and drank again.

When he was finished, he sat down on the bank, with his side to the pool, so that he could watch the trail's entrance. He embraced his knees and laid his chin down on his knees.

The light climbed on out of the valley, and as it went, the tops of the mountains seemed to blaze with increasing brightness.

Lennie said softly, "I di'n't forget, you bet, God damn. Hide in the brush an' wait for George." He pulled his hat down low over his eyes. "George gonna give me hell," he said. "George gonna wish he was alone an' not have me botherin' him." He turned his head and looked at the bright mountain tops. "I can go right off there an' find a cave," he said. And he continued sadly, "—an' never have no ketchup—but I won't care. If George don't want me . . . . I'll go away. I'll go away."

And then from out of Lennie's head there came a little fat old woman. She wore thick bull's-eye glasses and she wore a huge gingham apron with pockets, and she was starched and clean. She stood in front of Lennie and put her hands on her hips, and she frowned disapprovingly at him.

And when she spoke, it was in Lennie's voice. "I tol' you an' tol' you," she said. "I tol' you, 'Min' George because he's such a nice fella an' good to you.' But you don't never take no care. You do bad things."

And Lennie answered her, "I tried, Aunt Clara, ma'am. I tried and tried. I couldn' help it."

"You never give a thought to George," she went on in Lennie's voice. "He been doin' nice things for you alla time. When he got a piece of pie you always got half or more'n half. An' if they was any ketchup, why he'd give it all to you."

"I know," said Lennie miserably. "I tried, Aunt Clara, ma'am. I tried and tried."

She interrupted him. "All the time he coulda had such a good time if it wasn't for you. He woulda took his pay an' raised hell in a whore house, and he coulda set in a pool room an' played snooker. But he got to take care of you."

Lennie moaned with grief. "I know, Aunt Clara, ma'am. I'll go right off in the hills an' I'll fin' a cave an' I'll live there so I won't be no more trouble to George."

"You jus' say that," she said sharply. "You're always sayin' that, an' you know sonofabitching well you ain't never gonna do it. You'll jus' stick around an' stew the b'Jesus outa George all the time."

Lennie said, "I might jus' as well go away. George ain't gonna let me tend no rabbits now."

Aunt Clara was gone, and from out of Lennie's head there came a gigantic rabbit. It sat on its haunches in front of him, and it waggled its ears and crinkled its nose at him. And it spoke in Lennie's voice too.

"Tend rabbits," it said scornfully. "You crazy bastard. You ain't fit to lick the boots of no rabbit. You'd forget 'em and let 'em go hungry. That's what you'd do. An' then what would George think?"

"I would *not* forget," Lennie said loudly.

"The hell you wouldn'," said the rabbit. "You ain't worth a greased jack-pin to ram you into hell. Christ knows George done ever'thing he could to jack you outa the sewer, but it don't do no good. If you think George gonna let you tend rabbits, you're even crazier'n usual. He ain't. He's gonna beat hell outa you with a stick, that's what he's gonna do."

Now Lennie retorted belligerently, "He ain't neither. George won't do nothing like that. I've knew George since—I forget when—and he ain't never raised his han' to me with a stick. He's nice to me. He ain't gonna be mean."

"Well, he's sick of you," said the rabbit. "He's gonna beat hell outa you an' then go away an' leave you."

"He won't," Lennie cried frantically. "He won't do nothing like that. I know George. Me an' him travels together."

But the rabbit repeated softly over and over, "He gonna leave you, ya crazy bastard. He gonna leave ya all alone. He gonna leave ya, crazy bastard."

Lennie put his hands over his ears. "He ain't, I tell ya he ain't." And he cried, "Oh! George—George—George!"

George came quietly out of the brush and the rabbit scuttled back into Lennie's brain.

George said quietly, "What the hell you yellin' about?"

Lennie got up on his knees. "You ain't gonna leave me, are ya, George? I know you ain't."

George came stiffly near and sat down beside him. "No."

"I knowed it," Lennie cried. "You ain't that kind."

George was silent.

Lennie said, "George."

"Yeah?"

"I done another bad thing."

"It don't make no difference," George said, and he fell silent again.

Only the topmost ridges were in the sun now. The shadow in the valley was blue and soft. From the distance

came the sound of men shouting to one another. George
turned his head and listened to the shouts.

Lennie said, "George."

"Yeah?"

"Ain't you gonna give me hell?"

"Give ya hell?"

"Sure, like you always done before. Like, 'If I di'n't
have you I'd take my fifty bucks——'"

"Jesus Christ, Lennie! You can't remember nothing
that happens, but you remember ever' word I say."

"Well, ain't you gonna say it?"

George shook himself. He said woodenly, "If I was
alone I could live so easy." His voice was monotonous,
had no emphasis. "I could get a job an' not have no mess."
He stopped.

"Go on," said Lennie. "An' when the enda the month
come——"

"An' when the end of the month came I could take
my fifty bucks an' go to a . . . . cat house . . . ." He
stopped again.

Lennie looked eagerly at him. "Go on, George. Ain't
you gonna give me no more hell?"

"No," said George.

"Well, I can go away," said Lennie. "I'll go right off in
the hills an' find a cave if you don' want me."

George shook himself again. "No," he said. "I want
you to stay with me here."

Lennie said craftily—"Tell me like you done before."

"Tell you what?"

"'Bout the other guys an' about us."

George said, "Guys like us got no fambly. They make a
little stake an' then they blow it in. They ain't got nobody in the worl' that gives a hoot in hell about 'em——"

"*But not us*," Lennie cried happily. "Tell about us
now."

George was quiet for a moment. "But not us," he said. "Because——"

"Because I got you an'——"

"An' I got you. We got each other, that's what, that gives a hoot in hell about us," Lennie cried in triumph.

The little evening breeze blew over the clearing and the leaves rustled and the wind waves flowed up the green pool. And the shouts of men sounded again, this time much closer than before.

George took off his hat. He said shakily, "Take off your hat, Lennie. The air feels fine."

Lennie removed his hat dutifully and laid it on the ground in front of him. The shadow in the valley was bluer, and the evening came fast. On the wind the sound of crashing in the brush came to them.

Lennie said, "Tell how it's gonna be."

George had been listening to the distant sounds. For a moment he was business-like. "Look acrost the river, Lennie, an' I'll tell you so you can almost see it."

Lennie turned his head and looked off across the pool and up the darkening slopes of the Gabilans. "We gonna get a little place," George began. He reached in his side pocket and brought out Carlson's Luger; he snapped off the safety, and the hand and gun lay on the ground behind Lennie's back. He looked at the back of Lennie's head, at the place where the spine and skull were joined.

A man's voice called from up the river, and another man answered.

"Go on," said Lennie.

George raised the gun and his hand shook, and he dropped his hand to the ground again.

"Go on," said Lennie. "How's it gonna be. We gonna get a little place."

"We'll have a cow," said George. "An' we'll have maybe a pig an' chickens . . . . an' down the flat we'll have a . . . . little piece alfalfa——"

"For the rabbits," Lennie shouted.

"For the rabbits," George repeated.

"And I get to tend the rabbits."

"An' you get to tend the rabbits."

Lennie giggled with happiness. "An' live on the fatta the lan'."

"Yes."

Lennie turned his head.

"No, Lennie. Look down there acrost the river, like you can almost see the place."

Lennie obeyed him. George looked down at the gun.

There were crashing footsteps in the brush now. George turned and looked toward them.

"Go on, George. When we gonna do it?"

"Gonna do it soon."

"Me an' you."

"You . . . . an' me. Ever'body gonna be nice to you. Ain't gonna be no more trouble. Nobody gonna hurt nobody nor steal from 'em."

Lennie said, "I thought you was mad at me, George."

"No," said George. "No, Lennie. I ain't mad. I never been mad, an' I ain't now. That's a thing I want ya to know."

The voices came close now. George raised the gun and listened to the voices.

Lennie begged, "Le's do it now. Le's get that place now."

"Sure, right now. I gotta. We gotta."

And George raised the gun and steadied it, and he brought the muzzle of it close to the back of Lennie's head. The hand shook violently, but his face set and his hand steadied. He pulled the trigger. The crash of the shot rolled up the hills and rolled down again. Lennie jarred, and then settled slowly forward to the sand, and he lay without quivering.

George shivered and looked at the gun, and then he threw it from him, back up on the bank, near the pile of old ashes.

The brush seemed filled with cries and with the sound of running feet. Slim's voice shouted, "George. Where you at, George?"

But George sat stiffly on the bank and looked at his right hand that had thrown the gun away. The group burst into the clearing, and Curley was ahead. He saw Lennie lying on the sand. "Got him, by God." He went over and looked down at Lennie, and then he looked back at George. "Right in the back of the head," he said softly.

Slim came directly to George and sat down beside him, sat very close to him. "Never you mind," said Slim. "A guy got to sometimes."

But Carlson was standing over George. "How'd you do it?" he asked.

"I just done it," George said tiredly.

"Did he have my gun?"

"Yeah. He had your gun."

"An' you got it away from him and you took it an' you killed him?"

"Yeah. Tha's how." George's voice was almost a whisper. He looked steadily at his right hand that had held the gun.

Slim twitched George's elbow. "Come on, George. Me an' you'll go in an' get a drink."

George let himself be helped to his feet. "Yeah, a drink."

Slim said, "You hadda, George. I swear you hadda.

Come on with me." He led George into the entrance of the trail and up toward the highway.

Curley and Carlson looked after them. And Carlson said, "Now what the hell ya suppose is eatin' them two guys?"

The Red Pony

The complete work, first published as a separate volume in 1945.. The original Red Pony, issued in a limited edition in 1937, consisted of only the first three parts. The fourth part was added when the story was reprinted in the volume called The Long Valley, 1938.

THE RED PONY

I. THE GIFT

AT daybreak Billy Buck emerged from the bunkhouse and stood for a moment on the porch looking up at the sky. He was a broad, bandy-legged little man with a walrus mustache, with square hands, puffed and muscled on the palms. His eyes were a contemplative, watery gray and the hair which protruded from under his Stetson hat was spiky and weathered. Billy was still stuffing his shirt into his blue jeans as he stood on the porch. He unbuckled his belt and tightened it again. The belt showed, by the worn shiny places opposite each hole, the gradual increase of Billy's middle over a period of years. When he had seen to the weather, Billy cleared each nostril by holding its mate closed with his forefinger and blowing fiercely. Then he walked down to the barn, rubbing his hands together. He curried and brushed two saddle horses in the stalls, talking quietly to them all the time; and he had hardly finished when the iron triangle started ringing at the ranch house. Billy stuck the brush and currycomb together and laid them on the rail, and went up to breakfast. His action had been so deliberate and yet so wasteless of time that he came to the house while Mrs. Tiflin was still ringing the triangle. She nodded her gray head to him and withdrew into the kitchen. Billy Buck sat down on the steps, because he was a cow-hand, and it wouldn't be fitting that he should go first into the dining-room. He heard Mr. Tiflin in the house, stamping his feet into his boots.

The high jangling note of the triangle put the boy Jody in motion. He was only a little boy, ten years old, with hair like dusty yellow grass and with shy polite gray eyes, and with a mouth that worked when he thought. The triangle picked him up out of sleep. It didn't occur to him to disobey the harsh note. He never had: no one he knew ever had. He brushed the tangled hair out of his eyes and skinned his nightgown off. In a moment he was dressed—blue chambray shirt and overalls. It was late in the summer, so of course there were no shoes to bother with. In the kitchen he waited until his mother got from in front of the sink and went back to the stove. Then he washed himself and brushed back his wet hair with his fingers. His mother turned sharply on him as he left the sink. Jody looked shyly away.

"I've got to cut your hair before long," his mother said. "Breakfast's on the table. Go on in, so Billy can come."

Jody sat at the long table which was covered with white oilcloth washed through to the fabric in some places. The fried eggs lay in rows on their platter. Jody took three eggs on his plate and followed with three thick slices of crisp bacon. He carefully scraped a spot of blood from one of the egg yolks.

Billy Buck clumped in. "That won't hurt you," Billy explained. "That's only a sign the rooster leaves."

Jody's tall stern father came in then and Jody knew from the noise on the floor that he was wearing boots, but he looked under the table anyway, to make sure. His father turned off the oil lamp over the table, for plenty of morning light now came through the windows.

Jody did not ask where his father and Billy Buck were riding that day, but he wished he might go along. His father was a disciplinarian. Jody obeyed him in everything without questions of any kind. Now, Carl Tiflin sat down and reached for the egg platter.

"Got the cows ready to go, Billy?" he asked.

"In the lower corral," Billy said. "I could just as well take them in alone."

"Sure you could. But a man needs company. Besides your throat gets pretty dry." Carl Tiflin was jovial this morning.

Jody's mother put her head in the door. "What time do you think to be back, Carl?"

"I can't tell. I've got to see some men in Salinas. Might be gone till dark."

The eggs and coffee and big biscuits disappeared rapidly. Jody followed the two men out of the house. He watched them mount their horses and drive six old milk cows out of the corral and start over the hill toward Salinas. They were going to sell the old cows to the butcher.

When they had disappeared over the crown of the ridge Jody walked up the hill in back of the house. The dogs trotted around the house corner hunching their shoulders and grinning horribly with pleasure. Jody patted their heads—Doubletree Mutt with the big thick tail and yellow eyes, and Smasher, the shepherd, who had killed a coyote and lost an ear in doing it. Smasher's one good ear stood up higher than a collie's ear should. Billy Buck said that always happened. After the frenzied greeting the dogs lowered their noses to the ground in a businesslike way and went ahead, looking back now and then to make sure that the boy was coming. They walked up through the chicken yard and saw the quail eating with the chickens. Smasher chased the chickens a little to keep in practice in case there should ever be sheep to herd. Jody continued on through the large vegetable patch where the green corn was higher than his head. The cowpumpkins were green and small yet. He went on to the sagebrush line where the cold spring ran out of its pipe and fell into a round wooden tub. He leaned over and drank close to the green mossy wood where the water tasted best. Then he turned and looked back on the ranch, on the low, whitewashed house girded with red geraniums, and on the long bunkhouse by the cypress tree where Billy Buck lived alone. Jody could see the great black kettle under the cypress tree. That was where the pigs were scalded. The sun was coming over the ridge now, glaring on the whitewash of the houses and barns, making the wet grass blaze softly. Behind him, in the tall sagebrush, the birds were scampering on the ground, making a great noise among the dry leaves; the squirrels piped shrilly on the side-hills. Jody looked along at the farm buildings. He felt an uncertainty in the air, a feeling of change and of loss and of the gain of new and unfamiliar things. Over the hillside two big black buzzards sailed low to the ground and their shadows slipped smoothly and quickly ahead of them. Some animal had died in the vicinity. Jody knew it. It might be a cow or it might be the remains of a rabbit. The buzzards overlooked nothing. Jody hated them as all decent things hate them, but they could not be hurt because they made away with carrion.

After a while the boy sauntered down hill again. The dogs had long ago given him up and gone into the brush to do things in their own way. Back through the vegetable garden he went, and he paused for a moment to smash a green muskmelon with his heel, but he was not happy about it. It was a bad thing to do, he knew perfectly well. He kicked dirt over the ruined melon to conceal it.

Back at the house his mother bent over his rough hands, inspecting his fingers and nails. It did little good to start him clean to school for too many things could happen on the way. She sighed over the black cracks on his fingers, and then gave him his books and his lunch and started him on the mile walk to school. She noticed that his mouth was working a good deal this morning.

Jody started his journey. He filled his pockets with little pieces of white quartz that lay in the road, and every so often he took a shot at a bird or at some rabbit that had stayed sunning itself in the road too long. At the cross-roads over the bridge he met two friends and the three of them walked to school together, making ridiculous strides and being rather silly. School had just opened two weeks before. There was still a spirit of revolt among the pupils.

It was four o'clock in the afternoon when Jody topped the hill and looked down on the ranch again. He looked for the saddle horses, but the corral was empty. His father was not back yet. He went slowly, then, toward the afternoon chores. At the ranch house, he found his mother sitting on the porch, mending socks.

"There's two doughnuts in the kitchen for you," she said. Jody slid to the kitchen, and returned with half of one of the doughnuts already eaten and his mouth full. His mother asked him what he had learned in school that day, but she didn't listen to his doughnut-muffled answer. She interrupted, "Jody, tonight see you fill the wood-box clear full. Last night you crossed the sticks and it wasn't only about half full. Lay the sticks flat tonight. And Jody, some of the hens are hiding eggs, or else the dogs are eating them. Look about in the grass and see if you can find any nests."

Jody, still eating, went out and did his chores. He saw the quail come down to eat with the chickens when he threw out the grain. For some reason his father was proud to have them come. He never allowed any shooting near the house for fear the quail might go away.

When the wood-box was full, Jody took his twenty-two rifle up to the cold spring at the brush line. He drank again and then aimed the gun at all manner of things, at rocks, at birds on the wing, at the big black pig kettle under the cypress tree, but he didn't shoot for he had no cartridges and wouldn't have until he was twelve. If his father had seen him aim the rifle in the direction of the house he would have put the cartridges off another year. Jody remembered this and did not point the rifle down the hill again. Two years was enough to wait for cartridges. Nearly all of his father's presents were given with reservations which hampered their value somewhat. It was good discipline.

The supper waited until dark for his father to return. When at last he came in with Billy Buck, Jody could smell the delicious brandy on their breaths. Inwardly he rejoiced, for his father sometimes talked to him when he smelled of brandy, sometimes even told things he had done in the wild days when he was a boy.

After supper, Jody sat by the fireplace and his shy polite eyes sought the room corners, and he waited for his father to tell what it was he contained, for Jody knew he had news of some sort. But he was disappointed. His father pointed a stern finger at him.

"You'd better go to bed, Jody. I'm going to need you in the morning."

That wasn't so bad. Jody liked to do the things he had to do as long as they weren't routine things. He looked at the floor and his mouth worked out a question before he spoke it. "What are we going to do in the morning, kill a pig?" he asked softly.

"Never you mind. You better get to bed."

When the door was closed behind him, Jody heard his father and Billy Buck chuckling and he knew it was a joke of some kind. And later, when he lay in bed, trying to make words out of the murmurs in the other room, he heard his father protest, "But, Ruth, I didn't give much for him."

Jody heard the hoot-owls hunting mice down by the barn, and he heard a fruit tree limb tap-tapping against the house. A cow was lowing when he went to sleep.

When the triangle sounded in the morning, Jody dressed more quickly even than usual. In the kitchen, while he washed his face and combed back his hair, his mother addressed him irritably. "Don't you go out until you get a good breakfast in you."

He went into the dining-room and sat at the long white table. He took a steaming hotcake from the platter, arranged two fried eggs on it, covered them with another hotcake and squashed the whole thing with his fork.

His father and Billy Buck came in. Jody knew from the sound on the floor that both of them were wearing flat-heeled shoes, but he peered under the table to make sure. His father turned off the oil lamp, for the day had arrived, and he looked stern and disciplinary, but Billy Buck didn't look at Jody at all. He avoided the shy questioning eyes of the boy and soaked a whole piece of toast in his coffee.

Carl Tiflin said crossly, "You come with us after breakfast!"

Jody had trouble with his food then, for he felt a kind of doom in the air. After Billy had tilted his saucer and drained the coffee which had slopped into it, and had wiped his hands on his jeans, the two men stood up from the table and went out into the morning light together, and Jody respectfully followed a little behind them. He tried to keep his mind from running ahead, tried to keep it absolutely motionless.

His mother called, "Carl! Don't you let it keep him from school."

They marched past the cypress, where a singletree hung from a limb to butcher the pigs on, and past the black iron kettle, so it was not a pig killing. The sun shone over the hill and threw long, dark shadows of the trees and buildings. They crossed a stubble-field to shortcut to the barn. Jody's father unhooked the door and they went in. They had been walking toward the sun on the way down. The barn was black as night in contrast and warm from the hay and from the beasts. Jody's father moved over toward the one box stall. "Come here!" he ordered. Jody could begin to see things now. He looked into the box stall and then stepped back quickly.

A red pony colt was looking at him out of the stall. Its tense ears were forward and a light of disobedience was in its eyes. Its coat was rough and thick as an airedale's fur and its mane was long and tangled. Jody's throat collapsed in on itself and cut his breath short.

"He needs a good currying," his father said, "and if I ever hear of you not feeding him or leaving his stall dirty, I'll sell him off in a minute."

Jody couldn't bear to look at the pony's eyes any more. He gazed down at his hands for a moment, and he asked very shyly, "Mine?" No one answered him. He put his hand out toward the pony. Its gray nose came close, sniffing loudly, and then the lips drew back and the strong teeth closed on Jody's fingers. The pony shook its head up and down and seemed to laugh with amusement. Jody regarded his bruised fingers. "Well," he said with pride— "Well, I guess he can bite all right." The two men laughed, somewhat in relief. Carl Tiflin went out of the barn and walked up a side-hill to be by himself, for he was embarrassed, but Billy Buck stayed. It was easier to talk to Billy Buck. Jody asked again—"Mine?"

Billy became professional in tone. "Sure! That is, if you look out for him and break him right. I'll show you how. He's just a colt. You can't ride him for some time."

Jody put out his bruised hand again, and this time the red pony let his nose be rubbed. "I ought to have a carrot," Jody said. "Where'd we get him, Billy?"

"Bought him at a sheriff's auction," Billy explained. "A show went broke in Salinas and had debts. The sheriff was selling off their stuff."

The pony stretched out his nose and shook the forelock from his wild eyes. Jody stroked the nose a little. He said softly, "There isn't a—saddle?"

Billy Buck laughed. "I'd forgot. Come along."

In the harness room he lifted down a little saddle of red morocco leather. "It's just a show saddle," Billy Buck said disparagingly. "It isn't practical for the brush, but it was cheap at the sale."

Jody couldn't trust himself to look at the saddle either, and he couldn't speak at all. He brushed the shining red leather with his fingertips, and after a long time he said, "It'll look pretty on him though." He thought of the grandest and prettiest things he knew. "If he hasn't a name already, I think I'll call him Gabilan Mountains," he said.

Billy Buck knew how he felt. "It's a pretty long name. Why don't you just call him Gabilan? That means hawk. That would be a fine name for him." Billy felt glad. "If you will collect tail hair, I might be able to make a hair rope for you sometime. You could use it for a hackamore."

Jody wanted to go back to the box stall. "Could I lead him to school, do you think—to show the kids?"

But Billy shook his head. "He's not even halter-broke yet. We had a time getting him here. Had to almost drag him. You better be starting for school though."

"I'll bring the kids to see him here this afternoon," Jody said.

Six boys came over the hill half an hour early that afternoon, running hard, their heads down, their forearms working, their breath whistling. They swept by the house and cut across the stubble-field to the barn. And then they stood self-consciously before the pony, and then they looked at Jody with eyes in which there was a new admiration and a new respect. Before today Jody had been a boy, dressed in overalls and a blue shirt—quieter than most, even suspected of being a little cowardly. And now he was different. Out of a thousand centuries they drew the ancient admiration of the footman for the horseman. They knew instinctively that a man on a horse is spiritually as well as physically bigger than a man on foot. They knew that Jody had been miraculously lifted out of equality with them, and had been placed over them. Gabilan put his head out of the stall and sniffed them.

"Why'n't you ride him?" the boys cried. "Why'n't you braid his tail with ribbons like in the fair?" "When you going to ride him?"

Jody's courage was up. He too felt the superiority of the horseman. "He's not old enough. Nobody can ride him for a long time. I'm going to train him on the long halter. Billy Buck is going to show me how."

"Well, can't we even lead him around a little?"

"He isn't even halter broke," Jody said. He wanted to be completely alone when he took the pony out the first time. "Come and see the saddle."

They were speechless at the red morocco saddle, completely shocked out of comment. "It isn't much use in the brush," Jody explained. "It'll look pretty on him though. Maybe I'll ride bareback when I go into the brush."

"How you going to rope a cow without a saddle horn?"

"Maybe I'll get another saddle for every day. My father might want me to help him with the stock." He let them feel the red saddle, and showed them the brass chain

throat-latch on the bridle and the big brass buttons at
each temple where the headstall and brow band crossed.
The whole thing was too wonderful. They had to go away
after a little while, and each boy, in his mind, searched
among his possessions for a bribe worthy of offering in return for a ride on the red pony when the time should
come.

Jody was glad when they had gone. He took brush and
currycomb from the wall, took down the barrier of the
box stall and stepped cautiously in. The pony's eyes glittered, and he edged around into kicking position. But
Jody touched him on the shoulder and rubbed his high
arched neck as he had always seen Billy Buck do, and he
crooned, "So-o-o Boy," in a deep voice. The pony gradually relaxed his tenseness. Jody curried and brushed until
a pile of dead hair lay in the stall and until the pony's coat
had taken on a deep red shine. Each time he finished he
thought it might have been done better. He braided the
mane into a dozen little pigtails, and he braided the forelock, and then he undid them and brushed the hair out
straight again.

Jody did not hear his mother enter the barn. She was
angry when she came, but when she looked in at the pony
and at Jody working over him, she felt a curious pride rise
up in her. "Have you forgot the wood-box?" she asked
gently. "It's not far off from dark and there's not a stick
of wood in the house, and the chickens aren't fed."

Jody quickly put up his tools. "I forgot, ma'am."

"Well, after this do your chores first. Then you won't
forget. I expect you'll forget lots of things now if I don't
keep an eye on you."

"Can I have carrots from the garden for him, ma'am?"

She had to think about that. "Oh—I guess so, if you
only take the big tough ones."

"Carrots keep the coat good," he said, and again she felt the curious rush of pride.

Jody never waited for the triangle to get him out of bed after the coming of the pony. It became his habit to creep out of bed even before his mother was awake, to slip into his clothes and to go quietly down to the barn to see Gabilan. In the gray quiet mornings when the land and the brush and the houses and the trees were silver-gray and black like a photograph negative, he stole toward the barn, past the sleeping stones and the sleeping cypress tree. The turkeys, roosting in the tree out of coyotes' reach, clicked drowsily. The fields glowed with a gray frost-like light and in the dew the tracks of rabbits and of field mice stood out sharply. The good dogs came stiffly out of their little houses, hackles up and deep growls in their throats. Then they caught Jody's scent, and their stiff tails rose up and waved a greeting—Doubletree Mutt with the big thick tail, and Smasher, the incipient shepherd—then went lazily back to their warm beds.

It was a strange time and a mysterious journey, to Jody —an extension of a dream. When he first had the pony he liked to torture himself during the trip by thinking Gabilan would not be in his stall, and worse, would never have been there. And he had other delicious little self-induced pains. He thought how the rats had gnawed ragged holes in the red saddle, and how the mice had nibbled Gabilan's tail until it was stringy and thin. He usually ran the last little way to the barn. He unlatched the rusty hasp of the barn door and stepped in, and no matter how quietly he opened the door, Gabilan was always looking at him over the barrier of the box stall and Gabilan whinnied softly and stamped his front foot, and his eyes had big sparks of red fire in them like oakwood embers.

Sometimes, if the work horses were to be used that day,

Jody found Billy Buck in the barn harnessing and currying. Billy stood with him and looked long at Gabilan and he told Jody a great many things about horses. He explained that they were terribly afraid for their feet, so that one must make a practice of lifting the legs and patting the hooves and ankles to remove their terror. He told Jody how horses love conversation. He must talk to the pony all the time, and tell him the reasons for everything. Billy wasn't sure a horse could understand everything that was said to him, but it was impossible to say how much was understood. A horse never kicked up a fuss if some one he liked explained things to him. Billy could give examples, too. He had known, for instance, a horse nearly dead beat with fatigue to perk up when told it was only a little farther to his destination. And he had known a horse paralyzed with fright to come out of it when his rider told him what it was that was frightening him. While he talked in the mornings, Billy Buck cut twenty or thirty straws into neat three-inch lengths and stuck them into his hatband. Then during the whole day, if he wanted to pick his teeth or merely to chew on something, he had only to reach up for one of them.

Jody listened carefully, for he knew and the whole country knew that Billy Buck was a fine hand with horses. Billy's own horse was a stringy cayuse with a hammer head, but he nearly always won the first prizes at the stock trials. Billy could rope a steer, take a double half-hitch about the horn with his riata, and dismount, and his horse would play the steer as an angler plays a fish, keeping a tight rope until the steer was down or beaten.

Every morning, after Jody had curried and brushed the pony, he let down the barrier of the stall, and Gabilan thrust past him and raced down the barn and into the corral. Around and around he galloped, and sometimes he jumped forward and landed on stiff legs. He stood quivering, stiff ears forward, eyes rolling so that the whites showed, pretending to be frightened. At last he walked snorting to the water-trough and buried his nose in the water up to the nostrils. Jody was proud then, for he knew that was the way to judge a horse. Poor horses only touched their lips to the water, but a fine spirited beast put his whole nose and mouth under, and only left room to breathe.

Then Jody stood and watched the pony, and he saw things he had never noticed about any other horse, the sleek, sliding flank muscles and the cords of the buttocks, which flexed like a closing fist, and the shine the sun put on the red coat. Having seen horses all his life, Jody had never looked at them very closely before. But now he noticed the moving ears which gave expression and even inflection of expression to the face. The pony talked with his ears. You could tell exactly how he felt about everything by the way his ears pointed. Sometimes they were stiff and upright and sometimes lax and sagging. They went back when he was angry or fearful, and forward when he was anxious and curious and pleased; and their exact position indicated which emotion he had.

Billy Buck kept his word. In the early fall the training began. First there was the halter-breaking, and that was the hardest because it was the first thing. Jody held a carrot and coaxed and promised and pulled on the rope. The pony set his feet like a burro when he felt the strain. But before long he learned. Jody walked all over the ranch leading him. Gradually he took to dropping the rope until the pony followed him unled wherever he went.

And then came the training on the long halter. That was slower work. Jody stood in the middle of a circle, holding the long halter. He clucked with his tongue and the pony started to walk in a big circle, held in by the long rope. He clucked again to make the pony trot, and again to make him gallop. Around and around Gabilan went thundering and enjoying it immensely. Then he called, "Whoa," and the pony stopped. It was not long until Gabilan was perfect at it. But in many ways he was a bad pony. He bit Jody in the pants and stomped on Jody's feet. Now and then his ears went back and he aimed a tremendous kick at the boy. Every time he did one of these bad things, Gabilan settled back and seemed to laugh to himself.

Billy Buck worked at the hair rope in the evenings before the fireplace. Jody collected tail hair in a bag, and he sat and watched Billy slowly constructing the rope, twisting a few hairs to make a string and rolling two strings together for a cord, and then braiding a number of cords to make the rope. Billy rolled the finished rope on the floor under his foot to make it round and hard.

The long halter work rapidly approached perfection. Jody's father, watching the pony stop and start and trot and gallop, was a little bothered by it.

"He's getting to be almost a trick pony," he complained. "I don't like trick horses. It takes all the—dignity out of a horse to make him do tricks. Why, a trick horse is kind of like an actor—no dignity, no character of his own." And his father said, "I guess you better be getting him used to the saddle pretty soon."

Jody rushed for the harness-room. For some time he had been riding the saddle on a sawhorse. He changed the stirrup length over and over, and could never get it just right. Sometimes, mounted on the sawhorse in the harness-room, with collars and hames and tugs hung all about him, Jody rode out beyond the room. He carried his rifle across the pommel. He saw the fields go flying by, and he heard the beat of the galloping hoofs.

It was a ticklish job, saddling the pony the first time.

Gabilan hunched and reared and threw the saddle off before the cinch could be tightened. It had to be replaced again and again until at last the pony let it stay. And the cinching was difficult, too. Day by day Jody tightened the girth a little more until at last the pony didn't mind the saddle at all.

Then there was the bridle. Billy explained how to use a stick of licorice for a bit until Gabilan was used to having something in his mouth. Billy explained, "Of course we could force-break him to everything, but he wouldn't be as good a horse if we did. He'd always be a little bit afraid, and he wouldn't mind because he wanted to."

The first time the pony wore the bridle he whipped his head about and worked his tongue against the bit until the blood oozed from the corners of his mouth. He tried to rub the headstall off on the manger. His ears pivoted about and his eyes turned red with fear and with general rambunctiousness. Jody rejoiced, for he knew that only a mean-souled horse does not resent training.

And Jody trembled when he thought of the time when he would first sit in the saddle. The pony would probably throw him off. There was no disgrace in that. The disgrace would come if he did not get right up and mount again. Sometimes he dreamed that he lay in the dirt and cried and couldn't make himself mount again. The shame of the dream lasted until the middle of the day.

Gabilan was growing fast. Already he had lost the long-leggedness of the colt; his mane was getting longer and blacker. Under the constant currying and brushing his coat lay as smooth and gleaming as orange-red lacquer. Jody oiled the hoofs and kept them carefully trimmed so they would not crack.

The hair rope was nearly finished. Jody's father gave him an old pair of spurs and bent in the side bars and cut down the strap and took up the chainlets until they fitted. And then one day Carl Tiflin said:

"The pony's growing faster than I thought. I guess you can ride him by Thanksgiving. Think you can stick on?"

"I don't know," Jody said shyly. Thanksgiving was only three weeks off. He hoped it wouldn't rain, for rain would spot the red saddle.

Gabilan knew and liked Jody by now. He nickered when Jody came across the stubble-field, and in the pasture he came running when his master whistled for him. There was always a carrot for him every time.

Billy Buck gave him riding instructions over and over. "Now when you get up there, just grab tight with your knees and keep your hands away from the saddle, and if you get throwed, don't let that stop you. No matter how good a man is, there's always some horse can pitch him. You just climb up again before he gets to feeling smart about it. Pretty soon, he won't throw you no more, and pretty soon he *can't* throw you no more. That's the way to do it."

"I hope it don't rain before," Jody said.

"Why not? Don't want to get throwed in the mud?"

That was partly it, and also he was afraid that in the flurry of bucking Gabilan might slip and fall on him and break his leg or his hip. He had seen that happen to men before, had seen how they writhed on the ground like squashed bugs, and he was afraid of it.

He practiced on the sawhorse how he would hold the reins in his left hand and a hat in his right hand. If he kept his hands thus busy, he couldn't grab the horn if he felt himself going off. He didn't like to think of what would happen if he did grab the horn. Perhaps his father and Billy Buck would never speak to him again, they would be so ashamed. The news would get about and his mother would be ashamed too. And in the school yard—it was too awful to contemplate.

He began putting his weight in a stirrup when Gabilan was saddled, but he didn't throw his leg over the pony's back. That was forbidden until Thanksgiving.

Every afternoon he put the red saddle on the pony and cinched it tight. The pony was learning already to fill his stomach out unnaturally large while the cinching was going on, and then to let it down when the straps were fixed. Sometimes Jody led him up to the brush line and let him drink from the round green tub, and sometimes he led him up through the stubble-field to the hilltop from which it was possible to see the white town of Salinas and the geometric fields of the great valley, and the oak trees clipped by the sheep. Now and then they broke through the brush and came to little cleared circles so hedged in that the world was gone and only the sky and the circle of brush were left from the old life. Gabilan liked these trips and showed it by keeping his head very high and by quivering his nostrils with interest. When the two came back from an expedition they smelled of the sweet sage they had forced through.

Time dragged on toward Thanksgiving, but winter came fast. The clouds swept down and hung all day over the land and brushed the hilltops, and the winds blew shrilly at night. All day the dry oak leaves drifted down from the trees until they covered the ground, and yet the trees were unchanged.

Jody had wished it might not rain before Thanksgiving, but it did. The brown earth turned dark and the trees glistened. The cut ends of the stubble turned black with mildew; the haystacks grayed from exposure to the damp, and on the roofs the moss, which had been all summer as gray as lizards, turned a brilliant yellow-green. During

the week of rain, Jody kept the pony in the box stall out
of the dampness, except for a little time after school when
he took him out for exercise and to drink at the water-
trough in the upper corral. Not once did Gabilan get wet.

The wet weather continued until little new grass appeared. Jody walked to school dressed in a slicker and
short rubber boots. At length one morning the sun came
out brightly. Jody, at his work in the box stall, said to
Billy Buck, "Maybe I'll leave Gabilan in the corral when
I go to school today."

"Be good for him to be out in the sun," Billy assured
him. "No animal likes to be cooped up too long. Your
father and me are going back on the hill to clean the
leaves out of the spring." Billy nodded and picked his
teeth with one of his little straws.

"If the rain comes, though—" Jody suggested.

"Not likely to rain today. She's rained herself out."
Billy pulled up his sleeves and snapped his arm bands.
"If it comes on to rain—why a little rain don't hurt a
horse."

"Well, if it does come to rain, you put him in, will you,
Billy? I'm scared he might get cold so I couldn't ride him
when the time comes."

"Oh sure! I'll watch out for him if we get back in time.
But it won't rain today."

And so Jody, when he went to school left Gabilan
standing out in the corral.

Billy Buck wasn't wrong about many things. He
couldn't be. But he was wrong about the weather that
day, for a little after noon the clouds pushed over the hills
and the rain began to pour down. Jody heard it start on
the schoolhouse roof. He considered holding up one finger
for permission to go to the outhouse and, once outside,
running for home to put the pony in. Punishment would
be prompt both at school and at home. He gave it up and

took ease from Billy's assurance that rain couldn't hurt a horse. When school was finally out, he hurried home through the dark rain. The banks at the sides of the road spouted little jets of muddy water. The rain slanted and swirled under a cold and gusty wind. Jody dog-trotted home, slopping through the gravelly mud of the road.

From the top of the ridge he could see Gabilan standing miserably in the corral. The red coat was almost black, and streaked with water. He stood head down with his rump to the rain and wind. Jody arrived running and threw open the barn door and led the wet pony in by his forelock. Then he found a gunny sack and rubbed the soaked hair and rubbed the legs and ankles. Gabilan stood patiently, but he trembled in gusts like the wind.

When he had dried the pony as well as he could, Jody went up to the house and brought hot water down to the barn and soaked the grain in it. Gabilan was not very hungry. He nibbled at the hot mash, but he was not very much interested in it, and he still shivered now and then. A little steam rose from his damp back.

It was almost dark when Billy Buck and Carl Tiflin came home. "When the rain started we put up at Ben Herche's place, and the rain never let up all afternoon," Carl Tiflin explained. Jody looked reproachfully at Billy Buck and Billy felt guilty.

"You said it wouldn't rain," Jody accused him.

Billy looked away. "It's hard to tell, this time of year," he said, but his excuse was lame. He had no right to be fallible, and he knew it.

"The pony got wet, got soaked through."

"Did you dry him off?"

"I rubbed him with a sack and I gave him hot grain."

Billy nodded in agreement.

"Do you think he'll take cold, Billy?"

"A little rain never hurt anything," Billy assured him.

Jody's father joined the conversation then and lectured the boy a little. "A horse," he said, "isn't any lap-dog kind of thing." Carl Tiflin hated weakness and sickness, and he held a violent contempt for helplessness.

Jody's mother put a platter of steaks on the table and boiled potatoes and boiled squash, which clouded the room with their steam. They sat down to eat. Carl Tiflin still grumbled about weakness put into animals and men by too much coddling.

Billy Buck felt bad about his mistake. "Did you blanket him?" he asked.

"No. I couldn't find any blanket. I laid some sacks over his back."

"We'll go down and cover him up after we eat, then." Billy felt better about it then. When Jody's father had gone in to the fire and his mother was washing dishes, Billy found and lighted a lantern. He and Jody walked through the mud to the barn. The barn was dark and warm and sweet. The horses still munched their evening hay. "You hold the lantern!" Billy ordered. And he felt the pony's legs and tested the heat of the flanks. He put his cheek against the pony's gray muzzle and then he rolled up the eyelids to look at the eyeballs and he lifted the lips to see the gums, and he put his fingers inside his ears. "He don't seem so chipper," Billy said. "I'll give him a rub-down."

Then Billy found a sack and rubbed the pony's legs violently and he rubbed the chest and the withers. Gabilan was strangely spiritless. He submitted patiently to the rubbing. At last Billy brought an old cotton comforter from the saddle-room, and threw it over the pony's back and tied it at neck and chest with string.

"Now he'll be all right in the morning," Billy said.

Jody's mother looked up when he got back to the house.

"You're late up from bed," she said. She held his chin in her hard hand and brushed the tangled hair out of his eyes and she said, "Don't worry about the pony. He'll be all right. Billy's as good as any horse doctor in the country."

Jody hadn't known she could see his worry. He pulled gently away from her and knelt down in front of the fireplace until it burned his stomach. He scorched himself through and then went in to bed, but it was a hard thing to go to sleep. He awakened after what seemed a long time. The room was dark but there was a grayness in the window like that which precedes the dawn. He got up and found his overalls and searched for the legs, and then the clock in the other room struck two. He laid his clothes down and got back into bed. It was broad daylight when he awakened again. For the first time he had slept through the ringing of the triangle. He leaped up, flung on his clothes and went out of the door still buttoning his shirt. His mother looked after him for a moment and then went quietly back to her work. Her eyes were brooding and kind. Now and then her mouth smiled a little but without changing her eyes at all.

Jody ran on toward the barn. Halfway there he heard the sound he dreaded, the hollow rasping cough of a horse. He broke into a sprint then. In the barn he found Billy Buck with the pony. Billy was rubbing its legs with his strong thick hands. He looked up and smiled gaily. "He just took a little cold," Billy said. "We'll have him out of it in a couple of days."

Jody looked at the pony's face. The eyes were half closed and the lids thick and dry. In the eye corners a crust of hard mucus stuck. Gabilan's ears hung loosely sideways and his head was low. Jody put out his hand, but the pony did not move close to it. He coughed again and his whole body constricted with the effort. A little stream of thin fluid ran from his nostrils.

Jody looked back at Billy Buck. "He's awful sick, Billy."

"Just a little cold, like I said," Billy insisted. "You go get some breakfast and then go back to school. I'll take care of him."

"But you might have to do something else. You might leave him."

"No, I won't. I won't leave him at all. Tomorrow's Saturday. Then you can stay with him all day." Billy had failed again, and he felt badly about it. He had to cure the pony now.

Jody walked up to the house and took his place listlessly at the table. The eggs and bacon were cold and greasy, but he didn't notice it. He ate his usual amount. He didn't even ask to stay home from school. His mother pushed his hair back when she took his plate. "Billy'll take care of the pony," she assured him.

He moped through the whole day at school. He couldn't answer any questions nor read any words. He couldn't even tell anyone the pony was sick, for that might make him sicker. And when school was finally out he started home in dread. He walked slowly and let the other boys leave him. He wished he might continue walking and never arrive at the ranch.

Billy was in the barn, as he had promised, and the pony was worse. His eyes were almost closed now, and his breath whistled shrilly past an obstruction in his nose. A film covered that part of the eyes that was visible at all. It was doubtful whether the pony could see any more. Now and then he snorted, to clear his nose, and by the action seemed to plug it tighter. Jody looked dispiritedly at the pony's coat. The hair lay rough and unkempt and seemed to have lost all of its old luster. Bill stood quietly beside the stall. Jody hated to ask, but he had to know.

"Billy, is he—is he going to get well?"

Billy put his fingers between the bars under the pony's

jaw and felt about. "Feel here," he said and he guided
Jody's fingers to a large lump under the jaw. "When that
gets bigger, I'll open it up and then he'll get better."

Jody looked quickly away, for he had heard about that
lump. "What is it the matter with him?"

Billy didn't want to answer, but he had to. He couldn't
be wrong three times. "Strangles," he said shortly, "but
don't you worry about that. I'll pull him out of it. I've seen
them get well when they were worse than Gabilan is. I'm
going to steam him now. You can help."

"Yes," Jody said miserably. He followed Billy into the
grain room and watched him make the steaming bag
ready. It was a long canvas nose bag with straps to go over
a horse's ears. Billy filled it one-third full of bran and then
he added a couple of handfuls of dried hops. On top of the
dry substance he poured a little carbolic acid and a little
turpentine. "I'll be mixing it all up while you run to the
house for a kettle of boiling water," Billy said.

When Jody came back with the steaming kettle, Billy
buckled the straps over Gabilan's head and fitted the bag
tightly around his nose. Then through a little hole in the
side of the bag he poured the boiling water on the mixture. The pony started away as a cloud of strong steam
rose up, but then the soothing fumes crept through his
nose and into his lungs, and the sharp steam began to
clear out the nasal passages. He breathed loudly. His legs
trembled in an ague, and his eyes closed against the biting
cloud. Billy poured in more water and kept the steam rising for fifteen minutes. At last he set down the kettle and
took the bag from Gabilan's nose. The pony looked better.
He breathed freely, and his eyes were open wider than
they had been.

"See how good it makes him feel," Billy said. "Now
we'll wrap him up in the blanket again. Maybe he'll be
nearly well by morning."

"I'll stay with him tonight," Jody suggested.

"No. Don't you do it. I'll bring my blankets down here and put them in the hay. You can stay tomorrow and steam him if he needs it."

The evening was falling when they went to the house for their supper. Jody didn't even realize that some one else had fed the chickens and filled the wood-box. He walked up past the house to the dark brush line and took a drink of water from the tub. The spring water was so cold that it stung his mouth and drove a shiver through him. The sky above the hills was still light. He saw a hawk flying so high that it caught the sun on its breast and shone like a spark. Two blackbirds were driving him down the sky, glittering as they attacked their enemy. In the west, the clouds were moving in to rain again.

Jody's father didn't speak at all while the family ate supper, but after Billy Buck had taken his blankets and gone to sleep in the barn, Carl Tiflin built a high fire in the fireplace and told stories. He told about the wild man who ran naked through the country and had a tail and ears like a horse, and he told about the rabbit-cats of Moro Cojo that hopped into the trees for birds. He revived the famous Maxwell brothers who found a vein of gold and hid the traces of it so carefully that they could never find it again.

Jody sat with his chin in his hands; his mouth worked nervously, and his father gradually became aware that he wasn't listening very carefully. "Isn't that funny?" he asked.

Jody laughed politely and said, "Yes, sir." His father was angry and hurt, then. He didn't tell any more stories. After a while, Jody took a lantern and went down to the barn. Billy Buck was asleep in the hay, and, except that his breath rasped a little in his lungs, the pony seemed to be much better. Jody stayed a little while, running his fingers over the red rough coat, and then he took up the lantern and went back to the house. When he was in bed, his mother came into the room.

"Have you enough covers on? It's getting winter."

"Yes, ma'am."

"Well, get some rest tonight." She hesitated to go out, stood uncertainly. "The pony will be all right," she said.

Jody was tired. He went to sleep quickly and didn't awaken until dawn. The triangle sounded, and Billy Buck came up from the barn before Jody could get out of the house.

"How is he?" Jody demanded.

Billy always wolfed his breakfast. "Pretty good. I'm going to open that lump this morning. Then he'll be better maybe."

After breakfast, Billy got out his best knife, one with a needle point. He whetted the shining blade a long time on a little carborundum stone. He tried the point and the blade again and again on his calloused thumb-ball, and at last he tried it on his upper lip.

On the way to the barn, Jody noticed how the young grass was up and how the stubble was melting day by day into the new green crop of volunteer. It was a cold sunny morning.

As soon as he saw the pony, Jody knew he was worse. His eyes were closed and sealed shut with dried mucus. His head hung so low that his nose almost touched the straw of his bed. There was a little groan in each breath, a deep-seated, patient groan.

Billy lifted the weak head and made a quick slash with the knife. Jody saw the yellow pus run out. He held up the head while Billy swabbed out the wound with weak carbolic acid salve.

"Now he'll feel better," Billy assured him. "That yellow poison is what makes him sick."

Jody looked unbelieving at Billy Buck. "He's awful sick."

Billy thought a long time what to say. He nearly tossed off a careless assurance, but he saved himself in time. "Yes, he's pretty sick," he said at last. "I've seen worse ones get well. If he doesn't get pneumonia, we'll pull him through. You stay with him. If he gets worse, you can come and get me."

For a long time after Billy went away, Jody stood beside the pony, stroking him behind the ears. The pony didn't flip his head the way he had done when he was well. The groaning in his breathing was becoming more hollow.

Doubletree Mutt looked into the barn, his big tail waving provocatively, and Jody was so incensed at his health that he found a hard black clod on the floor and deliberately threw it. Doubletree Mutt went yelping away to nurse a bruised paw.

In the middle of the morning, Billy Buck came back and made another steam bag. Jody watched to see whether the pony improved this time as he had before. His breathing eased a little, but he did not raise his head.

The Saturday dragged on. Late in the afternoon Jody went to the house and brought his bedding down and made up a place to sleep in the hay. He didn't ask permission. He knew from the way his mother looked at him that she would let him do almost anything. That night he left a lantern burning on a wire over the box stall. Billy had told him to rub the pony's legs every little while.

At nine o'clock the wind sprang up and howled around the barn. And in spite of his worry, Jody grew sleepy. He got into his blankets and went to sleep, but the breathy groans of the pony sounded in his dreams. And in his sleep he heard a crashing noise which went on and on until it awakened him. The wind was rushing through the barn. He sprang up and looked down the lane of stalls. The barn door had blown open, and the pony was gone.

He caught the lantern and ran outside into the gale, and he saw Gabilan weakly shambling away into the darkness, head down, legs working slowly and mechanically. When Jody ran up and caught him by the forelock, he allowed himself to be led back and put into his stall. His groans were louder, and a fierce whistling came from his nose. Jody didn't sleep any more then. The hissing of the pony's breath grew louder and sharper.

He was glad when Billy Buck came in at dawn. Billy looked for a time at the pony as though he had never seen him before. He felt the ears and flanks. "Jody," he said, "I've got to do something you won't want to see. You run up to the house for a while."

Jody grabbed him fiercely by the forearm. "You're not going to shoot him?"

Billy patted his hand. "No. I'm going to open a little hole in his windpipe so he can breathe. His nose is filled up. When he gets well, we'll put a little brass button in the hole for him to breathe through."

Jody couldn't have gone away if he had wanted to. It was awful to see the red hide cut, but infinitely more terrible to know it was being cut and not to see it. "I'll stay right here," he said bitterly. "You sure you got to?"

"Yes. I'm sure. If you stay, you can hold his head. If it doesn't make you sick, that is."

The fine knife came out again and was whetted again just as carefully as it had been the first time. Jody held the pony's head up and the throat taut, while Billy felt up and down for the right place. Jody sobbed once as the bright knife point disappeared into the throat. The pony plunged weakly away and then stood still, trembling violently. The blood ran thickly out and up the knife and across Billy's hand and into his shirtsleeve. The sure square hand sawed out a round hole in the flesh, and the breath came bursting out of the hole, throwing a fine spray of blood. With the rush of oxygen, the pony took a sudden strength. He lashed out with his hind feet and tried to rear, but Jody held his head down while Billy mopped the new wound with carbolic salve. It was a good job. The blood stopped flowing and the air puffed out the hole and sucked it in regularly with a little bubbling noise.

The rain brought in by the night wind began to fall on the barn roof. Then the triangle rang for breakfast. "You go up and eat while I wait," Billy said. "We've got to keep this hole from plugging up."

Jody walked slowly out of the barn. He was too dispirited to tell Billy how the barn door had blown open and let the pony out. He emerged into the wet gray morning and sloshed up to the house, taking a perverse pleasure in splashing through all the puddles. His mother fed him and put dry clothes on. She didn't question him. She seemed to know he couldn't answer questions. But when he was ready to go back to the barn she brought him a pan of steaming meal. "Give him this," she said.

But Jody did not take the pan. He said, "He won't eat anything," and ran out of the house. At the barn, Billy showed him how to fix a ball of cotton on a stick, with which to swab out the breathing hole when it became clogged with mucus.

Jody's father walked into the barn and stood with them in front of the stall. At length he turned to the boy. "Hadn't you better come with me? I'm going to drive over the hill." Jody shook his head. "You better come on, out of this," his father insisted.

Billy turned on him angrily. "Let him alone. It's his pony, isn't it?"

Carl Tiflin walked away without saying another word. His feelings were badly hurt.

All morning Jody kept the wound open and the air passing in and out freely. At noon the pony lay wearily down on his side and stretched his nose out.

Billy came back. "If you're going to stay with him tonight, you better take a little nap," he said. Jody went absently out of the barn. The sky had cleared to a hard thin blue. Everywhere the birds were busy with worms that had come to the damp surface of the ground.

Jody walked to the brush line and sat on the edge of the mossy tub. He looked down at the house and at the old bunkhouse and at the dark cypress tree. The place was familiar, but curiously changed. It wasn't itself any more, but a frame for things that were happening. A cold wind blew out of the east now, signifying that the rain was over for a little while. At his feet Jody could see the little arms of new weeds spreading out over the ground. In the mud about the spring were thousands of quail tracks.

Doubletree Mutt came sideways and embarrassed up through the vegetable patch, and Jody, remembering how he had thrown the clod, put his arm about the dog's neck and kissed him on his wide black nose. Doubletree Mutt sat still, as though he knew some solemn thing was happening. His big tail slapped the ground gravely. Jody pulled a swollen tick out of Mutt's neck and popped it dead between his thumb-nails. It was a nasty thing. He washed his hands in the cold spring water.

Except for the steady swish of the wind, the farm was very quiet. Jody knew his mother wouldn't mind if he didn't go in to eat his lunch. After a little while he went slowly back to the barn. Mutt crept into his own little house and whined softly to himself for a long time.

Billy Buck stood up from the box and surrendered the cotton swab. The pony still lay on his side and the wound in his throat bellowsed in and out. When Jody saw how dry and dead the hair looked, he knew at last that there was no hope for the pony. He had seen the dead hair before on dogs and on cows, and it was a sure sign. He sat heavily on the box and let down the barrier of the box stall. For a long time he kept his eyes on the moving wound, and at last he dozed, and the afternoon passed quickly. Just before dark his mother brought a deep dish of stew and left it for him and went away. Jody ate a little of it, and, when it was dark, he set the lantern on the floor by the pony's head so he could watch the wound and keep it open. And he dozed again until the night chill awakened him. The wind was blowing fiercely, bringing the north cold with it. Jody brought a blanket from his bed in the hay and wrapped himself in it. Gabilan's breathing was quiet at last; the hole in his throat moved gently. The owls flew through the hayloft, shrieking and looking for mice. Jody put his hands down on his head and slept. In his sleep he was aware that the wind had increased. He heard it slamming about the barn.

It was daylight when he awakened. The barn door had swung open. The pony was gone. He sprang up and ran out into the morning light.

The pony's tracks were plain enough, dragging through the frostlike dew on the young grass, tired tracks with little lines between them where the hoofs had dragged. They headed for the brush line halfway up the ridge. Jody broke into a run and followed them. The sun shone on the sharp white quartz that stuck through the ground here and there. As he followed the plain trail, a shadow cut across in front of him. He looked up and saw a high circle of black buzzards, and the slowly revolving circle dropped lower and lower. The solemn birds soon disappeared over the ridge. Jody ran faster then, forced on by panic and rage. The trail entered the brush at last and followed a winding route among the tall sage brushes.

At the top of the ridge Jody was winded. He paused, puffing noisily. The blood pounded in his ears. Then he saw what he was looking for. Below, in one of the little clearings in the brush, lay the red pony. In the distance, Jody could see the legs moving slowly and convulsively. And in a circle around him stood the buzzards, waiting for the moment of death they know so well.

Jody leaped forward and plunged down the hill. The wet ground muffled his steps and the brush hid him. When he arrived, it was all over. The first buzzard sat on the pony's head and its beak had just risen dripping with dark eye fluid. Jody plunged into the circle like a cat. The black brotherhood arose in a cloud, but the big one on the pony's head was too late. As it hopped along to take off, Jody caught its wing tip and pulled it down. It was nearly as big as he was. The free wing crashed into his face with the force of a club, but he hung on. The claws fastened on his leg and the wing elbows battered his head on either side. Jody groped blindly with his free hand. His fingers found the neck of the struggling bird. The red eyes looked into his face, calm and fearless and fierce; the naked head turned from side to side. Then the beak opened and vomited a stream of putrefied fluid. Jody brought up his knee and fell on the great bird. He held the neck to the ground with one hand while his other found a piece of sharp white quartz. The first blow broke the beak sideways and black blood spurted from the twisted, leathery mouth corners. He struck again and missed. The red fearless eyes still looked at him, impersonal and unafraid and detached. He struck again and again, until the buzzard lay dead, until its head was a red pulp. He was still beating the dead bird when Billy Buck pulled him off and held him tightly to calm his shaking.

Carl Tiflin wiped the blood from the boy's face with a red bandana. Jody was limp and quiet now. His father moved the buzzard with his toe. "Jody," he explained, "the buzzard didn't kill the pony. Don't you know that?"

"I know it," Jody said wearily.

It was Billy Buck who was angry. He had lifted Jody in his arms, and had turned to carry him home. But he turned back on Carl Tiflin. " 'Course he knows it," Billy said furiously, "Jesus Christ! man, can't you see how he'd feel about it?"

II. THE GREAT MOUNTAINS

IN the humming heat of a midsummer afternoon the little boy Jody listlessly looked about the ranch for something to do. He had been to the barn, had thrown rocks at the swallows' nests under the eaves until every one of the little mud houses broke open and dropped its lining of straw and dirty feathers. Then at the ranch house he baited a rat trap with stale cheese and set it where Doubletree Mutt, that good big dog, would get his nose snapped. Jody was not moved by an impulse of cruelty; he was bored with the long hot afternoon. Doubletree Mutt put his stupid nose in the trap and got it smacked, and shrieked with agony and limped away with blood on his nostrils. No matter where he was hurt, Mutt limped. It was just a way he had. Once when he was young, Mutt got caught in a coyote trap, and always after that he limped, even when he was scolded.

When Mutt yelped, Jody's mother called from inside the house, "Jody! Stop torturing that dog and find something to do."

Jody felt mean then, so he threw a rock at Mutt. Then he took his slingshot from the porch and walked up toward the brush line to try to kill a bird. It was a good slingshot, with store-bought rubbers, but while Jody had often shot at birds, he had never hit one. He walked up through the vegetable patch, kicking his bare toes into the dust. And on the way he found the perfect slingshot stone, round and slightly flattened and heavy enough to carry through the air. He fitted it into the leather pouch of his weapon and proceeded to the brush line. His eyes narrowed, his mouth worked strenuously; for the first time that afternoon he was intent. In the shade of the sagebrush the little birds were working, scratching in the leaves, flying restlessly a few feet and scratching again. Jody pulled back the rubbers of the sling and advanced cautiously. One little thrush paused and looked at him and crouched, ready to fly. Jody sidled nearer, moving one foot slowly after the other. When he was twenty feet away, he carefully raised the sling and aimed. The stone whizzed; the thrush started up and flew right into it. And down the little bird went with a broken head. Jody ran to it and picked it up.

"Well, I got you," he said.

The bird looked much smaller dead than it had alive. Jody felt a little mean pain in his stomach, so he took out his pocket-knife and cut off the bird's head. Then he disemboweled it, and took off its wings; and finally he threw all the pieces into the brush. He didn't care about the bird, or its life, but he knew what older people would say if they had seen him kill it; he was ashamed because of their potential opinion. He decided to forget the whole thing as quickly as he could, and never to mention it.

The hills were dry at this season, and the wild grass was golden, but where the spring-pipe filled the round tub and the tub spilled over, there lay a stretch of fine green grass, deep and sweet and moist. Jody drank from the mossy tub and washed the bird's blood from his hands in cold water. Then he lay on his back in the grass and looked up at the dumpling summer clouds. By closing one eye and destroying perspective he brought them down within reach so that he could put up his fingers and stroke them. He helped the gentle wind push them down the sky; it seemed to him that they went faster for his help. One fat white cloud he helped clear to the mountain rims and pressed it firmly over, out of sight. Jody wondered what it was seeing, then. He sat up the better to look at the great mountains where they went piling back, growing darker and more savage until they finished with one jagged ridge, high up against the west. Curious secret mountains; he thought of the little he knew about them.

"What's on the other side?" he asked his father once.

"More mountains, I guess. Why?"

"And on the other side of them?"

"More mountains. Why?"

"More mountains on and on?"

"Well, no. At last you come to the ocean."

"But what's in the mountains?"

"Just cliffs and brush and rocks and dryness."

"Were you ever there?"

"No."

"Has anybody ever been there?"

"A few people, I guess. It's dangerous, with cliffs and things. Why, I've read there's more unexplored country in the mountains of Monterey County than any place in the United States." His father seemed proud that this should be so.

"And at last the ocean?"

"At last the ocean."

"But," the boy insisted, "but in between? No one knows?"

"Oh, a few people do, I guess. But there's nothing there to get. And not much water. Just rocks and cliffs and greasewood. Why?"

"It would be good to go."

"What for? There's nothing there."

Jody knew something was there, something very wonderful because it wasn't known, something secret and mysterious. He could feel within himself that this was so. He said to his mother, "Do you know what's in the big mountains?"

She looked at him and then back at the ferocious range, and she said, "Only the bear, I guess."

"What bear?"

"Why the one that went over the mountain to see what he could see."

Jody questioned Billy Buck, the ranch hand, about the possibility of ancient cities lost in the mountains, but Billy agreed with Jody's father.

"It ain't likely," Billy said. "There'd be nothing to eat unless a kind of people that can eat rocks live there."

That was all the information Jody ever got, and it made the mountains dear to him, and terrible. He thought often of the miles of ridge after ridge until at last there was the sea. When the peaks were pink in the morning they invited him among them: and when the sun had gone over the edge in the evening and the mountains were a purple-like despair, then Jody was afraid of them; then they were so impersonal and aloof that their very imperturbability was a threat.

Now he turned his head toward the mountains of the east, the Gabilans, and they were jolly mountains, with hill ranches in their creases, and with pine trees growing on the crests. People lived there, and battles had been fought against the Mexicans on the slopes. He looked back for an instant at the Great Ones and shivered a little at the contrast. The foothill cup of the home ranch below him was sunny and safe. The house gleamed with white light and the barn was brown and warm. The red cows on the farther hill ate their way slowly toward the north. Even the dark cypress tree by the bunkhouse was usual and safe. The chickens scratched about in the dust of the farm-yard with quick waltzing steps.

Then a moving figure caught Jody's eye. A man walked slowly over the brow of the hill, on the road from Salinas, and he was headed toward the house. Jody stood up and moved down toward the house too, for if someone was coming, he wanted to be there to see. By the time the boy had got to the house the walking man was only halfway down the road, a lean man, very straight in the shoulders. Jody could tell he was old only because his heels struck the ground with hard jerks. As he approached nearer, Jody saw that he was dressed in blue jeans and in a coat of the same material. He wore clodhopper shoes and an old flat-brimmed Stetson hat. Over his shoulder he carried a gunny sack, lumpy and full. In a few moments he had trudged close enough so that his face could be seen. And his face was as dark as dried beef. A mustache, blue-white against the dark skin, hovered over his mouth, and his hair was white, too, where it showed at his neck. The skin of his face had shrunk back against the skull until it defined bone, not flesh, and made the nose and chin seem sharp and fragile. The eyes were large and deep and dark, with eyelids stretched tightly over them. Irises and pupils were one, and very black, but the eyeballs were brown. There were no wrinkles in the face at all. This old man wore a blue denim coat buttoned to the throat with brass buttons, as all men do who wear no shirts. Out of the sleeves came strong bony wrists and hands gnarled and knotted and hard as peach branches. The nails were flat and blunt and shiny.

The old man drew close to the gate and swung down his sack when he confronted Jody. His lips fluttered a little and a soft impersonal voice came from between them.

"Do you live here?"

Jody was embarrassed. He turned and looked at the house, and he turned back and looked toward the barn where his father and Billy Buck were. "Yes," he said, when no help came from either direction.

"I have come back," the old man said. "I am Gitano, and I have come back."

Jody could not take all this responsibility. He turned abruptly, and ran into the house for help, and the screen door banged after him. His mother was in the kitchen poking out the clogged holes of a colander with a hairpin, and biting her lower lip with concentration.

"It's an old man," Jody cried excitedly. "It's an old *paisano* man, and he says he's come back."

His mother put down the colander and stuck the hairpin behind the sink board. "What's the matter now?" she asked patiently.

"It's an old man outside. Come on out."

"Well, what does he want?" She untied the strings of her apron and smoothed her hair with her fingers.

"I don't know. He came walking."

His mother smoothed down her dress and went out, and Jody followed her. Gitano had not moved.

"Yes?" Mrs. Tiflin asked.

Gitano took off his old black hat and held it with both hands in front of him. He repeated, "I am Gitano, and I have come back."

"Come back? Back where?"

Gitano's whole straight body leaned forward a little. His right hand described the circle of the hills, the sloping fields and the mountains, and ended at his hat again. "Back to the rancho. I was born here, and my father, too."

"Here?" she demanded. "This isn't an old place."

"No, there," he said, pointing to the western ridge. "On the other side there, in a house that is gone."

At last she understood. "The old 'dobe that's washed almost away, you mean?"

"Yes, *señora*. When the rancho broke up they put no more lime on the 'dobe, and the rains washed it down."

Jody's mother was silent for a little, and curious homesick thoughts ran through her mind, but quickly she cleared them out. "And what do you want here now, Gitano?"

"I will stay here," he said quietly, "until I die."

"But we don't need an extra man here."

"I can not work hard any more, *señora*. I can milk a cow, feed chickens, cut a little wood; no more. I will stay here." He indicated the sack on the ground beside him. "Here are my things."

She turned to Jody. "Run down to the barn and call your father."

Jody dashed away, and he returned with Carl Tiflin and Billy Buck behind him. The old man was standing as he had been, but he was resting now. His whole body had sagged into a timeless repose.

"What is it?" Carl Tiflin asked. "What's Jody so excited about?"

Mrs. Tiflin motioned to the old man. "He wants to stay here. He wants to do a little work and stay here."

"Well, we can't have him. We don't need any more men. He's too old. Billy does everything we need."

They had been talking over him as though he did not

exist, and now, suddenly, they both hesitated and looked at Gitano and were embarrassed.

He cleared his throat. "I am too old to work. I come back where I was born."

"You weren't born here," Carl said sharply.

"No. In the 'dobe house over the hill. It was all one rancho before you came."

"In the mud house that's all melted down?"

"Yes. I and my father. I will stay here now on the rancho."

"I tell you you won't stay," Carl said angrily. "I don't need an old man. This isn't a big ranch. I can't afford food and doctor bills for an old man. You must have relatives and friends. Go to them. It is like begging to come to strangers."

"I was born here," Gitano said patiently and inflexibly.

Carl Tiflin didn't like to be cruel, but he felt he must. "You can eat here tonight," he said. "You can sleep in the little room of the old bunkhouse. We'll give you your breakfast in the morning, and then you'll have to go along. Go to your friends. Don't come to die with strangers."

Gitano put on his black hat and stooped for the sack. "Here are my things," he said.

Carl turned away. "Come on, Billy, we'll finish down at the barn. Jody, show him the little room in the bunk-house."

He and Billy turned back toward the barn. Mrs. Tiflin went into the house, saying over her shoulder, "I'll send some blankets down."

Gitano looked questioningly at Jody. "I'll show you where it is," Jody said.

There was a cot with a shuck mattress, an apple box holding a tin lantern, and a backless rocking-chair in the little room of the bunkhouse. Gitano laid his sack carefully on the floor and sat down on the bed. Jody stood shyly in the room, hesitating to go. At last he said,

"Did you come out of the big mountains?"

Gitano shook his head slowly. "No, I worked down the Salinas Valley."

The afternoon thought would not let Jody go. "Did you ever go into the big mountains back there?"

The old dark eyes grew fixed, and their light turned inward on the years that were living in Gitano's head. "Once—when I was a little boy. I went with my father."

"Way back, clear into the mountains?"

"Yes."

"What was there?" Jody cried. "Did you see any people or any houses?"

"No."

"Well, what was there?"

Gitano's eyes remained inward. A little wrinkled strain came between his brows.

"What did you see in there?" Jody repeated.

"I don't know," Gitano said. "I don't remember."

"Was it terrible and dry?"

"I don't remember."

In his excitement, Jody had lost his shyness. "Don't you remember anything about it?"

Gitano's mouth opened for a word, and remained open while his brain sought the word. "I think it was quiet— I think it was nice."

Gitano's eyes seemed to have found something back in the years, for they grew soft and a little smile seemed to come and go in them.

"Didn't you ever go back in the mountains again?" Jody insisted.

"No."

"Didn't you ever want to?"

But now Gitano's face became impatient. "No," he

said in a tone that told Jody he didn't want to talk about it any more. The boy was held by a curious fascination. He didn't want to go away from Gitano. His shyness returned.

"Would you like to come down to the barn and see the stock?" he asked.

Gitano stood up and put on his hat and prepared to follow.

It was almost evening now. They stood near the watering trough while the horses sauntered in from the hillsides for an evening drink. Gitano rested his big twisted hands on the top rail of the fence. Five horses came down and drank, and then stood about, nibbling at the dirt or rubbing their sides against the polished wood of the fence. Long after they had finished drinking an old horse appeared over the brow of the hill and came painfully down. It had long yellow teeth; its hooves were flat and sharp as spades, and its ribs and hip-bones jutted out under its skin. It hobbled up to the trough and drank water with a loud sucking noise.

"That's old Easter," Jody explained. "That's the first horse my father ever had. He's thirty years old." He looked up into Gitano's old eyes for some response.

"No good any more," Gitano said.

Jody's father and Billy Buck came out of the barn and walked over.

"Too old to work," Gitano repeated. "Just eats and pretty soon dies."

Carl Tiflin caught the last words. He hated his brutality toward old Gitano, and so he became brutal again.

"It's a shame not to shoot Easter," he said. "It'd save him a lot of pains and rheumatism." He looked secretly at Gitano, to see whether he noticed the parallel, but the big bony hands did not move, nor did the dark eyes turn from the horse. "Old things ought to be put out of their misery," Jody's father went on. "One shot, a big noise, one big pain in the head maybe, and that's all. That's better than stiffness and sore teeth."

Billy Buck broke in. "They got a right to rest after they worked all of their life. Maybe they like to just walk around."

Carl had been looking steadily at the skinny horse. "You can't imagine now what Easter used to look like," he said softly. "High neck, deep chest, fine barrel. He could jump a five-bar gate in stride. I won a flat race on him when I was fifteen years old. I could of got two hundred dollars for him any time. You wouldn't think how pretty he was." He checked himself, for he hated softness. "But he ought to be shot now," he said.

"He's got a right to rest," Billy Buck insisted.

Jody's father had a humorous thought. He turned to Gitano. "If ham and eggs grew on a side-hill I'd turn you out to pasture too," he said. "But I can't afford to pasture you in my kitchen."

He laughed to Billy Buck about it as they went on toward the house. "Be a good thing for all of us if ham and eggs grew on the side-hills."

Jody knew how his father was probing for a place to hurt in Gitano. He had been probed often. His father knew every place in the boy where a word would fester.

"He's only talking," Jody said. "He didn't mean it about shooting Easter. He likes Easter. That was the first horse he ever owned."

The sun sank behind the high mountains as they stood there, and the ranch was hushed. Gitano seemed to be more at home in the evening. He made a curious sharp sound with his lips and stretched one of his hands over the fence. Old Easter moved stiffly to him, and Gitano rubbed the lean neck under the mane.

"You like him?" Jody asked softly.

"Yes—but he's no damn good."

The triangle sounded at the ranch house. "That's supper," Jody cried. "Come on up to supper."

As they walked up toward the house Jody noticed again that Gitano's body was as straight as that of a young man. Only by a jerkiness in his movements and by the scuffling of his heels could it be seen that he was old.

The turkeys were flying heavily into the lower branches of the cypress tree by the bunkhouse. A fat sleek ranch cat walked across the road carrying a rat so large that its tail dragged on the ground. The quail on the side-hills were still sounding the clear water call.

Jody and Gitano came to the back steps and Mrs. Tiflin looked out through the screen door at them.

"Come running, Jody. Come in to supper, Gitano."

Carl and Billy Buck had started to eat at the long oilcloth-covered table. Jody slipped into his chair without moving it, but Gitano stood holding his hat until Carl looked up and said, "Sit down, sit down. You might as well get your belly full before you go on." Carl was afraid he might relent and let the old man stay, and so he continued to remind himself that this couldn't be.

Gitano laid his hat on the floor and diffidently sat down. He wouldn't reach for food. Carl had to pass it to him. "Here, fill yourself up." Gitano ate very slowly, cutting tiny pieces of meat and arranging little pats of mashed potato on his plate.

The situation would not stop worrying Carl Tiflin. "Haven't you got any relatives in this part of the country?" he asked.

Gitano answered with some pride, "My brother-in-law is in Monterey. I have cousins there, too."

"Well, you can go and live there, then."

"I was born here," Gitano said in gentle rebuke.

Jody's mother came in from the kitchen, carrying a large bowl of tapioca pudding.

Carl chuckled to her, "Did I tell you what I said to him? I said if ham and eggs grew on the side-hills I'd put him out to pasture, like old Easter."

Gitano stared unmoved at his plate.

"It's too bad he can't stay," said Mrs. Tiflin.

"Now don't you start anything," Carl said crossly.

When they had finished eating, Carl and Billy Buck and Jody went into the living-room to sit for a while, but Gitano, without a word of farewell or thanks, walked through the kitchen and out the back door. Jody sat and secretly watched his father. He knew how mean his father felt.

"This country's full of these old *paisanos*," Carl said to Billy Buck.

"They're damn good men," Billy defended them. "They can work older than white men. I saw one of them a hundred and five years old, and he could still ride a horse. You don't see any white men as old as Gitano walking twenty or thirty miles."

"Oh, they're tough, all right," Carl agreed. "Say, are you standing up for him too? Listen, Billy," he explained, "I'm having a hard enough time keeping this ranch out of the Bank of Italy without taking on anybody else to feed. You know that, Billy."

"Sure, I know," said Billy. "If you was rich, it'd be different."

"That's right, and it isn't like he didn't have relatives to go to. A brother-in-law and cousins right in Monterey. Why should I worry about him?"

Jody sat quietly listening, and he seemed to hear Gitano's gentle voice and its unanswerable, "But I was born here." Gitano was mysterious like the mountains.

There were ranges back as far as you could see, but behind the last range piled up against the sky there was a great unknown country. And Gitano was an old man, until you got to the dull dark eyes. And in behind them was some unknown thing. He didn't ever say enough to let you guess what was inside, under the eyes. Jody felt himself irresistibly drawn toward the bunkhouse. He slipped from his chair while his father was talking and he went out the door without making a sound.

The night was very dark and far-off noises carried in clearly. The hamebells of a wood team sounded from way over the hill on the county road. Jody picked his way across the dark yard. He could see a light through the window of the little room of the bunkhouse. Because the night was secret he walked quietly up to the window and peered in. Gitano sat in the rocking-chair and his back was toward the window. His right arm moved slowly back and forth in front of him. Jody pushed the door open and walked in. Gitano jerked upright and, seizing a piece of deerskin, he tried to throw it over the thing in his lap, but the skin slipped away. Jody stood overwhelmed by the thing in Gitano's hand, a lean and lovely rapier with a golden basket hilt. The blade was like a thin ray of dark light. The hilt was pierced and intricately carved.

"What is it?" Jody demanded.

Gitano only looked at him with resentful eyes, and he picked up the fallen deerskin and firmly wrapped the beautiful blade in it.

Jody put out his hand. "Can't I see it?"

Gitano's eyes smoldered angrily and he shook his head.

"Where'd you get it? Where'd it come from?"

Now Gitano regarded him profoundly, as though he pondered. "I got it from my father."

"Well, where'd he get it?"

Gitano looked down at the long deerskin parcel in his hand. "I don' know."

"Didn't he ever tell you?"

"No."

"What do you do with it?"

Gitano looked slightly surprised. "Nothing. I just keep it."

"Can't I see it again?"

The old man slowly unwrapped the shining blade and let the lamplight slip along it for a moment. Then he wrapped it up again. "You go now. I want to go to bed." He blew out the lamp almost before Jody had closed the door.

As he went back toward the house, Jody knew one thing more sharply than he had ever known anything. He must never tell anyone about the rapier. It would be a dreadful thing to tell anyone about it, for it would destroy some fragile structure of truth. It was a truth that might be shattered by division.

On the way across the dark yard Jody passed Billy Buck. "They're wondering where you are," Billy said.

Jody slipped into the living-room, and his father turned to him. "Where have you been?"

"I just went out to see if I caught any rats in my new trap."

"It's time you went to bed," his father said.

Jody was first at the breakfast table in the morning. Then his father came in, and last, Billy Buck. Mrs. Tiflin looked in from the kitchen.

"Where's the old man, Billy?" she asked.

"I guess he's out walking," Billy said. "I looked in his room and he wasn't there."

"Maybe he started early to Monterey," said Carl. "It's a long walk."

"No," Billy explained. "His sack is in the little room."

After breakfast Jody walked down to the bunkhouse. Flies were flashing about in the sunshine. The ranch seemed especially quiet this morning. When he was sure no one was watching him, Jody went into the little room, and looked into Gitano's sack. An extra pair of long cotton underwear was there, an extra pair of jeans and three pairs of worn socks. Nothing else was in the sack. A sharp loneliness fell on Jody. He walked slowly back toward the house. His father stood on the porch talking to Mrs. Tiflin.

"I guess old Easter's dead at last," he said. "I didn't see him come down to water with the other horses."

In the middle of the morning Jess Taylor from the ridge ranch rode down.

"You didn't sell that old gray crowbait of yours, did you, Carl?"

"No, of course not. Why?"

"Well," Jess said. "I was out this morning early, and I saw a funny thing. I saw an old man on an old horse, no saddle, only a piece of rope for a bridle. He wasn't on the road at all. He was cutting right up straight through the brush. I think he had a gun. At least I saw something shine in his hand."

"That's old Gitano," Carl Tiflin said. "I'll see if any of my guns are missing." He stepped into the house for a second. "Nope, all here. Which way was he heading, Jess?"

"Well, that's the funny thing. He was heading straight back into the mountains."

Carl laughed. "They never get too old to steal," he said. "I guess he just stole old Easter."

"Want to go after him, Carl?"

"Hell no, just save me burying that horse. I wonder

where he got the gun. I wonder what he wants back there."

Jody walked up through the vegetable patch, toward the brush line. He looked searchingly at the towering mountains—ridge after ridge after ridge until at last there was the ocean. For a moment he thought he could see a black speck crawling up the farthest ridge. Jody thought of the rapier and of Gitano. And he thought of the great mountains. A longing caressed him, and it was so sharp that he wanted to cry to get it out of his breast. He lay down in the green grass near the round tub at the brush line. He covered his eyes with his crossed arms and lay there a long time, and he was full of a nameless sorrow.

III. THE PROMISE

IN a mid-afternoon of spring, the little boy Jody walked martially along the brush-lined road toward his home ranch. Banging his knee against the golden lard bucket he used for school lunch, he contrived a good bass drum, while his tongue fluttered sharply against his teeth to fill in snare drums and occasional trumpets. Some time back the other members of the squad that walked so smartly from the school had turned into the various little canyons and taken the wagon roads to their own home ranches. Now Jody marched seemingly alone, with high-lifted knees and pounding feet; but behind him there was a phantom army with great flags and swords, silent but deadly.

The afternoon was green and gold with spring. Underneath the spread branches of the oaks the plants grew pale and tall, and on the hills the. feed was smooth and thick. The sagebrushes shone with new silver leaves and the oaks wore hoods of golden green. Over the hills there hung such a green odor that the horses on the flats galloped madly, and then stopped, wondering; lambs, and even old sheep jumped in the air unexpectedly and landed on stiff legs, and went on eating; young clumsy calves butted their heads together and drew back and butted again.

As the gray and silent army marched past, led by Jody, the animals stopped their feeding and their play and watched it go by.

Suddenly Jody stopped. The gray army halted, bewildered and nervous. Jody went down on his knees. The army stood in long uneasy ranks for a moment, and then, with a soft sigh of sorrow, rose up in a faint gray mist and disappeared. Jody had seen the thorny crown of a horny-toad moving under the dust of the road. His grimy hand went out and grasped the spiked halo and held firmly while the little beast struggled. Then Jody turned the horny-toad over, exposing its pale gold stomach. With a gentle forefinger he stroked the throat and chest until the horny-toad relaxed, until its eyes closed and it lay languorous and asleep.

Jody opened his lunch pail and deposited the first game inside. He moved on now, his knees bent slightly, his shoulders crouched; his bare feet were wise and silent. In his right hand there was a long gray rifle. The brush along the road stirred restively under a new and unexpected population of gray tigers and gray bears. The hunting was very good, for by the time Jody reached the fork of the road where the mail box stood on a post, he had captured two more horny-toads, four little grass lizards, a blue snake, sixteen yellow-winged grasshoppers and a brown damp newt from under a rock. This assortment scrabbled unhappily against the tin of the lunch bucket.

At the road fork the rifle evaporated and the tigers and bears melted from the hillsides. Even the moist and uncomfortable creatures in the lunch pail ceased to exist, for the little red metal flag was up on the mail box, signifying that some postal matter was inside. Jody set his pail on the ground and opened the letter box. There was a Montgomery Ward catalog and a copy of the *Salinas Weekly Journal*. He slammed the box, picked up his lunch pail and trotted over the ridge and down into the cup of the ranch. Past the barn he ran, and past the used-up haystack and the bunkhouse and the cypress tree. He banged through the front screen door of the ranch house calling, "Ma'am, ma'am, there's a catalog."

Mrs. Tiflin was in the kitchen spooning clabbered milk into a cotton bag. She put down her work and rinsed her hands under the tap. "Here in the kitchen, Jody. Here I am."

He ran in and clattered his lunch pail on the sink. "Here it is. Can I open the catalog, ma'am?"

Mrs. Tiflin took up the spoon again and went back to her cottage cheese. "Don't lose it, Jody. Your father will want to see it." She scraped the last of the milk into the bag. "Oh, Jody, your father wants to see you before you go to your chores." She waved a cruising fly from the cheese bag.

Jody closed the new catalog in alarm. "Ma'am?"

"Why don't you ever listen? I say your father wants to see you."

The boy laid the catalog gently on the sink board. "Do you—is it something I did?"

Mrs. Tiflin laughed. "Always a bad conscience. What did you do?"

"Nothing, ma'am," he said lamely. But he couldn't remember, and besides it was impossible to know what action might later be construed as a crime.

His mother hung the full bag on a nail where it could drip into the sink. "He just said he wanted to see you when you got home. He's somewhere down by the barn."

Jody turned and went out the back door. Hearing his mother open the lunch pail and then gasp with rage, a memory stabbed him and he trotted away toward the barn, conscientiously not hearing the angry voice that called him from the house.

Carl Tiflin and Billy Buck, the ranch hand, stood against the lower pasture fence. Each man rested one foot on the lowest bar and both elbows on the top bar. They were talking slowly and aimlessly. In the pasture half a dozen horses nibbled contentedly at the sweet grass. The mare, Nellie, stood backed up against the gate, rubbing her buttocks on the heavy post.

Jody sidled uneasily near. He dragged one foot to give an impression of great innocence and nonchalance. When he arrived beside the men he put one foot on the lowest fence rail, rested his elbows on the second bar and looked into the pasture too. The two men glanced sideways at him.

"I wanted to see you," Carl said in the stern tone he reserved for children and animals.

"Yes, sir," said Jody guiltily.

"Billy, here, says you took good care of the pony before it died."

No punishment was in the air. Jody grew bolder. "Yes, sir, I did."

"Billy says you have a good patient hand with horses."

Jody felt a sudden warm friendliness for the ranch hand.

Billy put in, "He trained that pony as good as anybody I ever seen."

Then Carl Tiflin came gradually to the point. "If you could have another horse would you work for it?"

Jody shivered. "Yes, sir."

"Well, look here, then. Billy says the best way for you to be a good hand with horses is to raise a colt."

"It's the *only* good way," Billy interrupted.

"Now, look here, Jody," continued Carl. "Jess Taylor, up to the ridge ranch, has a fair stallion, but it'll cost five dollars. I'll put up the money, but you'll have to work it out all summer. Will you do that?"

Jody felt that his insides were shriveling. "Yes, sir," he said softly.

"And no complaining? And no forgetting when you're told to do something?"

"Yes, sir."

"Well, all right, then. Tomorrow morning you take Nellie up to the ridge ranch and get her bred. You'll have to take care of her, too, till she throws the colt."

"Yes, sir."

"You better get to the chickens and the wood now."

Jody slid away. In passing behind Billy Buck he very nearly put out his hand to touch the blue-jeaned legs. His shoulders swayed a little with maturity and importance.

He went to his work with unprecedented seriousness. This night he did not dump the can of grain to the chickens so that they had to leap over each other and struggle to get it. No, he spread the wheat so far and so carefully that the hens couldn't find some of it at all. And in the house, after listening to his mother's despair over boys who filled their lunch pails with slimy, suffocated reptiles, and bugs, he promised never to do it again. Indeed, Jody felt that all such foolishness was lost in the past. He was far too grown up ever to put horny-toads in his lunch pail any more. He carried in so much wood and built such a high structure with it that his mother walked in fear of an avalanche of oak. When he was done, when he had gathered eggs that had remained hidden for weeks, Jody walked down again past the cypress tree, and past the bunkhouse toward the pasture. A fat warty toad that looked out at him from under the watering trough had no emotional effect on him at all.

Carl Tiflin and Billy Buck were not in sight, but from a metallic ringing on the other side of the barn Jody knew that Billy Buck was just starting to milk a cow.

The other horses were eating toward the upper end of the pasture, but Nellie continued to rub herself nervously against the post. Jody walked slowly near, saying, "So, girl, so-o, Nellie." The mare's ears went back naughtily and her lips drew away from her yellow teeth. She turned her head around; her eyes were glazed and mad. Jody climbed to the top of the fence and hung his feet over and looked paternally down on the mare.

The evening hovered while he sat there. Bats and nighthawks flicked about. Billy Buck, walking toward the house carrying a full milk bucket, saw Jody and stopped. "It's a long time to wait," he said gently. "You'll get awful tired waiting."

"No I won't, Billy. How long will it be?"

"Nearly a year."

"Well, I won't get tired."

The triangle at the house rang stridently. Jody climbed down from the fence and walked to supper beside Billy Buck. He even put out his hand and took hold of the milk bucket to help carry it.

The next morning after breakfast Carl Tiflin folded a five-dollar bill in a piece of newspaper and pinned the package in the bib pocket of Jody's overalls. Billy Buck haltered the mare Nellie and led her out of the pasture.

"Be careful now," he warned. "Hold her up short here so she can't bite you. She's crazy as a coot."

Jody took hold of the halter leather itself and started

up the hill toward the ridge ranch with Nellie skittering and jerking behind him. In the pasturage along the road the wild oat heads were just clearing their scabbards. The warm morning sun shone on Jody's back so sweetly that he was forced to take a serious stiff-legged hop now and then in spite of his maturity. On the fences the shiny blackbirds with red epaulets clicked their dry call. The meadowlarks sang like water, and the wild doves, concealed among the bursting leaves of the oaks, made a sound of restrained grieving. In the fields the rabbits sat sunning themselves, with only their forked ears showing above the grass heads.

After an hour of steady uphill walking, Jody turned into a narrow road that led up a steeper hill to the ridge ranch. He could see the red roof of the barn sticking up above the oak trees, and he could hear a dog barking unemotionally near the house.

Suddenly Nellie jerked back and nearly freed herself. From the direction of the barn Jody heard a shrill whistling scream and a splintering of wood, and then a man's voice shouting. Nellie reared and whinnied. When Jody held to the halter rope she ran at him with bared teeth. He dropped his hold and scuttled out of the way, into the brush. The high scream came from the oaks again, and Nellie answered it. With hoofs battering the ground the stallion appeared and charged down the hill trailing a broken halter rope. His eyes glittered feverishly. His stiff, erected nostrils were as red as flame. His black, sleek hide shone in the sunlight. The stallion came on so fast that he couldn't stop when he reached the mare. Nellie's ears went back; she whirled and kicked at him as he went by. The stallion spun around and reared. He struck the mare with his front hoof, and while she staggered under the blow, his teeth raked her neck and drew an ooze of blood.

Instantly Nellie's mood changed. She became coquet-tishly feminine. She nibbled his arched neck with her lips. She edged around and rubbed her shoulders against his shoulder. Jody stood half-hidden in the brush and watched. He heard the step of a horse behind him, but before he could turn, a hand caught him by the overall straps and lifted him off the ground. Jess Taylor sat the boy behind him on the horse.

"You might have got killed," he said. "Sundog's a mean devil sometimes. He busted his rope and went right through a gate."

Jody sat quietly, but in a moment he cried, "He'll hurt her, he'll kill her. Get him away!"

Jess chuckled. "She'll be all right. Maybe you'd better climb off and go up to the house for a little. You could get maybe a piece of pie up there."

But Jody shook his head. "She's mine, and the colt's going to be mine. I'm going to raise it up."

Jess nodded. "Yes, that's a good thing. Carl has good sense sometimes."

In a little while the danger was over. Jess lifted Jody down and then caught the stallion by its broken halter rope. And he rode ahead, while Jody followed, leading Nellie.

It was only after he had unpinned and handed over the five dollars, and after he had eaten two pieces of pie, that Jody started for home again. And Nellie followed docilely after him. She was so quiet that Jody climbed on a stump and rode her most of the way home.

The five dollars his father had advanced reduced Jody to peonage for the whole late spring and summer. When the hay was cut he drove a rake. He led the horse that pulled on the Jackson-fork tackle, and when the baler came he drove the circling horse that put pressure on the bales. In addition, Carl Tiflin taught him to milk and put a cow under his care, so that a new chore was added night and morning.

The bay mare Nellie quickly grew complacent. As she walked about the yellowing hillsides or worked at easy tasks, her lips were curled in a perpetual fatuous smile. She moved slowly, with the calm importance of an empress. When she was put to a team, she pulled steadily and unemotionally. Jody went to see her every day. He studied her with critical eyes and saw no change whatever.

One afternoon Billy Buck leaned the many-tined manure fork against the barn wall. He loosened his belt and tucked in his shirt-tail and tightened the belt again. He picked one of the little straws from his hatband and put it in the corner of his mouth. Jody, who was helping Doubletree Mutt, the big serious dog, to dig out a gopher, straightened up as the ranch hand sauntered out of the barn.

"Let's go up and have a look at Nellie," Billy suggested.

Instantly Jody fell into step with him. Doubletree Mutt watched them over his shoulder; then he dug furiously, growled, sounded little sharp yelps to indicate that the gopher was practically caught. When he looked over his shoulder again, and saw that neither Jody nor Billy was interested, he climbed reluctantly out of the hole and followed them up the hill.

The wild oats were ripening. Every head bent sharply under its load of grain, and the grass was dry enough so that it made a swishing sound as Jody and Billy stepped through it. Halfway up the hill they could see Nellie and the iron-gray gelding, Pete, nibbling the heads from the wild oats. When they approached, Nellie looked at them and backed her ears and bobbed her head up and down rebelliously. Billy walked to her and put his hand under her mane and patted her neck, until her ears came forward again and she nibbled delicately at his shirt.

Jody asked, "Do you think she's really going to have a colt?"

Billy rolled the lids back from the mare's eyes with his thumb and forefinger. He felt the lower lip and fingered the black, leathery teats. "I wouldn't be surprised." he said.

"Well, she isn't changed at all. It's three months gone."

Billy rubbed the mare's flat forehead with his knuckle while she grunted with pleasure. "I told you you'd get tired waiting. It'll be five months more before you can even see a sign, and it'll be at least eight months more before she throws the colt, about next January."

Jody sighed deeply. "It's a long time, isn't it?"

"And then it'll be about two years more before you can ride."

Jody cried out in despair, "I'll be grown up."

"Yep, you'll be an old man," said Billy.

"What color do you think the colt'll be?"

"Why, you can't ever tell. The stud is black and the dam is bay. Colt might be black or bay or gray or dappled. You can't tell. Sometimes a black dam might have a white colt."

"Well, I hope it's black, and a stallion."

"If it's a stallion, we'll have to geld it. Your father wouldn't let you have a stallion."

"Maybe he would," Jody said. "I could train him not to be mean."

Billy pursed his lips, and the little straw that had been in the corner of his mouth rolled down to the center. "You can't ever trust a stallion," he said critically. "They're mostly fighting and making trouble. Sometimes when they're feeling funny they won't work. They make the mares uneasy and kick hell out of the geldings. Your father wouldn't let you keep a stallion."

Nellie sauntered away, nibbling the drying grass. Jody skinned the grain from a grass stem and threw the handful into the air, so that each pointed, feathered seed sailed out like a dart. "Tell me how it'll be, Billy. Is it like when the cows have calves?"

"Just about. Mares are a little more sensitive. Sometimes you have to be there to help the mare. And sometimes if it's wrong, you have to——" he paused.

"Have to what, Billy?"

"Have to tear the colt to pieces to get it out, or the mare'll die."

"But it won't be that way this time, will it, Billy?"

"Oh, no. Nellie's thrown good colts."

"Can I be there, Billy? Will you be certain to call me? It's my colt."

"Sure, I'll call you. Of course I will."

"Tell me how it'll be."

"Why, you've seen the cows calving. It's almost the same. The mare starts groaning and stretching, and then, if it's a good right birth, the head and forefeet come out, and the front hoofs kick a hole just the way the calves do. And the colt starts to breathe. It's good to be there, 'cause if its feet aren't right maybe he can't break the sack, and then he might smother."

Jody whipped his leg with a bunch of grass. "We'll have to be there, then, won't we?"

"Oh, we'll be there, all right."

They turned and walked slowly down the hill toward the barn. Jody was tortured with a thing he had to say, although he didn't want to. "Billy," he began miserably, "Billy, you won't let anything happen to the colt, will you?"

And Billy knew he was thinking of the red pony,

Gabilan, and of how it died of strangles. Billy knew he had been infallible before that, and now he was capable of failure. This knowledge made Billy much less sure of himself than he had been. "I can't tell," he said roughly. "All sorts of things might happen, and they wouldn't be my fault. I can't do everything." He felt badly about his lost prestige, and so he said, meanly, "I'll do everything I know, but I won't promise anything. Nellie's a good mare. She's thrown good colts before. She ought to this time." And he walked away from Jody and went into the saddle-room beside the barn, for his feelings were hurt.

Jody traveled often to the brushline behind the house. A rusty iron pipe ran a thin stream of spring water into an old green tub. Where the water spilled over and sank into the ground there was a patch of perpetually green grass. Even when the hills were brown and baked in the summer that little patch was green. The water whined softly into the trough all the year round. This place had grown to be a center-point for Jody. When he had been punished the cool green grass and the singing water soothed him. When he had been mean the biting acid of meanness left him at the brushline. When he sat in the grass and listened to the purling stream, the barriers set up in his mind by the stern day went down to ruin.

On the other hand, the black cypress tree by the bunk-house was as repulsive as the water-tub was dear; for to this tree all the pigs came, sooner or later, to be slaughtered. Pig killing was fascinating, with the screaming and the blood, but it made Jody's heart beat so fast that it hurt him. After the pigs were scalded in the big iron tripod kettle and their skins were scraped and white, Jody had to go to the water-tub to sit in the grass until his heart grew quiet. The water-tub and the black cypress were opposites and enemies.

When Billy left him and walked angrily away, Jody turned up toward the house. He thought of Nellie as he walked, and of the little colt. Then suddenly he saw that he was under the black cypress, under the very singletree where the pigs were hung. He brushed his dry-grass hair off his forehead and hurried on. It seemed to him an unlucky thing to be thinking of his colt in the very slaughter place, especially after what Billy had said. To counteract any evil result of that bad conjunction he walked quickly past the ranch house, through the chicken yard, through the vegetable patch, until he came at last to the brush-line.

He sat down in the green grass. The trilling water sounded in his ears. He looked over the farm buildings and across at the round hills, rich and yellow with grain. He could see Nellie feeding on the slope. As usual the water place eliminated time and distance. Jody saw a black, long-legged colt, butting against Nellie's flanks, demanding milk. And then he saw himself breaking a large colt to halter. All in a few moments the colt grew to be a magnificent animal, deep of chest, with a neck as high and arched as a sea-horse's neck, with a tail that tongued and rippled like black flame. This horse was terrible to everyone but Jody. In the schoolyard the boys begged rides, and Jody smilingly agreed. But no sooner were they mounted than the black demon pitched them off. Why, that was his name, Black Demon! For a moment the trilling water and the grass and the sunshine came back, and then . . .

Sometimes in the night the ranch people, safe in their beds, heard a roar of hoofs go by. They said, "It's Jody, on Demon. He's helping out the sheriff again." And then . . .

The golden dust filled the air in the arena at the Salinas Rodeo. The announcer called the roping contests. When

Jody rode the black horse to the starting chute the other contestants shrugged and gave up first place, for it was well known that Jody and Demon could rope and throw and tie a steer a great deal quicker than any róping team of two men could. Jody was not a boy any more, and Demon was not a horse. The two together were one glorious individual. And then . . .

The President wrote a letter and asked them to help catch a bandit in Washington. Jody settled himself comfortably in the grass. The little stream of water whined into the mossy tub.

The year passed slowly on. Time after time Jody gave up his colt for lost. No change had taken place in Nellie. Carl Tiflin still drove her to a light cart, and she pulled on a hay rake and worked the Jackson-fork tackle when the hay was being put into the barn.

The summer passed, and the warm bright autumn. And then the frantic morning winds began to twist along the ground, and a chill came into the air, and the poison oak turned red. One morning in September, when he had finished his breakfast, Jody's mother called him into the kitchen. She was pouring boiling water into a bucket full of dry midlings and stirring the materials to a steaming paste.

"Yes, ma'am?" Jody asked.

"Watch how I do it. You'll have to do it after this every other morning."

"Well, what is it?"

"Why, it's warm mash for Nellie. It'll keep her in good shape."

Jody rubbed his forehead with a knuckle. "Is she all right?" he asked timidly.

Mrs. Tiflin put down the kettle and stirred the mash with a wooden paddle. "Of course she's all right, only you've got to take better care of her from now on. Here, take this breakfast out to her!"

Jody seized the bucket and ran, down past the bunk-house, past the barn, with the heavy bucket banging against his knees. He found Nellie playing with the water in the trough, pushing waves and tossing her head so that the water slopped out on the ground.

Jody climbed the fence and set the bucket of steaming mash beside her. Then he stepped back to look at her. And she was changed. Her stomach was swollen. When she moved, her feet touched the ground gently. She buried her nose in the bucket and gobbled the hot break-fast. And when she had finished and had pushed the bucket around the ground with her nose a little, she stepped quietly over to Jody and rubbed her cheek against him.

Billy Buck came out of the saddle-room and walked over. "Starts fast when it starts, doesn't it?"

"Did it come all at once?"

"Oh, no, you just stopped looking for a while." He pulled her head around toward Jody. "She's goin' to be nice, too. See how nice her eyes are! Some mares get mean, but when they turn nice, they just love every-thing." Nellie slipped her head under Billy's arm and rubbed her neck up and down between his arm and his side. "You better treat her awful nice now," Billy said.

"How long will it be?" Jody demanded breathlessly.

The man counted in whispers on his fingers. "About three months," he said aloud. "You can't tell exactly. Sometimes it's eleven months to the day, but it might be two weeks early, or a month late, without hurting any-thing."

Jody looked hard at the ground. "Billy," he began nervously, "Billy, you'll call me when it's getting born, won't you? You'll let me be there, won't you?"

Billy bit the tip of Nellie's ear with his front teeth. "Carl says he wants you to start right at the start. That's the only way to learn. Nobody can tell you anything. Like my old man did with me about the saddle blanket. He was a government packer when I was your size, and I helped him some. One day I left a wrinkle in my saddle blanket and made a saddle-sore. My old man didn't give me hell at all. But the next morning he saddled me up with a forty-pound stock saddle. I had to lead my horse and carry that saddle over a whole damn mountain in the sun. It darn near killed me, but I never left no wrinkles in a blanket again. I couldn't. I never in my life since then put on a blanket but I felt that saddle on my back."

Jody reached up a hand and took hold of Nellie's mane. "You'll tell me what to do about everything, won't you? I guess you know everything about horses, don't you?"

Billy laughed. "Why I'm half horse myself, you see," he said. "My ma died when I was born, and being my old man was a government packer in the mountains, and no cows around most of the time, why he just gave me mostly mare's milk." He continued seriously, "And horses know that. Don't you know it, Nellie?"

The mare turned her head and looked full into his eyes for a moment, and this is a thing horses practically never do. Billy was proud and sure of himself now. He boasted a little. "I'll see you get a good colt. I'll start you right. And if you do like I say, you'll have the best horse in the county."

That made Jody feel warm and proud, too; so proud that when he went back to the house he bowed his legs and swayed his shoulders as horsemen do. And he whispered, "Whoa, you Black Demon, you! Steady down there and keep your feet on the ground."

The winter fell sharply. A few preliminary gusty showers, and then a strong steady rain. The hills lost their straw color and blackened under the water, and the winter streams scrambled noisily down the canyons. The mushrooms and puffballs popped up and the new grass started before Christmas.

But this year Christmas was not the central day to Jody. Some undetermined time in January had become the axis day around which the months swung. When the rains fell, he put Nellie in a box stall and fed her warm food every morning and curried her and brushed her.

The mare was swelling so greatly that Jody became alarmed. "She'll pop wide open," he said to Billy.

Billy laid his strong square hand against Nellie's swollen abdomen. "Feel here," he said quietly. "You can feel it move. I guess it would surprise you if there were twin colts."

"You don't think so?" Jody cried. "You don't think it will be twins, do you, Billy?"

"No, I don't, but it does happen, sometimes."

During the first two weeks of January it rained steadily. Jody spent most of his time, when he wasn't in school, in the box stall with Nellie. Twenty times a day he put his hand on her stomach to feel the colt move. Nellie became more and more gentle and friendly to him. She rubbed her nose on him. She whinnied softly when he walked into the barn.

Carl Tiflin came to the barn with Jody one day. He looked admiringly at the groomed bay coat, and he felt the firm flesh over ribs and shoulders. "You've done a good job," he said to Jody. And this was the greatest praise he knew how to give. Jody was tight with pride for hours afterward.

The fifteenth of January came, and the colt was not

born. And the twentieth came; a lump of fear began to form in Jody's stomach. "Is it all right?" he demanded of Billy.

"Oh, sure."

And again, "Are you sure it's going to be all right?"

Billy stroked the mare's neck. She swayed her head uneasily. "I told you it wasn't always the same time, Jody. You just have to wait."

When the end of the month arrived with no birth, Jody grew frantic. Nellie was so big that her breath came heavily, and her ears were close together and straight up, as though her head ached. Jody's sleep grew restless, and his dreams confused.

On the night of the second of February he awakened crying. His mother called to him, "Jody, you're dreaming. Wake up and start over again."

But Jody was filled with terror and desolation. He lay quietly a few moments, waiting for his mother to go back to sleep, and then he slipped his clothes on, and crept out in his bare feet.

The night was black and thick. A little misting rain fell. The cypress tree and the bunkhouse loomed and then dropped back into the mist. The barn door screeched as he opened it, a thing it never did in the daytime. Jody went to the rack and found a lantern and a tin box of matches. He lighted the wick and walked down the long straw-covered aisle to Nellie's stall. She was standing up. Her whole body weaved from side to side. Jody called to her, "So, Nellie, so-o, Nellie," but she did not stop her swaying nor look around. When he stepped into the stall and touched her on the shoulder she shivered under his hand. Then Billy Buck's voice came from the hayloft right above the stall.

"Jody, what are you doing?"

Jody started back and turned miserable eyes up toward

the nest where Billy was lying in the hay. "Is she all right, do you think?"

"Why sure, I think so."

"You won't let anything happen, Billy, you're sure you won't?"

Billy growled down at him, "I told you I'd call you, and I will. Now you get back to bed and stop worrying that mare. She's got enough to do without you worrying her."

Jody cringed, for he had never heard Billy speak in such a tone. "I only thought I'd come and see," he said. "I woke up."

Billy softened a little then. "Well, you get to bed. I don't want you bothering her. I told you I'd get you a good colt. Get along now."

Jody walked slowly out of the barn. He blew out the lantern and set it in the rack. The blackness of the night, and the chilled mist struck him and enfolded him. He wished he believed everything Billy said as he had before the pony died. It was a moment before his eyes, blinded by the feeble lantern-flame, could make any form of the darkness. The damp ground chilled his bare feet. At the cypress tree the roosting turkeys chattered a little in alarm, and the two good dogs responded to their duty and came charging out, barking to frighten away the coyotes they thought were prowling under the tree.

As he crept through the kitchen, Jody stumbled over a chair. Carl called from his bedroom, "Who's there? What's the matter there?"

And Mrs. Tiflin said sleepily, "What's the matter, Carl?"

The next second Carl came out of the bedroom carrying a candle, and found Jody before he could get into bed. "What are you doing out?"

Jody turned shyly away. "I was down to see the mare."

For a moment anger at being awakened fought with approval in Jody's father. "Listen," he said, finally, "there's not a man in this country that knows more about colts than Billy. You leave it to him."

Words burst out of Jody's mouth. "But the pony died——"

"Don't you go blaming that on him," Carl said sternly. "If Billy can't save a horse, it can't be saved."

Mrs. Tiflin called, "Make him clean his feet and go to bed, Carl. He'll be sleepy all day tomorrow."

It seemed to Jody that he had just closed his eyes to try to go to sleep when he was shaken violently by the shoulder. Billy Buck stood beside him, holding a lantern in his hand. "Get up," he said. "Hurry up." He turned and walked quickly out of the room.

Mrs. Tiflin called, "What's the matter? Is that you, Billy?"

"Yes, ma'am."

"Is Nellie ready?"

"Yes, ma'am."

"All right, I'll get up and heat some water in case you need it."

Jody jumped into his clothes so quickly that he was out the back door before Billy's swinging lantern was halfway to the barn. There was a rim of dawn on the mountain-tops, but no light had penetrated into the cup of the ranch yet. Jody ran frantically after the lantern and caught up to Billy just as he reached the barn. Billy hung the lantern to a nail on the stall-side and took off his blue denim coat. Jody saw that he wore only a sleeveless shirt under it.

Nellie was standing rigid and stiff. While they watched, she crouched. Her whole body was wrung with a spasm. The spasm passed. But in a few moments it started over again, and passed.

Billy muttered nervously, "There's something wrong." His bare hand disappeared. "Oh, Jesus," he said. "It's wrong."

The spasm came again, and this time Billy strained, and the muscles stood out on his arm and shoulder. He heaved strongly, his forehead beaded with perspiration. Nellie cried with pain. Billy was muttering, "It's wrong. I can't turn it. It's way wrong. It's turned all around wrong."

He glared wildly toward Jody. And then his fingers made a careful, careful diagnosis. His cheeks were growing tight and gray. He looked for a long questioning minute at Jody standing back of the stall. Then Billy stepped to the rack under the manure window and picked up a horseshoe hammer with his wet right hand.

"Go outside, Jody," he said.

The boy stood still and stared dully at him.

"Go outside, I tell you. It'll be too late."

Jody didn't move.

Then Billy walked quickly to Nellie's head. He cried, "Turn you face away, damn you, turn your face."

This time Jody obeyed. His head turned sideways. He heard Billy whispering hoarsely in the stall. And then he heard a hollow crunch of bone. Nellie chuckled shrilly. Jody looked back in time to see the hammer rise and fall again on the flat forehead. Then Nellie fell heavily to her side and quivered for a moment.

Billy jumped to the swollen stomach; his big pocket-knife was in his hand. He lifted the skin and drove the knife in. He sawed and ripped at the tough belly. The air filled with the sick odor of warm living entrails. The other horses reared back against their halter chains and squealed and kicked.

Billy dropped the knife. Both of his arms plunged into the terrible ragged hole and dragged out a big, white, dripping bundle. His teeth tore a hole in the covering. A little black head appeared through the tear, and little slick, wet ears. A gurgling breath was drawn, and then another. Billy shucked off the sac and found his knife and cut the string. For a·moment he held the little black colt in his arms and looked at it. And then he walked slowly over and laid it in the straw at Jody's feet.

Billy's face and arms and chest were dripping red. His body shivered and his teeth chattered. His voice was gone; he spoke in a throaty whisper. "There's your colt. I promised. And there it is. I had to do it—had to." He stopped and looked over his shoulder into the box stall. "Go get hot water and a sponge," he whispered. "Wash him and dry him the way his mother would. You'll have to feed him by hand. But there's your colt, the way I promised."

Jody stared stupidly at the wet, panting foal. It stretched out its chin and tried to raise its head. Its blank eyes were navy blue.

"God damn you," Billy shouted, "will you go now for the water? *Will you go?*"

Then Jody turned and trotted out of the barn into the dawn. He ached from his throat to his stomach. His legs were stiff and heavy. He tried to be glad because of the colt, but the bloody face, and the haunted, tired eyes of Billy Buck hung in the air ahead of him.

IV. THE LEADER OF THE PEOPLE

ON Saturday afternoon Billy Buck, the ranch-hand, raked together the last of the old year's haystack and pitched small forkfuls over the wire fence to a few mildly interested cattle. High in the air small clouds like puffs of cannon smoke were driven eastward by the March wind. The wind could be heard whishing in the brush on the ridge crests, but no breath of it penetrated down into the ranch-cup.

The little boy, Jody, emerged from the house eating a thick piece of buttered bread. He saw Billy working on the last of the haystack. Jody tramped down scuffing his shoes in a way he had been told was destructive to good shoe-leather. A flock of white pigeons flew out of the black cypress tree as Jody passed, and circled the tree and landed again. A half-grown tortoise-shell cat leaped from the bunkhouse porch, galloped on stiff legs across the road, whirled and galloped back again. Jody picked up a stone to help the game along, but he was too late, for the cat was under the porch before the stone could be discharged. He threw the stone into the cypress tree and started the white pigeons on another whirling flight.

Arriving at the used-up haystack, the boy leaned against the barbed wire fence. "Will that be all of it, do you think?" he asked.

The middle-aged ranch-hand stopped his careful raking and stuck his fork into the ground. He took off his black hat and smoothed down his hair. "Nothing left of it that isn't soggy from ground moisture," he said. He replaced his hat and rubbed his dry leathery hands together.

"Ought to be plenty mice," Jody suggested.

"Lousy with them," said Billy. "Just crawling with mice."

"Well, maybe, when you get all through, I could call the dogs and hunt the mice."

"Sure, I guess you could," said Billy Buck. He lifted a forkful of the damp ground-hay and threw it into the air. Instantly three mice leaped out and burrowed frantically under the hay again.

Jody sighed with satisfaction. Those plump, sleek, arrogant mice were doomed. For eight months they had lived and multiplied in the haystack. They had been immune from cats, from traps, from poison and from Jody. They had grown smug in their security, overbearing and fat. Now the time of disaster had come; they would not survive another day.

Billy looked up at the top of the hills that surrounded the ranch. "Maybe you better ask your father before you do it," he suggested.

"Well, where is he? I'll ask him now."

"He rode up to the ridge ranch after dinner. He'll be back pretty soon."

Jody slumped against the fence post. "I don't think he'd care."

As Billy went back to his work he said ominously, "You'd better ask him anyway. You know how he is."

Jody did know. His father, Carl Tiflin, insisted upon giving permission for anything that was done on the ranch, whether it was important or not. Jody sagged farther against the post until he was sitting on the ground. He looked up at the little puffs of wind-driven cloud. "Is it like to rain, Billy?"

"It might. The wind's good for it, but not strong enough."

"Well, I hope it don't rain until after I kill those damn mice." He looked over his shoulder to see whether Billy had noticed the mature profanity. Billy worked on without comment.

Jody turned back and looked at the side-hill where the road from the outside world came down. The hill was washed with lean March sunshine. Silver thistles, blue lupins and a few poppies bloomed among the sage bushes. Halfway up the hill Jody could see Doubletree Mutt, the black dog, digging in a squirrel hole. He paddled for a while and then paused to kick bursts of dirt out between his hind legs, and he dug with an earnestness which belied the knowledge he must have had that no dog had ever caught a squirrel by digging in a hole.

Suddenly, while Jody watched, the black dog stiffened, and backed out of the hole and looked up the hill toward the cleft in the ridge where the road came through. Jody looked up too. For a moment Carl Tiflin on horseback stood out against the pale sky and then he moved down the road toward the house. He carried something white in his hand.

The boy started to his feet. "He's got a letter," Jody cried. He trotted away toward the ranch house, for the letter would probably be read aloud and he wanted to be there. He reached the house before his father did, and ran in. He heard Carl dismount from his creaking saddle and slap the horse on the side to send it to the barn where Billy would unsaddle it and turn it out.

Jody ran into the kitchen. "We got a letter!" he cried.

His mother looked up from a pan of beans. "Who has?"

"Father has. I saw it in his hand."

Carl strode into the kitchen then, and Jody's mother asked, "Who's the letter from, Carl?"

He frowned quickly. "How did you know there was a letter?"

She nodded her head in the boy's direction. "Big-Britches Jody told me."

Jody was embarrassed.

His father looked down at him contemptuously. "He *is*

getting to be a Big-Britches," Carl said. "He's minding everybody's business but his own. Got his big nose into everything."

Mrs. Tiflin relented a little. "Well, he hasn't enough to keep him busy. Who's the letter from?"

Carl still frowned on Jody. "I'll keep him busy if he isn't careful." He held out a sealed letter. "I guess it's from your father."

Mrs. Tiflin took a hairpin from her head and slit open the flap. Her lips pursed judiciously. Jody saw her eyes snap back and forth over the lines. "He says," she translated, "he says he's going to drive out Saturday to stay for a little while. Why, this is Saturday. The letter must have been delayed." She looked at the postmark. "This was mailed day before yesterday. It should have been here yesterday." She looked up questioningly at her husband, and then her face darkened angrily. "Now what have you got that look on you for? He doesn't come often."

Carl turned his eyes away from her anger. He could be stern with her most of the time, but when occasionally her temper arose, he could not combat it.

"What's the matter with you?" she demanded again.

In his explanation there was a tone of apology Jody himself might have used. "It's just that he talks," Carl said lamely. "Just talks."

"Well, what of it? You talk yourself."

"Sure I do. But your father only talks about one thing."

"Indians!" Jody broke in excitedly. "Indians and crossing the plains!"

Carl turned fiercely on him. "You get out, Mr. Big-Britches! Go on, now! Get out!"

Jody went miserably out the back door and closed the screen with elaborate quietness. Under the kitchen window his shamed, downcast eyes fell upon a curiously shaped stone, a stone of such fascination that he squatted down and picked it up and turned it over in his hands.

The voices came clearly to him through the open kitchen window. "Jody's damn well right," he heard his father say. "Just Indians and crossing the plains. I've heard that story about how the horses got driven off about a thousand times. He just goes on and on, and he never changes a word in the things he tells."

When Mrs. Tiflin answered her tone was so changed that Jody, outside the window, looked up from his study of the stone. Her voice had become soft and explanatory. Jody knew how her face would have changed to match the tone. She said quietly, "Look at it this way, Carl. That was the big thing in my father's life. He led a wagon train clear across the plains to the coast, and when it was finished, his life was done. It was a big thing to do, but it didn't last long enough. Look!" she continued, "it's as though he was born to do that, and after he finished it, there wasn't anything more for him to do but think about it and talk about it. If there'd been any farther west to go, he'd have gone. He's told me so himself. But at last there was the ocean. He lives right by the ocean where he had to stop."

She had caught Carl, caught him and entangled him in her soft tone.

"I've seen him," he agreed quietly. "He goes down and stares off west over the ocean." His voice sharpened a little. "And then he goes up to the Horseshoe Club in Pacific Grove, and he tells people how the Indians drove off the horses."

She tried to catch him again. "Well, it's everything to him. You might be patient with him and pretend to listen."

Carl turned impatiently away. "Well, if it gets too bad,

I can always go down to the bunkhouse and sit with
Billy," he said irritably. He walked through the house and
slammed the front door after him.

Jody ran to his chores. He dumped the grain to the
chickens without chasing any of them. He gathered the
eggs from the nests. He trotted into the house with the
wood and interlaced it so carefully in the wood-box that
two armloads seemed to fill it to overflowing.

His mother had finished the beans by now. She stirred
up the fire and brushed off the stove-top with a turkey
wing. Jody peered cautiously at her to see whether any
rancor toward him remained. "Is he coming today?" Jody
asked.

"That's what his letter said."

"Maybe I better walk up the road to meet him."

Mrs. Tiflin clanged the stove-lid shut. "That would be
nice," she said. "He'd probably like to be met."

"I guess I'll just do it then."

Outside, Jody whistled shrilly to the dogs. "Come on
up the hill," he commanded. The two dogs waved their
tails and ran ahead. Along the roadside the sage had
tender new tips. Jody tore off some pieces and rubbed
them on his hands until the air was filled with the sharp
wild smell. With a rush the dogs leaped from the road and
yapped into the brush after a rabbit. That was the last
Jody saw of them, for when they failed to catch the rabbit, they went back home.

Jody plodded on up the hill toward the ridge top. When
he reached the little cleft where the road came through,
the afternoon wind struck him and blew up his hair and
ruffled his shirt. He looked down on the little hills and
ridges below and then out at the huge green Salinas Valley. He could see the white town of Salinas far out in the
flat and the flash of its windows under the waning sun.
Directly below him, in an oak tree, a crow congress had

convened. The tree was black with crows all cawing at once.

Then Jody's eyes followed the wagon road down from the ridge where he stood, and lost it behind a hill, and picked it up again on the other side. On that distant stretch he saw a cart slowly pulled by a bay horse. It disappeared behind the hill. Jody sat down on the ground and watched the place where the cart would reappear again. The wind sang on the hilltops and the puff-ball clouds hurried eastward.

Then the cart came into sight and stopped. A man dressed in black dismounted from the seat and walked to the horse's head. Although it was so far away, Jody knew he had unhooked the check-rein, for the horse's head dropped forward. The horse moved on, and the man walked slowly up the hill beside it. Jody gave a glad cry and ran down the road toward them. The squirrels bumped along off the road, and a road-runner flirted its tail and raced over the edge of the hill and sailed out like a glider.

Jody tried to leap into the middle of his shadow at every step. A stone rolled under his foot and he went down. Around a little bend he raced, and there, a short distance ahead, were his grandfather and the cart. The boy dropped from his unseemly running and approached at a dignified walk.

The horse plodded stumble-footedly up the hill and the old man walked beside it. In the lowering sun their giant shadows flickered darkly behind them. The grandfather was dressed in a black broadcloth suit and he wore kid congress gaiters and a black tie on a short, hard collar. He carried his black slouch hat in his hand. His white beard was cropped close and his white eyebrows overhung his eyes like mustaches. The blue eyes were sternly merry. About the whole face and figure there was a granite dignity, so that every motion seemed an impossible thing. Once at rest, it seemed the old man would be stone, would never move again. His steps were slow and certain. Once made, no step could ever be retraced; once headed in a direction, the path would never bend nor the pace increase nor slow.

When Jody appeared around the bend, Grandfather waved his hat slowly in welcome, and he called, "Why, Jody! Come down to meet me, have you?"

Jody sidled near and turned and matched his step to the old man's step and stiffened his body and dragged his heels a little. "Yes, sir," he said. "We got your letter only today."

"Should have been here yesterday," said Grandfather. "It certainly should. How are all the folks?"

"They're fine, sir." He hesitated and then suggested shyly, "Would you like to come on a mouse hunt tomorrow, sir?"

"Mouse hunt, Jody?" Grandfather chuckled. "Have the people of this generation come down to hunting mice? They aren't very strong, the new people, but I hardly thought mice would be game for them."

"No, sir. It's just play. The haystack's gone. I'm going to drive out the mice to the dogs. And you can watch, or even beat the hay a little."

The stern, merry eyes turned down on him. "I see. You don't eat them, then. You haven't come to that yet."

Jody explained, "The dogs eat them, sir. It wouldn't be much like hunting Indians, I guess."

"No, not much—but then later, when the troops were hunting Indians and shooting children and burning teepees, it wasn't much different from your mouse hunt."

They topped the rise and started down into the ranch cup, and they lost the sun from their shoulders. "You've grown," Grandfather said. "Nearly an inch, I should say."

"More," Jody boasted. "Where they mark me on the door, I'm up more than an inch since Thanksgiving even."

Grandfather's rich throaty voice said, "Maybe you're getting too much water and turning to pith and stalk. Wait until you head out, and then we'll see."

Jody looked quickly into the old man's face to see whether his feelings should be hurt, but there was no will to injure, no punishing nor putting-in-your-place light in the keen blue eyes. "We might kill a pig," Jody suggested.

"Oh, no! I couldn't let you do that. You're just humoring me. It isn't the time and you know it."

"You know Riley, the big boar, sir?"

"Yes. I remember Riley well."

"Well, Riley ate a hole into that same haystack, and it fell down on him and smothered him."

"Pigs do that when they can," said Grandfather.

"Riley was a nice pig, for a boar, sir. I rode him sometimes, and he didn't mind."

A door slammed at the house below them, and they saw Jody's mother standing on the porch waving her apron in welcome. And they saw Carl Tiflin walking up from the barn to be at the house for the arrival.

The sun had disappeared from the hills by now. The blue smoke from the house chimney hung in flat layers in the purpling ranch-cup. The puff-ball clouds, dropped by the falling wind, hung listlessly in the sky.

Billy Buck came out of the bunkhouse and flung a wash basin of soapy water on the ground. He had been shaving in mid-week, for Billy held Grandfather in reverence, and Grandfather said that Billy was one of the few men of the new generation who had not gone soft. Although Billy was in middle age, Grandfather considered him a boy. Now Billy was hurrying toward the house too.

When Jody and Grandfather arrived, the three were waiting for them in front of the yard gate.

Carl said, "Hello, sir. We've been looking for you."

Mrs. Tiflin kissed Grandfather on the side of his beard, and stood still while his big hand patted her shoulder. Billy shook hands solemnly, grinning under his straw mustache. "I'll put up your horse," said Billy, and he led the rig away.

Grandfather watched him go, and then, turning back to the group, he said as he had said a hundred times before, "There's a good boy. I knew his father, old Mule-tail Buck. I never knew why they called him Mule-tail except he packed mules."

Mrs. Tiflin turned and led the way into the house. "How long are you going to stay, Father? Your letter didn't say."

"Well, I don't know. I thought I'd stay about two weeks. But I never stay as long as I think I'm going to."

In a short while they were sitting at the white oilcloth table eating their supper. The lamp with the tin reflector hung over the table. Outside the dining-room windows the big moths battered softly against the glass.

Grandfather cut his steak into tiny pieces and chewed slowly. "I'm hungry," he said. "Driving out here got my appetite up. It's like when we were crossing. We all got so hungry every night we could hardly wait to let the meat get done. I could eat about five pounds of buffalo meat every night."

"It's moving around does it," said Billy. "My father was a government packer. I helped him when I was a kid. Just the two of us could about clean up a deer's ham."

"I knew your father, Billy," said Grandfather. "A fine man he was. They called him Mule-tail Buck. I don't know why except he packed mules."

"That was it," Billy agreed. "He packed mules."

Grandfather put down his knife and fork and looked around the table. "I remember one time we ran out of meat—" His voice dropped to a curious low sing-song, dropped into a tonal groove the story had worn for itself. "There was no buffalo, no antelope, not even rabbits. The hunters couldn't even shoot a coyote. That was the time for the leader to be on the watch. I was the leader, and I kept my eyes open. Know why? Well, just the minute the people began to get hungry they'd start slaughtering the team oxen. Do you believe that? I've heard of parties that just ate up their draft cattle. Started from the middle and worked toward the ends. Finally they'd eat the lead pair, and then the wheelers. The leader of a party had to keep them from doing that."

In some manner a big moth got into the room and circled the hanging kerosene lamp. Billy got up and tried to clap it between his hands. Carl struck with a cupped palm and caught the moth and broke it. He walked to the window and dropped it out.

"As I was saying," Grandfather began again, but Carl interrupted him. "You'd better eat some more meat. All the rest of us are ready for our pudding."

Jody saw a flash of anger in his mother's eyes. Grandfather picked up his knife and fork. "I'm pretty hungry, all right," he said. "I'll tell you about that later."

When supper was over, when the family and Billy Buck sat in front of the fireplace in the other room, Jody anxiously watched Grandfather. He saw the signs he knew. The bearded head leaned forward; the eyes lost their sternness and looked wonderingly into the fire; the big lean fingers laced themselves on the black knees. "I wonder," he began, "I just wonder whether I ever told you how those thieving Piutes drove off thirty-five of our horses."

"I think you did," Carl interrupted. "Wasn't it just before you went up into the Tahoe country?"

Grandfather turned quickly toward his son-in-law.

"That's right. I guess I must have told you that story."

"Lots of times," Carl said cruelly, and he avoided his wife's eyes. But he felt the angry eyes on him, and he said, " 'Course I'd like to hear it again."

Grandfather looked back at the fire. His fingers unlaced and laced again. Jody knew how he felt, how his insides were collapsed and empty. Hadn't Jody been called a Big-Britches that very afternoon? He arose to heroism and opened himself to the term Big-Britches again. "Tell about Indians," he said softly.

Grandfather's eyes grew stern again. "Boys always want to hear about Indians. It was a job for men, but boys want to hear about it. Well, let's see. Did I ever tell you how I wanted each wagon to carry a long iron plate?"

Everyone but Jody remained silent. Jody said, "No. You didn't."

"Well, when the Indians attacked, we always put the wagons in a circle and fought from between the wheels. I thought that if every wagon carried a long plate with rifle holes, the men could stand the plates on the outside of the wheels when the wagons were in the circle and they would be protected. It would save lives and that would make up for the extra weight of the iron. But of course the party wouldn't do it. No party had done it before and they couldn't see why they should go to the expense. They lived to regret it, too."

Jody looked at his mother, and knew from her expression that she was not listening at all. Carl picked at a callus on his thumb and Billy Buck watched a spider crawling up the wall.

Grandfather's tone dropped into its narrative groove again. Jody knew in advance exactly what words would fall. The story droned on, speeded up for the attack, grew sad over the wounds, struck a dirge at the burials on the great plains. Jody sat quietly watching Grandfather. The stern blue eyes were detached. He looked as though he were not very interested in the story himself.

When it was finished, when the pause had been politely respected as the frontier of the story, Billy Buck stood up and stretched and hitched his trousers. "I guess I'll turn in," he said. Then he faced Grandfather. "I've got an old powder horn and a cap and ball pistol down to the bunkhouse. Did I ever show them to you?"

Grandfather nodded slowly. "Yes, I think you did, Billy. Reminds me of a pistol I had when I was leading the people across." Billy stood politely until the little story was done, and then he said, "Good night," and went out of the house.

Carl Tiflin tried to turn the conversation then. "How's the country between here and Monterey? I've heard it's pretty dry."

"It is dry," said Grandfather. "There's not a drop of water in the Laguna Seca. But it's a long pull from '87. The whole country was powder then, and in '61 I believe all the coyotes starved to death. We had fifteen inches of rain this year."

"Yes, but it all came too early. We could do with some now." Carl's eye fell on Jody. "Hadn't you better be getting to bed?"

Jody stood up obediently. "Can I kill the mice in the old haystack, sir?"

"Mice? Oh! Sure, kill them all off. Billy said there isn't any good hay left."

Jody exchanged a secret and satisfying look with Grandfather. "I'll kill every one tomorrow," he promised.

Jody lay in his bed and thought of the impossible world of Indians and buffaloes, a world that had ceased to be forever. He wished he could have been living in the heroic time, but he knew he was not of heroic timber. No one living now, save possibly Billy Buck, was worthy to do the things that had been done. A race of giants had lived then, fearless men, men of a staunchness unknown in this day. Jody thought of the wide plains and of the wagons moving across like centipedes. He thought of Grandfather on a huge white horse, marshaling the people. Across his mind marched the great phantoms, and they marched off the earth and they were gone.

He came back to the ranch for a moment, then. He heard the dull rushing sound that space and silence make. He heard one of the dogs, out in the doghouse, scratching a flea and bumping his elbow against the floor with every stroke. Then the wind arose again and the black cypress groaned and Jody went to sleep.

He was up half an hour before the triangle sounded for breakfast. His mother was rattling the stove to make the flames roar when Jody went through the kitchen. "You're up early," she said. "Where are you going?"

"Out to get a good stick. We're going to kill the mice today."

"Who is 'we'?"

"Why, Grandfather and I."

"So you've got him in it. You always like to have someone in with you in case there's blame to share."

"I'll be right back," said Jody. "I just want to have a good stick ready for after breakfast."

He closed the screen door after him and went out into the cool blue morning. The birds were noisy in the dawn and the ranch cats came down from the hill like blunt snakes. They had been hunting gophers in the dark, and although the four cats were full of gopher meat, they sat in a semi-circle at the back door and mewed piteously for milk. Doubletree Mutt and Smasher moved sniffing along the edge of the brush, performing the duty with rigid ceremony, but when Jody whistled, their heads jerked up and their tails waved. They plunged down to him, wriggling their skins and yawning. Jody patted their heads seriously, and moved on to the weathered scrap pile. He selected an old broom handle and a short piece of inch-square scrap wood. From his pocket he took a shoelace and tied the ends of the sticks loosely together to make a flail. He whistled his new weapon through the air and struck the ground experimentally, while the dogs leaped aside and whined with apprehension.

Jody turned and started down past the house toward the old haystack ground to look over the field of slaughter, but Billy Buck, sitting patiently on the back steps, called to him, "You better come back. It's only a couple of minutes till breakfast."

Jody changed his course and moved toward the house. He leaned his flail against the steps. "That's to drive the mice out," he said. "I'll bet they're fat. I'll bet they don't know what's going to happen to them today."

"No, nor you either," Billy remarked philosophically, "nor me, nor anyone."

Jody was staggered by this thought. He knew it was true. His imagination twitched away from the mouse hunt. Then his mother came out on the back porch and struck the triangle, and all thoughts fell in a heap.

Grandfather hadn't appeared at the table when they sat down. Billy nodded at his empty chair. "He's all right? He isn't sick?"

"He takes a long time to dress," said Mrs. Tiflin. "He combs his whiskers and rubs up his shoes and brushes his clothes."

Carl scattered sugar on his mush. "A man that's led a wagon train across the plains has got to be pretty careful how he dresses."

Mrs. Tiflin turned on him. "Don't do that, Carl! Please don't!" There was more of threat than of request in her tone. And the threat irritated Carl.

"Well, how many times do I have to listen to the story of the iron plates, and the thirty-five horses? That time's done. Why can't he forget it, now it's done?" He grew angrier while he talked, and his voice rose. "Why does he have to tell them over and over? He came across the plains. All right! Now it's finished. Nobody wants to hear about it over and over."

The door into the kitchen closed softly. The four at the table sat frozen. Carl laid his mush spoon on the table and touched his chin with his fingers.

Then the kitchen door opened and Grandfather walked in. His mouth smiled tightly and his eyes were squinted. "Good morning," he said, and he sat down and looked at his mush dish.

Carl could not leave it there. "Did—did you hear what I said?"

Grandfather jerked a little nod.

"I don't know what got into me, sir. I didn't mean it. I was just being funny."

Jody glanced in shame at his mother, and he saw that she was looking at Carl, and that she wasn't breathing. It was an awful thing that he was doing. He was tearing himself to pieces to talk like that. It was a terrible thing to him to retract a word, but to retract it in shame was infinitely worse.

Grandfather looked sidewise. "I'm trying to get right side up," he said gently. "I'm not being mad. I don't mind what you said, but it might be true, and I would mind that."

"It isn't true," said Carl. "I'm not feeling well this morning. I'm sorry I said it."

"Don't be sorry, Carl. An old man doesn't see things sometimes. Maybe you're right. The crossing is finished. Maybe it should be forgotten, now it's done."

Carl got up from the table. "I've had enough to eat. I'm

going to work. Take your time, Billy!" He walked quickly out of the dining-room. Billy gulped the rest of his food and followed soon after. But Jody could not leave his chair.

"Won't you tell any more stories?" Jody asked.

"Why, sure I'll tell them, but only when—I'm sure people want to hear them."

"I like to hear them, sir."

"Oh! Of course you do, but you're a little boy. It was a job for men, but only little boys like to hear about it."

Jody got up from his place. "I'll wait outside for you, sir. I've got a good stick for those mice."

He waited by the gate until the old man came out on the porch. "Let's go down and kill the mice now," Jody called.

"I think I'll just sit in the sun, Jody. You go kill the mice."

"You can use my stick if you like."

"No, I'll just sit here a while."

Jody turned disconsolately away, and walked down toward the old haystack. He tried to whip up his enthusiasm with thoughts of the fat juicy mice. He beat the ground with his flail. The dogs coaxed and whined about him, but he could not go. Back at the house he could see Grandfather sitting on the porch, looking small and thin and black.

Jody gave up and went to sit on the steps at the old man's feet.

"Back already? Did you kill the mice?"

"No, sir. I'll kill them some other day."

The morning flies buzzed close to the ground and the ants dashed about in front of the steps. The heavy smell of sage slipped down the hill. The porch boards grew warm in the sunshine.

Jody hardly knew when Grandfather started to talk. "I

shouldn't stay here, feeling the way I do." He examined his strong old hands. "I feel as though the crossing wasn't worth doing." His eyes moved up the side-hill and stopped on a motionless hawk perched on a dead limb. "I tell those old stories, but they're not what I want to tell. I only know how I want people to feel when I tell them.

"It wasn't Indians that were important, nor adventures, nor even getting out here. It was a whole bunch of people made into one big crawling beast. And I was the head. It was westering and westering. Every man wanted something for himself, but the big beast that was all of them wanted only westering. I was the leader, but if I hadn't been there, someone else would have been the head. The thing had to have a head.

"Under the little bushes the shadows were black at white noonday. When we saw the mountains at last, we cried—all of us. But it wasn't getting here that mattered, it was movement and westering.

"We carried life out here and set it down the way those ants carry eggs. And I was the leader. The westering was as big as God, and the slow steps that made the movement piled up and piled up until the continent was crossed.

"Then we came down to the sea, and it was done." He stopped and wiped his eyes until the rims were red. "That's what I should be telling instead of stories."

When Jody spoke, Grandfather started and looked down at him. "Maybe I could lead the people some day," Jody said.

The old man smiled. "There's no place to go. There's the ocean to stop you. There's a line of old men along the shore hating the ocean because it stopped them."

"In boats I might, sir."

"No place to go, Jody. Every place is taken. But that's not the worst—no, not the worst. Westering has died out of the people. Westering isn't a hunger any more. It's all done. Your father is right. It is finished." He laced his fingers on his knee and looked at them.

Jody felt very sad. "If you'd like a glass of lemonade I could make it for you."

Grandfather was about to refuse, and then he saw Jody's face. "That would be nice," he said. "Yes, it would be nice to drink a lemonade."

Jody ran into the kitchen where his mother was wiping the last of the breakfast dishes. "Can I have a lemon to make a lemonade for Grandfather?"

His mother mimicked—"And another lemon to make a lemonade for you."

"No, ma'am. I don't want one."

"Jody! You're sick!" Then she stopped suddenly. "Take a lemon out of the cooler," she said softly. "Here, I'll reach the squeezer down to you."

◇◇◇

BREAKFAST

This episode, discussed in the Introduction, first appeared in The Long Valley (1938) *and then (with a few minor changes) in* Chapter 22 *of* The Grapes of Wrath (1939).

THIS thing fills me with pleasure. I don't know why, I can see it in the smallest detail. I find myself recalling it again and again, each time bringing more detail out of a sunken memory, remembering brings the curious warm pleasure.

It was very early in the morning. The eastern mountains were black-blue, but behind them the light stood up faintly colored at the mountain rims with a washed red, growing colder, grayer and darker as it went up and overhead until, at a place near the west, it merged with pure night.

And it was cold, not painfully so, but cold enough so that I rubbed my hands and shoved them deep into my pockets, and I hunched my shoulders up and scuffled my feet on the ground. Down in the valley where I was, the earth was that lavender gray of dawn. I walked along a country road and ahead of me I saw a tent that was only a little lighter gray than the ground. Beside the tent there was a flash of orange fire seeping out of the cracks of an old rusty iron stove. Gray smoke spurted up out of the stubby stovepipe, spurted up a long way before it spread out and dissipated.

I saw a young woman beside the stove, really a girl. She was dressed in a faded cotton skirt and waist. As I came close I saw that she carried a baby in a crooked arm and

417

the baby was nursing, its head under her waist out of the cold. The mother moved about, poking the fire, shifting the rusty lids of the stove to make a greater draft, opening the oven door; and all the time the baby was nursing, but that didn't interfere with the mother's work, nor with the light quick gracefulness of her movements. There was something very precise and practiced in her movements. The orange fire flicked out of the cracks in the stove and threw dancing reflections on the tent.

I was close now and I could smell frying bacon and baking bread, the warmest, pleasantest odors I know. From the east the light grew swiftly. I came near to the stove and stretched my hands out to it and shivered all over when the warmth struck me. Then the tent flap jerked up and a young man came out and an older man followed him. They were dressed in new blue dungarees and in new dungaree coats with the brass buttons shining. They were sharp-faced men, and they looked much alike.

The younger had a dark stubble beard and the older had a gray stubble beard. Their heads and faces were wet, their hair dripped with water, and water stood out on their stiff beards and their cheeks shone with water. Together they stood looking quietly at the lightening east; they yawned together and looked at the light on the hill rims. They turned and saw me.

"Morning," said the older man. His face was neither friendly nor unfriendly.

"Morning, sir," I said.

"Morning," said the young man.

The water was slowly drying on their faces. They came to the stove and warmed their hands at it.

The girl kept to her work, her face averted and her eyes on what she was doing. Her hair was tied back out of her eyes with a string and it hung down her back and swayed as she worked. She set tin cups on a big packing box, set

tin plates and knives and forks out too. Then she scooped
fried bacon out of the deep grease and laid it on a big tin
platter, and the bacon cricked and rustled as it grew crisp.
She opened the rusty oven door and took out a square pan
full of high big biscuits.

When the smell of that hot bread came out, both of the
men inhaled deeply. The young man said softly, "Kee-
rist!"

The elder man turned to me, "Had your breakfast?"

"No."

"Well, sit down with us, then."

That was the signal. We went to the packing case and
squatted on the ground about it. The young man asked,
"Picking cotton?"

"No."

"We had twelve days' work so far," the young man said.

The girl spoke from the stove. "They even got new
clothes."

The two men looked down at their new dungarees and
they both smiled a little.

The girl set out the platter of bacon, the brown high
biscuits, a bowl of bacon gravy and a pot of coffee, and
then she squatted down by the box too. The baby was still
nursing, its head up under her waist out of the cold. I
could hear the sucking noises it made.

We filled our plates, poured bacon gravy over our biscuits and sugared our coffee. The older man filled his
mouth full and he chewed and chewed and swallowed.
Then he said, "God Almighty, it's good," and he filled his
mouth again.

The young man said, "We been eating good for twelve
days."

We all ate quickly, frantically, and refilled our plates
and ate quickly again until we were full and warm. The
hot bitter coffee scalded our throats. We threw the last

little bit with the grounds in it on the earth and refilled our cups.

There was color in the light now, a reddish gleam that made the air seem colder. The two men faced the east and their faces were lighted by the dawn, and I looked up for a moment and saw the image of the mountain and the light coming over it reflected in the older man's eyes.

Then the two men threw the grounds from their cups on the earth and they stood up together. "Got to get going," the older man said.

The younger turned to me. " 'Fyou want to pick cotton, we could maybe get you on."

"No. I got to go along. Thanks for breakfast."

The older man waved his hand in a negative. "O. K. Glad to have you." They walked away together. The air was blazing with light at the eastern skyline. And I walked away down the country road.

That's all. I know, of course, some of the reasons why it was pleasant. But there was some element of great beauty there that makes the rush of warmth when I think of it.

FROM

The Grapes of Wrath

THE TURTLE

"THE LAST CLEAR DEFINITE FUNCTION OF MAN"

MIGRANT PEOPLE

LIFE AND DEATH

BREAKFAST AND WORK

MA AND TOM

THE FLOOD

Chapters and excerpts from the novel of one man's developing consciousness amidst the struggles of the "Okies"—the migrant workers from the Oklahoma dust bowl—as they move to California, published in 1939. Pulitzer Prize novel, 1940.

THE TURTLE

THE concrete highway was edged with a mat of tangled, broken, dry grass, and the grass heads were heavy with oat beards to catch on a dog's coat, and foxtails to tangle in a horse's fetlocks, and clover burrs to fasten in sheep's wool; sleeping life waiting to be spread and dispersed, every seed armed with an appliance of dispersal, twisting darts and parachutes for the wind, little spears and balls of tiny thorns, and all waiting for animals and for the wind, for a man's trouser cuff or the hem of a woman's skirt, all passive but armed with appliances of activity, still, but each possessed of the anlage of movement.

The sun lay on the grass and warmed it, and in the shade under the grass the insects moved, ants and ant lions to set traps for them, grasshoppers to jump into the air and flick their yellow wings for a second, sow bugs like little armadillos, plodding restlessly on many tender feet. And over the grass at the roadside a land turtle crawled, turning aside for nothing, dragging his high-domed shell over the grass. His hard legs and yellow-nailed feet threshed slowly through the grass, not really walking, but boosting and dragging his shell along. The barley beards slid off his shell, and the clover burrs fell on him and rolled to the ground. His horny beak was partly open, and his fierce, humorous eyes, under brows like fingernails, stared straight ahead. He came over the grass leaving a beaten trail behind him, and the hill, which was the highway embankment, reared up ahead of him. For a moment he stopped, his head held high. He blinked and looked up and down. At last he started to climb the embankment. Front clawed feet reached forward but did not touch. The hind feet kicked his shell along, and it scraped on the grass, and on the gravel. As the embankment grew steeper and steeper, the more frantic were the efforts of the land turtle. Pushing hind legs strained and slipped, boosting the shell along, and the horny head protruded as far as the neck could stretch. Little by little the shell slid up the embankment until at last a parapet cut straight across its line of march, the shoulder of the road, a concrete wall four inches high. As though they worked independently the hind legs pushed the shell against the wall. The head upraised and peered over the wall to the broad smooth plain of cement. Now the hands, braced on top of the wall, strained and lifted, and the shell came slowly up and rested its front end on the wall. For a moment the turtle rested. A red ant ran into the shell, into the soft skin inside the shell, and suddenly head and legs snapped in, and the armored tail clamped in sideways. The red ant was crushed between body and legs. And one head of wild oats was clamped into the shell by a front leg. For a long moment the turtle lay still, and then the neck crept out and the old humorous frowning eyes looked about and the legs and tail came out. The back legs went to work, straining like elephant legs, and the shell tipped to an angle so that the front legs could not reach the level cement plain. But higher and higher the hind legs boosted it, until at last the center of balance was reached, the front tipped down, the front legs scratched at the pavement, and it was up. But the head of wild oats was held by its stem around the front legs.

Now the going was easy, and all the legs worked, and the shell boosted along, waggling from side to side. A sedan driven by a forty-year old woman approached. She saw the turtle and swung to the right, off the highway, the wheels screamed and a cloud of dust boiled up. Two wheels lifted for a moment and then settled. The car skidded back onto the road, and went on, but more slowly. The turtle had jerked into its shell, but now it hurried on, for the highway was burning hot.

And now a light truck approached, and as it came near, the driver saw the turtle and swerved to hit it. His front wheel struck the edge of the shell, flipped the turtle like a tiddly-wink, spun it like a coin, and rolled it off the highway. The truck went back to its course along the right side. Lying on its back, the turtle was tight in its shell for a long time. But at last its legs waved in the air, reaching for something to pull it over. Its front foot caught a piece of quartz and little by little the shell pulled over and flopped upright. The wild oat head fell out and three of the spearhead seeds stuck in the ground. And as the turtle crawled on down the embankment, its shell dragged dirt over the seeds. The turtle entered a dust road and jerked itself along, drawing a wavy shallow trench in the dust with its shell. The old humorous eyes looked ahead, and the horny beak opened a little. His yellow toe nails slipped a fraction in the dust.

"THE LAST CLEAR DEFINITE FUNCTION OF MAN"

THE western land, nervous under the beginning change. The Western States, nervous as horses before a thunder storm. The great owners, nervous, sensing a change, knowing nothing of the nature of the change. The great owners, striking at the immediate thing, the widening government, the growing labor unity; striking at new taxes, at plans; not knowing these things are results, not causes. Results, not causes; results, not causes. The causes lie deep and simply—the causes are a hunger in a stomach, multiplied a million times; a hunger in a single soul, hunger for joy and some security, multiplied a million times; muscles and mind aching to grow, to work, to create, multiplied a million times. The last clear definite function of man—muscles aching to work, minds aching to create beyond the single need—this is man. To build a wall, to build a house, a dam, and in the wall and house and dam to put something of Manself, and to Manself take back something of the wall, the house, the dam; to take hard muscles from the lifting, to take the clear lines and form from conceiving. For man, unlike any other thing organic or inorganic in the universe, grows beyond his work, walks up the stairs of his concepts, emerges ahead of his accomplishments. This you may say of man—when theories change and crash, when schools, philosophies, when narrow dark alleys of thought, national, religious, economic, grow and disintegrate, man reaches, stumbles forward, painfully, mistakenly sometimes. Having stepped forward, he may slip back, but only half a step, never the full step back. This you may say and know it and know it. This you may know when the bombs plummet out of the black planes on the market place, when prisoners are stuck like pigs, when the crushed bodies drain filthily in the dust. You may know it in this way. If the step were not being taken, if the stumbling-forward ache were not alive, the bombs would not fall, the throats would not be cut. Fear the time when the bombs stop falling while the bombers live—for every bomb is proof that the spirit has not died. And fear the time when the strikes stop while the great owners live—for every little beaten strike is proof that the step is being taken. And this you can know—fear the time when Manself will not suffer and die for a concept, for this one quality is the foundation of Manself, and this one quality is man, distinctive in the universe.

The Western States nervous under the beginning change. Texas and Oklahoma, Kansas and Arkansas, New Mexico, Arizona, California. A single family moved from the land. Pa borrowed money from the bank, and now the bank wants the land. The land company— that's the bank when it has land—wants tractors, not families on the land. Is a tractor bad? Is the power that turns the long furrows wrong? If this tractor were ours it would be good—not mine, but ours. If our tractor turned the long furrows of our land, it would be good. Not my land, but ours. We could love that tractor then as we have loved this land when it was ours. But this tractor does two things—it turns the land and turns us off the land. There is little difference between this tractor and a tank. The people are driven, intimidated, hurt by both. We must think about this.

One man, one family driven from the land; this rusty car creaking along the highway to the west. I lost my land, a single tractor took my land. I am alone and I am bewildered. And in the night one family camps in a ditch and another family pulls in and the tents come out. The two men squat on their hams and the women and children listen. Here is the node, you who hate change and fear revolution. Keep these two squatting men apart; make them hate, fear, suspect each other. Here is the anlage of the thing you fear. This is the zygote. For here "I lost my land" is changed; a cell is split and from its splitting grows the thing you hate—"We lost *our* land." The danger is here, for two men are not as lonely and perplexed as one. And from this first "we" there grows a still more dangerous thing: "I have a little food" plus "I have none." If from this problem the sum is "We have a little food," the thing is on its way, the movement has direction. Only a little multiplication now, and this land, this tractor are ours. The two men squatting in a ditch, the little fire, the side-meat stewing in a single pot, the silent, stone-eyed women; behind, the children listening with their souls to words their minds do not understand. The night draws down. The baby has a cold. Here, take this blanket. It's wool. It was my mother's blanket—take it for the baby. This is the thing to bomb. This is the beginning—from "I" to "we."

If you who own the things people must have could understand this, you might preserve yourself. If you could separate causes from results, if you could know that Paine, Marx, Jefferson, Lenin, were results, not causes, you might survive. But that you cannot know.

For the quality of owning freezes you forever into "I," and cuts you off forever from the "we."

The Western States are nervous under the beginning change. Need is the stimulus to concept, concept to action. A half-million people moving over the country; a million more restive, ready to move; ten million more feeling the first nervousness.

And tractors turning the multiple furrows in the vacant land.

(Chapter 14)

MIGRANT PEOPLE

THE cars of the migrant people crawled out of the side roads onto the great cross-country highway, and they took the migrant way to the West. In the daylight they scuttled like bugs to the westward; and as the dark caught them, they clustered like bugs near to shelter and to water. And because they were lonely and perplexed, because they had all come from a place of sadness and worry and defeat, and because they were all going to a new mysterious place, they huddled together; they talked together; they shared their lives, their food, and the things they hoped for in the new country. Thus it might be that one family camped near a spring, and another camped for the spring and for company, and a third because two families had pioneered the place and found it good. And when the sun went down, perhaps twenty families and twenty cars were there.

In the evening a strange thing happened: the twenty families became one family, the children were the children of all. The loss of home became one loss, and the golden time in the West was one dream. And it might be that a sick child threw despair into the hearts of twenty families, of a hundred people; that a birth there in a tent kept a hundred people quiet and awestruck through the night and filled a hundred people with the birth-joy in the morning. A family which the night before had been lost and fearful might search its goods to find a present for a new baby. In the evening, sitting about the fires, the twenty were one. They grew to be units of the camps, units of the evenings and the nights. A guitar unwrapped from a blanket and tuned—and the songs, which were all of the people, were sung in the nights. Men sang the words, and women hummed the tunes.

Every night a world created, complete with furniture—friends made and enemies established; a world complete with braggarts and with cowards, with quiet men, with humble men, with kindly men. Every night relationships that make a world, established; and every morning the world torn down like a circus.

At first the families were timid in the building and tumbling worlds, but gradually the technique of building worlds became their technique. Then leaders emerged, then laws were made, then codes came into being. And as the worlds moved westward they were more complete and better furnished, for their builders were more experienced in building them.

The families learned what rights must be observed— the right of privacy in the tent; the right to keep the past black hidden in the heart; the right to talk and to listen; the right to refuse help or to accept, to offer help or to decline it; the right of son to court and daughter to be courted; the right of the hungry to be fed; the rights of the pregnant and the sick to transcend all other rights.

And the families learned, although no one told them, what rights are monstrous and must be destroyed: the right to intrude upon privacy, the right to be noisy while the camp slept, the right of seduction or rape, the right of adultery and theft and murder. These rights were crushed, because the little worlds could not exist for even a night with such rights alive.

And as the worlds moved westward, rules became

laws, although no one told the families. It is unlawful to foul near the camp; it is unlawful in any way to foul the drinking water; it is unlawful to eat good rich food near one who is hungry, unless he is asked to share.

And with the laws, the punishments—and there were only two—a quick and murderous fight or ostracism; and ostracism was the worst. For if one broke the laws his name and face went with him, and he had no place in any world, no matter where created.

In the worlds, social conduct became fixed and rigid, so that a man must say "Good morning" when asked for it, so that a man might have a willing girl if he stayed with her, if he fathered her children and protected them. But a man might not have one girl one night and another the next, for this would endanger the worlds.

The families moved westward, and the technique of building the worlds improved so that the people could be safe in their worlds; and the form was so fixed that a family acting in the rules knew it was safe in the rules.

There grew up government in the worlds, with leaders, with elders. A man who was wise found that his wisdom was needed in every camp; a man who was a fool could not change his folly with his world. And a kind of insurance developed in these nights. A man with food fed a hungry man, and thus insured himself against hunger. And when a baby died a pile of silver coins grew at the door flap, for a baby must be well buried, since it has had nothing else of life. An old man may be left in a potter's field, but not a baby.

A certain physical pattern is needed for the building of a world—water, a river bank, a stream, a spring, or even a faucet ungarded. And there is needed enough flat land to pitch the tents, a little brush or wood to build the fires. If there is a garbage dump not too far

off, all the better; for there can be found equipment—
stove tops, a curved fender to shelter the fire, and cans
to cook in and to eat from.

And the worlds were built in the evening. The people, moving in from the highways, made them with
their tents and their hearts and their brains.

In the morning the tents came down, the canvas was
folded, the tent poles tied along the running board, the
beds put in place on the cars, the pots in their places.
And as the families moved westward, the technique of
building up a home in the evening and tearing it down
with the morning light became fixed; so that the folded
tent was packed in one place, the cooking pots counted
in their box. And as the cars moved westward, each
member of the family grew into his proper place, grew
into his duties; so that each member, old and young,
had his place in the car; so that in the weary, hot evenings, when the cars pulled into the camping places,
each member had his duty and went to it without instruction: children to gather wood, to carry water; men
to pitch the tents and bring down the beds; women to
cook the supper and to watch while the family fed. And
this was done without command. The families, which
had been units of which the boundaries were a house
at night, a farm by day, changed their boundaries. In
the long hot light, they were silent in the cars moving
slowly westward; but at night they integrated with any
group they found.

Thus they changed their social life—changed as in
the whole universe only man can change. They were
not farm men any more, but migrant men. And the
thought, the planning, the long staring silence that had
gone out to the fields, went now to the roads, to the
distance, to the West. That man whose mind had been
bound with acres lived with narrow concrete miles. And

his thought and his worry were not any more with rainfall, with wind and dust, with the thrust of the crops. Eyes watched the tires, ears listened to the clattering motors, and minds struggled with oil, with gasoline, with the thinning rubber between air and road. Then a broken gear was tragedy. Then water in the evening was the yearning, and food over the fire. Then health to go on was the need and strength to go on, and spirit to go on. The wills thrust westward ahead of them, and fears that had once apprehended drought or flood now lingered with anything that might stop the westward crawling.

The camps became fixed—each a short day's journey from the last.

And on the road the panic overcame some of the families, so that they drove night and day, stopped to sleep in the cars, and drove on to the West, flying from the road, flying from movement. And these lusted so greatly to be settled that they set their faces into the West and drove toward it, forcing the clashing engines over the roads.

But most of the families changed and grew quickly into the new life. And when the sun went down——

Time to look out for a place to stop.

And—there's some tents ahead.

The car pulled off the road and stopped, and because others were there first, certain courtesies were necessary. And the man, the leader of the family, leaned from the car.

Can we pull up here an' sleep?

Why, sure, be proud to have you. What State you from?

Come all the way from Arkansas.

They's Arkansas people down that fourth tent.

That so?

And the great question, How's the water?

Well, she don't taste so good, but they's plenty.

Well, thank ya.

No thanks to me.

But the courtesies had to be. The car lumbered over the ground to the end tent, and stopped. Then down from the car the weary people climbed, and stretched stiff bodies. Then the new tent sprang up; the children went for water and the older boys cut brush or wood. The fires started and supper was put on to boil or to fry. Early comers moved over, and States were exchanged, and friends and sometimes relatives discovered.

Oklahoma, huh? What county?

Cherokee.

Why, I got folks there. Know the Allens? They's Allens all over Cherokee. Know the Willises?

Why, sure.

And a new unit was formed. The dusk came, but before the dark was down the new family was of the camp. A word had been passed with every family. They were known people—good people.

I knowed the Allens all my life. Simon Allen, ol' Simon, had trouble with his first wife. She was part Cherokee. Purty as—as a black colt.

Sure, an' young Simon, he married a Rudolph, didn' he? That's what I thought. They went to live in Enid an' done well—real well.

Only Allen that ever done well. Got a garage.

When the water was carried and the wood cut, the children walked shyly, cautiously among the tents. And they made elaborate acquaintanceship gestures. A boy stopped near another boy and studied a stone, picked it up, examined it closely, spat on it, and rubbed it clean and inspected it until he forced the other to demand, What you got there?

And casually, Nothin'. Jus' a rock.

Well, what you lookin' at it like that for?

Thought I seen gold in it.

How'd you know? Gold ain't gold, it's black in a rock.

Sure, ever'body knows that.

I bet it's fool's gold, an' you figgered it was gold.

That ain't so, 'cause Pa, he's foun' lots a gold an' he tol' me how to look.

How'd you like to pick up a big ol' piece a gold?

Sa-a-ay! I'd git the bigges' old son-a-bitchin' piece a candy you ever seen.

I ain't let to swear, but I do, anyways.

Me too. Let's go to the spring.

And young girls found each other and boasted shyly of their popularity and their prospects. The women worked over the fire, hurrying to get food to the stomachs of the family—pork if there was money in plenty, pork and potatoes and onions. Dutch-oven biscuits or cornbread, and plenty of gravy to go over it. Side-meat or chops and a can of boiled tea, black and bitter. Fried dough in drippings if money was slim, dough fried crisp and brown and the drippings poured over it.

Those families which were very rich or very foolish with their money ate canned beans and canned peaches and packaged bread and bakery cake; but they ate secretly, in their tents, for it would not have been good to eat such fine things openly. Even so, children eating their fried dough smelled the warming beans and were unhappy about it.

When supper was over and the dishes dipped and

wiped, the dark had come, and then the men squatted down to talk.

And they talked of the land behind them. I don' know what it's coming to, they said. The country's spoilt.

It'll come back though, on'y we won't be there.

Maybe, they thought, maybe we sinned some way we didn't know about.

Fella says to me, gov'ment fella, an' he says, she's gullied up on ya. Gov'ment fella. He says, if ya plowed 'cross the contour, she won't gully. Never did have no chance to try her. An' the new super' ain't plowin' 'cross the contour. Runnin' a furrow four miles long that ain't stoppin' or goin' aroun' Jesus Christ Hisself.

And they spoke softly of their homes: They was a little cool-house under the win'mill. Use' ta keep milk in there ta cream up, an' watermelons. Go in there midday when she was hotter'n a heifer, an' she'd be jus' as cool, as cool as you'd want. Cut open a melon in there an' she'd hurt your mouth, she was so cool. Water drippin' down from the tank.

They spoke of their tragedies: Had a brother Charley, hair as yella as corn, an' him a growed man. Played the 'cordeen nice too. He was harrowin' one day an' he went up to clear his lines. Well, a rattlesnake buzzed an' them horses bolted an' the harrow went over Charley, an' the points dug into his guts an' his stomach, an' they pulled his face off an'—God Almighty!

They spoke of the future: Wonder what it's like out there?

Well, the pitchers sure do look nice. I seen one where it's hot an' fine, an' walnut trees an' berries; an' right behind, close as a mule's ass to his withers, they's a tall up mountain covered with snow. That was a pretty thing to see.

If we can get work it'll be fine. Won't have no cold in the winter. Kids won't freeze on the way to school. I'm gonna take care my kids don't miss no more school. I can read good, but it ain't no pleasure to me like with a fella that's used to it.

And perhaps a man brought out his guitar to the front of his tent. And he sat on a box to play, and everyone in the camp moved slowly in toward him, drawn in toward him. Many men can chord a guitar, but perhaps this man was a picker. There you have something —the deep chords beating, beating, while the melody runs on the strings like little footsteps. Heavy hard fingers marching on the frets. The man played and the people moved slowly in on him until the circle was closed and tight, and then he sang "Ten-Cent Cotton and Forty-Cent Meat." And the circle sang softly with him. And he sang "Why Do You Cut Your Hair, Girls?" And the circle sang. He wailed the song, "I'm Leaving Old Texas," that eerie song that was sung before the Spaniards came, only the words were Indian then.

And now the group was welded to one thing, one unit, so that in the dark the eyes of the people were inward, and their minds played in other times, and their sadness was like rest, like sleep. He sang the "McAlester Blues" and then, to make up for it to the older people, he sang "Jesus Calls Me to His Side." The children drowsed with the music and went into the tents to sleep, and the singing came into their dreams.

And after a while the man with the guitar stood up and yawned. Good night, folks, he said.

And they murmured, Good night to you.

And each wished he could pick a guitar, because it is a gracious thing. Then the people went to their beds, and the camp was quiet. And the owls coasted overhead, and the coyotes gabbled in the distance, and

into the camp skunks walked, looking for bits of food—
waddling, arrogant skunks afraid of nothing.

The night passed, and with the first streak of dawn
the women came out of the tents, built up the fires, and
put the coffee to boil. And the men came out and talked
softly in the dawn.

When you cross the Colorado river, there's the desert, they say. Look out for the desert. See you don't
get hung up. Take plenty water, case you get hung up.

I'm gonna take her at night.

Me too. She'll cut the living Jesus outa you.

The families ate quickly, and the dishes were dipped
and wiped. The tents came down. There was a rush to
go. And when the sun arose, the camping place was
vacant, only a little litter left by the people. And the
camping place was ready for a new world in a new
night.

But along the highway the cars of the migrant people crawled out like bugs, and the narrow concrete
miles stretched ahead.

(Chapter 17)

LIFE AND DEATH

THE truck took the road and moved up the long hill, through the broken, rotten rock. The engine boiled very soon and Tom slowed down and took it easy. Up the long slope, winding and twisting through dead country, burned white and gray, and no hint of life in it. Once Tom stopped for a few moments to let the engine cool, and then he traveled on. They topped the pass while the sun was still up, and looked down on the desert—black cinder mountains in the distance, and the yellow sun reflected on the gray desert. The little starved bushes, sage and greasewood, threw bold shadows on the sand and bits of rock. The glaring sun was straight ahead. Tom held his hand before his eyes to see at all. They passed the crest and coasted down to cool the engine. They coasted down the long sweep to the floor of the desert, and the fan turned over to cool the water in the radiator. In the driver's seat, Tom and Al and Pa, and Winfield on Pa's knee, looked into the bright descending sun; and their eyes were stony, and their brown faces were damp with perspiration. The burnt land and the black, cindery hills broke the even distance and made it terrible in the reddening light of the setting sun.

Al said, "Jesus, what a place. How'd you like to walk acrost her?"

"People done it," said Tom. "Lots a people done it; an' if they could, we could."

"Lots must a died," said Al.

"Well, we ain't come out exac'ly clean."

Al was silent for a while, and the reddening desert swept past. "Think we'll ever see them Wilsons again?" Al asked.

Tom flicked his eyes down to the oil gauge. "I got a hunch nobody ain't gonna see Mis' Wilson for long. Jus' a hunch I got."

Winfield said, "Pa, I wanta get out."

Tom looked over at him. "Might's well let ever'-body out 'fore we settle down to drivin' tonight." He slowed the car and brought it to a stop. Winfield scrambled out and urinated at the side of the road. Tom leaned out. "Anybody else?"

"We're holdin' our water up here," Uncle John called.

Pa said, "Winfiel', you crawl up on top. You put my legs to sleep a-settin' on 'em." The little boy buttoned his overalls and obediently crawled up the back board and on his hands and knees crawled over Granma's mattress and forward to Ruthie.

The truck moved on into the evening, and the edge of the sun struck the rough horizon and turned the desert red.

Ruthie said, "Wouldn' leave you set up there, huh?"

"I didn' want to. It wasn't so nice as here. Couldn' lie down."

"Well, don' you bother me, a-squawkin' an' a-talkin'," Ruthie said, "'cause I'm goin' to sleep, an' when I wake up, we gonna be there! 'Cause Tom said so! Gonna seem funny to see pretty country."

The sun went down and left a great halo in the sky. And it grew very dark under the tarpaulin, a long cave with light at each end—a flat triangle of light.

Connie and Rose of Sharon leaned back against the cab, and the hot wind tumbling through the tent struck the backs of their heads, and the tarpaulin whipped and drummed above them. They spoke together in low tones, pitched to the drumming canvas, so that no one could hear them. When Connie spoke he turned his head and spoke into her ear, and she did the same to him. She said, "Seems like we wasn't never gonna do nothin' but move. I'm so tar'd."

He turned his head to her ear. "Maybe in the mornin'. How'd you like to be alone now?" In the dusk his hand moved out and stroked her hip.

She said, "Don't. You'll make me crazy as a loon. Don't do that." And she turned her head to hear his response.

"Maybe—when ever'body's asleep."

"Maybe," she said. "But wait till they get to sleep. You'll make me crazy, an' maybe they won't get to sleep."

"I can't hardly stop," he said.

"I know. Me neither. Le's talk about when we get there; an' you move away 'fore I get crazy."

He shifted away a little. "Well, I'll get to studyin' nights right off," he said. She sighed deeply. "Gonna get one a them books that tells about it an' cut the coupon, right off."

"How long, you think?" she asked.

"How long what?"

"How long 'fore you'll be makin' big money an' we got ice?"

"Can't tell," he said importantly. "Can't really rightly tell. Fella oughta be studied up pretty good 'fore Christmus."

"Soon's you get studied up we could get ice an' stuff, I guess."

He chuckled. "It's this here heat," he said. "What you gonna need ice roun' Christmus for?"

She giggled. "Tha's right. But I'd like ice any time. Now don't. You'll get me crazy!"

The dusk passed into dark and the desert stars came out in the soft sky, stars stabbing and sharp, with few points and rays to them, and the sky was velvet. And the heat changed. While the sun was up, it was a beating, flailing heat, but now the heat came from below, from the earth itself, and the heat was thick and muffling. The lights of the truck came on, and they illuminated a little blur of highway ahead, and a strip of desert on either side of the road. And sometimes eyes gleamed in the lights far ahead, but no animal showed in the lights. It was pitch dark under the canvas now. Uncle John and the preacher were curled in the middle of the truck, resting on their elbows, and staring out the back triangle. They could see the two bumps that were Ma and Granma against the outside. They could see Ma move occasionally, and her dark arm moving against the outside.

Uncle John talked to the preacher. "Casy," he said, "you're a fella oughta know what to do."

"What to do about what?"

"I dunno," said Uncle John.

Casy said, "Well, that's gonna make it easy for me!"

"Well, you been a preacher."

"Look, John, ever'body takes a crack at me 'cause I been a preacher. A preacher ain't nothin' but a man."

"Yeah, but—he's—a *kind* of a man, else he wouldn' be a preacher. I wanna ast you—well, you think a fella could bring bad luck to folks?"

"I dunno," said Casy. "I dunno."

"Well—see—I was married—fine, good girl. An' one night she got a pain in her stomach. An' she says, 'You better get a doctor.' An' I says, 'Hell, you jus' et too much.'" Uncle John put his hand on Casy's knee and he peered through the darkness at him. "She give me a *look*. An' she groaned all night, an' she died the next afternoon." The preacher mumbled something. "You see," John went on, "I kil't her. An' sence then I tried to make it up—mos'ly to kids. An' I tried to be good, an' I can't. I get drunk, an' I go wild."

"Ever'body goes wild," said Casy. "I do too."

"Yeah, but you ain't got a sin on your soul like me."

Casy said gently, "Sure I got sins. Ever'body got sins. A sin is somepin you ain't sure about. Them people that's sure about ever'thing an' ain't got no sin—well, with that kind a son-of-a-bitch, if I was God I'd kick their ass right outa heaven! I couldn' stand 'em!"

Uncle John said, "I got a feelin' I'm bringin' bad luck to my own folks. I got a feelin' I oughta go away an' let 'em be. I ain't comf'table bein' like this."

Casy said quickly, "I know this—a man got to do what he got to do. I can't tell you. I can't tell you. I don't think they's luck or bad luck. On'y one thing in this worl' I'm sure of, an' that's I'm sure nobody got a right to mess with a fella's life. He got to do it all his-self. Help him, maybe, but not tell him what to do."

Uncle John said disappointedly, "Then you don' know?"

"I don' know."

"You think it was a sin to let my wife die like that?"

"Well," said Casy, "for anybody else it was a mistake, but if you think it was a sin—then it's a sin. A fella builds his own sins right up from the groun'."

"I got to give that a goin'-over," said Uncle John, and he rolled on his back and lay with his knees pulled up.

The truck moved on over the hot earth, and the hours passed. Ruthie and Winfield went to sleep. Connie loosened a blanket from the load and covered himself and Rose of Sharon with it, and in the heat they struggled together, and held their breaths. And after a time Connie threw off the blanket and the hot tunneling wind felt cool on their wet bodies.

On the back of the truck Ma lay on the mattress beside Granma, and she could not see with her eyes, but she could feel the struggling body and the struggling heart; and the sobbing breath was in her ear. And Ma said over and over, "All right. It's gonna be all right." And she said hoarsely, "You know the family got to get acrost. You know that."

Uncle John called, "You all right?"

It was a moment before she answered. "All right. Guess I dropped off to sleep." And after a time Granma was still, and Ma lay rigid beside her.

The night hours passed, and the dark was in against the truck. Sometimes cars passed them, going west and away; and sometimes great trucks came up out of the west and rumbled eastward. And the stars flowed down in a slow cascade over the western horizon. It was near midnight when they neared Daggett, where the inspection station is. The road was floodlighted there, and a sign illuminated, "KEEP RIGHT AND STOP." The officers loafed in the office, but they came out and stood under the long covered shed when Tom pulled in. One officer put down the license number and raised the hood.

Tom asked, "What's this here?"

"Agricultural inspection. We got to look over your stuff. Got any vegetables or seeds?"

"No," said Tom.

"Well, we got to look over your stuff. You got to unload."

Now Ma climbed heavily down from the truck. Her face was swollen and her eyes were hard. "Look, mis-

ter. We got a sick ol' lady. We got to get her to a doctor. We can't wait." She seemed to fight with hysteria.
"You can't make us wait."

"Yeah? Well, we got to look you over."

"I swear we ain't got any thing!" Ma cried. "I swear
it. An' Granma's awful sick."

"You don't look so good yourself," the officer said.

Ma pulled herself up the back of the truck, hoisted
herself with huge strength. "Look," she said.

The officer shot a flashlight beam up on the old
shrunken face. "By God, she is," he said. "You swear
you got no seeds or fruits or vegetables, no corn, no
oranges?"

"No, no. I swear it!"

"Then go ahead. You can get a doctor in Barstow.
That's only eight miles. Go on ahead."

Tom climbed in and drove on.

The officer turned to his companion. "I couldn' hold
'em."

"Maybe it was a bluff," said the other.

"Oh, Jesus, no! You should of seen that ol' woman's
face. That wasn't no bluff."

Tom increased his speed to Barstow, and in the little town he stopped, got out, and walked around the
truck. Ma leaned out. "It's awright," she said. "I didn'
wanta stop there, fear we wouldn' get acrost."

"Yeah! But how's Granma?"

"She's awright—awright. Drive on. We got to get
acrost." Tom shook his head and walked back.

"Al," he said, "I'm gonna fill her up, an' then you
drive some." He pulled to an all-night gas station and
filled the tank and the radiator, and filled the crank
case. Then Al slipped under the wheel and Tom took
the outside, with Pa in the middle. They drove away

into the darkness and the little hills near Barstow were behind them.

Tom said, "I don' know what's got into Ma. She's flighty as a dog with a flea in his ear. Wouldn' a took long to look over the stuff. An' she says Granma's sick; an' now she says Granma's awright. I can't figger her out. She ain't right. S'pose she wore her brains out on the trip."

Pa said, "Ma's almost like she was when she was a girl. She was a wild one then. She wasn' scairt of nothin'. I thought havin' all the kids an' workin' took it out a her, but I guess it ain't. Christ! When she got that jack handle back there, I tell you I wouldn' wanna be the fella took it away from her."

"I dunno what's got into her," Tom said. "Maybe she's jus' tar'd out."

Al said, "I won't be doin' no weepin' an' a-moanin' to get through. I got this goddamn car on my soul."

Tom said, "Well, you done a damn good job a pickin'. We ain't had hardly no trouble with her at all."

All night they bored through the hot darkness, and jack-rabbits scuttled into the lights and dashed away in long jolting leaps. And the dawn came up behind them when the lights of Mojave were ahead. And the dawn showed high mountains to the west. They filled with water and oil at Mojave and crawled into the mountains, and the dawn was about them.

Tom said, "Jesus, the desert's past! Pa, Al, for Christ sakes! The desert's past!"

"I'm too goddamn tired to care," said Al.

"Want me to drive?"

"No, wait awhile."

They drove through Tehachapi in the morning glow, and the sun came up behind them, and then—suddenly they saw the great valley below them. Al jammed on the brake and stopped in the middle of the road, and, "Jesus Christ! Look!" he said. The vineyards, the orchards, the great flat valley, green and beautiful, the trees set in rows, and the farm houses.

And Pa said, "God Almighty!" The distant cities, the little towns in the orchard land, and the morning sun, golden on the valley. A car honked behind them. Al pulled to the side of the road and parked.

"I want ta look at her." The grain fields golden in the morning, and the willow lines, the eucalyptus trees in rows.

Pa sighed, "I never knowed they was anything like her." The peach trees and the walnut groves, and the dark green patches of oranges. And red roofs among the trees, and barns—rich barns. Al got out and stretched his legs.

He called, "Ma—come look. We're there!"

Ruthie and Winfield scrambled down from the car, and then they stood, silent and awestruck, embarrassed before the great valley. The distance was thinned with haze, and the land grew softer and softer in the distance. A windmill flashed in the sun, and its turning blades were like a little heliograph, far away. Ruthie and Winfield looked at it, and Ruthie whispered, "It's California."

Winfield moved his lips silently over the syllables. "There's fruit," he said aloud.

Casy and Uncle John, Connie and Rose of Sharon climbed down. And they stood silently. Rose of Sharon had started to brush her hair back, when she caught sight of the valley and her hand dropped slowly to her side.

Tom said, "Where's Ma? I want Ma to see it. Look, Ma! Come here, Ma." Ma was climbing slowly, stiffly, down the back board. Tom looked at her. "My God, Ma, you sick?" Her face was stiff and putty-like, and her eyes seemed to have sunk deep into her head, and the rims were red with weariness. Her feet touched the ground and she braced herself by holding the truckside.

Her voice was a croak. "Ya say we're acrost?"

Tom pointed to the great valley. "Look!"

She turned her head, and her mouth opened a little. Her fingers went to her throat and gathered a little pinch of skin and twisted gently. "Thank God!" she said. "The fambly's here." Her knees buckled and she sat down on the running board.

"You sick, Ma?"

"No, jus' tar'd."

"Didn' you get no sleep?"

"No."

"Was Granma bad?"

Ma looked down at her hands, lying together like tired lovers in her lap. "I wisht I could wait an' not tell you. I wisht it could be all—nice."

Pa said, "Then Granma's bad."

Ma raised her eyes and looked over the valley. "Granma's dead."

They looked at her, all of them, and Pa asked, "When?"

"Before they stopped us las' night."

"So that's why you didn' want 'em to look."

"I was afraid we wouldn' get acrost," she said. "I tol' Granma we couldn' he'p her. The fambly had ta get acrost. I tol' her, tol' her when she was a-dyin'. We couldn' stop in the desert. There was the young ones —an' Rosasharn's baby. I tol' her." She put up her hands and covered her face for a moment. "She can get buried in a nice green place," Ma said softly. "Trees aroun' an' a nice place. She got to lay her head down in California."

The family looked at Ma with a little terror at her strength.

Tom said, "Jesus Christ! You layin' there with her all night long!"

"The fambly hadda get acrost," Ma said miserably.

Tom moved close to put his hand on her shoulder.

"Don' touch me," she said. "I'll hol' up if you don' touch me. That'd get me."

Pa said, "We got to go on now. We got to go on down."

Ma looked up at him. "Can—can I set up front? I don' wanna go back there no more—I'm tar'd. I'm awful tar'd."

They climbed back on the load, and they avoided the long stiff figure covered and tucked in a comforter, even the head covered and tucked. They moved to their places and tried to keep their eyes from it—from the hump on the comfort that would be the nose, and the steep cliff that would be the jut of the chin. They tried to keep their eyes away, and they could not. Ruthie and Winfield, crowded in a forward corner as far away from the body as they could get, stared at the tucked figure.

And Ruthie whispered, "Tha's Granma, an' she's dead."

Winfield nodded solemnly. "She ain't breathin' at all. She's awful dead."

And Rose of Sharon said softly to Connie, "She was a-dyin' right when we——"

"How'd we know?" he reassured her.

Al climbed on the load to make room for Ma in the seat. And Al swaggered a little because he was sorry. He plumped down beside Casy and Uncle John. "Well, she was ol'. Guess her time was up," Al said. "Ever'-body got to die." Casy and Uncle John turned eyes expressionlessly on him and looked at him as though he were a curious talking bush. "Well, ain't they?" he demanded. And the eyes looked away, leaving Al sullen and shaken.

Casy said in wonder, "All night long, an' she was alone." And he said, "John, there's a woman so great with love—she scares me. Makes me afraid an' mean."

John asked, "Was it a sin? Is they any part of it you might call a sin?"

Casy turned on him in astonishment, "A sin? No, there ain't no part of it that's a sin."

"I ain't never done nothin' that wasn't part sin," said John, and he looked at the long wrapped body.

Tom and Ma and Pa got into the front seat. Tom let the truck roll and started on compression. And the heavy truck moved, snorting and jerking and popping down the hill. The sun was behind them, and the valley golden and green before them. Ma shook her head slowly from side to side. "It's purty," she said. "I wisht they could of saw it."

"I wisht so too," said Pa.

Tom patted the steering wheel under his hand. "They was too old," he said. "They wouldn't of saw nothin' that's here. Grampa would a been a-seein' the Injuns an' the prairie country when he was a young fella. An' Granma would a remembered an' seen the first home she lived in. They was too ol'. Who's really seein' it is Ruthie an' Winfiel'."

Pa said, "Here's Tommy talkin' like a growed-up man, talkin' like a preacher almos'."

And Ma smiled sadly. "He is. Tommy's growed way up—way up so I can't get aholt of 'im sometimes."

They popped down the mountain, twisting and looping, losing the valley sometimes, and then finding it again. And the hot breath of the valley came up to them, with hot green smells on it, and with resinous sage and tarweed smells. The crickets crackled along the road. A rattlesnake crawled across the road and Tom hit it and broke it and left it squirming.

Tom said, "I guess we got to go to the coroner, wherever he is. We got to get her buried decent. How much money might be lef', Pa?"

"'Bout forty dollars," said Pa.

Tom laughed. "Jesus, are we gonna start clean! We sure ain't bringin' nothin' with us." He chuckled a moment, and then his face straightened quickly. He pulled the visor of his cap down low over his eyes. And the truck rolled down the mountain into the great valley.

(*From* Chapter 18)

BREAKFAST AND WORK

TOM climbed up over the tail-board of the truck. He lay down on his back on the wooden floor and he pillowed his head on his crossed hands, and his forearms pressed against his ears. The night grew cooler. Tom buttoned his coat over his chest and settled back again. The stars were clear and sharp over his head.

It was still dark when he awakened. A small clashing noise brought him up from sleep. Tom listened and heard again the squeak of iron on iron. He moved stiffly and shivered in the morning air. The camp still slept. Tom stood up and looked over the side of the truck. The eastern mountains were blue-black, and as he watched, the light stood up faintly behind them, colored at the mountain rims with a washed red, then growing colder, grayer, darker, as it went up overhead, until at a place near the western horizon it merged with pure night. Down in the valley the earth was the lavender-gray of dawn.

The clash of iron sounded again. Tom looked down the line of tents, only a little lighter gray than the ground. Beside a tent he saw a flash of orange fire seeping from the cracks in an old iron stove. Gray smoke spurted up from a stubby smoke-pipe.

Tom climbed over the truck side and dropped to the ground. He moved slowly toward the stove. He saw a girl working about the stove, saw that she carried a baby on her crooked arm, and that the baby was nursing, its head up under the girl's shirtwaist. And the girl moved about, poking the fire, shifting the rusty stove lids to make a better draft, opening the oven door; and all the time the baby sucked, and the mother shifted it deftly from arm to arm. The baby didn't interfere with her work or with the quick gracefulness of her movements. And the orange fire licked out of the stove cracks and threw flickering reflections on the tent.

Tom moved closer. He smelled frying bacon and baking bread. From the east the light grew swiftly. Tom came near to the stove and stretched out his hands to it. The girl looked at him and nodded, so that her two braids jerked.

"Good mornin'," she said, and she turned the bacon in the pan.

The tent flap jerked up and a young man came out and an older man followed him. They were dressed in new blue dungarees and in dungaree coats, stiff with filler, the brass buttons shining. They were sharp-faced men, and they looked much alike. The younger man had a dark stubble beard and the older man a white stubble beard. Their heads and faces were wet, their hair dripped, water stood in drops on their stiff beards. Their cheeks shone with dampness. Together they stood looking quietly into the lightening east. They yawned together and watched the light on the hill rims. And then they turned and saw Tom.

"Mornin'," the older man said, and his face was neither friendly nor unfriendly.

"Mornin'," said Tom.

And, "Mornin'," said the younger man.

The water slowly dried on their faces. They came to the stove and warmed their hands at it.

The girl kept to her work. Once she set the baby

down and tied her braids together in back with a string, and the two braids jerked and swung as she worked. She set tin cups on a big packing box, set tin plates and knives and forks out. Then she scooped bacon from the deep grease and laid it on a tin platter, and the bacon cricked and rustled as it grew crisp. She opened the rusty oven door and took out a square pan full of big high biscuits.

When the smell of the biscuits struck the air both of the men inhaled deeply. The younger said, "Kee-rist!" softly.

Now the older man said to Tom, "Had your breakfast?"

"Well, no, I ain't. But my folks is over there. They ain't up. Need the sleep."

"Well, set down with us, then. We got plenty—thank God!"

"Why, thank ya," Tom said. "Smells so darn good I couldn' say no."

"Don't she?" the younger man asked. "Ever smell anything so good in ya life?" They marched to the packing box and squatted around it.

"Workin' around here?" the young man asked.

"Aim to," said Tom. "We jus' got in las' night. Ain't had no chance to look aroun'."

"We had twelve days' work," the young man said.

The girl, working by the stove, said, "They even got new clothes." Both men looked down at their stiff blue clothes, and they smiled a little shyly. The girl set out the platter of bacon and the brown, high biscuits and a bowl of bacon gravy and a pot of coffee, and then she squatted down by the box too. The baby still nursed, its head up under the girl's shirtwaist.

They filled their plates, poured bacon gravy over the biscuits, and sugared their coffee.

The older man filled his mouth full, and he chewed

and chewed and gulped and swallowed. "God Almighty, it's good!" he said, and he filled his mouth again.

The younger man said, "We been eatin' good for twelve days now. Never missed a meal in twelve days —none of us. Workin' an' gettin' our pay an' eatin'." He fell to again, almost frantically, and refilled his plate. They drank the scalding coffee and threw the grounds to the earth and filled their cups again.

There was color in the light now, a reddish gleam. The father and son stopped eating. They were facing to the east and their faces were lighted by the dawn. The image of the mountain and the light coming over it were reflected in their eyes. And then they threw the grounds from their cups to the earth, and they stood up together.

"Got to git goin'," the older man said.

The younger turned to Tom. "Lookie," he said. "We're layin' some pipe. 'F you want to walk over with us, maybe we could get you on."

Tom said, "Well, that's mighty nice of you. An' I sure thank ya for the breakfast."

"Glad to have you," the older man said. "We'll try to git you workin' if you want."

"Ya goddamn right I want," Tom said. "Jus' wait a minute. I'll tell my folks." He hurried to the Joad tent and bent over and looked inside. In the gloom under the tarpaulin he saw the lumps of sleeping figures. But a little movement started among the bedclothes. Ruthie came wriggling out like a snake, her hair down over her eyes and her dress wrinkled and twisted. She crawled carefully out and stood up. Her gray eyes were clear and calm from sleep, and mischief was not in them. Tom moved off from the tent and beckoned her to follow, and when he turned, she looked up at him.

"Lord God, you're growin' up," he said.

She looked away in sudden embarrassment. "Listen here," Tom said. "Don't you wake nobody up, but when they get up, you tell 'em I got a chancet at a job, an' I'm a-goin' for it. Tell Ma I et breakfas' with some neighbors. You hear that?"

Ruthie nodded and turned her head away, and her eyes were little girl's eyes. "Don't you wake 'em up," Tom cautioned. He hurried back to his new friends. And Ruthie cautiously approached the sanitary unit and peeked in the open doorway.

The two men were waiting when Tom came back. The young woman had dragged a mattress out and put the baby on it while she cleaned up the dishes.

Tom said, "I wanted to tell my folks where-at I was. They wasn't awake." The three walked down the street between the tents.

The camp had begun to come to life. At the new fires the women worked, slicing meat, kneading the dough for the morning's bread. And the men were stirring about the tents and about the automobiles. The sky was rosy now. In front of the office a lean old man raked the ground carefully. He so dragged his rake that the tine marks were straight and deep.

"You're out early, Pa," the young man said as they went by.

"Yep, yep. Got to make up my rent."

"Rent, hell!" the young man said. "He was drunk last Sat'dy night. Sung in his tent all night. Committee give him work for it." They walked along the edge of the oiled road; a row of walnut trees grew beside the way. The sun shoved its edge over the mountains.

Tom said, "Seems funny. I've et your food, an' I ain't tol' you my name—nor you ain't mentioned yours. I'm Tom Joad."

The older man looked at him, and then he smiled a little. "You ain't been out here long?"

"Hell, no! Jus' a couple days."

"I knowed it. Funny, you git outa the habit a mentionin' your name. They's so goddamn many. Jist fellas. Well, sir—I'm Timothy Wallace, an' this here's my boy Wilkie."

"Proud to know ya," Tom said. "You been out here long?"

"Ten months," Wilkie said. "Got here right on the tail a the floods las' year. Jesus! We had *a* time, *a* time! Goddamn near starve' to death." Their feet rattled on the oiled road. A truckload of men went by, and each man was sunk into himself. Each man braced himself in the truck bed and scowled down.

"Goin' out for the Gas Company," Timothy said. "They got a nice job of it."

"I could of took our truck," Tom suggested.

"No." Timothy leaned down and picked up a green walnut. He tested it with his thumb and then shied it at a blackbird sitting on a fence wire. The bird flew up, let the nut sail under it, and then settled back on the wire and smoothed its shining black feathers with its beak.

Tom asked, "Ain't you got no car?"

Both Wallaces were silent, and Tom, looking at their faces, saw that they were ashamed.

Wilkie said, "Place we work at is on'y a mile up the road."

Timothy said angrily, "No, we ain't got no car. We sol' our car. Had to. Run outa food, run outa ever'thing. Couldn' git no job. Fellas come aroun' ever' week, buyin' cars. Come aroun', an' if you're hungry, why, they'll buy your car. An' if you're hungry enough, they don't hafta pay nothin' for it. An'—we was hungry enough. Give us ten dollars for her." He spat into the road.

Wilkie said quietly, "I was in Bakersfiel' las' week. I seen her—a-settin' in a use'-car lot—settin' right there, an' seventy-five dollars was the sign on her."

"We had to," Timothy said. "It was either us let 'em steal our car or us steal somepin from them. We ain't had to steal yet, but, goddamn it, we been close!"

Tom said, "You know, 'fore we lef' home, we heard they was plenty work out here. Seen han'bills askin' folks to come out."

"Yeah," Timothy said. "We seen 'em too. An' they ain't much work. An' wages is comin' down all a time. I git so goddamn tired jus' figgerin' how to eat."

"You got work now," Tom suggested.

"Yeah, but it ain't gonna las' long. Workin' for a nice fella. Got a little place. Works 'longside of us. But, hell —it ain't gonna las' no time."

Tom said, "Why in hell you gonna git me on? I'll make it shorter. What you cuttin' your own throat for?"

Timothy shook his head slowly. "I dunno. Got no sense, I guess. We figgered to get us each a hat. Can't do it, I guess. There's the place, off to the right there. Nice job, too. Gettin' thirty cents an hour. Nice frien'ly fella to work for."

They turned off the highway and walked down a graveled road, through a small kitchen orchard; and behind the trees they came to a small white farm house, a few shade trees, and a barn; behind the barn a vineyard and a field of cotton. As the three men walked past the house a screen door banged, and a stocky sunburned man came down the back steps. He wore a paper sun helmet, and he rolled up his

sleeves as he came across the yard. His heavy sunburned eyebrows were drawn down in a scowl. His
cheeks were sunburned a beef red.

"Mornin', Mr. Thomas," Timothy said.

"Morning." The man spoke irritably.

Timothy said, "This here's Tom Joad. We wondered if you could see your way to put him on?"

Thomas scowled at Tom. And then he laughed
shortly, and his brows still scowled. "Oh, sure! I'll put
him on. I'll put everybody on. Maybe I'll get a hundred men on."

"We jus' thought—" Timothy began apologetically.

Thomas interrupted him. "Yes, I been thinkin' too."
He swung around and faced them. "I've got some things
to tell you. I been paying you thirty cents an hour—
that right?"

"Why, sure, Mr. Thomas—but——"

"And I been getting thirty cents' worth of work."
His heavy hard hands clasped each other.

"We try to give a good day of work."

"Well, goddamn it, this morning you're getting
twenty-five cents an hour, and you take it or leave it."
The redness of his face deepened with anger.

Timothy said, "We've give you good work. You said
so yourself."

"I know it. But it seems like I ain't hiring my own
men any more." He swallowed. "Look," he said. "I got
sixty-five acres here. Did you ever hear of the Farmers'
Association?"

"Why, sure."

"Well, I belong to it. We had a meeting last night.
Now, do you know who runs the Farmers' Association?
I'll tell you. The Bank of the West. That bank owns
most of this valley, and it's got paper on everything it

don't own. So last night the member from the bank told me, he said, 'You're paying thirty cents an hour. You'd better cut it down to twenty-five.' I said, 'I've got good men. They're worth thirty.' And he says, 'It isn't that,' he says. 'The wage is twenty-five now. If you pay thirty, it'll only cause unrest. And by the way,' he says, 'you going to need the usual amount for a crop loan next year?'" Thomas stopped. His breath was panting through his lips. "You see? The rate is twenty-five cents—and like it."

"We done good work," Timothy said helplessly.

"Ain't you got it yet? Mr. Bank hires two thousand men an' I hire three. I've got paper to meet. Now if you can figure some way out, by Christ, I'll take it! They got me."

Timothy shook his head. "I don' know what to say."

"You wait here." Thomas walked quickly to the house. The door slammed after him. In a moment he was back, and he carried a newspaper in his hand. "Did you see this? Here, I'll read it: 'Citizens, angered at red agitators, burn squatters' camp. Last night a band of citizens, infuriated at the agitation going on in a local squatters' camp, burned the tents to the ground and warned agitators to get out of the county.'"

Tom began, "Why, I—" and then he closed his mouth and was silent.

Thomas folded the paper carefully and put it in his pocket. He had himself in control again. He said quietly, "Those men were sent out by the Association. Now I'm giving 'em away. And if they ever find out I told, I won't have a farm next year."

"I jus' don't know what to say," Timothy said. "If they was agitators, I can see why they was mad."

Thomas said, "I watched it a long time. There's always red agitators just before a pay cut. Always. God-damn it, they got me trapped. Now, what are you go-ing to do? Twenty-five cents?"

Timothy looked at the ground. "I'll work," he said.

"Me too," said Wilkie.

Tom said, "Seems like I walked into somepin. Sure, I'll work. I got to work."

Thomas pulled a bandanna out of his hip pocket and wiped his mouth and chin. "I don't know how long it can go on. I don't know how you men can feed a family on what you get now."

"We can while we work," Wilkie said. "It's when we don't git work."

Thomas looked at his watch. "Well, let's go out and dig some ditch. By God," he said, "I'm a-gonna tell you. You fellas live in that government camp, don't you?"

Timothy stiffened. "Yes, sir."

"And you have dances every Saturday night?"

Wilkie smiled. "We sure do."

"Well, look out next Saturday night."

Suddenly Timothy straightened. He stepped close. "What you mean? I belong to the Central Committee. I got to know."

Thomas looked apprehensive. "Don't you ever tell I told."

"What is it?" Timothy demanded.

"Well, the Association don't like the government camps. Can't get a deputy in there. The people make their own laws, I hear, and you can't arrest a man without a warrant. Now if there was a big fight and maybe shooting—a bunch of deputies could go in and clean out the camp."

Timothy had changed. His shoulders were straight and his eyes cold. "What you mean?"

"Don't you ever tell where you heard," Thomas said uneasily. "There's going to be a fight in the camp Saturday night. And there's going to be deputies ready to go in."

Tom demanded, "Why, for God's sake? Those folks ain't bothering nobody."

"I'll tell you why," Thomas said. "Those folks in the camp are getting used to being treated like humans. When they go back to the squatters' camps they'll be hard to handle." He wiped his face again. "Go on out to work now. Jesus, I hope I haven't talked myself out of my farm. But I like you people."

Timothy stepped in front of him and put out a hard lean hand, and Thomas took it. "Nobody won't know who tol'. We thank you. They won't be no fight."

"Go on to work," Thomas said. "And it's twenty-five cents an hour."

"We'll take it," Wilkie said, "from you."

Thomas walked away toward the house. "I'll be out in a piece," he said. "You men get to work." The screen door slammed behind him.

The three men walked out past the little whitewashed barn, and along a field edge. They came to a long narrow ditch with sections of concrete pipe lying beside it.

"Here's where we're a-workin'," Wilkie said.

His father opened the barn and passed out two picks and three shovels. And he said to Tom, "Here's your beauty."

Tom hefted the pick. "Jumping Jesus! If she don't feel good!"

"Wait'll about 'leven o'clock," Wilkie suggested. "See how good she feels then."

They walked to the end of the ditch. Tom took off his coat and dropped it on the dirt pile. He pushed up his cap and stepped into the ditch. Then he spat on his hands. The pick arose into the air and flashed down. Tom grunted softly. The pick rose and fell, and the grunt came at the moment it sank into the ground and loosened the soil.

Wilkie said, "Yes, sir, Pa, we got here a first-grade muck-stick man. This here boy been married to that there little digger."

Tom said, "I put in time (*umph*). Yes, sir, I sure did (*umph*). Put in my years (*umph!*). Kinda like the feel (*umph!*)." The soil loosened ahead of him. The sun cleared the fruit trees now and the grape leaves were golden green on the vines. Six feet along and Tom stepped aside and wiped his forehead. Wilkie came behind him. The shovel rose and fell and the dirt flew out to the pile beside the lengthening ditch.

"I heard about this here Central Committee," said Tom. "So you're one of 'em."

"Yes, sir," Timothy replied. "And it's a responsibility. All them people. We're doin' our best. An' the people in the camp a-doin' their best. I wisht them big farmers wouldn' plague us so. I wisht they wouldn'.'"

Tom climbed back into the ditch and Wilkie stood aside. Tom said, "How 'bout this fight (*umph!*) at the dance, he tol' about (*umph*)? What they wanta do that for?"

Timothy followed behind Wilkie, and Timothy's shovel beveled the bottom of the ditch and smoothed it ready for the pipe. "Seems like they got to drive us," Timothy said. "They're scairt we'll organize, I guess. An' maybe they're right. This here camp is a organization. People there look out for theirselves. Got the nicest strang band in these parts. Got a little charge account in the store for folks that's hungry. Fi' dollars—you can git that much food an' the camp'll stan' good. We ain't never had no trouble with the law. I guess the big farmers is scairt of that. Can't throw us in jail—why, it scares 'em. Figger maybe if we can gove'n ourselves, maybe we'll do other things."

Tom stepped clear of the ditch and wiped the sweat out of his eyes. "You hear what that paper said 'bout agitators up north a Bakersfiel'?"

"Sure," said Wilkie. "They do that all a time."

"Well, I was there. They wasn't no agitators. What they call reds. What the hell is these reds anyways?"

Timothy scraped a little hill level in the bottom of the ditch. The sun made his white bristle beard shine. "They's a lot a fellas wanta know what reds is." He laughed. "One of our boys foun' out." He patted the piled earth gently with his shovel. "Fella named Hines —got 'bout thirty thousan' acres, peaches and grapes— got a cannery an' a winery. Well, he's all a time talkin' about 'them goddamn reds.' 'Goddamn reds is drivin' the country to ruin,' he says, an' 'We got to drive these here red bastards out.' Well, they were a young fella jus' come out west here, an' he's listenin' one day. He kinda scratched his head an' he says, 'Mr. Hines, I ain't been here long. What is these goddamn reds?' Well, sir, Hines says, 'A red is any son-of-a-bitch that wants thirty cents an hour when we're payin' twenty-five!' Well, this young fella he thinks about her, an' he scratches his head, an' he says, 'Well, Jesus, Mr. Hines. I ain't a son-of-a-bitch, but if that's what a red is—why, I want thirty cents an hour. Ever'body does. Hell, Mr. Hines, we're all reds.' " Timothy drove his shovel along the ditch bottom, and the solid earth shone where the shovel cut it.

Tom laughed. "Me too, I guess." His pick arced up and drove down, and the earth cracked under it. The sweat rolled down his forehead and down the sides of his nose, and it glistened on his neck. "Damn it," he said, "a pick is a nice tool (*umph*), if you don' fight it (*umph*). You an' the pick (*umph*) workin' together (*umph*)."

In line, the three men worked, and the ditch inched along, and the sun shone hotly down on them in the growing morning.

(*From* Chapter 22)

MA AND TOM

O N the stream side of the boxcars, the tents were pitched close together, their guy ropes crossing one another, and the pegs of one at the canvas line of the next. The lights shone through the cloth, and all the chimneys belched smoke. Men and women stood in the doorways talking. Children ran feverishly about. Ma moved majestically down the line of tents. Here and there she was recognized as she went by. "Evenin', Mis' Joad."

"Evenin'."

"Takin' somepin out, Mis' Joad?"

"They's a frien'. I'm takin' back some bread."

She came at last to the end of the line of tents. She stopped and looked back. A glow of light was on the camp, and the soft overtone of a multitude of speakers. Now and then a harsher voice cut through. The smell of smoke filled the air. Someone played a harmonica softly, trying for an effect, one phrase over and over.

Ma stepped in among the willows beside the stream. She moved off the trail and waited, silently, listening to hear any possible follower. A man walked down the trail toward the camp, boosting his suspenders and buttoning his jeans as he went. Ma sat very still, and he passed on without seeing her. She waited five minutes and then she stood up and crept on up the trail beside the stream. She moved quietly, so quietly that she could hear the murmur of the water above her soft steps on

467

the willow leaves. Trail and stream swung to the left and then to the right again until they neared the highway. In the gray starlight she could see the embankment and the black round hole of the culvert where she always left Tom's food. She moved forward cautiously, thrust her package into the hole, and took back the empty tin plate which was left there. She crept back among the willows, forced her way into a thicket, and sat down to wait. Through the tangle she could see the black hole of the culvert. She clasped her knees and sat silently. In a few moments the thicket crept to life again. The field mice moved cautiously over the leaves. A skunk padded heavily and unself-consciously down the trail, carrying a faint effluvium with him. And then a wind stirred the willows delicately, as though it tested them, and a shower of golden leaves coasted down to the ground. Suddenly a gust boiled in and racked the trees, and a cricking downpour of leaves fell. Ma could feel them on her hair and on her shoulders. Over the sky a plump black cloud moved, erasing the stars. The fat drops of rain scattered down, splashing loudly on the fallen leaves, and the cloud moved on and unveiled the stars again. Ma shivered. The wind blew past and left the thicket quiet, but the rushing of the trees went on down the stream. From back at the camp came the thin penetrating tone of a violin feeling about for a tune.

Ma heard a stealthy step among the leaves far to her left, and she grew tense. She released her knees and straightened her head, the better to hear. The movement stopped, and after a long moment began again. A vine rasped harshly on the dry leaves. Ma saw a dark figure creep into the open and draw near to the culvert. The black round hole was obscured for a moment, and then the figure moved back. She called softly, "Tom!" The figure stood still, so still, so low to the ground that it might have been a stump. She called again, "Tom, oh, Tom!" Then the figure moved.

"That you, Ma?"

"Right over here." She stood up and went to meet him.

"You shouldn' of came," he said.

"I got to see you, Tom. I got to talk to you."

"It's near the trail," he said. "Somebody might come by."

"Ain't you got a place, Tom?"

"Yeah—but if—well, s'pose somebody seen you with me—whole fambly'd be in a jam."

"I got to, Tom."

"Then come along. Come quiet." He crossed the little stream, wading carelessly through the water, and Ma followed him. He moved through the brush, out into a field on the other side of the thicket, and along the plowed ground. The blackening stems of the cotton were harsh against the ground, and a few fluffs of cotton clung to the stems. A quarter of a mile they went along the edge of the field, and then he turned into the brush again. He approached a great mound of wild blackberry bushes, leaned over and pulled a mat of vines aside. "You got to crawl in," he said.

Ma went down on her hands and knees. She felt sand under her, and then the black inside of the mound no longer touched her, and she felt Tom's blanket on the ground. He arranged the vines in place again. It was lightless in the cave.

"Where are you, Ma?"

"Here. Right here. Talk soft, Tom."

"Don't worry. I been livin' like a rabbit some time."

She heard him unwrap his tin plate.

"Pork chops," she said. "And fry potatoes."

"God Awmighty, an' still warm."

Ma could not see him at all in the blackness, but she could hear him chewing, tearing at the meat and swallowing.

"It's a pretty good hide-out," he said.

Ma said uneasily, "Tom—Ruthie tol' about you." She heard him gulp.

"Ruthie? What for?"

"Well, it wasn' her fault. Got in a fight, an' says her brother'll lick that other girl's brother. You know how they do. An' she tol' that her brother killed a man an' was hidin'."

Tom was chuckling. "With me I was always gonna get Uncle John after 'em, but he never would do it. That's jus' kid talk, Ma. That's awright."

"No, it ain't," Ma said. "Them kids'll tell it aroun' an' then the folks'll hear, an' they'll tell aroun', an' pretty soon, well, they liable to get men out to look, jus' in case. Tom, you got to go away."

"That's what I said right along. I was always scared somebody'd see you put stuff in that culvert, an' then they'd watch."

"I know. But I wanted you near. I was scared for you. I ain't seen you. Can't see you now. How's your face?"

"Gettin' well quick."

"Come clost, Tom. Let me feel it. Come clost." He crawled near. Her reaching hand found his head in the blackness and her fingers moved down to his nose, and then over his left cheek. "You got a bad scar, Tom. An' your nose is all crooked."

"Maybe tha's a good thing. Nobody wouldn't know me, maybe. If my prints wasn't on record, I'd be glad." He went back to his eating.

"Hush," she said. "Listen!"

"It's the wind, Ma. Jus' the wind." The gust poured

down the stream, and the trees rustled under its passing.

She crawled close to his voice. "I wanta touch ya again, Tom. It's like I'm blin', it's so dark. I wanta remember, even if it's on'y my fingers that remember. You got to go away, Tom."

"Yeah! I knowed it from the start."

"We made purty good," she said. "I been squirrelin' money away. Hol' out your han', Tom. I got seven dollars here."

"I ain't gonna take ya money," he said. "I'll get 'long all right."

"Hol' out ya han', Tom. I ain't gonna sleep none if you got no money. Maybe you got to take a bus, or somepin. I want you should go a long ways off, three-four hunderd miles."

"I ain't gonna take it."

"Tom," she said sternly. "You take this money. You hear me? You got no right to cause me pain."

"You ain't playin' fair," he said.

"I thought maybe you could go to a big city. Los Angeles, maybe. They wouldn' never look for you there."

"Hm-m," he said. "Lookie, Ma. I been all day an' all night hidin' alone. Guess who I been thinkin' about? Casy! He talked a lot. Used ta bother me. But now I been thinkin' what he said, an' I can remember—all of it. Says one time he went out in the wilderness to find his own soul, an' he foun' he didn' have no soul that was his'n. Says he foun' he jus' got a little piece of a great big soul. Says a wilderness ain't no good, 'cause his little piece of a soul wasn't no good 'less it was with the rest, an' was whole. Funny how I remember. Didn' think I was even listenin'. But I know now a fella ain't no good alone."

"He was a good man," Ma said.

Tom went on, "He spouted out some Scripture once, an' it didn' soun' like no hell-fire Scripture. He tol' .it twicet, an' I remember it. Says it's from the Preacher."

"How's it go, Tom?"

"Goes, 'Two are better than one, because they have a good reward for their labor. For if they fall, the one will lif' up his fellow, but woe to him that is alone when he falleth, for he hath not another to help him up.' That's part of her."

"Go on," Ma said. "Go on, Tom."

"Jus' a little bit more. 'Again, if two lie together, then they have heat: but how can one be warm alone? And if one prevail against him, two shall withstand him, and a three-fold cord is not quickly broken.' "

"An' that's Scripture?"

"Casy said it was. Called it the Preacher."

"Hush—listen."

"On'y the wind, Ma. I know the wind. An' I got to thinkin', Ma—most of the preachin' is about the poor we shall have always with us, an' if you got nothin', why, jus' fol' your hands an' to hell with it, you gonna get ice cream on gol' plates when you're dead. An' then this here Preacher says two get a better reward for their work."

"Tom," she said. "What you aimin' to do?"

He was quiet for a long time. "I been thinkin' how it was in that gov'ment camp, how our folks took care a theirselves, an' if they was a fight they fixed it theirself; an' they wasn't no cops wagglin' their guns, but they was better order than them cops ever give. I been a-wonderin' why we can't do that all over. Throw out the cops that ain't our people. All work together for our own thing—all farm our own lan'."

"Tom," Ma repeated, "what you gonna do?"

"What Casy done," he said.

"But they killed him."

"Yeah," said Tom. "He didn' duck quick enough. He wasn' doing nothin' against the law, Ma. I been thinkin' a hell of a lot, thinkin' about our people livin' like pigs, an' the good rich lan' layin' fallow, or maybe one fella with a million acres, while a hunderd thousan' good farmers is starvin'. An' I been wonderin' if all our folks got together an' yelled, like them fellas yelled, only a few of 'em at the Hooper ranch——"

Ma said, "Tom, they'll drive you, an' cut you down like they done to young Floyd."

"They gonna drive me anyways. They drivin' all our people."

"You don't aim to kill nobody, Tom?"

"No. I been thinkin', long as I'm a outlaw anyways, maybe I could— Hell, I ain't thought it out clear, Ma. Don' worry me now. Don' worry me."

They sat silent in the coal-black cave of vines. Ma said, "How'm I gonna know 'bout you? They might kill ya an' I wouldn' know. They might hurt ya. How'm I gonna know?"

Tom laughed uneasily, "Well, maybe like Casy says, a fella ain't got a soul of his own, but on'y a piece of a big one—an' then——"

"Then what, Tom?"

"Then it don' matter. Then I'll be all aroun' in the dark. I'll be ever'where—wherever you look. Wherever they's a fight so hungry people can eat, I'll be there. Wherever they's a cop beatin' up a guy, I'll be there. If Casy knowed, why, I'll be in the way guys yell when they're mad an'—I'll be in the way kids laugh when they're hungry an' they know supper's ready. An' when our folks eat the stuff they raise an' live in the houses they build—why, I'll be there. See? God, I'm talkin' like Casy. Comes of thinkin' about him so much. Seems like I can see him sometimes."

"I don' un'erstan'," Ma said. "I don' really know."

"Me neither," said Tom. "It's jus' stuff I been thinkin' about. Get thinkin' a lot when you ain't movin' aroun'. You got to get back, Ma."

"You take the money then."

He was silent for a moment. "Awright," he said.

"An', Tom, later—when it's blowed over, you'll come back. You'll find us?"

"Sure," he said. "Now you better go. Here, gimme your han'." He guided her toward the entrance. Her fingers clutched his wrist. He swept the vines aside and followed her out. "Go up to the field till you come to a sycamore on the edge, an' then cut acrost the stream. Good-by."

"Good-by," she said, and she walked quickly away. Her eyes were wet and burning, but she did not cry. Her footsteps were loud and careless on the leaves as she went through the brush. And as she went, out of the dim sky the rain began to fall, big drops and few, splashing on the dry leaves heavily. Ma stopped and stood still in the dripping thicket. She turned about— took three steps back toward the mound of vines; and then she turned quickly and went back toward the box- car camp.

(*From* Chapter 28)

THE FLOOD

OVER the high coast mountains and over the valleys the gray clouds marched in from the ocean. The wind blew fiercely and silently, high in the air, and it swished in the brush, and it roared in the forests. The clouds came in brokenly, in puffs, in folds, in gray crags; and they piled in together and settled low over the west. And then the wind stopped and left the clouds deep and solid. The rain began with gusty showers, pauses and downpours; and then gradually it settled to a single tempo, small drops and a steady beat, rain that was gray to see through, rain that cut midday light to evening. And at first the dry earth sucked the moisture down and blackened. For two days the earth drank the rain, until the earth was full. Then puddles formed, and in the low places little lakes formed in the fields. The muddy lakes rose higher, and the steady rain whipped the shining water. At last the mountains were full, and the hillsides spilled into the streams, built them to freshets, and sent them roaring down the canyons into the valleys. The rain beat on steadily. And the streams and the little rivers edged up to the bank sides and worked at willows and tree roots, bent the willows deep in the current, cut out the roots of cottonwoods and brought down the trees. The muddy water whirled along the bank sides and crept up the banks until at last it spilled over, into the fields, into the orchards, into the cotton patches where the black stems stood. Level fields became lakes, broad and gray, and the rain whipped up the surfaces. Then the water poured over the highways, and cars moved slowly, cutting the water ahead, and leaving a boiling muddy wake behind. The earth whispered under the beat of the rain, and the streams thundered under the churning freshets.

When the first rain started, the migrant people huddled in their tents, saying, It'll soon be over, and asking, How long's it likely to go on?

And when the puddles formed, the men went out in the rain with shovels and built little dikes around the tents. The beating rain worked at the canvas until it penetrated and sent streams down. And then the little dikes washed out and the water came inside, and the streams wet the beds and the blankets. The people sat in wet clothes. They set up boxes and put planks on the boxes. Then, day and night, they sat on the planks.

Beside the tents the old cars stood, and water fouled the ignition wires and water fouled the carburetors. The little gray tents stood in lakes. And at last the people had to move. Then the cars wouldn't start because the wires were shorted; and if the engines would run, deep mud engulfed the wheels. And the people waded away, carrying their wet blankets in their arms. They splashed along, carrying the children, carrying the very old, in their arms. And if a barn stood on high ground, it was filled with people, shivering and hopeless.

Then some went to the relief offices, and they came sadly back to their own people.

They's rules—you got to be here a year before you can git relief. They say the gov'ment is gonna help. They don' know when.

And gradually the greatest terror of all came along.

They ain't gonna be no kinda work for three months.

In the barns; the people sat huddled together; and

the terror came over them, and their faces were gray with terror. The children cried with hunger, and there was no food.

Then the sickness came, pneumonia, and measles that went to the eyes and to the mastoids.

And the rain fell steadily, and the water flowed over the highways, for the culverts could not carry the water.

Then from the tents, from the crowded barns, groups of sodden men went out, their clothes slopping rags, their shoes muddy pulp. They splashed out through the water, to the towns, to the country stores, to the relief offices, to beg for food, to cringe and beg for food, to beg for relief, to try to steal, to lie. And under the begging, and under the cringing, a hopeless anger began to smolder. And in the little towns pity for the sodden men changed to anger, and anger at the hungry people changed to fear of them. Then sheriffs swore in deputies in droves, and orders were rushed for rifles, for tear gas, for ammunition. Then the hungry men crowded the alleys behind the stores to beg for bread, to beg for rotting vegetables, to steal when they could.

Frantic men pounded on the doors of the doctors; and the doctors were busy. And sad men left word at country stores for the coroner to send a car. The coroners were not too busy. The coroners' wagons backed up through the mud and took out the dead.

And the rain pattered relentlessly down, and the streams broke their banks and spread out over the country.

Huddled under sheds, lying in wet hay, the hunger and the fear bred anger. Then boys went out, not to beg, but to steal; and men went out weakly, to try to steal.

The sheriffs swore in new deputies and ordered new rifles; and the comfortable people in tight houses felt pity at first, and then distaste, and finally hatred for the migrant people.

In the wet hay of leaking barns babies were born to women who panted with pneumonia. And old people curled up in corners and died that way, so that the coroners could not straighten them. At night the frantic men walked boldly to hen roosts and carried off the squawking chickens. If they were shot at, they did not run, but splashed sullenly away; and if they were hit, they sank tiredly in the mud.

The rain stopped. On the fields the water stood, reflecting the gray sky, and the land whispered with moving water. And the men came out of the barns, out of the sheds. They squatted on their hams and looked out over the flooded land. And they were silent. And sometimes they talked very quietly.

No work till spring. No work.

And if no work—no money, no food.

Fella had a team of horses, had to use 'em to plow an' cultivate an' mow, wouldn' think a turnin' 'em out to starve when they wasn't workin'.

Them's horses—we're men.

The women watched the men, watched to see whether the break had come at last. The women stood silently and watched. And where a number of men gathered together, the fear went from their faces, and anger took its place. And the women sighed with relief, for they knew it was all right—the break had not come; and the break would never come as long as fear could turn to wrath.

Tiny points of grass came through the earth, and in a few days the hills were pale green with the beginning year.

(Chapter 29)

FROM

Sea of Cortez

Written in Collaboration with Edward F. Ricketts

"IS" THINKING AND "LIVING INTO"

THE PEARL OF LA PAZ

PARABLE OF LAZINESS

DIFFERENCES

"IT MIGHT BE SO"

Speculation from the record of a scientific collecting expedition in the Gulf of California, published in 1941.

"IS" THINKING AND
"LIVING INTO"

March 24, Easter Sunday

THE beach was hot and yellow. We swam, and then walked along on the sand and went inland along the ridge between the beach and a large mangrove-edged lagoon beyond. On the lagoon side of the ridge there were thousands of burrows, presumably of large land-crabs, but it was hopeless to dig them out. The shores of the lagoon teemed with the little clicking bubbling fiddler crabs and estuarian snails. Here we could smell the mangrove flowers without the foul root smell, and the odor was fresh and sweet, like that of new-cut grass. From where we waded there was a fine picture, still reflecting water and the fringing green mangroves against the burnt red-brown of the distant mountains, all like some fantastic Doré drawing of a pressed and embattled heaven. The air was hot and still and the lagoon rippleless. Now and then the surface was ringed as some lagoon fish came to the air. It was a curious quiet resting-place and perhaps because of the quiet we heard in our heads the children singing in the church at La Paz. We did not collect strongly or very efficiently, but rather we half dozed through the day, thinking of old things, each one in himself. And later we discussed manners of thinking and methods of thinking, speculation which is not stylish any more. On a day like this the mind goes outward and touches in all directions. We discussed intellectual methods and approaches, and we thought that through inspection of thinking technique a kind of purity of approach might be consciously achieved—that non-teleological or "is" thinking might be substituted in part for the usual cause-effect methods.

The hazy Gulf, with its changes of light and shape, was rather like us, trying to apply our thoughts, but finding them always pushed and swayed by our bodies and our needs and our satieties. It might be well here to set down some of the discussions of non-teleological thinking.

During the depression there were, and still are, not only destitute but thriftless and uncareful families, and we have often heard it said that the county had to support them because they were shiftless and negligent. If they would only perk up and be somebody everything would be all right. Even Henry Ford in the depth of the depression gave as his solution to that problem, "Everybody ought to roll up his sleeves and get to work."

This view may be correct as far as it goes, but we wonder what would happen to those with whom the shiftless would exchange places in the large pattern— those whose jobs would be usurped, since at that time there was work for only about seventy percent of the total employable population, leaving the remainder as government wards.

This attitude has no bearing on what might be or could be if so-and-so happened. It merely considers conditions "as is." No matter what the ability or aggressiveness of the separate units of society, at that time there were, and still there are, great numbers necessarily out of work, and the fact that those numbers comprised the incompetent or maladjusted or unlucky units is in one sense beside the point. No causality is involved in that; collectively it's just "so"; collectively it's related to the fact that animals produce more offspring than the world can support. The units may be blamed as individuals, but as members of society they cannot be blamed. Any given individual very possibly may transfer from the underprivileged into the more fortunate group by better luck or by improved aggressiveness or competence, but all cannot be so benefited whatever their strivings, and the large population will be unaffected. The seventy-thirty ratio will remain, with merely a reassortment of the units. And no blame, at least no social fault, imputes to these people; they are where they are "because" natural conditions are what they are. And so far as we selfishly are concerned we can rejoice that they, rather than we, represent the low extreme, since there must be one.

So if one is very aggressive he will be able to obtain work even under the most sub-normal economic conditions, but only because there are others, less aggressive than he, who serve in his stead as potential government wards. In the same way, the sight of a half-wit should never depress us, since his extreme, and the extreme of his kind, so affects the mean standard that we, hatless, coatless, often bewhiskered, thereby will be regarded only as a little odd. And similarly, we cannot justly approve the success manuals that tell our high school graduates how to get a job—there being jobs for only half of them!

This type of thinking unfortunately annoys many people. It may especially arouse the anger of women, who regard it as cold, even brutal, although actually it would seem to be more tender and understanding, certainly more real and less illusionary and even less blaming, than the more conventional methods of consideration.

And the value of it as a tool in increased understanding cannot be denied.

As a more extreme example, consider the sea-hare *Tethys*, a shell-less, flabby sea-slug, actually a marine snail, which may be seen crawling about in tidal estuaries, somewhat resembling a rabbit crouched over. A California biologist estimated the number of eggs produced by a single animal during a single breeding season to be more than 478 million. And the adults sometimes occur by the hundred! Obviously all these eggs cannot mature, all this potential cannot, *must not*, become reality, else the ocean would soon be occupied exclusively by sea-hares. There would be no kindness in that, even for the sea-hares themselves, for in a few generations they would overflow the earth; there would be nothing for the rest of us to eat, and nothing for them unless they turned cannibal. On the average, probably no more than the biblical one or two attain full maturity. Somewhere along the way all the rest will have been eaten by predators whose life cycle is postulated upon the presence of abundant larvae of sea-hares and other forms as food—as all life itself is based on such a postulate. Now picture the combination mother-father sea-hare (the animals are hermaphroditic, with the usual cross-fertilization) parentally blessing its offspring with these words: "Work hard and be aggressive, so you can grow into a nice husky *Tethys* like your ten-pound parent." Imagine it, the hypocrite, the illusionist, the Pollyanna, the genial liar, saying that to its millions of eggs *en masse*, with the dice loaded at such a ratio! Inevitably, 99.999 percent are destined to fall by the wayside. No prophet could foresee which specific individuals are to survive, but the most casual student could state confidently that no more than a few are likely to do so; any given individual has *almost* no chance at all—but still there is the "almost," since the race persists. And there is even a semblance of truth in the parent sea-hare's admonition, since even here, with this almost infinitesimal differential, the race is still to the swift and/or to the lucky.

What we personally conceive by the term "teleological thinking," as exemplified by the notion about the shiftless unemployed, is most frequently associated with the evaluating of causes and effects, the purposiveness of events. This kind of thinking considers changes and cures—what "should be" in the terms of an end pattern (which is often a subjective or an anthropomorphic projection); it presumes the bettering of conditions, often, unfortunately, without achieving more than a most superficial understanding of those conditions. In their sometimes intolerant refusal to face facts as they are, teleological notions may substitute a fierce but ineffectual attempt to change conditions which are assumed to be undesirable, in place of the understanding-acceptance which would pave the way for a more sensible attempt at any change which might still be indicated.

Non-teleological ideas derive through "is" thinking, associated with natural selection as Darwin seems to have understood it. They imply depth, fundamentalism, and clarity—seeing beyond traditional or personal projections. They consider events as outgrowths and expressions rather than as results; conscious acceptance as a desideratum, and certainly as an all-important prerequisite. Non-teleological thinking concerns itself primarily not with what should be, or could be, or might be, but rather with what actually "is"—attempting at most to answer the already sufficiently difficult questions *what* or *how*, instead of *why*.

An interesting parallel to these two types of thinking

is afforded by the microcosm with its freedom or indeterminacy, as contrasted with the morphologically inviolable pattern of the macrocosm. Statistically, the electron is free to go where it will. But the destiny pattern of any aggregate, comprising uncountable billions of these same units, is fixed and certain, however much that inevitability may be slowed down. The eventual disintegration of a stick of wood or a piece of iron through the departure of the presumably immortal electrons is assured, even though it may be delayed by such protection against the operation of the second law of thermodynamics as is afforded by painting and rust-proofing.

Examples sometimes clarify an issue better than explanations or definitions. Here are three situations considered by the two methods.

A. *Why are some men taller than others?*

Teleological "answer": because of the underfunctioning of the growth-regulating ductless glands. This seems simple enough. But the simplicity is merely a function of inadequacy and incompleteness. The finality is only apparent. A child, being wise and direct, would ask immediately if given this answer: "Well, why do the glands underfunction?" hinting instantly towards non-teleological methods, or indicating the rapidity with which teleological thinking gets over into the stalemate of first causes.

In the non-teleological sense there can be no "answer." There can be only pictures which become larger and more significant as one's horizon increases. In this given situation, the steps might be something like this:

(1) Variation is a universal and truly primitive trait. It occurs in any group of entities—razor blades, measuring-rods, rocks, trees, horses, matches, or men.

(2) In this case, the apropos variations will be to-wards shortness or tallness from a mean standard—the height of adult men as determined by the statistics of measurements, or by common-sense observation.

(3) In men varying towards tallness there seems to be a constant relation with an underfunctioning of the growth-regulating ductless glands, of the sort that one can be regarded as an index of the other.

(4) There are other known relations consistent with tallness, such as compensatory adjustments along the whole chain of endocrine organs. There may even be other factors, separately not important or not yet dis-covered, which in the aggregate may be significant, or the integration of which may be found to wash over some critical threshold.

(5) The men in question are taller "because" they fall in a group within which there are the above-men-tioned relations. In other words, "they're tall because they're tall."

This is the statistical, or "is," picture to date, more complex than the teleological "answer"—which is really no answer at all—but complex only in the sense that reality is complex; actually simple, inasmuch as the simplicity of the word "is" can be comprehended.

Understandings of this sort can be reduced to this deep and significant summary: "It's so because it's so." But exactly the same words can also express the hasty or superficial attitude. There seems to be no explicit method for differentiating the deep and participating understanding, the "all-truth" which admits infinite change or expansion as added relations become ap-parent, from the shallow dismissal and implied lack of further interest which may be couched in the very same words.

B. *Why are some matches larger than others?*

Examine similarly a group of matches. At first they seem all to be of the same size. But to turn up differences, one needs only to measure them carefully with calipers or to weigh them with an analytical balance. Suppose the extreme comprises only a .001 percent departure from the mean (it will be actually much more); even so slight a differential we know can be highly significant, as with the sea-hares. The differences will group into plus-minus variations from a hypothetical mean to which not one single example will be found exactly to conform. Now the ridiculousness of the question becomes apparent. There is no *particular* reason. It's just so. There may be in the situation some factor or factors more important than the others: owing to the universality of variation (even in those very factors which "cause" variation), there surely *will* be, some even predominantly so. But the question as put is seen to be beside the point. The good answer is: "It's just in the nature of the beast." And this needn't imply belittlement; to have understood the "nature" of a thing is in itself a considerable achievement.

But if the size variations should be quite obvious—and especially if uniformity were to be a desideratum—then there might be a particularly dominant "causative" factor which could be searched out. Or if a person must have a stated "cause"—and many people must, in order to get an emotional understanding, a sense of relation to the situation and to give a name to the thing in order to "settle" it so it may not bother them any more—he can examine the automatic machinery which fabricates the products, and discover in it the variability which results in variation in the matches. But in doing so, he will become involved with a larger principle or pattern, the universality of variation, which has little to do with causality as we think of it.

C. *Leadership*.

The teleological notion would be that those in the forefront are leaders in a given movement and actually direct and consciously lead the masses in the sense that an army corporal orders "Forward march" and the squad marches ahead. One speaks in such a way of church leaders, of political leaders, and of leaders in scientific thought, and of course there is some limited justification for such a notion.

Non-teleological notion: that the people we call leaders are simply those who, at the given moment, are moving in the direction behind which will be found the greatest weight, and which represents a future mass movement.

For a more vivid picture of this state of affairs, consider the movements of an ameba under the microscope. Finger-like processes, the pseudopodia, extend at various places beyond the confines of the chief mass. Locomotion takes place by means of the animal's flowing into one or into several adjacent pseudopodia. Suppose that the molecules which "happened" to be situated in the forefront of the pseudopodium through which the animal is progressing, or into which it will have flowed subsequently, should be endowed with consciousness and should say to themselves and to their fellows: "We are directly leading this great procession, our leadership 'causes' all the rest of the population to move this way, the mass follows the path we blaze." This would be equivalent to the attitude with which we commonly regard leadership.

As a matter of fact there are three distinct types of thinking, two of them teleological. Physical teleology, the type we have been considering, is by far the commonest today. Spiritual teleology is rare. Formerly predominant, it now occurs metaphysically and in most religions, especially as they are popularly understood (but not, we suspect, as they were originally enunciated or as they may still be known to the truly adept). Occasionally the three types may be contrasted in a single problem. Here are a couple of examples:

(1) Van Gogh's feverish hurrying in the Arles epoch, culminating in epilepsy and suicide.

Teleological "answer": Improper care of his health during times of tremendous activity and exposure to the sun and weather brought on his epilepsy out of which discouragement and suicide resulted.

Spiritual teleology: He hurried because he innately foresaw his imminent death, and wanted first to express as much of his essentiality as possible.

Non-teleological picture: Both the above, along with a good many other symptoms and expressions (some of which could probably be inferred from his letters), were parts of his essentiality, possibly glimpsable as his "lust for life."

(2) The thyroid-neurosis syndrome.

Teleological "answer": Over-activity of the thyroid gland irritates and over-stimulates the patient to the point of nervous breakdown.

Spiritual teleology: The neurosis is causative. Something psychically wrong drives the patient on to excess mental irritation which harries and upsets the glandular balance, especially the thyroid, through shock-resonance in the autonomic system, in the sense that a purely psychic shock may spoil one's appetite, or may even result in violent illness. In this connection, note the army's acceptance of extreme homesickness as a reason for disability discharge.

Non-teleological picture: Both are discrete segments of a vicious circle, which may also include other factors as additional more or less discrete segments, symbols or maybe parts of an underlying but non-teleological pattern which comprises them and many others, the ramifications of which are *n*, and which has to do with causality only reflectedly.

Teleological thinking may even be highly fallacious, especially where it approaches the very superficial but quite common *post hoc, ergo propter hoc* pattern. Consider the situation with reference to dynamiting in a quarry. Before a charge is set off, the foreman toots warningly on a characteristic whistle. People living in the neighborhood come to associate the one with the other, since the whistle is almost invariably followed within a few seconds by the shock and sound of an explosion for which one automatically prepares oneself. Having experienced this many times without closer contact, a very naïve and unthinking person might justly conclude not only that there was a cause-effect relation, but that the whistle actually caused the explosion. A slightly wiser person would insist that the explosion caused the whistle, but would be hard put to explain the transposed time element. The normal adult would recognize that the whistle no more caused the explosion than the explosion caused the whistle, but that both were parts of a larger pattern out of which a "why" could be postulated for both, but more immediately and particularly for the whistle. Determined to chase the thing down in a cause-effect sense, an observer would have to be very wise indeed who could follow the intricacies of cause through more fundamental cause to primary cause, even in this largely man-made series about which we presumably know most of the motives, causes, and ramifications. He would eventually find himself in a welter of thoughts on production, and ownership of the means of production, and economic whys and wherefores about which there is little agreement.

The example quoted is obvious and simple. Most things are far more subtle than that, and have many of their relations and most of their origins far back in things more difficult of access than the tooting of a whistle calculated to warn bystanders away from an explosion. We know little enough even of a man-made series like this—how much less of purely natural phenomena about which also there is apt to be teleological pontificating!

Usually it seems to be true that when even the most definitely apparent cause-effect situations are examined in the light of wider knowledge, the cause-effect aspect comes to be seen as less rather than more significant, and the statistical or relational aspects acquire larger importance. It seems safe to assume that non-teleological is more "ultimate" than teleological reasoning. Hence the latter would be expected to prove to be limited and constricting except when used provisionally. But while it is true that the former is more open, for that very reason its employment necessitates greater discipline and care in order to allow for the dangers of looseness and inadequate control.

Frequently, however, a truly definitive answer seems to arise through teleological methods. Part of this is due to wish-fulfillment delusion. When a person asks "Why?" in a given situation, he usually deeply expects, and in any case receives, only a relational answer in place of the definitive "because" which he thinks he

wants. But he customarily accepts the actually relational answer (it couldn't be anything else unless it
comprised the whole, which is unknowable except by
"living into") as a definitive "because." Wishful thinking probably fosters that error, since everyone continually searches for absolutisms (hence the value placed
on diamonds, the most permanent physical things in
the world) and imagines continually that he finds them.
More justly, the relational picture should be regarded
only as a glimpse—a challenge to consider also the rest
of the relations as they are available—to envision the
whole picture as well as can be done with given abil-
ities and data. But one accepts it instead of a real "because," considers it settled, and, having named it, loses
interest and goes on to something else.

Chiefly, however, we seem to arrive occasionally at
definitive answers through the workings of another
primitive principle: the universality of quanta. No one
thing ever merges gradually into anything else; the
steps are discontinuous, but often so very minute as to
seem truly continuous. If the investigation is carried
deep enough, the factor in question, instead of being
graphable as a continuous process, will be seen to
function by discrete quanta with gaps or synapses between, as do quanta of energy, undulations of light.
The apparently definitive answer occurs when causes
and effects both arise on the same large plateau which
is bounded a great way off by the steep rise which an-
nounces the next plateau. If the investigation is extended
sufficiently, that distant rise will, however, inevitably
be encountered; the answer which formerly seemed definitive now will be seen to be at least slightly inadequate and the picture will have to be enlarged so as to
include the plateau next further out. Everything impinges on everything else, often into radically different

systems, although in such cases faintly. We doubt very much if there are any truly "closed systems." Those so called represent kingdoms of a great continuity bounded by the sudden discontinuity of great synapses which eventually must be bridged in any unified-field hypothesis. For instance, the ocean, with reference to waves of water, might be considered as a closed system. But anyone who has lived in Pacific Grove or Carmel during the winter storms will have felt the house tremble at the impact of waves half a mile or more away impinging on a totally different "closed" system.

But the greatest fallacy in, or rather the greatest objection to, teleological thinking is in connection with the emotional content, the belief. People get to believing and even to professing the apparent answers thus arrived at, suffering mental constrictions by emotionally closing their minds to any of the further and possibly opposite "answers" which might otherwise be unearthed by honest effort—answers which, if faced realistically, would give rise to a struggle and to a possible rebirth which might place the whole problem in a new and more significant light. Grant for a moment that among students of endocrinology a school of thought might arise, centering upon some belief as to etiology— upon the belief, for instance, that all abnormal growth is caused by glandular imbalance. Such a clique, becoming formalized and powerful, would tend, by scorn and opposition, to wither any contrary view which, if untrammeled, might discover a clue to some opposing "causative" factor of equal medical importance. That situation is most unlikely to arise in a field so lusty as endocrinology, with its relational insistence, but the principle illustrated by a poor example is thought nevertheless to be sound.

Significant in this connection is the fact that conflicts

may arise between any two or more of the "answers" brought forth by either of the teleologies, or between the two teleologies themselves. But there can be no conflict between any of these and the non-teleological picture. For instance, in the condition called hyperthyroidism, the treatments advised by believers in the psychic or neurosis etiology very possibly may conflict with those arising out of a belief in the purely physical cause. Or even within the physical teleology group there may be conflicts between those who believe the condition due to a strictly thyroid upset and those who consider causation derived through a general imbalance of the ductless glands. But there can be no conflict between any or all of these factors and the non-teleological picture, because the latter includes them—evaluates them relationally or at least attempts to do so, or maybe only accepts them as time-place truths. Teleological "answers" necessarily must be included in the non-teleological method—since they are part of the picture even if only restrictedly true—and as soon as their qualities of relatedness are recognized. Even erroneous beliefs are real things, and have to be considered proportional to their spread or intensity. "Alltruth" must embrace all extant apropos errors also, and know them as such by relation to the whole, and allow for their effects.

The criterion of validity in the handling of data seems to be this: that the summary shall say in substance, significantly and understandingly, "It's so because it's so." Unfortunately the very same words might equally derive through a most superficial glance, as any child could learn to repeat from memory the most abstruse of Dirac's equations. But to know a thing emergently and significantly is something else again, even though the understanding may be expressed in the self-same words that were used superficially. In the following example[1] note the deep significance of the emergent as contrasted with the presumably satisfactory but actually incorrect original naïve understanding. At one time an important game bird in Norway, the willow grouse, was so clearly threatened with extinction that it was thought wise to establish protective regulations and to place a bounty on its chief enemy, a hawk which was known to feed heavily on it. Quantities of the hawks were exterminated, but despite such drastic measures the grouse disappeared actually more rapidly than before. The naïvely applied customary remedies had obviously failed. But instead of becoming discouraged and quietistically letting this bird go the way of the great auk and the passenger pigeon, the authorities enlarged the scope of their investigations until the anomaly was explained. An ecological analysis into the relational aspects of the situation disclosed that a parasitic disease, coccidiosis, was epizootic among the grouse. In its incipient stages, this disease so reduced the flying speed of the grouse that the mildly ill individuals became easy prey for the hawks. In living largely off the slightly ill birds, the hawks prevented them from developing the disease in its full intensity and so spreading it more widely and quickly to otherwise healthy fowl. Thus the presumed enemies of the grouse, by controlling the epizootic aspects of the disease, proved to be friends in disguise.

In summarizing the above situation, the measure of validity wouldn't be to assume that, even in the well-understood factor of coccidiosis, we have the real "cause" of any beneficial or untoward condition, but to say, rather, that in this phase we have a highly signif-

---

[1] Abstracted from the article on ecology by Elton, *Encyclopaedia Britannica*, 14th Edition, Vol. VII, p. 916.

icant and possibly preponderantly important relational aspect of the picture.

However, many people are unwilling to chance the sometimes ruthless-appearing notions which may arise through nonteleological treatments. They fear even to use them in that they may be left dangling out in space, deprived of such emotional support as had been afforded them by an unthinking belief in the proved value of pest control in the conservation of game birds; in the institutions of tradition; religion; science; in the security of the home or the family; or in a comfortable bank account. But for that matter emancipations in general are likely to be held in terror by those who may not yet have achieved them, but whose thresholds in those respects are becoming significantly low. Think of the fascinated horror, or at best tolerance, with which little girls regard their brothers who have dispensed with the Santa Claus belief; or the fear of the devout young churchman for his university senior who has grown away from depending on the security of religion.

As a matter of fact, whoever employs this type of thinking with other than a few close friends will be referred to as detached, hard-hearted, or even cruel. Quite the opposite seems to be true. Non-teleological methods more than any other seem capable of great tenderness, of an all-embracingness which is rare otherwise. Consider, for instance, the fact that, once a given situation is deeply understood, no apologies are required. There are ample difficulties even to understanding conditions "as is." Once that has been accomplished, the "why" of it (known now to be simply a relation, though probably a near and important one) seems no longer to be preponderantly important. It needn't be condoned or extenuated, it just "is." It is seen merely as part of a more or less dim whole picture. As an example: A woman near us in the Carmel woods was upset when her dog was poisoned—frightened at the thought of passing the night alone after years of companionship with the animal. She phoned to ask if, with our windows on that side of the house closed as they were normally, we could hear her ringing a dinner bell as a signal during the night that marauders had cut her phone wires preparatory to robbing her. Of course that was, in fact, an improbable contingency to be provided against; a man would call it a foolish fear, neurotic. And so it was. But one could say kindly, "We can hear the bell quite plainly, but if desirable we can adjust our sleeping arrangements so as to be able to come over there instantly in case you need us," without even stopping to consider whether or not the fear was foolish, or to be concerned about it if it were, correctly regarding all that as secondary. And if the woman had said apologetically, "Oh, you must forgive me; I know my fears are foolish, but I am so upset!" the wise reply would have been, "Dear person, nothing to forgive. If you have fears, they *are;* they are real things and to be considered. Whether or not they're foolish is beside the point. *What* they are is unimportant alongside the fact *that* they are." In other words, the badness or goodness, the teleology of the fears, was decidedly secondary. The whole notion could be conveyed by a smile or by a pleasant intonation more readily than by the words themselves. Teleological treatment which one might have been tempted to employ under the circumstances would first have stressed the fact that the fear was foolish—would say with a great show of objective justice, "Well, there's no use in *our* doing anything; the fault is that *your* fear is foolish and improbable. Get over that" (as a judge would say, "Come into court with clean hands"); "then if there's anything *sensible* we can do, we'll see," with smug blame implied in every word. Or, more kindly, it would try to reason with the woman in an attempt to help her get over it—the business of propaganda directed towards change even before the situation is fully understood (maybe as a lazy substitute for understanding). Or, still more kindly, the teleological method would try to understand the fear causally. But with the non-teleological treatment there is only the love and understanding of instant acceptance; after that fundamental has been achieved, the next step, if any should be necessary, can be considered more sensibly.

Strictly, the term non-teleological thinking ought not to be applied to what we have in mind. Because it involves more than thinking, that term is inadequate. *Modus operandi* might be better—a method of handling data of any sort. The example cited just above concerns feeling more than thinking. The method extends beyond thinking even to living itself; in fact, by inferred definition it transcends the realm of thinking possibilities, it postulates "living into."

In the destitute-unemployed illustration, thinking, as being the evaluatory function chiefly concerned, was the point of departure, "the crust to break through." There the "blame approach" considered the situation in the limited and inadequate teleological manner. The non-teleological method included that viewpoint as correct but limited. But when it came to the feeling aspects of a human relation situation, the non-teleological method would probably ameliorate the woman's fears in a loving, truly mellow, and adequate fashion, whereas the teleological would have tended to bungle things by employing the limited and sophisticated approach.

Incidentally, there is in this connection a remarkable etiological similarity to be noted between cause in thinking and blame in feeling. One feels that one's neighbors are to be blamed for their hate or anger or fear. One thinks that poor pavements are "caused" by politics. The non-teleological picture in either case is the larger one that goes beyond blame or cause. And the non-causal or non-blaming viewpoint seems to us very often relatively to represent the "new thing," the Hegelian "Christ-child" which arises emergently from the union of two opposing viewpoints, such as those of physical and spiritual teleologies, especially if there is conflict as to causation between the two or within either. The new viewpoint very frequently sheds light over a larger picture, providing a key which may unlock levels not accessible to either of the teleological viewpoints. There are interesting parallels here: to the triangle, to the Christian ideas of trinity, to Hegel's dialectic, and to Swedenborg's metaphysic of divine love (feeling) and divine wisdom (thinking).

The factors we have been considering as "answers" seem to be merely symbols or indices, relational aspects of things—of which they are integral parts—not to be considered in terms of causes and effects. The truest reason for anything's being so is that it *is*. This is actually and truly a reason, more valid and clearer than all the other separate reasons, or than any group of them short of the whole. Anything less than the whole forms part of the picture only, and the infinite whole is unknowable except by *being* it, by living into it.

A thing may be *so* "because" of a thousand and one reasons of greater or lesser importance, such as the man oversized because of glandular insufficiency. The integration of these many reasons which are in the nature of relations rather than reasons is that he *is*. The separate reasons, no matter how valid, are only fragmentary parts of the picture. And the whole necessarily includes all that it impinges on as object and subject, in ripples fading with distance or depending upon the original intensity of the vortex.

The frequent allusions to an underlying pattern have no implication of mysticism—except inasmuch as a pattern which comprises infinity in factors and symbols might be called mystic. But infinity as here used occurs also in the mathematical aspects of physiology and physics, both far away from mysticism as the term is ordinarily employed. Actually, the underlying pattern is probably nothing more than an integration of just such symbols and indices and mutual reference points as are already known, except that its power is n. Such an integration might include nothing more spectacular than we already know. But, equally, it *could* include anything, even events and entities as different from those already known as the vectors, tensors, scalars, and ideas of electrical charges in mathematical physics are different from the mechanical-model world of the Victorian scientists.

In such a pattern, causality would be merely a name for something that exists only in our partial and biased mental reconstructings. The pattern which it indexes, however, would be real, but not intellectually apperceivable because the pattern goes everywhere and is everything and cannot be encompassed by finite mind or by anything short of life—which it is.

The psychic or spiritual residua remaining after the most careful physical analyses, or the physical remnants obvious, particularly to us of the twentieth century, in the most honest and disciplined spiritual speculations of medieval philosophers, all bespeak such a pattern. Those residua, those most minute differentials, the

0.001 percentages which suffice to maintain the races of sea animals, are seen finally to be the most important things in the world, not because of their sizes, but because they are everywhere. The differential is the true universal, the true catalyst, the cosmic solvent. Any investigation carried far enough will bring to light these residua, or rather will leave them still unassailable as Emerson remarked a hundred years ago in "The Oversoul"—will run into the brick wall of the *impossibility* of perfection while at the same time insisting on the *validity* of perfection. Anomalies especially testify to that framework; they are the commonest intellectual vehicles for breaking through; all are solvable in the sense that any *one* is understandable, but that one leads with the power n to still more and deeper anomalies.

This deep underlying pattern inferred by non-teleological thinking crops up everywhere—a relational thing, surely, relating opposing factors on different levels, as reality and potential are related. But it must not be considered as causative, it simply exists, it *is*, things are merely expressions of it as it is expressions of them. And they *are* it, also. As Swinburne, extolling Hertha, the earth goddess, makes her say: "Man, equal and one with me, man that is made of me, man that is I," so all things which are *that*—which is all—equally may be extolled. That pattern materializes everywhere in the sense that Eddington finds the non-integer q "number" appearing everywhere, in the background of all fundamental equations,[2] in the sense that the speed of light, constant despite compoundings or subtractions, seemed at one time almost to be conspiring against investigation.

The whole is necessarily everything, the whole world of fact and fancy, body and psyche, physical fact and

---

[2] *The Nature of the Physical World*, pp. 208-10.

spiritual truth, individual and collective, life and death, macrocosm and microcosm (the greatest quanta here, the greatest synapse between these two), conscious and unconscious, subject and object. The whole picture is portrayed by *is*, the deepest word of deep ultimate reality, not shallow or partial as reasons are, but deeper and participating, possibly encompassing the Oriental concept of *being*.

And all this against the hot beach on an Easter Sunday, with the passing day and the passing time. This little trip of ours was becoming a thing and a dual thing, with collecting and eating and sleeping merging with the thinking-speculating activity. Quality of sunlight, blueness and smoothness of water, boat engines, and ourselves were all parts of a larger whole and we could begin to feel its nature but not its size.

(Chapter 15)

THE PEARL OF LA PAZ

THE Gulf and Gulf ports have always been unfriendly to colonization. Again and again attempts
were made before a settlement would stick. Humans
are not much wanted on the Peninsula. But at La Paz
the pearl oysters drew men from all over the world. And,
as in all concentrations of natural wealth, the terrors of
greed were let loose on the city again and again. An
event which happened at La Paz in recent years is
typical of such places. An Indian boy by accident found
a pearl of great size, an unbelievable pearl. He knew
its value was so great that he need never work again.
In his one pearl he had the ability to be drunk as long
as he wished, to marry any one of a number of girls,
and to make many more a little happy too. In his great
pearl lay salvation, for he could in advance purchase
masses sufficient to pop him out of Purgatory like a
squeezed watermelon seed. In addition he could shift
a number of dead relatives a little nearer to Paradise.
He went to La Paz with his pearl in his hand and his
future clear into eternity in his heart. He took his pearl
to a broker and was offered so little that he grew angry,
for he knew he was cheated. Then he carried his pearl
to another broker and was offered the same amount.
After a few more visits he came to know that the bro-
kers were only the many hands of one head and that
he could not sell his pearl for more. He took it to the
beach and hid it under a stone, and that night he was
clubbed into unconsciousness and his clothing was

searched. The next night he slept at the house of a friend and his friend and he were injured and bound and the whole house searched. Then he went inland to lose his pursuers and he was waylaid and tortured. But he was very angry now and he knew what he must do. Hurt as he was he crept back to La Paz in the night and he skulked like a hunted fox to the beach and took out his pearl from under the stone. Then he cursed it and threw it as far as he could into the channel. He was a free man again with his soul in danger and his food and shelter insecure. And he laughed a great deal about it.

This seems to be a true story, but it is so much like a parable that it almost can't be. This Indian boy is too heroic, too wise. He knows too much and acts on his knowledge. In every way, he goes contrary to human direction. The story is probably true, but we don't believe it; it is far too reasonable to be true.

La Paz, the great city, was only a little way from us now, we could almost see its towers and smell its perfume. And it was right that it should be so hidden here out of the world, inaccessible except to the galleons of a small boy's imagination.

(*From* Chapter 11)

PARABLE OF LAZINESS

March 28

AFTER the collecting on Coronado Island, on the twenty-seventh, and the preservation and labeling, we found that we were very tired. We had worked constantly. On the morning of the twenty-eighth we slept. It was a good thing, we told ourselves; the eyes grow weary with looking at new things; sleeping late, we said, has its genuine therapeutic value; we would be better for it, would be able to work more effectively. We have little doubt that all this was true, but we wish we could build as good a rationalization every time we are lazy. For in some beastly way this fine laziness has got itself a bad name. It is easy to see how it might have come into disrepute, if the result of laziness were hunger. But it rarely is. Hunger makes laziness impossible. It has even become sinful to be lazy. We wonder why. One could argue, particularly if one had a gift for laziness, that it is a relaxation pregnant of activity, a sense of rest from which directed effort may arise, whereas most busy-ness is merely a kind of nervous tic. We know a lady who is obsessed with the idea of ashes in an ashtray. She is not lazy. She spends a good half of her waking time making sure that no ashes remain in any ashtray, and to make sure of keeping busy she has a great many ashtrays. Another acquaintance, a man, straightens rugs and pictures and arranges books and magazines in neat piles. He is not lazy, either; he is very busy. To what end? If he should relax, perhaps with his feet up on a chair and a glass of cool beer beside him—not cold, but cool—if he should examine from this position a rumpled rug or a crooked picture, saying to himself between sips of beer (preferably Carta Blanca beer), "This rug irritates me for some reason. If it were straight, I should be comfortable; but there is only one straight position (and this is, of course, only my own personal discipline of straightness) among all possible positions. I am, in effect, trying to impose my will, my insular sense of rightness, on a rug, which of itself can have no such sense, since it seems equally contented straight or crooked. Suppose I should try to straighten people," and here he sips deeply. "Helen C., for instance, is not neat, and Helen C."—here he goes into a reverie—"how beautiful she is with her hair messy, how lovely when she is excited and breathing through her mouth." Again he raises his glass, and in a few minutes he picks up the telephone. He is happy; Helen C. may be happy; and the rug is not disturbed at all.

How can such a process have become a shame and a sin? Only in laziness can one achieve a state of contemplation which is a balancing of values, a weighing of oneself against the world and the world against itself. A busy man cannot find time for such balancing. We do not think a lazy man can commit murders, nor great thefts, nor lead a mob. He would be more likely to think about it and laugh. And a nation of lazy contemplative men would be incapable of fighting a war unless their very laziness were attacked. Wars are the activities of busy-ness.

With such a background of reasoning, we slept until nine A.M. And then the engines started and we moved toward Concepción Bay. The sea, with the exception of one blow outside of La Paz, had been very calm. This day, a little wind blew over the ultramarine water. The swordfish in great numbers jumped and played about us. We set up our lightest harpoon on the bow with a coil of cotton line beside it, and for hours we stood watch. The helmsman changed course again and again to try to bring the bow over a resting fish, but they seemed to wait until we were barely within throwing range and then they sounded so quickly that they seemed to snap from view. We made many wild casts and once we got the iron in, near the tail of a monster. But he flicked his tail and tore it out and was gone. We could see schools of leaping tuna all about us, and whenever we crossed the path of a school, our lines jumped and snapped under the strikes, and we brought the beautiful fish in.

We had set up a salt barrel near the stern, and we cut the fish into pieces and put them into brine to take home. It developed after we got home that several of us had added salt to the brine and the whole barrel was hopelessly salty and inedible.

(From Chapter 18)

DIFFERENCES

April 5

WE sailed in the morning on the short trip to Guaymas. It was the first stop in a town that had anything like communication since we had left San Diego. The world and the war had become remote to us; all the immediacies of our usual lives had slowed up. Far from welcoming a return, we rather resented going back to newspapers and telegrams and business. We had been drifting in some kind of dual world—a parallel realistic world; and the preoccupations of the world we came from, which are considered realistic, were to us filled with mental mirage. Modern economies; war drives; party affiliations and lines; hatreds, political, and social and racial, cannot survive in dignity the perspective of distance. We could understand, because we could feel, how the Indians of the Gulf, hearing about the great ant-doings of the north, might shake their heads sadly and say, "But it is crazy. It would be nice to have new Ford cars and running water, but not at the cost of insanity." And in us the factor of time had changed: the low tides were our clock and the throbbing engine our second hand.

Now, approaching Guaymas, we were approaching an end. We planned only two or three collecting stations beyond, and then the time of charter-end would be crowding us, and we would have to run for it to be back when the paper said we would. The charter at least fixed our place in time. And already our crew was trying to think of ways to come back to the Gulf. This trip had been like a dreaming sleep, a rest from immediacies. And in our contacts with Mexican people we had been faced with a change in expediencies. Perhaps—even surely—these people are expedient, but on some other plane than our ordinary one. What they did for us was without hope or plan of profit. We suppose there must have been some kind of profit involved, but not the kind we are used to, not of material things changing hands. And yet some trade took place at every contact—something was exchanged, some unnamable of great value. Perhaps these people are expedient in the unnamables. Maybe they bargain in feelings, in pleasures, even in simple contacts. When the Indians came to the *Western Flyer* and sat timelessly on the rail, perhaps they were taking something. We gave them presents, but it is sure they had not come for presents. When they helped us, it was with no idea of material payment. There were material prices for material things, but one couldn't buy kindness with money, as one can in our country. It was so in every contact, and they were so used to the spiritual transaction that they had difficulty translating material things into money. If we wanted to buy a harpoon, there was difficulty immediately. What was the price? An Indian had paid three pesos for the harpoon several years ago. Obviously, since that had been paid, that was the price. But he had not yet learned to give time a money value. If he had to go three days in a canoe to get another harpoon, he could not add his time to the price, because he had never thought of time as a medium of exchange. At first we tried to explain the feeling we all had that time is a salable article, but we had to give it up. Time, these Indians said, went on. If one could stop time, or take it away, or hoard it, then one might sell it. One might as well sell air or heat or cold or health or beauty. And we thought of the great businesses in our country—the sale of clean air, of heat and cold, the scrabbling bargains in health offered over the radio, the boxed and bottled beauty, all for a price. This was not bad or good, it was only different. Time and beauty, they thought, could not be captured and sold, and we knew they not only *could* be, but that time could be warped and beauty made ugly. And again it was not good or bad. Our people would pay more for pills in a yellow box than in a white box—even the refraction of light had its price. They would buy books because they should rather than because they wanted to. They bought immunity from fear in salves to go under their arms. They bought romantic adventure in bars of tomato-colored soaps. They bought education by the foot and hefted the volumes to see that they were not short-weighted. They purchased pain, and then analgesics to put down the pain. They bought courage and rest and had neither. And they are vastly amused at the Indian who, with his silver, bought Heaven and ransomed his father from Hell. These Indians were far too ignorant to understand the absurdities merchandising can really achieve when it has an enlightened people to work on.

One can go from race to race. It is coming back that has its violation. As we feel greatness, we feel that these people are very great. It seems to us that the repose of an Indian woman sitting in the gutter is beyond our achievement. But even these people wish for our involvement in temporal and material things. Once we thought that the bridge between cultures might be through education, public health, good housing, and through political vehicles—democracy, Nazism, communism—but now it seems much simpler than that.

The invasion comes with good roads and high-tension wires. Where those two go, the change takes place very quickly. Any of the political forms can come in once the radio is hooked up, once the concrete highway irons out the mountains and destroys the "localness" of a community. Once the Gulf people are available to contact, they too will come to consider clean feet more important than clean minds. These are the factors of civilization and their paths, good roads, high-voltage wires, and possibly canned foods. A local 110-volt power unit and a winding dirt road may leave a people for a long time untouched, but high-voltage operating day and night, the network of wires, will draw the people into the civilizing web, whether it be in Asiatic Russia, in rural England, or in Mexico. That *Zeitgeist* operates everywhere, and there is no escape from it.

Again, this is not to be considered good or bad. To us, a little weary of the complication and senselessness of a familiar picture, the Indian seems a rested, simple man. If we should permit ourselves to remain in ignorance of his complications, then we might long for his condition, thinking it superior to ours. The indian on the other hand, subject to constant hunger and cold, mourning a grandfather and set of uncles in Purgatory, pained by the aching teeth and sore eyes of malnutrition, may well envy us our luxury. It is easy to remember how, when we were in the terrible complication of childhood, we longed for easy and uncomplicated adulthood. Then we would have only to reach into our pockets for money, then all problems would be ironed out. The ranch-owner had said, "There is no poverty in your country and no misery. Everyone has a Ford."

(*From* Chapter 26)

"IT MIGHT BE SO"

April 11

AT ten o'clock we moved toward the northern side of the entrance of Agiabampo estuary. The sand-bars were already beginning to show with the lowering tide. Tiny used the leadline on the bow while Sparky was again on the crow's-nest where he could watch for the shallow water. Tony would not approach closer than a mile from the entrance, leaving as always a margin of safety.

When we anchored, five of us got into the little skiff, filling it completely. Any rough water would have swamped us. Sparky and Tiny rowed us in, competing violently with each other, which gave a curious twisting course to the boat.

Agiabampo is a great lagoon with a narrow seaward entrance. There is a little town ten miles in on the northern shore which we did not even try to reach. The entrance is intricate and obstructed with many shoals and sand-bars. It would be difficult without local knowledge to bring in a boat of any draft. We moved in around the northern shore; there were dense thickets of mangrove with little river-like entrances winding away into them. We saw great expanses of sand flat and the first extensive growth of eel-grass we had found.[1] But the eel-grass, which ordinarily shelters a great

---

[1] The true Zostera marina according to Dr. Dawson, botanist at the University of California, who remarks that it had not been reported previously so far south.

variety of animal life, was here not very rich at all. We saw the depressions where *botete*, the poison fish, lay. And there were great numbers of sting-rays, which made us walk very carefully, even in rubber boots, for a slash with the tail-thorn of a sting-ray can easily pierce a boot.

The sand banks near the entrance were deeply cut by currents. High in the intertidal many grapsoid crabs[2] lived in slanting burrows about eighteen inches deep. There were a great many of the huge stalk-eyed conchs and the inevitable big hermit crabs living in the cast-off conch shells. Farther in, there were numbers of *Chione* and the blue-clawed swimming crabs. They seemed even cleverer and fiercer here than at other places. Some of the eel-grass was sexually mature, and we took it for identification. On this grass there were clusters of snail eggs, but we saw none of the snails that had laid them. We found one scale-worm,[3] a magnificent specimen in a *Cerianthus*-like tube. There were great numbers of tube-worms in the sand. The wind was light or absent while we collected, and we could see the bottom everywhere. On the exposed sand-bars birds were feeding in multitudes, possibly on the tube-worms. Along the shore, oyster-catchers hunted the burrowing crabs, diving at them as they sat at the entrances of their houses. It was not a difficult collecting station; the pattern, except for the eel-grass, was by now familiar to us although undoubtedly there were many things we did not see. Perhaps our eyes were tired with too much looking.

As soon as the tide began its strong ebb we got into the skiff and started back to the *Western Flyer*. Collecting in narrow-mouthed estuaries, we are always wrong with the currents, for we come in against an ebb-

---

[2] *Ocypode occidentalis.*
[3] *Polyodontes oculea.*

ing tide and we go out against the flow. It was heavy work to defeat this current. The Sea-Cow gave us a hand and we rowed strenuously to get outside.

That night we intended to run across the Gulf and start for home. It was good to be running at night again, easier to sleep with the engine beating. Tiny at the wheel inveighed against the waste of fish by the Japanese. To him it was a waste complete, a loss of something. We discussed the widening and narrowing picture. To Tiny the fisherman, having as his function not only the catching of fish but the presumption that they would be eaten by humans, the Japanese were wasteful. And in that picture he was very correct. But all the fish actually were eaten; if any small parts were missed by the birds they were taken by the detritus-eaters, the worms and cucumbers. And what they missed was reduced by the bacteria. What was the fisherman's loss was a gain to another group. We tried to say that in the macrocosm nothing is wasted, the equation always balances. The elements which the fish elaborated into an individuated physical organism, a microcosm, go back again into the undifferentiated macrocosm which is the great reservoir. There is not, nor can there be, any actual waste, but simply varying forms of energy. To each group, of course, there must be waste—the dead fish to man, the broken pieces to gulls, the bones to some and the scales to others—but to the whole, there is no waste. The great organism, Life, takes it all and uses it all. The large picture is always clear and the smaller can be clear—the picture of eater and eaten. And the large equilibrium of the life of a given animal is postulated on the presence of abundant larvae of just such forms as itself for food. Nothing is wasted; "no star is lost."

And in a sense there is no over-production, since every living thing has its niche, *a posteriori*, and God, in a real, non-mystical sense, sees every sparrow fall and every cell utilized. What is called "over-production" even among us in our manufacture of articles is only over-production in terms of a status quo, but in the history of the organism, it may well be a factor or a function in some great pattern of change or repetition. Perhaps some cells, even intellectual ones, must be sickened before others can be well. And perhaps with us these production climaxes are the therapeutic fevers which cause a rush of curative blood to the sickened part. Our history is as much a product of torsion and stress as it is of unilinear drive. It is amusing that at any given point of time we haven't the slightest idea of what is happening to us. The present wars and ideological changes of nervousness and fighting seem to have direction, but in a hundred years it is more than possible it will be seen that the direction was quite different from the one we supposed. The limitation of the seeing point in time, as well as in space, is a warping lens.

Among men, it seems, historically at any rate, that processes of co-ordination and disintegration follow each other with great regularity, and the index of the co-ordination is the measure of the disintegration which follows. There is no mob like a group of well-drilled soldiers when they have thrown off their discipline. And there is no lostness like that which comes to a man when a perfect and certain pattern has dissolved about him. There is no hater like one who has greatly loved.

We think these historical waves may be plotted and the harmonic curves of human group conduct observed. Perhaps out of such observation a knowledge of the function of war and destruction might emerge. Little enough is known about the function of individual pain and suffering, although from its profound organization it is suspected of being necessary as a survival mechanism. And nothing whatever is known of the group pains of the species, although it is not unreasonable to suppose that they too are somehow functions of the surviving species. It is too bad that against even such investigation we build up a hysterical and sentimental barrier. Why do we so dread to think of our species as a species? Can it be that we are afraid of what we may find? That human self-love would suffer too much and that the image of God might prove to be a mask? This could be only partly true, for if we could cease to wear the image of a kindly, bearded, interstellar dictator, we might find ourselves true images of his kingdom, our eyes the nebulae, and universes in our cells.

The safety-valve of all speculation is: *It might be so.* And as long as that *might* remains, a variable deeply understood, then speculation does not easily become dogma, but remains the fluid creative thing it might be. Thus, a valid painter, letting color and line, observed, sift into his eyes, up the nerve trunks, and mix well with his experience before it flows down his hand to the canvas, has made his painting say, "It might be so." Perhaps his critic, being not so honest and not so wise, will say, "It is not so. The picture is damned." If this critic could say, "It is not so with me, but that might be because my mind and experience are not identical with those of the painter," that critic would be the better critic for it, just as that painter is a better painter for knowing he himself is in the pigment.

We tried always to understand that the reality we observed was partly us; the speculation, our product. And yet if somehow, "The laws of thought must be the laws of things," one can find an index of reality even in insanity.

(*From* Chapter 28)

◇◇◇◇◇◇◇◇◇◇◇◇◇◇◇◇◇◇◇◇◇◇◇◇◇◇◇◇◇◇◇◇◇◇◇◇◇

FROM

"About Ed Ricketts"

"KNOWING ED RICKETTS"

"SPECULATIVE METAPHYSICS"

The death of Ed Ricketts in 1948 moved John Steinbeck to write this memorial-tribute to his closest friend. It appeared as a preface to The Log from the Sea of Cortez in 1951. Ed Ricketts has often been seen as the prototype of Steinbeck's wisely observant characters Doc Burton of In Dubious Battle, Doc of Cannery Row and Sweet Thursday, and even Jim Casy of The Grapes of Wrath and Pippin in The Short Reign of Pippin IV.

◇◇◇◇◇◇◇◇◇◇◇◇◇◇◇◇◇◇◇◇◇◇◇◇◇◇◇◇◇◇◇◇◇◇◇◇◇

"KNOWING ED RICKETTS"

KNOWING Ed Ricketts was instant. After the first moment I knew him, and for the next eighteen years I knew him better than I knew anyone, and perhaps I did not know him at all. Maybe it was that way with all of his friends. He was different from anyone and yet so like that everyone found himself in Ed, and that might be one of the reasons his death had such an impact. It wasn't Ed who had died but a large and important part of oneself.

When I first knew him, his laboratory was an old house in Cannery Row which he had bought and transformed to his purposes. The entrance was a kind of showroom with mounted marine specimens in glass jars on shelves around the walls. Next to this room was a small office, where for some reason the rattlesnakes were kept in cages between the safe and the filing cabinets. The top of the safe was piled high with stationery and filing cards. Ed loved paper and cards. He never ordered small amounts but huge supplies of it.

On the side of the building toward the ocean were two more rooms, one with cages for white rats—hundreds of white rats, and reproducing furiously. This room used to get pretty smelly if it was not cleaned with great regularity—which it never was. The other rear room was set up with microscopes and slides and the equipment for making and mounting and baking the delicate microorganisms which were so much a part of the laboratory income. In the basement there was a big stockroom with jars and tanks for preserving the larger animals, and also the equipment for embalming and injecting the cats, dogfish, frogs, and other animals that were used by dissection classes.

This little house was called Pacific Biological Laboratories, Inc., as strange an operation as ever outraged the corporate laws of California. When, after Ed's death, the corporation had to be liquidated, it was impossible to find out who owned the stock, how much of it there was, or what it was worth. Ed kept the most careful collecting notes on record, but sometimes he would not open a business letter for weeks.

How the business ran for twenty years no one knows, but it did run even though it staggered a little sometimes. At times it would spurt ahead with system and efficiency and then wearily collapse for several months. Orders would pile up on the desk. Once during a weary period someone sent Ed a cheesecake by parcel post. He thought it was preserved material of some kind, and when he finally opened it three months later we could not have identified it had it not been that a note was enclosed which said, "Eat this cheesecake at once. It's very delicate."

Often the desk was piled so high with unopened letters that they slid tiredly to the floor. Ed believed completely in the theory that a letter unanswered for a week usually requires no answer, but he went even farther. A letter unopened for a month does not require opening.

Every time some definite statement like that above is set down I think of exceptions. Ed carried on a large and varied correspondence with a number of people. He answered letters quickly and at length, using a typewriter with elite type to save space. The purchase of a typewriter was a long process with him, for much of the type had to be changed from business signs to biologic signs, and he also liked to have some foreign-language signs on his typewriter, tilde for Spanish, accents and cedilla for French, umlaut for German. He rarely used them but he liked to have them.

The days of the laboratory can be split into two periods. The era before the fire and that afterwards. The fire was interesting in many respects.

One night something went wrong with the electric current on the whole water front. Where 220 volts were expected and prepared for, something like two thousand volts suddenly came through. Since in the subsequent suits the electric company was found blameless by the courts, this must be set down to an act of God. What happened was that a large part of Cannery Row burst into flames in a moment. By the time Ed awakened, the laboratory was a sheet of fire. He grabbed his typewriter, rushed to the basement, and got his car out just in time, and just before the building was about ready to crash into its own basement. He had no pants but he had transportation and printing. He always admired his choice. The scientific library, accumulated with such patience and some of it irreplaceable, was gone. All the fine equipment, the microscopes, the museum jars, the stock—everything was gone. Besides typewriter and automobile, only one thing was saved.

Ed had a remarkably fine safe. It was so good that he worried for fear some misguided and romantic burglar might think there was something of value in it and, trying to open it, might abuse and injure its beautiful mechanism. Consequently he not only never

locked the safe but contrived a wood block so that
it could not be locked. Also, he pasted a note above
the combination, assuring all persons that the safe
was not locked. Then it developed that there was
nothing to put in the safe anyway. Thus the safe
became the repository of foods which might attract
the flies of Cannery Row, and there were clouds of
them drawn to the refuse of the fish canneries but willing to come to other foods. And it must be said that
no fly was ever able to negotiate the safe.

But to get back to the fire. After the ashes had
cooled, there was the safe lying on its side in the
basement where it had fallen when the floor above gave
way. It must have been an excellent safe, for when
we opened it we found half a pineapple pie, a quarter
of a pound of Gorgonzola cheese, and an open can of
sardines—all of them except the sardines in good
condition. The sardines were a little dry. Ed admired
that safe and used to refer to it with affection. He
would say that if there *had* been valuable things in the
safe it would surely have protected them. "Think
how delicate Gorgonzola is," he said. "It couldn't
have been very hot inside that safe. The cheese is
still delicious."

In spite of a great erudition, or perhaps because of
it, Ed had some naïve qualities. After the fire there
were a number of suits against the electric company,
based on the theory, later proved wrong, that if the
fires were caused by error or negligence on the part
of the company, the company should pay for the
damage.

Pacific Biological Laboratories, Inc., was one of the
plaintiffs in this suit. Ed went over to Superior Court
in Salinas to testify. He told the truth as clearly and as
fully as he could. He loved true things and believed

in them. Then he became fascinated by the trial and
the jury and he spent much time in court, inspecting
the legal system with the same objective care he would
have lavished on a new species of marine animal.

Afterwards he said calmly and with a certain wonder, "You see how easy it is to be completely wrong
about a simple matter. It was always my conviction—
or better, my impression—that the legal system was
designed to arrive at the truth in matters of human
and property relationships. You see, I had forgotten or
never considered one thing. Each side wants to win,
and that factor warps any original intent to the extent
that the objective truth of the matter disappears in
emphasis. Now you take the case of this fire," he went
on. "Both sides wanted to win, and neither had any
interest in, indeed both sides seemed to have a kind
of abhorrence for, the truth." It was an amazing
discovery to him and one that required thinking out.
Because he loved true things, he thought everyone
did. The fact that it was otherwise did not sadden
him. It simply interested him. And he set about re-
building his laboratory and replacing his books with
an antlike methodicalness.

Ed's use of words was unorthodox and, until you
knew him, somewhat startling. Once, in getting a
catalogue ready, he wanted to advise the trade that
he had plenty of hagfish available. Now the hagfish
is a most disgusting animal both in appearance and
texture, and some of its habits are nauseating. It is a
perfect animal horror. But Ed did not feel this, because the hagfish has certain functions which he found
fascinating. In his catalogue he wrote, "Available in
some quantities, delightful and beautiful hagfish."

He admired worms of all kinds and found them so
desirable that, searching around for a pet name for a

girl he loved, he called her "Wormy." She was a little huffy until she realized that he was using not the adjective but a diminutive of the noun. His use of this word meant that he found her pretty, interesting, and desirable. But still it always sounded to the girl like an adjective.

Ed loved food, and many of the words he used were eating words. I have heard him refer to a girl, a marine animal, and a plain song as "delicious."

His mind had no horizons. He was interested in everything. And there were very few things he did not like. Perhaps it would be well to set down the things he did not like. Maybe they would be some kind of key to his personality, although it is my conviction that there is no such key.

Chief among his hatreds was old age. He hated it in other people and did not even conceive of it in himself. He hated old women and would not stay in a room with them. He said he could smell them. He had a remarkable sense of smell. He could smell a mouse in a room, and I have seen him locate a rattlesnake in the brush by smell.

He hated women with thin lips. "If the lips are thin —where will there be any fullness?" he would say. His observation was certainly physical and open to verification, and he seemed to believe in its accuracy and so do I, but with less vehemence.

He loved women too much to take any nonsense from the thin-lipped ones. But if a girl with thin lips painted on fuller ones with lipstick, he was satisfied. "Her intentions are correct," he said. "There is a psychic fullness, and sometimes that can be very fine."

He hated hot soup and would pour cold water into the most beautifully prepared bisque.

He unequivocally hated to get his head wet. Collecting animals in the tide pools, he would be soaked by the waves to his eyebrows, but his head was invariably covered and safe. In the shower he wore an oilskin sou'wester—a ridiculous sight.

He hated one professor whom he referred to as "old jingle ballicks." It never developed why he hated "old jingle ballicks."

He hated pain inflicted without good reason. Driving through the streets one night, he saw a man beating a red setter with a rake handle. Ed stopped the car and attacked the man with a monkey wrench and would have killed him if the man had not run away.

Although slight in build, when he was angry Ed had no fear and could be really dangerous. On an occasion one of our cops was pistol-whipping a drunk in the middle of the night. Ed attacked the cop with his bare hands, and his fury was so great that the cop released the drunk.

This hatred was only for reasonless cruelty. When the infliction of pain was necessary, he had little feeling about it. Once during the depression we found we could buy a live sheep for three dollars. This may seem incredible now but it was so. It was a great deal of food and even for those days a great bargain. Then we had the sheep and none of us could kill it. But Ed cut its throat with no emotion whatever, and even explained to the rest of us who were upset that bleeding to death is quite painless if there is no fear involved. The pain of opening a vein is slight if the instrument is sharp, and he had opened the jugular with a scalpel and had not frightened the animal, so that our secondary or empathic pain was probably much greater than that of the sheep.

His feeling for psychic pain in normal people also was philosophic. He would say that nearly everything that can happen to people not only does happen but has happened for a million years. "Therefore," he would say, "for everything that can happen there is a channel or mechanism in the human to take care of it —a channel worn down in prehistory and transmitted in the genes."

He disliked time intensely unless it was part of an observation or an experiment. He was invariably and consciously late for appointments. He said he had once worked for a railroad where his whole life had been regulated by a second hand and that he had then conceived his disgust, a disgust for exactness in time. To my knowledge, that is the only time he ever spoke of the railroad experience. If you asked him to dinner at seven, he might get there at nine. On the other hand, if a good low collecting tide was at 6:53, he would be in the tide pool at 6:52.

The farther I get into this the more apparent it becomes to me that no rule was final. He himself was not conscious of any rules of behavior in himself, although he observed behavior patterns in other people with delight.

For many years he wore a beard, not large, and slightly pointed, which accentuated his half-goat, half-Christ appearance. He had started wearing the beard because some girl he wanted thought he had a weak chin. He didn't have a weak chin, but as long as she thought so he cultivated his beard. This was probably during the period of the prognathous Arrow Collar men in the advertising pages. Many girls later he was still wearing the beard because he was used to it. He kept it until the Army made him shave it off in the Second World War. His beard sometimes caused a disturbance. Small boys often followed Ed, baaing like sheep. He developed a perfect defense against this. He would turn and baa back at them, which invariably so embarrassed the boys that they slipped shyly away.

Ed had a strange and courteous relationship with dogs, although he never owned one or wanted to. Passing a dog on the street, he greeted it with dignity and, when driving, often tipped his hat and smiled and waved at dogs on the sidewalk. And damned if they didn't smile back at him. Cats, on the other hand, did not arouse any enthusiasm in him. However, he always remembered one cat with admiration. It was in the old days before the fire when Ed's father was still alive and doing odd jobs about the laboratory. The cat in question took a dislike to Ed's father and developed a spite tactic which charmed Ed. The cat would climb up on a shelf and pee on Ed's father when he went by—the cat did it not once but many times.

He regarded his father with affection. "He has one quality of genius," Ed would say. "He is always wrong. If a man makes a million decisions and judgments at random, it is perhaps mathematically tenable to suppose that he will be right half the time and wrong half the time. But you take my father—he is wrong all of the time about everything. That is a matter not of luck but of selection. That requires genius."

"SPECULATIVE
METAPHYSICS"

WE had a game which we playfully called speculative metaphysics. It was a sport consisting of
lopping off a piece of observed reality and letting it
move up through the speculative process like a tree
growing tall and bushy. We observed with pleasure
how the branches of thought grew away from the
trunk of external reality. We believed, as we must,
that the laws of thought parallel the laws of things.
In our game there was no stricture of rightness. It
was an enjoyable exercise on the instruments of our
minds, improvisations and variations on a theme,
and it gave the same delight and interest that discovered music does. No one can say, "This music is
the only music," nor would we say, "This thought is
the only thought," but rather, "This is *a* thought,
perhaps well or ill formed, but *a* thought which is a
real thing in nature."

Once a theme was established we subjected observ-
able nature to it. The following is an example of our
game—one developed quite a long time ago.

We thought that perhaps our species thrives best
and most creatively in a state of semi-anarchy, governed
by loose rules and half-practiced mores. To this we
added the premise that over-integration in human
groups might parallel the law in paleontology that
over-armor or over-ornamentation are symptoms of
decay and disappearance. Indeed, we thought, over-

integration *might be* the symptom of human decay. We thought: there is no creative unit in the human save the individual working alone. In pure creativeness, in art, in music, in mathematics, there are no true collaborations. The creative principle is a lonely and an individual matter. Groups can correlate, investigate, and build, but we could not think of any group that has ever created or invented anything. Indeed, the first impulse of the group seems to be to destroy the creation and the creator. But integration, or the designed group, seems to be highly vulnerable.

Now with this structure of speculation we would slip examples on the squares of the speculative graphing paper.

Consider, we would say, the Third Reich or the Politburo-controlled Soviet. The sudden removal of twenty-five key men from either system could cripple it so thoroughly that it would take a long time to recover, if it ever could. To preserve itself in safety such a system must destroy or remove all opposition as a danger to itself. But opposition is creative and restriction is non-creative. The force that feeds growth is therefore cut off. Now, the tendency to integration must constantly increase. And this process of integration must destroy all tendencies toward improvisation, must destroy the habit of creation, since this is sand in the bearings of the system. The system then must, if our speculation is accurate, grind to a slow and heavy stop. Thought and art must be forced to disappear and a weighty traditionalism take its place. Thus we would play with thinking. A too greatly integrated system or society is in danger of destruction since the removal of one unit may cripple the whole.

Consider the blundering anarchic system of the

United States, the stupidity of some of its lawmakers, the violent reaction, the slowness of its ability to change. Twenty-five key men destroyed could make the Soviet Union stagger, but we could lose our congress, our president, and our general staff and nothing much would have happened. We would go right on. In fact we might be better for it.

That is an example of the game we played. Always our thinking was prefaced with, "It might be so!" Often a whole night would draw down to a moment while we pursued the fireflies of our thinking.

FROM

Cannery Row

FROG HUNT

Two passages forming one episode from the novel, published in
1945. Mack and the boys have gone up into the mountains behind
Monterey to find frogs for Doc's laboratory. The sale of the frogs
is to pay for Doc's birthday party.

◇◇◇◇◇◇◇◇◇◇◇◇◇◇◇◇◇◇◇◇◇◇◇◇◇◇◇◇◇◇◇◇◇◇◇

FROG HUNT

M ACK and the boys slept peacefully on the pine
needles. Some time before dawn Eddie came
back. He had gone a long way before he found a
Model T. And then when he did, he wondered whether
or not it would be a good idea to take the needle out
of its seat. It might not fit. So he took the whole carburetor. The boys didn't wake up when he got back.
He lay down beside them and slept under the pine
trees. There was one nice thing about Model T's. The
parts were not only interchangeable, they were un-
identifiable.

There is a beautiful view from the Carmel grade,
the curving bay with the waves creaming on the sand,
the dune country around Seaside and right at the bottom of the hill, the warm intimacy of the town.

Mack got up in the dawn and hustled his pants
where they bound him and he stood looking down on
the bay. He could see some of the purse-seiners coming
in. A tanker stood over against Seaside, taking on oil.
Behind him the rabbits stirred in the bush. Then the
sun came up and shook the night chill out of the air
the way you'd shake a rug. When he felt the first sun
warmth, Mack shivered.

The boys ate a little bread while Eddie installed the
new carburetor. And when it was ready they didn't
bother to crank it. They pushed it out to the highway
and coasted in gear until it started. And then Eddie
driving, they backed up over the rise, over the top and

turned and headed forward and down past Hatton
Fields. In Carmel Valley the artichoke plants stood
gray green, and the willows were lush along the river.
They turned left up the valley. Luck blossomed from
the first. A dusty Rhode Island red rooster who had
wandered too far from his own farmyard crossed the
road and Eddie hit him without running too far off
the road. Sitting in the back of the truck, Hazel picked
him as they went and let the feathers fly from his
hand, the most widely distributed evidence on record,
for there was a little breeze in the morning blowing
down from Jamesburg and some of the red chicken
feathers were deposited on Pt. Lobos and some even
blew out to sea.

The Carmel is a lovely little river. It isn't very
long but in its course it has everything a river should
have. It rises in the mountains, and tumbles down a
while, runs through shallows, is dammed to make a
lake, spills over the dam, crackles among round
boulders, wanders lazily under sycamores, spills into
pools where trout live, drops in against banks where
crayfish live. In the winter it becomes a torrent, a
mean little fierce river, and in the summer it is a
place for children to wade in and for fishermen to
wander in. Frogs blink from its banks and the deep
ferns grow beside it. Deer and foxes come to drink
from it, secretly in the morning and evening, and now
and then a mountain lion crouched flat laps its water.
The farms of the rich little valley back up to the river
and take its water for the orchards and the vegetables.
The quail call beside it and the wild doves come
whistling in at dusk. Raccoons pace its edges looking
for frogs. It's everything a river should be.

A few miles up the valley the river cuts in under a
high cliff from which vines and ferns hang down. At
the base of this cliff there is a pool, green and deep,

and on the other side of the pool there is a little sandy place where it is good to sit and to cook your dinner.

Mack and the boys came down to this place happily. It was perfect. If frogs were available, they would be here. It was a place to relax, a place to be happy. On the way out they had thriven. In addition to the big red chicken there was a sack of carrots which had fallen from a vegetable truck, half a dozen onions which had not. Mack had a bag of coffee in his pocket. In the truck there was a five-gallon can with the top cut off. The wining jug was nearly half full. Such things as salt and pepper had been brought. Mack and the boys would have thought anyone who traveled without salt, pepper, and coffee very silly indeed.

Without effort, confusion, or much thought, four round stones were rolled together on the little beach. The rooster who had challenged the sunrise of this very day lay dismembered and clean in water in the five-gallon can with peeled onions about him, while a little fire of dead willow sticks sputtered between the stones, a very little fire. Only fools build big fires. It would take a long time to cook this rooster, for it had taken him a long time to achieve his size and muscularity. But as the water began to boil gently about him, he smelled good from the beginning.

Mack gave them a pep talk. "The best time for frogs is at night," he said, "so I guess we'll just lay around 'til it gets dark." They sat in the shade and gradually one by one they stretched out and slept.

Mack was right. Frogs do not move around much in the daytime; they hide under ferns and they look secretly out of holes under rocks. The way to catch frogs is with a flashlight at night. The men slept knowing they might have a very active night. Only Hazel stayed awake to replenish the little fire under the cooking chicken.

There is no golden afternoon next to the cliff. When the sun went over it at about two o'clock a whispering shade came to the beach. The sycamores rustled in the afternoon breeze. Little water snakes slipped down to the rocks and then gently entered the water and swam along through the pool, their heads held up like little periscopes and a tiny wake spreading behind them. A big trout jumped in the pool. The gnats and mosquitoes which avoid the sun came out and buzzed over the water. All of the sun bugs, the flies, the dragonflies, the wasps, the hornets, went home. And as the shadow came to the beach, as the first quail began to call, Mack and the boys awakened. The smell of the chicken stew was heartbreaking. Hazel had picked a fresh bay leaf from a tree by the river and he had dropped it in. The carrots were in now. Coffee in its own can was simmering on its own rock, far enough from the flame so that it did not boil too hard. Mack awakened, started up, stretched, staggered to the pool, washed his face with cupped hands, hacked, spat, washed out his mouth, broke wind, tightened his belt, scratched his legs, combed his wet hair with his fingers, drank from the jug, belched and sat down by the fire. "By God that smells good," he said.

Men all do about the same things when they wake up. Mack's process was loosely the one all of them followed. And soon they had all come to the fire and complimented Hazel. Hazel stuck his pocket knife into the muscles of the chicken.

"He ain't going to be what you'd call tender," said Hazel. "You'd have to cook him about two weeks to get him tender. How old about do you judge he was, Mack?"

"I'm forty-eight and I ain't as tough as he is," said Mack.

Eddie said, "How old can a chicken get, do you think—that's if nobody pushes him around or he don't get sick?"

"That's something nobody isn't ever going to find out," said Jones.

It was a pleasant time. The jug went around and warmed them.

Jones said, "Eddie, I don't mean to complain none. I was just thinkin'. S'pose you had two or three jugs back of the bar. S'pose you put all the whisky in one and all the wine in another and all the beer in another—"

A slightly shocked silence followed the suggestion. "I didn't mean nothing," said Jones quickly. "I like it this way—" Jones talked too much then because he knew he had made a social blunder and he wasn't able to stop. "What I like about it this way is you never know what kind of a drunk you're going to get out of it," he said. "You take whisky," he said hurriedly. "You more or less know what you'll do. A fightin' guy fights and a cryin' guy cries, but this—" he said magnanimously —"why you don't know whether it'll run you up a pine tree or start you swimming to Santa Cruz. It's more fun that way," he said weakly.

"Speaking of swimming," said Mack to fill in the indelicate place in the conversation and to shut Jones up. "I wonder whatever happened to that guy McKinley Moran. Remember that deep sea diver?"

"I remember him," said Hughie. "I and him used to hang around together. He just didn't get much work and then he got to drinking. It's kind of tough on you divin' and drinkin'. Got to worryin' too. Finally he sold his suit and helmet and pump and went on a hell of a drunk and then he left town. I don't know where he went. He wasn't no good after he went down after that Wop that got took down with the anchor from the

Twelve Brothers. McKinley just dove down. Bust his eardrums, and he wasn't no good after that. Didn't hurt the Wop a bit."

Mack sampled the jug again. "He used to make a lot of dough during Prohibition," Mack said. "Used to get twenty-five bucks a day from the government to dive lookin' for liquor on the bottom and he got three dollars a case from Louie for not findin' it. Had it worked out so he brought up one case a day to keep the government happy. Louie didn't mind that none. Made it so they didn't get in no new divers. McKinley made a lot of dough."

"Yeah," said Hughie. "But he's like everybody else—gets some dough and he wants to get married. He got married three times before his dough run out. I could always tell. He'd buy a white fox fur piece and bang!—next thing you'd know, he's married."

"I wonder what happened to Gay," Eddie asked. It was the first time they had spoken of him.

"Same thing, I guess," said Mack. "You just can't trust a married guy. No matter how much he hates his old lady why he'll go back to her. Get to thinkin' and broodin' and back he'll go. You can't trust him no more. Take Gay," said Mack. "His old lady hits him. But I bet you when Gay's away from her three days, he gets it figured out that it's his fault and he goes back to make it up to her."

They ate long and daintily, spearing out pieces of chicken, holding the dripping pieces until they cooled and then gnawing the muscled meat from the bone. They speared the carrots on pointed willow switches and finally they passed the can and drank the juice. And around them the evening crept in as delicately as music. The quail called each other down to the water. The trout jumped in the pool. And the moths came down and fluttered about the pool as the daylight mixed into the darkness. They passed the coffee can about and they were warm and fed and silent. At last Mack said, "God damn it. I hate a liar."

"Who's been lyin' to you?" Eddie asked.

"Oh, I don't mind a guy that tells a little one to get along or to hop up a conversation, but I hate a guy that lies to himself."

"Who done that?" Eddie asked.

"Me," said Mack. "And maybe you guys. Here we are," he said earnestly, "the whole God damned shabby lot of us. We worked it out that we wanted to give Doc a party. So we come out here and have a hell of a lot of fun. Then we'll go back and get the dough from Doc. There's five of us, so we'll drink five times as much liquor as he will. And I ain't sure we're doin' it for Doc. I ain't sure we ain't doin' it for ourselves. And Doc's too nice a fella to do that to. Doc is the nicest fella I ever knew. I don't want to be the kind of a guy that would take advantage of him. You know one time I put the bee on him for a buck. I give him a hell of a story. Right in the middle I seen he knew God damn well the story was so much malarky. So right in the middle I says, 'Doc, that's a fuggin' lie!' And he put his hand in his pocket and brought out a buck. 'Mack,' he says, 'I figure a guy that needs it bad enough to make up a lie to get it, really needs it,' and he give me the buck. I paid him that buck back the next day. I never did spend it. Just kept it overnight and then give it back to him."

Hazel said, "There ain't nobody likes a party better than Doc. We're givin' him the party. What the hell is the beef?"

"I don't know," said Mack. "I'd just like to give him something when I didn't get most of it back."

"How about a present?" Hughie suggested. "S'pose we just bought the whisky and give it to him and let him do what he wants."

"Now you're talkin'," said Mack. "That's just what we'll do. We'll just give him the whisky and fade out."

"You know what'll happen," said Eddie. "Henri and them people from Carmel will smell that whisky out and then instead of only five of us there'll be twenty. Doc told me one time himself they can smell him fryin' a steak from Cannery Row clear down to Point Sur. I don't see the percentage. He'd come out better if we give him the party ourselves."

Mack considered this reasoning. "Maybe you're right," he said at last. "But s'pose we give him something except whisky, maybe cuff links with his initials."

"Oh, horse shit," said Hazel. "Doc don't want stuff like that."

The night was in by now and the stars were white in the sky. Hazel fed the fire and it put a little room of light on the beach. Over the hill a fox was barking sharply. And now in the night the smell of sage came down from the hills. The water chuckled on the stones where it went out of the deep pool.

Mack was mulling over the last piece of reasoning when the sound of footsteps on the ground made them turn. A man dark and large stalked near and he had a shotgun over his arm and a pointer walked shyly and delicately at his heel.

"What the hell are you doing here?" he asked.

"Nothing," said Mack.

"The land's posted. No fishing, hunting, fires, camping. Now you just pack up and put that fire out and get off this land."

Mack stood up humbly. "I didn't know, Captain," he said. "Honest we never seen the sign, Captain."

"There's signs all over. You couldn't have missed them."

"Look, Captain, we made a mistake and we're sorry," said Mack. He paused and looked closely at the slouching figure. "You are a military man, aren't you, sir? I can always tell. Military man don't carry his shoulders the same as ordinary people. I was in the army so long, I can always tell."

Imperceptibly the shoulders of the man straightened, nothing obvious, but he held himself differently.

"I don't allow fires on my place," he said.

"Well, we're sorry," said Mack. "We'll get right out, Captain. You see, we're workin' for some scientists. We're tryin' to get some frogs. They're workin' on cancer and we're helpin' out getting some frogs."

The man hesitated for a moment. "What do they do with the frogs?" he said.

"Well, sir," said Mack, "they give cancer to the frogs and then they can study and experiment and they got it nearly licked if they can just get some frogs. But if you don't want us on your land, Captain, we'll get right out. Never would of come in if we knew." Suddenly Mack seemed to see the pointer for the first time. "By God that's a fine-lookin' bitch," he said enthusiastically. "She looks like Nola that win the field trials in Virginia last year. She a Virginia dog, Captain?"

The captain hesitated and then he lied. "Yes," he said shortly. "She's lame. Tick got her right on her shoulder."

Mack was instantly solicitous. "Mind if I look, Captain? Come, girl. Come on, girl." The pointer looked up at her master and then sidled up to Mack. "Pile on some twigs so I can see," he said to Hazel.

"It's up where she can't lick it," said the captain and he leaned over Mack's shoulder to look.

Mack pressed some pus out of the evil-looking crater

on the dog's shoulder. "I had a dog once had a thing like this and it went right in and killed him. She just had pups, didn't she?"

"Yes," said the captain, "six. I put iodine on that place."

"No," said Mack, "that won't draw. You got any epsom salts up at your place?"

"Yes—there's a big bottle."

"Well you make a hot poultice of epsom salts and put it on there. She's weak, you know, from the pups. Be a shame if she got sick now. You'd lose the pups too." The pointer looked deep into Mack's eyes and then she licked his hand.

"Tell you what I'll do, Captain. I'll look after her myself. Epsom salts'll do the trick. That's the best thing."

The captain stroked the dog's head. "You know, I've got a pond up by the house that's so full of frogs I can't sleep nights. Why don't you look up there? They bellow all night. I'd be glad to get rid of them."

"That's mighty nice of you," said Mack. "I'll bet those docs would thank you for that. But I'd like to get a poultice on this dog." He turned to the others. "You put out this fire," he said. "Make sure there ain't a spark left and clean up around. You don't want to leave no mess. I and the captain will go and take care of Nola here. You fellows follow along when you get cleared up." Mack and the captain walked away together.

Hazel kicked sand on the fire. "I bet Mack could of been president of the U.S. if he wanted," he said.

"What could he do with it if he had it?" Jones asked. "There wouldn't be no fun in that."

(Chapter 13)

By the time the boys got up to the farmhouse Mack was in the kitchen. The pointer bitch lay on her

side, and Mack held a cloth saturated with epsom salts
against her tick bite. Among her legs the big fat wiener
pups nuzzled and bumped for milk and the bitch looked
patiently up into Mack's face saying, "You see how it is?
I try to tell him but he doesn't understand."

The captain held a lamp and looked down on Mack.
"I'm glad to know about that," he said.

Mack said, "I don't want to tell you about your business, sir, but these pups ought to be weaned. She ain't
got a hell of a lot of milk left and them pups are chew-
in' her to pieces."

"I know," said the captain. "I s'pose I should have
drowned them all but one. I've been so busy trying to
keep the place going. People don't take the interest in
bird dogs they used to. It's all poodles and boxers and
Dobermans."

"I know," said Mack. "And there ain't no dog like a
pointer for a man. I don't know what's come over people. But you wouldn't of drowned them, would you, sir?"

"Well," said the captain, "since my wife went into
politics, I'm just running crazy. She got elected to the
Assembly for this district and when the Legislature
isn't in session, she's off making speeches. And when
she's home she's studying all the time and writing bills."

"Must be lousy in—I mean it must be pretty lonely,"
said Mack. "Now if I had a pup like this—" he picked
up a squirming fuzz-faced pup—"why I bet I'd have
a real bird dog in three years. I'd take a bitch every
time."

"Would you like to have one?" the captain asked.

Mack looked up. "You mean you'd let me have one?
Oh! Jesus Christ yes."

"Take your pick," said the captain. "Nobody seems
to understand bird dogs any more."

The boys stood in the kitchen and gathered quick
impressions. It was obvious that the wife was away—

the opened cans, the frying pan with lace from fried eggs still sticking to it, the crumbs on the kitchen table, the open box of shotgun shells on the bread box all shrieked of the lack of a woman, while the white curtains and the papers on the dish shelves and the too small towels on the rack told them a woman had been there. And they were unconsciously glad she wasn't there. The kind of women who put papers on shelves and had little towels like that instinctively distrusted and disliked Mack and the boys. Such women knew that they were the worst threats to a home, for they offered ease and thought and companionship as opposed to neatness, order, and properness. They were very glad she was away.

Now the captain seemed to feel that they were doing him a favor. He didn't want them to leave. He said hesitantly, "S'pose you boys would like a little something to warm you up before you go out for the frogs?"

The others looked at Mack. Mack was frowning as though he was thinking it through. "When we're out doin' scientific stuff, we make it a kind of a rule not to touch nothin'," he said, and then quickly as though he might have gone too far, "But seein' as how you been so nice to us—well I wouldn't mind a short one myself. I don't know about the boys."

The boys agreed that they wouldn't mind a short one either. The captain got a flashlight and went down in the cellar. They could hear him moving lumber and boxes about and he came back upstairs with a five-gallon oak keg in his arms. He set it on the table. "During Prohibition I got some corn whisky and laid it away. I just got to thinking I'd like to see how it is. It's pretty old now. I'd almost forgot it. You see—my wife—" he let it go at that because it was apparent that they understood. The captain knocked out the oak plug from the end of the keg and got glasses down from the shelf that had scallop-edged paper laid on it. It is a hard job to pour a small drink from a five-gallon keg. Each of them got half a water glass of the clear brown liquor. They waited ceremoniously for the captain and then they said, "Over the river," and tossed it back. They swallowed, tasted their tongues, sucked their lips, and there was a faraway look in their eyes.

Mack peered into his empty glass as though some holy message were written in the bottom. And then he raised his eyes. "You can't say nothin' about that," he said. "They don't put that in bottles." He breathed in deeply and sucked his breath as it came out. "I don't think I ever tasted nothin' as good as that," he said.

The captain looked pleased. His glance wandered back to the keg. "It is good," he said. "You think we might have another little one?"

Mack stared into his glass again. "Maybe a short one," he agreed. "Wouldn't it be easier to pour out some in a pitcher? You're liable to spill it that way."

Two hours later they recalled what they had come for.

The frog pool was square—fifty feet wide and seventy feet long and four feet deep. Lush soft grass grew about its edge and a little ditch brought the water from the river to it and from it little ditches went out to the orchards. There were frogs there all right, thousands of them. Their voices beat the night, they boomed and barked and croaked and rattled. They sang to the stars, to the waning moon, to the waving grasses. They bellowed love songs and challenges. The men crept through the darkness toward the pool. The captain carried a nearly filled pitcher of whisky and every man had his own glass. The captain had found them flashlights that worked. Hughie and Jones carried gunny sacks. As they drew quietly near, the frogs heard them coming. The night had been roaring with frog song and

CANNERY ROW

then suddenly it was silent. Mack and the boys and the captain sat down on the ground to have one last short one and to map their campaign. And the plan was bold.

During the millennia that frogs and men have lived in the same world, it is probable that men have hunted frogs. And during that time a pattern of hunt and parry has developed. The man with net or bow or lance or gun creeps noiselessly, as he thinks, toward the frog. The pattern requires that the frog sit still, sit very still and wait. The rules of the game require the frog to wait until the final flicker of a second, when the net is descending, when the lance is in the air, when the finger squeezes the trigger, then the frog jumps, plops into the water, swims to the bottom and waits until the man goes away. That is the way it is done, the way it has always been done. Frogs have every right to expect it will always be done that way. Now and then the net is too quick, the lance pierces, the gun flicks and that frog is gone, but it is all fair and in the framework. Frogs don't resent that. But how could they have anticipated Mack's new method? How could they have foreseen the horror that followed? The sudden flashing of lights, the shouting and squealing of men, the rush of feet. Every frog leaped, plopped into the pool, and swam frantically to the bottom. Then into the pool plunged the line of men, stamping, churning, moving in a crazy line up the pool, flinging their feet about. Hysterically the frogs displaced from their placid spots swam ahead of the crazy thrashing feet and the feet came on. Frogs are good swimmers but they haven't much endurance. Down the pool they went until finally they were bunched and crowded against the end. And the feet and wildly plunging bodies followed them. A few frogs lost their heads and floundered among the feet and got through and these were saved. But the majority decided to leave this pool forever, to find a new home in a new country where this kind of thing didn't happen. A wave of frantic, frustrated frogs, big ones, little ones, brown ones, green ones, men frogs and women frogs, a wave of them broke over the bank, crawled, leaped, scrambled. They clambered up the grass, they clutched at each other, little ones rode on big ones. And then— horror on horror—the flashlights found them. Two men gathered them like berries. The line came out of the water and closed in on their rear and gathered them like potatoes. Tens and fifties of them were flung into the gunny sacks, and the sacks filled with tired, frightened, and disillusioned frogs, with dripping, whimpering frogs. Some got away, of course, and some had been saved in the pool. But never in frog history had such an execution taken place. Frogs by the pound, by the fifty pounds. They weren't counted but there must have been six or seven hundred. Then happily Mack tied up the necks of the sacks. They were soaking, dripping wet and the air was cool. They had a short one in the grass before they went back to the house so they wouldn't catch cold.

It is doubtful whether the captain had ever had so much fun. He was indebted to Mack and the boys. Later when the curtains caught fire and were put out with the little towels, the captain told the boys not to mind it. He felt it was an honor to have them burn his house clear down, if they wanted to. "My wife is a wonderful woman," he said in a kind of peroration. "Most wonderful woman. Ought to of been a man. If she was a man I wouldn' of married her." He laughed a long time over that and repeated it three or four times and resolved to remember it so he could tell' it to a lot of other people. He filled a jug with whisky and gave it to Mack. He wanted to go to live with them in the

Palace Flophouse. He decided that his wife would like Mack and the boys if she only knew them. Finally he went to sleep on the floor with his head among the puppies. Mack and the boys poured themselves a short one and regarded him seriously.

Mack said, "He give me that jug of whisky, didn't he? You heard him?"

"Sure he did," said Eddie. "I heard him."

"And he give me a pup?"

"Sure, pick of the litter. We all heard him. Why?"

"I never did roll a drunk and I ain't gonna start now," said Mack. "We got to get out of here. He's gonna wake up feelin' lousy and it's goin' to be all our fault. I just don't want to be here." Mack glanced at the burned curtains, at the floor glistening with whisky and puppy dirt, at the bacon grease that was coagulating on the stove front. He went to the pups, looked them over carefully, felt bone and frame, looked in eyes and regarded jaws, and he picked out a beautifully spotted bitch with a liver-colored nose and a fine dark yellow eye. "Come on, darling," he said.

They blew out the lamp because of the danger of fire. It was just turning dawn as they left the house.

"I don't think I ever had such a fine trip," said Mack. "But I got to thinkin' about his wife comin' back and it gave me the shivers." The pup whined in his arms and he put it under his coat. "He's a real nice fella," said Mack. "After you get him feelin' easy, that is." He strode on toward the place where they had parked the Ford. "We shouldn't go forgettin' we're doin' all this for Doc," he said. "From the way things are pannin' out, it looks like Doc is a pretty lucky guy."

(Chapter 15)

FROM

East of Eden

ADAM AND HIS SONS

CHOICE AND RESPONSIBILITY

TECHNOLOGY AND A TECHNOCRAT

TIMSHEL

This long novel, published in 1952, traces the interaction of the Trask and Hamilton families in John Steinbeck's valley. With the working title of "The Salinas Valley," it began as a history of the author's own family (the Hamiltons). Then the title changed to reflect the emerging moral focus of the book, represented by three of the following passages. Of almost equal interest is the novel's presentation of American life (including the coming of the automobile) over the half-century that joined the ending of the Civil War with the beginning of World War I. Chapter 29 briefly suggests this flavor.

ADAM AND HIS SONS

[1]

ON the Trask place Adam drew into himself. The unfinished Sanchez house lay open to wind and rain, and the new floorboards buckled and warped with moisture. The laid-out vegetable gardens rioted with weeds.

Adam seemed clothed in a viscosity that slowed his movements and held his thoughts down. He saw the world through gray water. Now and then his mind fought its way upward, and when the light broke in it brought him only a sickness of the mind, and he retired into the grayness again. He was aware of the twins because he heard them cry and laugh, but he felt only a thin distaste for them. To Adam they were symbols of his loss. His neighbors drove up into his little valley, and every one of them would have understood anger or sorrow—and so helped him. But they could do nothing with the cloud that hung over him. Adam did not resist them. He simply did not see them, and before long the neighbors stopped driving up the road under the oaks.

For a time Lee tried to stimulate Adam to awareness, but Lee was a busy man. He cooked and washed, he bathed the twins and fed them. Through his hard and constant work he grew fond of the two little boys. He talked to them in Cantonese, and Chinese words were the first they recognized and tried to repeat.

Samuel Hamilton went back twice to try to wedge Adam up and out of his shock. Then Liza stepped in.

"I want you to stay away from there," she said. "You come back a changed man. Samuel, you don't change him. He changes you. I can see the look of him in your face."

"Have you thought of the two little boys, Liza?" he asked.

"I've thought of your own family," she said snappishly. "You lay a crepe on us for days after."

"All right, Mother," he said, but it saddened him because Samuel could not mind his own business when there was pain in any man. It was no easy thing for him to abandon Adam to his desolation.

Adam had paid him for his work, had even paid him for the windmill parts and did not want the windmills. Samuel sold the equipment and sent Adam the money. He had no answer.

He became aware of an anger at Adam Trask. It seemed to Samuel that Adam might be pleasuring himself with sadness. But there was little leisure to brood. Joe was off to college—to that school Leland Stanford had built on his farm near Palo Alto. Tom worried his father, for Tom grew deeper and deeper into books. He did his work well enough, but Samuel felt that Tom had not joy enough.

Will and George were doing well in business, and Joe was writing letters home in rhymed verse and making as smart an attack on all the accepted verities as was healthful.

Samuel wrote to Joe, saying, "I would be disappointed if you had not become an atheist, and I read pleasantly that you have, in your age and wisdom, accepted agnosticism the way you'd take a cookie on a full stomach. But I would ask you with all my understanding heart

not to try to convert your mother. Your last letter only
made her think you are not well. Your mother does not
believe there are many ills uncurable by good strong
soup. She puts your brave attack on the structure of our
civilization down to a stomach ache. It worries her. Her
faith is a mountain, and you, my son, haven't even got
a shovel yet."

Liza was getting old. Samuel saw it in her face, and
he could not feel old himself, white beard or no. But
Liza was living backwards, and that's the proof.

There was a time when she looked on his plans and
prophecies as the crazy shoutings of a child. Now she
felt that they were unseemly in a grown man. They
three, Liza and Tom and Samuel, were alone on the
ranch. Una was married to a stranger and gone away.
Dessie had her dressmaking business in Salinas. Olive
had married her young man, and Mollie was married
and living, believe it or not, in an apartment in San Francisco. There was perfume, and a white bearskin rug
in the bedroom in front of the fireplace, and Mollie
smoked a gold-tipped cigarette—Violet Milo—with
her coffee after dinner.

One day Samuel strained his back lifting a bale of
hay, and it hurt his feelings more than his back, for
he could not imagine a life in which Sam Hamilton was
not privileged to lift a bale of hay. He felt insulted by
his back, almost as he would have been if one of his
children had been dishonest.

In King City, Dr. Tilson felt him over. The doctor
grew more testy with his overworked years.

"You sprained your back."

"That I did," said Samuel.

"And you drove all the way in to have me tell you
that you sprained your back and charge you two dollars?"

"Here's your two dollars."

"And you want to know what to do about it?"

"Sure I do."

"Don't sprain it any more. Now take your money back. You're not a fool, Samuel, unless you're getting childish."

"But it hurts."

"Of course it hurts. How would you know it was strained if it didn't?"

Samuel laughed. "You're good for me," he said. "You're more than two dollars good for me. Keep the money."

The doctor looked closely at him. "I think you're telling the truth, Samuel. I'll keep the money."

Samuel went in to see Will in his fine new store. He hardly knew his son, for Will was getting fat and prosperous and he wore a coat and vest and a gold ring on his little finger.

"I've got a package made up for Mother," Will said. "Some little cans of things from France. Mushrooms and liver paste and sardines so little you can hardly see them."

"She'll just send them to Joe," said Samuel.

"Can't you make her eat them?"

"No," said his father. "But she'll enjoy sending them to Joe."

Lee came into the store and his eyes lighted up. "How do, Missy," he said.

"Hello, Lee. How are the boys?"

"Boys fine."

Samuel said, "I'm going to have a glass of beer next door, Lee. Be glad to have you join me."

Lee and Samuel sat at the little round table in the barroom and Samuel drew figures on the scrubbed wood with the moisture of his beer glass. "I've wanted to go to see you and Adam but I didn't think I could do any good."

"Well, you can't do any harm. I thought he'd get over it. But he still walks around like a ghost."

"It's over a year, isn't it?" Samuel asked.

"Three months over."

"Well, what do you think I can do?"

"I don't know," said Lee. "Maybe you could shock him out of it. Nothing else has worked."

"I'm not good at shocking. I'd probably end up by shocking myself. By the way, what did he name the twins?"

"They don't have any names."

"You're making a joke, Lee."

"I am not making jokes."

"What does he call them?"

"He calls them 'they.'"

"I mean when he speaks to them."

"When he speaks to them he calls them 'you,' one or both."

"This is nonsense," Samuel said angrily. "What kind of a fool is the man?"

"I've meant to come and tell you. He's a dead man unless you can wake him up."

Samuel said, "I'll come. I'll bring a horse whip. No names! You're damn right I'll come, Lee."

"When?"

"Tomorrow."

"I'll kill a chicken," said Lee. "You'll like the twins, Mr. Hamilton. They're fine-looking boys. I won't tell Mr. Trask you're coming."

[2]

Shyly Samuel told his wife he wanted to visit the Trask place. He thought she would pile up strong walls of objection, and for one of the few times in his life he would disobey her wish no matter how strong her objection. It gave him a sad feeling in the stomach to think of disobeying his wife. He explained his purpose almost as though he were confessing. Liza put her hands on her hips during the telling and his heart sank. When he was finished she continued to look at him, he thought, coldly.

Finally she said, "Samuel, do you think you can move this rock of a man?"

"Why, I don't know, Mother." He had not expected this. "I don't know."

"Do you think it is such an important matter that those babies have names right now?"

"Well, it seemed so to me," he said lamely.

"Samuel, do you think why you want to go? Is it your natural incurable nosiness? Is it your black inability to mind your own business?"

"Now, Liza, I know my failings pretty well. I thought it might be more than that."

"It had better be more than that," she said. "This man has not admitted that his sons live. He has cut them off mid-air."

"That's the way it seems to me, Liza."

"If he tells you to mind your own business—what then?"

"Well, I don't know."

Her jaw snapped shut and her teeth clicked. "If you do not get those boys named, there'll be no warm place in this house for you. Don't you dare come whining back, saying he wouldn't do it or he wouldn't listen. If you do I'll have to go myself."

"I'll give him the back of my hand," Samuel said.

"No, that you won't do. You fall short in savagery, Samuel. I know you. You'll give him sweet-sounding words and you'll come dragging back and try to make me forget you ever went."

"I'll beat his brains out," Samuel shouted.

He slammed into the bedroom, and Liza smiled at the panels.

He came out soon in his black suit and his hard shiny shirt and collar. He stooped down to her while she tied his black string tie. His white beard was brushed to shining.

"You'd best take a swab at your shoes with a blacking brush," she said.

In the midst of painting the blacking on his worn shoes he looked sideways up at her. "Could I take the Bible along?" he asked. "There's no place for getting a good name like the Bible."

"I don't much like it out of the house," she said uneasily. "And if you're late coming home, what'll I have for my reading? And the children's names are in it." She saw his face fall. She went into the bedroom and came back with a small Bible, worn and scuffed, its cover held on by brown paper and glue. "Take this one," she said.

"But that's your mother's."

"She wouldn't mind. And all the names but one in here have two dates."

"I'll wrap it so it won't get hurt," said Samuel.

Liza spoke sharply, "What my mother would mind is what I mind, and I'll tell you what I mind. You're never

satisfied to let the Testament alone. You're forever picking at it and questioning it. You turn it over the way a
'coon turns over a wet rock, and it angers me."

"I'm just trying to understand it, Mother."

"What is there to understand? Just read it. There
it is in black and white. Who wants you to understand
it? If the Lord God wanted you to understand it He'd
have given you to understand or He'd have set it down
different."

"But, Mother—"

"Samuel," she said, "you're the most contentious
man this world has ever seen."

"Yes, Mother."

"Don't agree with me all the time. It hints of
insincerity. Speak up for yourself."

She looked after his dark figure in the buggy as he
drove away. "He's a sweet husband," she said aloud,
"but contentious."

And Samuel was thinking with wonder, Just when I
think I know her she does a thing like that.

[3]

On the last half-mile, turning out of the Salinas Valley
and driving up the unscraped road under the great
oak trees, Samuel tried to plait a rage to take care of
his embarrassment. He said heroic words to himself.

Adam was more gaunt than Samuel remembered. His
eyes were dull, as though he did not use them much for
seeing. It took a little time for Adam to become aware
that Samuel was standing before him. A grimace of
displeasure drew down his mouth.

Samuel said, "I feel small now—coming uninvited
as I have."

Adam said, "What do you want? Didn't I pay you?"

"Pay?" Samuel asked. "Yes, you did. Yes, by God, you did. And I'll tell you that pay has been more than I've merited by the nature of it."

"What? What are you trying to say?"

Samuel's anger grew and put out leaves. "A man, his whole life, matches himself against pay. And how, if it's my whole life's work to find my worth, can you, sad man, write me down instant in a ledger?"

Adam exclaimed, "I'll pay. I tell you I'll pay. How much? I'll pay."

"You have, but not to me."

"Why did you come then? Go away!"

"You once invited me."

"I don't invite you now."

Samuel put his hands on his hips and leaned forward. "I'll tell you now, quiet. In a bitter night, a mustard night that was last night, a good thought came and the dark was sweetened when the day sat down. And this thought went from evening star to the late dipper on the edge of the first light—that our betters spoke of. So I invite myself."

"You are not welcome."

Samuel said, "I'm told that out of some singular glory your loins got twins."

"What business is that of yours?"

A kind of joy lighted Samuel's eyes at the rudeness. He saw Lee lurking inside the house and peeking out at him. "Don't, for the love of God, put violence on me. I'm a man hopes there'll be a picture of peace on my hatchments."

"I don't understand you."

"How could you? Adam Trask, a dog wolf with a pair of cubs, a scrubby rooster with sweet paternity for a fertilized egg! A dirty clod!"

A darkness covered Adam's cheeks and for the first

time his eyes seemed to see. Samuel joyously felt hot rage in his stomach. He cried, "Oh, my friend, retreat from me! Please, I beg of you!" The saliva dampened the corners of his mouth. "Please!" he cried. "For the love of any holy thing you can remember, step back from me. I feel murder nudging my gizzard."

Adam said, "Get off my place. Go on—get off. You're acting crazy. Get off. This is my place. I bought it."

"You bought your eyes and nose," Samuel jeered. "You bought your uprightness. You bought your thumb on sideways. Listen to me, because I'm like to kill you after. You bought! You bought out of some sweet inheritance. Think now—do you deserve your children, man?"

"Deserve them? They're here—I guess. I don't understand you."

Samuel wailed, "God save me, Liza! It's not the way you think. Adam! Listen to me before my thumb finds the bad place at your throat. The precious twins —untried, unnoticed, undirected—and I say it quiet with my hands down—undiscovered."

"Get off," said Adam hoarsely. "Lee, bring a gun! This man is crazy. Lee!"

Then Samuel's hands were on Adam's throat, pressing the throbbing up to his temples, swelling his eyes with blood. And Samuel was snarling at him. "Tear away with your jelly fingers. You have not bought these boys, nor stolen them, nor passed any bit for them. You have them by some strange and lovely dispensation." Suddenly he plucked his hard thumbs out of his neighbor's throat.

Adam stood panting. He felt his throat where the blacksmith hands had been. "What is it you want of me?"

"You have no love."

"I had—enough to kill me."

"No one ever had enough. The stone orchard celebrates too little, not too much."

"Stay away from me. I can fight back. Don't think I can't defend myself."

"You have two weapons, and they not named."

"I'll fight you, old man. You are an old man."

Samuel said, "I can't think in my mind of a dull man picking up a rock, who before evening would not put a name to it—like Peter. And you—for a year you've lived with your heart's draining and you've not even laid a number to the boys."

Adam said, "What I do is my own business."

Samuel struck him with a work-heavy fist, and Adam sprawled out in the dust. Samuel asked him to rise, and when Adam accepted struck him again, and this time Adam did not get up. He looked stonily at the menacing old man.

The fire went out of Samuel's eyes and he said quietly, "Your sons have no names."

Adam replied, "Their mother left them motherless."

"And you have left them fatherless. Can't you feel the cold at night of a lone child? What warm is there, what bird song, what possible morning can be good? Don't you remember, Adam, how it was, even a little?"

"I didn't do it," Adam said.

"Have you undone it? Your boys have no names." He stooped down and put his arms around Adam's shoulders and helped him to his feet. "We'll give them names," he said. "We'll think long and find good names to clothe them." He whipped the dust from Adam's shirt with his hands.

Adam wore a faraway yet intent look, as though he were listening to some wind-carried music, but his eyes were not dead as they had been. He said, "It's

hard to imagine I'd thank a man for insults and for shaking me out like a rug. But I'm grateful. It's a hurty
thanks, but it's thanks."

Samuel smiled, crinkle-eyed. "Did it seem natural?
Did I do it right?" he asked.

"What do you mean?"

"Well, in a way I promised my wife I'd do it. She
didn't believe I would. I'm not a fighting man, you see.
The last time I clobbered a human soul it was over a
red-nosed girl and a schoolbook in County Derry."

Adam stared at Samuel, but in his mind he saw and
felt his brother Charles, black and murderous, and that
sight switched to Cathy and the quality of her eyes
over the gun barrel. "There wasn't any fear in it,"
Adam said. "It was more like a weariness."

"I guess I was not angry enough."

"Samuel, I'll ask just once and then no more. Have
you heard anything? Has there been any news of her—
any news at all?"

"I've heard nothing."

"It's almost a relief," said Adam.

"Do you have hatred?"

"No. No—only a kind of sinking in the heart. Maybe
later I'll sort it out to hatred. There was no interval
from loveliness to horror, you see. I'm confused, confused."

Samuel said, "One day we'll sit and you'll lay it out
on the table, neat like a solitaire deck, but now—why,
you can't find all the cards."

From behind the shed there came the indignant
shrieking of an outraged chicken and then a dull thump.

"There's something at the hens," said Adam.

A second shrieking started. "It's Lee at the hens,"
said Samuel. "You know, if chickens had government
and church and history, they would take a distant and

distasteful view of human joy. Let any gay and hopeful thing happen to a man, and some chicken goes howling to the block."

Now the two men were silent, breaking it only with small false courtesies—meaningless inquiries about health and weather, with answers unlistened to. And this might have continued until they were angry at each other again if Lee had not interfered.

Lee brought out a table and two chairs and set the chairs facing each other. He made another trip for a pint of whisky and two glasses and set a glass on the table in front of each chair. Then he carried out the twins, one under each arm, and put them on the ground beside the table and gave each boy a stick for his hand to shake and make shadows with.

The boys sat solemnly and looked about, stared at Samuel's beard and searched for Lee. The strange thing about them was their clothing, for the boys were dressed in the straight trousers and the frogged and braided jackets of the Chinese. One was in turquoise blue and the other in a faded rose pink, and the frogs and braid were black. On their heads sat round black silken hats, each with a bright red button on its flat top.

Samuel asked, "Where in the world did you get those clothes, Lee?"

"I didn't get them," Lee said testily. "I had them. The only other clothes they have I made myself, out of sail cloth. A boy should be well dressed on his naming day."

"You've dropped the pidgin, Lee."

"I hope for good. Of course I use it in King City." He addressed a few short sung syllables to the boys on the ground, and they both smiled up at him and waved their sticks in the air. Lee said, "I'll pour you a drink. It's some that was here."

"It's some you bought yesterday in King City," said Samuel.

Now that Samuel and Adam were seated together and the barriers were down, a curtain of shyness fell on Samuel. What he had beaten in with his fists he could not supplement easily. He thought of the virtues of courage and forbearance, which become flabby when there is nothing to use them on. His mind grinned inward at itself.

The two sat looking at the twin boys in their strange bright-colored clothes. Samuel thought, Sometimes your opponent can help you more than your friend. He lifted his eyes to Adam.

"It's hard to start," he said. "And it's like a put-off letter that gathers difficulties to itself out of the minutes. Could you give me a hand?"

Adam looked up for a moment and then back at the boys on the ground. "There's a crashing in my head," he said. "Like sounds you hear under water. I'm having to dig myself out of a year."

"Maybe you'll tell me how it was and that will get us started."

Adam tossed down his drink and poured another and rolled the glass at an angle in his hand. The amber whisky moved high on the side and the pungent fruit odor of its warming filled the air. "It's hard to remember," he said. "It was not agony but a dullness. But no—there were needles in it. You said I had not all the cards in the deck—and I was thinking of that. Maybe I'll never have all the cards."

"Is it herself trying to come out? When a man says he does not want to speak of something he usually means he can think of nothing else."

"Maybe it's that. She's all mixed up with the dullness, and I can't remember much except the last picture drawn in fire."

"She did shoot you, didn't she, Adam?"

His lips grew thin and his eyes black.

Samuel said, "There's no need to answer."

"There's no reason not to," Adam replied. "Yes, she did."

"Did she mean to kill you?"

"I've thought of that more than anything else. No, I don't think she meant to kill me. She didn't allow me that dignity. There was no hatred in her, no passion at all. I learned about that in the army. If you want to kill a man, you shoot at head or heart or stomach. No, she hit me where she intended. I can see the gun barrel moving over. I guess I wouldn't have minded so much if she had wanted my death. That would have been a kind of love. But I was an annoyance, not an enemy."

"You've given it a lot of thought," said Samuel.

"I've had lots of time for it. I want to ask you something. I can't remember behind the last ugly thing. Was she very beautiful, Samuel?"

"To you she was because you built her. I don't think you ever saw her—only your own creation."

Adam mused aloud, "I wonder who she was—what she was. I was content not to know."

"And now you want to?"

Adam dropped his eyes. "It's not curiosity. But I would like to know what kind of blood is in my boys. When they grow up—won't I be looking for something in them?"

"Yes, you will. And I will warn you now that not their blood but your suspicion might build evil in them. They will be what you expect of them."

"But their blood—"

"I don't very much believe in blood," said Samuel. "I think when a man finds good or bad in his children he is seeing only what he planted in them after they cleared the womb."

"You can't make a race horse of a pig."

"No," said Samuel, "but you can make a very fast pig."

"No one hereabouts would agree with you. I think even Mrs. Hamilton would not."

"That's exactly right. She most of all would disagree, and so I would not say it to her and let loose the thunder of her disagreement. She wins all arguments by the use of vehemence and the conviction that a difference of opinion is a personal affront. She's a fine woman, but you have to learn to feel your way with her. Let's speak of the boys."

"Will you have another drink?"

"That I will, thank you. Names are a great mystery. I've never known whether the name is molded by the child or the child changed to fit the name. But you can be sure of this—whenever a human has a nickname it is a proof that the name given him was wrong. How do you favor the standard names—John or James or Charles?"

Adam was looking at the twins and suddenly with the mention of the name he saw his brother peering out of the eyes of one of the boys. He leaned forward.

"What is it?" Samuel asked.

"Why," Adam cried, "these boys are not alike! They don't look alike."

"Of course they don't. They're not identical twins."

"That one—that one looks like my brother. I just saw it. I wonder if the other looks like me."

"Both of them do. A face has everything in it right back to the beginning."

"It's not so much now," said Adam. "But for a moment I thought I was seeing a ghost."

"Maybe that's what ghosts are," Samuel observed.

Lee brought dishes out and put them on the table.

"Do you have Chinese ghosts?" Samuel asked.

"Millions," said Lee. "We have more ghosts than any-thing else. I guess nothing in China ever dies. It's very crowded. Anyway, that's the feeling I got when I was there."

Samuel said, "Sit down, Lee. We're trying to think of names."

"I've got chicken frying. It will be ready pretty soon."

Adam looked up from the twins and his eyes were warmed and softened. "Will you have a drink, Lee?"

"I'm nipping at the ng-ka-py in the kitchen," said Lee and went back to the house.

Samuel leaned down and gathered up one of the boys and held him on his lap. "Take that one up," he said to Adam. "We ought to see whether there's something that draws names to them."

Adam held the other child awkwardly on his knee. "They look some alike," he said, "but not when you look close. This one has rounder eyes than that one."

"Yes, and a rounder head and bigger ears," Samuel added. "But this one is more like—like a bullet. This one might go farther but not so high. And this one is going to be darker in the hair and skin. This one will be shrewd, I think, and shrewdness is a limitation on the mind. Shrewdness tells you what you must not do be-cause it would not be shrewd. See how this one supports himself! He's farther along than that one—better de-veloped. Isn't it strange how different they are when you look close?"

Adam's face was changing as though he had opened and come out on his surface. He held up his finger, and the child made a lunge for it and missed and nearly fell off his lap. "Whoa!" said Adam. "Take it easy. Do you want to fall?"

"It would be a mistake to name them for qualities

we think they have," Samuel said. "We might be wrong —so wrong. Maybe it would be good to give them a high mark to shoot at—a name to live up to. The man I'm named for had his name called clear by the Lord God, and I've been listening all my life. And once or twice I've thought I heard my name called—but not clear, not clear."

Adam, holding the child by his upper arm, leaned over and poured whisky in both glasses. "I thank you for coming, Samuel," he said. "I even thank you for hitting me. That's a strange thing to say."

"It was a strange thing for me to do. Liza will never believe it, and so I'll never tell her. An unbelieved truth can hurt a man much more than a lie. It takes great courage to back truth unacceptable to our times. There's a punishment for it, and it's usually crucifixion. I haven't the courage for that."

Adam said, "I've wondered why a man of your knowledge would work a desert hill place."

"It's because I haven't courage," said Samuel. "I could never quite take the responsibility. When the Lord God did not call my name, I might have called His name—but I did not. There you have the difference between greatness and mediocrity. It's not an uncommon disease. But it's nice for a mediocre man to know that greatness must be the loneliest state in the world."

"I'd think there are degrees of greatness," Adam said.

"I don't think so," said Samuel. "That would be like saying there is a little bigness. No. I believe when you come to that responsibility the hugeness and you are alone to make your choice. On one side you have warmth and companionship and sweet understanding, and on the other—cold, lonely greatness. There you make your choice. I'm glad I chose mediocrity, but how am I to say what reward might have come with the other? None of my children will be great either, except perhaps Tom. He's suffering over the choosing right now. It's a painful thing to watch. And somewhere in me I want him to say yes. Isn't that strange? A father to want his son condemned to greatness! What selfishness that must be."

Adam chuckled. "This naming is no simple business, I see."

"Did you think it would be?"

"I didn't know it could be so pleasant," said Adam.

Lee came out with a platter of fried chicken, a bowl of smoking boiled potatoes, and a deep dish of pickled beets, all carried on a pastry board. "I don't know how good it will be," he said. "The hens are a little old. We don't have any pullets. The weasels got the baby chicks this year."

"Pull up," said Samuel.

"Wait until I get my ng-ka-py," said Lee.

While he was gone Adam said, "It's strange to me—he used to speak differently."

"He trusts you now," Samuel said. "He has a gift of resigned loyalty without hope of reward. He's maybe a much better man than either of us could dream of being."

Lee came back and took his seat at the end of the table. "Just put the boys on the ground," he said.

The twins protested when they were set down. Lee spoke to them sharply in Cantonese and they were silent.

The men ate quietly as nearly all country people do. Suddenly Lee got up and hurried into the house. He came back with a jug of red wine. "I forgot it," he said. "I found it in the house."

Adam laughed. "I remember drinking wine here before I bought the place. Maybe I bought the place because of the wine. The chicken's good, Lee. I don't think I've been aware of the taste of food for a long time."

"You're getting well," Samuel said. "Some people think it's an insult to the glory of their sickness to get well. But the time poultice is no respecter of glories. Everyone gets well if he waits around."

[4]

Lee cleared the table and gave each of the boys a clean drumstick. They sat solemnly holding their greasy batons and alternately inspecting and sucking them. The wine and the glasses stayed on the table.

"We'd best get on with the naming," Samuel said. "I can feel a little tightening on my halter from Liza."

"I can't think what to name them," Adam said.

"You have no family name you want—no inviting trap for a rich relative, no proud name to re-create?"

"No, I'd like them to start fresh, insofar as that is possible."

Samuel knocked his forehead with his knuckles. "What a shame," he said. "What a shame it is that the proper names for them they cannot have."

"What do you mean?" Adam asked.

"Freshness, you said. I thought last night—" He paused. "Have you thought of your own name?"

"Mine?"

"Of course. Your first-born—Cain and Abel."

Adam said. "Oh, no. No, we can't do that."

"I know we can't. That would be tempting whatever fate there is. But isn't it odd that Cain is maybe the best-known name in the whole world and as far as I know only one man has ever borne it?"

Lee said, "Maybe that's why the name has never changed its emphasis."

Adam looked into the ink-red wine in his glass. "I got a shiver when you mentioned it," he said.

"Two stories have haunted us and followed us from our beginning," Samuel said. "We carry them along with us like invisible tails—the story of original sin and the story of Cain and Abel. And I don't understand either of them. I don't understand them at all but I feel them. Liza gets angry with me. She says I should not try to understand them. She says why should we try to explain a verity. Maybe she's right—maybe she's right. Lee, Liza says you're a Presbyterian—do you understand the Garden of Eden and Cain and Abel?"

"She thought I should be something, and I went to Sunday School long ago in San Francisco. People like you to be something, preferably what they are."

Adam said, "He asked you if you understood."

"I think I understand the Fall. I could perhaps feel that in myself. But the brother murder—no. Well, maybe I don't remember the details very well."

Samuel said, "Most people don't read the details. It's the details that astonish me. And Abel had no children." He looked up at the sky. "Lord, how the day passes! It's like a life—so quickly when we don't watch it and so slowly when we do. No," he said, "I'm having enjoyment. And I made a promise to myself that I would not consider enjoyment a sin. I take a pleasure in inquiring into things. I've never been content to pass a stone without looking under it. And it is a black disappointment to me that I can never see the far side of the moon."

"I don't have a Bible," Adam said. "I left the family one in Connecticut."

"I have," said Lee. "I'll get it."

"No need," said Samuel. "Liza let me take her mother's. It's here in my pocket." He took out the package and unwrapped the battered book. "This one has been scraped and gnawed at," he said. "I wonder what agonies have settled here. Give me a used Bible and I will, I think, be able to tell you about a man by the places that are edged with the dirt of seeking fingers. Liza wears a Bible down evenly. Here we are—this oldest story. If it troubles us it must be that we find the trouble in ourselves."

"I haven't heard it since I was a child," said Adam.

"You think it's long then, and it's very short," said Samuel. "I'll read it through and then we'll go back. Give me a little wine, my throat's dried out with wine. Here it is—such a little story to have made so deep a wound." He looked down at the ground. "See!" he said. "The boys have gone to their sleep, there in the dust."

Lee got up. "I'll cover them," he said.

"The dust is warm," said Samuel. "Now it goes this way. 'And Adam knew Eve his wife; and she conceived, and bare Cain, and said, "I have gotten a man from the Lord." '"

Adam started to speak and Samuel looked up at him and he was silent and covered his eyes with his hand. Samuel read, " 'And she again bare his brother Abel. And Abel was a keeper of sheep, but Cain was a tiller of the ground. And in the process of time it came to pass that Cain brought of the fruit of the ground an offering unto the Lord. And Abel, he also brought of the firstlings of his flock and of the fat thereof. And the Lord had respect unto Abel and to his offering. But unto Cain and to his offering he had not respect.' "

Lee said, "Now there—no, go on, go on. We'll come back."

Samuel read, " 'And Cain was very wroth, and his countenance fell. And the Lord said unto Cain, "Why art thou wroth? And why is thy countenance fallen? If thou doest well, shalt thou not be accepted? And if thou doest not well, sin lieth at the door. And unto thee shall be his desire, and thou shalt rule over him."

" 'And Cain talked with Abel his brother: and it came to pass, when they were in the field, that Cain rose up against Abel his brother and slew him. And the Lord said unto Cain, "Where is Abel thy brother?" And he said, "I know not. Am I my brother's keeper?" And he said, "What hast thou done? The voice of thy brother's blood crieth unto me from the ground. And now art thou cursed from the earth, which hath opened her mouth to receive thy brother's blood from thy hand. When thou tillest the ground it shall not henceforth yield unto thee her strength; a fugitive and a vagabond shalt thou be in the earth." And Cain said unto the Lord, "My punishment is greater than I can bear. Behold, thou hast driven me out this day from the face of the earth, and from thy face shall I be hid. And I shall be a fugitive and a vaga-bond in the earth; and it shall come to pass that every-one that findeth me shall slay me." And the Lord said unto him, "Therefore whosoever slayeth Cain, venge-ance shall be taken on him sevenfold." And the Lord set a mark upon Cain, lest any finding him should kill him. And Cain went out from the presence of the Lord and dwelt in the land of Nod on the east of Eden.' "

Samuel closed the loose cover of the book almost with weariness. "There it is," he said. "Sixteen verses, no more. And oh, Lord! I had forgotten how dreadful it is—no single tone of encouragement. Maybe Liza's right. There's nothing to understand."

Adam sighed deeply. "It's not a comforting story, is it?"

Lee poured a tumbler full of dark liquor from his round stone bottle and sipped it and opened his mouth to get the double taste on the back of his tongue. "No story has power, nor will it last, unless we feel in ourselves that it is true and true of us. What a great burden of guilt men have!"

Samuel said to Adam, "And you have tried to take it all."

Lee said, "So do I, so does everyone. We gather our arms full of guilt as though it were precious stuff. It must be that we want it that way."

Adam broke in, "It makes me feel better, not worse."

"How do you mean?" Samuel asked.

"Well, every little boy thinks he invented sin. Virtue we think we learn, because we are told about it. But sin is our own designing."

"Yes, I see. But how does this story make it better?"

"Because," Adam said excitedly, "we are descended from this. This is our father. Some of our guilt is absorbed in our ancestry. What chance did we have? We are the children of our father. It means we aren't the first. It's an excuse, and there aren't enough excuses in the world."

"Not convincing ones anyway," said Lee. "Else we would long ago have wiped out guilt, and the world would not be filled with sad, punished people."

Samuel said, "But do you think of another frame to this picture? Excuse or not, we are snapped back to our ancestry. We have guilt."

Adam said, "I remember being a little outraged at God. Both Cain and Abel gave what they had, and God accepted Abel and rejected Cain. I never thought that was a just thing. I never understood it. Do you?"

"Maybe we think out of a different background," said Lee. "I remember that this story was written by and for a shepherd people. They were not farmers. Wouldn't the god of shepherds find a fat lamb more valuable than a sheaf of barley? A sacrifice must be the best and most valuable."

"Yes, I can see that," said Samuel. "And Lee, let

me caution you about bringing your Oriental reasoning to Liza's attention."

Adam was excited. "Yes, but why did God condemn Cain? That's an injustice."

Samuel said, "There's an advantage to listening to the words. God did not condemn Cain at all. Even God can have a preference, can't he? Let's suppose God liked lamb better than vegetables. I think I do myself. Cain brought him a bunch of carrots maybe. And God said, 'I don't like this. Try again. Bring me something I like and I'll set you up alongside your brother.' But Cain got mad. His feelings were hurt. And when a man's feelings are hurt he wants to strike at something, and Abel was in the way of his anger."

Lee said, "St. Paul says to the Hebrews that Abel had faith."

"There's no reference to it in Genesis," Samuel said. "No faith or lack of faith. Only a hint of Cain's temper."

Lee asked, "How does Mrs. Hamilton feel about the paradoxes of the Bible?"

"Why, she does not feel anything because she does not admit they are there."

"But—"

"Hush, man. Ask her. And you'll come out of it older but not less confused."

Adam said, "You two have studied this. I only got it through my skin and not much of it stuck. Then Cain was driven out for murder?"

"That's right—for murder."

"And God branded him?"

"Did you listen? Cain bore the mark not to destroy him but to save him. And there's a curse called down on any man who shall kill him. It was a preserving mark."

Adam said, "I can't get over a feeling that Cain got the dirty end of the stick."

"Maybe he did," said Samuel. "But Cain lived and had children, and Abel lives only in the story. We are Cain's children. And isn't it strange that three grown men, here in a century so many thousands of years away, discuss this crime as though it happened in King City yesterday and hadn't come up for trial?"

One of the twins awakened and yawned and looked at Lee and went to sleep again.

Lee said, "Remember, Mr. Hamilton, I told you I was trying to translate some old Chinese poetry into English? No, don't worry. I won't read it. Doing it, I found some of the old things as fresh and clear as this morning. And I wondered why. And, of course, people are interested only in themselves. If a story is not about the hearer he will not listen. And I here make a rule—a great and lasting story is about everyone or it will not last. The strange and foreign is not interesting—only the deeply personal and familiar."

Samuel said, "Apply that to the Cain-Abel story."

And Adam said, "I didn't kill my brother—" Suddenly he stopped and his mind went reeling back in time.

"I think I can," Lee answered Samuel. "I think this is the best-known story in the world because it is everybody's story. I think it is the symbol story of the human soul. I'm feeling my way now—don't jump on me if I'm not clear. The greatest terror a child can have is that he is not loved, and rejection is the hell he fears. I think everyone in the world to a large or small extent has felt rejection. And with rejection comes anger, and with anger some kind of crime in revenge for the rejection, and with the crime guilt—and there is the story of mankind. I think that if rejection could be amputated, the human would not be what he is. Maybe there would be fewer crazy people. I am sure in myself there would not be many jails. It is all there—the start, the beginning. One child, refused the love he craves, kicks the cat and hides his secret guilt; and another steals so that money will make him loved; and a third conquers the world—and always the guilt and revenge and more guilt. The human is the only guilty animal. Now wait! Therefore I think this old and terrible story is important because it is a chart of the soul—the secret, rejected, guilty soul. Mr. Trask, you said you did not kill your brother and then you remembered something. I don't want to know what it was, but was it very far apart from Cain and Abel? And what do you think of my Oriental patter, Mr. Hamilton? You know I am no more Oriental than you are."

Samuel had leaned his elbows on the table and his hands covered his eyes and his forehead. "I want to think," he said. "Damn you, I want to think. I'll want to take this off alone where I can pick it apart and see. Maybe you've tumbled a world for me. And I don't know what I can build in my world's place."

Lee said softly, "Couldn't a world be built around accepted truth? Couldn't some pains and insanities be rooted out if the causes were known?"

"I don't know, damn you. You've disturbed my pretty universe. You've taken a contentious game and made an answer of it. Let me alone—let me think! Your damned bitch is having pups in my brain already. Oh, I wonder what my Tom will think of this! He'll cradle it in the palm of his mind. He'll turn it slow in his brain like a roast of pork before the fire. Adam, come out now. You've been long enough in whatever memory it was."

Adam started. He sighed deeply. "Isn't it too simple?" he asked. "I'm always afraid of simple things."

"It isn't simple at all," said Lee. "It's desperately complicated. But at the end there's light."

"There's not going to be light long," Samuel said. "We've sat and let the evening come. I drove over to help name the twins and they're not named. We've swung ourselves on a pole. Lee, you better keep your complications out of the machinery of the set-up churches or there might be a Chinese with nails in his hands and feet. They like complications but they like their own. I'll have to be driving home."

Adam said desperately, "Name me some names."

"From the Bible?"

"From anyplace."

"Well, let's see. Of all the people who started out of Egypt only two came to the Promised Land. Would you like them for a symbol?"

"Who?"

"Caleb and Joshua."

"Joshua was a soldier—a general. I don't like soldiering."

"Well, Caleb was a captain."

"But not a general. I kind of like Caleb—Caleb Trask."

One of the twins woke up and without interval began to wail.

"You called his name," said Samuel. "You don't like Joshua, and Caleb's named. He's the smart one—the dark one. See, the other one is awake too. Well, Aaron I've always liked, but he didn't make it to the Promised Land."

The second boy almost joyfully began to cry.

"That's good enough," said Adam.

Suddenly Samuel laughed. "In two minutes," he said, "and after a waterfall of words. Caleb and Aaron —now you are people and you have joined the fraternity and you have the right to be damned."

Lee took the boys up under his arms. "Have you got them straight?" he asked.

"Of course," said Adam. "That one is Caleb and you are Aaron."

Lee lugged the yelling twins toward the house in the dusk.

"Yesterday I couldn't tell them apart," said Adam. "Aaron and Caleb."

"Thank the good Lord we had produce from our patient thought," Samuel said. "Liza would have preferred Joshua. She loves the crashing walls of Jericho. But she likes Aaron too, so I guess it's all right. I'll go and hitch up my rig."

Adam walked to the shed with him. "I'm glad you came," he said. "There's a weight off me."

Samuel slipped the bit in Doxology's reluctant mouth, set the brow band, and buckled the throatlatch. "Maybe you'll now be thinking of the garden in the flat land," he said. "I can see it there the way you planned it."

Adam was long in answering. At last he said, "I think that kind of energy is gone out of me. I can't feel the pull of it. I have money enough to live. I never wanted it for myself. I have no one to show a garden to."

Samuel wheeled on him and his eyes were filled with tears. "Don't think it will ever die," he cried. "Don't expect it. Are you better than other men? I tell you it won't ever die until you do." He stood panting for a moment and then he climbed into the rig and whipped Doxology and he drove away, his shoulders hunched, without saying good-by.

(Chapter 22)

CHOICE AND
RESPONSIBILITY

PLACES were very important to Samuel. The ranch was a relative, and when he left it he plunged a knife into a darling. But having made up his mind, Samuel set about doing it well. He made formal calls on all of his neighbors, the old-timers who remembered how it used to be and how it was. And when he drove away from his old friends they knew they would not see him again, although he did not say it. He took to gazing at the mountains and the trees, even at faces, as though to memorize them for eternity.

He saved his visit to the Trask place for last. He had not been there for months. Adam was not a young man any more. The boys were eleven years old, and Lee—well, Lee did not change much. Lee walked to the shed with Samuel.

"I've wanted to talk to you for a long time," said Lee. "But there's so much to do. And I try to get to San Francisco at least once a month."

"You know how it is," Samuel said. "When you know a friend is there you do not go to see him. Then he's gone and you blast your conscience to shreds that you did not see him."

"I heard about your daughter. I'm sorry."

"I got your letter, Lee. I have it. You said good things."

"Chinese things," said Lee. "I seem to get more Chinese as I get older."

"There's something changed about you, Lee. What is it?"

"It's my queue, Mr. Hamilton. I've cut off my queue."

"That's it."

"We all did. Haven't you heard? The dowager Empress is gone. China is free. The Manchus are not overlords and we do not wear queues. It was a proclamation of the new government. There's not a queue left anywhere."

"Does it make a difference, Lee?"

"Not much. It's easier. But there's a kind of looseness on the scalp that makes me uneasy. It's hard to get used to the convenience of it."

"How is Adam?"

"He's all right. But he hasn't changed much. I wonder what he was like before."

"Yes, I've wondered about that. It was a short flowering. The boys must be big."

"They are big. I'm glad I stayed here. I learned a great deal from seeing the boys grow and helping a little."

"Did you teach them Chinese?"

"No. Mr. Trask didn't want me to. And I guess he was right. It would have been a needless complication. But I'm their friend—yes, I'm their friend. They admire their father, but I think they love me. And they're very different. You can't imagine how different."

"In what way, Lee?"

"You'll see when they come home from school. They're like two sides of a medal. Cal is sharp and dark and watchful, and his brother—well, he's a boy you like before he speaks and like more afterwards."

"And you don't like Cal?"

"I find myself defending him—to myself. He's

fighting for his life and his brother doesn't have to fight."

"I have the same thing in my brood," said Samuel. "I don't understand it. You'd think with the same training and the same blood they'd be alike, but they're not—not at all."

Later Samuel and Adam walked down the oak-shadowed road to the entrance to the draw where they could look out at the Salinas Valley.

"Will you stay to dinner?" Adam asked.

"I will not be responsible for the murder of more chickens," said Samuel.

"Lee's got a pot roast."

"Well, in that case—"

Adam still carried one shoulder lower than the other from the old hurt. His face was hard and curtained, and his eyes looked at generalities and did not inspect details. The two men stopped in the road and looked out at the valley, green tinged from the early rains.

Samuel said softly, "I wonder you do not feel a shame at leaving that land fallow."

"I had no reason to plant it," Adam said. "We had that out before. You thought I would change. I have not changed."

"Do you take pride in your hurt?" Samuel asked. "Does it make you seem large and tragic?"

"I don't know."

"Well, think about it. Maybe you're playing a part on a great stage with only yourself as audience."

A slight anger came into Adam's voice. "Why do you come to lecture me? I'm glad you've come, but why do you dig into me?"

"To see whether I can raise a little anger in you. I'm a nosy man. But there's all that fallow land, and here beside me is all that fallow man. It seems a waste.

And I have a bad feeling about waste because I could never afford it. Is it a good feeling to let your life lie fallow?"

"What else could I do?"

"You could try again."

Adam faced him. "I'm afraid to, Samuel," he said. "I'd rather just go about it this way. Maybe I haven't the energy or the courage."

"How about your boys—do you love them?"

"Yes—yes."

"Do you love one more than the other?"

"Why do you say that?"

"I don't know. Something about your tone."

"Let's go back to the house," said Adam. They strolled back under the trees. Suddenly Adam said, "Did you ever hear that Cathy was in Salinas? Did you ever hear such a rumor?"

"Did you?"

"Yes—but I don't believe it. I can't believe it."

Samuel walked silently in the sandy wheel rut of the road. His mind turned sluggishly in the pattern of Adam and almost wearily took up a thought he had hoped was finished. He said at last, "You have never let her go."

"I guess not. But I've let the shooting go. I don't think about it any more."

"I can't tell you how to live your life," Samuel said, "although I do be telling you how to live it. I know that it might be better for you to come out from under your might-have-beens, into the winds of the world. And while I tell you, I am myself sifting my memories, the way men pan the dirt under a barroom floor for the bits of gold dust that fall between the cracks. It's small mining—small mining. You're too young a man to be panning memories, Adam. You should be getting yourself some new ones, so that the mining will be richer when you come to age."

Adam's face was bent down, and his jawbone jutted below his temples from clenching.

Samuel glanced at him. "That's right," he said. "Set your teeth in it. How we do defend a wrongness! Shall I tell you what you do, so you will not think you invented it? When you go to bed and blow out the lamp—then she stands in the doorway with a little light behind her, and you can see her nightgown stir. And she comes sweetly to your bed, and you, hardly breathing, turn back the covers to receive her and move your head over on the pillow to make room for her head beside yours. You can smell the sweetness of her skin, and it smells like no other skin in the world—"

"Stop it," Adam shouted at him. "Goddam you, stop it! Stop nosing over my life! You're like a coyote sniffing around a dead cow."

"The way I know," Samuel said softly, "is that one came to me that selfsame way—night after month after year, right to the very now. And I think I should have double-bolted my mind and sealed off my heart against her, but I did not. All of these years I've cheated Liza. I've given her an untruth, a counterfeit, and I've saved the best for those dark sweet hours. And now I could wish that she may have had some secret caller too. But I'll never know that. I think she would maybe have bolted her heart shut and thrown the key to hell."

Adam's hands were clenched and the blood was driven out of his white knuckles. "You make me doubt myself," he said fiercely. "You always have. I'm afraid of you. What should I do, Samuel? Tell me! I don't know how you saw the thing so clear. What should I do?"

"I know the 'shoulds,' although I never do them, Adam. I always know the 'shoulds.' You should try to find a new Cathy. You should let the new Cathy kill the dream Cathy—let the two of them fight it out. And you, sitting by, should marry your mind to the winner. That's the second-best should. The best would be to search out and find some fresh new loveliness to cancel out the old."

"I'm afraid to try," said Adam.

"That's what you've said. And now I'm going to put a selfishness on you. I'm going away, Adam. I came to say good-by."

"What do you mean?"

"My daughter Olive has asked Liza and me to visit with her in Salinas, and we're going—day after tomorrow."

"Well, you'll be back."

Samuel went on, "After we've visited with Olive for maybe a month or two, there will come a letter from George. And his feelings will be hurt if we don't visit him in Paso Robles. And after that Mollie will want us in San Francisco, and then Will, and maybe even Joe in the East, if we should live so long."

"Well, won't you like that? You've earned it. You've worked hard enough on that dust heap of yours."

"I love that dust heap," Samuel said. "I love it the way a bitch loves her runty pup. I love every flint, the plow-breaking outcroppings, the thin and barren topsoil, the waterless heart of her. Somewhere in my dust heap there's a richness."

"You deserve a rest."

"There, you've said it again," said Samuel. "That's what I had to accept, and I have accepted. When you say I deserve a rest, you are saying that my life is over."

"Do you believe that?"

"That's what I have accepted."

Adam said excitedly, "You can't do that. Why, if you accept that you won't live!"

"I know," said Samuel.

"But you can't do that."

"Why not?"

"I don't want you to."

"I'm a nosy old man, Adam. And the sad thing to me is that I'm losing my nosiness. That's maybe how I know it's time to visit my children. I'm having to pretend to be nosy a good deal of the time."

"I'd rather you worked your guts out on your dust heap."

Samuel smiled at him. "What a nice thing to hear! And I thank you. It's a good thing to be loved, even late."

Suddenly Adam turned in front of him so that Samuel had to stop. "I know what you've done for me," Adam said. "I can't return anything. But I can ask you for one more thing. If I asked you, would you do me one more kindness, and maybe save my life?"

"I would if I could."

Adam swung out his hand and made an arc over the west. "That land out there—would you help me to make the garden we talked of, the windmills and the wells and the flats of alfalfa? We could raise flower-seeds. There's money in that. Think what it would be like, acres of sweet peas and gold squares of calendulas. Maybe ten acres of roses for the gardens of the West. Think how they would smell on the west wind!"

"You're going to make me cry," Samuel said, "and that would be an unseemly thing in an old man." And indeed his eyes were wet. "I thank you, Adam," he said. "The sweetness of your offer is a good smell on the west wind."

"Then you'll do it?"

"No, I will not do it. But I'll see it in my mind when I'm in Salinas, listening to William Jennings Bryan. And maybe I'll get to believe it happened."

"But I want to do it."

"Go and see my Tom. He'll help you. He'd plant the world with roses, poor man, if he could."

"You know what you're doing, Samuel?"

"Yes, I know what I'm doing, know so well that it's half done."

"What a stubborn man you are!"

"Contentious," said Samuel. "Liza says I am contentious, but now I'm caught in a web of my children—and I think I like it."

[2]

The dinner table was set in the house. Lee said, "I'd have liked to serve it under the tree like the other times, but the air is chilly."

"So it is, Lee," said Samuel.

The twins came in silently and stood shyly staring at their guest.

"It's a long time since I've seen you, boys. But we named you well. You're Caleb, aren't you?"

"I'm Cal."

"Well, Cal then." And he turned to the other. "Have you found a way to rip the backbone out of your name?"

"Sir?"

"Are you called Aaron?"

"Yes, sir."

Lee chuckled. "He spells it with one *a*. The two *a*'s seem a little fancy to his friends."

"I've got thirty-five Belgian hares, sir," Aron said. "Would you like to see them, sir? The hutch is up by the spring. I've got eight newborns—just born yesterday."

"I'd like to see them, Aron." His mouth twitched. "Cal, don't tell me you're a gardener?"

Lee's head snapped around and he inspected Samuel. "Don't do that," Lee said nervously.

Cal said, "Next year my father is going to let me have an acre in the flat."

Aron said, "I've got a buck rabbit weighs fifteen pounds. I'm going to give it to my father for his birthday."

They heard Adam's bedroom door opening. "Don't tell him," Aron said quickly. "It's a secret."

Lee sawed at the pot roast. "Always you bring trouble for my mind, Mr. Hamilton," he said. "Sit down, boys."

Adam came in, turning down his sleeves, and took his seat at the head of the table. "Good evening, boys," he said, and they replied in unison, "Good evening, Father."

And, "Don't you tell," said Aron.

"I won't," Samuel assured him.

"Don't tell what?" Adam asked.

Samuel said, "Can't there be a privacy? I have a secret with your son."

Cal broke in, "I'll tell you a secret too, right after dinner."

"I'll like to hear it," said Samuel. "And I do hope I don't know already what it is."

Lee looked up from his carving and glared at Samuel. He began piling meat on the plates.

The boys ate quickly and quietly, wolfed their food. Aron said, "Will you excuse us, Father?"

Adam nodded, and the two boys went quickly out. Samuel looked after them. "They seem older than eleven," he said. "I seem to remember that at eleven my brood were howlers and screamers and runners in circles. These seem like grown men."

"Do they?" Adam asked.

Lee said, "I think I see why that is. There is no woman in the house to put a value on babies. I don't think men care much for babies, and so it was never an advantage to these boys to be babies. There was nothing to gain by it. I don't know whether that is good or bad."

Samuel wiped up the remains of gravy in his plate with a slice of bread. "Adam, I wonder whether you know what you have in Lee. A philosopher who can cook, or a cook who can think? He has taught me a great deal. You must have learned from him, Adam."

Adam said, "I'm afraid I didn't listen enough—or maybe he didn't talk."

"Why didn't you want the boys to learn Chinese, Adam?"

Adam thought for a moment. "It seems a time for honesty," he said at last. "I guess it was plain jealousy. I gave it another name, but maybe I didn't want them to be able so easily to go away from me in a direction I couldn't follow."

"That's reasonable enough and almost too human," said Samuel. "But knowing it—that's a great jump. I wonder whether I have ever gone so far."

Lee brought the gray enameled coffeepot to the table and filled the cups and sat down. He warmed the palm of his hand against the rounded side of his cup. And then Lee laughed. "You've given me great trouble, Mr. Hamilton, and you've disturbed the tranquillity of China."

"How do you mean, Lee?"

"It almost seems that I have told you this," said Lee. "Maybe I only composed it in my mind, meaning to tell you. It's an amusing story anyway."

"I want to hear," said Samuel, and he looked at Adam. "Don't you want to hear, Adam? Or are you slipping into your cloud bath?"

"I was thinking of that," said Adam. "It's funny— a kind of excitement is coming over me."

"That's good," said Samuel. "Maybe that's the best of all good things that can happen to a human. Let's hear your story, Lee."

The Chinese reached to the side of his neck and he smiled. "I wonder whether I'll ever get used to the lack of a queue," he said. "I guess I used it more than I knew. Yes, the story. I told you, Mr. Hamilton, that I was growing more Chinese. Do you ever grow more Irish?"

"It comes and goes," said Samuel.

"Do you remember when you read us the sixteen verses of the fourth chapter of Genesis and we argued about them?"

"I do indeed. And that's a long time ago."

"Ten years nearly," said Lee. "Well, the story bit deeply into me and I went into it word for word. The more I thought about the story, the more profound it became to me. Then I compared the translations we have—and they were fairly close. There was only one place that bothered me. The King James version says this—it is when Jehovah has asked Cain why he is angry. Jehovah says, 'If thou doest well, shalt thou not be accepted? and if thou doest not well, sin lieth at the door. And unto thee shall be his desire, and *thou shalt* rule over him,' It was the 'thou shalt' that struck me, because it was a promise that Cain would conquer sin."

Samuel nodded. "And his children didn't do it entirely," he said.

Lee sipped his coffee. "Then I got a copy of the American Standard Bible. It was very new then. And it was different in this passage. It says, '*Do thou* rule over him.' Now this is very different. This is not a promise, it is an order. And I began to stew about it. I wondered what the original word of the original writer had been that these very different translations could be made."

Samuel put his palms down on the table and leaned forward and the old young light came into his eyes. "Lee," he said, "don't tell me you studied Hebrew!"

Lee said, "I'm going to tell you. And it's a fairly long story. Will you have a touch of ng-ka-py?"

"You mean the drink that tastes of good rotten apples?"

"Yes. I can talk better with it."

"Maybe I can listen better," said Samuel.

While Lee went to the kitchen Samuel asked, "Adam, did you know about this?"

"No," said Adam. "He didn't tell me. Maybe I wasn't listening."

Lee came back with his stone bottle and three little porcelain cups so thin and delicate that the light shone through them. "Dlinkee Chinee fashion," he said and poured the almost black liquor. "There's a lot of wormwood in this. It's quite a drink," he said. "Has about the same effect as absinthe if you drink enough of it."

Samuel sipped the drink. "I want to know why you were so interested," he said.

"Well, it seemed to me that the man who could conceive this great story would know exactly what he wanted to say and there would be no confusion in his statement."

"You say 'the man.' Do you then not think this is a divine book written by the inky finger of God?"

"I think the mind that could think this story was a curiously divine mind. We have had a few such minds in China too."

"I just wanted to know," said Samuel. "You're not a Presbyterian after all."

"I told you I was getting more Chinese. Well, to go on, I went to San Francisco to the headquarters of our family association. Do you know about them? Our great families have centers where any member can get help or give it. The Lee family is very large. It takes care of its own."

"I have heard of them," said Samuel.

"You mean Chinee hatchet man fightee Tong war over slave girl?"

"I guess so."

"It's a little different from that, really," said Lee. "I went there because in our family there are a number of ancient reverend gentlemen who are great scholars. They are thinkers in exactness. A man may spend many years pondering a sentence of the scholar you call Confucius. I thought there might be experts in meaning who could advise me.

"They are fine old men. They smoke their two pipes of opium in the afternoon and it rests and sharpens them, and they sit through the night and their minds are wonderful. I guess no other people have been able to use opium well."

Lee dampened his tongue in the black brew. "I respectfully submitted my problem to one of these sages, read him the story, and told him what I understood from it. The next night four of them met and called me in. We discussed the story all night long."

Lee laughed. "I guess it's funny," he said. "I know I wouldn't dare tell it to many people. Can you imagine four old gentlemen, the youngest is over ninety now, taking on the study of Hebrew? They engaged a learned rabbi. They took to the study as though they were children. Exercise books, grammar, vocabulary, simple sentences. You should see Hebrew written in Chinese ink with a brush! The right to left didn't bother them as much as it would you, since we write up to down. Oh, they were perfectionists! They went to the root of the matter."

"And you?" said Samuel.

"I went along with them, marveling at the beauty of their proud clean brains. I began to love my race, and for the first time I wanted to be Chinese. Every two weeks I went to a meeting with them, and in my room here I covered pages with writing. I bought every known Hebrew dictionary. But the old gentlemen were always ahead of me. It wasn't long before they were ahead of our rabbi; he brought a colleague in. Mr. Hamilton, you should have sat through some of those nights of argument and discussion. The questions, the inspection, oh, the lovely thinking—the beautiful thinking.

"After two years we felt that we could approach your sixteen verses of the fourth chapter of Genesis. My old gentlemen felt that these words were very important too—'Thou shalt' and 'Do thou.' And this was the gold from our mining: *Thou mayest.*' 'Thou mayest rule over sin.' The old gentlemen smiled and nodded and felt the years were well spent. It brought them out of their Chinese shells too, and right now they are studying Greek."

Samuel said, "It's a fantastic story. And I've tried to follow and maybe I've missed somewhere. Why is this word so important?"

Lee's hand shook as he filled the delicate cups. He drank his down in one gulp. "Don't you see?" he cried. "The American Standard translation *orders* men to triumph over sin, and you can call sin ignorance. The King James translation makes a promise in 'Thou shalt,' meaning that men will surely triumph over sin. But the Hebrew word, the word *timshel*—'Thou mayest'—that gives a choice. It might be the most important word in the world. That says the way is open. That throws it right back on a man. For if 'Thou mayest'—it is also true that 'Thou mayest not.' Don't you see?"

"Yes, I see. I do see. But you do not believe this is divine law. Why do you feel its importance?"

"Ah!" said Lee. "I've wanted to tell you this for a long time. I even anticipated your questions and I am well prepared. Any writing which has influenced the thinking and the lives of innumerable people is important. Now, there are many millions in their sects and churches who feel the order, 'Do thou,' and throw their weight into obedience. And there are millions more who feel predestination in 'Thou shalt.' Nothing they may do can interfere with what will be. But 'Thou mayest'! Why, that makes a man great, that gives him stature with the gods, for in his weakness and his filth and his murder of his brother he has still the great choice. He can choose his course and fight it through and win." Lee's voice was a chant of triumph.

Adam said, "Do you believe that, Lee?"

"Yes, I do. Yes, I do. It is easy out of laziness, out of weakness, to throw oneself into the lap of deity, saying, 'I couldn't help it; the way was set.' But think of the glory of the choice! That makes a man a man. A cat has no choice, a bee must make honey. There's no godliness there. And do you know, those old gentlemen who were sliding gently down to death are too interested to die now?"

Adam said, "Do you mean these Chinese men believe the Old Testament?"

Lee said, "These old men believe a true story, and they know a true story when they hear it. They are critics of truth. They know that these sixteen verses are a history of humankind in any age or culture or race. They do not believe a man writes fifteen and three-quarter verses of truth and tells a lie with one verb. Confucius tells men how they should live to have good and successful lives. But this—this is a ladder to climb to the stars." Lee's eyes shone. "You can never lose that. It cuts the feet from under weakness and cowardliness and laziness."

Adam said, "I don't see how you could cook and raise the boys and take care of me and still do all this."

"Neither do I," said Lee. "But I take my two pipes in the afternoon, no more and no less, like the elders. And I feel that I am a man. And I feel that a man is a very important thing—maybe more important than a star. This is not theology. I have no bent toward gods. But I have a new love for that glittering instrument, the human soul. It is a lovely and unique thing in the universe. It is always attacked and never destroyed— because 'Thou mayest.'"

[3]

Lee and Adam walked out to the shed with Samuel to
see him off. Lee carried a tin lantern to light the
way, for it was one of those clear early winter nights
when the sky riots with stars and the earth seems
doubly dark because of them. A silence lay on the
hills. No animal moved about, neither grass-eater
nor predator, and the air was so still that the dark
limbs and leaves of the live oaks stood unmoving
against the Milky Way. The three men were silent.
The bail of the tin lantern squeaked a little as the light
swung in Lee's hand.

Adam asked, "When do you think you'll be back
from your trip?"

Samuel did not answer.

Doxology stood patiently in the stall, head down,
his milky eyes staring at the straw under his feet.

"You've had that horse forever," Adam said.

"He's thirty-three," said Samuel. "His teeth are worn
off. I have to feed him warm mash with my fingers.
And he has bad dreams. He shivers and cries sometimes in his sleep."

"He's about as ugly a crow bait as I ever saw,"
Adam said.

"I know it. I think that's why I picked him when
he was a colt. Do you know I paid two dollars for
him thirty-three years ago? Everything was wrong
with him, hoofs like flapjacks, a hock so thick and
short and straight there seems no joint at all. He's
hammerheaded and swaybacked. He has a pinched
chest and a big behind. He has an iron mouth and he
still fights the crupper. With a saddle he feels as though
you were riding a sled over a gravel pit. He can't trot
and he stumbles over his feet when he walks. I have

never in thirty-three years found one good thing about him. He even has an ugly disposition. He is selfish and quarrelsome and mean and disobedient. To this day I don't dare walk behind him because he will surely take a kick at me. When I feed him mash he tries to bite my hand. And I love him."

Lee said, "And you named him 'Doxology.' "

"Surely," said Samuel, "so ill endowed a creature deserved, I thought, one grand possession. He hasn't very long now."

Adam said, "Maybe you should put him out of his misery."

"What misery?" Samuel demanded. "He's one of the few happy and consistent beings I've ever met."

"He must have aches and pains."

"Well, he doesn't think so. Doxology still thinks he's one hell of a horse. Would you shoot him, Adam?"

"Yes, I think I would. Yes, I would."

"You'd take the responsibility?"

"Yes, I think I would. He's thirty-three. His lifespan is long over."

Lee had set his lantern on the ground. Samuel squatted beside it and instinctively stretched his hands for warmth to the bufferfly of yellow light.

"I've been bothered by something, Adam," he said.

"What is that?"

"You would really shoot my horse because death might be more comfortable?"

"Well, I meant—"

Samuel said quickly, "Do you like your life, Adam?"

"Of course not."

"If I had a medicine that might cure you and also might kill you, should I give it to you? Inspect yourself, man."

"What medicine?"

"No," said Samuel. "If I tell you, believe me when I say it may kill you."

Lee said, "Be careful, Mr. Hamilton. Be careful."

"What is this?" Adam demanded. "Tell me what you're thinking of."

Samuel said softly, "I think for once I will not be careful. Lee, if I am wrong—listen—if I am mistaken, I accept the responsibility and I will take what blame there is to take."

"Are you sure you're right?" Lee asked anxiously.

"Of course I'm not sure. Adam, do you want the medicine?"

"Yes. I don't know what it is but give it to me."

"Adam, Cathy is in Salinas. She owns a whorehouse, the most vicious and depraved in this whole end of the country. The evil and ugly, the distorted and slimy, the worst things humans can think up are for sale there. The crippled and crooked come there for satisfaction. But it is worse than that. Cathy, and she is now called Kate, takes the fresh and young and beautiful and so maims them that they can never be whole again. Now, there's your medicine. Let's see what it does to you."

"You're a liar!" Adam said.

"No, Adam. Many things I am, but a liar I am not."

Adam whirled on Lee. "Is this true?"

"I'm no antidote," said Lee. "Yes. It's true."

Adam stood swaying in the lantern light and then he turned and ran. They could hear his heavy steps running and tripping. They heard him falling over the brush and scrambling and clawing his way upward on the slope. The sound of him stopped only when he had gone over the brow of the hill.

Lee said, "Your medicine acts like poison."

"I take responsibility," said Samuel. "Long ago I

learned this: When a dog has eaten strychnine and is going to die, you must get an ax and carry him to a chopping block. Then you must wait for his next convulsion, and in that moment—chop off his tail. Then, if the poison has not gone too far, your dog may recover. The shock of pain can counteract the poison. Without the shock he will surely die."

"But how do you know this is the same?" Lee asked.

"I don't. But without it he would surely die."

"You're a brave man," Lee said.

"No, I'm an old man. And if I should have anything on my conscience it won't be for long."

Lee asked, "What do you suppose he'll do?"

"I don't know," said Samuel, "but at least he won't sit around and mope. Here, hold the lantern for me, will you?"

In the yellow light Samuel slipped the bit in Doxology's mouth, a bit worn so thin that is was a flake of steel. The check rein had been abandoned long ago. The old hammerhead was free to drag his nose if he wished, or to pause and crop grass beside the road. Samuel didn't care. Tenderly he buckled the crupper, and the horse edged around to try to kick him.

When Dox was between the shafts of the cart Lee asked, "Would you mind if I rode along with you a little? I'll walk back."

"Come along," said Samuel, and he tried not to notice that Lee helped him up into the cart.

The night was very dark, and Dox showed his disgust for night-traveling by stumbling every few steps.

Samuel said, "Get on with it, Lee. What is it you want to say?"

Lee did not appear surprised. "Maybe I'm nosy the way you say you are. I get to thinking. I know proba-

bilities, but tonight you fooled me completely. I would
have taken any bet that you of all men would not have
told Adam."

"Did you know about her?"

"Of course," said Lee.

"Do the boys know?"

"I don't think so, but that's only a matter of time.
You know how cruel children are. Someday in the
schoolyard it will be shouted at them."

"Maybe he ought to take them away from here,"
said Samuel. "Think about that, Lee."

"My question isn't answered, Mr. Hamilton. How
were you able to do what you did?"

"Do you think I was that wrong?"

"No, I don't mean that at all. But I've never thought
of you as taking any strong unchanging stand on anything. This has been my judgment. Are you interested?"

"Show me the man who isn't interested in discussing
himself," said Samuel. "Go on."

"You're a kind man, Mr. Hamilton. And I've always
thought it was the kindness that comes from not
wanting any trouble. And your mind is as facile as a
young lamb leaping in a daisy field. You have never
to my knowledge taken a bulldog grip on anything.
And then tonight you did a thing that tears down my
whole picture of you."

Samuel wrapped the lines around a stick stuck in
the whip socket, and Doxology stumbled on down
the rutty road. The old man stroked his beard, and it
shone very white in the starlight. He took off his black
hat and laid it in his lap. "I guess it surprised me as
much as it did you," he said. "But if you want to know
why—look into yourself."

"I don't understand you."

"If you had only told me about your studies earlier it might have made a great difference, Lee."

"I still don't understand you."

"Careful, Lee, you'll get me talking. I told you my Irish came and went. It's coming now."

Lee said, "Mr. Hamilton, you're going away and you're not coming back. You do not intend to live very much longer."

"That's true, Lee. How did you know?"

"There's death all around you. It shines from you."

"I didn't know anyone could see it," Samuel said. "You know, Lee, I think of my life as a kind of music, not always good music but still having form and melody. And my life has not been a full orchestra for a long time now. A single note only—and that note unchanging sorrow. I'm not alone in my attitude, Lee. It seems to me that too many of us conceive of a life as ending in defeat."

Lee said, "Maybe everyone is too rich. I have noticed that there is no dissatisfaction like that of the rich. Feed a man, clothe him, put him in a good house, and he will die of despair."

"It was your two-word retranslation, Lee—'Thou mayest.' It took me by the throat and shook me. And when the dizziness was over, a path was open, new and bright. And my life which is ending seems to be going on to an ending wonderful. And my music has a new last melody like a bird song in the night."

Lee was peering at him through the darkness. "That's what it did to those old men of my family."

" 'Thou mayest rule over sin,' Lee. That's it. I do not believe all men are destroyed. I can name you a dozen who were not, and they are the ones the world lives by. It is true of the spirit as it is true of battles

—only the winners are remembered. Surely most men are destroyed, but there are others who like pillars of fire guide frightened men through the darkness. *'Thou mayest, Thou mayest!'* What glory! It is true that we are weak and sick and quarrelsome, but if that is all we ever were, we would, millenniums ago, have disappeared from the face of the earth. A few remnants of fossilized jawbone, some broken teeth in strata of limestone, would be the only mark man would have left of his existence in the world. But the choice, Lee, the choice of winning! I had never understood it or accepted it before. Do you see now why I told Adam tonight? I exercised the choice. Maybe I was wrong, but by telling him I also forced him to live or get off the pot. What is that word, Lee?"

"*Timshel*," said Lee. "Will you stop the cart?"

"You'll have a long walk back."

Lee climbed down. "Samuel!" he said.

"Here am I." The old man chuckled. "Liza hates for me to say that."

"Samuel, you've gone beyond me."

"It's time, Lee."

"Good-by, Samuel," Lee said, and he walked hurriedly back along the road. He heard the iron tires of the cart grinding on the road. He turned and looked after it, and on the slope he saw old Samuel against the sky, his white hair shining with starlight.

(*From* Chapter 24)

TECHNOLOGY AND
A TECHNOCRAT

[1]

AFTER his first letter to his brother in over ten years was mailed Adam became impatient for an answer. He forgot how much time had elapsed. Before the letter got as far as San Francisco he was asking aloud in Lee's hearing, "I wonder why he doesn't answer. Maybe he's mad at me for not writing. But he didn't write either. No—he didn't know where to write. Maybe he's moved away."

Lee answered, "It's only been gone a few days. Give it time."

"I wonder whether he would really come out here?" Adam asked himself, and he wondered whether he wanted Charles. Now that the letter was gone, Adam was afraid Charles might accept. He was like a restless child whose fingers stray to every loose article. He interfered with the twins, asked them innumerable questions about school.

"Well, what did you learn today?"

"Nothing!"

"Oh, come! You must have learned something. Did you read?"

"Yes, sir."

"What did you read?"

"That old one about the grasshopper and the ant."

"Well, that's interesting."

"There's one about an eagle carries a baby away."

"Yes, I remember that one. I forget what happens."

"We aren't to it yet. We saw the pictures."

The boys were disgusted. During one of Adam's moments of fatherly bungling Cal borrowed his pocketknife, hoping he would forget to ask for it back. But the sap was beginning to run freely in the willows. The bark would slip easily from a twig. Adam got his knife back to teach the boys to make willow whistles, a thing Lee had taught them three years before. To make it worse, Adam had forgotten how to make the cut. He couldn't get a peep out of his whistles.

At noon one day Will Hamilton came roaring and bumping up the road in a new Ford. The engine raced in its low gear, and the high top swayed like a storm-driven ship. The brass radiator and the Prestolite tank on the running board were blinding with brass polish.

Will pulled up the brake lever, turned the switch straight down, and sat back in the leather seat. The car backfired several times without ignition because it was overheated.

"Here she is!" Will called with a false enthusiasm. He hated Fords with a deadly hatred, but they were daily building his fortune.

Adam and Lee hung over the exposed insides of the car while Will Hamilton, puffing under the burden of his new fat, explained the workings of a mechanism he did not understand himself.

It is hard now to imagine the difficulty of learning to start, drive, and maintain an automobile. Not only was the whole process complicated, but one had to start from scratch. Today's children breathe in the theory, habits, and idiosyncrasies of the internal combustion engine in their cradles, but then you started with the blank belief that it would not run at all, and sometimes you were right. Also, to start the engine of a modern car you do just two things, turn a key and touch the starter. Everything else is automatic. The process used to be more complicated. It required not only a good memory, a strong arm, an angelic temper, and a blind hope, but also a certain amount of practice of magic, so that a man about to turn the crank of a Model T might be seen to spit on the ground and whisper a spell.

Will Hamilton explained the car and went back and explained it again. His customers were wide-eyed, interested as terriers, cooperative, and did not interrupt, but as he began for the third time Will saw that he was getting no place.

"Tell you what!" he said brightly. "You see, this isn't my line. I wanted you to see her and listen to her before I made delivery. Now, I'll go back to town and tomorrow I'll send out this car with an expert, and he'll tell you more in a few minutes than I could in a week. But I just wanted you to see her."

Will had forgotten some of his own instructions. He cranked for a while and then borrowed a buggy and a horse from Adam and drove to town, but he promised to have a mechanic out the next day.

[2]

There was no question of sending the twins to school the next day. They wouldn't have gone. The Ford stood tall and aloof and dour under the oak tree where Will had stopped it. Its new owners circled it and touched it now and then, the way you touch a dangerous horse to soothe him.

Lee said, "I wonder whether I'll ever get used to it."

"Of course you will," Adam said without conviction. "Why, you'll be driving all over the county first thing you know."

"I will try to understand it," Lee said. "But drive it I will not."

The boys made little dives in and out, to touch something and leap away. "What's this do-hickey, Father?"

"Get your hands off that."

"But what's it for?"

"I don't know, but don't touch it. You don't know what might happen."

"Didn't the man tell you?"

"I don't remember what he said. Now you boys get away from it or I'll have to send you to school. Do you hear me, Cal? Don't open that."

They had got up and were ready very early in the morning. By eleven o'clock hysterical nervousness had set in. The mechanic drove up in the buggy in time for the midday meal. He wore boxtoed shoes and Duchess trousers and his wide square coat came almost to his knees. Beside him in the buggy was a satchel in which were his working clothes and tools. He was nineteen and chewed tobacco, and from his three months in automobile school he had gained a great though weary contempt for human beings. He spat and threw the lines at Lee.

"Put this hayburner away," he said. "How do you tell which end is the front?" And he climbed down from the rig as an ambassador comes out of a state train. He sneered at the twins and turned coldly to Adam. "I hope I'm in time for dinner," he said.

Lee and Adam stared at each other. They had forgotten about the noonday meal.

In the house the godling grudgingly accepted cheese and bread and cold meat and pie and coffee and a piece of chocolate cake.

"I'm used to a hot dinner," he said. "You better keep those kids away if you want any car left." After a leisurely meal and a short rest on the porch the mechanic took his satchel into Adam's bedroom. In a few minutes he emerged, dressed in striped overalls and a white cap which had "Ford" printed on the front of its crown.

"Well," he said. "Done any studying?"

"Studying?" Adam asked.

"Ain't you even read the litature in the book under the seat?"

"I didn't know it was there," said Adam.

"Oh, Lord," said the young man disgustedly. With a courageous gathering of his moral forces he moved with decision toward the car. "Might as well get started," he said. "God knows how long it's going to take if you ain't studied."

Adam said, "Mr. Hamilton couldn't start it last night."

"He always tries to start it on the magneto," said the sage. "All right! All right, come along. Know the principles of a internal combustion engine?"

"No," said Adam.

"Oh, Jesus Christ!" He lifted the tin flaps. "This-here is a internal combustion engine," he said.

Lee said quietly, "So young to be so erudite."

The boy swung around toward him, scowling. "What did you say?" he demanded, and he asked Adam, "What did the Chink say?"

Lee spread his hands and smiled blandly. "Say velly smaht fella," he observed quietly. "Mebbe go college. Velly wise."

"Just call me Joe!" the boy said for no reason at all, and he added, "College! What do them fellas know? Can they set a timer, huh? Can they file a point? College!" And he spat a brown disparaging comment on the ground. The twins regarded him with admiration, and Cal collected spit on the back of his tongue to practice.

Adam said, "Lee was admiring your grasp of the subject."

The truculence went out of the boy and a magnanimity took its place. "Just call me Joe," he said. "I *ought* to know it. Went to automobile school in Chicago. That's a real school—not like no college." And he said, "My old man says you take a good Chink, I mean a good one—why, he's about as good as anybody. They're honest."

"But not the bad ones," said Lee.

"Hell, no! Not no highbinders nor nothing like that. But good Chinks."

"I hope I may be included in that group?"

"You look like a good Chink to me. Just call me Joe."

Adam was puzzled at the conversation, but the twins weren't. Cal said experimentally to Aron, "Jus' call me Joe," and Aron moved his lips, trying out, "Jus' call me Joe."

The mechanic became professional again but his tone was kinder. An amused friendliness took the place of his former contempt. "This-here," he said, "is a internal combustion engine." They looked down at the ugly lump of iron with a certain awe.

Now the boy went on so rapidly that the words ran together into a great song of the new era. "Operates through the explosion of gases in a enclosed space. Power of explosion is exerted on piston and through connecting rod and crankshaft through transmission thence to rear wheels. Got that?" They nodded blankly, afraid to stop the flow. "They's two kinds, two cycle and four cycle. This-here is four cycle. Got that?"

Again they nodded. The twins, looking up into his face with adoration, nodded.

"That's interesting," said Adam.

Joe went on hurriedly, "Main difference of a Ford automobile from other kinds is its planetary transmission which operates on a rev-rev-a-lu-shun-ary principle." He pulled up for a moment, his face showing strain. And when his four listeners nodded again he cautioned them, "Don't get the idea you know it all. The planetary system is, don't forget, rev-a-lu-shun-ary. You better study up on it in the book. Now, if you got all that we'll go on to Operation of the Automobile," He said this in boldface type, capital letters. He was obviously glad to be done with the first part of his lecture, but he was no gladder than his listeners. The strain of concentration was beginning to tell on them, and it was not made any better by the fact that they had not understood one single word.

"Come around here," said the boy. "Now you see that-there? That's the ignition key. When you turn that-there you're ready to go ahead. Now, you push this do-hickey to the left. That puts her on battery— see, where it says Bat. That means battery." They craned their necks into the car. The twins were standing on the running board.

"No—wait. I got ahead of myself. First you got to retard the spark and advance the gas, else she'll kick your goddam arm off. This-here—see it?—this-here's the spark. You push it up—get it?—*up*. Clear up. And this-here's the gas—you push her down. Now I'm going to explain it and then I'm going to do it. I want you to pay attention. You kids get off the car. You're in my light. Get down, goddam it." The boys reluctantly climbed down from the running board; only their eyes looked over the door.

He took a deep breath. "Now you ready? Spark retarded, gas advanced. Spark up, gas down. Now switch to battery—left, remember—left." A buzzing like that of a gigantic bee sounded. "Hear that? That's the contact in one of the coil boxes. If you don't get that, you got to adjust the points or maybe file them." He noticed a look of consternation on Adam's face. "You can study up on that in the book," he said kindly.

He moved to the front of the car. "Now this-here is the crank and—see this little wire sticking out of the radiator?—that's the choke. Now watch careful while I show you. You grab the crank like this and push till she catches. See how my thumb is turned down? If I grabbed her the other way with my thumb around her, and she was to kick, why, she'd knock my thumb off. Got it?"

He didn't look up but he knew they were nodding.

"Now," he said, "look careful. I push in and bring her up until I got compression, and then, why, I pull out this wire and I bring her around careful to suck gas in. Hear that sucking sound? That's choke. But don't pull her too much or you'll flood her. Now, I let go the wire and I give her a hell of a spin, and as soon as she catches I run around and advance the spark and retard the gas and I reach over and throw the switch quick over to magneto—see where it says Mag?—and there you are."

His listeners were limp. After all this they had just got the engine started.

The boy kept at them. "I want you to say after me now so you learn it. Spark up—gas down."

They repeated in chorus, "Spark up—gas down."

"Switch to Bat."

"Switch to Bat."

"Crank to compression, thumb down."

"Crank to compression, thumb down."

"Easy over—choke out."

"Easy over—choke out."

"Spin her."

"Spin her."

"Spark down—gas up."
"Spark down—gas up."
"Switch to Mag."
"Switch to Mag."
"Now, we'll go over her again. Just call me Joe."
"Just call you Joe."
"Not that. Spark up—gas down."

A kind of weariness settled on Adam as they went over the litany for the fourth time. The process seemed silly to him. He was relieved when a short time later Will Hamilton drove up in his low sporty red car. The boy looked at the approaching vehicle. "That-there's got sixteen valves," he said in a reverent tone. "Special job."

Will leaned out of his car. "How's it going?" he asked.

"Just fine," said the mechanic. "They catch on quick."

"Look, Roy, I've got to take you in. The new hearse knocked out a bearing. You'll have to work late to get it ready for Mrs. Hawks at eleven tomorrow."

Roy snapped to efficient attention. "I'll get my clos'," he said and ran for the house. As he tore back with his satchel Cal stood in his way.

"Hey," Cal said, "I thought your name was Joe."

"How do you mean, Joe?"

"You told us to call you Joe. Mr. Hamilton says you're Roy."

Roy laughed and jumped into the roadster. "Know why I say call me Joe?"

"No. Why?"

"Because my name is Roy." In the midst of his laughter he stopped and said sternly to Adam, "You get that book under the seat and you study up. Hear me?"

"I will," said Adam.

(Chapter 29)

TIMSHEL

L EE said, "Adam!"
The blue wide eyes looked for the voice and finally
found Lee's brown and shining eyes.

Lee said, "Adam, I don't know what you can hear
or understand. When you had the numbness in your
hand and your eyes refused to read, I found out
everything I could. But some things no one but you
can know. You may, behind your eyes, be alert and
keen, or you may be living in a confused gray dream.
You may, like a newborn child, perceive only light
and movement.

"There's damage in your brain, and it may be that
you are a new thing in the world. Your kindness may
be meanness now, and your bleak honesty fretful
and conniving. No one knows these things except
you. Adam! Can you hear me?"

The blue eyes wavered, closed slowly, then opened.

Lee said, "Thank you Adam. I know how hard it is.
I'm going to ask you to do a much harder thing. Here
is your son—Caleb—your only son. Look at him,
Adam!"

The pale eyes looked until they found Cal. Cal's
mouth moved dryly and made no sound.

Lee's voice cut in, "I don't know how long you will
live, Adam. Maybe a long time. Maybe an hour. But

your son will live. He will marry and his children will
be the only remnant left of you." Lee wiped his eyes
with his fingers.

"He did a thing in anger, Adam, because he thought
you had rejected him. The result of his anger is that
his brother and your son is dead."

Cal said, "Lee—you can't."

"I have to," said Lee. "If it kills him I have to. I
have the choice," and he smiled sadly and quoted, " 'If
there's blame, it's my blame.' " Lee's shoulders straightened. He said sharply, "Your son is marked with guilt
out of himself—out of himself—almost more than he
can bear. Don't crush him with rejection. Don't crush
him, Adam."

Lee's breath whistled in his throat. "Adam, give him
your blessing. Don't leave him alone with his guilt.
Adam, can you hear me? Give him your blessing!"

A terrible brightness shone in Adam's eyes and he
closed them and kept them closed. A wrinkle formed
between his brows.

Lee said, "Help him, Adam—help him. Give him
his chance. Let him be free. That's all a man has over
the beasts. Free him! Bless him!"

The whole bed seemed to shake under the concentration. Adam's breath came quick with his effort
and then, slowly, his right hand lifted—lifted an inch
and then fell back.

Lee's face was haggard. He moved to the head of the
bed and wiped the sick man's damp face with the edge
of the sheet. He looked down at the closed eyes. Lee
whispered, "Thank you, Adam—thank you, my friend.
Can you move your lips? Make your lips form his
name."

Adam looked up with sick weariness. His lips parted
and failed and tried again. Then his lungs filled. He

expelled the air and his lips combed the rushing sigh. His whispered word seemed to hang in the air:

"*Timshel!*"

His eyes closed and he slept.

(*From* Chapter 55)

Two Uncollected Stories

THE AFFAIR AT 7, RUE DE M——

HOW MR. HOGAN ROBBED A BANK

"The Affair at 7, rue de M——," *a modern version of a Poe thriller, first appeared in Harper's Bazaar in 1955. Its original title, "The Affair at 1 Avenue de M——," honored the Steinbecks' Paris address. Anticipating The Winter of Our Discontent, Mr. Hogan's exploit appeared in The Atlantic Monthly in March 1956.*

THE AFFAIR AT 7
RUE DE M——

I HAD hoped to withhold from public scrutiny those rather curious events which have given me some concern for the past month. I knew of course that there was talk in the neighborhood. I have even heard some of the distortions current in my district, stories, I hasten to add, in which there is no particle of truth. However, my desire for privacy was shattered yesterday by a visit of two members of the fourth estate who assured me that the story, or rather *a* story, had escaped the boundaries of my *arrondissement*.

In the light of impending publicity I think it only fair to issue the true details of those happenings which have come to be known as The Affair at 7, rue de M——, in order that nonsense may not be added to a set of circumstances which are not without their *bizarrerie*. I shall set down the events as they happened without comment, thereby allowing the public to judge of the situation.

At the beginning of the summer I carried my family to Paris and took up residence in a pretty little house at 7, rue de M——, a building which in another period had been the mews of the great house beside it. The whole property is now owned and part of it inhabited by a noble French family of such age and purity that its members still consider the Bourbons unacceptable as claimants to the throne of France.

To this pretty little converted stable with three

floors of rooms above a well-paved courtyard, I brought my immediate family, consisting of my wife, my three children, two small boys and a grown daughter, and of course myself. Our domestic arrangement in addition to the concierge who, as you might say, came with the house, consists of a French cook of great ability, a Spanish maid and my own secretary, a girl of Swiss nationality whose high attainments and ambitions are only equaled by her moral altitude. This then was our little family group when the events I am about to chronicle were ushered in.

If one must have an agency in this matter, I can find no alternative to placing not the blame but rather the authorship, albeit innocent, on my younger son John who has only recently attained his eighth year, a lively child of singular beauty and buck teeth.

This young man has, during the last several years in America, become not so much an addict as an aficionado of that curious American practice, the chewing of bubble gum, and one of the pleasanter aspects of the early summer in Paris lay in the fact that the Cadet John had neglected to bring any of the atrocious substance with him from America. The child's speech became clear and unobstructed and the hypnotized look went out of his eyes.

Alas, this delightful situation was not long to continue. An old family friend traveling in Europe brought as a present to the children a more than adequate supply of this beastly gum, thinking to do them a kindness. Thereupon the old familiar situation reasserted itself. Speech fought its damp way past a huge wad of the gum and emerged with the sound of a faulty water trap. The jaws were in constant motion, giving the face at best a look of agony while the eyes took on a glaze like those of a pig with a recently severed jugular. Since I do not believe in inhibiting my children I resigned myself to a summer not quite so pleasant as I had at first hoped.

On occasion I do not follow my ordinary practice of laissez-faire. When I am composing the material for a book or play or essay, in a word, when the utmost of concentration is required, I am prone to establish tyrannical rules for my own comfort and effectiveness. One of these rules is that there shall be neither chewing nor bubbling while I am trying to concentrate. This rule is so thoroughly understood by the Cadet John that he accepts it as one of the laws of nature and does not either complain or attempt to evade the ruling. It is his pleasure and my solace for my son to come sometimes into my workroom, there to sit quietly beside me for a time. He knows he must be silent and when he has remained so for as long a time as his character permits, he goes out quietly, leaving us both enriched by the wordless association.

Two weeks ago in the late afternoon I sat at my desk composing a short essay for *Figaro Littéraire,* an essay which later aroused some controversy when it was printed under the title "Sartre Resartus.". I had come to that passage concerning the proper clothing for the soul when to my astonishment and chagrin I heard the unmistakable soft plopping sound of a bursting balloon of bubble gum. I looked sternly at my offspring and saw him chewing away. His cheeks were colored with embarrassment and the muscles of his jaws stood rigidly out.

"You know the rule," I said coldly.

To my amazement tears came into his eyes and while his jaws continued to masticate hugely, his blubbery voice forced its way past the huge lump of bubble gum in his mouth.

"I didn't do it," he cried.

"What do you mean, you didn't do it?" I demanded in a rage. "I distinctly heard and now I distinctly see."

"Oh sir!" he moaned, "I really didn't. I'm not chewing it, sir. It's chewing me."

For a moment I inspected him closely. He is an honest child, only under the greatest pressure of gain permitting himself an untruth. I had the horrible thought that the bubble gum had finally had its way and that my son's reason was tottering. If this were so, it were better to tread softly. Quietly I put out my hand. "Lay it here," I said kindly.

My child manfully tried to disengage the gum from his jaws. "It won't let me go," he sputtered.

"Open up," I said and then inserting my fingers in his mouth I seized hold of the large lump of gum and after a struggle in which my fingers slipped again and again, managed to drag it forth and to deposit the ugly blob on my desk on top of a pile of white manuscript paper.

For a moment it seemed to shudder there on the paper and then with an easy slowness it began to undulate, to swell and recede with the exact motion of being chewed while my son and I regarded it with popping eyes.

For a long time we watched it while I drove through my mind for some kind of explanation. Either I was dreaming or some principle as yet unknown had taken its seat in the pulsing bubble gum on the desk. I am not unintelligent. While I considered the indecent thing, a hundred little thoughts and glimmerings of understanding raced through my brain. At last I asked, "How long has it been chewing you?"

"Since last night," he replied.

"And when did you first notice this, this propensity on its part?"

He spoke with perfect candor. "I will ask you to believe me, sir," he said. "Last night before I went to sleep I put it under my pillow as is my invariable custom. In the night I was awakened to find that it was in my mouth. I again placed it under my pillow and this morning it was again in my mouth, lying very quietly. When, however, I became thoroughly awakened, I was conscious of a slight motion and shortly afterward the situation dawned on me that I was no longer master of the gum. It had taken its head. I tried to remove it, sir, and could not. You yourself with all of your strength have seen how difficult it was to extract. I came to your workroom to await your first disengagement, wishing to acquaint you with my difficulty. Oh, Daddy, what do you think has happened?"

The cancerous thing held my complete attention.

"I must think," I said. "This is something a little out of the ordinary, and I do not believe it should be passed over without some investigation."

As I spoke a change came over the gum. It ceased to chew itself and seemed to rest for a while, and then with a flowing movement like those monocellular animals of the order Paramecium, the gum slid across the desk straight in the direction of my son. For a moment I was stricken with astonishment and for an even longer time I failed to discern its intent. It dropped to his knee, climbed horribly up his shirt front. Only then did I understand. It was trying to get back into his mouth. He looked down on it paralyzed with fright.

"Stop," I cried, for I realized that my third-born was in danger and at such times I am capable of a violence which verges on the murderous. I seized the monster from his chin and striding from my work-room, entered the salon, opened the window and hurled the thing into the busy traffic on the rue de M——.

I believe it is the duty of a parent to ward off those shocks which may cause dreams or trauma whenever possible. I went back to my study to find young John sitting where I had left him. He was staring into space. There was a troubled line between his brows.

"Son," I said, "you and I have seen something which, while we know it to have happened, we might find difficult to describe with any degree of success to others. I ask you to imagine the scene if we should tell this story to the other members of the family. I greatly fear we should be laughed out of the house."

"Yes, sir," he said passively.

"Therefore I am going to propose to you, my son, that we lock the episode deep in our memories and never mention it to a soul as long as we live." I waited for his assent and when it did not come, glanced up at his face to see it a ravaged field of terror. His eyes were starting out of his head. I turned in the direction of his gaze. Under the door there crept a paper-thin sheet which, once it had entered the room, grew to a gray blob and rested on the rug, pulsing and chewing. After a moment it moved again by pseudopodian pro-gression toward my son.

I fought down panic as I rushed at it. I grabbed it up and flung it on my desk, then seizing an African war club from among the trophies on the wall, a dreadful instrument studded with brass, I beat the gum until I was breathless and it a torn piece of plastic fabric. The moment I rested, it drew itself together and for a few moments chewed very rapidly as though it chuckled at my impotence, and then inexorably it moved toward my son, who by this time was crouched in a corner moaning with terror.

Now a coldness came over me. I picked up the filthy thing and wrapped it in my handkerchief, strode out of the house, walked three blocks to the Seine and flung the handkerchief into the slowly moving current.

I spent a good part of the afternoon soothing my son and trying to reassure him that his fears were over. But such was his nervousness that I had to give him half a barbiturate tablet to get him to sleep that night, while my wife insisted that I call a doctor. I did not at that time dare to tell her why I could not obey her wish.

I was awakened, indeed the whole house was awakened, in the night by a terrified muffled scream from the children's room. I took the stairs two at a time and burst in the room, flicking the light switch as I went. John sat up in bed squalling, while with his fingers he dug at his half-open mouth, a mouth which horrifyingly went right on chewing. As I looked a bubble emerged between his fingers and burst with a wet plopping sound.

What chance of keeping our secret now! All had to be explained, but with the plopping gum pinned to a breadboard with an ice pick the explanation was easier than it might have been. And I am proud of the help and comfort given me. There is no strength like that of the family. Our French cook solved the problem by refusing to believe it even when she saw it. It was not reasonable, she explained, and she was a reasonable member of a reasonable people. The Spanish maid ordered and paid for an exorcism by the parish priest who, poor man, after two hours of strenuous effort went away muttering that this was more a matter of the stomach than the soul.

For two weeks we were besieged by the monster. We burned it in the fireplace, causing it to splutter in blue flames and melt in a nasty mess among the ashes. Before morning it had crawled through the keyhole of the children's room, leaving a trail of wood ash on the door, and again we were awakened by screams from the Cadet.

In despair I drove far into the country and threw it from my automobile. It was back before morning. Apparently it had crept to the highway and placed itself in the Paris traffic until picked up by a truck tire. When we tore it from John's mouth it had still the nonskid marks of Michelin imprinted in its side.

Fatigue and frustration will take their toll. In exhaustion, with my will to fight back sapped, and after we had tried every possible method to lose or destroy the bubble gum, I placed it at last under a bell jar which I ordinarily use to cover my microscope. I collapsed in a chair to gaze at it with weary defeated eyes. John slept in his little bed under the influence of sedatives backed by my assurance that I would not let the Thing out of my sight.

I lighted a pipe and settled back to watch it. Inside the bell jar the gray tumorous lump moved restlessly about searching for some means of exit from its prison. Now and then it paused as though in thought and emitted a bubble in my direction. I could feel the hatred it had for me. In my weariness I found my mind slipping into an analysis which had so far escaped me.

The background I had been over hurriedly. It must be that from constant association with the lambent life which is my son, the magic of life had been created in the bubble gum. And with life had come intelligence, not the manly open intelligence of the boy, but an evil calculating wiliness.

How could it be otherwise? Intelligence without the soul to balance it must of necessity be evil. The gum had not absorbed any part of John's soul.

Very well, said my mind, now we have a hypothesis of its origin, let us consider its nature. What does it think? What does it want? What does it need? My mind leaped like a terrier. It needs and wants to get back to its host, my son. It wants to be chewed. It must be chewed to survive.

Inside the bell jar the gum inserted a thin wedge of itself under the heavy glass foot and constricted so that the whole jar lifted a fraction of an inch. I laughed as I drove it back. I laughed with almost insane triumph. I had the answer.

In the dining room I procured a clear plastic plate, one of a dozen my wife had bought for picnics in the country. Then turning the bell jar over and securing the monster in its bottom, I smeared the mouth of it with a heavy plastic cement guaranteed to be water-, alcohol- and acid-proof. I forced the plate over the opening and pressed it down until the glue took hold and bound the plate to the glass, making an airtight container. And last I turned the jar upright again and adjusted the reading light so that I could observe every movement of my prisoner.

Again it searched the circle for escape. Then it faced me and emitted a great number of bubbles very rapidly. I could hear the little bursting plops through the glass.

"I have you, my beauty," I cried. "I have you at last."

That was a week ago. I have not left the side of the bell jar since, and have only turned my head to accept a cup of coffee. When I go to the bathroom, my wife takes my place. I can now report the following hopeful news.

During the first day and night, the bubble gum tried every means to escape. Then for a day and a night it seemed to be agitated and nervous as though it had for the first time realized its predicament. The third day it went to work with its chewing motion, only the action was speeded up greatly, like the chewing of a baseball fan. On the fourth day it began to weaken and I observed with joy a kind of dryness on its once slick and shiny exterior.

I am now in the seventh day and I believe it is almost over. The gum is lying in the center of the plate. At intervals it heaves and subsides. Its color has turned to a nasty yellow. Once today when my son entered the room, it leaped up excitedly, then seemed to realize its hopelessness and collapsed on the plate. It will die tonight I think and only then will I dig a deep hole in the garden, and I will deposit the sealed bell jar and cover it up and plant geraniums over it.

It is my hope that this account will set straight some of the silly tales that are being hawked in the neighborhood.

HOW MR. HOGAN
ROBBED A BANK

[1]

ON the Saturday before Labor Day, 1955, at 9:04½ A.M., Mr. Hogan robbed a bank. He was forty-two years old, married, and the father of a boy and a girl, named John and Joan, twelve and thirteen respectively. Mrs. Hogan's name was Joan and Mr. Hogan's was John, but since they called themselves Papa and Mama that left their names free for the children, who were considered very smart for their ages, each having jumped a grade in school. The Hogans lived at 215 East Maple Street, in a brown-shingle house with white trim—there are two. 215 is the one across from the street light and it is the one with the big tree in the yard, either oak or elm—the biggest tree in the whole street, maybe in the whole town.

John and Joan were in bed at the time of the robbery, for it was Saturday. At 9:10 A.M., Mrs. Hogan was making the cup of tea she always had. Mr. Hogan went to work early. Mrs. Hogan drank her tea slowly, scalding hot, and read her fortune in the tea leaves. There was a cloud and a five-pointed star with two short points in the bottom of the cup, but that was at 9:12 and the robbery was all over by then.

The way Mr. Hogan went about robbing the bank was very interesting. He gave it a great deal of thought and had for a long time, but he did not discuss it with anyone. He just read his newspaper and kept his own counsel. But he worked it out to his own satisfaction that people went to too much trouble robbing banks and that got them in a mess. The simpler the better, he always thought. People went in for too much hullabaloo and hanky-panky. If you didn't do that, if you left hanky-panky out, robbing a bank would be a relatively sound venture—barring accidents, of course, of an improbable kind, but then they could happen to a man crossing the street or anything. Since Mr. Hogan's method worked fine, it proved that his thinking was sound. He often considered writing a little booklet on his technique when the how-to rage was running so high. He figured out the first sentence, which went: "To successfully rob a bank, forget all about hanky-panky."

Mr. Hogan was not just a clerk at Fettucci's grocery store. He was more like the manager. Mr. Hogan was in charge, even hired and fired the boy who delivered groceries after school. He even put in orders with the salesmen, sometimes when Mr. Fettucci was right in the store too, maybe talking to a customer. "You do it, John," he would say and he would nod at the customer, "John knows the ropes. Been with me—how long you been with me, John?"

"Sixteen years."

"Sixteen years. Knows the business as good as me. John, why he even banks the money."

And so he did. Whenever he had a moment, Mr. Hogan went into the storeroom on the alley, took off his apron, put on his necktie and coat, and went back through the store to the cash register. The checks and bills would be ready for him inside the bankbook with a rubber band around it. Then he went next door and stood at the teller's window and handed the checks and bankbook through to Mr. Cup and passed the time of day with him too. Then, when the bankbook was handed back, he checked the entry, put the rubber band around it, and walked next door to Fettucci's grocery and put the bankbook in the cash register, continued on to the storeroom, removed his coat and tie, put on his apron, and went back into the store ready for business. If there was no line at the teller's window, the whole thing didn't take more than five minutes, even passing the time of day.

Mr. Hogan was a man who noticed things, and when it came to robbing the bank, this trait stood him in good stead. He had noticed, for instance, where the big bills were kept right in the drawer under the counter and he had noticed also what days there were likely to be more than other days. Thursday was payday at the American Can Company's local plant, for instance, so there would be more then. Some Fridays people drew more money to tide them over the weekend. But it was even Steven, maybe not a thousand dollars' difference, between Thursdays and Fridays and Saturday mornings. Saturdays were not terribly good because people didn't come to get money that early in the morning, and the bank closed at noon. But he thought it over and came to the conclusion that the Saturday before a long weekend in the summer would be the best of all. People going on trips, vacations, people with relatives visiting, and the bank closed Monday. He thought it out and looked, and sure enough the Saturday morning before Labor Day the cash drawer had twice as much money in it—he saw it when Mr. Cup pulled out the drawer.

Mr. Hogan thought about it during all that year, not all the time, of course, but when he had some moments. It was a busy year too. That was the year John and Joan had the mumps and Mrs. Hogan got her teeth pulled and was fitted for a denture. That was the year when Mr. Hogan was Master of the Lodge, with all the time that takes. Larry Shield died that year—he was Mrs. Hogan's brother and was buried from the Hogan house at 215 East Maple. Larry was a bachelor and had a room in the Pine Tree House and he played pool nearly every night. He worked at the Silver Diner but that closed at nine and so Larry would go to Louie's and play pool for an hour. Therefore, it was a surprise when he left enough so that after funeral expenses there were twelve hundred dollars left. And even more surprising that he left a will in Mrs. Hogan's favor, but his double-barreled twelve-gauge shotgun he left to John Hogan, Jr. Mr. Hogan was pleased, although he never hunted. He put the shotgun away in the back of the closet in the bathroom, where he kept his things, to keep it for young John. He didn't want children handling guns and he never bought any shells. It was some of that twelve hundred that got Mrs. Hogan her dentures. Also, she bought a bicycle for John and a doll buggy and walking-talking doll for Joan—a doll with three changes of dresses and a little suitcase, complete with play make-up. Mr. Hogan thought it might spoil the children, but it didn't seem to. They made just as good marks in school and John even got a job delivering papers. It was a very busy year. Both John and Joan wanted to enter the W. R. Hearst National "I Love America" Contest and Mr. Hogan thought it was almost too much, but they promised to do the work during their summer vacation, so he finally agreed.

[2]

During that year, no one noticed any difference in Mr. Hogan. It was true, he was thinking about robbing the bank, but he only thought about it in the evening when there was neither a Lodge meeting nor a movie they wanted to go to, so it did not become an obsession and people noticed no change in him.

He had studied everything so carefully that the approach of Labor Day did not catch him unprepared or nervous. It was hot that summer and the hot spells were longer than usual. Saturday was the end of two weeks heat without a break and people were irritated with it and anxious to get out of town, although the country was just as hot. They didn't think of that. The children were excited because the "I Love America" Essay Contest was due to be concluded and the winners announced, and the first prize was an all-expense-paid two days trip to Washington, D.C., with every fixing— hotel room, three meals a day, and side trips in a limousine—not only for the winner, but for an accompanying chaperone; visit to the White House—shake hands with the President—everything. Mr. Hogan thought they were getting their hopes too high and he said so.

"You've got to be prepared to lose," he told his children. "There're probably thousands and thousands entered. You get your hopes up and it might spoil the whole autumn. Now I don't want any long faces in this house after the contest is over."

"I was against it from the start," he told Mrs. Hogan. That was the morning she saw the Washington Monument in her teacup, but she didn't tell anybody about that except Ruth Tyler, Bob Tyler's wife. Ruthie brought over her cards and read them in the Hogan kitchen, but she didn't find a journey. She did tell Mrs. Hogan that the cards were often wrong. The cards had said Mrs. Winkle was going on a trip to Europe and the next week Mrs. Winkle got a fishbone in her throat and choked to death. Ruthie, just thinking out loud, wondered if there was any connection between the fishbone and the ocean voyage to Europe. "You've got to interpret them right." Ruthie did say she saw money coming to the Hogans.

"Oh, I got that already from poor Larry," Mrs. Hogan explained.

"I must have got the past and future cards mixed," said Ruthie. "You've got to interpret them right."

Saturday dawned a blaster. The early morning weather report on the radio said "Continued hot and humid, light scattered rain Sunday night and Monday." Mrs. Hogan said, "Wouldn't you know? Labor Day." And Mr. Hogan said, "I'm sure glad we didn't plan anything." He finished his egg and mopped the plate with his toast. Mrs. Hogan said, "Did I put coffee on the list?" He took the paper from his handkerchief pocket and consulted it. "Yes, coffee, it's here."

"I had a crazy idea I forgot to write it down," said Mrs. Hogan. "Ruth and I are going to Altar Guild this afternoon. It's at Mrs. Alfred Drake's. You know, they just came to town. I can't wait to see their furniture."

"They trade with us," said Mr. Hogan. "Opened an account last week. Are the milk bottles ready?"

"On the porch."

Mr. Hogan looked at his watch just before he picked up the bottles and it was five minutes 'o eight. He was about to go down the stairs, when he turned and looked back through the opened door at Mrs. Hogan. She said, "Want something, Papa?"

"No," he said. "No," and he walked down the steps.

He went down to the corner and turned right on Spooner, and Spooner runs into Main Street in two blocks, and right across from where it runs in, there is Fettucci's and the bank around the corner and the alley beside the bank. Mr. Hogan picked up a handbill in front of Fettucci's and unlocked the door. He went through to the storeroom, opened the door to the alley, and looked out. A cat tried to force its way in, but Mr. Hogan blocked it with his foot and leg and closed the door. He took off his coat and put on his long apron, tied the strings in a bowknot behind his back. Then he got the broom from behind the counter and swept out behind the counters and scooped the sweepings into a dustpan; and, going through the storeroom, he opened the door to the alley. The cat had gone away. He emptied the dustpan into the garbage can and tapped it smartly to dislodge a piece of lettuce leaf. Then he went back to the store and worked for a while on the order sheet. Mrs. Clooney came in for a half a pound of bacon. She said it was hot and Mr. Hogan agreed. "Summers are getting hotter," he said.

"I think so myself," said Mrs. Clooney. "How's Mrs. standing up?"

"Just fine," said Mr. Hogan. "She's going to Altar Guild."

"So am I. I just can't wait to see their furniture," said Mrs. Clooney, and she went out.

[3]

Mr. Hogan put a five-pound hunk of bacon on the slicer and stripped off the pieces and laid them on wax paper and then he put the wax-paper-covered squares in the cooler cabinet. At ten minutes to nine, Mr. Hogan went to a shelf. He pushed a spaghetti box aside and took down a cereal box, which he emptied in the little closet toilet. Then, with a banana knife, he cut out the Mickey Mouse mask that was on the back. The rest of the box he took to the toilet and tore up the cardboard and flushed it down. He went into the store then and yanked a piece of string loose and tied the ends through the side holes of the mask and then he looked at his watch—a large silver Hamilton with black hands. It was two minutes to nine.

Perhaps the next four minutes were his only time of nervousness at all. At one minute to nine, he took the broom and went out to sweep the sidewalk and he swept it very rapidly—was sweeping it, in fact, when Mr. Warner unlocked the bank door. He said good morning to Mr. Warner and a few seconds later the bank staff of four emerged from the coffee shop. Mr. Hogan saw them across the street and he waved at them and they waved back. He finished the sidewalk and went back in the store. He laid his watch on the little step of the cash register. He sighed very deeply, more like a deep breath than a sigh. He knew that Mr. Warner would have the safe open now and he would be carrying the cash trays to the teller's window. Mr. Hogan looked at the watch on the cash register step. Mr. Kenworthy paused in the store entrance, then shook his head vaguely and walked on and Mr. Hogan let out his breath gradually. His left hand went behind his back and pulled the bowknot on his apron, and then the black hand on his watch crept up on the four-minute mark and covered it.

Mr. Hogan opened the charge account drawer and took out the store pistol, a silver-colored Iver Johnson .38. He moved quickly to the storeroom, slipped off his apron, put on his coat, and stuck the revolver in his side pocket. The Mickey Mouse mask he shoved up under his coat where it didn't show. He opened the alley door and looked up and down and stepped quickly out, leaving the door slightly ajar. It is sixty feet to where the alley enters Main Street, and there he paused and looked up and down and then he turned his head toward the center of the street as he passed the bank window. At the bank's swinging door, he took out the mask from under his coat and put it on. Mr. Warner was just entering his office and his back was to the door. The top of Will Cup's head was visible through the teller's grill.

Mr. Hogan moved quickly and quietly around the end of the counter and into the teller's cage. He had the revolver in his right hand now. When Will Cup turned his head and saw the revolver, he froze. Mr. Hogan slipped his toe under the trigger of the floor alarm and he motioned Will Cup to the floor with the revolver and Will went down quick. Then Mr. Hogan opened the cash drawer and with two quick movements he piled the large bills from the tray together. He made a whipping motion to Will on the floor, to indicate that he should turn over and face the wall, and Will did. Then Mr. Hogan stepped back around the counter. At the door of the bank, he took off the mask, and as he passed the window he turned his head toward the middle of the street. He moved into the alley, walked quickly to the storeroom, and entered. The cat had got in. It watched him from a pile of canned goods cartons. Mr. Hogan went to the toilet closet and tore up the mask and flushed it. He took off his coat and put on his apron. He looked out into the store and then moved to the cash register. The revolver went back into the charge account drawer. He punched No Sale and, lifting the top drawer, distributed the stolen money underneath the top tray and then pulled the tray forward and closed the register, and only then did he look at his watch and it was 9:07½.

He was trying to get the cat out of the storeroom when the commotion boiled out of the bank. He took his broom and went out on the sidewalk. He heard all about it and offered his opinion when it was asked for. He said he didn't think the fellow could get away— where could he get to? Still, with the holiday coming up—

It was an exciting day. Mr. Fettucci was as proud as though it were his bank. The sirens sounded around town for hours. Hundreds of holiday travelers had to stop at the roadblocks set up all around the edge of town and several sneaky-looking men had their cars searched.

Mrs. Hogan heard about it over the phone and she dressed earlier than she would have ordinarily and came to the store on her way to Altar Guild. She hoped Mr. Hogan would have seen or heard something new, but he hadn't. "I don't see how the fellow can get away," he said.

Mrs. Hogan was so excited, she forgot her own news. She only remembered when she got to Mrs. Drake's house, but she asked permission and phoned the store the first moment she could. "I forgot to tell you. John's won honorable mention."

"What?"

"In the 'I Love America' Contest."

"What did he win?"

"Honorable mention."

"Fine. Fine—Anything come with it?"

"Why, he'll get his picture and his name all over the country. Radio too. Maybe even television. They've already asked for a photograph of him."

"Fine," said Mr. Hogan. "I hope it don't spoil him." He put up the receiver and said to Mr. Fettucci, "I guess we've got a celebrity in the family."

Fettucci stayed open until nine on Saturdays. Mr. Hogan ate a few snacks from cold cuts, but not much, because Mrs. Hogan always kept his supper warming.

It was 9:05, or :06, or :07, when he got back to the brown-shingle house at 215 East Maple. He went in through the front door and out to the kitchen where the family was waiting for him.

"Got to wash up," he said, and went up to the bathroom. He turned the key in the bathroom door and then he flushed the toilet and turned on the water in the basin and tub while he counted the money. Eight thousand three hundred and twenty dollars. From the top shelf of the storage closet in the bathroom, he took down the big leather case that held his Knight Templar's uniform. The plumed hat lay there on its form. The white ostrich feather was a little yellow and needed changing. Mr. Hogan lifted out the hat and pried the form up from the bottom of the case. He put the money in the form and then he thought again and removed two bills and shoved them in his side pocket. Then he put the form back over the money and laid the hat on top and closed the case and shoved it back on the top shelf. Finally he washed his hands and turned off the water in the tub and the basin.

In the kitchen, Mrs. Hogan and the children faced him, beaming. "Guess what some young man's going on?"

"What?" asked Mr. Hogan.

"Radio," said John. "Monday night. Eight o'clock."

"I guess we got a celebrity in the family," said Mr. Hogan.

Mrs. Hogan said, "I just hope some young lady hasn't got her nose out of joint."

Mr. Hogan pulled up to the table and stretched his legs. "Mama, I guess I got a fine family," he said. He reached in his pocket and took out two five-dollar bills. He handed one to John. "That's for winning," he said. He poked the other bill at Joan. "And that's for being a good sport. One celebrity and one good sport. What a fine family!" He rubbed his hands together and lifted the lid of the covered dish. "Kidneys," he said. "Fine."

And that's how Mr. Hogan did it.

FROM

Travels with Charley
in Search of America

PEOPLE

TEXAN OSTENTATION

SOUTHERN TROUBLES

LAST LEG

A 1960 trip across America and back, in Rocinante, the small house-truck for this contemporary Don Quixote and his dog, led to this record, published in 1962.

PEOPLE

*His feet comfortably in a cold stream, the author muses,
then enjoys an interruption.*

I HAD been keen to hear what people thought politically. Those whom I had met did not talk about the subject, didn't seem to want to talk about it. It seemed to me partly caution and partly a lack of interest, but strong opinions were just not stated. One storekeeper did admit to me that he had to do business with both sides and could not permit himself the luxury of an opinion. He was a graying man in a little gray store, a crossroads place where I stopped for a box of dog biscuits and a can of pipe tobacco. This man, this store might have been anywhere in the nation, but actually it was back in Minnesota. The man had a kind of gray wistful twinkle in his eyes as though he remembered humor when it was not against the law, so that I dared go out on a limb. I said, "It looks then as though the natural contentiousness of people had died. But I don't believe that. It'll just take another channel. Can you think, sir, of what that channel might be?"

"You mean where will they bust out?"

"Where do they bust out?"

I was not wrong, the twinkle was there, the precious, humorous twinkle. "Well, sir," he said, "we've got a murder now and then, or we can read about them. Then we've got the World Series. You can raise a wind any time over the Pirates or the Yankees, but I guess the best of all is we've got the Russians."

"Feelings pretty strong there?"

"Oh, sure! Hardly a day goes by somebody doesn't take a belt at the Russians." For some reason he was getting a little easier, even permitted himself a chuckle that could have turned to throat-clearing if he saw a bad reaction from me.

I asked, "Anybody know any Russians around here?"

And now he went all out and laughed. "Course not. That's why they're valuable. Nobody can find fault with you if you take out after the Russians."

"Because we're not doing business with them?"

He picked up a cheese knife from the counter and carefully ran his thumb along the edge and laid the knife down. "Maybe that's it. By George, maybe that's it. We're not doing business."

"You think then we might be using the Russians as an outlet for something else, for other things."

"I didn't think that at all, sir, but I bet I'm going to. Why, I remember when people took everything out on Mr. Roosevelt. Andy Larsen got red in the face about Roosevelt one time when his hens got the croup. Yes, sir," he said with growing enthusiasm, "those Russians got quite a load to carry. Man has a fight with his wife, he belts the Russians."

"Maybe everybody needs Russians. I'll bet even in Russia they need Russians. Maybe they call it Americans."

He cut a sliver of cheese from a wheel and held it out to me on the knife blade. "You've give me something to think about in a sneaking kind of way."

"I thought you gave it to me."

"How?"

"About business and opinions."

"Well, maybe so. Know what I'm going to do? Next time Andy Larsen comes in red in the face, I'm going to see if the Russians are bothering his hens. It was a great loss to Andy when Mr. Roosevelt died."

Now I don't say that an awful lot of people have this man's sense of things. Maybe they don't, but maybe they do—also in their privacy or in non-business areas.

Charley raised his head and roared a warning without bothering to get to his feet. Then I heard a motor approaching, and trying to get up found my feet were long gone in sleep in the cold water. I couldn't feel them at all. While I rubbed and massaged them and they awakened to painful pins and needles, a vintage sedan pulling a short coupled trailer like a box turtle lumbered down from the road and took a position on the water about fifty yards away. I felt annoyance at this invasion of my privacy, but Charley was delighted. He moved on stiff legs with little delicate mincing steps to investigate the newcomer and in the manner of dogs and people did not look directly at the object of his interest. If I seem to be ridiculing Charley, look you at what I was doing in the next half hour and also what my neighbor was doing. Each of us went about our business, with slow deliberateness, each being very careful not to stare at the other and at the same time sneaking glances, appraising, evaluating. I saw a man, not young, not old, but with a jaunty springy step. He was dressed in olive-drab trousers and a leather jacket, and he wore a cowboy hat but with a flat crown and the brim curled and held to a peak by the chin strap. He had a classic profile, and even in the distance I could see that he wore a beard that tied into his sideburns and so found his hair. My own beard is restricted to my chin. The air had grown quickly chill. And I don't

know whether my head was cold or that I didn't want
to remain uncovered in the presence of a stranger. At
any rate, I put on my old naval cap, made a pot of coffee, and sat on my back steps glancing with great interest at everything except my neighbor, who swept
out his trailer and threw out a dishpan of soapy water
while he pointedly unwatched me. Charley's interest
was captured and held by various growlings and bark-
ings that came from inside the trailer.

There must be in everyone a sense of proper and
civil timing, for I had just resolved to speak to my neighbor, in fact had just stood up to move toward him, when
he strolled toward me. He too had felt that the
period of waiting was over. He moved with a strange
gait reminiscent to me of something I couldn't place.
There was a seedy grandeur about the man. In the time
of chivalric myth this would be the beggar who turns
out to be a king's son. As he came near I stood up from
my iron back stoop to greet him.

He did not give me a sweeping bow, but I had the
impression that he might have—either that or a full
regimental salute.

"Good afternoon," he said. "I see you are of the
profession."

I guess my mouth fell open. It's years since I have
heard the term. "Well, no. No, I'm not."

Now it was his turn to look puzzled. "Not? But—
my dear chap, if you're not, how do you know the expression?"

"I guess I've been on the fringes."

"Ah! Fringes. Of course. Backstage no doubt—direction, stage manager?"

"Flops," I said. "Would you like a cup of coffee?"

"Delighted." He never let down. That's one nice
thing about those of the profession—they rarely do. He

folded himself on the divan seat behind my table with
a grace I never achieved in all my traveling. And I
set out two plastic mugs and two glasses, poured coffee,
and set a bottle of whisky within easy reach. It seemed
to me a mist of tears came into his eyes, but it might
be that they were in mine.

"Flops," he said. "Who hasn't known them hasn't
played."

"Shall I pour for you?"

"Please do—no, no water." He cleared his palate
with black coffee and then munched delicately on the
whisky while his eye swept my abode. "Nice place you
have here, very nice."

"Tell me, please, what made you think I was in the
theater?"

He chuckled dryly. "Very simple, Watson. You know
I've played that. Both parts. Well, first I saw your poo-
dle, and then I observed your beard. Then on approaching I saw that you wore a naval cap with the British
Royal Arms."

"Was that what broadened your *a*'s?"

"That might be, old chap. That certainly might be.
I fall into such things, hardly knowing I'm doing it."
Now, close up, I saw that he was not young. His movements were pure youth but there was that about his
skin texture and the edges of his lips that was middle-
aged or past it. And his eyes, large warm brown irises
set on whites that were turning yellow, corroborated
this.

"Your health," I said. We emptied our plastic glasses,
chased with coffee, and I refilled.

"If it isn't too personal or too painful—what did you
do in the theater?"

"I wrote a couple of plays."

"Produced?"

"Yes. They flopped."

"Would I know your name?"

"I doubt it. Nobody else did."

He sighed. "It's a hard business. But if you're hooked, you're hooked. I was hooked by my granddaddy and my daddy set the hook."

"Both actors?"

"And my mother and grandmother."

"Lord. That *is* show business. Are you"—I searched for the old word—"resting now?"

"Not at all. I'm playing."

"What, for God's sake, and where?"

"Wherever I can trap an audience. Schools, churches, service clubs. I bring culture, give readings. I guess you can hear my partner over there complaining. He's very good too. Part Airedale and part coyote. Steals the show when he feels like it."

I began to feel delighted with this man. "I didn't know such things went on."

"They don't, some of the time."

"Been at it long?"

"Three years less two months."

"All over the country?"

"Wherever two or three are gathered together. I hadn't worked for over a year—just tramped the agencies and casting calls and lived up my benefits. With me there's no question of doing something else. It's all I know—all I ever have known. Once long ago there was a community of theater people on Nantucket island. My daddy bought a nice lot there and put up a frame house. Well, I sold that and bought my outfit there and I've been moving ever since, and I like it. I don't think I'll ever go back to the grind. Of course, if there should be a part—but hell, who'd remember me for a part—any part?"

"You're striking close to home there."

"Yes, it's a hard business."

"I hope you won't think I'm inquisitive even if I am. I'd like to know how you go about it. What happens? How do people treat you?"

"They treat me very well. And I don't know how I go about it. Sometimes I even have to rent a hall and advertise, sometimes I speak to the principal of the high school."

"But aren't people scared of gypsies, vagabonds, and actors?"

"I guess they are at first. At the beginning they take me for a kind of harmless freak. But I'm honest and I don't charge much, and after a little the material takes over and gets into them. You see, I respect the material. That makes the difference. I'm not a charlatan, I'm an actor—good or bad, an actor." His color had deepened with whisky and vehemence, and perhaps at being able to talk to someone with a little likeness of experience. I poured more into his glass this time and watched with pleasure his enjoyment of it. He drank and sighed. "Don't get something like this very often," he said. "I hope I haven't given you the impression that I'm rolling in receipts. Sometimes it's a little rough."

"Go on about it. Tell more."

"Where was I?"

"You were saying you respected your material and that you were an actor."

"Oh, yes. Well, there's one more thing. You know when show people come into what they call the sticks, they have a contempt for the yokels. It took me a little time, but when I learned that there aren't any yokels I began to get on fine. I learned respect for my audience. They feel that and they work with me, and not against me. Once you respect them, they can understand anything you can tell them."

"Tell about your material. What do you use?"

He looked down at his hands and I saw that they were well-kept and very white, as though he wore gloves most of the time. "I hope you won't think I'm stealing material," he said. "I admire the delivery of Sir John Gielgud. I heard him do his monologue of Shakespeare—*The Ages of Man*. And then I bought a record of it to study. What he can do with words, with tones, and inflections!"

"You use that?"

"Yes, but I don't steal it. I tell about hearing Sir John, and what it did to me, and then I say I'm going to try to give an impression of how he did it."

"Clever."

"Well, it does help, because it gives authority to the performance, and Shakespeare doesn't need billing, and that way I'm not stealing his material. It's like I'm celebrating him, which I do."

"How do they respond?"

"Well, I guess I'm pretty much at home with it now, because I can watch the words sink in, and they forget about me and their eyes kind of turn inward and I'm not a freak to them any more. Well—what do you think?"

"I think Gielgud would be pleased."

"Oh! I wrote to him and told him what I was doing and how I was doing it, a long letter." He brought a lumpy wallet from his hip pocket and extracted a carefully folded piece of aluminum foil, opened it, and with careful fingers unfolded a small sheet of notepaper with the name engraved at the top. The message was typed. It said, "Dear . . . : Thank you for your kind and interesting letter. I would not be an actor if I were not aware of the sincere flattery implied in your work. Good luck and God bless you. John Gielgud."

I sighed, and I watched his reverent fingers fold the note and close it in its armor of foil and put it away. "I never show that to anyone to get a show," he said. "I wouldn't think of doing that."

And I'm sure he wouldn't.

He whirled his plastic glass in his hand and regarded the rinse of whisky left in it, a gesture often designed to draw emptiness to the attention of a host. I uncorked the bottle.

"No," he said. "No more for me. I learned long ago that the most important and valuable of acting techniques is the exit."

"But I'd like to ask more questions."

"All the more reason for the exit." He drained the last drop. "Keep them asking," he said, "and exit clean and sharp. Thank you and good afternoon."

I watched him swing lightly toward his trailer and I knew I would be haunted by one question. I called out,—"Wait a moment."

He paused and turned back to me.

"What does the dog do?"

"Oh, a couple of silly tricks," he said. "He keeps the performance simple. He picks it up when it goes stale." And he continued on to his home.

So it went on—a profession older than writing and one that will probably survive when the written word has disappeared. And all the sterile wonders of movies and television and radio will fail to wipe it out—a living man in communication with a living audience. But how did he live? Who were his companions? What was his hidden life? He was right. His exit whetted the questions.

(*From* Part Three)

TEXAN OSTENTATION

WHEN I started this narrative, I knew that sooner or later I would have to have a go at Texas, and I dreaded it. I could have bypassed Texas about as easily as a space traveler can avoid the Milky Way. It sticks its big old Panhandle up north and it slops and slouches along the Rio Grande. Once you are in Texas it seems to take forever to get out, and some people never make it.

Let me say in the beginning that even if I wanted to avoid Texas I could not, for I am wived in Texas and mother-in-lawed and uncled and aunted and cousined within an inch of my life. Staying away from Texas geographically is no help whatever, for Texas moves through our house in New York, our fishing cottage at Sag Harbor, and when we had a flat in Paris, Texas was there too. It permeates the world to a ridiculous degree. Once, in Florence, on seeing a lovely little Italian princess, I said to her father, "But she doesn't look Italian. It may seem strange, but she looks like an American Indian." To which her father replied, "Why shouldn't she? Her grandfather married a Cherokee in Texas."

Writers facing the problem of Texas find themselves floundering in generalities, and I am no exception. Texas is a state of mind. Texas is an obsession. Above all, Texas is a nation in every sense of the word. And there's an opening covey of generalities. A Texan outside of Texas is a foreigner. My wife refers to herself as the Texan that got away, but that is only partly true. She has virtually no accent until she talks to a Texan, when she instantly reverts. You would not have to scratch deep to find her origin. She says such words as yes, air, hair, guess, with two syllables—yayus, ayer, hayer, gayus. And sometimes in a weary moment the word ink becomes ank. Our daughter, after a stretch in Austin, was visiting New York friends. She said, "Do you have a pin?"

"Certainly, dear," said her host. "Do you want a straight pin or a safety pin?"

"Aont a fountain pin," she said.

I've studied the Texas problem from many angles and for many years. And of course one of my truths is inevitably canceled by another. Outside their state I think Texans are a little frightened and very tender in their feelings, and these qualities cause boasting, arrogance, and noisy complacency—the outlets of shy children. At home Texans are none of these things. The ones I know are gracious, friendly, generous, and quiet. In New York we hear them so often bring up their treasured uniqueness. Texas is the only state that came into the Union by treaty. It retains the right to secede at will. We have heard them threaten to secede so often that I formed an enthusiastic organization— The American Friends for Texas Secession. This stops the subject cold. They want to be able to secede but they don't want anyone to want them to.

Like most passionate nations Texas has its own private history based on, but not limited by, facts. The tradition of the tough and versatile frontiersman is true but not exclusive. It is for the few to know that in the great old days of Virginia there were three punishments for high crimes—death, exile to Texas, and imprisonment, in that order. And some of the deportees must have descendants.

Again—the glorious defense to the death of the Alamo against the hordes of Santa Anna is a fact. The brave bands of Texans did indeed wrest their liberty from Mexico, and freedom, liberty, are holy words. One must go to contemporary observers in Europe for a non-Texan opinion as to the nature of the tyranny that raised need for revolt. Outside observers say the pressure was twofold. The Texans, they say, didn't want to pay taxes and, second, Mexico had abolished slavery in 1829, and Texas, being part of Mexico, was required to free its slaves. Of course there were other causes of revolt, but these two are spectacular to a European, and rarely mentioned here.

I have said that Texas is a state of mind, but I think it is more than that. It is a mystique closely approximating a religion. And this is true to the extent that people either passionately love Texas or passionately hate it and, as in other religions, few people dare to inspect it for fear of losing their bearings in mystery and paradox. Any observations of mine can be quickly cancelled by opinion or counter-observation. But I think there will be little quarrel with my feeling that Texas is one thing. For all its enormous range of space, climate, and physical appearance, and for all the internal squabbles, contentions, and strivings, Texas has a tight cohesiveness perhaps stronger than any other section of America. Rich, poor, Panhandle, Gulf, city, country, Texas is the obsession, the proper study and the passionate possession of all Texans. Some years ago, Edna Ferber wrote a book about a very tiny group of very rich Texans. Her description was accurate, so far as my knowledge extends, but the emphasis was one of disparagement. And instantly the book was attacked by Texans of all groups, classes, and possessions. To attack one Texan is to draw fire from all Texans. The Texas joke, on the other hand, is a revered institution, beloved and in many cases originating in Texas.

The tradition of the frontier cattleman is as tenderly nurtured in Texas as is the hint of Norman blood in England. And while it is true that many families are descended from contract colonists not unlike the present-day braceros, all hold to the dream of the longhorn steer and the unfenced horizon. When a man makes his fortune in oil or government contracts, in chemicals or wholesale groceries, his first act is to buy a ranch, the largest he can afford, and to run some cattle. A candidate for public office who does not own a ranch is said to have little chance of election. The tradition of the land is deep fixed in the Texas psyche. Businessmen wear heeled boots that never feel a stirrup, and men of great wealth who have houses in Paris and regularly shoot grouse in Scotland refer to themselves as little old country boys. It would be easy to make sport of their attitude if one did not know that in this way they try to keep their association with the strength and simplicity of the land. Instinctively they feel that this is the source not only of wealth but of energy. And the energy of Texans is boundless and explosive. The successful man with his traditional ranch, at least in my experience, is no absentee owner. He works at it, oversees his herd and adds to it. The energy, in a climate so hot as to be staggering, is also staggering. And the tradition of hard work is maintained whatever the fortune or lack of it.

The power of an attitude is amazing. Among other tendencies to be noted, Texas is a military nation. The armed forces of the United States are loaded with Texans and often dominated by Texans. Even the dearly loved spectacular sports are run almost like military operations. Nowhere are there larger bands or more marching organizations, with corps of costumed girls whirling glittering batons. Sectional football games have the glory and the despair of war, and when a Texas team takes the field against a foreign state, it is an army with banners.

If I keep coming back to the energy of Texas, it is because I am so aware of it. It seems to me like that thrust of dynamism which caused and permitted whole peoples to migrate and to conquer in earlier ages. The land mass of Texas is rich in recoverable spoil. If this had not been so, I think I believe the relentless energy of Texans would have moved out and conquered new lands. This conviction is somewhat borne out in the restless movement of Texas capital. But now, so far, the conquest has been by purchase rather than by warfare. The oil deserts of the Near East, the opening lands of South America have felt the thrust. Then there are new islands of capital conquest: factories in the Middle West, food-processing plants, tool and die works, lumber and pulp. Even publishing houses have been added to the legitimate twentieth-century Texas spoil. There is no moral in these observations, nor any warning. Energy must have an outlet and will seek one.

In all ages, rich, energetic, and successful nations, when they have carved their place in the world, have felt hunger for art, for culture, even for learning and beauty. The Texas cities shoot upward and outward. The colleges are heavy with gifts and endowments. Theaters and symphony orchestras sprout overnight. In any huge and boisterous surge of energy and enthusiasm there must be errors and miscalculations, even breach of judgment and taste. And there is always the non-productive brotherhood of critics to disparage and to satirize, to view with horror and contempt. My own interest is attracted to the fact that these things are done at all. There will doubtless be thousands of ribald failures, but in the world's history artists have always been drawn where they are welcome and well treated.

By its nature and its size Texas invites generalities, and the generalities usually end up as paradox—the "little ol' country boy" at a symphony, the booted and blue-jeaned ranchman in Neiman-Marcus, buying Chinese jades.

Politically Texas continues its paradox. Traditionally and nostalgically it is Old South Democrat, but this does not prevent its voting conservative Republican in national elections while electing liberals to city and county posts. My opening statement still holds—everything in Texas is likely to be canceled by something else.

Most areas in the world may be placed in latitude and longitude, described chemically in their earth, sky and water, rooted and fuzzed over with identified flora and peopled with known fauna, and there's an end to it. Then there are others where fable, myth, preconception, love, longing, or prejudice step in and so distort a cool, clear appraisal that a kind of high-colored magical confusion takes permanent hold. Greece is such an area, and those parts of England where King Arthur walked. One quality of such places as I am trying to define is that a very large part of them is personal and subjective. And surely Texas is such a place.

I have moved over a great part of Texas and I know that within its borders I have seen just about as many kinds of country, contour, climate, and conformation as there are in the world saving only the Arctic, and a good north wind can even bring the icy breath down.

The stern horizon-fenced plains of the Panhandle are foreign to the little wooded hills and sweet streams in the Davis Mountains. The rich citrus orchards of the Rio Grande valley do not relate to the sagebrush grazing of South Texas. The hot and humid air of the Gulf Coast has no likeness in the cool crystal in the northwest of the Panhandle. And Austin on its hills among the bordered lakes might be across the world from Dallas.

What I am trying to say is that there is no physical or geographical unity in Texas. Its unity lies in the mind. And this is not only in Texans. The word Texas becomes a symbol to everyone in the world. There's no question that this Texas-of-the-mind fable is often synthetic, sometimes untruthful, and frequently romantic, but that in no way diminishes its strength as a symbol.

The foregoing investigation into the nature of the idea of Texas is put down as a prelude to my journeying across Texas with Charley in Rocinante. It soon became apparent that this stretch had to be different from the rest of the trip. In the first place I knew the countryside, and in the second I had friends and relatives by marriage, and such a situation makes objectivity practically impossible, for I know no place where hospitality is practiced so fervently as in Texas.

But before that most pleasant and sometimes exhausting human trait took hold, I had three days of namelessness in a beautiful motor hotel in the middle of Amarillo. A passing car on a gravel road had thrown up pebbles and broken out the large front window of Rocinante and it had to be replaced. But, more important, Charley had been taken with his old ailment again, and this time he was in bad trouble and great pain. I remembered the poor incompetent veterinary in the Northwest, who did not know and did not care. And I remembered how Charley had looked at him with pained wonder and contempt.

In Amarillo the doctor I summoned turned out to be a young man. He drove up in a medium-priced convertible. He leaned over Charley. "What's his problem?" he asked. I explained Charley's difficulty. Then the young vet's hands went down and moved over hips and distended abdomen—trained and knowing hands. Charley sighed a great sigh and his tail wagged slowly up from the floor and down again. Charley put himself in this man's care, completely confident. I've seen this instant rapport before, and it is good to see.

The strong fingers probed and investigated and then the vet straightened up. "It can happen to any little old boy," he said.

"Is it what I think it is?"

"Yep. Prostatitis."

"Can you treat it?"

"Sure. I'll have to relax him first, and then I can give him medication for it. Can you leave him for maybe four days?"

"Whether I can or not, I will."

He lifted Charley in his arms and carried him out and laid him in the front seat of the convertible, and the tufted tail twittered against the leather. He was content and confident, and so was I. And that is how I happened to stay around Amarillo for a while. To complete the episode, I picked up Charley four days later, completely well. The doctor gave me pills to give at intervals while traveling so that the ailment never came back. There's absolutely nothing to take the place of a good man.

I do not intend to dwell long on Texas. Since the death of Hollywood the Lone Star State has taken its place at the top for being interviewed, inspected, and discussed. But no account of Texas would be complete without a Texas orgy, showing men of great wealth squandering their millions on tasteless and impassioned exhibitionism. My wife had come from New York to join me, and we were invited to a Texas ranch for Thanksgiving. It is owned by a friend who sometimes comes to New York, where we give him an orgy. I shall not name him, following the tradition of letting the reader guess. I presume that he is rich, although I have never asked him about it. As invited, we arrived at the ranch on the afternoon before the Thanksgiving orgy. It is a beautiful ranch, rich in water and trees and grazing land. Everywhere bulldozers had pushed up earth dams to hold back the water, making a series of life-giving lakes down the center of the ranch. On well-grassed flats the blooded Herefords grazed, only looking up as we drove by in a cloud of dust. I don't know how big the ranch is. I didn't ask my host.

The house, a one-story brick structure, stood in a grove of cottonwoods on a little eminence over a pool made by a dammed-up spring. The dark surface of the water was disturbed by trout that had been planted there. The house was comfortable, had three bedrooms, each room with a bath—both tub and shower. The living room, paneled in stained pine, served also as a dining room, with a fireplace at one end and a glass-fronted gun case against the side. Through the open kitchen door the staff could be seen—a large dark lady and a giggleful girl. Our host met us and helped carry our bags in.

The orgy began at once. We had a bath and on emerging were given scotch and soda, which we drank thirstily. After that we inspected the barn across the way, the kennels in which there were three pointers, one of them not feeling so well. Then to the corral, where the daughter of the house was working on the training of a quarter horse, an animal of parts named Specklebottom. After that we inspected two new dams with water building slowly behind them, and at several drinking stations communed with a small herd of recently purchased cattle. This violence exhausted us and we went back to the house for a short nap.

We awakened from this to find neighboring friends arriving; they brought a large pot of chili con carne, made from a family recipe, the best I have ever tasted. Now other rich people began to arrive, concealing their status in blue jeans and riding boots. Drinks were passed and a gay conversation ensued having to do with hunting, riding, and cattle-breeding, with many bursts of laughter. I reclined on a window seat and in the gathering dusk watched the wild turkeys come in to roost in the cottonwood trees. They fly up clumsily and distribute themselves and then suddenly they blend with the tree and disappear. At least thirty of them came in to roost.

As the darkness came the window became a mirror in which I could watch my host and his guests without their knowledge. They sat about the little paneled room, some in rocking chairs and three of the ladies on a couch. And the subtlety of their ostentation drew my attention. One of the ladies was making a sweater while another worked a puzzle, tapping her teeth with the eraser of a yellow pencil. The men talked casually of grass and water, of So-and-So who had bought a new champion bull in England and flown it home. They were dressed in jeans of that light blue, lighter and a little frayed at the seams, that can be achieved only by a hundred washings.

But the studied detail did not stop there. Boots were scuffed on the inside and salted with horse sweat, and the heels run over. The open collars of the men's shirts showed dark red lines of sunburn on their throats, and one guest had gone to the trouble and expense of breaking his forefinger, which was splinted and covered with laced leather cut from a glove. My host went to the extreme of serving his guests from a bar which consisted of a tub of ice, quart bottles of soda, two bottles of whisky and a case of pop.

The smell of money was everywhere. The daughter of the house, for example, sat on the floor cleaning a .22 rifle, telling a sophisticated and ribald story of how Specklebottom, her stallion, had leaped a five-bar corral gate and visited a mare in the next county. She thought she had property rights in the foal, Specklebottom's blood line being what it was. The scene verified what we have all heard about fabulous Texas millionaires.

I was reminded of a time in Pacific Grove when I was painting the inside of a cottage my father had built there before I was born. My hired helper worked beside me, and neither of us being expert we were well splattered. Suddenly we found ourselves out of paint. I said, "Neal, run up to Holman's and get a half-gallon of paint and a quart of thinner."

"I'll have to clean up and change my clothes," he said.

"Nuts! Go as you are."

"I can't do it."

"Why not? I would."

Then he said a wise and memorable thing. "You got to be awful rich to dress as bad as you do," he said.

And this isn't funny. It's true. And it was true at the orgy. How unthinkably rich these Texans must be to live as simply as they were.

I took a walk with my wife, around the trout pool

and over against the hill. The air was chill and the wind blowing from the north had winter in it. We listened for frogs, but they had shacked up for the winter. But we heard a coyote howl upwind and we heard a cow bawling for her late weaned bairn. The pointers came to the wire mesh of the kennel, wriggling like happy snakes and sneezing with enthusiasm, and even the sickly one came out of his house and fleered at us. Then we stood in the high entrance of the great barn and smelled at the sweetness of alfalfa and the bready odor of rolled barley. At the corral the stock horses snorted at us and rubbed their heads against the bars, and Specklebottom took a kick at a gelded friend just to keep in practice. Owls were flying this night, shrieking to start their prey, and a nighthawk made soft rhythmic whoops in the distance. I wished that Able Baker Charley Dog could have been with us. He would have admired this night. But he was resting under sedatives in Amarillo curing his prostatitis. The sharp north wind clashed the naked branches of the cottonwoods. It seemed to me that winter, which had been on my tail during the whole trip, had finally caught up with me. Somewhere in our, or at least my, recent zoologic past, hibernation must have been a fact of being. Else why does cold night air make me so sleepy? It does and it did, and we went into the house where the ghosts had already retired and we went to bed.

I awakened early. I had seen two trout rods leaning against the screen outside our room. I went down the grassed hill, slipping in the frost to the edge of the dark pool. A fly was ready fastened on the line, a black gnat, a little frayed but still hairy enough. And as it touched the surface of the pool the water boiled and churned. I brought in a ten-inch rainbow trout and skidded him up on the grass and knocked him on the head. I cast four times and had four trout. I cleaned them and threw the innards to their friends.

In the kitchen the cook gave me coffee and I sat in an alcove while she dipped my fish in corn meal and fried them crisp in bacon fat and served them to me under a coverlet of bacon that crumbled in my mouth. It was a long time since I had eaten trout like that, five minutes from water to pan. You take him in your fingers delicately by head and tail and nibble him from off his backbone, and finally you eat the tail, crisp as a potato chip. Coffee has a special taste of a frosty morning, and the third cup is as good as the first. I would have lingered in the kitchen discussing nothing with the staff, but she cleared me out because she had to stuff two turkeys for the Thanksgiving orgy.

In the mid-morning sunshine we went quail-hunting, I with my old and shiny 12-bore with the dented barrel, which I carried in Rocinante. That gun was no great shakes when I bought it second-hand fifteen years ago, and it has never got any better. But I suppose it is as good as I am. If I can hit them the gun will pull them down. But before we started I looked with a certain longing through the glass door at a Luigi Franchi 12-gauge double with a Purdy lock so beautiful that I was filled with covetousness. The carving on the steel had the pearly gleam of a Damascus blade, while the stock flowed into lock and lock into barrels as though they had grown that way from a magic planted seed. I'm sure that if my host had seen my envy he would have loaned me the beauty, but I didn't ask. Suppose I tripped and fell, or dropped it, or knocked its lovely tubes against a rock? No, it would be like carrying the crown jewels through a mine field. My old beat-up gun is no bargain, but at least anything that can happen to it has, and there's no worrying.

For a week our host had noted where the coveys were gathering. We spread out and moved through brush and thicket, down into water, out, and up, while the spring-steel pointers worked ahead of us and a fat old bitch pointer named Duchess with flame in her eyes outworked them all, and us too. We found quail tracks in the dust, quail tracks in the sand and mud of stream beds, bits of quail-feather fluff in the dry tips of the sage. We walked for miles, slowly, guns up and ready to throw shot at a drumming flight. And we never saw a quail. The dogs never saw or smelled a quail. We told stories and some lies about previous quail hunts, but it did no good. The quail had gone, really gone. I am only a reasonable quail shot but the men with me were excellent, the dogs were professional, keen, hard, and hard-working. No quail. But there's one nice thing about hunting. Even with no birds, you'd rather go than not.

My host thought my heart was breaking. He said, "Look. You take that little 222 of yours this afternoon and shoot yourself a wild turkey."

"How many are there?" I asked.

"Well, two years ago I planted thirty. I think there are about eighty now."

"I counted thirty in the band that flew up near the house last night."

"There's two other bands," he said.

I really didn't want a turkey. What would I do with it in Rocinante? I said, "Wait a year. When they top a hundred birds, I'll come down and hunt with you."

We came back to the house and showered and shaved, and because it was Thanksgiving we put on white shirts and jackets and ties. The orgy came off on schedule at two o'clock. I'll skip through the details quickly in order not to shock the readers, and also I see no reason to hold these people up to scorn. After two good drinks of whisky, the two brown and glazed turkeys were brought in, carved by our host and served by us. We said grace and afterward drank a toast all around and ate ourselves into a proper insensibility. Then, like decadent Romans at Petronius's board, we took a walk and retired for the necessary and inevitable nap. And that was my Thanksgiving orgy in Texas.

Of course I don't think they do it every day. They couldn't. And somewhat the same thing happens when they visit us in New York. Of course they want to see shows and go to night clubs. And at the end of a few days of this they say, "We just don't see how you can live like this." To which we reply, "We don't. And when you go home, we won't."

And now I feel better for having exposed to the light of scrutiny the decadent practices of the rich Texans I know. But I don't for one moment think they eat chili con carne or roast turkey every day.

(*From* Part Four)

SOUTHERN TROUBLES

N OW I had moved through a galaxy of states, each
with its own character, and through clouds and
myriads of people, and ahead of me lay an area, the
South, that I dreaded to see and yet knew I must see
and hear. I am not drawn to pain and violence. I never
gaze at accidents unless I can help, or attend street
fights for kicks. I faced the South with dread. Here, I
knew, were pain and confusion and all the manic results of bewilderment and fear. And the South being a
limb of the nation, its pain spreads out to all America.

I knew, as everyone knows, the true but incomplete
statement of the problem—that an original sin of the
fathers was being visited on the children of succeeding
generations. I have many Southern friends, both Negro
and white, many of them of superb minds and characters,
and often, when not the problem but the mere suggestion of the Negro-white subject has come up, I have
seen and felt them go into a room of experience into
which I cannot enter.

Perhaps I, more than most people from the so-called
North, am kept out of real and emotional understanding of the agony not because I, a white, have no experience with Negroes but because of the nature of
my experience.

In Salinas in California, where I was born and grew
and went to school gathering the impressions that
formed me, there was only one Negro family. The
name was Cooper and the father and mother were

there when I was born, but they had three sons, one a little older than I, one my age, and one a year younger, so that in grade school and high school there was always a Cooper in the grade ahead, one in my class, and one in the class below. In a word, I was bracketed with Coopers. The father, universally called Mr. Cooper, ran a little trucking business—ran it well and made a good living. His wife was a warm and friendly woman who was good for a piece of gingerbread any time we wanted to put the hustle on her.

If there was any color prejudice in Salinas I never heard or felt a breath of it. The Coopers were respected, and their self-respect was in no way forced. Ulysses, the oldest, was one of the best pole-vaulters our town ever developed, a tall, quiet boy. I remember the lean grace of his movements in a track suit and I remember envying his smooth and perfect timing. He died in his third year in high school and I was one of his pallbearers, and I think I was guilty of the sin of pride at being chosen. The second son, Ignatius, my classmate, was not my favorite, I discover now, because he was far and away the best student. In arithmetic and later in mathematics he topped our grades, and in Latin he not only was a better student but he didn't cheat. And who can like a classmate like that? The youngest Cooper—the baby—was all smiles. It's odd that I do not remember his first name. He was a musician from the start, and when I last saw him he was deep in composition which seemed, to my partially in- structed ear, bold and original and good. But beyond this giftedness, the Cooper boys were my friends.

Now, these were the only Negroes I knew or had contact with in the days of my flypaper childhood, and you can see how little I was prepared for the great world. When I heard, for example, that Negroes were an inferior race, I thought the authority was misinformed. When I heard that Negroes were dirty I remembered Mrs. Cooper's shining kitchen. Lazy? The drone and clop of Mr. Cooper's horse-drawn dray in the street outside used to awaken us in the dawn. Dishonest? Mr. Cooper was one of the very few Salinians who never let a debt cross the fifteenth of the month.

I realize now that there was something else about the Coopers that set them apart from other Negroes I have seen and met since. Because they were not hurt or insulted, they were not defensive or combative. Because their dignity was intact, they had no need to be overbearing, and because the Cooper boys had never heard that they were inferior, their minds could grow to their true limits.

That was my Negro experience until I was well grown, perhaps too far grown to reform the inflexible habits of childhood. Oh, I have seen plenty since and have felt the shattering waves of violence and despair and confusion. I have seen Negro children who really cannot learn, particularly those who in their gelatin plate of babyness have been told they were inferior. And, remembering the Coopers and how we felt about them, I think my main feeling is sorrow at the curtain of fear and anger drawn down between us. And I've just thought of an amusing possibility. If in Salinas anyone from a wiser and more sophisticated world had asked, "How would you like your sister to marry a Cooper?" I think we would have laughed. For it might have occurred to us that a Cooper might not have wanted to marry our sister, good friends though we all were.

Thus it remains that I am basically unfitted to take sides in the racial conflict. I must admit that cruelty and force exerted against weakness turn me sick with rage, but this would be equally true in the treatment of any weak by any strong.

Beyond my failings as a racist, I knew I was not wanted in the South. When people are engaged in something they are not proud of, they do not welcome witnesses. In fact, they come to believe the witness causes the trouble.

In all this discussion of the South I have been speaking only about the violence set loose by the desegregation movements—the children going to school, the young Negroes demanding the questionable privilege of lunch counters, buses, and toilets. But I am particularly interested in the school business, because it seems to me that the blight can disappear only when there are millions of Coopers.

Recently a dear Southern friend instructed me passionately in the theory of "equal but separate." "It just happens," he said, "that in my town there are three new Negro schools not equal but superior to the white schools. Now wouldn't you think they would be satisfied with that? And in the bus station the washrooms are exactly the same. What's your answer to that?"

I said, "Maybe it's a matter of ignorance. You could solve it and really put them in their places if you switched schools and toilets. The moment they realized that your schools weren't as good as theirs, they would realize their error."

And do you know what he said? He said, "You trouble-making son of a bitch." But he said it smiling.

While I was still in Texas, late in 1960, the incident most reported and pictured in the newspapers was the matriculation of a couple of tiny Negro children in a

New Orleans school. Behind these small dark mites were the law's majesty and the law's power to enforce —both the scales and the sword were allied with the infants—while against them were three hundred years of fear and anger and terror of change in a changing world. I had seen photographs in the papers every day and motion pictures on the television screen. What made the newsmen love the story was a group of stout middle-aged women who, by some curious definition of the word "mother," gathered every day to scream invectives at children. Further, a small group of them had become so expert that they were known as the Cheerleaders, and a crowd gathered every day to enjoy and to applaud their performance.

This strange drama seemed so improbable that I felt I had to see it. It had the same draw as a five-legged calf or a two-headed foetus at a sideshow, a distortion of normal life we have always found so interesting that we will pay to see it, perhaps to prove to ourselves that we have the proper number of legs or heads. In the New Orleans show, I felt all the amusement of the improbable abnormal, but also a kind of horror that it could be so.

At this time the winter which had been following my track ever since I left home suddenly struck with a black norther. It brought ice and freezing sleet and sheeted the highways with dark ice. I gathered Charley from the good doctor. He looked half his age and felt wonderful, and to prove it he ran and jumped and rolled and laughed and gave little yips of pure joy. It felt very good to have him with me again, sitting up right in the seat beside me, peering ahead at the unrolling road, or curling up to sleep with his head in my lap and his silly ears available for fondling. That dog can sleep through any amount of judicious caresses.

Now we stopped dawdling and laid our wheels to

the road and went. We could not go fast because of the ice, but we drove relentlessly, hardly glancing at the passing of Texas beside us. And Texas was achingly endless—Sweetwater and Balinger and Austin. We bypassed Houston. We stopped for gasoline and coffee and slabs of pie. Charley had his meals and his walks in gas stations. Night did not stop us, and when my eyes ached and burned from peering too long and my shoulders were side hills of pain, I pulled into a turnout and crawled like a mole into my bed, only to see the highway writhe along behind my closed lids. No more than two hours could I sleep, and then out into the bitter cold night and on and on. Water beside the road was frozen solid, and people moved about with shawls and sweaters wrapped around their ears.

Other times I have come to Beaumont dripping with sweat and lusting for ice and air-conditioning. Now Beaumont with all its glare of neon signs was what they called froze up. I went through Beaumont at night, or rather in the dark well after midnight. The blue-fingered man who filled my gas tank looked in at Charley and said, "Hey, it's a dog! I thought you had a nigger in there." And he laughed delightedly. It was the first of many repetitions. At least twenty times I heard it—"Thought you had a nigger in there." It was an unusual joke—always fresh—and never Negro or even Nigra, always Nigger or rather Niggah. That word seemed terribly important, a kind of safety word to cling to lest some structure collapse.

And then I was in Louisiana, with Lake Charles away to the side in the dark, but my lights glittered on ice and glinted on diamond frost, and those people who forever trudge the roads at night were mounded over with cloth against the cold. I dogged it on through La Fayette and Morgan City and came in the early dawn to Houma, which is pronounced Homer and is in my memory one of the pleasantest places in the world. There lives my old friend Doctor St. Martin, a gentle, learned man, a Cajun who has lifted babies and cured colic among the shell-heap Cajuns for miles around. I guess he knows more about Cajuns than anyone living, but I remembered with longing other gifts of Doctor St. Martin. He makes the best and most subtle martini in the world by a process approximating magic. The only part of his formula I know is that he uses distilled water for his ice and distills it himself to be sure. I have eaten black duck at his table—two St. Martin martinis and a brace of black duck with a burgundy delivered from the bottle as a baby might be delivered, and this in a darkened house where the shades have been closed at dawn and the cool night air preserved. At that table with its silver soft and dull, shining as pewter, I remember the raised glass of the grape's holy blood, the stem caressed by the doctor's strong artist fingers, and even now I can hear the sweet little health and welcome in the singing language of Acadia which once was French and now is itself. This picture filled my frosty windshield, and if there had been traffic would have made me a dangerous driver. But it was pale yellow frozen dawn in Houma and I knew that if I stopped to pay my respects, my will and my determination would drift away on the particular lotus St. Martin purveys and we would be speaking of timeless matters when the evening came, and another evening. And so I only bowed in the direction of my friend and scudded on toward New Orleans, for I wanted to catch a show of the Cheerleaders.

Even I know better than to drive a car near trouble, particularly Rocinante, with New York license plates. Only yesterday a reporter had been beaten and his camera smashed, for even convinced voters are reluctant to have their moment of history recorded and preserved.

674 TRAVELS WITH CHARLEY

So, well on the edge of town I drove into a parking lot. The attendant came to my window. "Man, oh man, I thought you had a nigger in there. Man, oh man, it's a dog. I see that big old black face and I think it's a big old nigger."

"His face is blue-gray when he's clean," I said coldly.

"Well I see some blue-gray niggers and they wasn't clean. New York, eh?"

It seemed to me a chill like the morning air came into his voice. "Just driving through," I said. "I want to park for a couple of hours. Think you can get me a taxi?"

"Tell you what I bet. I bet you're going to see the Cheerleaders."

"That's right."

"Well, I hope you're not one of those trouble-makers or reporters."

"I just want to see it."

"Man, oh man, you going to see something. Ain't those Cheerleaders something? Man, oh man, you never heard nothing like it when they get going."

I locked Charley in Rocinante's house after giving the attendant a tour of the premises, a drink of whisky, and a dollar. "Be kind of careful about opening the door when I'm away," I said. "Charley take his job pretty seriously. You might lose a hand." This was an outrageous lie, of course, but the man said, "Yes, sir. You don't catch me fooling around with no strange dog."

The taxi driver, a sallow, yellowish man, shriveled like a chickpea with the cold, said, "I wouldn't take you more than a couple of blocks near. I don't go to have my cab wrecked."

"Is it that bad?"

"It ain't is it. It's can it get. And it can get that bad."

"When do they get going?"

He looked at his watch. "Except it's cold, they been

coming in since dawn. It's quarter to. You get along and you won't miss nothing except it's cold."

I had camouflaged myself in an old blue jacket and my British navy cap on the supposition that in a seaport no one ever looks at a sailor any more than a waiter is inspected in a restaurant. In his natural haunts a sailor has no face and certainly no plans beyond getting drunk and maybe in jail for fighting. At least that's the general feeling about sailors. I've tested it. The most that happens is a kindly voice of authority saying, "Why don't you go back to your ship, sailor? You wouldn't want to sit in the tank and miss your tide, now would you, sailor?" And the speaker wouldn't recognize you five minutes later. And the Lion and Unicorn on my cap made me even more anonymous. But I must warn anyone testing my theory, never try it away from a shipping port.

"Where you from?" the driver asked with a complete lack of interest.

"Liverpool."

"Limey, huh? Well, you'll be all right. It's the goddamn New York Jews cause all the trouble."

I found myself with a British inflection and by no means one of Liverpool. "Jews—what? How do they cause trouble?"

"Why, hell, mister. We know how to take care of this. Everybody's happy and getting along fine. Why, I *like* niggers. And them goddamn New York Jews come in and stir the niggers up. They just stay in New York there wouldn't be no trouble. Ought to take them out."

"You mean lynch them?"

"I don't mean nothing else, mister."

He let me out and I started to walk away. "Don't try to get too close, mister," he called after me. "Just you enjoy it but don't mix in."

"Thanks," I said, and killed the "awfully" that came to my tongue.

As I walked toward the school I was in a stream of people all white and all going in my direction. They walked intently like people going to a fire after it has been burning for some time. They beat their hands against their hips or hugged them under coats, and many men had scarves under their hats and covering their ears.

Across the street from the school the police had set up wooden barriers to keep the crowd back, and they paraded back and forth, ignoring the jokes called to them. The front of the school was deserted but along the curb United States marshals were spaced, not in uniform but wearing armbands to identify them. Their guns bulged decently under their coats but their eyes darted about nervously, inspecting faces. It seemed to me that they inspected me to see if I was a regular, and then abandoned me as unimportant.

It was apparent where the Cheerleaders were, because people shoved forward to try to get near them. They had a favored place at the barricade directly across from the school entrance, and in that area a concentration of police stamped their feet and slapped their hands together in unaccustomed gloves.

Suddenly I was pushed violently and a cry went up: "Here she comes. Let her through . . . Come on, move back. Let her through. Where you been? You're late for school. Where you been, Nellie?"

The name was not Nellie. I forget what it was. But she shoved through the dense crowd quite near enough to me so that I could see her coat of imitation fleece and her gold earrings. She was not tall, but her body was ample and full-busted. I judge she was about fifty. She was heavily powdered, which made the line of her double chin look very dark.

She wore a ferocious smile and pushed her way through the milling people, holding a fistful of clippings high in her hand to keep them from being crushed. Since it was her left hand I looked particularly for a wedding ring, and saw that there was none. I slipped in behind her to get carried along by her wave, but the crush was dense and I was given a warning too. "Watch it, sailor. Everybody wants to hear."

Nellie was received with shouts of greeting. I don't know how many Cheerleaders there were. There was no fixed line between the Cheerleaders and the crowd behind them. What I could see was that a group was passing newspaper clippings back and forth and reading them aloud with little squeals of delight.

Now the crowd grew restless, as an audience does when the clock goes past curtain time. Men all around me looked at their watches. I looked at mine. It was three minutes to nine.

The show opened on time. Sound of sirens. Motorcycle cops. Then two big black cars filled with big men in blond felt hats pulled up in front of the school. The crowd seemed to hold its breath. Four big marshals got out of each car and from somewhere in the automobiles they extracted the littlest Negro girl you ever saw, dressed in shining starchy white, with new white shoes on feet so little they were almost round. Her face and little legs were very black against the white.

The big marshals stood her on the curb and a jangle of jeering shrieks went up from behind the barricades. The little girl did not look at the howling crowd but from the side the whites of her eyes showed like those of a frightened fawn. The men turned her around like a doll, and then the strange procession moved up the broad walk toward the school, and the child was even more a mite because the men were so big. Then the girl made a curious hop, and I think I know what it was. I think in her whole life she had not gone ten steps without skipping, but now in the middle of her first skip the weight bore her down and her little round feet took measured, reluctant steps between the tall guards. Slowly they climbed the steps and entered the school.

The papers had printed that the jibes and jeers were cruel and sometimes obscene, and so they were, but this was not the big show. The crowd was waiting for the white man who dared to bring his white child to school. And here he came along the guarded walk, a tall man dressed in light gray, leading his frightened child by the hand. His body was tensed as a strong leaf spring drawn to the breaking strain; his face was grave and gray, and his eyes were on the ground immediately ahead of him. The muscles of his cheeks stood out from clenched jaws, a man afraid who by his will held his fears in check as a great rider directs a panicked horse.

A shrill, grating voice rang out. The yelling was not in chorus. Each took a turn and at the end of each the crowd broke into howls and roars and whistles of applause. This is what they had come to see and hear.

No newspaper had printed the words these women shouted. It was indicated that they were indelicate, some even said obscene. On television the sound track was made to blur or had crowd noises cut in to cover. But now I heard the words, bestial and filthy and degenerate. In a long and unprotected life I have seen and heard the vomitings of demoniac humans before. Why then did these screams fill me with a shocked and sickened sorrow?

The words written down are dirty, carefully and selectedly filthy. But there was something far worse here than dirt, a kind of frightening witches' Sabbath. Here was no spontaneous cry of anger, of insane rage.

Perhaps that is what made me sick with weary nausea. Here was no principle good or bad, no direction. These blowzy women with their little hats and their clippings hungered for attention. They wanted to be admired. They simpered in happy, almost innocent triumph when they were applauded. Theirs was the demented cruelty of egocentric children, and somehow this made their insensate beastliness much more heartbreaking. These were not mothers, not even women. They were crazy actors playing to a crazy audience.

The crowd behind the barrier roared and cheered and pounded one another with joy. The nervous strolling police watched for any break over the barrier. Their lips were tight but a few of them smiled and quickly unsmiled. Across the street the U.S. marshals stood unmoving. The gray-clothed man's legs had speeded for a second, but he reined them down with his will and walked up the school pavement.

The crowd quieted and the next cheer lady had her turn. Her voice was the bellow of a bull, a deep and powerful shout with flat edges like a circus barker's voice. There is no need to set down her words. The pattern was the same; only the rhythm and tonal quality were different. Anyone who has been near the theater would know that these speeches were not spontaneous. They were tried and memorized and carefully rehearsed. This was theater. I watched the intent faces of the listening crowd and they were the faces of an audience. When there was applause, it was for a performer.

My body churned with weary nausea, but I could not let an illness blind me after I had come so far to look and to hear. And suddenly I knew something was wrong and distorted and out of drawing. I knew New Orleans, I have over the years had many friends there, thoughtful, gentle people, with a tradition of kindness and courtesy. I remembered Lyle Saxon, a huge man of soft laughter. How many days I have spent with Roark Bradford, who took Louisiana sounds and sights and created God and the Green Pastures to which He leadeth us. I looked in the crowd for such faces of such people and they were not there. I've seen this kind bellow for blood at a prize fight, have orgasms when a man is gored in the bull ring, stare with vicarious lust at a highway accident, stand patiently in line for the privilege of watching any pain or any agony. But where were the others—the ones who would be proud they were of a species with the gray man—the ones whose arms would ache to gather up the small, scared black mite?

I don't know where they were. Perhaps they felt as helpless as I did, but they left New Orleans misrepresented to the world. The crowd, no doubt, rushed home to see themselves on television, and what they saw went out all over the world, unchallenged by the other things I know are there.

The show was over and the river of us began to move away. Second show would be when school-closing bell rang and the little black face had to look out at her accusers again. I was in New Orleans of the great restaurants. I know them all and most of them know me. And I could no more have gone to Gallatoir's for an omelet and champagne than I could have danced on a grave. Even setting this down on paper has raised the weary, hopeless nausea in me again. It is not written to amuse. It does not amuse me.

(*From* Part Four)

LAST LEG

IT is very strange. Up to Abingdon, Virginia, I can reel back the trip like film. I have almost total recall, every face is there, every hill and tree and color, and sound of speech and small scenes ready to replay themselves in my memory. After Abingdon—nothing. The way was a gray, timeless, eventless tunnel, but at the end of it was the one shining reality—my own wife, my own house in my own street, my own bed. It was all there, and I lumbered my way toward it. Rocinante could be fleet, but I had not driven her fast. Now she leaped under my heavy relentless foot, and the wind shrieked around the corners of the house. If you think I am indulging in fantasy about the trip, how can you explain that Charley knew it was over too? He at least is no dreamer, no coiner of moods. He went to sleep with his head in my lap, never looked out the window, never said "Ftt," never urged me to a turn-out. He carried out his functions like a sleepwalker, ignored whole rows of garbage cans. If that doesn't prove the truth of my statement, nothing can.

New Jersey was another turnpike. My body was in a nerveless, tireless vacuum. The increasing river of traffic for New York carried me along, and suddenly there was the welcoming maw of Holland Tunnel and at the other end home.

A policeman waved me out of the snake of traffic

and flagged me to a stop. "You can't go through the tunnel with that butane," he said.

"But officer, it's turned off."

"Doesn't matter. It's the law. Can't take gas into the tunnel."

And suddenly I fell apart, collapsed into a jelly of weariness. "But I want to get home," I wailed. "How am I going to get home?"

He was very kind to me, and patient too. Maybe he had a home somewhere. "You can go up and take George Washington Bridge, or you can take a ferry."

It was rush hour, but the gentle-hearted policeman must have seen a potential maniac in me. He held back the savage traffic and got me through and directed me with great care. I think he was strongly tempted to drive me home.

Magically I was on the Hoboken ferry and then ashore, far downtown with the daily panic rush of commuters leaping and running and dodging in front, obeying no signals. Every evening is Pamplona in lower New York. I made a turn and then another, entered a one-way street the wrong way and had to back out, got boxed in the middle of a crossing by a swirling rapids of turning people.

Suddenly I pulled to the curb in a no-parking area, cut my motor, and leaned back in the seat and laughed, and I couldn't stop. My hands and arms and shoulders were shaking with road jitters.

An old-fashioned cop with a fine red face and a frosty blue eye leaned in toward me. "What's the matter with you, Mac, drunk?" he asked.

I said, "Officer, I've driven this thing all over the country—mountains, plains, deserts. And now I'm back in my own town, where I live—and I'm lost."

He grinned happily. "Think nothing of it, Mac," he said. "I got lost in Brooklyn only Saturday. Now where is it you were wanting to go?"

And that's how the traveler came home again.

(*From* Part Four)

◇◇◇

The Language of Awareness

From *EAST OF EDEN*

NOBEL PRIZE ACCEPTANCE SPEECH

*Two representative statements of belief and commitment, from the
1952 novel and the 1962 address.*

◇◇◇

From *EAST OF EDEN*

[1]

SOMETIMES a kind of glory lights up the mind of a man. It happens to nearly everyone. You can feel it growing or preparing like a fuse burning toward dynamite. It is a feeling in the stomach, a delight of the nerves, of the forearms. The skin tastes the air, and every deep-drawn breath is sweet. Its beginning has the pleasure of a great stretching yawn; it flashes in the brain and the whole world glows outside your eyes. A man may have lived all of his life in the gray, and the land and trees of him dark and somber. The events, even the important ones, may have trooped by faceless and pale. And then—the glory —so that a cricket song sweetens his ears, the smell of the earth rises chanting to his nose, and dappling light under a tree blesses his eyes. Then a man pours outward, a torrent of him, and yet he is not diminished. And I guess a man's importance in the world can be measured by the quality and number of his glories. It is a lonely thing but it relates us to the world. It is the mother of all creativeness, and it sets each man separate from all other men.

I don't know how it will be in the years to come. There are monstrous changes taking place in the world, forces shaping a future whose face we do not know. Some of these forces seem evil to us, perhaps not in themselves but because their tendency is to eliminate other things we hold good. It is true that two men can lift a bigger stone than one man. A group can build automobiles quicker and better than one man, and bread from a huge factory is cheaper and more uniform. When our food and clothing and housing all are born in the complication of mass production, mass method is bound to get into our thinking and to eliminate all other thinking. In our time mass or collective production has entered our economics, our politics, and even our religion, so that some nations have substituted the idea collective for the idea God. This in my time is the danger. There is great tension in the world, tension toward a breaking point, and men are unhappy and confused.

At such a time it seems natural and good to me to ask myself these questions. What do I believe in? What must I fight for and what must I fight against?

Our species is the only creative species, and it has only one creative instrument, the individual mind and spirit of a man. Nothing was ever created by two men. There are no good collaborations, whether in music, in art, in poetry, in mathematics, in philosophy. Once the miracle of creation has taken place, the group can build and extend it, but the group never invents anything. The preciousness lies in the lonely mind of a man.

And now the forces marshaled around the concept of the group have declared a war of extermination on that preciousness, the mind of man. By disparagement, by starvation, by repressions, forced direction, and the stunning hammerblows of conditioning, the free, roving mind is being pursued, roped, blunted, drugged. It is a sad suicidal course our species seems to have taken.

And this I believe: that the free, exploring mind of the individual human is the most valuable thing in the world. And this I would fight for: the freedom of the mind to take any direction it wishes, undirected. And this I must fight against: any idea, religion, or government which limits or destroys the individual. This is what I am and what I am about. I can understand why a system built on a pattern must try to destroy the free mind, for that is one thing which can by inspection destroy such a system. Surely I can understand this, and I hate it and I will fight against it to preserve the one thing that separates us from the uncreative beasts. If the glory can be killed, we are lost.

(*From* Chapter 13)

NOBEL PRIZE
ACCEPTANCE SPEECH

I THANK the Swedish Academy for finding my work worthy of this highest honor. In my heart there may be doubt that I deserve the Nobel Award over other men of letters whom I hold in respect and reverence— but there is no question of my pleasure and pride in having it for myself.

It is customary for the recipient of this award to offer scholarly or personal comment on the nature and the direction of literature. However, I think it would be well at this particular time to consider the high duties and the responsibilities of the makers of literature.

Such is the prestige of the Nobel Award and of this place where I stand that I am impelled, not to squeak like a grateful and apologetic mouse, but to roar like a lion out of pride in my profession and in the great and good men who have practiced it through the ages.

Literature was not promulgated by a pale and emasculated critical priesthood singing their litanies in empty churches—nor is it a game for the cloistered elect, the tin-horn mendicants of low-calorie despair.

Literature is as old as speech. It grew out of human need for it and it has not changed except to become more needed. The skalds, the bards, the writers are not separate and exclusive. From the beginning, their functions, their duties, their responsibilities have been decreed by our species.

Humanity has been passing through a gray and desolate time of confusion. My great predecessor,

William Faulkner, speaking here, referred to it as a tragedy of universal physical fear, so long sustained that there were no longer problems of the spirit, so that only the human heart in conflict with itself seemed worth writing about. Faulkner, more than most men, was aware of human strength as well as of human weakness. He knew that the understanding and the resolution of fear are a large part of the writer's reason for being.

This is not new. The ancient commission of the writer has not changed. He is charged with exposing our many grievous faults and failures, with dredging up to the light our dark and dangerous dreams for the purpose of improvement.

Furthermore, the writer is delegated to declare and to celebrate man's proven capacity for greatness of heart and spirit—for gallantry in defeat, for courage, compassion and love. In the endless war against weakness and despair, these are the bright rally flags of hope and of emulation. I hold that a writer who does not passionately believe in the perfectibility of man has no dedication nor any membership in literature.

The present universal fear has been the result of a forward surge in our knowledge and manipulation of certain dangerous factors in the physical world. It is true that other phases of understanding have not yet caught up with this great step, but there is no reason to presume that they cannot or will not draw abreast. Indeed, it is a part of the writer's responsibility to make sure that they do. With humanity's long, proud history of standing firm against all of its natural enemies, sometimes in the face of almost certain defeat and extinction, we would be cowardly and stupid to leave the field on the eve of our greatest potential victory.

Understandably, I have been reading the life of

Alfred Nobel; a solitary man, the books say, a thoughtful man. He perfected the release of explosive forces capable of creative good or of destructive evil, but lacking choice, ungoverned by conscience or judgment.

Nobel saw some of the cruel and bloody misuses of his inventions. He may even have foreseen the end result of his probing—access to ultimate violence, to final destruction. Some say that he became cynical, but I do not believe this. I think he strove to invent a control—a safety valve. I think he found it finally only in the human mind and the human spirit.

To me, his thinking is clearly indicated in the categories of these awards. They are offered for increased and continuing knowledge of man and of his world—for *understanding* and *communication,* which are the functions of literature. And they are offered for demonstrations of the capacity for peace—the culmination of all the others.

Less than fifty years after his death, the door of nature was unlocked and we were offered the dreadful burden of choice. We have usurped many of the powers we once ascribed to God. Fearful and unprepared, we have assumed lordship over the life and death of the whole world of all living things. The danger and the glory and the choice rest finally in man. The test of his perfectibility is at hand.

Having taken God-like power, we must seek in ourselves for the responsibility and the wisdom we once prayed some deity might have. Man himself has become our greatest hazard and our only hope. So that today, Saint John the Apostle may well be paraphrased: In the end is the *word,* and the word is *man,* and the word is *with* man.